CHARLOTTE
BRONTË

CHARLOTTE BRONTË, detail of group by Branwell Brontë, *c.* 1838

WINIFRED GÉRIN

CHARLOTTE BRONTË

THE EVOLUTION OF GENIUS

OXFORD
AT THE CLARENDON PRESS

Oxford University Press, Ely House, London W. 1

GLASGOW NEW YORK TORONTO MELBOURNE WELLINGTON
CAPE TOWN SALISBURY IBADAN NAIROBI LUSAKA ADDIS ABABA
BOMBAY CALCUTTA MADRAS KARACHI LAHORE DACCA
KUALA LUMPUR HONG KONG TOKYO

FIRST PUBLISHED 1967
REPRINTED (WITH CORRECTIONS) 1968

TO MY HUSBAND

my dear partner in Brontë studies

ACKNOWLEDGEMENTS

I wish to thank the following for their help and kindness in supplying me with, or giving me access to, material necessary to the writing of this book: Geoffrey Beard, former Curator and Secretary of the Brontë Parsonage Museum, for his unfailing courtesy, knowledge, and advice in seconding my researches there; the Council of the Brontë Society for authority to quote from Brontë source material; Mrs. Bonnell, of Philadelphia, for her interest, encouragement, and generosity in making manuscripts in her private collection available to me; Dr. J. D. Gordon, Curator of the H. W. and A. A. Berg Collection, New York Public Library, Miss E. C. Ford, Curator of the Harry Elkins Widener Memorial Library, Harvard University, Cambridge, Mass., the Curators of the Henry Huntington Library, San Marino, California, the Wrenn Library, University of Texas, and the J. Pierpont Morgan Library, New York City, for making photostat copies of Brontë manuscripts in their collections and allowing quotation from them; the Keeper of Rare Manuscripts, British Museum, for access to Brontë letters and juvenilia and permission to quote from them; the Headmistress of Casterton School, Lancashire, for facilities to examine the school's ledgers, records, and registers from its foundation in 1824; Mrs. Seton Gordon, granddaughter of George Smith, for her generous loan of family documents; my friend Mrs. Moorman for the correspondence of her grandmother Mrs. Humphry Ward with Arthur Bell Nicholls; Mrs. Trevor Jones, Mrs. Gaskell's great-granddaughter, for the permission to reproduce the family portraits; Dr. Tyson, Librarian of Manchester University Library, for access to Charlotte Brontë's letters to Mrs. Gaskell; the Curator of the Enthoven Collection, Victoria & Albert Museum; Miss Maidie Rathbone, of Ashford, Kent, for putting the Dixon family letters at my disposal, and supplying photographs of the Dixon and Taylor families; the Keeper of the Leeds City Museum, for permission to quote from the Dixon Papers in its possession; the Librarian of the Fitzwilliam Museum Library, for making the letters of Charlotte to the Miss Woolers (the Allbutt Bequest) available to me; the Curator of the Brotherton Library, Leeds, for similar permission to examine and quote from the letters of Charlotte in its collection; the Librarian of Sheffield University Library, for access to the Diaries of Elizabeth Firth; and Walter Cunliffe, Esq., of Uckfield, Sussex, for lending me the originals of fourteen letters from M. and Mme Heger to the ladies of his family, former pupils of the Pensionnat Heger.

I am grateful to several people who allowed me to visit their homes, where Charlotte Brontë at one time lived or worked: Mrs. Greenwood of

Swarcliffe, for very helpful family data, the loan of documents, and delightful hospitality at Swarcliffe; Mrs. Holroyd of Stonegappe, for hospitality throughout a long day when she allowed me to roam freely over the house and grounds where CB was governess; Miss L. Harper, the present owner of Mrs. Gaskell's house in Plymouth Grove, Manchester; Major Hedley of Briary Close, Windermere; Mrs. Everatt of the Green House, Mirfield; the Father Superior of the Verona Fathers, Roe Head, Mirfield, for permission to go over the house, and for access to the deeds; and the tenants of Harriet Martineau's house, the Knoll, Ambleside.

In Brussels I received invaluable help from: Mlle Mina Martens, Curator of the Archives of the Town of Brussels; the Revd. H. Isherwood, Chaplain to the United Anglican Churches, and the Revd. Mathieu Schyns, Protestant Pastor of Brussels, who searched their registers for entries of the burials of Martha Taylor and Julia Wheelwright, etc.; the Keeper and Librarians of the Bibliothèque Royale, in my research into the historical and topographical background of Charlotte Brontë's Brussels; and I wish particularly to acknowledge the scholarly help of my nephew, Paul-Eugène Gérin, Lecturer in History at the University of Liége, in all my Brussels research, which, without his preparation, and introduction to the relevant academical bodies, libraries, museums, and collections, could not have been carried out.

I should like also particularly to acknowledge the help, and salute the memory, of the late Mme Beckers-Heger, who laid the whole of the family records, photographs, and press-cuttings entirely at my disposal, and accorded me several hours' interview at her beautiful house at Uccle, where the family portraits and furniture were still preserved.

The incumbents of the following parishes have kindly allowed me access to their registers: Tunstall, Casterton, Lothersdale, Kildwick, Mirfield, Appleby, and Keighley; the Chief Librarians of the following places have helped me with much topographical material: Bridlington, Mirfield, Batley, Cleckheaton, Kensington, and Keighley; and I want especially to mention the research undertaken for me by Doreen Jackson, of the Manchester Central Library, in preparing my investigations into Gaskell material.

Finally, my heartfelt gratitude to the Revd. R. H. Boyle, Rector of Banagher, Co. Offaly, who, with his wife, made my research into the Bell family history such a pleasure, and helped me so materially with his transcripts of the memorials in his church; to Captain Landon of Banagher and Miss Valerie Landon, for the photograph of Cuba House and permission to reproduce it; to Miss R. O'Neill, solicitor, of Belfast, for the data concerning Arthur Bell Nicholls.

CONTENTS

LIST OF PLATES

ABBREVIATIONS

AB	Anne Brontë
BM	British Museum
BPM	Brontë Parsonage Museum
BST	*Brontë Society Transactions*
CB	Charlotte Brontë
CBN	(after her marriage) Charlotte Brontë Nicholls
Chadwick	*In the Footsteps of the Brontës*, London, 1914
EJB	Emily Jane Brontë
EN	Ellen Nussey, 'Reminiscences of Charlotte Brontë', *Scribner's Magazine*, May 1871; quoted in *SLL* and *W & S*
Gaskell	*The Life of Charlotte Brontë*, London, 1857
GMS	George Murray Smith
Hopkins	*Elizabeth Gaskell: Her Life and Work*, John Lehmann, 1952
LW	Laetitia Wheelwright
MT	Mary Taylor, reminiscencs of Charlotte Brontë in a letter to Mrs. Gaskell, 18 January 1856; quoted in *SLL* and *W & S*
PBB	Patrick Branwell Brontë
Revd. PB	Revd. Patrick Brontë
SBC	Shorter, C. K.: *The Brontës and their Circle*, London, 1914
SLL	Shorter, C. K.: *The Brontës: Life and Letters*, 2 vols., London, 1908
W & S	Wise, T. J. & Symington, J. A., *The Brontës: Their Lives, Friendships and Correspondence*, 4 vols., Oxford, 1932 (Shakespeare Head Press)
W & S *PCPBB*	Wise, T. J. & Symington, J. A., *The Poems of Charlotte Brontë and Patrick Branwell Brontë*, Oxford, 1934 (Shakespeare Head Press)
W & S *PEJAB*	Wise, T. J. & Symington, J. A., *The Poems of Emily Jane and Anne Brontë*, Oxford, 1934 (Shakespeare Head Press)
WSW	William Smith Williams

References to Charlotte Brontë's letters have been made to *W & S*, to *SLL*, and to *SBC*—but in all cases where the autograph originals are available they have been consulted, or photostat copies of them made for comparison.

The quotations from Gaskell are from the Everyman edition (Dent).

INTRODUCTION

CHARLOTTE BRONTË has been the subject of many books, so many indeed that to add to their number with yet another work of this size lays a particular obligation on the biographer to make his purpose plain.

The truth is that the majority of these books are repetitive; and where they have broken new ground it has been over a limited field, treating of specific aspects and phases of Charlotte's life and work. No serious attempt has been made in recent years to present her *whole*.

It is paradoxical that the standard work is still Mrs. Gaskell's *Life*. This remains a great biography, but published two years after its subject's death it suffered from the outset from the inevitable limitations thus imposed. It was not bettered by its immediate followers—far from it indeed—and the long line of monographs, beginning with that of T. Wemyss-Reid in 1879, which in turn gave place to a spate of works of a semi-fictional order, added little.

The main contributions to Brontë studies in this century have been on the editorial plane, with such invaluable pioneer work as the deciphering of the Brontë juvenilia by Professor Fannie Ratchford and the collecting, collating, and editing of the Brontë Poems by C. W. Hatfield in successive volumes, culminating in *The Complete Poems* of Emily Jane Brontë in 1941.

To the student in search of facts, however, what emerges from this ocean of print is that the one reliable source of truth upon Charlotte Brontë are the letters of Charlotte herself, collected and published under the enthusiastic direction of Clement Shorter in the first place (between 1896 and 1908), and of T. J. Wise and J. A. Symington in the corrected and more comprehensive texts of the Shakespeare Head Press edition of 1932—a labour not yet complete.

The letters to M. Heger, which his son donated to the British Museum in 1913, still remain the greatest single contribution to our knowledge of Charlotte Brontë. But though they have been made the subject of countless commentaries, theories, and fictions, they have not yet been fitted into the overall framework of her life, or shown as the logical outcome of her romantic upbringing, and the forerunner of her literary achievements—as the epitome, in short, of just such a woman's evolution towards fulfilment. In the case of Charlotte Brontë, 'ful-filment' was something more than literary achievement; it was creation of character. During her short life she suffered exceptional griefs; their mere relation would be intolerable but for the manner in which she bore them—a manner that places them upon the plane of tragedy.

The growth of Charlotte's moral and artistic stature deeply con-cerns the biographer. Though her experience was limited, this was more than compensated for by her receptive, impressible, responsive nature. Hence it is essential to know what influences were working from within and from without upon her childhood and adolescence; and hence the obligation on the biographer to examine not only the background of her home, but of the literary, pictorial, and romantic fashions of her youth, with particular reference to the poetry of Byron and the painting of John Martin. The emotional contents of her novels can only be fairly judged (as Harriet Martineau could not judge them) if the peculiar influences affecting her girlhood are defined and recog-nized.

The importance of Charlotte's childish writings as a key to her mature productions has long been realized; even more revealing, how-ever, are the narratives of her early twenties, of which enough remain to indicate the gradual mastery over self, over passion and temper that she achieved. The value of such tales as 'Caroline Vernon', 'Mina Laury', 'Julia', 'Henry Hastings' (left untitled by her) lies in the analyses of motive, of character, and in the precocious understanding of the sufferings of love. They are the direct precursors of the master-pieces to come. They also bear witness to their author's long struggle towards perfection; their heroines, unlike their later sisters in tempta-tion, inevitably fall victim to their love for the all-pervading 'Zamorna'. The emotional content of these novelettes has here been considered in depth for the first time in any Brontë study.

Similarly, given Charlotte's response to environment, it is of the first importance to see the actual places, to enter the houses where, at various times, she lived; and I have spared no effort in following her physically from the earliest scenes at Thornton and Cowan Bridge to the home in Ireland where her husband took her on their honeymoon —the noble ruin that is Cuba House today. In between these are the schools, the friends' houses, the employers' mansions that have all a contribution to make towards our realization of her development. Much time and research were devoted to Brussels where the major experience of Charlotte's life occurred. There I received from the late

Madame Beckers-Heger the first, full biographical account of her grand-parents and the Pensionnat Heger to be published in English. My gratitude to the many people, descendants of those families with whom Charlotte had greater or lesser contacts, who have generously placed family data at my disposal is expressed elsewhere.

Above all, it seems to me, the biographer of Charlotte Brontë should know the horizons that swept round her home; the tremendous skies and illimitable moors that enlarged her vision and experience. I have now lived ten years in Haworth and found—however barren it may appear to some—why to Charlotte and her sisters it was the only place on earth where they felt free and at one with those universal natural forces from which they derived such lasting joy.

This familiarity with Charlotte Brontë's background, this wider study of her unpublished works, has allowed, I hope, a closer, more continuous examination of her life than any since Mrs. Gaskell published the first biography.

WINIFRED GÉRIN

Haworth, 1955–65

FIRST LESSONS

'READS tolerably—Writes indifferently—Ciphers a little and works neatly—Knows nothing of Grammar, Geography, History or Accomplishments—Altogether clever of her age but knows nothing systematically—.'[1]

Such were the headmistress's findings after a first rapid examination of the new scholar's capacities which were neatly entered into the school's register on the day of her arrival, 10 August 1824. The gaps in knowledge, the lack of all system in learning, were glaring indeed, and almost obscured the evidence of a natural intelligence 'altogether' remarkable in a child of her age. Her age, as the Superintendent entered in the appropriate column, was 8. The child was tiny, and as yet the youngest to be admitted to the school. Her name, Charlotte Brontë (written with an acute accent), was duly entered in the register, the new clean register of the Clergy Daughters' School, only recently opened at Cowan Bridge near Tunstall in Lancashire.

Everything was orderly in the school registers; a child's individuality was to be summed up by a glance at the appropriate columns under which the facts relating to her must be entered: her origin and parenthood, by 'whom supported' at the school, 'diseases had', the purpose ('for what educated'), the dates of her entry and departure, her ultimate destination; all were to be specified, and there was a column for 'General Remarks', permitting of some elaboration of the more elusive elements composing a child's identity.

Charlotte Brontë was lucky in having a father to 'support' her at the school; numbers of her fellow pupils were orphans, as the registers show, and paid for by patrons. He was—as her presence in that place denoted—a clergyman of the Established Church, Perpetual Curate of the chapelry of Haworth in the parish of Bradford, and of sufficiently limited means to benefit by the boon the school conferred upon the daughters of clergy in the way of board and education, at a fee of £14 per annum. It was a small sum, even for those days of cheap living,

---

[1] Register, Clergy Daughters' School, Cowan Bridge, 1824.

and hardly representative of the value received. The real cost of board and education was made up by the charity of the founder and of the institution's patrons and subscribers, who had annually to find something like £300 to supplement the fees for the 60 to 70 pupils for whom the school was designed. In August 1824 there were, as yet, only 29 scholars in the place, Charlotte Brontë bringing the number up to 30.

Opened on the previous 30 January, the school was still 'in its infancy', as Charlotte herself later recorded;[1] and however 'sad and rickety' that infancy proved, the school had been conceived with vision and daring by its founder, and was enthusiastically supported by most of the progressive educationists of the day. The names of William Wilberforce, Hannah More, and the Rev. Charles Simeon headed the list of its subscribers, next to those of the local members of Parliament and the surrounding clergy, who welcomed the chance of a really comprehensive education for their daughters. The girls' prospects in the changed society of the post-Napoleonic era were precarious indeed, and called for a more solid and practical training than their mothers had ever had, if they were to be assured of even a modest livelihood.

The generally low level of female education at the time can be seen by a glance at the school's registers, where girls admitted in their teens were recorded as 'reading vilely', or only 'tolerably', or 'pretty well', and where scarcely any had a smattering of history or geography. The lowest record was reached by a Jane Abbot (Charlotte Brontë did not forget the name and used it in *Jane Eyre*) who entered the school at 14, shortly after Maria and Elizabeth Brontë, and on whom the comment was: 'Reads most abominably and is perfectly ignorant in all else besides.'

With the Hon. Mrs. Howard as Patroness (a post soon to be filled by Royalty), 16 Vice-Patronesses, and 12 Trustees, the school got off to a propitious start. The name of its founder, moreover, seemed a guarantee of success. He was the Rev. William Carus Wilson, Vicar of Tunstall, a considerable landowner in the district; because he resided at Casterton Hall near by, he was left by the other Trustees in virtual control of the domestic as well as the scholastic administration of the school. Mr. Wilson was known far beyond the confines of his county and parish as an ardent educationist and had, as the list of his patrons and supporters shows, important contacts in both universities and in London's philanthropic circles. He had already founded one school in

---

[1] See letter to Miss Wooler, 28th Aug. 1848, Fitzwilliam Museum.

his parish for prospective governesses, and he was generally reputed a great lover of children. With such a circle of influential acquaintances, with such a fortune to command, and such natural propensities for doing good, who could doubt his success?

The whole plan had been put through with remarkable speed. Premises had only been found the previous year and these, though hardly suitable for the object in hand, were hastily converted under Mr. Wilson's impetus. They were a row of cottages at Cowan Bridge, belonging to a local family named Picard, dating back to the beginning of the eighteenth century (the two-foot thickness of the walls suggests their antiquity), and lying at water-level on the banks of the Leck about seventy yards from the old stone bridge (A.D. 1200) that gave the place its name. The cottages stood at a bend in the road, the 'turnpike' from Leeds to Kendal, with a daily coach-service passing the door. But passengers for the school had either to go on a further three miles to Kirkby Lonsdale, or to stop short of their destination at Ingleton.

The existing cottages were converted to hold the school dining-room (whose graceful pillars, though partially encased today, are still visible), the Superintendent's lodging on the first floor, and bedrooms for the teachers. The ornate wrought-iron banisters of the staircase in the central cottage, leading direct to the largest first-floor room, still indicate where the Superintendent's lodging was—the room described in *Jane Eyre* as being reached after the girls had 'threaded some intricate passages' from their own quarters and mounted a staircase.

At either end of the original cottages Mr. Wilson built on a wing, projecting at right-angles, in one of which he built a schoolroom with four dormitories over it, and in the other he made a covered veranda where in bad weather the children could take daily exercise and yet be in shelter. In the central square left vacant by the enclosure a garden was planned, or rather a number of little plots, which in due course were allotted to the scholars for individual cultivation. The bill for these alterations and for the fitting-out of the school was £2,333. 17s. 9d. —a very considerable sum for the time, and it says much for the generosity of the promoters that the school was able to open with only £31. 5s. 0d. to find.

A staff of six teachers, two under-teachers, a Superintendent, and six servants, as well as a visiting music-master was engaged. The 'accomplishments', indeed, were catered for—music, French, drawing—but all at an additional cost. Investigation into the salaries paid the teaching staff shows that while the Superintendent received £60 the other teachers were paid only £20 per annum. The school's first Superintendent was Miss Ann Evans.[1]

The district, contrary to much that has been said, is distinguished by grand and beautiful scenery. It is in sight of the high Cumberland fells, and the whole valley through which the Leck runs tributary to the Lune is verdant and smiling, with extensive pasture lands, wooded heights, and ancient farmsteads reached by winding lanes with sheltering hedges. For three seasons of the year it might be said to rival in beauty the neighbouring and better-known Eden valley. The winters were long and harsh. Of its charms in summer Charlotte Brontë wrote later, notably of the 'raving sound' of the beck at the school's boundaries,[2] still an arresting feature of the place today.

But neither with the school's situation nor with its structure or curriculum would Charlotte Brontë be concerned that August evening of her first arrival. She had been brought by her father fifty miles by coach from Keighley. She had left home for the first time and was suffering all the terrors usual in her situation, as well as many others provoked by her inordinately shy and shrinking nature. One thought alone can have sustained her as she stood at the massive door in the outer wall awaiting admittance (the spiked wall enclosing the school upon three sides struck her then and later as preternaturally high): the thought that waiting for her inside would be her incomparable sisters, Maria and Elizabeth, who had preceded her to Cowan Bridge the previous month.

To realize the meaning of such a reunion both to the elder girls inside and to the young one now joining them, the peculiar quality of their home-life must be considered, and the exceptional ties which bound these children together.

Bereft of their mother so young that Charlotte could remember no more than a shadowy image seen on the single occasion,[3] the little Brontës were driven in upon each other's affections, like shelterless sheep huddled together to keep out the cold. The fierceness and passion of their mutual devotion, enhanced no doubt by their Celtic parenthood, was the outcome of that terrifying sense of insecurity awakened in them by the early death of their mother. Throughout life, strangers who met them—even at home—remarked on the clinging nature of their love for each other: 'clinging' in the real physical sense of holding tight together when confronted by an intruder. They seemed to feel

---

[1] Ann Evans: see below, Additional Notes.   [2] *Jane Eyre*, ch. 4.
[3] Gaskell 33; Leyland i. 62.

the need to form a defensive 'square', as it were, against a hostile world.

In their home, the children were, nevertheless, supremely happy; not perhaps as other children are happy, but in ways of their own, and they had early reached a maturity of mind that would have been exceptional in children twice their age. They were so advanced in their tastes and judgements and had already read so widely, especially the political news of the day which was their father's passion, that he could make of them, and of his eldest daughter in particular (Maria was 10 when she went to Cowan Bridge), intellectual companions whom he considered his equals in many things, and treated with the consideration due to adults.[1] Aflame with educational ardour, both for himself and his children, he was concerned with them primarily as intellects in need of nurture—and vigorous nurture they got. The five girls and one boy of his 'sweet but small little family'[2] (as he saw them) responded with rapture to the treatment; only the maiden aunt who had come to take the mother's place and the young servants, Nancy and Sarah Garrs (brought over from Thornton, their former home), saw them as infants in need of care and constant correction.

But Papa was master in his own house, and to Papa they looked for all the joys of life: the books, the stories, the pictures, the stimulus of imaginative conversation, laced with Irish humour and couched in vigorous eighteenth-century language. The mental freedom of their early childhood—a freedom hardly ever enjoyed by girls of the period —could only be measured by its sudden loss on their being sent away to school. Then, indeed, did they feel their childish state, their impotent subjection to a feminine régime which sought to compress their already opening minds into a set mould, and divert the force of their native energy into a narrow—and purely practical—conduit. Poets as these children already were, by the ardour of their feelings and the extravagance of their imaginations, they must surely have suffered more than the other children exposed to a like regimentation.

The eight-year-old Charlotte, ignominiously placed at the bottom of a school because she was the youngest, had already written her first book before leaving home—written and illustrated it in water-colours, for her baby sister Anne, whom she made its heroine. Minute as the offering was (it measures $2\frac{1}{2} \times 1\frac{1}{2}$ inches), 'indifferent' the writing, and non-existent the spelling, it already shows powers of observation by no means ordinary. There are tiny drawings representing in precise detail

[1] Gaskell 36. [2] Burder letters: *SBC* 37.

familiar objects of the home—bed, table, chairs, and curtained windows. A passion for landscape is revealed in the obviously copied scenes of a lakeside, of a ruined Gothic castle, of a towered church, and of the ladies in poke-bonnets leisurely promenading their dogs. It was a labour of love, like many subsequent drawings inscribed 'for Anne', and the sense of accomplishment in the author is evident in the fact of her sewing the pages neatly together and binding the whole with brown paper for a cover.[1]

When Mr. Brontë brought Charlotte to Cowan Bridge, Maria and Elizabeth had already been there three weeks (they were entered on 21 July), and nothing that he then saw or that either of them had to tell him altered his original conception of the school as an unqualified blessing to a poor clergyman like himself with five daughters to educate. Maria, his trusted companion, the pride and delight of his widower's heart, had far too deep a respect for learning to rebel at the way it was disseminated at the Clergy Daughters' School, alien though it was to everything she had hitherto experienced. Elizabeth, a stoic at nine as she was shortly to prove, was not likely to complain of the material miseries of an establishment designed to do her and her sisters nothing but good. In three weeks they would barely have realized the extent of the change in their lives nor in the joy of reunion with Charlotte, would they have begged to be removed. Mr. Brontë, it must also not be forgotten, had nothing but the highest recommendations for the school; his colleague and neighbour, the Revd. Theodore Dury, Rector of Keighley, was one of the Trustees, and the benevolent Miss Currer of Eshton Hall, former patroness of Mr. Brontë's best friend William Morgan, was a Vice-Patroness. He was so convinced that everything was for the best that, after spending the night at the school, he returned home fully resolved to bring his fourth daughter, Emily, to share in her sisters' advantages as soon as she was fit to travel.

The sad fact was that the health of all his children, at that crucial moment in their lives, was poor, in consequence of a year of epidemics in Haworth during which they had, successively, caught chicken-pox, whooping-cough, and measles. Maria and Elizabeth, indeed, should have joined the school at its opening in January, but had been too ill then and for some time afterwards to be sent from home. How they might have fared at Cowan Bridge had they gone there in good health is the abiding question, and the one avidly seized upon by the school's defenders when its imperfections were ultimately brought to public

[1] 'There was a little girl and her name was Ane:' BPM.

notice. In 1824 questions of hygiene were not paramount anywhere, and particularly not so at a school like Cowan Bridge, where the whole bias of education was towards the suppression of physical claims, however fiercely they might make themselves felt in young and growing girls.

Charlotte Brontë made herself the mouthpiece of those clamours long after the ordeal was over and time had put the whole experience into perspective. The long days' lessons, the close routine, the unremitting order of work into which the child of eight was now caught up, she related in *Jane Eyre*. Much, necessarily, had to be omitted since it was a work of fiction. But the true details derived from other sources, however pedestrian they may sound, are essential in recapturing the atmosphere into which the children were now plunged.

Every girl had to take with her an outfit prescribed in the school's regulations. Its comprehensive character was dictated by the fact that there was only one annual holiday (five weeks at midsummer) and for some pupils not even that. Few parents could afford the coach-fare (as much as £6 for the girls who lived at a distance) and it was assumed in very many cases that the girls would spend long years at the school.

In the case of the little Brontës a peculiar interest attaches to the outfit of underwear, because of the evidence of Nancy Garrs, the parsonage servant who lived to be an old woman, and who remembered with sorrow the many weeks of painstaking application during which Maria and Elizabeth stitched away in their aunt's airless bedroom, instead of running on the moors like their younger sisters, after their severe illnesses in the spring.[1] The effort and the poor result can be gauged from the entry in the school registers on their arrival, where both girls were noted as 'working (sewing) very badly'.

The outfit specified in Rule III of the School Prospectus comprised, besides 'a Bible and Prayer-Book, a work-bag with necessary sewing-implements, Combs, Brushes, Pair of Pattens, Gloves', etc., '4 Day shifts, 3 Night do, 3 Night Caps, 2 Pairs of Stays, 2 Flannel Petticoats, 3 White Upper Petticoats, Grey Stuff do, 2 Pairs of Pockets, 4 White Cotton Stockings, 3 Pair Black Worsted do, 1 Nankeen Spencer, 4 Brown Holland Pinafores, 2 White do, 1 Short coloured Dressing-gown, 2 Pair of Shoes'.[2]

In addition to the half-year's fee of £7 upon each girl's entry, Mr. Brontë paid £4 for each, made up of £1 for books and £3 for outer clothing supplied by the school as a uniform. In winter the girls wore

[1] Chadwick 64 65, 81.　　　　　[2] School Records, 1829.

purple merino frocks with a matching cape, brown holland pinafores, black stockings, and plaid cloaks out of doors. In summer the uniform was a buff-coloured nankeen dress (with short sleeves and low neck) with matching tippets, white straw bonnets trimmed with green calico, and white stockings. Sundays they wore white dresses, white muslin 'frills', and white bonnets. By order of Mr. Wilson every girl wore her hair close cropped. Though 'Pattens' were provided for (later replaced by 'clogs') Charlotte Brontë recorded walking to church in shoes that got soaked on rainy Sundays and in which they sat for the rest of the day. The whole outfit she recalled as 'insufficient to protect us from the severe cold; we had no boots, the snow got into our shoes and melted there; our ungloved hands became numbed and covered with chilblains, as were our feet; I remember well the distracting irritation I endured from this cause every evening, when my feet inflamed; and the torture of thrusting the swelled, raw, and stiff toes into my shoes in the morning . . .'[1] Mornings, in the arctic dormitories, meant too the misery of frozen pitchers of water in which the children were expected to wash.

The evidence of the school's records corroborates Charlotte's account both of the meals and of the day's routine. The rising-bell was at 6; from 7–8 there was Bible-reading, followed by the learning and repetition of texts and hymns; 8 o'clock breakfast consisted of milk and a slice of dry bread (a 'thin scraping of butter' was given only on Sundays at tea), or milk and porridge. Lessons from 9 to 12. At 12 the girls were turned out for exercise, for a walk in fine weather, or, if wet, to play in the covered veranda. Dinner was at 1, at which a pudding was served (mostly baked rice) as the *first* course—doubtless to take the edge off the girls' appetites—and a meat course with vegetables served second. The meat is variously catalogued as 'Hot Roast', 'Pie of Odds & Ends', 'Hotch-Potch', or 'Boiled Beef'. Afternoon lessons were from 2 to 5; tea came at 5, consisting again of milk and dry bread. The older girls, who worked on from 7 to 8, had a supper of bread and milk.

Monotonous and scanty as it was, the food was, moreover, constantly spoilt by the carelessness of the cook, whose neglect even of rudimentary rules of hygiene was a prime factor in the typhoid epidemic which broke out in the spring of 1825. On all too many days the porridge was burnt, the milk 'turned', and the meat was a greasy stew with alien bodies floating in it. It was the horrible quality of the food, not

[1] *Jane Eyre*, ch. 7.

its nature, which turned the fastidious stomachs of the little Brontës and prevented their eating even such meals as were provided.[1]

Both the hunger and the cold were aggravated for Charlotte by the fact that she was the youngest and the smallest girl in the school. Most of the girls were in their middle teens (14 or 15, as the registers show, was the general age of admittance) and from this arose the abuse, of which Charlotte wrote in *Jane Eyre*, '. . . which pressed hardly on the younger pupils; whenever the famished girls had an opportunity, they would coax or menace the little ones out of their portion. Many a time I have shared between two claimants the precious morsel of brown bread distributed at tea-time; and after relinquishing to a third half the contents of my mug of coffee, I have swallowed the remainder with an accompaniment of secret tears, forced from me by the exigency of hunger. . . .'[2] It was the same thing with the fires at either end of the long schoolroom; 'the great girls' crowded round them, she wrote, in 'a double row . . . and behind them the younger children crouched in groups, wrapping their starved arms in their pinafores'.

But not all were so brutal. The oldest girl in Charlotte's day was Charlotte Hayne, aged 22, whose sister Mellany, 17, Mr. Brontë remembered years later Charlotte speaking of with affection and amusement.[3] Mrs. Gaskell, applying to the former Superintendent for the recollections she might have of the Brontë girls, was told that Mellany Hane [*sic*] was a great friend of Charlotte's, '. . . a hungry, good-natured, ordinary girl, . . . ever-ready to protect her from petty tyranny . . .'. The Haynes were orphans and came from the West Indies, their fees at school being paid by a brother. They were certainly Charlotte's first contact with people from that part of the world, which she later developed to such point in the Masons of *Jane Eyre*.

The worst ordeal of the winter was the two-mile walk to church and back on Sundays across open country, when, as Charlotte recorded, the children 'set out cold . . . arrived at church colder . . .', and 'during the morning service became almost paralysed'. The distance to Tunstall church made it too far to return to dinner and get back in time for afternoon church, so 'an allowance of cold meat and bread, in the same penurious proportion observed in our ordinary meals, was served round between the services. At the close of the afternoon service we returned by an exposed and hilly road, where the bitter winter

[1] Charlotte's widower, the Revd. A. B. Nicholls, in the controversy carried on in the *Halifax Guardian*, June–Aug. 1857, quoted the school doctor, a Kirkby Lonsdale surgeon, as saying of the food in the early days of the school that 'it was unfit for pigs'. *SLL* ii, Appendix VIII.　　　[2] *Jane Eyre*, ch. 7.　　　[3] Gaskell 48.

wind, blowing over a range of snowy summits to the north, almost
flayed the skin from our faces. . . .'[1]

As Charlotte's widower[2] related in after years, it was the sitting
through the two church services in sodden shoes that was the origin
of so many of the children's illnesses. Not only the little Brontës, but
many other girls, as the school records show, succumbed to the treatment. No fewer than six children died of tuberculosis during the
Brontës' period at Cowan Bridge, quite apart from those who died in
the typhoid epidemic of 1825.

On 25 November Emily joined her sisters at the school. She was the
44th pupil to be admitted and was found to read 'very prettily' for her
6¼ years. We cannot help wondering whether she was sent in charge of
the guard, like Jane Eyre, and whether, for some cause not known, Mr.
Brontë did not in her case go to Cowan Bridge and see for himself the
actual condition of his other daughters. For by November it would
seem probable that some of the symptoms undermining the health of
Maria and Elizabeth must have been apparent. No provisions were
made in the school's regulations for holidays at Christmas; only a few
days' break in lessons, and those spent at the school, marked the festivity. As late as 26 January, when Mr. Brontë received the half-year's
account for Maria and Elizabeth's board, he was charged 'extras' for
Maria; thirty shillings for a half-year's French and the same sum for
'Drawing', both to be paid in advance. Apparently no notice was
taken of Maria's worsening condition till mid February, when a letter
was sent to her father. Mr. Brontë, acting immediately (14 February),
hurried to the school and fetched Maria away.

Mr. Nicholls, in after years, quoted the case of a contemporary
of the Brontës who told him that, though she was very ill at school and
considered far gone in consumption, the authorities never notified her
mother; and that it was only by the merest chance, her mother being
ill and sending for her to come home, that her condition was discovered
and she was permanently removed.[3]

The evidence of the first pupils of the Clergy Daughters' School
remains conflicting; there were many who stayed there for years,
moving to the healthy and pleasant new surroundings at Casterton to
which the school transferred in 1833, and who extolled its régime and
witnessed to its many excellencies after the publication of *Jane Eyre*

[1] *Jane Eyre*, ch. 7.
[2] Letters to the *Halifax Guardian*, June–Aug. 1857: *SLL* ii. 447–62.
[3] Mr. Nicholls's evidence: *Halifax Guardian*, June–Aug. 1857.

Eng. by O. JEWITT, PUBLISHED BY DERBY

THE CLERGY DAUGHTERS' SCHOOL, COWAN BRIDGE, engraving of 1824 by O. Jewitt of Derby

brought discredit on its early days. Charlotte herself was among those who recognized the immense improvement after the removal to Casterton. Writing in 1848 to Miss Wooler, she said: '. . . I understand it is very much altered for the better since those days; the accommodation, the diet, the discipline, the system of tuition, all are, I believe, entirely altered and greatly improved . . .'. But of the school as she had known it she did not alter her opinion. Her widower gave evidence that 'to the day of her death . . . she maintained that the picture drawn in *Jane Eyre* was on the whole a true picture of the Cowan Bridge school as she knew it by experience'.[1]

On the question of Cowan Bridge Charlotte Brontë left the world in no doubt: she believed the harshness of the régime to be responsible for the deaths of her sisters and she never forgave the institution for that. And there were other pupils who corroborated the evidence of *Jane Eyre*, and who said that conditions had been even worse than Charlotte Brontë had painted them.

Charlotte's knowledge of the school extended over only ten months, but during that time she saw enough to record in after life, in a letter to her publishers: '. . . My career was a very quiet one. I was plodding and industrious, perhaps I was very grave, for I suffered to see my sisters perishing.'[2] Seldom, if ever, in disgrace herself—according to the recollections of Miss Evans, who remembered her as 'a bright, clever, happy little girl'—Charlotte perceived, with a penetration rare in a child of her age, that the humiliations and punishments to which her sisters were subjected were sufferings of the spirit as much as of the body.

Of these there were all too many. As the months passed their recurrence wore down the feeble reserves of strength of Maria and Elizabeth. Of Maria's treatment by 'Miss Scatcherd' (a Miss Andrews in real life), when the condition of her lungs required a blister to be applied, Mrs. Gaskell[3] heard from other witnesses than Charlotte. Maria, already so weak as to be incapable of getting up when the morning bell rang, and still suffering from the open blister on her side, was violently jerked out of bed by Miss Andrews, thrown on to the dormitory floor,

---

[1] The defenders of the school and its founder sought to invalidate CB's evidence on the score of her extreme youth. Evidence of her exceptional memory and keen observation is supplied by EN, who first met CB at 13. She was still then weeping and grieving for her sisters' deaths. '. . . When surprise was expressed that she should know so much about her sisters when they were so young, and she herself still younger, she said she began to analyse character when she was five years old . . .': EN, Reminiscence of CB: *SLL* i. 89.

[2] CB to W. S. Williams, 5 Nov. 1849.   [3] Gaskell 45.

abused for 'dirty and untidy habits', and ordered downstairs as on every other day. This scene and many others Charlotte witnessed. Quite apart from Miss Andrews's personal venom against Maria, the fact emerges that, though a doctor had obviously been called and had prescribed the blister, there was no question of Maria's being treated as an invalid. The all-too-frequent incidence of tuberculosis in the school would make her case the less remarkable. It must also be remembered that Maria's fortitude was of no ordinary nature; she asked for no indulgence. In any case, indulgence of physical weakness was, at that time, no policy of the school, though the Superintendent seems on many occasions to have taken the law into her own hands and shown mercy.

How illness and death were envisaged by the Rev. Carus Wilson can be seen by all who care to read his numerous writings intended for the instruction—and amusement—of the very young. To compensate for the ban on all fiction and fairy tales in the girls' spare-time reading (Scott's novels were surreptitiously read by the bolder spirits, and Helen Burns is described as reading *Rasselas* in her playtime), Mr. Wilson compiled a series of monthly magazines which he called *The Children's Friend* and published in Kirkby Lonsdale at the price of a penny a copy. (Their monthly issues varied from 20,000 to 30,000 copies.)

In them the very language of Mr. Brocklehurst repeatedly appears. Death, as the goal towards which good children should hurry joyfully, is the burden of every tale. Only the wicked child need fear death— hence the awfulness of accidental death and the certainty of damnation. In the story of Edward, aged 5, who died of a mad-dog bite, the author exclaims: 'My dear young friends, how necessary it is to be prepared to die: when Edward rose in the morning he little thought what would happen to him. . . . Dear Edward's papa and mamma felt much at losing him, but they were enabled to bless God amidst their tears, and to rejoice that their beloved child was taken from the evil to come . . .'.[1]

A Calvinist, Mr. Wilson left his young readers in no doubt about the eternity of damnation for the wicked, among whom must be classed the naughty child—like the bad boy who skates on thin ice and is drowned: 'He left his school. He took his play on the Sunday. And he thought he should go to hell for this. I fear he would go there. How sad it is to think of!'[2]

In a little volume of 114 tales, *The Child's First Tales*, 1836, illustrated by the crudest woodcuts, showing criminals being hanged, men

[1] *The Children's Friend*, May 1834.   [2] *The Child's First Tales*, 1836.

in chains, and children in their coffins, Mr. Wilson wrote in words of one syllable, for the child who had just learnt to read, tales of death and torture intended to console and elevate the infant mind. To the little child grieving by its mother's death-bed he argued: 'Well, if you love her, you would wish her to have what will do her most good.' 'Yes,' eagerly replies the grieving child, 'that I would.' 'Well, to die will do her the most good.'[1]

Death is the great protector from sin and hence something to be desired by the yet innocent child. Mr. Wilson's stories were not mere cautionary tales, they reflected his own profound beliefs. Writing in *The Children's Friend* for December 1826 of the real death of one of his girls at Cowan Bridge, his thankfulness for her early removal from a world of temptation is a genuine sentiment that cannot be in doubt. Rather dead than in danger of committing sin—that was his attitude towards the children placed under his care. As the case concerns a contemporary of the Brontës at Cowan Bridge, Mr. Wilson's account of it is revealing. It concerns eleven-year-old Sarah Bicker who, as the registers show, entered the school on 21 February 1824, being, indeed, the third girl to be admitted.

'On the 28th of last September', writes Mr. Wilson in *The Children's Friend* for 1826, 'died in the Clergy School at Cowen Bridge [*sic*] Sarah Bicker, aged 11 years. . . . Her complaint was inflammation in the bowels, and her sufferings were very great. . . . I had heard from the teachers that she had expressed a desire to depart and to be with Christ and I was anxious to assure myself that her hopes were well founded.' The following conversation took place. 'Sarah, are you happy?' 'Yes, very happy, Sir.' 'And what is it makes you happy?' 'Because Jesus Christ died to save me and he will take me to heaven.' 'And he will save all men?' 'No, Sir, only those that trust in him. . . .' He goes on to relate her virtues, how very industrious in her work, how very tidy in her person, how she had only once ever been punished, how she used to pray with her schoolfellows on Saturday nights—offering up long prayers, especially for three naughty girls. On the Sunday evening she was taken ill she was asked by Miss R—'If she should like to die?' She answered 'Not yet.' 'Why?' 'I should wish to have time to repent, and be a better child.' The school housekeeper nursed her night and day till she died, and Mr. Wilson's final comment upon her death was: '*I bless God that he has taken from us the child of whose salvation we have the best hope and may her death be the means of rousing many of her school-*

[1] Ibid., Kirkby Lonsdale, 1836.

fellows to seek the Lord while he may be found.[1] Such an attitude to the death of a child was not rare by any means at the time; Mr. Wilson's Calvinist tenets were very generally held. But not all his scholars had such keen sensibilities as Charlotte, upon whom his teaching left a mark for life.

Of Maria Brontë's salvation Mr. Wilson had no such clear conviction. The reports he would receive of her, particularly if they came from Miss Andrews, would be highly prejudicial. Her incurable 'untidyness', the result of constant absorption in her own thoughts (her mind was undoubtedly of the calibre of her sister Emily's and mystical abstractions must have been responsible for much of the 'absent-mindedness' for which she was punished), was a failing peculiarly hateful to Mr. Wilson. He mentions it as a very bad trait in a girl in many stories.

Of Miss Andrews's cruelty to Maria not only Charlotte gave evidence, as has been seen, but Mr. Nicholls later testified that the portrait of Helen Burns was true, *in all particulars*, of Maria Brontë.[2] That Maria met the injustice of her teachers with a fortitude rare in adults, and unique in one so young, only heightened Charlotte's heartbreak at her treatment. Her sense of Maria's superiority to all around her made her ill-treatment at the hands of such people doubly intolerable. Writing many years later to her publishers, Charlotte said that it would not be surprising if schoolmates of Maria remembered her; '. . . her prematurely-developed and remarkable intelligence, as well as the mildness, wisdom and fortitude of her character, *might* have left an indelible impression on them . . .'[3]

At her second school, when Charlotte met other girls they were strongly impressed with the fervour of her love for this exceptional sister. 'She would speak of her elder sisters', said Mary Taylor, 'till I used to believe them to have been wonders of talent and kindness.' 'Her love for them', recalled Ellen Nussey, 'was most intense; a kind of adoration dwelt in her feelings which, as she conversed, almost imparted itself to her listeners. She described Maria as a little mother among the rest, superhuman in goodness and cleverness. But the most touching of all were the revelation of her sufferings—how she suffered with the sensibility of a grown-up person and endured with a patience and fortitude that were Christ-like . . .'[4]

Of Elizabeth Brontë, of whom so little is remembered, Miss Evans

[1] *The Children's Friend,* 1826.

[2] Mr. Nicholls to *Halifax Guar.*: *SLL.* ii, Appendix VIII; June-Aug. 1857. See also CB to WSW, 28 Oct. 1847: *W & S* ii; and 5 Nov. 1849: *SLL* ii. 81.

[3] CB to WSW, 5 Nov. 1849: *SLL* ii. 81.   [4] *SLL* i. 89.

recalled an incident that showed her equal in spirit to her elder sister. In reply to inquiries from Mrs. Gaskell she wrote: 'The second, Elizabeth, is the only one of the family of whom I have a vivid recollection from her meeting with a somewhat alarming accident, in consequence of which I had her for some days and nights in my bed-room, not only for the sake of the greater quiet, but that I might watch over her myself. Her head was severely cut, but she bore all the consequent suffering with exemplary patience, and by it won much upon my esteem . . .'[1]

From these two admired sisters Charlotte was now shortly to be separated for ever. On 14 February 1825 Mr. Brontë fetched Maria home 'in ill health', as the school's registers recorded it, and by 6 May she was dead. That some news of the progress of her illness was received at the school—and consequently by her remaining sisters—is shown by a quotation from a letter of Mr. Brontë's copied into the registers, in which he told the Superintendent that 'She exhibited during her illness many symptoms of a heart under divine influence'.[2] By the time the actual news of Maria's death reached her sisters, the whole atmosphere of the school was redolent of death.

The 'low fever', described in *Jane Eyre*, which had so many of the symptoms of typhoid, broke out in early April and caused the death or removal of a number of girls. Its causes, variously debated, and to which the low physical condition of the girls certainly contributed, were ascribed to the cook's dirty ways and the dampness of the school-buildings. It might also be added that the school's only privy, a stone hut belonging to the original eighteenth-century cottages, was hardly adequate to a growing community which, by the spring of 1825, already numbered over seventy girls and adults.

The school registers record the removals and deaths, at their homes or at the school, of the victims of the epidemic. Some of the girls were buried in Tunstall churchyard (like Helen Burns in Charlotte's account) their funerals being attended by their playmates, dressed in their white Sunday frocks. The daily familiarity with death—or its approaches—may in a sense have blunted Charlotte's actual grief when the news of Maria's death came; the whole of life had taken on a morbid meaning by then, into which even the departure of her dearest seemed to fit as into an accepted pattern.

At the same time the upheaval caused by the epidemic in the school routine brought nothing but alleviations to Charlotte's lot. Lessons were totally suspended; those children who, like herself, escaped the

[1] Gaskell 48. [2] Registers, Clergy Daughters' School, 1825.

infection were given complete liberty and, the spring weather helping, were ordered to keep out and encouraged to roam the woods and play in the fields all day. Mr. Wilson, contrary to his custom, paid no more visits to the school; the slovenly cook was dismissed; and more plentiful meals were given to the healthy children. Paradoxically, Charlotte probably owed her survival to the typhus epidemic.

Not so Elizabeth. She escaped the infection only to fall into a sudden 'decline' towards the end of May. A letter dispatched to Haworth broke the news to her father. She was sent home on 31 May in charge of a trusted local woman, a Mrs. Hardacre, who was employed at the school and whose husband repaired the children's shoes.

The repetition of the tragedy of Maria so alarmed the school authorities that straightway on the day Elizabeth was sent home Charlotte and Emily were sent to Mr. Wilson's seaside house at Silverdale on Morecambe Bay, called 'The Cove'. There they spent the night and there, on 1 June, Mr. Brontë found them and immediately took them home. A fortnight later Elizabeth died.

Mr. Brontë, with characteristically muddled memory when it came to relating these events to Mrs. Gaskell thirty years later, overlooked the important fact that Charlotte and Emily never returned to Cowan Bridge. He gave Mrs. Gaskell the impression that they stayed there until the following autumn, thus incurring her condemnation, and that of posterity, as a callous father. The registers prove, however, that the children left the school for good on 1 June. Moreover, on the following 23 September, Mr. Brontë was refunded the amounts paid in advance for his daughters' board.

Charlotte Brontë's first educational experience was over. It was not from the lessons learnt from the text-books in use at the Clergy Daughters' School that she emerged enlightened; it was those other lessons, learnt from adversity, that permanently shaped her mind and that she carried with her through life and the marks of which she bore with her to the grave. 'Stunted' in figure, she spoke of herself to Mrs. Gaskell, permanently 'undeveloped';[1] a condition she did not hesitate to ascribe to the privations of Cowan Bridge.[2] To Cowan Bridge, also, must be ascribed her lack of hope, so noticeable in youth,[3] her sceptical incredulity about good fortune that characterized her adult life. She grew up to expect nothing but the 'mixed cup' in human prospects and to be exceptionally vulnerable to pain.

---

[1] Gaskell 310. [2] Mrs. Gaskell to Mrs. Froude, Aug. 1850: *Letters of Mrs. Gaskell*, ed. Chapple and Pollard, M.U.P. 1966, p. 128. [3] Gaskell 77.

SLAVE OF THE LAMP

In the fragment of a story written in her teens Charlotte reverted to the experience that awaited her on her return from Cowan Bridge: the death and burial of Elizabeth. There she described the heroine of her story, Jane Moore, falling into 'an abstracted reverie' and recalling former days. She remembers 'the death of her eldest sister who died when she was a child', and thinks of 'the rigid corpse laid in its coffin on the hall table, of the servants pressing round to gaze on Miss Harriet for the last time, of the kiss that she herself was bidden to give the corpse, of the feeling which then first gushed into her childish and volatile heart that Harriet had left them for ever . . .'[1]

Just so Branwell described the funeral-day of Maria years after the event with hallucinating detail, showing how the Brontë children were exempted from none of the ghoulish rites attending funerals at the time. For him, moreover, the ordeal was twice repeated; he saw Maria and Elizabeth carried into the same vault where his mother had been laid only four years before.[2]

No children were less endowed with 'childish and volatile hearts' than the little Brontës, and just because of the maturity and intensity of their feelings the effect of the successive deaths of their mother and sisters was to drive them far from all thought of mortality—as far as the wings of invention could bear them—towards the creation of an existence of which they held the key and of whose permanence they themselves could be the guarantors. It was not for mere love of magic that, for years after, in their games and dramatized stories, they claimed 'to make alive again' the casualties of the day.

Upon Charlotte, the eldest of the surviving children, the blow fell with greatest force. The need for prompt care and comfort was apparent, and evidence has recently come to light that former Thornton friends of Mr. Brontë's, the Kayes of Allerton Hall, fetched her to stay with them. There she was seen by a visiting niece, who was amused by

---

[1] Roe Head MSS.: Fragment of a tale: BPM, Bonnell 98(5).
[2] PBB, 'Caroline', Leyland i. 217–22.

C

the sight of the very small girl, wearing a night-cap, sitting up in a great four-poster bed.[1]

Mr. Brontë had spent five happy years at Thornton before going to Haworth, and had made a whole circle of friends at Kipping House, the home of the wealthy and pious Firths. It was at a dinner at Allerton Hall, a previous possession of the Firths, and then newly leased to Mercy and Benjamin Kaye, that Mr. and Mrs. Brontë had first met Elizabeth Firth and her father, and it is thanks to young Elizabeth's diary that so much relating to the Brontës' life at Thornton is known.

From those first contacts some lasting connexions were made and in due course Mr. Brontë's friends stood sponsors to his children. Charlotte's godparents were a cousin of Elizabeth Firth's, Frances Walker, and her husband, the Revd. Thomas Atkinson, Vicar of Hartshead, Mr. Brontë's previous incumbency. Tradition in the Firth family[2] had it that Elizabeth was Charlotte's other godmother (she was already godmother to Elizabeth Brontë and would be so again later to Anne). The fact that Charlotte was called after her mother's sister, Charlotte Branwell of Penzance, suggests that her aunt was her godmother, for whom Miss Firth may have stood proxy. Mr. Firth and his second wife were Branwell's godparents, while a close friend of Elizabeth Firth's, Fanny Outhwaite, daughter of a Bradford doctor, became Anne's second godmother. Emily's godparents were the Bradford relatives of her mother, the Fennels and the Morgans. The children thus carried with them into the very different world of Haworth early influences formed at Thornton that would still come to bear upon their adult life.

It was not surprising, therefore, that, upon the death of his wife in September 1821, Mr. Brontë should turn for consolation to the Thornton friends, and make Elizabeth Firth an offer of marriage. The fact that she refused him did not put an end to the friendship. Three years later she married the Revd. J. C. Franks, Vicar of Huddersfield, from whence she continued to take a practical and charitable interest in Mr. Brontë's children.[3]

The home to which Charlotte returned in the midsummer of 1825 was not the home she had left the year before. The deaths of Maria and Elizabeth caused not the only radical changes; the children's aunt, Miss

[1] Holgate, 'The Brontës at Thornton': *BST*, 1959.
[2] For fuller data concerning Elizabeth Firth, see Gérin, *Anne Brontë*, 1–16.
[3] On her honeymoon Mrs. Franks visited the little Brontës at Cowan Bridge, Sept. 1824: Firth Diaries, Sheffield Univ. Lib.

Branwell, whose presence had been necessitated by the death of their mother, was now a permanent inmate of the parsonage at Haworth. The children may or may not have divined the deeper reasons why, hitherto, her régime had been on a temporary footing: had Mr. Brontë succeeded in finding a second wife Miss Branwell would have returned to her native Cornwall, whose genial climate and genteel society she never ceased to regret. But none of Mr. Brontë's proposals (and he made three of them) met with a kind response; by the time Charlotte returned from Cowan Bridge he had given up all hopes of a remarriage, and Miss Branwell had become the permanent mistress of his house. The full effect of such an arrangement would only be felt later. That Miss Branwell had an uncertain temper and rigid notions on social and domestic conventions had already been apparent to the children; like the black silk gown, the lace cap, and 'front' of auburn curls, they made up their aunt's identity in their young eyes.

A view of Miss Branwell as seen by the parsonage servants has been preserved. Visited in old age by enthusiastic Americans, Nancy Wainwright, formerly Nancy Garrs, the children's nurse, described her in forceful Yorkshire idiom, as 'so crosslike an' fault findin' and so close, she ga'e us, my sister Sarah an' me, but a gill o' beer a day, an' she gi'e it to us hersel, did Miss Branwell, to our dinner, she wouldn't let us go to draw it oursel' in t' cellar. A pint a day, she gi'e us, that were half a pint for me an' half a pint for Sarah . . .'. In summing up the character of her late employer in one all-inclusive Yorkshire word, Nancy opined that Miss Branwell had been 'a bit of a tyke'.[1]

Charlotte must have felt the change in her father on her return home even more. He was no longer the same keen companionable Papa she had known before; the joyous ring had gone out of the Irish voice and, for the time at least, he was less disposed to delight the children with his tales. Thankful not to be constantly reminded of the gaps in the family circle, he diverted most of his energies out of the house upon his parish duties.

There were other changes: in place of kind Nancy and Sarah Garrs, the Thornton servants, an elderly woman had been engaged, Tabitha Aykroyd, whose immense importance to the children's happiness Charlotte could not yet foresee. 'Tabby' was a disciplinarian and had a rough tongue, and didn't hesitate on occasions, when a kind of bacchic frenzy informed her young charges, to think and say that 'yon

---

[1] Cortazzo: *BST* (1958), 227. Interview with Nancy Wainwright.

childer was mad'; but Tabby it was and not their aunt who supplanted the dead mother in their hearts.

Coming home to the depleted family circle, Charlotte had also to take fresh stock of those that remained—especially those from whom she had been separated for a year. Closest to her in age was Branwell, the only boy of the family—'little Bany' to himself—passionate and uncontrolled, violent in nursery games, but so inventive in his wilfulness, so avid a reader, so quick a learner that, despite the fifteen months separating them, Charlotte soon recognized in him her mental equal. To Branwell, the close partner in all her childish pursuits, she soon transferred the heart's allegiance once dedicated to Maria—though never so blindly. Bany was not perfect like Maria—and well Charlotte knew it from the start[1]—but her need to love was compelling and she made him the focal point of her existence. He was carroty-haired like their father, and there exists a series of tiny drawings of him by Charlotte, showing the tousled mop of hair hanging round a pinched and pointed face, the frilled shirt of the little boys of the period worn carelessly open at the neck, perhaps to convey the poetic character of the wearer, for before he could write at all Branwell was making rhymes and claiming for himself the name and style of poet.

At the return from Cowan Bridge Emily was still very young—just turned seven—and already bound by a twin-like sympathy of character to Anne, the baby of the family. Towards Anne Charlotte was at first inclined to adopt Branwell's contemptuous attitude: she was 'a queer little thing' who lisped and stuttered in her valiant attempts to keep pace with her elders, to read their books, and pronounce the difficult words they currently employed—often without knowledge of their meaning. In the quartette's new relationships after their elder sisters' deaths, Anne found a champion in Emily and Branwell in Charlotte, who was for many years to come his *alter ego*.

At no time did Miss Branwell accept the full responsibility for her nieces' education (which now ostensibly devolved on Mr. Brontë), but she was an adept at establishing a domestic time-table and seeing that children and servants alike stuck to it. Since even Anne was long past initiating into the rudiments of reading, writing, and arithmetic, Miss Branwell's training of her nieces was focused mainly upon two subjects: religion and sewing. The latter accomplishment was not easy in days when so many things were made at home—sheets, bolster-

---

[1] In 'Tales of the Islanders', 1829, Branwell figures as 'Little King', an imperious, unreliable, spoilt and lazy boy, given to unpredictable acts of violence.

cases, towels, and every article of female apparel from pelisses to shifts, as well as the gentlemen's frilled shirts, wrist-bands, and neckerchiefs. There are specimens of finest stitchery still preserved in the Brontës' old home. Remembering Charlotte's indifferent marks for 'working' on her arrival at Cowan Bridge, the eventual perfection she attained in every branch of sewing must be laid to her aunt's credit. Upon Emily the same admirable instructions seem not to have borne fruit, and Anne, long after reaching adult age and being herself a governess, was very dubious of 'what sort of a hand' she would make at turning 'a grey figured silk'.[1]

The need for close economy in that clerical household made the 'turning' of garments, the mending and altering to fit younger sisters with the elders' cast-offs, a constant task, even more than that of hemming long yards of calico for new night-shifts or frills to petticoats. Anne herself related in *Agnes Grey* how she acquired a knowledge of 'Worsted Work', required of most governesses, only after going out in the world. Embroidery in coloured silks—a lady's leisure occupation—both Charlotte and Anne practised without much enthusiasm but with sufficient skill to make saleable objects for the 'Jews Basket'. All three girls, like Maria and Elizabeth before them, completed a sampler by their tenth year. Charlotte's, composed of three lines of alphabet in capitals, two lines of small lettering, and a short text, appears to have been less arduous in execution than either Emily's or Anne's, composed throughout of a closely stitched biblical text. Charlotte's, finished on 20 June 1826, must have occupied the major part of her sewing lessons during the year immediately following her return from Cowan Bridge.

Miss Branwell instructed her nieces in these mysteries every afternoon in her large bedroom overlooking the garden, on the first floor of the parsonage, where she spent the greater part of her time. In all the twenty-one years of her residence at Haworth it is said she was never once seen in the village except at church; yet her presence, by a rigorous enforcement of punctuality in the ordering of domestic affairs, was made so apparent that all Haworth set its clocks by her routine.[2]

The girls were brought up to do house-work, as Emily's and Anne's diary-papers show; they were expected, for instance, to make their own beds and sweep the carpets. But fire-laying, grate-polishing, cooking, and laundry were not considered a lady's occupation—and

[1] AB Diary Paper, 31 July 1845.
[2] Gaskell, 124-5.

their aunt herself was not more jealous of her social status than the girls grew up to be. Not until Charlotte was 20 did an accident to Tabby lay any of these menial tasks upon her; and then, in her first attempts at ironing, she singed the sheets.

In her kitchen, where she reigned supreme, Tabby's office was no sinecure. The household bread was baked at home, as were all 'cakes and pastry', and sometimes there were three separate dinners to cook for the family—that meal being taken by Mr. Brontë and Miss Branwell in their several apartments, with separate dishes suited to their dyspeptic requirements. Mrs. Gaskell's accusations of vegetarian under-nourishment of the children were discredited by the discoveries of the girls' diary-papers.

'... We are going to have for Dinner', Emily noted on a November Monday morning, when the three girls had invaded Tabby's kitchen, more from bravado than a desire to help, 'Boiled Beef Turnips potatoes and apple-pudding . . .'; adding as the corollary to their disrupting presence '. . . the kitchen is in a very untidy state. . . .'[1] '. . . While I write this', recorded Charlotte, aged 12, 'I am in the kitchen of the Parsonage Haworth; Tabby, the servant, is washing up the breakfast things, and Anne my youngest sister (Maria was my eldest) is kneeling on a chair looking at some cakes which Tabby has been baking for us. Emily is in the parlour brushing the carpet. . . .'[2]

For the heavy household wash, always performed at home, Tabby was given help; a village girl was brought in for the day, and an outside 'wash-house' with copper was built by Mr. Brontë for the purpose. On the Monday morning for which she detailed the dinner Emily reported '. . . Sally Mosley is washing in the back kitchen . . .'.[1] As the six daughters of Mr. Brontë's sexton, John Brown, grew out of childhood, they became Tabby's chief adjutants in the house, Martha Brown beginning her long and faithful association with the parsonage at the age of 10.

By Miss Branwell's routine the girls, after making their beds and performing the light household tasks required of them, spent the remainder of the morning with Branwell in learning the lessons set by their father. With constant calls upon his time from his parish duties Mr. Brontë's short-cut to teaching his daughters was to set them a task—a portion of the Bible, of Mangnall's *Historical Questions*, of Lindley Murray's *Grammar*, of Goldsmith's *Geography*. But he very well

[1] EJB Diary Paper, 24 Nov. 1834: BPM.
[2] 'History of the Year 1829': BPM; Gaskell 55.

knew that when the lesson was learnt the text-book would hurriedly be exchanged for reading of a more stimulating character. Flesh of his flesh and bone of his bone, his children needed no enforcements to learning: they shared his appetite for knowledge.

The morning ended with a short walk before dinner, which was taken at 2 o'clock, very often with Tabby in the kitchen. After play in the garden or a walk on the moors in summer, the girls spent the afternoon as already mentioned, at their sewing in their aunt's room. On afternoons when Mr. Brontë was at home this dreary hour was transformed for the children by readings aloud, either from the weekly papers or from *Blackwood's*, intended principally by Miss Branwell to spare her brother-in-law's failing sight. The elders' heated discussions upon current topics (Miss Branwell, we are told, would 'tilt arguments against Mr. Brontë without fear')[1] were carried over into the ensuing tea-hour, usually taken downstairs in the parlour, adding further fuel to the children's already fierce partisan passion for politics, art, literature, and every other palpitating question of the day.

Just how palpitating those questions appeared to them is indicated by a record Charlotte wrote, at 12 years, upon the issues of the Catholic Emancipation Bill.[2]

... O those 3 months from the time of the Kings speech to the end! nobody could think speak or write of anything but the catholic question and the Duke of Wellington or Mr. Peel. I remember the Sunday when the Intelligence extraordinary came with Mr. Peels speech in it containing the terms on which the catholics were to be let in with what eagerness papa tore off the cover and how we all gathered round him and with what breathless anxiety we listened as one by one they were disclosed explained and argued upon so ably and so well and then when it was all out how aunt said she thought it was excellent and that the catholics [could] do no harm with such good security and I remember the doubts as to whether it would pass into the house of Lords and the prophesys that it would not and when the paper came which was to decide the question the anxiety was almost dreadful with which we listened to the whole affair—the opening of the doors . . . The Royal Dukes in their robes and the Great Duke in green sash and waistcoat the rising of all the peeresses when he rose the reading of his speech papa saying that his words were like precious gold and lastly the majority one to 4 in favour of the bill. . . .[3]

---

[1] Nussey: 'Reminiscences of CB', *Scribner's Mag.*, May 1871: *SLL* i. 102.
[2] Mrs. Gaskell 67, quoting Mary Taylor's evidence on CB's intense interest in politics ever since she was 5 yrs old'.
[3] CB, 'Tales of the Islanders', vol. 2, 1829: Berg Coll.

Paramount as was the influence of their father in shaping the children's tastes, such a familiarity with the events and great names in current affairs was not derived at second-hand from his reading of the weekly press; it came from the children's own enchanted reading over an unlimited field of literature, beginning with the monthly numbers of *Blackwood's Magazine*. These ranged over subjects as various as the late Napoleonic campaigns; the successive explorations into the interior of Africa; the literary scene dominated by the *Edinburgh* reviewers; the Memoirs of exiled French royalty; English Court news; art criticism; reviews of current exhibitions, etc. In article after article on these and related subjects in the *Blackwood's* issues of the 1820s the origin of the children's early enthusiasms and information is to be found. To John Wilson, *Blackwood's* editor, Branwell wrote many years later: '. . . I cannot express the heavenliness of associations Connected with such articles as Professor Wilson's, *read and re-read while a little child*, with all their poetry of language and divine flight into that visionary region of imagination which one very young would believe reality. . . . I speak so, Sir, because while a child 'Blackwood's' formed my chief delight. . . .'[1]

Few boys remembering their school-days in later life could write with such a recollected rapture of their lessons; to the Brontë children, however, such 'lessons' were the very stuff of life. In Mr. Brontë's library, small as it was, there were books enough to exercise the energy of eager minds and they had access to all of them. Besides Homer and Virgil in the original there were Milton's works, Johnson's *Lives of the Poets*, Thomson's *Seasons*, Goldsmith's *History of Rome*, Hume's *History of England*, Scott's *Life of Napoleon Bonaparte* (Branwell's earliest favourite), and, last but not least, the works of Byron, Southey, and Cowper. With Byron's works Charlotte was fully acquainted at 13; from *Childe Harold* and *Manfred* she quoted freely, which says something for Mr. Brontë's breadth of mind. They were also able to borrow books from the Heatons' library at Ponden House,[2] to which they had early access, and which accounts for their precocious knowledge of French history and literature and of the Elizabethan dramatists, and there were Mr. Brontë's subscription volumes from the Keighley Mechanics' Institute Library. Something of the range

---

[1] PBB to ed. of *Blackwood's*, 7 Dec. 1835; Oliphant, *Annals of a Publishing House*, 1897.
[2] Vide Catalogue of Ponden House Library, Heaton Collection, Cartwright Memorial Hall, Bradford.

of the children's reading can be grasped from this, and the origin
of incidents and allusions in their earliest writings can be traced.

Of their own earliest childish books Aesop's *Fables* and *The Arabian
Nights' Entertainments* appear to have been their favourites. Thousands
of children before and since the Brontës—Thackeray and Beckford
among them—read these books, but in few can they have generated so
lively a creative impulse. So intense was their immersion in a book that
they had only to read to identify themselves with the characters; from
this to *acting* the parts in dramatized reconstructions of the stories
was but a step (this they called 'establishing a play'), and then to add to
the original plots was a natural consequence of their tireless invention.
At the age of 12 Charlotte wrote:

Our Plays were established: Young Men June 1826; Our Fellows, July
1827; Islanders, December 1827. These are our three great plays, they are
not kept secret . . . the Young Men play took its rise from some wooden
soldiers Branwell had Our Fellows from Esops fables and the Islanders from
several events which happened I will sketch out the origin of our plays more
explicitly if I can. . . .
The origin of the O'Deays was as follows we pretended we had each
a large island inhabited by people 6 miles high the people we took out of
Esops fable Hay Man was my Cheif Man Boaster Branwell's, Hunter Anne's
and Clown Emily's our Cheif Men where 10 miles high except Emily's who
was only 4. . . .[1]

Examination of the old editions available to the children gives the
key to this somewhat cabalistic statement. The characters of 'Boaster'
(by which name Branwell signed several of his early tales), of 'Clown',
and the others appeared in the titles of the 1825 edition of Aesop's
Fables, in the translation of Samuel Croxall, D.D.—but not in other
editions. Branwell's momentous acquisition of a box of toy soldiers in
June 1826 is well-known. It provided the *dramatis personae* not only
for the children's 'Plays' of the 'Young Men' noted by Charlotte, but
for the lasting and significant invention—their 'Glass Town' literature.
From the names given the soldiers at the children's first rapturous
reception of them grew the characters that occupied their creative
energies for the next thirteen years. '. . . The truth respecting the
Young Men', wrote Branwell in his *History of the Young Men* in
December 1830,

is when I first saw them in the morning after they were bought, I carried
them to Emily Charlotte and Anne. They each took up a soldier, gave them

[1] CB, 'History of the Year 1829'; BPM.

names, which I consented to, and I gave Charlotte Twemy (Wellington) to Emily Pare (Parry) and to Anne Trott (Ross) to take care of them though they were to be mine and I to have the disposal of them as I would—shortly after this I gave them to them as their own. . . .

Emily's and Anne's heroes of the day were the explorers Captain Edward Parry and William Ross—and Branwell was mocking Anne's lisp in his spelling.[1] The wooden soldiers, acquired at the same time as the children's passion for the *Arabian Nights*, were incorporated into a magical background derived as much from the Arabian tales as from their current studies of the geography of Africa, with particular relation to the Guinea coast. The resultant amalgam, with the soldiers become explorers and adventurers into the interior of the Gold Coast, was the magical city of Glass Town—raised by the Genii of the *Arabian Nights*.[2] Tiny as were the children themselves, one wonders if the attraction of the Genii was not their gigantic stature; certainly the little Brontës revelled in the attribution of their supernal powers. To Branwell at 12 the power of the Genii was ubiquitous—though somewhat confused with that of the Body Snatchers, then much to the fore in the press reports of the trials of Burke and Hare. The following 'Song' is one of his many tributes to them:

> If you live by the sunny fountain
> If you live in the streets of a town
> If you live on the top of a mountain
> Or if you wear a crown
>   The Genii will meddle with you
>
> Think not that in your graves
> You will be quiet there
> For Genii come with spades
> To dig you up they dare
>   Genii will meddle with you
>
> Even if in your palaces—
> Among your Courteirs there
> The Genii meddle with you
> For mischeif is their care
>   Genii will meddle with you
>   etc., etc.[3]

---

[1] PBB, 'History of the Young Men,' Dec. 1830: BM.

[2] The edition of the *Arabian Nights* accessible to the Brontë children was a translation of the French text by Galland, pub. 1706 (the definitive was that of 1787).

[3] 'Branwell's Blackwood's Magazine', June 1829: BPM.

As with Beckford, upon whom an early reading of the *Arabian Nights* is said to have had momentous consequences (was not his Fonthill the equivalent of the Brontës' Glass Town?), the children's vision became imbued with the Arabian imagery. They moved in deserts of undulating sands, slept under palm trees, drank from fountains, were intoxicated with the scent of lotus and of lilies, erected thrones set with diamonds and rubies for themselves, from which they dictated the laws governing all their games. As ruling spirits, renamed Cheif Genius Tallii (Charlotte), Cheif Genius Brannii, Cheif Genius Emmii, and Cheif Genius Annii, they invested themselves with powers of life and death and of the restoration of life over the characters in their plays and stories, into which, as in the authentic *Arabian Nights*, they erupted in *propria persona* to intervene in desperate situations and to restore order when Chaos was come. On Charlotte the influence of this early belief in magical powers was deep and lasting; the effort to combat it became more than the adolescent's usual painful squaring with reality; the creative artist in her suffered a life-long struggle to overcome the lure of the fabulous, in which she had not only believed but *participated* in childhood.

Among her earliest stories is 'The Country of the Genii', written under the influence not only of the *Arabian Nights* but of the *Tales of the Genii* published in 1764 and purporting to be an authentic translation from the Persian by the British Ambassador, Sir Charles Morell, but in reality another literary hoax, in the style of the *Rowley Papers*, by a certain James Ridley. Passages like the following show Charlotte's indebtedness to Ridley's text:

[A party of Charlotte's heroes have landed in a strange country.]

. . . We were now about the middle of the desert. Nothing was to be seen far and near but vast plains of sand under a burning sun and cloudless sky. . . . We travelled a long way till the sun went down. . . . The night-wind had some what cooled the sands of the desert so that we walked with more ease than before; but now a mist arose. . . . As the mist cleared . . . the light grew more distinct till it burst upon us in almost insufferable splendour. Out of the barren desert arose a palace of diamonds, the pillars of which were ruby and emerald illuminated with lamps too bright to look upon. The Genius led us into a hall of sapphire in which were thrones of gold. On the thrones sat the princes of the Genii. . . . Around it stood genii and fairies whose robes were of beaten gold sparkling with diamonds. . . .[1]

[1] CB, 'Twelve Adventurers', 1829: Hodder, 1925.

In Ridley's passage we read:

> . . . as soon as they arrived at the Palace, Moang (the Genius in charge) led her little charges into a spacious Saloon, where on 28 Thrones of Gold sat the good race of the Genii; and, beneath, on carpets covering the whole saloon, were numberless of the lower class of Genii, each with 2 or more of the Faithful under their charge. . . .[1]

It was inevitable that between children growing and creating in such close collaboration the stream of influence affecting one should have its indirect influence upon the others. So, to the various influences shaping Charlotte's earliest tastes must be added the stream of influence affecting Branwell, which was predominantly French in origin, and that affecting Emily, which was predominantly Scots. To the latter taste Miss Branwell contributed in 1828 by a 'New Year's Gift' to her 'dear little Nephew and Nieces' of Scott's *Tales of a Grandfather*.[2]

Branwell's early readings of Scott's *Life of the Emperor Napoleon* and of Chateaubriand's *Travels through Greece and the Holy Land* awakened such an enthusiasm for everything French that for years he wrote under a French pseudonym, 'Young Soult'. He introduced French subject-matters into all his stories and claimed that they were 'published' in Paris, with editorial notes by 'Chateubriand'. Among Charlotte's youthful manuscripts is a page of her drawings of Branwell, drawn to illustrate a list of Napoleon's Marshals and relatives, with the prefix 'Young' to their names; which gives the obvious origin of his pseudonym—'Young Soult' being chosen from the list that included: 'Young Murat', 'Young Ney', 'Young Lucien Bonaparte', 'Young Eugène Beauharnais'. For *Old Soult*, Wellington's opponent in the Peninsular campaign, the children had a preference based on his chivalrous conduct towards Sir John Moore; and as Charlotte chose Wellington's sons, the Marquis of Douro and Lord Charles Wellesley, born 1807 and 1808 respectively, for her special heroes and pseudonyms, so Branwell chose Soult's for his.

In microscopic magazines written in imitation of *Blackwood's* Charlotte and Branwell collaborated in an intensive literary output for a couple of years (1829–31), during which they pooled every influence affecting their fertile minds. In 'A Frenchman's Journal' in one of Charlotte's magazines Branwell introduced himself thus: 'I am Alexander Soult the Rhymer son of the Great Marshal of that name—have you never heard me spoken of?' Again, in articles imitated from

---

[1] *Tales of the Genii*, London, 1764.
[2] Copy preserved in the BPM, Haworth.

Blackwood's 'Noctes Ambrosianae', which the children called 'Nights at Bravey's Inn', 'Young Soult, the Emperor Napoleon and Lucien Bonaparte, Wellington, Sir Edward Parry and Captain Ross' (the children's special heroes) are listed among the speakers assembled at supper. Further illustrative of the children's enthusiasm for everything French are the titles of Charlotte's tales and serials running through several numbers of their miniature magazines: 'The Enfant', 'The Adventures of Mon. Edouard de Crack', 'The Journal of a Frenchman', all of which are set in Paris with *dramatis personae* constantly in and out of the 'Thuillierys'.[1]

Everything that went to the making of books, the writing, illustrating, editing, sewing, and binding into paper covers, constituted these children's chief delight. What the acquisition of a new book meant to them, or the writing of a commentary on a favourite author, can still be felt today in deciphering the minute script of their miniature magazines. 'Sir,' Branwell addressed the Editor of his own 'Branwell's Blackwood's Magazine' for 1 July 1820—his spelling suffering somewhat from the excitement of the moment—

I write to accwaint you of a circumstance which has happened to me and which is of great importance to the world at large. On May 22 1829 the Cheif Genius Taly [Charlotte] came to me with a small yellow book in her hand—she gave it to me saying it was the POEMS of that Ossian of whom so much has been said about whose works could never be got. Upon a attentive perusal of the above said works I found they were most sublime and excellent I am engaged in publishing an edition of them. Quarto 3 vols with notes commentary etc. I am fully convinced that it is the work of OSSIAN who lived 1000 years ago—and of no other there is a most intense anxiety prevailing amongst literary men to know its contents in & about they shall be gratified for it will be published on the 1st July 1829. . . .

Further on in the same issue of the magazine, in the dialogue between famous men modelled on the *'Noctes Ambrosianae'*, the young editor returns to the theme of Ossian:

Young Soult. You have heard of Ossian's poems
Duke. I have
Lord Charles Wellesley. We should very much like to see them

[1] 'The Enfant', 13 July 1829: BPM. 'Adventures of Mon. Edouard de Crack.'
22 Feb. 1830: Harvard; 'Adventures of Ernest d'Alembert', New York, Pforzheimer Coll.

Bud (Branwell himself in yet another role). Very well to make a short cut
   the Genius Taly has made me a present of it
Lucien Bonaparte. Has she no doubt it will contain some passages worth
   remembering
Bud. It does I will read a few (reads)[1]

When barely 14 Charlotte catalogued her writings to date;[2] they
numbered already twenty-two, irrespective of the poems, dialogues,
and tales running through the issues of the 'Young Men's Magazine'
in which she collaborated with Branwell. If it be asked how children of
their ages came to have leisure and opportunity to write so much thus
early the answer must lie in the character of their father and in the
unchanging routine of their home. Thanks to its seclusion and to their
father's peculiar passion for letters, Charlotte was given a liberty to
evolve such as few children—and particularly her own contemporaries
—ever enjoyed. To the disaster of Cowan Bridge—after which there
could be no question of sending the girls away again to school—must
be attributed the precocious development of her talents. At no school
would Charlotte at that age have absorbed so many various and adult influences to shape her mind as she did at home playing with her little
sisters and brother. Typical of such an education was the opportunity
given her to evolve simultaneously upon two planes: a child still,
believing in fairies and the eastern genii, yet grasping the significance
of contemporary politics and taking an adult's interest in the world
about her. Its heroes, from Wellington downwards, were not mere
names, they were 'her friends', as she later claimed, as fully 'realized' as
the members of the home circle. It is in this respect that her childhood
was distinguished from that of other children. She did not turn away
from the real world in distaste; she hugged it to her heart, and integrated it into her dreams, investing the England of the early nineteenth century with all the magic of an *Arabian Nights*' entertainment.
Thus, as she grew, all the matter of which she gained knowledge became, like the old rusty lamp in the tale, a passport to fairyland.

Of the children's earliest processes of invention Charlotte left precious records, like that of the scene in Tabby's kitchen just two and a
half years after her return from Cowan Bridge.

The Play of the Islanders was formed in December 1827 in the following
manner.

   [1] 'Branwell's Blackwood's Magazine', 1 July 1829: BPM.
   [2] CB, 'Catalogue of my Books up to Aug. 3rd 1830': BPM.

One night about the time when the cold sleet and dreary fogs of November are succeeded by the snow storms, and high piercing winds of confirmed winter, we where all sitting round the warm blazing kitchen fire having just concluded a quarrel with Taby concerning the propriety of lighting a candle from which she came of victorious, no candle having been produced a long pause succeeded, which was at last broken by Bany saying, in a lazy maner I don't know what to do. This was re-echoed by E & A.

T. Wha ya may go t'bed
B. I'd rather do anything than that
C. Why are you so glum to-night? suppose we had each an island
B. If we had I would choose the Island of Man
C. And I would choose the Isle of Wight
E. The Isle of Aran for me
A. And mine should be Guernsey

We then chose who should be cheif men in our islands: Branwell chose John Bull, Astley Cooper, and Leigh Hunt; Emily, Walter Scott, Mr. Lockhart, Johnny Lockhart; Anne, Michael Sadler, Lord Bentinck, Sir Henry Halford. I chose the Duke of Wellington and sons, Christopher North and Co Mr. Abernethy. Here our conversation was interrupted by the, to us, dismal sound of the clock striking seven, and we where sumoned of to bed . . .[1]

Neither the 'dismal sound of the clock' nor the summons to bed, despite the momentary gloom they cast, could put an end to the day's delights. In the tiny nursery-bedroom Charlotte and Emily lay drowsing and adding new incidents to the scenes read or enacted during the day, directing from golden thrones with diamond canopies the morrow's campaigns. Noting down for future reference the 'establishment of our main plays' that they were not kept secret, Charlotte added the significant: 'Emily's and my bed plays were established the 1st December 1827, the others March 1828. Bed Plays mean secret plays: they are very nice ones . . .'[2] How the 'Bed Plays' operated she described elsewhere: 'A little while ago Emily and me one stormy night were going through the wood which leads to Strathfieldsays we saw by the light of the moon . . . the flashing of some bright substance . . . we heard a well known voice say O Arthur I wish you had never come what will my father say if he ever gets to know it and I am beginning to get very cold. . . .'[3] 'Emily and me' snugly laid in bed would appear to be

---

[1] CB's 'Tales of the Islanders', 1829: Berg Coll.
[2] CB, 'History of the Year 1829', Mar. 12: BPM.
[3] 'Tales of the Islanders', 1829, vol. 1.

frequently ranging the woods and moors by night, interposing just in the nick of time in many an adventure befalling the adored Night Friends—Arthur Augustus Adrian and Charles Florian Wellesley in particular.

On the morrow invention would proceed apace. Thus, by day and by night the ceaseless plot was spun. Creators of a fabulous universe, they were conscious of lacking nothing. For them life was a fairy-tale made up of magic hours.

THE VOICE OF CONSCIENCE

It must be a matter of wonder to any student of Brontë juvenilia to note the absence of all reference, either direct or indirect, to religious or clerical influences shaping their minds. This is the more striking because of the prodigal use they ultimately made of biblical allusions and quotations in their adult writings and correspondence. The knowledge of the Bible was there and early absorbed, as was to be expected of parsonage children. Yet their silence, on a subject occupying at least as much time as their other studies of history and literature, was complete.

In other children such a silence could be explained by a child's natural preference for frivolous subjects, by boredom, carelessness, or oblivion. But the little Brontës were the least frivolous of children, and their memory phenomenal. The explanation lies, rather, in the too great hold that religion took upon their inflammable imaginations, in the terrors it awakened, in the sorrows it recalled. In Charlotte's case, to the early deaths of her mother and sisters were added the harrowing experiences of Cowan Bridge.

The children's early religious training was in the hands of their aunt. Its influence exercised a far greater and more lasting hold than any subsequent teaching, even the far more enlightened and hopeful teaching of their father. By its deep impress on hypersensitive imaginations, it shocked, it frightened, it allured. It did everything, in short, but warm and comfort. Their response was to suppress the emotions it aroused, rather than to resist the teaching openly. They drove all thought of it underground. There it coiled, a black Cocytus, from which they withdrew their shuddering gaze. It is notable that three of the young Brontës underwent a severe adolescent crisis of religious melancholia, whose explanation lay not in their immediate circumstances but in causes closely connected with the religious training of their childhood.

From every reference it plainly appears that Miss Branwell's influence was repressive, her religion joyless and narrow, her outlook morbid. Lacking in vitality herself, she shared few of youth's illusions.

Bent on doing her duty by her nieces, she prepared them for a life devoid of pleasures, rather than for a life of self-expression. That heredity
should have sown seeds of genius in these perplexing children was a
freak of Fortune for which she was unprepared; she saw the 'wildness'
in their eyes, and even confided to the servants that she was alarmed
by what she saw—but understood nothing of it.[1]

Miss Branwell's religion was a joyless exercise, tinged by the melancholy of her own dry temperament, and so devoid of any warming
flame that when Anne, as an adolescent girl, fell ill at school and asked
for the comfort of a Moravian minister she had to confess to him that
religion had hitherto been presented to her as a Law to be obeyed, not
as an impulse of Love.[2] By precept and example Miss Branwell succeeded only in implanting in the malleable minds of her little nieces and
nephew a haunting sense of sin and dread of judgement that remained
long after their childhood. It left Anne, indeed, in permanent doubt
of her salvation; Branwell, scoff as he might, in a maze of terror;
Charlotte, during the years of adolescence at least, in a state of torment,
daring neither to indulge her dearest passion, creative writing, nor to
maintain hope in a personal forgiveness of sins. Calvinism, by her
own avowal wrung from her at 20, was the origin of this despair.
'. . . I am uncertain that I have ever felt true contrition . . .', she confided in her closest friend, 'smitten at times to the heart with the conviction that—ghastly Calvinistic doctrines are true, darkened in short,
by the very shadow of Spiritual Death! If Christian perfections be
necessary to Salvation, I shall never be saved . . .'[3] And again: '. . . I feel
in a strange state of mind still; gloomy but not despairing. I keep
trying to do right . . . I abhor myself, I despise myself—if the Doctrine
of Calvin be true I am already an outcast . . .'[4]

The poems of Branwell and Anne and the letters of Charlotte bear
painful witness to the harvest of unhappiness that their aunt's early
teaching left behind. Of Charlotte's ultimate reaction to the harshness
of such a creed, an eloquent commentary was left by her school-friend
Mary Taylor, who recorded of her: 'She had a larger religious tolera-
tion than a person would have who had never questioned, and *her
manner of recommending religion was always of offering comfort, not
fiercely enforcing a duty . . .*'[5]

[1] Chadwick 68.   [2] *BST* (1896), 26–27.
[3] CB to EN, 6 Dec. 1836: *W & S* i. 148.
[4] CB to EN, 1836. (*W & S*, No. 48): BPM.
[5] Mary Taylor, Reminiscences of CB: *SLL*, i. 118.

Immeasurably the worst effect of this training was to divide the young Brontës within themselves. From this division of soul Charlotte in particular was to be a victim all her life. The voice of conscience, however tardily roused, was to prove the most unrelenting of tyrants towards the creative artist she knew herself to be. The conflict of the two elements warring within her to tear her soul was made worse, no doubt, by the suppression of the religious experience of childhood. Rebel as she often would, she recognized the validity of the rival claims, and submitted to the dual tyranny. The urge to create was admittedly the dearest and strongest of tyrannic powers, the service of which brought her such delight that its excess rebuked her, and delivered her back into the thraldom of her *other* tyrant, Conscience. Certainly one of the lasting effects of Miss Branwell's religious training was to make her nieces extremely reserved about their beliefs—a reserve that may well have added further to their unhappiness, since it left even their father unaware of what tormented them.[1]

Mr. Brontë's position upon the heated debates of the day—Election and Reprobation—was made quite clear in sermons and letters, in one of which in particular he expressed his horror of the 'appalling doctrine of personal election and reprobation'.[2] In seeking a curate to work with him he was eloquent in refusing to work with a man who held Calvinistic tenets. In spite of his sorrows, Mr. Brontë preached a hopeful doctrine, and it was not from him that the children inherited the dark and gloomy creed in which they grew up.

So strong an impression was not achieved, it must be admitted, on Miss Branwell's side, by personal influence alone; much more potent were the children's readings in her complete set of the *Methodist Magazine*, which was sent after Mrs. Brontë from Penzance, salvaged from shipwreck on the way to Liverpool, and stained with the salt waves of the gales of 1812—a circumstance calculated to entice young readers with romantic minds, had the contents not drawn them irresistibly.

There was much curious reading in these magazines and selections from the religious verse of the last thirty years—Cowper's in particular —which permanently influenced their own versification. But what impressed the children most were the miraculous extravagant and supernatural tales appearing in a large proportion of the numbers. In

---

[1] For further data concerning Miss Branwell's religious outlook and influence on the Brontë children, see Gérin, *Anne Brontë* (1959), 28-39.

[2] Revd. P. Brontë's letter to Revd. J. C. Franks, 10 Jan. 1839: *Bookman* Oct. 1904. See further, T. P. Bunting, *Life of Jabez Bunting*, 197, note 1.

whatever Charlotte read at the time, it was the fabulous element she sought and integrated into her earliest writings. Looking back in wonder, after she was grown up, at her early infatuation with the Methodist literature, she wrote of the 'mad Methodist Magazines, full of miracles and apparitions, of preternatural warnings, ominous dreams and frenzied fanaticism . . .' But the miracles, the apparitions, and the warnings had been food and drink to her in her childhood and romantic youth; as she confessed in *Shirley* '. . . in her childhood she had extracted all the honey from them and found them tasteless now . . .' But *without* the apparitions and the preternatural warnings, it must be remembered, there would have been no ghostly nun in *Villette* and no disembodied voice in *Jane Eyre*.[1]

Interspersed among the miracles there were warnings of another character which left a more lasting dread. In a letter on 'The Absolute Eternity of the Torments of Hell' published in the *Methodist Magazine* for September 1801, Charlotte can have read of the proofs, based upon examination of the Scriptures, that there is no intimation of the least remission of the damned: 'This truth, therefore,' the editor added, 'awful as it is, we are bound in duty to declare . . .' And again, in the April issue of 1810, she might read:

> . . . All men are not created to the same end; but some are preordained to eternal life, others to eternal damnation. So, according as every man was created for the one end or the other . . . he was elected i.e. predestined to life or reprobated . . . to damnation. . . . Since salvation is impossible except to the elect none, before they are confident of their salvation, have any certain ground for believing that their salvation be even so much as possible. . . .

In recurrent crises of her adolescence these and similar tenets, read in childhood and brooded on in secret, took a veritable hold upon her outlook on life. At 20 she had to confess '. . . I have always taken a clouded and repulsive view of religious matters'.[2] The issue eluded in childhood was only deferred; it shook her for years.

Without these readings in the *Methodist Magazine* it is also possible that, moorland child as she was, she would not have been so observant of signs and portents in the weather, of which later she made such characteristic use in her novels. With her quicksilver temperament (she acknowledged the effect of being born in April, 'the month of cloud and sunshine'), Charlotte responded to every variation of wind and storm as surely few writers have ever done; her observation of

---

[1] *Shirley*, ch. 22.   [2] CB to EN, 1836: *W & S* i. 140.

the disturbances of Nature was exceptionally sharp, and must have owed something to her early readings of the *Methodist Magazine*.

On the practical side Miss Branwell's training of her nieces showed real insight into their needs. She knew her brother-in-law's circumstances well enough to guess that, in default of husbands, the girls would have to support themselves in life. At that period they had no alternative but to become teachers or governesses. To that end she bent her best endeavours to form in them habits of regularity and abstinence, which alone would stand the trial of inconsiderate and exacting employers.

In all fairness to Miss Branwell it must be said that whilst training them to accept a life of abnegation she hoped that better fortune might yet come their way, and with unobtrusive economy set aside year by year a sum for their benefit so that, when she died she was able to leave each of them—and a niece in Cornwall—something like £350 apiece. On more than one occasion during their youth Miss Branwell put her hand in her pocket for her nieces and nephew, and without her £100 loan Charlotte and Emily could not eventually have gone to Brussels.

For all these benefits her nieces were thankful to her; perhaps above all for the sense of order and punctuality she inculcated, since by nature they were untidy and careless—careless, that is, of all things not related to their secret passion for creative writing. Of that secret, shared among themselves with fanatical dedication, Miss Branwell had, of course, no inkling.

Robust Methodism,[1] as wholesome as it was engaging, the children met in Tabby, the servant engaged by Mr. Brontë as an economy to replace the two girls from Thornton. In her thirty years of loyal service to the family at the parsonage Tabby proved a treasure indeed. Her age on entering the family was 54, an attraction to children with their inquiring minds, for her memories reached back to times already departed, when everyday occurrences were invested with romance. Tabby remembered the days when the wool (which, with the stone-quarries, represented the livelihood of the village) was carried by packhorses with jangling bells on their bridles, along the Roman Way into Lancashire, across the hump-backed bridges spanning the becks. Tabby had known the 'hollows' before the building of the

---

[1] Tabby was a member of the Keighley Methodist Circuit, as the Registers for 1798–1825 show.

new mills, whose high chimneys had already become landmarks by the Brontës' day.

In her tales, where resentment yet burnt at the disfigurement of a beautiful landscape and the abolition of a centuries-old way of life, Tabby became an unconscious poet, filling the hills and woods and streams with an anthropomorphic life in which she believed with all the force of her good sense and rustic piety. In the golden age before the mills had come, there had been fairies by the beck-side in the hollows, and on certain mornings, when the milk-white mist overhanging the valleys cleared away, the traces of their midnight rings were clearly seen.

In the ears of children like the Brontës this was the language of enchantment—and of truth—to which their eager minds and fervent hearts went out in rapture. How Tabby's descriptions carried complete conviction can be seen by the semblance the child Charlotte gave the fairies, in her 'Tales of the Islanders' (written at 12)—their 'wands wreathed with ivy, by virtue of which they ruled the hearts of mortals . . .'[1]

Charlotte confessed the influence of those tales in the valedictory words of *Shirley*, when the nostalgia for her own vanished youth seemed to take the pen from her hand and write in her place, write even in Tabby's dialect:

'. . . I can tell,' says Martha the servant, '. . . where there was neither mill— nor cot nor hall . . . within 2 miles . . . I can tell, one summer evening fifty years syne, my mother coming running in just at the edge of dark, almost flayed [terrified] out of her wits, saying she had seen a fairish in Fieldhead Hollow; and that was the last fairish that ever was seen on this country side (though they've been heard within these forty years). A lonesome spot it is —and a bonnie spot—full of oak-trees and nut-trees. It is altered now. . .'[2]

Tabby could tell them tales bearing on a different aspect of Haworth's past: tales of the 'great and good Mr. Grimshaw', friend of the Wesleys and champion of all the Methodists in the north. He had been incumbent of the village for over twenty years and his death in 1763 had occurred less than ten years before Tabby's birth. Nothing in his life and ministry, packed with romantic incidents as they were, quite equalled the drama of his death and burial as Tabby related them. In the midst of a cholera epidemic, when all the local gentry fled and urged him to do the same, Grimshaw stuck by his people and died in

---

[1] 'Tales of the Islanders', Third Volume. Berg Coll.   [2] *Shirley*, ch. 37.

their midst. When his Will was opened it was found he had ordered all matters regarding his funeral. So great had been his love for his dead wife, buried long since at Luddenden, ten miles across the moors, that he directed that he should be carried there and laid beside her, no matter what the time of year and the impediments. As a child Tabby must have heard the tale from eye-witnesses on many a winter's night, and certain it is that Emily Brontë had not forgotten it when she brought Heathcliff, by an exercise of superhuman will, to lie by Cathy's side.

Nothing but good came to the children through Tabby's advent. She fed them generously, walked with them on the moors, cared for their frail bodies while, undoubtedly, not sparing their souls from wholesome admonitions. There would be many a night on which she reminded a naughty child of the pains of Hell, but there was nothing very fearsome in Tabby's threats and the Haworth dialect always provoked their merriment. For all her grumbling, they knew her to be their true friend.

The sanity of Tabby's influence could do much to counteract their aunt's while the children were little. The will to live that had brought Charlotte through the ordeal of Cowan Bridge could vigorously dispel the fear to die. Her very childhood was her strongest armour against the threat of judgement. With growth would come doubts; but a child's integrity of purpose is undivided. It is not surprising that Charlotte put into a child's mouth the retort direct to the forces of damnation— inevitably associated for her with the figure of Carus Wilson. In the long struggle ahead between the creative and destructive forces within her, at no time would Charlotte so uphold her right to be herself as in childhood. It was in perfect adherence to truth and her own experience that she painted the scene between Jane Eyre and Brocklehurst.

'Do you know where the wicked go after death?' began the catechism.
'They go to Hell . . .'
'What must you do to avoid it?'
'I must keep in good health, and not die.'[1]

Not so would Charlotte the adolescent have answered—even less the mature woman—but the artist remembered and unerringly recaptured the undivided courage of childhood. Life would never be so straightforward again.

[1] *Jane Eyre*, ch. 4.

CHAPTER IV

'THE BURNING CLIME'[1]

IF modern readers of the Brontë novels are struck by the intensity of the heroines' feelings, how much more were contemporary readers taken aback by the power and freedom of the treatment of love by writers whose identity, though unknown, was strongly suspected of being feminine? For what, in the final analysis, was *Wuthering Heights* but the apotheosis of love? and what the motivation of Currer Bell's novels, if not the *expectation of love*? The explanation of this temperamental kinship permeating the Bell novels lay not merely in the *fact* of their relationship and genius, but in the highly charged atmosphere in which they grew up; an atmosphere to which they became so accustomed that they could not afterwards live in any other without heartbreak, or without falling physically ill.

To understand the later Charlotte, it is vital to examine what constituted this peculiar atmosphere of the Brontës' youth. At 22 Charlotte began to realize that the atmosphere in which she had grown up, which had generated the excitement and heat of the phantasmal world of her childhood—the 'Burning clime' as she called it—was a serious threat to even a moderate expectation of happiness in a workaday world. Bravely she determined to combat its power, as if aware that the flame if unchecked would overpower her. Every influence of her formative years had fanned it, and try as she might there remained a furnace smouldering inside her, perpetually ready to leap into flame. Something of the vibration of intense heat that is visible to the naked eye in a scorching summer day would always palpitate from the pages of Charlotte Brontë. This quality of heat, which George Moore[2] noted as characteristic of Anne's writing, was common to all four Brontës and was generated in their youth through every extraneous influence acting on ultrareceptive senses and passionate hearts.

That such an emotional power-house existed within the confines of their father's parsonage was never suspected either by the elders of the

[1] From the fragment of an Angrian MS., *c.* 1839: BPM (Bonnell Coll. No. 125).
[2] George Moore, *Conversations in Ebury Street*, 1930.

family or by the children's teachers. Charlotte's girlhood has, indeed, been generally considered as lacking in all outside stimuli, and painfully circumscribed by the remote situation of her father's ministry in a moorland village. Mrs. Gaskell,[1] deploring the lack of cultivated feminine society in which the Brontë girls grew up, had no inkling to what an extent the echoes of the contemporary world reached Haworth Parsonage. Through every channel by which the mind is fed or the arts and fashions of an age disseminated, the young Brontës received the culture of their post-Napoleonic world in astounding measure. The extent, indeed, to which Charlotte was a child of her age can only become evident when the music, books, and pictures on which she fed her imagination are examined. It is essential to remember that her childhood spanned the 1820s and early 1830s—the height of the Romantic Movement in literature, art, and music—if the emotional ferment in which she passed from childhood to youth is to be understood.

Not only in serious periodicals, like *Blackwoods*, *Frasers*, and the *Edinburgh Magazine*, but also in the fashionable 'Annuals' just reaching England, the poetry of a period rich in exotic themes was poured into the receptive hearts and eager minds of the young Brontës. The anapaests of Byron were echoing yet as they emerged from childhood; the tamer metres of his emulators, the Moores, the Hunts, the Campbells, and the Southeys still perpetuated the passion and the pity of a love which, once enthroned as the supreme object of literature, was not easily displaced. Whether in the *Bride of Abydos* or the *Bride of Lammermoor*, in poetry and prose the passion of love was the constant theme placed before Charlotte and Branwell Brontë, who were allowed to read anything they wished.

They drank, unsuspicious of the poison lying hidden in the bottom of the cup. What could be more captivating than the imagery, part Gothic, part eastern Mediterranean, with which the followers of Byron decorated their romantic tales, or more fascinating than the heroes disguised as monks or pirates, and the heroines, swathed in their Albanian scarves, listening to whispered incitements to love under a moon suspended always at the full over a desolate and rocky shore? The pictorial aspect of this literature first reached the young Brontës through the new medium of the 'Annuals', whose engravings —or 'embellishments' as they were called—supplied a real craving in Charlotte's nature. She was, it must be remembered in passing, more sensitive to the plastic arts than her sisters and the importance to her

[1] Gaskell 33.

evolution of just such a stimulus as these romantic engravings cannot be over-estimated. Her greatest quality as a writer would ultimately be in the visual power of her descriptions. A token of her ardent pursuit of Ideal Beauty is to be found in the fragment in which she set down at 13 the 'List of the Painters whose Works I wish to see'. Her subsequent friend, Mary Taylor, reported of her also at 13 how 'Whenever an opportunity offered of examining a picture or cut of any kind she went over it piecemeal, with her eyes close to the paper, looking so long that we used to ask her "what she saw in it?" She could always see plenty and explained it very well.'[1]

The 'Annuals', already popular in Germany, were first introduced on to the English market by the Swiss engraver Rudolph Ackermann for the Christmas of 1822. He had already caused a furore by his illustrated 'Histories of the Universities of Oxford' (1814) and 'Cambridge' (1815), and with a special eye to pictorial reproduction he published his 'Forget Me Not: A Christmas and New Year's Present for 1823', with every attraction of binding and presentation.

The first of a whole spate of successors, the charming album measuring only $3\frac{1}{2} \times 5\frac{1}{2}$ inches, encased in its own protective box upon which was reproduced the design of the cover, was 'embellished' with twelve engravings and contained prose and verse selections from the fashionable authors and poets of the day. A luxury article, it yet sold at 12s., and was so instant a success that it was rapidly copied by other enterprising publishers and, in the immediate years following its first appearance, was followed by a score of others. Their titles were romantic, as was their intention, which was to convey to the recipient the homage of the donor; for these gracious little volumes were particularly directed towards the feminine public, as gifts from their masculine admirers.

'Friendship's Offering', 'The Keepsake', 'The Gem', 'The Amulet', 'The Literary Souvenir' were among some of the most successful titles of the 1820's. The demand for them was so great that in the first week of publication 'Friendship's Offering' sold 5,000 copies and had hurriedly to reprint 30,000 more. Not only fashionable society adopted the 'Annuals'; in the course of the 20s the sale for them became general, spread from the capital to the provinces and into every polite home, where, among other places, copies found their way into Haworth Parsonage.

As Thackeray described in *Pendennis*,[2] the attraction of the 'Annuals'

---

[1] MT, Recollections of CB: *SLL* i. 81.
[2] *Pendennis*, ch. 31, p. 307, ed. Smith, Elder, 1898.

was the engravings, around which a great part of the text was composed. The co-operation of such fashionable portrait painters as Westall and engravers like William Finden assured the early successes of the enterprise, but in time it was John Martin who, of all contemporary artists, became the most closely associated with the 'Annuals'.

The fact is of importance and has a direct bearing on the creative development of the Brontë children, upon whom Martin's imagery was to have a decisive influence. The character of Martin's paintings, representing vast perspectives of the lost cities of the ancient world— Babylon, Nineveh, the Cities of the Plain, Pompeii, seen at the apocalyptic hour of their destruction—satisfied and corresponded to a craving for the grandiose in Branwell and Charlotte Brontë. In his pictorial presentation of the biblical scenes of their early reading, the scale of the world was enlarged for them. The inordinate *feeling* awakened by the reading of Byron could alone be satisfied in the framework of a universe as conceived by Martin; so encompassed, their fervent hearts and overheated minds admitted of no limitations upon their imaginative powers; in this heroic world they alone were of a calibre to act their own heroes.

Between the years 1826 and 1837 Martin supplied twenty-seven designs from his pictures for the 'Annuals', several of which were known to the Brontë children and copied by them. Branwell's watercolour of Martin's 'Queen Esther' (published in the 'Forget Me Not' of 1830–1 and copied by Branwell in December 1830) and of Martin's 'The Hermit' can still be seen at the Brontë Parsonage Museum.

In 'The Keepsake' for 1828 appeared the engraving of Martin's 'Sadak in search of the Waters of Oblivion' illustrating a scene from Sir Charles Morell's 'Tales of the Genii', a subject already known to Charlotte from her previous reading. It drew a description from her pen the following April (when she turned 13) which, when compared with the illustration, shows not only her keen observation of pictorial detail, but, thus early, her command of language. '. . . I found myself encompassed by clouds and darkness. But soon this roar of mighty waters fell on my ear, and I saw some clouds of spray arising from high falls that rolled in awful majesty down tremendous precipices, and then foamed and thundered in the gulf beneath as if they had taken up their unquiet abode in some giant's cauldron . . .'[1]

This close and early scanning of every available picture is traceable

[1] CB, 'An Adventure in Ireland', 28 Apr. 1829: Hodder, 1925.

throughout Charlotte's juvenilia. The following passage from her 'The Search after Happiness', written at $13\frac{1}{2}$, is recognizably 'after' Martin's 'Deluge' (of which an engraving hung on the parsonage wall).

They were upon the top of a rock which was more than a thousand fathoms high. All beneath them were liquid mountains tossed to and fro' with horrible confusion, roaring and raging with a tremendous noise, and crowned with the waves of foam. All above them was a mighty firmament in one part covered with black clouds from which darted huge and terrible sheets of lightning. In another part an immense globe of light, like silver and hanging in the sky; and several smaller globes which sparkled exceedingly, surrounded it. . . .[1]

Mrs. Gaskell saw detailed notes made by Charlotte at 13 descriptive of the illustrations in the 1829 issue of 'Friendship's Offering' and commented that they showed 'How she had early formed those habits of close observation and patient analysis of cause and effect, which served so well in after-life as handmaids to her genius . . .'[2]

It was a quality, incidentally, so sufficiently rare among writers, as to receive recognition from one of the world's greatest modern painters, Van Gogh, who later instanced 'Ellis and Currer Bell' as being 'as potent in their plastic styles as Herkomer, or Fildes, or Israels . . .'[3]

Throughout the 1820s Martin's pictures were discussed and reviewed in the current periodicals, *Blackwood's*, *The Edinburgh*, *The Examiner*, *The European Magazine*, etc., as well as in the 'Annuals'; to these the Brontë children had access at the Keighley Mechanics' Institute of which their father was a member and from where they regularly borrowed books. Whether seen or described, Martin's pictures established a dominion over their childish imaginations and supplied a permanently splendid backcloth to their voluminous early writings.

The conclusive evidence of their close knowledge of Martin's masterpieces is to be found in the Catalogue of the Sale executed in the Brontës' old home on the death of Mr. Brontë in 1861 in which are listed four of Martin's engravings of the 1820s, 'Belshazzar's Feast', 'Joshua arresting the Sun', 'The Deluge', 'The Passage of the Red Sea'. The presence of these engravings on the walls of their home accounts for a distinctive characteristic of the children's 'Glasstown' sequence of tales;

[1] CB, 'The Search after Happiness', 17 Aug. 1829: BM.
[2] Gaskell 56.
[3] *Van Gogh Letters*, 38: Constable (1936).

THE FALL OF BABYLON, by John Martin

their very setting indeed is thus seen to be directly due to Martin's vast architectural perspective, to his 'Cyclopian pillars, the long vistas of terraces and towers', as becomes only too apparent when comparing the salient features of 'Glass Town' with 'Belshazzar's Feast', 'The Fall of Babylon', and 'The Fall of Nineveh' in particular.[1]

Charlotte herself gave a clue to the city's origin when she wrote that 'it bore the character of a dream or gorgeous fiction . . . few believed in its existence. It seemed as the cities of old: Nineveh and Babylon with the temples of their Gods . . .'.[2] In another allusion she wrote that one of the great features of their Glass Town was 'the Tower of Babylon'. The Tower of Babel featured in Martin's 'Fall of Babylon' and became 'The Tower of All Nations' in the children's stories, remaining a constant landmark in them over the years.

The significant features of 'Glass Town' were established in Charlotte's earliest descriptions of it: '. . . The city was lying in its splendour and magnificence surrounded by the broad stream of the Guadima. The palace was majestically towering in the midst of it, and all its pillars and battlements seemed in the light of the moon as if they were transformed into silver by the touch of a fairy's wand.'[3]

In a later yet still recognizably Martinian description of the city she apostrophizes it as 'The Queen of the Earth, who looks down on her majestic face mirrored in the noble Niger, and sees the far reflection of her valley and turrets caught by the flashing Guadima and flung with beauty unimaginable *on the glass that her harbour gives her* . . .'.[4]

'Glass Town' was without doubt an amalgam of the battlemented cities recurring in Martin's biblical scenes, with their hanging gardens and glassy river, their high-piled Assyrian terraces, massy gates, and colonnaded vistas. Charlotte herself, in a water-colour drawing of 'Glass Town', patently copied from a Martin original, blended the salient characteristics of them all, acknowledging the origin of the fabulous landscape of their tales.[5]

The country of the children's 'secret plays' had been recognizably 'lifted' from the *Arabian Nights* to begin with; Charlotte had not

---

[1] Catalogue of the Sale of Household Effects held at Haworth Parsonage, 1 Oct. 1861. John Cragg, Auctioneer: BPM. See also below Additional Notes.

[2] 'Albion and Marina', Oct. 1830.

[3] 'The Search after Happiness', 1829.

[4] For features of Martin's pictures especially influencing the Brontë juvenilia see Additional Notes.

[5] Professor A. L. Rowse (*The English Past: Evocations of Persons and Places* [1951], 157, 161) was the first to connect CB's 'Glass Town' drawings with Martin's pictures.

hesitated to call the scene of her first story 'The Country of the Genii'. Because Branwell acquired a box of twelve wooden soldiers it became 'The Country of the Twelves'—though still dominated by the Arabian Genii—with themselves playing the four permanent heroic roles named after Wellington, Napoleon, and the explorers Parry and Ross. Because of their readings of the explorations up the Niger of Mungo Park and their awakened interest in the coast of Guinea and the Ashantee country, Africa was substituted for Arabia. Now, under the impact of Martin's pictures, a city of barbaric splendour was created by the children for its capital, from which in due course a whole colonial empire spread, with farflung provinces each with its own smaller Glass Towns for capitals, called after the heroes of their games: Wellington's Glass Town, Parry's Glass Town, etc., to which the overall title of the Great Glass Town Confederacy was given.

Any reader of Charlotte's and Branwell's earliest writings must be struck by the structural reality of their architectural descriptions, the recurring landscapes, the recognizable *landmarks*, that gives to the whole such an air of solidity and permanence and is derived from the inspiration of Martin's pictures on their walls. The only change the years brought to the initial conception of the children's empire was to its title. As their studies progressed it pleased them to show off their learning and to call 'Glass Town' 'Vereopolis' and finally 'Verdopolis'. 'I have nothing to say,' wrote the 14-year-old Charlotte in a new serial called 'Visits in Vereopolis', 'except that Verreopolis means Glass Town being compounded of a Greek and French word to that effect, and that I fear the reader will find this the dullest and dryest book I have ever written . . .'. Of Verdopolis she would still be writing as a girl of twenty. Wemyss-Reid records how the image of a bright and beautiful city had hung before Charlotte's eyes since childhood when, after a first reading of 'Pilgrim's Progress' and, hearing constantly from the servants what a fine town Bradford was, she set off one day quite alone to find it. Though fatigue and fear overtook her long before she reached her goal, the resolution to reach it never quite abandoned her.[1] When she read of Paris as a little girl, she felt that she must see it 'or perish'.[2] The ideal persisted and haunted her into adult life, when an impulse stronger than reason drove her to Brussels to satisfy her hunger for great art and beautiful buildings.

[1] Wemyss-Reid, *Charlotte Bronte: A Monograph* (1877), 24–25.
[2] 'Adventures of Mon. Edouard de Crack', 1830: BPM.

Only, perhaps, because Glass Town derived from Babylon, Nine-veh, and the other departed cities of the ancient world, did Charlotte once contemplate its destruction. This was when she was 15 in a poem patently inspired by Byron's 'Sennacherib' and under the strong im-pression of Martin's 'Fall of Nineveh', about which she had read a critical and analytical description in *Blackwood's* for July 1828. The poem, for all that it owes to other works of art, contains lines of genuine poetry: already in her teens the visual arts had power to provoke an authentic artistic response.

The Trumpet hath Sounded

The Trumpet hath sounded, its voice is gone forth
From the plains of the south to the seas of the north
The great ocean groaned & the firm mountains shook
& the rivers in terror their channels forsook
The proud eagle quailed in her aerial dome
The gentle dove flew to her bowery home
The antelope trembled as onward she sprung
When hollow & death-like the trumpet-blast rung
It was midnight deep midnight & shrouded in sleep
Men heard not the roar of the terror struck deep
Nor the peal of the trumpet still sounding on high
They saw not the flashes that brightened the sky
All silent & tomb-like the great city lay
And fair rose her towers in their moonlight aray
'Twas the ruler of Spirits that sent forth the sound
To call his dread legions in myriads around

They heard him & from land and wave
The genii armies sprung
Some came from dim green ocean wave
Where thousand gems are flung

Some from the forests of the west
'Mid dark shades wandering
A giant host of winged forms
Rose round their mighty King

Some from the chill & ice-bound North
All swathed in snowy shrouds
With the wild howl of storms came forth
Sailing in compact clouds

The gentler fays in bright bands flew
    From each sweet woodland dell
All broidered with the violet blue
    & wild-flowers drooping bell

A sound of harps was on the blast
    Breathing faint melody
A dim light was from distance cast
    As their fair troop drew nigh

And mingling with stern genii forms
    Their tiny shapes are seen
Bright gleaming mid the gloom of storms
    Their gems & robes of green

The hall where they sat was the heart of the sky
And the stars to give light stooped their lamps from on high
The noise of the host rose like thunder around
The heavens gathered gloom at the hoarse sullen sound
No mortal may farther the vision reveal
Human eye cannot peirce what a spirit would seal
The secrets of Genii my tongue may not tell
But hoarsely they murmured bright city farewell
Then melted away like a dream of the night
While their palace evanished in oceans of light
Far beneath them the city lay silent and calm
The breath of the night-wind was softer than balm
As it sighed o'er its gardens & mourned in its bowers
And shook the bright dew drops from orient flowers
But still as the breeze on the myrtle groves fell
A voice was heard wailing bright city farewell
The morning arose o'er the far distant hill
And yet the great city lay silent and still
No chariot rode thunderous adown the wide street
Nor horse of Arabia impetuous & fleet
The river flowed on to the foam-crested sea
But unburdened by vessel its waves murmured free
The silence is dreadful. O city arise!
The sun is ascending the arch of the skies
Mute mute are the mighty & chilled is their breath
For at midnight passed o'er them the angel of death
The King & the peasant, the lord & the slave
Lie entombed in the depth of one wide solemn grave

Now Ruin daemon of the wild
    Her shadow round hath flung
And where the face of beauty smiled
    & where sweet music rung

The tigers' howl shall oft be heard
    Sounding through tower and dome
And to the moon the desert bird
    Shall make her thrilling moan

The murmur of the myrtle bowers
    The voice of waving trees
The fragrance of the sweet wild flower
    Shall mingle with the breeze

Unheard that gentle wind shall sweep
    The wide campaign of air
Unfelt the heavens their balm shall weep
    The living are not there[1]

To pictorial origins also must be traced the prototypes for the heroines of Charlotte's early tales. Besides reproducing the famous pictures of the day, the 'Annuals' published the portraits of the hostesses in the news. There exists a sketch-book of Charlotte's containing several copies of these.[2] She drew them with a loving care and close attention to every detail of fashion. There was no extravagance of feathered head-dress, bunched ringlets, flowered corsages, and leg-of-mutton sleeves with which she was not acquainted; she closely scrutinized the setting of their jewels, sometimes spending months over the task. Years later, describing Lucy Snowe bent over her desk, Charlotte recalled that early absorption of her own in 'copying an elaborate line-engraving, tediously working up my copy to the finish of the original, for that was my practical notion of art; and, strange to say I took extreme pleasure in the labour, and could even produce curiously finished facsimiles of steel or mezzotint plates. . . .'[3]

An artistic influence second only to Martin's in developing Charlotte's adolescent imagination, was the work of the engraver William Finden (1787–1852) whose 'Illustrations to the Life & Works of Lord Byron', published by Murray in 1833, were early acquired by Mr.

---

[1] 'The Trumpet hath Sounded', 11 Dec. 1831: Harvard.
[2] P. Bentley 'Charlotte Brontë's Sketch-book': *BST*, 1948.
[3] *Villette*, ch. 35.

Brontë. (Charlotte's copy of 'The Maid of Zaragossa', illustrating Canto I, st. 54–55 of *Childe Harold*, was dated 24 May 1833. The volumes also figure in the Catalogue of the Sale of Mr. Brontë's effects, after his death in 1861.) The impact of Finden's engravings on the young Brontës was instant and profound. Four meticulous copies made by Charlotte of Byronic landscapes and heroines—Finden's 'Lausanne', 'Geneva', 'Maid of Zaragossa', and 'Lady Jersey', and Emily's less slavish copy of the portrait of the Lady Charlotte Harley (Byron's 'Ianthe') remain to show how, during 1833 and 1834, when Mr. Brontë engaged an art-master to give his children lessons at home, the whole bent of their taste and training was towards copying mezzo-tint and copper-plate engravings.

Merely to copy pictures, however, was not enough for Charlotte; to satisfy her creative urge she must impart life to the portraits (in her own youthful manuscript 'A Peep into a Picture Book' written May–June 1834 Charlotte described the processes.) In the aristocratic features of the débutantes, the brides, and hostesses of the London scene she found the prototypes for her heroines, Zenobia Elrington, Mary Percy, Julia Wellesley, Jane Moore, Mina Laury, who for over ten years held the forefront of the stage in her Glass Town stories.

She wrote of them with a passionate conviction of their reality, as though actually living in their circle—the brunettes, the blondes, and the auburn-haired beauties—inventing dramas for them that stretched from their girlhood to their grave; characters and temperaments which, first conjectured from their physical traits, she amplified with a wealth of detail through dialogue and action that lent to each a recognizable and evolving personality. They may have begun as types of fashionable beauties, but they ended as recognizable individuals. '. . . Her features were regularly and finely formed,' Charlotte first wrote of Zenobia Elrington in 1830, 'with full and brilliant eyes, jetty black, as were the luxuriant tresses of her richly-curled hair. Her dark glowing complexion was set off by a robe of crimson velvet trimmed with ermine and a nodding plume of black ostrich feathers, added to the imposing dignity of her appearance. . . .'[1]

Four years later Zenobia Elrington is still recognizably the same haughty beauty. Charlotte had given her a decisive role to play in the complex plot. After vainly seeking the love of Zamorna (Arthur Augustus Adrian Wellesley, the hero of the Verdopolitan saga), Zenobia had submitted to marriage with his arch-enemy Alexander Percy

[1] 'Albion & Marina', 1830.

BELSHAZZAR'S FEAST, by John Martin

THE BAY OF GLASS TOWN, drawing by
Charlotte Brontë after Martin

Earl of Northangerland and held a prominent place in Angrian society.

> ... What eyes! what raven hair! What an imposing contour of form and countenance. She is perfectly grand in her velvet robes dark plume, and crown-like turban. The lady of Elrington House, the wife of Northangerland, the prima donna of the Angrian court, the most learned woman of her age, the modern Cleopatra, the Verdopolitan de Staël: in a word Zenobia Percy![1]

Incidentally, was it only coincidence or mere fashion that made her choose the name of Martin's daughter Zenobia for her heroine? The suggestion is teasing, especially as Charlotte's heroine began her career as 'Zelvia', to be changed three months later for the name of Martin's daughter.

In contrast to the imperious Zenobia, whose wit and learning 'and conversational talent not even Madame de Stael herself could have gone beyond', Charlotte drew the tender and ill-fated Marian Hume, Zamorna's girl-wife whose softer traits and less aggressive colouring, as first presented in the 'Annual's' pages, were made to suit the yielding role imposed on her by her author. First seen as a young bride, Marian did not appear 'to be above 15 years of age. . . .' She wore only a green silk frock and pearl necklace and a myrtle branch twined among her luxuriant auburn ringlets.[2] At the theatre, shortly afterwards, the portrait is enlarged; she is shown as 'a beautiful girl in a white dress and green sash without any ornament on her head except a profusion of chestnut curls. . . .'[3] As Marian Hume, abandoned and heart-broken, gradually engaged her creator's tenderest pity, the retrospective descriptions of her in youth and happiness are tinged with sweetness and compassion and with overtones recognizably Byronic. Auburn was the colour of Haidee's hair, and the long chain of alternating emeralds and gold, and the crescent of pearls in the hair belong to Finden's engraving of Lady Jersey, first published in Moore's *Life of Byron* (1830) already mentioned as having been copied by Charlotte.

> Her cheeks were tinted with a rich soft crimson . . . the clear light of her brilliant hazel eyes, and the soft waving of her auburn ringlets. . . . The only ornaments she wore were a long chain . . . which hung lower than her waist, composed of alternate beads of the finest emerald and gold . . . which, together with a small crescent of pearls glistening on her forehead, . . . betokened she had entered the path of married life. . . .[4]

---

[1] 'A Peep into a Picture Book', May–June 1834.
[2] 'The Foundling', 1833.
[3] 'The Tragedy & the Essay', Nov. 1833.
[4] 'The Bridal', Aug. 1832.

In some of Charlotte's descriptions the actual immobility of the inspiring model becomes apparent. This is especially noticeable in the first introduction of Julia Wellesley, the lively niece of the ubiquitous Zamorna. 'Her ivory fan and her as ivory arm were raised with an arch graceful gesture, and the scarlet plumes nodded proudly on her head as she bent it coquettishly to one side. . . .'[1]

The pictorial origin of Charlotte's early heroines explains why she, a provincial clergyman's daughter with few opportunities of seeing fashions even belatedly, and herself a girl noticeably uninterested in clothes, should give such prominence to the costumes of her heroines. Not alone their clothes but the very airs they played at their piano-fortes, on their harps and their guitars, were known to Charlotte. In Haworth Parsonage remain albums of music which show how, in their early teens, Charlotte and her sisters were laboriously practising—with fingering carefully pencilled in—not only the 'Sacred Oratorios' but the 'profane' music of the period; the fashionable arias and over-tures from the romantic operas of Bellini, Donizetti, and Auber then crowding the Parisian and London auditoriums, and rearranged as a requisite accomplishment for the young ladies of England as duets for four hands.

Upon the choice of setting for her tales, as on her choice of charac-ters, their pictorial origin played a decisive part. Series of engravings showing the interiors of Brighton Pavilion, of Apsley House, and other residences of the illustrious, were featured in many of the 'Annuals'. Hence the astounding assurance with which Charlotte made her heroes and heroines move through 'the brilliantly lit saloons' about which she read in the Annual Register, drive to the Glass Town Races in brightly painted curricles, attend the levees and military reviews about which she read in the Court Circular. Whether riding, dancing, or attending the Opera, she seldom presented them in a false light or out of their true element. 'I like high life,' comments her mouth-piece, Lord Charles Florian Wellesley, 'I like its manners, its splendours, the beings which move in its enchanted sphere. I like to consider the habits of those beings, their way of thinking, speaking and acting. Let fools talk about the artificial, voluptuous idle existence spun out by Dukes, Lords, Ladies, Knights and Esquires of high degree. Such cant is not for me. I despise it. . . .'[2]

Thus it was that without having entered a theatre Charlotte could

---

[1] 'My Angria & the Angrians', Oct. 1834: BPM (Bonnell 125).
[2] 'High Life in Verdopolis', 1834.

write at 16: '. . . . There are few sights more animated and inspiring than a crowded theatre. . . . More than a thousand of the lovliest women . . . sparkled in the dress circle, where the waving of plumes, the rustling of robes, the glitter of diamonds . . . were dazzling. . . . Zenobia Elrington sat in gorgeous purple, a star-like band of jewels gleaming among her rich raven locks: . . .'[1]

If her evocations of a Society about which she had only such hearsay information was surprisingly assured, her penetration into the recesses of the human heart was for a girl of her age also remarkable. Emotionally Charlotte was not only in advance of her age; her imagination and feeling were exercised to a degree that not many adults attain in a lifetime.

This can be seen in the heroic figure of Zamorna, the main achievement of her prentice hand, evolving over the years with the very movement of organic growth. Zamorna stands at the centre of the intricate complex of plots and characters constituting the literature of Glass Town. He was the amalgam of Charlotte's earliest love of Wellington for whose son he stood, inheriting his father's real title of Marquis of Douro, and of the Byronic Hero. Possessed of all the latter's treachery and courage, grace and melancholy, mystery and cunning, he achieves the dukedom of Zamorna and crown of Angria in a crescendo of triumphs, predominantly amatory. Zamorna reigns, indeed, by force of feeling, over the essentially feminine world of Angria. In him Charlotte displayed the romantic principle par excellence, the extreme personification of the Napoleonic and Byronic ideal. Here he is portrayed in one of the countless early descriptions of him:

. . . His figure was toweringly, overbearingly lofty, moulded in statue-like perfection, and invested with something which I cannot describe—something superb, impetuous, resistless. His hair was intensely black, curled luxuriantly, but the forehead underneath . . . looked white and smooth as ivory. His eye-brows were black and broad, but his long eye-lashes and large clear eyes were deep sepia brown. . . . The upper lip was very short— Grecian—and had a haughty curl. . . . At the first glance I discerned him to be a military man. . . .[2]

To ignore Zamorna is to lose the very concept from which Rochester sprang—the love not only of Charlotte's adolescence but, as time would show in all essential traits, of her life. Emotionally, Charlotte at

[1] 'The Tragedy & the Essay', 1833.
[2] 'My Angria & the Angrians', Oct. 1834: BPM.

fourteen was an adult with little more to discover of the workings of the heart.

There remained the hard lessons to learn of the difference between unbounded feeling and limited experience; between Ideal Life and Reality; between the radiant unrestricted visionary realm of poetry with its lovely inhabitants, and the dull prosaic figures with which the real world is filled—especially the industrial world spreading about her home, and from among whom the employers of governesses were drawn, and with whom it would be the lot of Miss Brontë to be concerned. For her the limiting lessons of experience began in her fifteenth year.

In the summer of 1830 an event occurred in the family which was fraught with consequences for Charlotte. Mr. Brontë fell gravely ill with congestion of the lungs and for a time his life was in danger. In the following spring he had still to report to Mrs. Franks (the former Miss Firth) '. . . I fear I shall never fully recover. . . .' The threat to his life was a threat also to his children's future; his death would leave them homeless and with little or no provision with which to go out into the world. The parsonage must automatically revert to his successor, and Miss Branwell with her annuity of £50 could hardly adopt the orphans, the eldest of whom was barely 14. The circumstance emphasized the urgent need of fitting the children to earn their livelihood and it is evident that Mr. Brontë's friends, and Charlotte's godparents in particular, came forward with some practical proposals. Mr. and Mrs. Atkinson offered to pay her fees at a new school opened in their district where she could receive a good education under the safest and happiest auspices. No repetition of Cowan Bridge need be feared; the Misses Wooler were personally known to them,[1] and 'Roe Head', the fine old house in which they had recently opened school, was barely a mile from their own pro-parsonage, the 'Green House', Mirfield. The offer was accepted and Charlotte was told to prepare herself for departure in the New Year 1831.

What such a decree meant to a girl of her temperament and habits can only too easily be guessed. Pocahontas cannot have felt the severance from her kingdom to receive the culture of her conquerors more acutely than the young Charlotte at that transplantation from the 'Burning Clime' to the salubrious situation of Roe Head, her new school. It was not the 20 miles distance from her home that made her

[1] Mrs. Franks's diary for 15 May 1829 mentions Miss Wooler taking tea with Mrs. Atkinson and herself, Sheffield Univ. Lib.

heart turn over in anguish so much as its immeasurable distance from the glorious secret country where she reigned as more than queen—as Creator as well as Ruler of her subjects.

For years she had directed her own studies, had been free to choose or to reject her reading, had been mistress of her own thoughts, the absolute disposer of her leisure, thinking and feeling less like a child than a creative artist whose universe took the shape of her own volition. She felt the prospective loss of freedom with a pang only a little less acute than the separation from those she loved. Submerged in grief she foresaw neither of the alleviations that came with her lot: the acquisition of knowledge for its own sake, and the love of friends.

CHAPTER V

THE PURSUIT OF KNOWLEDGE: ROE HEAD, 1831–1832

IT was on a stark January day that she set out for school. Mrs. Gaskell gave the date as 19 January, but the inscription repeated in three of her new school-books—'Roe Head January 17th 1831'—would rather point to the latter date being correct.

Roe Head, Mirfield Moor, was about 20 miles from Haworth, and two modes of conveyance were available to Charlotte, a hired gig or a covered cart that plied to the main centres on market days. She was sent in the latter.

As she would find when gradually, very gradually, she got to know her fellow pupils, she came from a greater distance than most and was, therefore, among the last to arrive. This put her at the disadvantage of a close scrutiny by the already-assembled girls crowding the wide bow-windows of the school's façade, whence the shrewdest of them all, Mary Taylor, noted her appearance. Years later Mary reported the scene to Mrs. Gaskell. Ten months younger than Charlotte, Mary shared neither her homesickness nor her shrinking fear of new faces and new surroundings. Forthright, pugnacious, curious, Mary's evidence bore not a trace of emotional bias towards the friend she afterwards greatly loved.

. . . I first saw her coming out of a covered cart, in very old-fashioned clothes, and looking very cold and miserable. . . . When she appeared in the schoolroom, her dress was changed, but just as old. She looked a little old woman, so short-sighted that she always appeared to be seeking something, and moving her head from side to side to catch sight of it. She was very shy and nervous, and spoke with a strong Irish accent. . . .[1]

The old-fashioned clothes and the short-sighted eyes, of which Charlotte was made doubly conscious in that vivacious concourse of well-dressed young persons—all addressed as 'Miss So and So' by their imposing teachers—only heightened the blighting timidity and the

[1] Mary Taylor's recollections of CB: *SLL* i. 80–83, derived from her letter to Mrs. Gaskell, 18 Jan. 1856.

Irish brogue. Mary Taylor found her downright ugly, and allowed no lapse of time to pass before telling her so. In later years, aware of the shock and hurt it had inflicted on supersensitive feelings, she apologized to Charlotte. On Charlotte it had the effect of a pail of ice-water on an arctic morning—salutary perhaps in bracing the nerves, but a blow to the heart all the same. 'You did me a great deal of good, Polly, so don't repent it', was all she ever said. But from then on the conscious-ness of her lack of beauty became one of the secret sorrows of her life.[1]

If she had been brought up to disregard externals in a home where mind reigned supreme, a deeper humiliation yet awaited her when her position in the school had to be decided by Miss Wooler. Better read at 14 than most women of the time in any part of the three kingdoms, she was found on examination to be ignorant on many subjects, of the theory of grammar in particular, and to possess very little geography. To have explained to Miss Wooler that she was a practised author with some scores of books to her credit, or that in the matter of geo-graphy she had not only penetrated darkest Africa but erected a king-dom there, would have availed her little. Despite her age, which placed her among the senior girls, Charlotte was relegated to the junior table in the pleasant schoolroom overlooking the gardens of Roe Head. The wound to her pride, following on a day of exhausting impressions and heart-ache, was too much to bear and she burst into a flood of tears. Miss Wooler, of whose good sense the following years would give many instances, realized then and there that there was more in the new girl than met the eye and, putting Charlotte on her mettle to catch up by private reading with the seniors' studies, admitted her to the senior class.

There were at that time no more than ten boarders at the Miss Woolers' school, which allowed not only considerable individual atten-tion but also plenty of living-space in the large comfortable house only recently acquired as a school. Of the three floors, all bow-fronted to the top, only two needed to be occupied by the Miss Woolers themselves, the servants, and the girls. The third floor, reached by a direct staircase from the kitchen-quarters and also by a door at the end of the first-floor gallery, remained uninhabited, a circumstance which tended greatly to heighten the girls' curiosity, for Roe Head was reputed to have its ghost. On certain nights—a slow-dying legend averred—the sound of a silk dress rustling over the floor-boards of the upper story could be distinctly heard.

[1] MT to Mrs. Gaskell, 18 Jan. 1856: *SLL* i. 81.

The evidence of a fellow pupil upon Charlotte's reaction to this story and to Miss Wooler's is typical of both: for Charlotte the tale had great charm; for Miss Wooler, the wish to discredit anything so fantastic as a ghost led to the practical course of sending any girl who mentioned it upstairs after dark to fetch her something that could be easily found. As 'no ghost made herself visible even to the frightened imaginations of the foolish and the timid . . . a general laugh soon set . . . all right again'.[1] Not only the ghost but the attraction of dormer windows opening on to the leads of the house and thence across a veritable switchback of old roofs presented a sore temptation to bold spirits on balmy summer nights.

Of the antiquity of the house the title-deeds give proof.[2] The land, bought from the surrounding Armytage estates in the 1620s, passed into the hands of the Marriott family in the early eighteenth century, the house itself being built before 1740. As tenants of the Marriotts (who did not part with the property till 1920) the Miss Woolers came to it in 1830.

Situated in pleasant grounds on the west side of the old Bradford and Huddersfield turnpike road, almost at the junction with the New Road from Leeds, with its high position commanding extensive views, Roe Head possessed considerable advantages as a school: it was a healthy place yet not far from the main industrial towns from which it sought its pupils.

To a romantic-minded girl like Charlotte Brontë its interior held also many attractive features. The walls of rooms and passages were oak-panelled throughout. Miss Wooler's parlour and the school-room occupied the ground-floor rooms, whose bow-windows with their deep window-seats had an uninterrupted view over the front lawns sloping down to Kirkleas Park in the foreground, to the Calder valley in the middle distance, and to the great gap in the surrounding hills that held Huddersfield on the far horizon. The view, with which Charlotte would become so familiar, held beauties for her eyes despite the chimneys and the smoke. There were the river-vapours rising in the valley, and the exposed highway upon which from so far off could be seen the country drays, the curricles, and the riders as they passed to and fro between Huddersfield and Leeds. In contrast to the nobility of the unchanging moors about her home, there was a stirring and restless energy infusing the Roe Head scene that opened her mind to worlds unsuspected in her reading.

---

[1] Ellen Nussey, Reminiscences of CB: *SLL* i. 90.
[2] By courtesy of the Verona Fathers.

The dining-room had its windows facing the school gates and the highroad, an advantage to girls on the look-out for a passing brother who from his curricle could throw letters and packets over the conventual wall secluding the young ladies. Out of character as it sounds, even Charlotte in her time was to benefit from this daring mode of communication with the outer world.

From the square entrance hall a fine oak staircase rose with massive banisters to a galleried first-floor. Here was the drawing-room with a flight of five steps leading up to its door, and corridors leading off to the various bedrooms. A rambling, roomy, solid, agreeable house, with enough winding passages and hidden doorways to kindle a budding novelist's imagination.

Always more difficult of approach and understanding for Charlotte than the natural scene were the inmates of the house, and they only gradually became distinct to her. There were, to begin with, the Miss Woolers, her teachers, with whom she had first to reckon.

There were four Miss Woolers then living at Roe Head, the fifth, Susanna, having left home to get married the previous 30 December. Her husband, the Rev. Edward Nicholl Carter, was curate of nearby Mirfield Parish Church, where the young ladies from Roe Head were expected to attend every Sunday during term. The Woolers were country women, their father and forebears being farmers with considerable property in Batley, where the family home, Rouse Mill, still was. Their status as landowners can be judged from the fact that as long before the Reform Bill as 1807 the Miss Woolers' father had a Parliamentary vote.[1]

The eldest Miss Wooler, Margaret, was the undoubted head of the family, spoken of with deference even by her brothers—of whom there were two, Dr. William Wooler, who achieved a considerable medical reputation, and Mr. John Wooler, the inheritor of Rouse Mill—and was invariably addressed as 'Sister' by them all. Born 10 June 1792 she was thus not 40 when Charlotte Brontë first knew her. She had a genuine love of learning and was an accomplished linguist, with a special preference for Italian, never failing to read a chapter in her Italian Testament each day as part of her devotions. As a girl she had lived for six years on the Isle of Wight with an uncle and aunt, a Dr. Moore and his wife, regimental doctor to the garrison stationed there, enjoying, in the recollection of a great-nephew,[2] 'the best society

[1] See the Manor Rolls of Batley. The Poll for the Knights of the Shire for Soothill in Batley, 1807.   [2] Revd. Max Blakeley: 'Memories of Margaret Wooler', *BST*, 1952.

in the Island'. Miss Wooler had great good sense allied to a firm mind and a kind heart, and though it took Charlotte years to appreciate her, she became eventually one of her most trusted friends.

In appearance she was thus described by another pupil whose acquaintance Charlotte would shortly make.

... She was short and stout, but graceful in her movements, very fluent in conversation and with a very sweet voice. .... Personally, Miss Wooler was like a lady abbess. She wore white, well-fitting dresses embroidered. Her long hair plaited, formed a coronet, and long large ringlets fell from her head to shoulders. She was not pretty or handsome, but her quiet dignity made her presence imposing. She was nobly scrupulous and conscientious—a woman of the greatest self-denial. Her income was small. She lived on half of it, and gave the remainder to charitable objects. . . .[1]

Next in age to Miss Wooler was 'Miss Catherine' (Catherine Harriet, born 3 August 1796), a highly intelligent but far less amiable character than Margaret. She chiefly taught French in the school. After her came Susan (Mrs. Carter, born 7 April 1800), who continued as a visiting teacher to the school for drawing until the birth of her first child in December 1832. After her came 'Miss Marianne' (born 1802), the only other sister eventually to marry; and finally 'Miss Eliza' (born 14 June 1808) who, though the youngest, was reputed to be the worst martinet of the sisters.

The evidence of all old pupils of Roe Head testifies to the humane atmosphere, to the agreeable and unforced programme of work, the plentiful food, playtime, and rest accorded the pupils, the regard paid to their health (daily walks and outdoor games, an innovation at that time, were essentials insisted on by Miss Wooler). But none of these things could console Charlotte for her lost empire.

The very healthiness of her robust companions only accentuated their difference from herself; her undersized frail body could not keep pace with them, her near-sighted eyes made all attempts at playing games a painful humiliation which made her shrink yet further within herself. As Mary Taylor remembered: '. . . In our play hours she sat or stood still, with a book, if possible. Some of us urged her to be on our side in a game of ball. She said she had never played, and could not play. We made her try, but soon found that she could not see the ball, so we put her out. . . .'[2] (Charlotte had, we are told, 'an invincible

---

[1] Ellen Nussey, Reminiscences of CB: *SLL* i. 84 et seq.
[2] Mary Taylor, Reminiscences of CB: *SLL* i. 81 et seq.

objection to wearing glasses at this time', which explains her blindness.)

It did not need many days for the proof to be made: Charlotte
Brontë was no good at games. Of her real worth, of course, the other
girls had as yet no inkling. Crushed by the sense of her own inadequacy
both as scholar and player, her misery was complete. Of her state of
mind after eight days at school a graphic account has been preserved by
a new girl who arrived at Roe Head on 25 January. The unprepared
encounter which found Ellen Nussey and Charlotte in unguarded
mood became the prelude to a lifelong friendship.

Charlotte with her load of incommunicable sorrow had once again
refused to join the other girls when they rushed out to play, and had
stayed behind in the schoolroom. From the great bow window she
could see them dashing about on the tree-studded lawns and hear
their cheerful shouts. Her desolation in that strange place, its distance
from home and the endless stretch of months ahead before June
brought the holidays and restored her there, was borne in upon her
with so intolerable an anguish that she was literally struck down to the
ground with grief. Ellen Nussey, just delivered into the Miss Woolers'
hands that morning by her brother Henry,[1] and left to recover herself in
what was believed to be the empty schoolroom, with feelings far less
acute perhaps than Charlotte but none the less in equal need of comfort,
stumbled upon her there in what was to prove the most momentous
encounter in her life. In old age she had not yet forgotten the scene.

Arriving at school about a week after the general assembly of the pupils,
I was not expected to accompany them when the time came for their daily
exercise, but while they were out, I was led into the schoolroom, and quietly
left to make my observations. I had come to the conclusion that it was very
nice and comfortable for a schoolroom, though I had little knowledge of
schoolrooms in general, when, turning to the window to observe the look-
out, I became aware for the first time that I was not alone; there was a silent,
weeping, dark little figure in the large bay-window; she must, I thought,
have risen from the floor. As soon as I had recovered from my surprise, I
went from the far end of the room, where the book-shelves were, the contents of which I must have contemplated with a little awe in anticipation of
coming studies. A crimson cloth covered the long table down the centre of
the room, which helped, no doubt, to hide the shrinking little figure from
my view. I was touched and troubled at once to see her so sad and so tearful.
I said shrinking, because her attitude, when I saw her, was that of one who

---

[1] Diary of Henry Nussey: Chadwick, 25 Jan. 1831.

wished to hide both herself and her grief. She did not shrink, however, when spoken to, but in very few words confessed she was homesick. After a little of such comfort as could be offered, it was suggested to her that there was a possibility of her too having to comfort the speaker by-and-by for the same cause. A faint quivering smile then lighted her face; the tear-drops fell; we silently took each other's hands, and at once we felt that genuine sympathy which always consoles, even though it be unexpressed. We did not talk nor stir till we heard the approaching footsteps of other pupils coming in from their play; it had been a game called 'French and English' which was always very vigorously played, but in which Charlote Bronte never could be induced to join. . . .[1]

How Charlotte appeared to her new-found friend, Ellen also remembered.

. . . Charlotte's appearance did not strike me at first as it did others. I saw her grief, not herself particularly, till afterwards. She never seemed to me the unattractive little person others designated her, but certainly she was at this time anything but *pretty*; even her good points were lost. Her naturally beautiful hair of soft silky brown being then dry and frizzy-looking, screwed up in tight little curls, showing features that were all the plainer for her exceeding thinness and want of complexion, she looked 'dried in'. A dark, rusty green stuff dress of old-fashioned make detracted still more from her appearance; but let her wear what she might or do what she would, she had ever the demeanour of a born gentle-woman; vulgarity was an element that never won the slightest affinity with her nature. . . .[2]

Ellen's own nature, as the wide-apart sleepy eyes of her portrait as a girl reveal, was soft and docile, as contrary to Charlotte's purposeful and passionate one as well might be. Yet irresistibly Ellen was drawn to Charlotte in that first hour of their meeting. Herself one of a family of twelve children, she was yet so much the youngest as to be very much in need of companionship and affection. The role of comforter, as novel perhaps as it was stimulating, the sense of her own composure in the presence of Charlotte's storm of anguish, then and there set the tone to a relationship in which, as of right, she assumed the part of gentle monitress that, to the end, she never wholly relinquished.

Many years later, discussing the long friendship in a letter to her publisher, Charlotte confessed: '. . . When I first saw Ellen I did not care for her; we were school-fellows. . . . We were contrasts . . . still, we suited. . . . She is without romance. If she attempts to read poetry, or

[1] Ellen Nussey, Reminiscences of CB: *SLL* i. 84 et seq.   [2] Idem.

'ENGLISH LADY', drawing by Charlotte Brontë from
Finden's engraving of the portrait of Lady Jersey

ELLEN NUSSEY, drawing by Charlotte Brontë

poetic prose, aloud, I am irritated and deprive her of the book . . . but she is good; she is true; she is faithful, and I love her. . . .'[1] As Charlotte herself later confessed, it sufficed if anybody liked her, for her to like them.[2]

The need to love and to be loved, never before so acutely realized as in those first days at school, inclined her to a thankful acceptance of the proffered friendship, however unlike she realized herself and Ellen to be—and however unlike her cherished sisters Ellen was. With Ellen's advent Charlotte's position improved; even towards the other girls it changed.

Ellen Nussey was in a manner a connexion of Mary Taylor's—an uncle of Ellen's having married a cousin of the Taylors called Dixon—and, living little more than a mile apart, Mary at Gomersal and Ellen at Birstall, had a common background, though standing politically poles apart. Ellen's family, established landowners for centuries in the district, was Tory to the core, while the violent Radicalism of the Taylors was matter of common knowledge throughout the Spen Valley. Both girls had backgrounds very different from Charlotte's, but at the moment of their meeting in 1831 their families were suffering under financial loss and obliged to live on a footing of strict economy. Ellen had lost her father five years before and her mother was reported to be 'not wise in business transactions', while Mary's father, a cloth-manufacturer and banker, had been bankrupt over an army contract. An honourable man, he only lived to pay off his debts.

What for Ellen and Mary were reduced circumstances were the normal condition of life for Charlotte, and perhaps the first shy approaches towards intimacy were made the easier for her by the fact that her new friends were not overbearingly smart and prosperous. Ellen Nussey, with her soft ringlets and innate elegance, could not forbear noticing that Mary Taylor and her younger sister Martha who accompanied her to Roe Head

'. . . were not dressed as well as other pupils, for economy at that time was the rule of their household. The girls had to stitch all over their new gloves before wearing them, by order of their mother, to make them wear longer. Their dark blue cloth coats were worn *when too short*, and black beaver bonnets quite plainly trimmed, with the ease and contentment of a fashionable costume. . . .'[3]

[1] CB to WSW, 3 Jan. 1850: *SLL* ii. 103.
[2] CB to EN, 4 Jan. 1838: *SLL* i. 145–6.   [3] EN, Reminiscences of CB: *SBC* 216.

Mary herself, Ellen remembered on first coming to school, as 'pretty, and very childish-looking, dressed in a red-coloured frock with short sleeves and low neck, as then worn by young girls. Miss Wooler in later years used to say that when Mary went to her as a pupil she thought her too pretty to live. . . .'.

The three girls were close in age. Charlotte was the eldest, 14 and nine months at the time, Mary was ten months younger, and Ellen exactly a year younger, her birthday being on 22nd April, the day after Charlotte's. Martha Taylor, two years younger than her sister, was a sparkling dare-devil of a girl, whose vitality then and later captivated Charlotte. Her originality, of a more comical nature than Mary's, enlivened the whole school. The other girls called her 'Miss Boisterous'. She was always a favourite, recalled Ellen Nussey, 'so piquant and fascinating were her ways. She was not in the least pretty, but something much better, full of change and variety, rudely out-spoken, lively and original, producing laughter with her own good humour and affection . . .'.[1] With these three girls Charlotte became fast friends. Something of the closeness and dearness of those fresh ties can be traced in the joining of their names in her new school-books. In her Mangnall's 'Questions', Lindley Murray's 'Grammar', her French Grammar and Exercise Books, can be seen with her own signature and date of arrival at Roe Head the signatures of her friends in their several hands.

The names of some of Charlotte's other fellow pupils are known to us; there were Susan Ledgard, Leah and Maria Brooke, Hannah Haigh, and 'Miss' Allison. The Brooke girls were daughters of a wealthy Dewsbury family well known to Mr. Brontë from his curate days twenty years before. They are mentioned in the correspondence between Charlotte, the Taylors, and Ellen Nussey. Another pupil whose presence at Roe Head might of itself explain Mrs. Atkinson's choice of the school for Charlotte was Amelia Walker, her own niece, younger daughter of Joseph Walker, Esq., of Lascelles Hall, Hudders-field, and Broadlands, Torquay. With Amelia Charlotte formed life-long contacts, though none of them cordial on her part, for Amelia was an arrogant young person whose uncertain temper, airs and graces, and countless affectations—changing character 'every half-hour' as Charlotte later told Ellen—helped Charlotte to a knowledge of the social butterfly which she later so brilliantly hit off in the character of Ginevra Fanshawe.

[1] C. Edgerley, 'Mary Taylor': *BST*, 1944.

Miss Wooler's curriculum was largely based on the prescriptions contained in Mrs. Chapone's *Letters on the Improvement of the Mind* (first published in 1773 and frequently reissued and enlarged), addressed to a little niece of 12—a copy of which, incidentally, Miss Wooler herself received at a precisely similar age. The advice contained therein very evidently took root for, like Mrs. Chapone, Miss Wooler advocated 'Rollin for Ancient History', Mangnall's 'Questions' for History and Biography—followed by the inescapable Hume—Lindley Murray for Grammar, Milton and Shakespeare for Poetry—the latter not merely for his poetry but because he was 'the most perfect characteriser of men and manners', and again for his historical plays which, declared Mrs. Chapone, 'if read in a series, will fix in your memory the reigns he has chosen more durably than any other history. . . .'[1]

Finding herself one of a group of friends and competitors did more to restore Charlotte's equanimity than anything else. She rapidly found her feet and very soon gained the respect of her classmates. Her clumsiness at games was forgotten in the admiration with which the slower-witted watched her catch up with their studies and, as swiftly, overtake their plodding efforts. Mary Taylor remembered:

. . . She would confound us, by knowing things that were out of our range altogether. She was acquainted with most of the short pieces of poetry that we had to learn by heart: would tell us the authors, the poems they were taken from, and sometimes repeat a page or two, and tell us the plot. . . .She made poetry and drawing . . . exceedingly interesting to me; and then I got into the habit, which I have yet, of referring mentally to her opinion on all matters of the kind. . . .[2]

It was Mary, it may be remembered, who was so impressed by Charlotte's knowledge of art and her taste in analysing pictures. Ellen wrote:

Some of the elder girls, who had been years at school, thought her ignorant. This was true in one sense; ignorant she was indeed in the elementary education which is given in schools, but she far surpassed her most advanced school-fellows in knowledge of what was passing in the world at large, and in the literature of her country. She knew a thousand things unknown to them. . . .

The breadth as well as the depth of her home education told in the long run. At the end of her first half at Roe Head, Charlotte bore off the three main prizes.

---

[1] Mrs. Chapone, *Letters on the Improvement of the Mind*, 1794.
[2] Mary Taylor, Reminiscences of CB: *SLL* i. 80–83.

To make the most of her chances became now her chief desire. That she had been sent to school with a purpose, to fit her to earn her living, was a thought seldom absent from her mind. 'She always seemed to feel', said Ellen Nussey, 'that a deep responsibility rested upon her; that she was an object of expense to those at home, and that she must use every moment to attain the purpose for which she was sent to school i.e. to fit herself for governess life. . . .'[1] How great a mental change such an acceptance of her lot implied, Ellen could not gauge, either then or later; she knew nothing of Charlotte's inner life and could have no inkling of the sacrifice entailed in her dedication to such an end. For Charlotte the new regimen of Roe Head marked not only the end of childhood, but the awakening of a tyrannical and enslaving conscience.

Ellen Nussey commented:

. . . She had almost too much opportunity for her conscientious diligence. We were so little restricted in our doings, the industrious might accomplish the appointed tasks of the day and enjoy a little leisure, but she chose in many things to do double lessons. . . . All her school-fellows regarded her, I believe, as a model of high rectitude, close application and great abilities. She did not play or amuse herself when others did. When her companions were merry round the fire, or otherwise enjoying themselves during the twilight, which was always a precious time of relaxation, she would be kneeling close to the window busy with her studies, and this would last so long that she was accused of seeing in the dark. . . .[2]

How resolutely she turned from all her former ways, such a picture shows. The twilight hour had been for her a time of poetic imaginings and extravagant invention; it was now dedicated to the one ideal of learning. The embargo she herself laid on creative writing is shown by the absence of any manuscripts for her first terms at Roe Head. For her, unlike her sisters, there can be no doubt that learning brought its own reward; had she not been a creative artist before all things she could with equal distinction have been a scholar, as her Brussels record would show. But of the pleasures of her age she knew nothing.

Pleasure of a kind that held little appeal for her was offered from time to time when she was invited to visit one or other of her god-mothers, Mrs. Atkinson and Mrs. Franks, who both lived within easy range of Roe Head. The Atkinsons' home, The Green House, was

---

[1] Ellen Nussey, Reminiscences of CB: *SLL* i. 86.
[2] Idem. et seq.

scarcely a mile away at the bottom of the turnpike road, on the corner of the lane over Stocks Bank into Mirfield. It was a house of character and considerable charm, dating from the early eighteenth century, with a great barn attached that went back to Tudor days. It lay back from the road in a large tangled garden with high walls bounding its orchard at the back. To the painfully shy girl Charlotte then was the daunting aspect of the stone-pillared gate and sweeping drive towards the front portico was an added ordeal. Mrs. Atkinson always sent one of her servants—Mrs. Abraham Hirst—to fetch Charlotte on the occasions of her week-end visits, and Mrs. Hirst remembered into old age Charlotte's unrelieved misery at the call.[1] All strangers alarmed her, but the sense of her own obligation to Mrs. Atkinson, who was paying her school-bills, made her doubly ill at ease in her company. To open her heart to her about the things she really cared for—poetry and novels—would have been impossible. Mrs. Atkinson, renowned for her piety and performing an act of charity in training a worthy clergyman's daughter for a career as governess, is not likely to have understood the artistic yearnings of her young protégée. In later years when she came to read *Jane Eyre* she was appalled at the secular nature of the work and the scant respect paid to the Cloth, and severed all connexion with the author.

Married 23 December 1817, the Atkinsons were a childless couple, wealthy and noted for their acts of benevolence. Mr. Atkinson, who had exchanged livings with Mr. Brontë in 1815 to be nearer Huddersfield and the current 'object' of his attentions, the wealthy Miss Frances Walker of Lascelles Hall, had remained on good terms with his former colleague. As godfather to Charlotte, he did not flinch now from his obligations: his watchful eye was constantly upon her. The Atkinsons kept open house and not the least of Charlotte's terrors in visiting them was the number and variety of the strangers she had to meet. Mrs. Atkinson had not only contingents of nephews and nieces from Lascelles Hall, but also invited her cousin's children from Huddersfield Vicarage, the children of the former Miss Firth of Thornton,[2] whose infantile prattle and frolics were supposed to be entertainment for young Charlotte Brontë. Her own very youthful appearance and diminutive size were matters of deep humiliation to her. As she

[1] W. W. Yates, 'The Father of the Brontës', Dewsbury, 1893; 'The Brontës at Dewsbury', *BST*, 1895.

[2] Mr. and Mrs. Franks (*née* Firth) had four children: John Firth, b. 6 Oct. 1826; Henry James, b. 17 Mar., 1830; Elizabeth, b. 1 June 1831; William Walker, b. 22 Mar. 1833.

confided to her new friend, Ellen Nussey, her godmothers 'took me for a child and treated me just like one—one tall lady *would* nurse me!'[1]

The Green House, with its deep-set Georgian windows, wide window-seats and high wooden shutters, its arched stairway and panelled recesses, its odd steps up and odd steps down into little side rooms, exhaled a grace and tranquillity that, could she have shared it with those she loved, would have held great attractions for Charlotte. As it was she sought refuge, whenever possible, in the garden which surrounded the house on all sides and afforded a fine hiding-place. Here, in the long grasses of the orchard, she might console herself among the buried pets of a bygone occupier who in the eighteenth century raised headstones to his faithful departed dogs, giving them the tribute of Latin memorials.[2]

The charitable ladies of the old Thornton circle, Mrs. Franks, her stepmother Mrs. Firth (Branwell's godmother), and Miss Outhwaite (Anne's godmother), were all assembled on one memorable visit to the Atkinsons, and found Mr. Brontë's 'little girl', whom they had not seen for ten years, an object of solicitude and interest. They noticed she had chilblains and they noticed furthermore that even the best frock which she donned for her visits to The Green House was deplorably shabby. On her return to Roe Head they sent her a parcel. Something of the burden this fresh obligation laid on her young shoulders can be sensed in the dutiful letter she addressed to Mrs. Franks. To accept charity under any guise was always bitter to the Brontë girls. Rather poverty and the rare pleasures of their own providing than be beholden to anyone.

Roe Head, May, 1831

Dear Madam,—I beg to acknowledge the receipt of the parcel, which arrived the other day from Huddersfield, and to thank yourself for the frock and muslin and Miss Outhwaite for the shawl which she has so kindly sent me. My chilblains are quite well. I am sorry I was out when Mr. Atkinson called the other day. Pray give my love to Mrs. Firth and present my thanks to her for her welcome note. The Miss Woolers desire their kind respects to you; they are much obliged to Mr. Franks for the loan of 'Keith on the Prophecies' with which they were greatly pleased. Accept, Dear Madam, my sincere thanks for all the kindnesses you have shown me, and permit me to subscribe myself, yours gratefully and affectionately,

C. Bronte.[3]

[1] EN, Reminiscences of CB: *SLL* i. 90.
[2] The author is much indebted to the present owners, Dr. and Mrs. Everatt of The Green House, Mirfield, for their permission to visit it.
[3] CB to Mrs. Franks: Moore-Smith Bequest, Sheffield Univ. Lib.

True pleasure, exceeding by its suddenness and surprise any happiness she had known since she left home, awaited her one May morning when she was called into Miss Wooler's parlour to be told that Branwell was there. He had walked the 20 miles from Haworth just to spend the day with her. The joy this visit gave her is fully reflected in the letter she wrote him afterwards, obviously adapted though it was to the censorship of the Miss Woolers:

Roe Head, May 17th 1831

Dear Branwell,—As usual I address my weekly letter to you, because to you I find the most to say. I feel exceedingly anxious to know how and in what state you arrived home after your long and (I should think) very fatiguing journey. I could perceive when you arrived at Roe Head that you were very much tired, though you refused to acknowledge it. After you were gone, many questions and subjects of conversation recurred to me which I had intended to mention to you, but quite forgot them in the agitation which I felt at the totally unexpected pleasure of seeing you. Lately I had begun to think that I had lost all the interest which I used formerly to take in politics, but the extreme pleasure I felt at the news of the Reform Bill's being thrown out by the House of Lords, and of the expulsion or resignation of Earl Grey, etc., etc., convinced me that I have not as yet lost *all* my penchant for politics. I am extremely glad that aunt has consented to take in 'Fraser's Magazine', for though, I know from your description of its general contents it will be rather uninteresting when compared with 'Blackwood', still it will be better than remaining the whole year without being able to obtain a sight of any periodical publication whatever; and such would assuredly be our case, as in the little wild moorland village where we reside, there would be no possibility of borrowing or obtaining a work of that description from a circulating library. I hope with you that the present delightful weather may contribute to the perfect restoration of our dear papa's health, and that it may give aunt pleasant reminiscences of the salubrious climate of her native place.

With love to all,—Believe me, dear Branwell, to remain your affectionate sister,

Charlotte.[1]

Branwell, the centre of her universe at that time, the lifeline that bound her yet to her most secret purposes, held in his person all the promise of life for her. She was convinced that whatever she might have to sacrifice of personal fulfilment, Branwell would accomplish in her place. To ramble arm-in-arm with him in Roe Head garden and to hear his latest addenda to the Glass Town Saga, was an inspiration, a reminder of holidays and home; where she might once again resume

[1] CB to PBB, 17 May 1831: *SBC* iii.

her real identity and pursue the promptings of her fancy without disloyalty to her teachers and benefactors.

Mary and Martha's family lived nearer the school than did Ellen's, which allowed them occasional visits home during the term. Charlotte was sometimes invited to join them, and this too was an entry into a new world, in which every value, save that of scrupulous regard for honour, was different from those she had been brought up to revere. The Taylors were Radicals, and very noisy aggressive ones at that—Republicans, Nonconformists, and Feminists. The strong-willed children (there were four boys as well as Mary and Martha) held as decided views as the parents, and were licensed to express themselves vociferously before their elders. So complete an absence of inhibitions was something of a novelty to Charlotte, but her inwardly courageous self responded at once to the stimulus, and she found visits to the Taylor family absorbingly interesting. A good listener, preferring to remain unobserved in any company, attentive to what was passing to the degree of remembering years later the looks, attitudes, and very phrases of speakers, her memories of those visits gave fresh and sparkling life to the pages of *Shirley*. '. . . At our house', Mary Taylor recalled, 'she had . . . little chance of a patient hearing, for though not schoolgirlish we were more intolerant. We had a rage for practicality, and laughed all poetry to scorn. Neither she nor we had any ideas but that our opinions were the opinions of all the *sensible* people in the world, and we used to astonish each other at every sentence. . . .'![1]

The scorn of poetry, so startling to a girl whose breath of life it was, was counterbalanced in this strange strifeful family by the rare and beautiful pictures, art-albums, and books collected by Mr. Taylor upon his continental travels. Himself the oddest mixture of uncouthness and culture, a cloth-manufacturer speaking the broadest Yorkshire and a dilettante, he travelled abroad not merely for business but to satisfy his profound love of art. He spoke French and Italian as fluently as his mother tongue. Joshua Taylor was a fascinating study to young Charlotte, so much so she introduced him into two of her novels—as Yorke Hunsdon in *The Professor*, and as Hiram Yorke in *Shirley*. Even so, his daughter Mary considered the portrait not good enough: '. . . he is not honest enough', she declared. '. . . It was from my father' she added, 'I learnt not to marry for money nor to tolerate any one who did. . . .' Mr. Taylor, who kept abreast of French literature all his life, was later of great use to Charlotte, lending her his latest acquisitions

[1] Mary Taylor, Reminiscences of CB: *SLL* i. 82–83.

from Paris, the novels of Paul de Kock, Eugene Sue, George Sand, and other modern writers.

Mrs. Taylor, *née* Ann Tickell, seems to have united in her person all the disagreeable qualities of Mrs. Gummidge, Mrs. Wilfer, and Mrs. Vardon; she was cordially disliked by Charlotte and not particularly loved by her daughters, whose life she oppressed with her gloom and tyranny. There were three brothers older than Mary—Joshua, John, and Joseph—and a brother younger than them all—Waring.[1]

The Taylors came of an old family established in the district since 1379. They lived at Gomersal in a charming house built by a forebear in 1660, whose red brick, contrasting with the prevailing 'dressed' stone of the houses in the region, earned it the name of 'The Red House'. It was a long and low structure, only two stories high, with high French windows reaching to the ground in front, five gables at the rear, its red walls trellised and covered with creepers, and surrounded back and front by lawns, and almost masked from the skirting highway by a sheltering grove of walnut trees.

Inside The Red House Charlotte quickly learned to feel at home. Across the entrance-hall, flagged with Dutch black and white tiles, and through an archway under the stairs, was the 'back parlour', 'the farthest to the right', where nightly the family foregathered and she found the conversation so entertaining. In that room were the stained glass windows described in *Shirley*: '. . . purple and amber the predominent hues, glittering round a grave-tinted medallion in the centre of each, representing the suave head of William Shakespeare, and the serene head of John Milton. . . .'[2] This noble window has now found its way to Charlotte Brontë's old home.

The stairs led up to a long-galleried first floor off which lay the bedrooms, and to an arched passage to the back of the house, in a room of which Charlotte placed the wounded Robert Moore in *Shirley*. Mary Taylor, reading the description years later, wrote: '. . . By the way, you have put him in the servant's bedroom. . . .'[3]

The more Charlotte knew the Taylors, the more she liked them. In after years she would write of them: '. . . the society of the Taylors is one of the most rousing pleasures I have ever known. . . .'[4]

A different atmosphere reigned in Ellen Nussey's home. Not until

---

[1] For the Taylor family, see *Cleckheaton Guardian*, 15 June 1894; *Bradford Daily Telegraph*, 2 Mar. 1892; Edgerley, *BST*, 1944; *Pall Mall Gazette*, 30 Oct., 1880; H. A. Cadman, *Gomersal Past & Present*.   [2] *Shirley*, ch. 9.
[3] Mary Taylor to CB, 13 Aug. 1850: *SLL* ii. 153.   [4] *BST*, 1944, p. 215.

she had left school did Charlotte stay there for any time, but on occasional half-holidays during her three terms at Roe Head she received invitations to visit there. Charlotte's very first letter to Ellen, probably written across the school-room, attests to this.

Roe Head May 11th 1831

Dear Ellen,

I take advantage of the earliest opportunity to thank you for the letter you favoured me with last week and to apologize for having so long neglected to write to you; indeed I believe this will be the first letter or note I have ever addressed to you. I am extremely obliged to your sister for her kind invitation and I assure you that I should very much have liked to hear Mr. Murray's lectures on Calvinism as they would doubtless have been both amusing and instructive. But we are often compelled 'to bend our inclinations to our duty' (as Miss Wooler observed the other day) and since there are so many holidays this half-year it would have appeared almost unreasonable to ask for an extra holiday; besides we should perhaps have got behind hand with our lessons. So that, everything considered it is perhaps as well that circumstances have deprived us of this pleasure.

Believe me to remain
Your affect friend
C. Brontë.[1]

Ellen's home, Rydings (without the definite article as its owner requested), lying in its own parkland off the main Birstall to Halifax road, was a fine building of very striking character, several of whose features Charlotte later incorporated into her descriptions of Thornfield Hall. A long, two-storied house, Rydings, like Thornfield, had a battlemented roof, a rookery, and a park of centenarian trees, including some double-thorns, mentioned in *Jane Eyre*, whose red and white blossoms flowered simultaneously on the same tree.

The title-deeds of Rydings go back to Edward IV, but the structure inherited by the Nusseys when Ellen was a little girl dated from the early eighteenth century, the rear being decidedly older than the front. It had belonged to Ellen's great-uncle Reuben Walker, who had lived there in great style, being the only Justice of the Peace for a very wide area that comprised Leeds, Bradford, Huddersfield, and Halifax. He had held his courts there and entertained the County candidate, Earl FitzWilliam, for a fortnight on the occasion of the 1809 parliamentary elections—the successful candidate be it added. Reuben Walker

[1] BPM.

was a retired Court Physician, a post in which four other members of Ellen's family would follow him, including her own brother John.

Ellen herself had been born at her father's home at Birstall Smithies, and as a little girl had been sent to a mixed school for boys and girls at Birstall kept by Benoni Elam. Her father's death in 1826 reduced the family finances, but the many wealthy relatives on both sides of the family—the Walkers and the Nusseys—who owned between them some of the best properties in the district—'Brookroyd', 'White Leas', 'Oakwell Hall', as well as 'Rydings'—ensured the widow's future and that of her daughters.[1]

At the time Charlotte met Ellen at Roe Head her mother was established at Rydings with her daughters Ann (then aged 35), Mercy (23), Sarah Walker (21), and her younger sons Richard (25), Henry (19, just about to go up to Cambridge), and George, Ellen's nearest in age, then 17. At nearby Oakwell Hall, an Elizabethan mansion later well known to Charlotte and described in *Shirley* as 'Fieldhead', lived other relatives of the Nusseys, a further branch of the Walker family. Through the marriage of her great-aunt Sarah with Sir George Armytage of Kirklees Priory, Ellen was also connected with the biggest landowner in the district whose estates, incidentally, adjoined Roe Head.

Her background was, therefore, at the same time wider and far narrower than that of Charlotte Brontë or Mary Taylor. Though Reuben Walker had collected some very fine pictures at Rydings, Ellen's home was neither essentially cultural, as was Charlotte's, nor liberal like the Taylors'. It lacked any distinctive character, in fact, and it was partly the mental dullness of her surroundings that made Ellen so intensely interested in Charlotte's. Though the threat of poverty never actually hung over her and she was not educated to earn her living, her prospects were yet less happy than either Charlotte's or Mary's. With none of the intellectual power of either friend, her family's exigencies wholly absorbed her vitality. She suffered their domestic tyranny with perfect docility, the one indulgence of her life being, perhaps, her friendship for Charlotte Brontë.

The first advances were made by her. It was her suggestion that, when their school-days were ended, a regular monthly correspondence should be pursued; and when that time arrived it was Ellen who first invited Charlotte for a long visit to her home, thus inaugurating the

[1] On the Nusseys and Rydings, see Cradock, *History of the Ancient Parish of Birstall*, 1933; *Cleckheaton Guardian*, 4 Dec. 1897; W. Scruton, Reminiscences of EN: *BST*, 1898; Edgerley, EN: *BST*, 1940.

regular exchange of visits between Haworth and Birstall which kept the
friendship alive.

Diffident at first, doubting in fact that she could secure so deep and
true an affection outside the family circle, Charlotte gradually succumbed to Ellen's proffered love. ' . . . The receipt of your letter gave
me an agreeable surprise . . .', she wrote in the Christmas holidays of
1831–2, 'for notwithstanding your faithful promises, you must excuse
me if I say I had little confidence in their fulfilment. . . .'[1]

By the following July, having just left school for good, she had
accepted the friendship and given her own in exchange. 'I have been
expecting to hear from you almost every day since my arrival home,
and I at length began to despair of receiving the wished-for letter. . . .'[2]

If it is difficult to find sufficient motive on Charlotte's side for this
attachment, it must be remembered that she met Ellen at an emotional
crisis in her youth. Impressed with the need to devote all her talents
to the purpose of earning a living, and prepared to make the sacrifice
of her personal hopes, loves, and ambitions to secure it, she found
nevertheless that it was not in her nature to submit without suffering
and struggle. She was bent on being good, on doing her duty, on
renouncing her plans of happiness, but she had to acknowledge with
shame how heavy was her soul at the necessity. Removed from the
siren voices of her spirit world, she resolved to stop her ears to their
appeal. In this resolve no one helped her so much as Ellen Nussey, all
unconscious as she was of the issue at stake. For Ellen the emptiness
of life was best filled by religion, and towards religion she gently drew
her friend. Charlotte's compliance was made all the easier in the pious
atmosphere of the Miss Woolers' school and of her own preparation for Confirmation by the Miss Woolers' brother-in-law, the Rev.
Edward Carter. In Ellen, a model of goodness in her sight, Charlotte
came to acknowledge the voice of conscience. As all her early correspondence with Ellen shows, she was subdued to a sense of high
seriousness of existence. Writing on 1 January 1833 to her new friend,
the reflection that came uppermost to her mind was: ' . . . The first day
of January always presents to my mind a train of very solemn and important reflections, and a question more easily asked than answered
frequently occurs, viz—How have I improved the past year . . . ?'[3]

It would be a significant feature of Ellen's hero-worship of Charlotte, and the chief article of her defence of Charlotte's memory after

[1] CB to EN, 13 Jan. 1832: *SBC* 192.
[2] CB to EN, 21 July 1832: *SLL* i. 94.   [3] CB to EN: *SLL* i. 99.

her death, that she emphasized above all other characteristics, qualities, and tastes, her friend's religion, the apparent absence of which in her writings was the object of the bitterest attacks on Currer Bell. The angle from which Ellen saw her friend and wished her to be seen by others was already displayed in her earliest recollections of their school-days together. 'I must not forget to state that no girl in the school was equal to Charlotte in Sunday lessons,' wrote Ellen. 'Her acquaintance with Holy Writ surpassed others in this as in everything else. She was very familiar with all the sublimest passages, especially those in Isaiah in which she took great delight. Her Confirmation took place while she was at school, and in her preparation for that, as in all other studies, she distinguished herself by application and proficiency. . . .'[1]

Charlotte gave Ellen a great measure of her love; during the emotional and religious crises of her youth she bared her soul to her, depending much on her for spiritual comfort. But never, throughout her girlhood, did she confide to Ellen a single matter relating to her writing and literary ambitions. Long after the secret was out and she had become a famous novelist, to Ellen her true self remained unknown. It was a region of the mind to which Charlotte never gave admittance save to Branwell, Emily, and Anne.

Within the limitations thus set, the friendship formed at Roe Head endured to the end of her life. The correspondence to which it led, stretching over nearly 25 years and piously preserved by Ellen, forms the basis of our knowledge of the outer circumstances of Charlotte's life. But it is as well to recognize at once that the correspondence of Charlotte Brontë and Ellen Nussey, invaluable as it is to any study of the former's life, is a deceptive document which leaves the essentials unsaid.

Very different may have been the letters addressed over the same years to Mary Taylor, but the reticent Mary, judging them 'unsafe' to preserve, destroyed them except for a few. How far Charlotte ever confided her literary activities can be deduced from a significant memory of Mary's: when the girls first met at Roe Head Charlotte's use of italic script greatly surprised Mary, to whom Charlotte confided about the miniature magazines and the wish to imitate print, and even promised to show her some numbers, 'but retracted it afterwards and would never be persuaded to do so', commented Mary.[2] The close collaboration, first between herself and Branwell, and then between her

---

[1] EN, Reminiscences of CB: *SLL* i. 91.
[2] Mary Taylor, Reminiscences of CB: *SLL* i. 80–83.

sisters and herself, bound her to secrecy even had she felt able to discuss the matter with her friends. Happily the great creative output of Charlotte's youth and maturity, her published and voluminous unpublished works, the fragments, echoes, visitations, trances, the appeals, pursuits, and struggles of her aspiring genius remain by which to know her potent spirit, as those who only knew her in the flesh could never do.

Enriched with the prescribed number of solid attainments and 'lady-like accomplishments' required of a governess, Charlotte was sent home after her three 'halves' at Roe Head in May 1832—a credit to her benefactors, her teachers, and herself. The first endurance test had been passed; over and above the new-found knowledge derived from books, she had learnt to conquer herself, a lesson in self-suppression which, in common with the heroines of her novels, she would often have to apply and which, suffer as she might, she would never forget.[1]

[1] See Additional Notes for further data concerning the district of Roe Head and of CB's friendships formed there.

CHAPTER VI

THE 'WEB OF SUNNY AIR'

A LAST echo of those school-days and a reflection of Charlotte's image as it remained in the mind of her friends is contained in a letter from Martha Taylor to Ellen Nussey, written shortly after the end-of-term dispersal. Charlotte and Mary Taylor had left school for good; Ellen's position remained characteristically undefined (she might or she might not return as a full boarder or only as a visiting pupil for extras); and the ebullient Martha, sobered temporarily at the prospect of a friendless return next 'Half', was prompt to take her dispositions. She wrote on 17 May:

Dear Miss Nussey, I asked Miss Wooler if she would allow me to sleep with you next half-year if you came to school and she said certainly and she said she hoped I would profit by your advice. Miss Susan Ledgard was asked to return home with us at the beginning of the holidays but she preferred going home first and coming to see us at haytime when I hope we shall have the pleasure of seeing you. . . . It is not quite settled whether my sister will come to take drawing lessons next half-year or not. . . . I wonder how we shall get on next half-year without you and Miss Bronte. I think the schoolroom will look strange without Miss Bronte at the head of the class. . . . I am going to try for the neatness prize but I am afraid if you come to school I shall not be able to obtain it. I think I shall feel Miss Bronte's loss very much as she has always been very kind to me. I must now conclude, and believe me to remain Yours very affectionately,

Martha Taylor.[1]

It remained a lifelong characteristic of Charlotte's to underestimate her powers to please; this early tribute from young Martha Taylor is the more noteworthy therefore.

The return home after the long absence at school was unalloyed delight for Charlotte. Her father's health was restored, and her present duty lay in nothing more arduous than in imparting her new-found knowledge to her sisters, so that in due course they too might be fitted

---

[1] Martha Taylor to EN: *W & S* i. 102.

to earn their livings. Few periods in her life would ever be so happy again—certainly none would be so free from care.

More than ever before Branwell was the undisputed lord of her life. He was the instigator, compeer, confidant of every creative thought, the astounding collaborator for whose speed, originality, and daring in composition her admiration was aflame. During their separation a new and exciting aspect of Branwell had evolved. His masculinity had found expression not only in his writing but in certain progressive tastes. He had become an addict of the Ring. With his new-found village cronies he went sparring in an upper room of the 'Black Bull' or the old 'White Lion'; he read Bell's sporting 'Life in London' as much now as he read Byron. The protagonists of his tales, especially Alexander Rogue, Viscount Elrington, whose treachery precipitated the civil wars throughout the Glass Town Confederacy, were no longer puppets, they were men, unscrupulous, scheming, tainted with all the love of quick-money, material prosperity, and political ambition that actuated the young Brontës' own contemporary parvenus. Branwell's prodigious literary output during Charlotte's absence at school, the six volumes of his 'Letters of an Englishman'[1] in particular, was an achievement the maturity of which, compared with the schoolgirl ambiance she herself had recently known, was particularly exciting. How to keep pace with Branwell was now the daily challenge.

Hardly less gratifying to her sense of importance in the family was the devotion of her sisters who, despite their twin-like absorption in each other, did not love her any the less and looked up to her as little short of a prodigy. How sweet their affection tasted after the months among strangers can be judged from the reactions of Ellen Nussey, the self-appointed keeper of Charlotte's conscience. Replying to a letter of Ellen's on 1 January 1833 Charlotte wrote: 'You very kindly caution me against being tempted by the fondness of my sisters to consider myself of too much importance, and then in parenthesis you beg me not to be offended. O Ellen, do you think I could be offended by any good advice you may give? No, I thank you heartily, and Love you, if possible, better for it. . . .'[2]

The perfect harmony existing between the four of them, alike in the intensity of their feelings, differing only in the degree of their endowments, was a singular blessing and one fully appreciated by Charlotte in retrospect. Writing in after years of that halcyon time she said:

[1] PBB, 'Letters of an Englishman', 6 vols. 1830–2: Brotherton Coll., Univ. of Leeds.
[2] CB to EN: *W & S* i. 108.

'. . . My home is humble and unattractive to strangers, but to me it contains what I shall find nowhere else in the world—the profound, the intense affection which brothers and sisters feel for each other when their minds are cast in the same mould, their ideas drawn from the same source—when they have clung to each other from childhood, and when disputes have never sprung up to divide them. . . .'[1] There were no disputes, though Charlotte could not explain to Ellen or any other outsider the source of their union.

Adolescence naturally worked differently in each of them. Emily and Anne were all for an outdoor life, playing the game of outlaws, exiles, of perilous escapes and trystings, as their 'Gondal' tales took form and substance among the hills of home. The heart of Charlotte was in advance of theirs; her thoughts were all turned to love. It suited them, as it suited her, to pursue a different track, create another landscape. They left to her the 'Burning Clime' of their 'Glass Town' creation, preferring the mists and wilds of 'Gondal' where their coltlike young limbs and boyish minds could range more freely. The difference between their closeness to the natural scene, their intimacy with the creatures inhabiting those high-ranging moors, and Charlotte's timidity is best conveyed in the recollections of Ellen Nussey after her first visit to Haworth. In their walks across the moors Ellen noted that it was 'Emily, Anne and Branwell who used to ford the streams, and who placed stepping stones for the other two' (herself and Charlotte). On the moors Ellen detected a 'spell of mischief' in Emily: 'she enjoyed leading Charlotte where she would not dare to go of her own free will. Charlotte had a mortal dread of unknown animals, and it was Emily's pleasure to lead her into close vicinity and then to tell her how and of what she had done, laughing at her terror with great amusement. . . .'[2]

The very nature of Charlotte's imaginings at the time, wholly amorous as they were, called for individual treatment rather than the old partnership pattern. The tales and poems of the three years following her return from school—left without titles as was her wont—have been listed for bibliographical purposes under such titles as: 'The Bridal', 'Love & Jealousy', 'The Rivals', 'Arthuriana'. The theme seldom departed from the wooing and wedding, the spurning and pursuit of her ideal hero, Arthur Adrian Augustus Wellesley, Marquis of Douro. While her little sisters were still playing the game of revolutions she brooded alone on love and jealousy.

[1] CB to Henry Nussey, 9 May 1841: *W & S* i. 232.
[2] EN, 'Reminiscences of CB': *Scribners Magazine*, May 1871.

Separate, yet blissfully close in the quality and nature of their happiness, the young authors spent every evening-hour poring over their writing desks in the dining-room. Only the completest confidence in each other's judgement, respect, and objectives could have released so simultaneous a flow of dissimilar narrative. While Emily was jotting down notes for herself and Anne on their evolving Gondal plot—'. . . The Gondals are discovering the interior of Gaaldine. . . .'[1] and Anne was apostrophizing Gondal's heroes and heroines in tender verses

> Why, when I hear the stormy breath
> Of the wild winter wind
> Rushing o'er the mountain heath,
> Does sadness fill my mind . . .?[2]

Charlotte, introducing her hero the newly created Duke of Zamorna and King of Angria to ever greater glory, was thrilling to the tale of his domestic infidelities in the hot-house atmosphere of court intrigue. '. . . My King, my Husband, my very Deity . . .' implores his second wife on behalf of her father Zamorna's arch-enemy, Percy, 'Am I to lie down on a sleepless pillow to-night Zamorna? Am I to eat the bread and drink the waters of bitterness, or blessed with the forgiving light of your countenance, am I to sleep in peace and awake in safety? . . .'[3]

Her enthusiasm as she knelt almost crouched in her earnest pleading at his feet, her sweet and swelling tones, her whole aspect, like Philippa supplicating for the Calaisians or Esther for the devoted Hebrews, quickly recalled Zamorna's absent thoughts. . . . The Monarch's hand shook through the influence of some strong internal emotion as he passed it over his broad white brow and then let it fall on his Queen's head bowed before him like a storm-beaten lily. . . . 'Be calm, love, be calm my dear Mary' said he in that still, dew-like voice of his. . . .[4]

Charlotte evoked later that time of inordinate indulgence in the lushest of visions, that period of magic union between sisters and brother, and between the four of them and the world of fantasy in which, too long for their subsequent peace, they prolonged their childhood. In verses of peculiar serenity she remembered how

> We wove a web in childhood,
> A web of sunny air;
> We dug a spring in infancy
> Of water pure and fair;

[1] EJB Diary Paper, 24 Nov. 1834: BPM.
[2] AB, 'Verses by Lady Geralda', Dec. 1836: *W & S PEJAB*.
[3] 'My Angria & the Angrians', 1834, op. cit.   [4] Idem.

We sowed in youth a mustard seed
We cut an almond rod;
We are now grown up to riper age—
Are they withered in the sod?

The mustard-seed in distant land
Bends down a mighty tree,
The dry unbudding almond wand
Has touched eternity . . .[1]

Her ability to live upon two planes of being is never more clearly
shown than in comparing her letters to Ellen with the substance of her
creative writing: to Ellen she wrote on 21 July 1832 in reply to queries
respecting her occupations:

. . . You ask me to give you a description of the manner in which I have
passed every day since I left school; this is soon done, as an account of one
day is an account of all. In the morning from 9 o'clock to half-past 12, I
instruct my sisters and draw, then we walk till dinner, after dinner I sew till
tea time, and after tea I either read, write, do a little fancy work, or draw, as I
please. Thus in one delightful, though somewhat monotonous course, my
life is passed. . . .[2]

In writing so to Ellen she practised no deceit; it was the truth—
though not the whole truth—just as the verses told the truth about a
life too responsive to romantic stimuli ever to be confined without
acute suffering within conventional limits.

For the time being she lived by *reflected* experiences and sentiments,
in a heightened state of being where, mentally, she was companioned
only by the great. Sending Ellen a list of recommended reading on
4 July 1834, she enjoined on her to avoid all poetry that was not first-
rate, and forestalled her objection to Shakespeare and Byron with the
argument: '. . . Now don't be startled at the names of Shakespeare and
Byron. Both these were great men, and their works are like themselves.
You will know how to choose the good, and avoid the evil. . . . Omit
the comedies of Shakespeare and the 'Don Juan'; perhaps the 'Cain' of
Byron, though the latter is a magnificent poem . . . and read the rest
fearlessly. . . .' (As has been seen, neither 'Manfred', nor 'Cain', nor
'Don Juan' were prohibited reading at Haworth parsonage, where

[1] CB, 'We Wove a Web in Childhood', 19 Dec. 1835: Huntington Univ. Lib., San
Marino, California.
[2] CB to EN: *W & S* i. 103.

echoes of the first poem had crept into Charlotte's tale 'The Foundling' the year before.) Byron and Lord Edward FitzGerald, whose bio-
graphies by Moore Ellen was further urged to read, were the gods of
Charlotte's current worship. Like Caroline Vernon, the heroine of one
of her later tales, 'her reading was Byron, and she thought Lord Byron
and Bonaparte, the Duke of Wellington and Lord Edward FitzGerald
the four best men that had ever lived . . .',[1] an opinion not without its
significance in the year that saw the creation of 'Angria'.

When it came to confiding in Ellen, however, the only passion of the
moment that seemed avowable was the passion for drawing. According
to F. A. Leyland, Branwell's later friend and biographer, '. . . Charlotte
even thought of art as a profession for herself; and so strong was this
intention, that she could scarcely be convinced that it was not her true
vocation. . . .'[2] If this was a seriously entertained project, she defeated
her own purpose by wearing out her eyes in the meticulous copying
of mezzotints, spending as much as six months on a single plate. As Mrs.
Gaskell later reported: '. . . her eyes . . . failed her in the minute and
useless labour which she had imposed upon herself . . . to this end. . . .'[3]
Artistically useless as she later realized these efforts to have been, the
long scrutiny of plates did, however, help to develop her natural gift
for analysis. The hope, maybe, of sharing Branwell's profession ultimately as an artist prompted her studies. To this period at any rate can
be assigned the drawing lessons given the young Brontës at home by
William Robinson, the Leeds artist, for which Mr. Brontë paid £2 a
lesson.[4] Certainly at no period was Branwell so much the overruling
influence in Charlotte's life as during the years immediately following
her return from school. In her development as a writer that influence
was paramount, shaping as it did, consciously or unconsciously, the
second self to which she gave a masculine name and which she endowed with Branwellian characteristics. She was 'C. W.' or more often
'Charles Thunder' (after her own name Brontë) or 'Charles Townsend',
and she assumed the 'Thersites'-type of character, the cynical onlooker
at the social scene, malicious, vain, cowardly, small-minded, inquisitive,
and withal deliciously comic, in whom she burlesqued the multiple
aspects of Branwell's variable nature. The happiest feature of her
devotion to Branwell was, indeed, her ability to laugh at him. Her

---

[1] Caroline Vernon, MS. fragment, July 1839: Harvard.
[2] Leyland i. 126–7.   [3] Gaskell 191.
[4] For further details respecting William Robinson and his lessons to the young
Brontës, see Gérin, *Branwell Brontë*, 79–81, 97–98. See also Chadwick 102.

admiration for his exceptional talents was at the same time so sane a
sentiment that she was not blind to his oddities—as her caricature of
him as 'Patrick Benjamin Wiggins' attests. The passage, among the
most purely comic ever written by Charlotte, shows all too plainly
what a humorous as well as dramatic writer she could have been had
home always been the happy place it was in 1834, and Branwell had
never disillusioned her. She introduced him as

a low slightly built man attired in a black coat and raven grey trousers, his
hat placed nearly at the back of his head, revealing a bush of carroty hair so
arranged that at the sides it projected almost like two spread hands, a pair of
spectacles placed across a prominent Roman nose, black neckerchief adjusted
with no attention to precision, and, to complete the picture, a little black
rattan flourished in his hand. His bearing as he walked was tolerably upright
and marked with that indescribable swing always assumed by those who
pride themselves on being good pedestrians. . . .[1]

This is Patrick Benjamin Wiggins, the comic relief of her long and
important fragment 'My Angria & the Angrians' written in October
1834. The swagger in Wiggins's gait is equally observed in his speech,
full as it is of the hesitancies in hyperbole of the braggart. Asked how
far he intended walking he replied:

'. . . Not *quite* to the end of the world, that is not altogether. I don't think of
walking much farther than Zamorna [the capital city]. Mr. Greenwood sent
for me. . . . The distance you know Lord Charles is forty miles and I did it
in twelve hours—indeed it's more than forty, nearer fifty. O yes, and above
sixty I daresay, or sixty-five. Now Sir, what do you-say to a man's walking
sixty-five miles in one day? . . .'[2]

As a nobleman on horseback overtakes them on the road, Wiggins
flings himself down in his path 'flat as a fluke, motionless as a Parsee
worshipping the new Risen Sun . . .', in sign of abject respect for
the gentleman's rank. From this posture only the passing of the Mail
Coach '. . . made Wiggins spring up pretty actively. . . .'[3]

Wiggins was on his way to a high musical festival, in connexion
with which the organizers had allowed him a humble role (music was
Branwell's passion of the moment and clearly he talked of it *ad nauseam*
to his family).

'. . . I hope,' said Wiggins, 'abundance of accommodation will be provided

1 'My Angria & the Angrians', 14 Oct. 1834: BPM.
2 Idem.   3 Idem.

for the bands of music, or else Mr. Greenwood'll not be pleased . . . by the
bye Lord Charles, there are to be five brass bands each consisting of two
trumpets, three bombardones four Cyclopedes, five Serpents, six Bugles,
seven French horns, eight gongs, nine Kettle drums, and ten Ramgalong-
tonas, a new kind of instrument that's never been blown in Africa before.
And then the five reed bands will contain eleven flutes . . . twelve clarinetts
(sic) thirteen piccolos. . . .'[1]

'Spare us Wiggins,' interrupted I, 'Why, man according to your calculation of musical instruments the Court-House will be entirely taken up by
them and their managers. . . .'

In ludicrous contrast to the polite, self-doubting, subservient Branwell that his family knew, was his assumption at times of worldly airs
and of manly prowess—be it only at eating and drinking. This aspect
of him Charlotte also showed in 'Wiggins'.

'. . . I'm rather thirsty' he said, 'and I think I'll call for a pot of porter or a
tumbler of brandy and water, at the Public yonder.' He bolted across the
road. A fat landlady met him at the door. 'Well, sir, what's your will?' she
said, for he stood a moment without speaking.

'If you please ma'am will you be kind enough to give me a ha'penny worth
of milk, or a gill of whey, or even a draught of ditch-water, if it would be
too much trouble to procure the other liquids for such a mere Tom-cat as I
am.'

The Hostess, who seemed to be a good-natured soul, was no doubt
accustomed to Wiggins' manner, as he is a frequent traveller on this
road. She laughed and said: 'You'd better step into the House, Sir,
and get a cup of warm tea into you. I've set the Breakfast things on the
table.'

Wiggins scraped his feet very carefully and followed her in. I could see
him through the open door, take a seat by the fireside, swallow two or three
cups of tea, with a due quantum of bread and butter very rapidly dismissed.
Then, rising from his seat he took from his pocket about 20 shillings in
silver (how he came by it I don't know) and offering it with an air to the
Landlady, said, 'Pay yourself, Ma'am . . .' and with a gallant 'Good
Morning' he quitted the House and rejoined me.

'Well!' was his first exclamation, 'I feel like a Lion now . . . Two bottles
of . . . ale, and a double quart of Porter, with cheese, bread, and cold beef
have I devoured since I left you Lord Charles. That's what I call doing the
thing in a handsome way, and I'm not a bit touched—only light and smart
and active. . . .'[2]

---

[1] 'My Angria & the Angrians', Oct. 1834: BPM.
[2] Idem.

Contempt of his sisters and of his home circumstances was the natural reflex of his 17 years and of his extravagant expectations in life.

'Why, you see Lord Charles' said Wiggins, 'my mind was always looking above my station. I was not satisfied with being a sign-painter at Howard, as Charlotte and them things were with being sempstresses. I set before myself the Grand Plan of Africa and I traced a path for my feet through it, which terminated at the door of a splendid Palace situated on Cock-hill [a local landmark] whose portal bore inscribed 'Residence of the Duke of Thorncliffe [born at Thornton Branwell often spoke of himself thus]. The inscription on his tombstone he predicted would bear the following: 'Erected to the memory of PATRICK BENJAMIN WIGGINS, Duke of Thorn-cliffe and Viscount Howard. As a Musician he was greater than Bach, as a Poet he surpassed Byron, as a Painter, Claude Lorraine yielded to him ... He erected the Obelisk of Baraliticus in Othaheite, to which country he also introduced the arts and science which now flourish there ... and last and greatest of his mighty acts, he built the stupendous Organ . . . now glorifying the Cathedral of St. Northangerland in his native Howard. . . .'[1]

The devotion of Charlotte to Branwell was a circumstance that greatly struck Ellen Nussey when she first saw the two together. In the autumn of 1832 (six months after the girls had left school) she invited Charlotte on a first visit to her home; describing Charlotte's arrival from Haworth in a two-wheeled gig she added:

... Mr. Brontë sent Branwell as an escort; he was *then* a very dear brother, as dear to Charlotte as her own soul; they were in perfect accord of taste and feeling, and it was mutual delight to be together. Branwell probably had never been far from home before! he was in wild ecstasy with everything. He walked about in unrestrained boyish enjoyment, taking views in every direction of the old turret-roofed house, the fine chestnut trees on the lawn ... and a large rookery, which gave to the house a good background—all these he noted and commented upon with perfect enthusiasm. He told his sister he was leaving her in Paradise, and if she were not intensely happy she never would be! Happy, indeed, she then was *in himself*, for she, with her own enthusiasm, looked forward to what her brother's great promise and talent might effect. . . .[2]

In the summer of the following year, 1833, Ellen paid a return visit to Haworth. Among a host of strong and strange impressions the intellectual calibre of the young Brontës, met in force, was among the clearest. Describing the interior of their home, 'the sanded floors, the

---

[1] Idem.
[2] EN, Reminiscences of CB: *SLL* i. 84 et seq.

sparse furnishings, the dove-coloured walls (no wall-paper) and book-lined recesses', she had the perception to note that '. . . Mind and thought, I had almost said elegance but certainly refinement, diffused themselves over all, and made nothing really wanting. . . .'[1]

The spiritual quality of her friend's home surprised Ellen in conjunction with its other simple aspects. A feature that impressed her then was the family's love of animals. This was a general sentiment shared by all (with the notable exception of Miss Branwell), stemming perhaps from Mr. Brontë's Irish origin and the need for the companionship and guardianship of a dog in those remote rural areas. But the Brontës' love of animals extended far beyond the house-dog—the known holders of which office were 'Grasper', 'Keeper', and 'Plato' (Anne's little spoilt spaniel 'Flossy' hardly qualifying for the post)—and included animals of every description and kind, from dogs and cats to ponies, donkeys, birds (wild and tame), and the hidden denizens of the moors. The tale of their adoptions, rescues, championings, and succouring is as long as their lives and finds an eloquent commentary in their writings. Immortality was conferred not only on 'Keeper' (and his prototype 'Tartar' in *Shirley*) but on 'Flossy', the innumerable cats headed by 'Snowflake' and 'Tom', the black tabby mentioned by Ellen as having received 'such gentle treatment it seemed to have lost cat's nature'; the canary 'Dick' and the privileged geese, called after the regnant queens of the Brontës' girlhood, 'Adelaide' and 'Victoria', who slept in the peat-room; and Emily's hawk 'Hero', rescued from the moors and lovingly nurtured in the parsonage. The doings of these dumb but not inarticulate creatures were recorded by Emily and Anne in their diaries over the years and reported in the family correspondence with the same interest that related to the humans of the family; their deaths were lamented with a depth of feeling their owners were quite unable to conceal. Conjuring up the image of her sisters as 'Mary' and 'Diana Rivers' in *Jane Eyre*, Charlotte saw the one with a mastiff's head pressed against her knee, and the other nursing a cat, and in doing so epitomized their domestic identities.[2] Summing up those first impressions, Ellen Nussey said: '. . . The Brontës' love of dumb creatures made them very sensitive of the treatment bestowed upon them. For any one to offend in this respect was with them an infallible bad sign on the disposition. . . .'[3]

Ellen would not appear at any time to have been blinded by Branwell's charm—despite the fact that he was the only boy in the family.

---

[1] EN, Reminiscences of CB: *Scribners*, op. cit.
[2] *Jane Eyre*, ch. 28.   [3] EN: *Scribners*, May 1871, op. cit.

She seems to have taken his family's assessment of his talents with a degree of scepticism. She was struck on the occasion of this visit how his future seemed an assured perspective towards which the whole family looked not only hopefully but enthusiastically: '. . . Branwell studied regularly with his father . . . and used to paint in oils, which was regarded as study for what might be eventually his profession. All the household entertained the idea of his becoming an artist, and hoped he would be a distinguished one. . . .'[1]

Branwell was endowed with all too many talents, was too much divided in his purposes, too febrile in his pursuit of each objective ever to attain the distinction so touchingly believed in by his family. Blinded as they were to his congenital weakness it was a pardonable misapprehension induced by the sheer brilliance of his boyhood.

During the year 1834 Charlotte and he worked out the scenario of their new plot relating to 'Angria', the African kingdom won from the Ashantees by the all-conquering Zamorna. For Branwell such a canvas offered unlimited scope for his favourite pursuit of cataloguing colossal forces, drawing up population returns, surveying territory, establishing boundaries, planning towns, appointing Governors. For Charlotte, the creation of a new court around the sovereign Adrian I, of a new society comprising every aspect of cultural life (writers, painters, singers), of a government whose members were increasingly drawn from observation and less from books, like the admirable study of General Thornton, the Yorkshire eccentric squire of the Taylor stamp,[2] such opportunities for descriptive writing constituted her best apprenticeship as a novelist. For this year alone her surviving manuscripts comprise a total of 141,000 words of prose narrative, and 400 lines of verse. Descriptive writing, the setting of a scene, the movement of crowds, was already bringing her aesthetic satisfaction and not merely romantic compensation, as the following passage, written in 1833, shows:

It was a bright and lovely afternoon in the midst of autumn. The saloons of Waterloo Place were thrown open for the admission of all the rank and fashion of Verdopolis. The doors of the great library were likewise unfolded, and there a knot of 'belesprits' the very flower of Africa's geniuses, had

[1] Idem. For Branwell's love of music, see Leyland, F. A., *The Brontë Family*, vol. i, 119. Also CB's letter to EN, 20 Feb. 1834, while in London: '. . . Will you be kind enough to inform me of the number of performers in the King's Military Band? Branwell wishes for this information . . .' *SLLT.* 109.

[2] For General Thornton see, in particular, 'Julia' narrative, dating from June 1837: Wrenn Lib., Univ. of Texas Lib.

gathered round a large open bow-window through which might be seen the
extensive pleasure grounds where groups of the brighter children of fashion
roamed idly about or reposed under the shade of sequestered bowers. Of
course my brother [Zamorna] and Lady Zenobia Elrington formed the
nucleus round which this literary party had assembled. While they were conversing Lord Lofty entered. . . . While he listened to the noble sentiment, the
brilliant wit, the exhaustless knowledge, and the varied information which,
clothed in the purest language and uttered in the soft subdued tones which
perfect refinement dictates, formed a conversazione of such fascinating brilliancy as he had never heard before, undefined longings arose in his heart to
become a more immediate partaker of the feast of reason and the flow of
soul he witnessed. . . .[1]

To become a 'more immediate partaker' of such circles, where
'exhaustless knowledge' was displayed, was all too patently the longing of the obscure young writer eating her heart out with dreams of
unattainable delight and devouring passion. Physical beauty allied to
exceptional mental powers were at that time essential prerequisites in
her characters; Angria abounded in every seduction of the senses, and
zestfully she allowed herself to be seduced!

Here the advantages of adopting the masculine pseudonym were
obvious: they afforded not only greater scope, but complete licence.
The transposition of sex in the writer allowed of such outspokenness as
characterized Zamorna when he told his mistress to her face that she
looked 'like an Angrian country-gentleman's Dolly'.[2] The disadvantages, on the other hand, were to make Charlotte self-conscious and to
exaggerate the cynical outlook and the licence of language which she
believed essential at that time to the masculine character she assumed.

In the long run the effect of this transposition of sex in the narrator
of Charlotte's tales (preserved as late as *The Professor*, the major
reason undoubtedly for its repeated rejection by publishers) showed
itself in her attitude to the masculine characters in the novels—as a man
speaking about men, in a manner borrowed from Branwell, she could
assume an equality of outlook that dispensed with judgement. Intended to be extremely 'blasé', it ended by becoming so unconscious a
part of her narrative style as to persist even into the wholly mature
creation of Rochester. To assess the degree of shock and incredulity
Rochester aroused in her first readers his natural evolution from the
heroes of Charlotte's youthful tales has to be remembered. Rochester,

[1] 'The Foundling', May–June 1833: Ashley Lib., BM.
[2] 'Mina Laury', 1836–8: *Tales from Angria*: Collins, 1956.

with his French mistresses and his illegitimate daughter, his unabashed confidences to that daughter's young governess, his scorn of bigamy and attempts at seducing virtue, was not only strong meat for the subscribers to the lending-libraries, but an object of scandal to the literary 'establishment'. Rochester was denounced by many, and even by some persons of taste, as a cad.[1] But to his creator Rochester was not only acceptable (and wholly lovable) but as familiar to her as her own brother. To be fairly judged, Rochester must be seen as the logical outcome of his author's earliest conceptions of a man.

Those conceptions, as has been seen, were deeply imbued with the Byronic model. The Ideal Hero must be saturnine, faithless, proud, disillusioned, masterful, melancholy, abrupt, a man of mystery with a past that can only be conjectured. Reading Charlotte's description of Zamorna written only two years after leaving school, it is impossible not to see the influence of Branwell—Branwell whose heated imagination often led to seizures that had the likeness of fits.

. . . There he stood with the red firelight flashing over him, one foot advanced, his head proudly raised, his kindled eyes fixed on the opposite wall and filled with a most inspired glory—that tinge of insanity which certainly mingles with his blood, was looking through their fierce dilated zones, as if it glared out at visions which itself had poured through the air. . . . Zamorna slowly paced the Saloon . . . and fixed upon them such an aspect, such eyes—it was evident he saw neither his father, his wife, nor Maxwell. The organs of vision were still and glazed; they looked through and beyond all solid objects with motionless intensity—motionless except an occasional fluttering of the eyelid and long lashes. . . . His face whitened more and more, something like foam became apparent on his lip—and he knitted his brow convulsively. . . .[2]

Above all, what distinguished Charlotte's conception of the hero, both in her juvenilia and adult writing, was her acceptance of his moral imperfections. Such an acceptance, though doubtless derived in part from the Calvinist creed in which she was reared, was present on every page of Byron, and in every embodiment of his heroes—Manfred the Giaour, the Corsair, Lara. But in the last resort it derived from the father-figure of all Byron's heroes—Milton's Satan himself.

The grandeur of the satanic figure (familiar to the young Brontës through Martin's illustrations to 'Paradise Lost' in particular), both in beauty of physique and force of mind, more than half captivated Byron

---

[1] Cf CB's astonishment at Mr. Williams's remarks on Rochester 14. 8. 48: *SLL* i. 446.
[2] 'My Angria & the Angrians', 1834, op. cit.

(as his Cain betrayed) and, be it admitted, captivated Charlotte Brontë as well. Was not Lara 'a stranger in this breathing world / An erring spirit from another hurl'd?' And, in a remarkable description for so young a girl to have written, Charlotte also came to acknowledge the demon part in her hero Zamorna. Presenting him as a portrait in an album, she laid him before her readers:

Fire! Light! What have we here? Zamorna's self, blazing in the frontispiece like the sun on his own standard. De Lisle has given him to us in full regimentals—plumed, epauletted and sabred . . . he stands as if a thunderbolt could neither blast the light of his eyes nor dash the effrontery of his brow. Keen, glorious being! O Zamorna! What eyes those are glancing under the deep shadow of that raven crest! They bode no good. Man nor woman could ever gather more than a troubled fitful happiness from their kindest light. Satan gave them their glory to deepen the midnight gloom that always follows where their lustre has fallen most lovingly. . . . All here is passion and fire unquenchable. Impetuous sin, stormy pride, diving and soaring enthusiasm, war and poetry, are kindling their fires in all his veins and his wild blood boils from his heart and back again like a torrent of new-sprung larva. Young Duke? Young demon![1]

The acceptance of imperfection as inseparable from the heroic role imparts a strangely hopeless tone to Charlotte's teenage romances. They are concerned with love but seldom for long with *happy* love. Infatuated couples, like Edward Sydney and Julia Wellesley in 'The Foundling' (1833), are soon shown, in 'A late Occurrence', 1834, to have drifted apart, and finally to have been resettled with other partners. The incidence of illicit connexions between the main characters is high. Both Zamorna and his rival Percy have liaisons resulting in illegitimate daughters. Such predicaments exercise the novelist's ingenuity, and Caroline Vernon, Percy's daughter by his French mistress Louisa, becomes the heroine of one of Charlotte's best adolescent tales. The similarities between the mother's character and the daughter's upbringing in Paris and Adèle's story in *Jane Eyre* are worth noting.

The sufferings of love are perhaps always more easily understood by the young than its felicities, but strangely haunting through all Charlotte's juvenilia is the unhappiness of her heroines. From her earliest 'Marina', whom separation from Albion killed, to Mina Laury, the last of the pre-publication heroines—the analysis of whose passion is a mature

[1] 'A Peep into a Picture Book', 1834.

achievement for a girl of 20—the lot of women is always one of suffering. The suffering, moreover, derives not only from their lover's infidelity and desertion but more deeply from their awareness of his moral imperfections. This is well understood by the young author to add to the heroines' sense of shame in their self-abasement before the hero. In a scene where Zamorna wounds and nearly kills a rival in his love for Mina Laury, Mina's reactions to his deed are thus described: '. . . so dark and profound are the mysteries of human nature, ever allying vice with virtue, that I fear this bloody proof of her master's love brought to her heart more rapture than horror. . . .'[1] (The early use here of the term 'master' for lover is an interesting forerunner of its habitual application to Rochester and Paul Emanuel.)

Sadly enough Mina acknowledges that her feelings for Zamorna are 'so fervid, so glowing in their colour that they effaced everything else. I lost the power of . . . appreciating the value of the world's opinion, of discerning the difference between right and wrong. . . .' Zamorna was 'something more to me than a human being. He superseded all things— all affections, all interests, all fears or hopes or principles. Unconnected with him my mind would be a blank. . . . I know the extent of my own infatuation. . . .'[2]

Already in the language of *Wuthering Heights* the sister of Ellis Bell at 20 indicated an awareness of the heart's excesses that cannot have come overnight. One would fear for such an ardent temperament a life of torment, and indeed no element of suffering was to be absent from it. But Charlotte's reaction to suffering when it came revealed a courage commensurate to her need.

The importance of her early acceptance of the mixed nature of man, however, is essential to an understanding of her relationship with her brother Branwell. Branwell's imperfections could be partially explained by the example of the Byronic hero for anyone living in an imaginary rather than a real world. By such standards Branwell might appear a perfect specimen of the artist-rebel at variance with a vulgar and materialistic society. So long as the norm by which Charlotte judged was derived from Byron, Branwell moved in a sacred aura. But doubly terrible for Branwell and for herself was the time when, no longer illumined by the glare of romantic sunsets but seen coldly in the sober light of reality, the brother's conduct appeared for what it was, not larger than life but miserably below even the common standard of

[1] 'Mina Laury' narrative dating from 28 Apr. 1836–17 Jan. 1838: Collins, 1958.
[2] Idem.

life. That would be the time of heartbreak for them both, the time to look back in incredulous wonder and exclaim 'Why! Why from such glorious beginnings should he have come to *this!*' That there had once been a time when sister and brother saw with an undivided vision would make her awakening all the worse for him to bear.

Charlotte's nineteenth birthday, 21 April 1835, was a milestone in her youth, for it almost coincided with a first opportunity for going out into the world to earn her living. From Miss Wooler, her former schoolmistress, came an offer of a post as assistant teacher at her old school Roe Head, and one or other of her sisters was offered free schooling in part payment for her services. No alternative to acceptance was even contemplated; the course of their future lives was clear and they might well consider themselves fortunate to have their livelihoods thus easily assured. The break-up of family life was the more admissible because Mr. Brontë had decided to send Branwell to the Academy Schools (if he could get in) and he would be going up that autumn. The drain on Mr. Brontë's resources as a result of such an arrangement (Branwell would need to live in London for three years) was considerable, and no greater incentive was needed to decide Charlotte to ensure her own independence and secure a free schooling for her sisters. On 2 July she wrote to tell Ellen of the great change in their family life:

... We are all about to divide, break up, separate. Emily is going to school, Branwell is going to London, and I am going to be a governess. This last determination I formed myself, knowing I should have to take the step sometime, and 'better sune as syne' to use the Scotch proverb; and knowing also that papa would have enough to do with his limited income, should Branwell be placed at the Royal Academy, and Emily go to Roe Head. ... Yes, I am going to teach in the very school where I was myself taught. Miss Wooler made me the offer, and I preferred it to one or two other proposals of private governess-ship which I had before received. I am sad—very sad—at the thought of leaving home; but *duty—necessity*—these are stern mistresses, who will not be disobeyed. ... Emily and I leave home on the 29th of this month; the idea of being together consoles us somewhat, and, in truth, since I must enter a situation, 'My lines have fallen in pleasant places.' I both love and respect Miss Wooler. ...[1]

For over three years Charlotte had enjoyed the absolute freedom of her home. She had savoured dominion over an imaginary world and

[1] CB to EN: *W & S* i. 129.

no restrictions had been imposed upon her creative powers. Every-thing in the quiet house had contributed to the evolution of her genius. In the tiny nursery-cum-playroom of their childhood overlooking the front garden and the old church tower, she could withdraw in summer twilights and give herself up to her obsessive dream. Only when the ex-ceptional privilege was lost did she fully grasp the magic of that time: She wrote in the coming months at Roe Head:

... Remembrance yields up many a fragment of past twilight hours spent in that little unfurnished room. There have I sat on the low bed—with my eyes fixed on the window, through which appeared no other landscape than a monotonous street—of moorland, a grey church tower, rising from the centre of a church-yard so filled with graves that the rank weed and coarse grass scarce had room to shoot up between the monuments. ... Such was the picture that threw its reflection upon my eye but communicated no impres-sion to my heart. The mind knew but did not feel its existence. It was away. It had launched on a distant voyage—haply it was nearing the shores of some far and unknown Island under whose cliffs no bark had ever cast anchor. In other words—in other words a long tale was perhaps evolving itself in my mind. . . .[1]

Verdopolis and Angria, Zamorna and Mary Percy his much-tried Queen, the beautiful devoted disillusioned mistresses with whom his fate was increasingly linked; the enemy Percy upon whose heart he could wreak double vengeance by tormenting the daughter who had become his wife—her enthralment in these themes was intense. She participated in the destinies of her characters, and the degree of her identification with them can be deciphered in the innumerable pages of minute writing. It may truly be said that these wholly absorbed her life. A passage like the following—a monologue by Mary Percy, Duchess of Zamorna and Queen of Angria—gives some indication of the agony of revolt when, in place of such high destinies as awaited her heroines, a post as assistant-teacher in a young ladies' seminary promised to be the extent of her own fulfilment.

Oh Adrianopolis! the joyous rapturous days I have spent in thee, the great men, the Giant Spirits! thy sons! thy Lords! I have had crowding round me from morning till night! the stirring, heroic air I breathed. The sounds of those voices, tones befitting warriors and leaders of my youthful Angria, how they used to strike my heart-strings—one rush of excitement scarce dying when another came to exhilarate the unwearied senses—with

[1] Fragment of Roe Head Journal: BPM, Bonnell 98 (6).

the joy of glory anticipated . . . the present unfolding in blinding glory around me, a chivalrous realm at my feet. . . .[1]

Duty and Necessity—the shadowy precepts of her aunt's long training become stern realities at last—supported her in the hurry and suddenness of the summons to Roe Head. Above all, the thought that what she did would materially help Branwell sustained her spirit. With Emily at her side she had courage enough for two as they set out from home on 29 July 1835—the day before Emily's seventeenth birthday: after all they were not going among strangers. There would be times each day when they could escape and be themselves. Angria and Gondal went with them; in leaving home they could carry with them, like other exiles, a little handful of their country's soil to remind them, even in their captors' power, that they were free, the self-elected citizens of another clime.

[1] 'Zamorna's Return', 1837–8.

THE DRUDGE'S LIFE

IN the space of a very few months every anticipation that buoyed Charlotte up in that departure from home was proved fallacious. Nothing turned out as she had hoped.

The opportunity of a thoroughly good education which was to be such an advantage to Emily proved utterly beyond her powers; she could not survive the alien atmosphere. What Charlotte had once borne and what Anne would bear after her, the great-souled Emily was incapable of enduring. The kindly atmosphere, the easy discipline, the unforced curriculum of the Miss Woolers' school were as pernicious to her spirit as forced labour under the most tyrannical of masters. Yet it was not really Roe Head but the loss of home that destroyed her. Too proud to complain she fell rapidly into a decline which Charlotte alone understood. In a famous passage written years later, Charlotte tried to rationalize her sister's predicament:

... Liberty was the breath of Emily's nostrils. The change from her own home to a school, from her own noiseless, very secluded, but unrestricted and inartificial mode of life, to one of disciplined routine ... was what she failed in enduring. Her nature proved here too strong for her fortitude. ... Nobody knew what ailed her but me—I knew only too well. ... I felt in my heart she would die, if she did not go home, and with this conviction obtained her recall. ...[1]

What Charlotte said of Emily applied to her own plight and it was her own profound suffering from a similar cause that enabled her to diagnose her sister's case. Even so, she held back what lay at the heart of the matter—Emily's inability to live outside her dream existence. Demanding a greater effort of herself than she did of Emily, she helped her sister to escape. By mid October Emily had been sent home (where she rapidly revived) and Anne had taken her place.

The substitution of sisters brought Charlotte little compensation. The loss of Emily, not only her favourite sister but the one nearest her

[1] Memoir of Ellis Bell, prefixing 1850 ed. of her *Poems*.

in age, materially altered her situation in school, for it left her without a confidante. Anne, four years her junior, whose fees were defrayed by Charlotte's services, became in a sense an innocent liability upon her sister, who held herself morally responsible for her education. From this circumstance an unhappy situation arose for both girls, emotionally dependent as they each were upon the absent Emily; the more so, as it turned out that Anne's schooling was to last for 2½ years.

Mary Taylor, commenting upon it years later to Mrs. Gaskell, saw the resultant harm to Charlotte's outlook.

... I heard that she had gone as a teacher to Miss Wooler's. I went to see her, and asked how she could give so much for so little money, when she could live without it. She owned that, after clothing herself and Anne, there was nothing left, though she had hoped to be able to save something. She confessed it was not brilliant, but what could she do? I had nothing to answer. She seemed to have no interest or pleasure beyond the feeling of duty, and, when she could get the opportunity, used to sit alone and 'make out'....[1]

Little enough leisure had Charlotte to 'sit alone and make out'; as the months passed the fortunes of the school entered upon an uneasy phase and the frequent absences of Miss Wooler upon family business laid increased responsibility on Charlotte's shoulders. Neither her loss of leisure nor the separation from Emily would have borne so heavily upon her spirits had not another and totally unexpected blow fallen at the same time: Branwell's all-important journey to London proved a fiasco. Not only was he not admitted to the Academy Schools—but he made no attempt to gain admittance. His failure, when the case was carefully gone into, proved something far worse than an artistic failure: it was a moral one, for which no amount of training in anatomy or drawing could compensate. Naïve as the whole family had been in supposing he would be received without these (a requisite to admittance at that time) it was his moral and even physical collapse when confronted with independence that had spelt defeat.

Generously supplied with money by his father, his godmother Mrs. Firth, and undoubtedly Miss Branwell (who had paid for his lessons at William Robinson's studio at Leeds) he went up to London in the autumn of 1835. By his own admission his pockets were full of letters of introduction to influential figures in the art world (Robinson had been a pupil of Lawrence, Leyland the sculptor had worked with

[1] MT: *SLL* i. 80–83, op. cit.

Chantrey, Westmacott, and B. R. Haydon, with whom, had Branwell been admitted, he would have studied anatomy), but none of these did he present, and upon none of the personalities competent to advance his interests did he call. The magnitude of London seemed to crush his spirit so that, 'little squibs of rum'[1] aiding, he went about in a daze, understanding nothing of what he saw. Left to his own resources for the first time in his life, he was incapable of rising to the occasion. When after several days of desultory wandering through the streets and of dreaming upon the Embankment as he watched the great India-men come and go, he eventually visited the National Gallery and saw the work of the great masters after which he had yearned all his life, his reaction was one of despair. He saw their perfection and realized his own incapacity in the same horrible and illuminating moment of truth. Afraid, as he later admitted, 'of ending his pleasure by approaching reality' he put off visiting St. Paul's for days and when finally he forced himself to the effort he dashed up the steps for fear of turning tail. The whole London experience was fraught with intense pain for him. London, he clearly saw after only a few days' trial, was no place for him; it made him feel his veritable stature, which was not much above five feet. Consoling himself in the hospitable 'snug' of the 'Castle Tavern' in Holborn, among painters and pugilists in search of engagements, he ran through his little patrimony of ready cash, and took the coach home with nothing to show for his great adventure, save an incurable sorrow, which only those who knew him intimately ever perceived.[2]

To his father and aunt he told a cock-and-bull story of being robbed of all his money on the journey out, and persuaded them that the pen and not the brush was his true medium. By the end of the year he was writing with his former jaunty self-confidence to the editor of *Black-wood's* demanding a post on his staff:

. . . Now, Sir, to you I appear writing with conceited assurance, but I am not; for I know myself so far as to believe in my own originality, and on that ground I desire of you admittance into your ranks and do not wonder that I apply so determinedly; for the remembrance I spoke of [earlier in the letter] have fixed you and your magazine in such a Manner upon my mind that the idea of striving to aid another periodical is *horribly* repulsive. . . .[3]

But again no answer was forthcoming.

---

[1] PBB: 'Adventures of Charles Wentworth', Brotherton Library, Leeds.
[2] For further details of Branwell's London journey see Gérin, *Branwell Brontë*, 98–110.
[3] PBB to Editor of *Blackwood's*, 7 Dec. 1835: Oliphant, *Annals of a Publishing House*, 1897.

The effect upon Charlotte of this major disappointment, though only gradually realized, was profound. Coinciding as it did with Emily's collapse, with the new and unaccustomed drudgery of teaching, with the sacrifice of her keenest pleasure, creative writing, it provoked a mental depression from which she became not only physically ill but spiritually scarred for years. The sacrifice to which she had consented, believing it to benefit the two beings she most loved in life, had lost its purpose. As Branwell's prospects of making a way for himself dwindled, and Emily's inability to live away from home became all too apparent, her own position suffered a radical change; what she was doing was no longer a voluntary gesture prompted by love, but an obligation to earn a living in place of others. As she found that she had neither patience nor talent for the work in hand, the role of teacher soon became abhorrent to her.

In this contingency, moreover, Anne's presence brought no alleviation. Living in the same house, assailed by the same degree of homesickness yet separate in their sorrow by the nature of their occupations —Charlotte an increasingly senior teacher, Anne a junior pupil—it hardly surprising they both drifted into deep depression. Subjected to the same influences in childhood it is also hardly surprising that their depression gradually assumed the form of religious melancholia. In Charlotte's case the contributing factor in this was the paramount influence of Ellen Nussey.

To understand the hold that her former schoolfellow now took upon Charlotte's whole outlook upon life, her severance from her habitual confidants—Branwell and Emily—has to be realized. Branwell himself confessed that communication with his sister, who was only twenty miles away, had well-nigh ceased at this period and was in any event strained and uneasy. The estrangement from the elders of the family, following his failure in London, and from his sisters too, plainly added to his misery at the time. In the character of his new prototype, 'Henry Hastings', he expressed the desperation and bravado that went with his sense of frustration. While scoffing at his family's old-fashioned standards of virtue on the subjects of drink and gambling—to both of which he was now becoming addicted—he suffered acutely at having lost those standards himself.[1]

Deprived of Branwell's complete confidence for the first time in her life, it was inevitable that Charlotte should turn for sympathy where sympathy was offered, to Ellen Nussey, living within four miles of Roe

[1] PBB, Angrian fragments dated 23 Jan. 1837, 12 July 1837: BPM.

Head. By 10 May 1836, the date of the first letter of the period to be
preserved, it is apparent that Ellen's moral ascendancy over Charlotte
had been established, though Charlotte's bitterness of heart and revolt
of spirit at the trials then afflicting her were far beyond the discernment
of the submissive Ellen. None too happy herself in her own family life,
in which she was all too often called upon to play the role of shuttle-
cock—Ellen could only preach acceptance of the will of God.

Charlotte's reactions to her friend's advocacy of doctrines in which, as
a clergyman's daughter, Ellen expected her to be better versed than herself, were as novel as they were violent. '. . . I won't play the hypocrite, I won't answer your kind, gentle, friendly questions in the way
you wish me to . . .'[1] Charlotte replied to a questionnaire from her
friend, intended to clarify her religious position.

> . . . Don't deceive your-self by imagining that I have a bit of real good-
> ness in me. . . . My Darling, if I were like you, I should turn my face Zion-
> ward. . . . But I am *not like you*. If you knew my thoughts; the dreams that
> absorb me; and the fiery imagination that at times eats me up and makes me
> feel society, as it *is*, wretchedly insipid, you would pity and I dare say despise
> me. . . .[2]

At no time did Charlotte expose her secret self so completely to the
unsuspecting friend taking her reformation in hand as in that passage,
though what Ellen made of it has never been recorded. As Charlotte
would not appear to have followed it up with a further revelation of the
fastness concealed within, Ellen's comprehension did not apparently
grasp the full meaning of the confession, and Charlotte let it alone;
it was useless to explain the nature of the 'fiery imagination' that made
the sterility of her present life a daily torment. Ellen could and did pity
her for the overwork and monotony of her teacher's life—for her
homesickness from so beloved a home, for her strivings after a closer
walk with God. For all these trials Ellen could show her genuine
sympathy. She believed she held the cure for them; and, just because
Ellen's sympathy was so guileless, Charlotte could not explain her predicament. She could only succumb to the kindness. '. . . I thank you
with energy for this kindness', she wrote in the following letter. 'I will
no longer shrink from your questions. I *do* wish to be better than I am.
I pray fervently sometimes to be made so. . . . Do not mistake me,
Ellen, do not think I am good, I only wish to be so. . . .'[3]

---

[1] This and the following quotations from CB's letters to EN cover the period 10 May
1836–May 1837 and are all written from Roe Head. The originals are at BPM.

[2] CB to EN, 10 May 1836: *W & S* i. 139.   [3] CB to EN: *W & S* i. 140.

From then on a correspondence was established, a moral climate was created, in which Ellen's role became that of Father Confessor and Charlotte's that of uneasy penitent. The more Ellen advanced her conventional tenets in order to console her friend, the further she drove Charlotte into a re-examination of her beliefs—a confrontation which brought nothing but distraction and misery in its wake. Examining what she believed, Charlotte found a tangle of contradictions in her mind, of doubts and fears, of remorse and terrors that dated back to her childhood, until she became afraid of life itself. '. . . O! I am no better than I ever was', she continues in the same letter. 'I am in a state of horrid, gloomy uncertainty, that at this moment I would submit to be old, grey-haired, to have passed all my youthful days of enjoyment and be tottering on the verge of the grave, if I could only thereby ensure the prospect of reconcilement to God. . . .'[1] Evoking the whole religious teaching of her childhood absorbed in the cold classrooms of Cowan Bridge and her aunt's stuffy bedroom, Ellen's fresh probings forced from her the confession: '. . . I never was exactly careless of these matters, but I have always taken a clouded and repulsive view of them; and now, if possible, the clouds are gathering darker, and a more oppressive despondency weighs continually on my spirits. . . .'[2]

Ellen, ignorant of what in reality ailed Charlotte, and recurring constantly to the one theme upon which she *could* be eloquent and Charlotte at a loss, had no idea that the very consolation she offered only deepened her friend's despair.

Her own placidity astonished Charlotte, torn as she was between two fiercely striving forces within her soul: the urge to create and the determination to do her duty. She saw Ellen as an embodiment of all goodness, immune from temptations, and wished at times to be like her. She wrote her friend after school-hours one day:

. . . It is a stormy evening, and the wind is uttering a continual moaning sound that makes me very melancholy. At such times, in such moods as these, Ellen, it is my nature to seek repose in some calm, tranquil idea [formerly the idea would have been of Verdopolis or Angria] and I have now summoned up your image to give me rest. There you sit upright and still in your black dress and white scarf, your pale, marble-like face looking so serene and kind—just like reality. I wish you would speak to me . . . It is from religion you derive your chief charm. . . .[3]

Increasingly, as the model of Ellen's goodness, kept constantly

---

[1] CB to EN, Roe Head letters: BPM (*W & S* i. 140).
[2] Idem.   [3] Idem: *W & S* i. 141.

before her by Ellen's letters and Ellen's visits, exposed her own short-comings, Charlotte lost heart of grace. '. . . What am I compared to you?' she wrote. 'I feel my own utter worthlessness when I make the comparison. I am a very coarse, commonplace wretch Ellen. I have some qualities which make me very miserable, some feelings that you can have no participation in, that few, very few people in the world can at all understand. . . .'[1]

This was a touch of the old Byronic boastfulness, suitable in the mouth of a discarded mistress of Zamorna, though influenced now by readings of the Bible. Convinced of her sinfulness by the severe probings of the spirit to which Ellen's exhortations prompted her, she began to sink under the recollected teachings of her childhood.

My eyes fill with tears when I contrast the bliss of a saintly life . . . with the melancholy state I now live in; uncertain that I have ever felt true contrition, wandering in thought and deed, longing for holiness which I shall *never*, *never* attain, smitten at times to the heart with the conviction that —'s ghastly Calvinistic doctrines are true, darkened, in short, by the very shadows of spiritual Death! If Christian perfection be necessary to Salvation, I shall never be saved. . . .[2]

At times, when the impress of Ellen's presence and of Ellen's arguments were less acute, when her own mind reasserted itself, Charlotte could still sanely judge her state of mind and the love of truth saved her from excess. She feared, before all things, to appear more committed than she was in the matter of religion. Around her, certainly in the homes of her godparents the Atkinsons and the Franks—if not in the study of Miss Wooler, an eminently balanced woman—she heard professions of virtue with which she could not honestly find herself in accord, and which, to her scrupulous mind, savoured uncommonly of hypocrisy. To become like *them* in her pursuit of salvation was more repellent than to confess herself already beyond redemption.

. . . I keep trying to do right, checking wrong feelings, repressing wrong thoughts—but still . . . I find myself going astray. I have a constant tendency to scorn people who are far better than I am, a horror at the idea of becoming one of a certain set—a dread lest, if I made the slightest profession, I should sink at once into Phariseeism, merge wholly into the ranks of the self-righteous. In writing at this moment I feel an irksome disgust at the idea of using a single phrase that sounds like religious cant. . . . If the Doctrine of Calvin be true I am already an outcast. . . .[3]

[1] CB to EN, Roe Head letters: BPM (*W & S* i. 141).
[2] Idem.   [3] CB to EN: *W & S* i. 143.

In far fewer words the single-minded Emily once and for all expressed her views on the debatable matter of religion. Mary Taylor, recalling the occurrence to Mrs. Gaskell, said she herself, when cross-examined upon her beliefs, had said that they were a matter between God and herself. '. . . Emily (who was lying on the hearth-rug) exclaimed "That's right". This was all I ever heard Emily say on religious subjects.'[1]

Of the Brontës' ultimate extreme reserve upon the subject of religion there is ample evidence. Even of Anne who, like Charlotte, experienced a severe religious crisis during her school-days at Roe Head, and of whose genuine and deep piety no doubt could possibly exist, Charlotte had yet to explain to one of the parsonage servants after Anne's death: '. . . It was not her custom to talk much about religion but she was very good. . . .'[2]

Thanks to their scrupulous regard for truth—as they each conceived it—the Brontës emerged from the harrowing lessons of childhood, from the despairs of adolescence, with an ennobling faith, strong enough to bear them through the exceptional ordeals of their adult life.

Charlotte's mental sufferings produced their own reaction: she revolted fiercely against the very tenets she sought to accept. '. . . You cannot imagine how hard, rebellious, and intractable all my feelings are', she wrote Ellen Nussey. 'When I begin to study on the subject, I almost grow blasphemous, atheistical in my sentiments. . . .'[3]

The rebellious feelings whose origin she could not avow to Ellen were prompted by much that had nothing to do with religion. In the first place, Miss Wooler was laying ever-increasing responsibility on her shoulders and her leisure-time was invaded by domestic obligations and the dreary correcting of her pupils' work. Far, far worse was the almost total suspension of creative writing which the packed routine of each day rendered well-nigh impossible. The disjointed jottings that form her Roe Head Journals over the two years 1835–7 show the distracted state of mind to which this privation had reduced her. Scribbled in almost illegible script upon the precious sheets of letter-paper brought from home, these descriptions of her drudgery and frustrations constitute an eloquent commentary not only upon her life at school but upon her correspondence with Ellen Nussey. Nothing

[1] MT to Mrs. Gaskell: *SLL* ii. 118, op. cit.
[2] CB to Martha Brown from Scarbro', June 1849: *SLL* ii. 53.
[3] CB to EN, 1836: BPM *W & S* i. 143.

could more feelingly convey the divided purpose of her life at the
period, torn as she was between the call of conscience and the creative
urge. 'I am just going to write because I cannot help it', she begins,
in a slanting and uneven script, the result, as she explains, of writing
with closed eyes:

. . . encompassed by bulls (query calves of Bashan) all wondering why I
write with my eyes shut—staring, gaping long their astonishment. A C[oo]k
on one side of me, E L[ister] on the other and Miss W[ooler] in the
background, stupidity the atmosphere, school-books the employment, asses
the society. What in all this is there to remind me of the divine, silent,
unseen land of thought, dim now and indefinite as the dream of a dream,
the shadow of a shade. There is a voice, there is an impulse that wakens
up that dormant power which in its torpidity I sometimes think dead.
That wind pouring in impetuous current through the air, sounding
wildly unremittingly from hour to hour, deepening its tone as the night
advances, coming not in gusts, but with a rapid gathering stormy swell,
that wind I know is heard at this moment far away on the moors at
Haworth. Branwell and Emily hear it and as it sweeps over our house
down the church-yard and round the old church, they think perhaps of me
and Anne—Glorious! that blast was mighty it reminded me of Northangerland, there was something so merciless in the heavier rush, that made
the very house groan as if it could scarce bear this acceleration of impetus.
O it has wakened a feeling that I cannot satisfy—a thousand wishes rose at
its call which must die with me for they will never be fulfilled. now I should
be agonised if I had not the dream to repose on—its existences, its forms its
scenes to fill a little of the craving vacancy—Hohenlinden! Childe Harold!
Flodden Field! the burial of Moore! why cannot the blood rouse the heart
the heart wake the head the head prompt the hand? to do things like
these? . . .[1]

Summer, like winter, in those unending scholastic 'halves', found
her spirit straining at the leash. Dated 11 August 1836 a long addition
to the journal reads:

All this day I have been in a dream half miserable and half ecstatic miserable because I could not follow it out uninterruptedly, and ecstatic because
it showed almost in the vivid light of reality the ongoings of the infernal
world. I had been toiling for nearly an hour with Miss Lister, Miss Marriott
and Ellen Cook striving to teach them the distinction between an article and
a substantive. The parsing lesson was completed, a dead silence had succeeded it in the school-room and I sat sinking from irritation and weariness
into a kind of lethargy. The thought came over me am I to spend all the

[1] Roe Head Journal: Bonnell Coll. (No. 98), BPM.

best part of my life in this wretched bondage forcibly suppressing my rage at the idleness the apathy and the hyperbolical and most assinine stupidity of those fat-headed oafs and on compulsion assuming an air of kindness patience and assiduity? Must I from day to day sit chained to this chair prisoned within these four bare walls, while these glorious summer suns are burning in heaven and the year is revolving in its richest glow, and declaring at the close of every summer's day, the time I am losing, will never come again? Stung to the heart with this reflection I started up and mechanically walked to the window—a sweet August morning was smiling without. The dew was not yet dried off the field, the early shadows were stretching cool and dim from the haystack and the roots of the grand old oaks and thorns scattered along the sunk fence. All was still except the murmur of the scrubs about me over their tasks, I flung up the sash, an uncertain sound of inexpressible sweetness came on a dying gale from the south, I looked in that direction—Huddersfield and the hills beyond it were all veiled in blue mist, the woods of Hopton and Heaton Lodge were clouding the water-edge and the Calder silent but bright was shooting among them like a silver arrow. . . . I shut the window and went back to my seat. Then came on me rushing impetuously all the mighty phantasm that we had conjured from nothing to a system strong as some religious creed. I felt as if I could have written gloriously—I longed to write . . . if I had had time to indulge it I felt that the vague sensations of that moment would have settled down into some narrative better at least than anything I ever produced before. But just then a Dolt came up with a lesson. I thought I should have vomited. . . .[1]

The fearful contrast between the primary level of the work required of her and the force of the visions that possessed her imagination, appears in the following passage. In the afternoon of the same day already chronicled, she was 'nearly killed' trying to instil French into the head of a pupil, 'between the violence of the irritation her horrid wilfulness excited and the labour it took to subdue it to a moderate appearance of calmness. My fingers trembled as if I had had twenty four hours of tooth-ache, and my spirits felt worn down to a degree of desperate despondency . . .'.[2] After the regulation walk and restoring her pupils to the school-room 'to do their exercises' she

crept up to the bed-room to be alone for the first time that day. Delicious was the sensation I experienced as I laid down on the spare-bed and resigned myself to the luxury of twilight and solitude. The stream of thought, checked all day came flowing free and calm along its channel. My ideas were too shattered to form any defined picture as they would have done in such

[1] Roe Head Journal, 'All this day', begun 11 Aug. 1836: Bonnell Coll. 98(8), BPM.
[2] Ibid.

circumstances at home, but detached thoughts soothingly flitted round me and unconnected scenes occurred to me then vanished producing an effect certainly strange but to me very pleasing. . . .[1]

As the vision wholly possesses her, while leaving a layer of consciousness free with which to observe the processes of invention, the reader participates in the actual creative moment in a manner quite rare in the annals of literature. It shows the inescapable dominance of her visionary world over her actual life. The part that *vision* takes in experience, the use of the verb 'to see' in the narrative, explains the pictorial nature of all Charlotte Brontë's descriptions, from childhood to literary maturity.

the toil of the day succeeded by this moment of divine leisure had acted on me like opium and was coiling about me a disturbed but fascinating spell such as I never felt before. What I imagined grew morbidly vivid. I remember I quite seemed to see with my bodily eyes a lady standing in the hall of a gentleman's house as if waiting for someone. It was dusk and there was the dim outline of antlers with a hat and rough great-coat upon them. She had a flat candle-stick in her hand and seemed coming from the kitchen or some such place. She was very handsome it is not often we can form from pure idea faces so individually fine she had black curls hanging rather low in her neck a very blooming skin and dark anxious looking eyes. I imagined it the sultry close of a summer's day and she was dressed in muslin not at all romantically a flimsy, printed fabric with large sleeves and a full skirt. As she waited I most distinctly heard the front door open and saw the soft moonlight disclosed upon a lawn outside, and beyond the lawn at a distance I saw a town with lights twinkling through the gloaming. Two or three gentlemen entered one of whom I knew by intuition to be called Dr. Charles Brandon. . . .[2]

The narrative, firmly established in scene and characters, progresses swiftly and dramatically, concerning a sick man, an operation, a removal from hospital—while each mention of place or of person, the writer notes, 'called up a certain set of reminiscences or rather fancies it would be endless to tell all that was at that moment suggested. . . . Lucy first appeared before me as sitting at the door of a lone cottage on a kind of moorish waste sorrowful and sickly . . .'.[3]

The scenes supersede each other, the characters come and go, and

[1] Roe Head Journal, contd. Bonnell Coll. 98(8), BPM.
[2] Idem.
[3] Roe Head Journal: Bonnell Coll. 98(8), BPM.

suddenly the stage is invaded by forces over which the writer has no control—reality irrupts in the form of her flesh and blood pupils.

> . . . No more I have not time to work out the vision. A thousand things were connected with it, a whole country, statesmen and Kings, a Revolution, thrones and princedoms subverted and reinstated—meantime the tall man washing his bloody hands in a bason and the dark beauty standing by with a light remained pictured in my mind's eye with irksome and alarming distinctness. I grew frightened at the vivid glow of the candle at the reality of the lady's erect and symmetrical figure. . . . I felt confoundedly annoyed I scarcely knew by what. At last I became aware of feeling like a heavy weight lying across me. I knew I was wide awake and that it was dark and that moreover the ladies were now come into the room to get their curl-papers they perceived me lying on the bed and I heard them talking about me. I wanted to speak, to rise it was impossible—I felt that this was a frightful predicament . . . I must get up I thought and I did so with a start. I have had enough of morbidity vivid realisations—every advantage has its corresponding disadvantages—tea's ready Miss Wooler is impatient. . . .[1]

The passive role of the dreamer possessed by her dream, of the eavesdropper, almost, having no right to what she sees and hears, is distinctly expressed in another entry of the journal. Watching an 'exquisitely beautiful' girl move through ranks of admiring 'patricians' to whom she is being presented, Charlotte adds:

> . . . I hear them speak as well as she does, I see distinctly their figures—and though alone, I experience all the feelings of one admitted for the first time into a grand circle of classic beings—recognising by tone, gesture and aspect hundreds whom I never saw before, but whom I have heard of many a time, and is not this enjoyment? I am not accustomed to such magnificence as surrounds me, to the gleam of such large mirrors, to the beauty of marble figures, to soft foreign carpets to long wide rooms and lofty gilded ceilings. I know nothing of people of rank and distinction, yet there they are before me. . . . There is one just now crossing—a lady I will not write her name though I know it—no history is connected with her identity, she is not one of the transcendantly fair and inaccessible sacred beings—whose fates are interwoven with the highest of the high—I cannot write of them except in total solitude I scarce dare think of them. . . .[2]

The hold these 'sacred beings' had upon her, even in the alien world of Roe Head, was so strong that when Branwell wrote, reporting fresh developments in the Angrian plot, she was bewitched for days.

[1] Roe Head Journal, Bonnell Coll. 98(8), BPM.   [2] Ibid.

'. . . About a week since,' she noted in an entry for the autumn of 1836, 'I got a letter from Branwell. . . . I lived on its contents for days . . . it came . . . bringing with it agreeable thoughts such as I had for many months been a stranger to—some representing scenes such as might arise in consequence of that unexpected letter some, unconnected with it, referring to other events. . . .'[1]

The purport of Branwell's letter had been to tell her that he had decided on killing Zamorna's wife, the neglected and heart-broken Mary Percy, a detailed account of which he wrote in September 1836. The news affected Charlotte like a family loss.

. . . I wonder if Branwell has really killed the Duchess. Is she dead? Is she buried is she alone in the cold earth on this dreary night with the ponderous coffin plate on her breast under the black pavement of a church in a vault closed up, with lime and mortar. No body near where she lies—she who was watched through months of suffering—as she lay on her bed of state. Now quite forsaken because her eyes are closed, her lips sealed and her limbs cold and rigid. . . . A set of wretched thoughts are rising in my mind, I hope she's alive still partly because I can't abide to think how hopelessly and cheerlessly she must have died, and partly because her removal if it has taken place, must have been to Northangerland like the quenching of the last spark that averted utter darkness. . . .[2]

Had Ellen Nussey had access to the spasmodic journal kept by her friend she might have had some insight into the nature of her misery as a governess at Roe Head. As it was, both she and Mary Taylor only pitied her for the drudgery and menial tasks for which she had so little aptitude, not for the spiritual severance from her source of life. In the hurried notes Charlotte scribbled to her friends she only gave glimpses of the avowable sources of her wretchedness: '. . . Ever since last Friday', she wrote Ellen on 14 December 1836, 'I have been as busy as I could be in finishing up the half-year's lessons, which concluded with a terrible fag in Geographical Problems (think of explaining that to Misses Marriott and Lister) and subsequently in mending Miss E. L's clothes [Ellen Lister] . . . Miss Wooler is calling for me—something about my protegee's nightcaps. . . .'[3]

Having found Miss Lister's nightcaps and packed her trunk, Miss

[1] Roe Head Journal: Bonnell Coll. 92, BPM.
[2] Ibid., Bonnell, 98.
[3] CB to EN: BPM: *W & S* i. 148.

Brontë was free to go home. It was hardly surprising that one of her actions during the Christmas holidays of 1836–7 should be to write to the poet Southey to inquire about the prospects awaiting a woman writer, and whether there were any likelihood of her ever earning her living. The alternative had proved very nearly intolerable.

The gesture was a sign not only of her desperation but of a renewal of family influence upon her—strong, energetic, concerted, as she found on her return after a five-months' absence. For the first time all four young Brontës took serious stock of their prospects as professional writers. Long as they had been writing poetry, fiction, drama, it was only in December 1836 that they made a serious attempt to collect and assess their work. It is from December 1836 that are dated Emily and Anne's first preserved manuscripts—in Anne's case it is a Gondal poem, 'Verses by Lady Geralda' ('Geralda' or 'Geraldine' was the middle name of Gondal's Queen, the Lady Macbeth-like 'Augusta Geraldine Almeida', the heroine of most of Emily's contributions to the saga). Emily's own lines 'High waving heather, 'neath stormy blasts bending' were also significantly dated 13 December 1836. It was the day before Charlotte and Anne's return home for the holidays—the date of Charlotte's letter to Ellen, and of Anne's end-of-term prize inscribed 'A Prize for good conduct presented to Miss A. Bronte with Miss Wooler's kind love, Roe Head, Dec. 14th 1836'.

Reunion with her brother and sister was like a reminder to Charlotte that the real purpose of life was pursued only at Haworth. There alone could the soul be nourished by celestial manna. At Roe Head it was the bread of slavery she swallowed. The dating of the transcript of Emily's poem reveals not only a joyful state of mind in the expectation of her sisters' return, but the decision already taken under Branwell's impetus to collect their forces for an assault on the literary establishment.

As already seen, Branwell had written twice to the editor of *Black-wood's* during the past year. He had written again in April '36 and during these Christmas holidays he wrote to suggest a visit to the Edinburgh offices of the journal. That letter, dated 9 January 1837, was followed ten days later by a letter to Wordsworth. In it Branwell voiced not only his own ambitions by implication but those of his sisters; in begging Wordsworth to read and pass judgement on a specimen of his writing, he explained that 'living among secluded hills' he had none to advise him on the value of what he had done 'since to this hour not half-a-dozen people in the world know that I have ever penned a line'.

But a change has taken place now, sir; and I am arrived at an age wherein I must do something for myself; the powers I possess must be exercised to a definite end. . . . But nothing of all this can be ever begun without means, and as I don't possess these, I must in every shape strive to gain them. . . . What I send you is the Prefatory Scene of a much longer subject . . . read it, sir; and, as you would hold a light to one in utter darkness—as you value your own kind-heartedness—*return* me an *answer*. . . . Forgive undue warmth, because my feelings in this matter cannot be cool. . . .[1]

The warmth of such feelings, shared to the full, had spurred Charlotte to write her letter to Southey on 29 December.

Strangely enough, had her existing plans for the Christmas holiday held, she might not have taken the step, however much she felt driven to it by her wretchedness at Roe Head. Before leaving school she had asked Ellen Nussey to come on a visit during the holiday, and only a serious accident to Tabby—who fell on the icy cobbles of the village street and broke her leg one night before Christmas—prevented it. In what a light of salvation, almost, Charlotte regarded her friend, is seen by the letter she wrote deferring her visit. '. . . After this disappointment', she wrote, 'I never dare reckon with certainty on the enjoyment of a pleasure again; it seems as if some fatality stood between you and me. I am not good enough for you, and you must be kept from the contamination of too intimate society. . . .'[2]

This letter, also dated 29 December, and the disappointment it expresses, perhaps drove Charlotte to the consolation of writing to Southey. The text of her letter is not preserved; only by his reply can its tenor be gauged.

He was 62 at the time and had lived for over 33 years in the same beautiful house near Keswick, Greta Hall, a man not only settled in his habits and beliefs, but undermined by sorrows. By a strange fatality Charlotte's letter, so full of 'ardour' and 'the generous desires of youth', reached him on the return from a long and saddening pilgrimage to the haunts of his childhood and youth in the West Country where he was born. The valedictory nature of this visit, recalling as it did so many of the disillusionments of his life—his unhappy marriage, the loss of beloved children, the friendship with Coleridge whose death had occurred only the previous year—had all induced an elegiac state

---

[1] PBB to Wordsworth, 19 Jan. 1837: *W & S.* i. 151–2. See Additional Notes.
[2] CB to EN, 29 Dec. 1836: *W & S* ii. 149.

of mind peculiarly out of harmony with the hopes and visions of his young and eager correspondent. Southey could never be anything but courteous and kind and, unlike Wordsworth who was disgusted with Branwell's letter and never answered it,[1] took great trouble to advise Charlotte against attempting the career of letters. He had astutely detected in what she had written an overheated imagination which, if indulged, would bring her nothing but misery. After apologizing for and explaining his delay in answering her letter, he wrote to her in March 1837:

... I, who have made literature my profession and devoted my life to it ... think myself, nevertheless, bound in duty to caution every young man who applies as an aspirant to me for encouragement and advice against taking so perilous a course. You will say that a woman has no need of such caution; there can be no peril in it for her. In a certain sense this is true; but there is a danger of which I would, with all kindness and all earnestness, warn you. The day dreams in which you habitually indulge are likely to induce a distempered state of mind and, in proportion as all the ordinary uses of the world seem to you flat and unprofitable, you will be unfitted for them without becoming fitted for anything else. Literature cannot be the business of a woman's life, and it ought not to be. The more she is engaged in her proper duties, the less leisure will she have for it, even as an accomplishment and a recreation. . . .

But do not suppose that I disparage the gift which you possess, nor that I would discourage you from exercising it. I only exhort you so to think of it, and so to use it, as to render it conducive to your own permanent good. Write poetry for its own sake; not in a spirit of emulation, and not with a view to celebrity; the less you aim at that the more likely you will be to deserve and finally to obtain it.

Farewell, madam. It is not because I have forgotten that I was once young myself, that I write to you in this strain; but because I remember it. . . .[2]

The receipt of this letter two and a half months after she had written to Southey in the first place and when she had, like Branwell, given up all hope of hearing from him, made an extraordinary impression on Charlotte. She could not resist writing by return of post to thank him for the genuine kindness he had shown and to demonstrate her own ability to learn by the experience and example of others. Her reply has a maturity, indeed, not found in any of her writings hitherto. Its good

---

[1] Letter of Southey to Caroline Bowles, Easter Monday, 1837: *W & S* i. 156.
[2] Southey to CB: *W & S* i. 87; i. 155–6; iv. 209.

sense—and good manners—contrasts forcibly with Branwell's conduct under similar circumstances. The letters to Southey and Wordsworth, indeed, mark a turning-point in the paths of brother and sister: from then on she would profit from the lessons of adversity, *he* wilfully reject them. She defended herself to Southey:

I am afraid, sir, you think me very foolish. I know the first letter I wrote you was all senseless trash from beginning to end, but I am not altogether the idle, dreaming being it would seem to denote.

My father is a clergyman of limited . . . income, and I am the eldest of his children. He expended quite as much in my education as he could afford in justice to the rest. I thought it therefore my duty, when I left school, to become a governess. In that capacity I find enough to occupy my thoughts all day long, and my head and hands too, without having a moment's time for one dream of the imagination. In the evenings, I confess, I do think, but I never trouble any one else with my thoughts. . . . Following my father's advice—who from my childhood has counselled me, just in the wise and friendly tone of your letter—I have endeavoured . . . to observe all the duties a woman ought to fulfil. . . . I don't always succeed, for sometimes when I'm teaching or sewing, I would rather be reading or writing; but I try to deny myself; and my father's approbation amply rewarded me for the privation.

In a postscript she added: '. . . I could not help writing, partly to tell you how thankful I am for your kindness, and partly to let you know that your advice shall not be wasted, however sorrowfully and reluctantly it may at first be followed.'[1]

Southey was genuinely touched by her reply and wrote to tell her so in a last letter dated 22 March. '. . . You have received admonition,' he said, 'as considerately and as kindly as it was given. Let me now request that, if you ever should come to these Lakes while I am living here, you will let me see you. . . .' His parting plea to her was: 'Take care of over-excitement, and endeavour to keep a quiet mind. . . .' How much she needed the advice, only she knew.

The two letters from the Poet Laureate, received at a time of heartsearching and bewilderment, were read and reread, 'again and again' as she later confessed, in search of covert encouragement, and when temporarily put away, on a momentous date in her life, endorsed: 'Southey's advice to be kept for ever. My twenty-first birthday. Roe Head. April 21, 1837.'

The bitter potion swallowed, with every attempt at belief in its powers to cure, the wretchedness of her life bore down on her more heavily than ever in the spring and summer of 1837. Every little

[1] CB to Southey: *W & S* i. 157–8.

change in the bleak monotony of her daily round proved a change for the worse. Ellen Nussey was suddenly summoned to London to make herself useful in her brother's house at No. 4 Cleveland Row, St. James's. On first hearing the news Charlotte wrote on 20 February: 'I read your letter with dismay, Ellen—What shall I do without you? . . .'[1] The return, first anxiously hoped for midsummer, was deferred until December in the end. The effect on Charlotte's spirits was doubly hurtful because without Ellen there was no pleasure to be had at Roe Head and, graver still, she fell back into the previous year's religious doubts and fears. Without Ellen her moral support had gone. '. . . You first pointed out to me that way in which I am so feebly endeavouring to travel, and now I cannot keep you by my side, I must proceed sorrowfully alone. . . .'

During the summer holidays of 1837 Miss Wooler moved her school to a smaller, altogether less consequential house on Dewsbury Moor, called after its previous owners, 'Heald's House'.[2] The Healds, father and son, successively vicars of Birstall, were well known to Charlotte.

The change was less the effect of a decline in the school's fortunes than of upheavals in the Wooler family itself, through which the importance of the school to the Miss Woolers gradually lessened. The illness of their father throughout the years 1836–7 (the cause of Miss Wooler's frequent absences from the school and of Miss Eliza's permanent return to her parents' home, Rouse Mill), and his death in April 1838, brought them added responsibilities and greater independence also. They could consider selling the goodwill of their school, but they had to provide a home for their widowed mother when their brother eventually took over Rouse Mill.

These upheavals in the family of her employers were the source of yet added responsibilities for Charlotte. During the first months at Heald's House Miss Wooler was almost constantly away and in addition to the teaching the domestic arrangements of the school were left to Charlotte. There were times, even, when the children of Miss Wooler's sister, Susan Carter, were left in her care. '. . . Miss Wooler is from home', she wrote Ellen in a typical account of her life, on 24 August 1837. 'Little Edward Carter and his baby sister are staying with us, so that between nursing and teaching I have my time pretty well occupied. . . .'[3]

---

[1] CB to EN, 20 Feb. 1837: *SLL* 136.
[2] For a fuller account of Heald's House, see the present author's *Anne Brontë*, ch. 10, pp. 103–14.   [3] CB to EN, 24 Aug. 1837: *SLL* i. 142–3.

A change affecting Charlotte more closely still occurred that autumn when Emily made a first attempt at earning her living in a big boarding-school at Southowram, near Halifax, kept by the Miss Patchetts. The conditions under which she worked both outraged and alarmed Char-lotte, who could not forget Emily's previous collapse at Roe Head. '. . . I have had one letter from her since her departure', she wrote Ellen on 2 October 1837; 'it gives an appalling account of her duties—hard labour from 6 in the morning until near 11 at night, with only one half-hour of exercise between. This is slavery. I fear she will never stand it. . . .'[1]

Contrasting their present situation and probable prospects in the ensuing years with the bright visions she had formerly entertained for Branwell, Emily, Anne, and herself, a new bitterness possessed her soul; her whole nature revolted against their destiny.

To crown all, Anne, who had been living at her side for over two years in silent endurance of an atmosphere no more congenial to her than to Charlotte, fell gravely ill from the effects of a neglected cold at the end of the school year. The dreaded signs of consumption, all too well known to Charlotte, roused her as nothing else could have done, at that time; she became a lion in Anne's defence, venting upon Miss Wooler, whom she held responsible for Anne's condition, the pent-up self-reproach and misery of the year. Writing after the event to Ellen Nussey—just returned home—she confessed her part in the quarrel that ensued.

. . . You were right in your conjectures respecting the cause of my sudden departure. Anne continued wretchedly ill—neither the pain nor the difficulty of breathing left her—and how could I feel otherwise than very miserable? I looked upon her case in a different light to what I could wish or expect any uninterested person to view it in. Miss Wooler thought me a fool, and by way of proving her opinion treated me with marked coldness. We came to a little eclaircissement one evening. I told her one or two rather plain truths, which set her a-crying, and the next day, unknown to me, she wrote to papa telling him that I had reproached her bitterly—taken her severely to task, etc. etc. Papa sent for us the day after he had received her letter. Meantime, I had formed a firm resolution—to quit Miss Wooler and her concerns for ever—but just before I went away she took me into her room, and giving way to her feelings, which in general she restrains far too rigidly, gave me to understand that in spite of her cold repulsive manners she had a considerable regard for me and would be very sorry to part with me. If anybody likes me I can't help liking them, and remembering that she had in general been very

[1] CB to EN, 2 Oct. 1837: BPM (*SLL* i. 138).

kind to me, I gave in and said I would come back if she wished me—so we're settled again for the present; but I am not satisfied. I should have respected her far more if she had turned me out of doors instead of crying for two days and two nights together. I was in a regular passion; my *'warm temper'* quite got the better of me—of which I don't boast, for it was a weakness; nor am I ashamed of it, for I had reason to be angry. Anne is now much better, though she still requires a great deal of care. However, I am relieved from my worst fears respecting her. . . .[1]

Commenting on the incident many decades later, a great-nephew of Miss Wooler, who remembered her well, said that she had been shocked 'as only a tender-hearted woman can be shocked, if she is thought to be lacking in understanding of other people's sufferings. . .'[2] The alarm provoked by Anne's illness decided the family to bring her school-days to an end. Alone, therefore, as she had not been since she first set out for Roe Head seven years ago, Charlotte returned to Dewsbury Moor on 30 January. With neither of her sisters beside her, and Ellen Nussey once again gone south to her brother's family in London, Charlotte entered upon the darkest period of her school-days.

Loneliness and loss of hope induced a mental and bodily prostration that she herself admitted afterwards to be nothing short of hypochondria. It was as though the liberating dream without which she had never lived and to whose access she was now debarred, turned in upon her in the likeness of a nightmare; the visual nature of her imagination induced a state of hallucination, the horrors of which she described unforgettably in *Villette*. To Miss Wooler herself some eight years after leaving school she wrote of that experience:

. . . I endured it [hypochondria] but a year, and assuredly I can never forget the concentrated anguish of certain insufferable moments, and the heavy gloom of many long hours, besides the preternatural horrors which seemed to clothe existence and nature and which made life a continual waking nightmare. . . . When I was at Dewsbury Moor I could have been no better company for you than a stalking ghost, and I remember I felt my incapacity to *impart* pleasure fully as much as my powerlessness to receive it. . . .[3]

Anne's illness and her own subsequent collapse made her loathe Dewsbury Moor: it became a 'poisoned place' to her. As the spring advanced she became so ill at last as to need a doctor. He told her that

[1] CB to EN, 4 Jan. 1838: *SLL* i. 145.
[2] Rev. Max Blakeley, 'Memoirs of Margaret Wooler and her Sisters': *BST*, 1952.
[3] CB to Miss Wooler: Allbutt Coll., FitzWilliam Museum, Cambridge.

if she valued her life she should go home. Aware that she had reached the limit of her endurance—and of her usefulness to those at home—she joyfully obeyed. A parting present from Miss Wooler, Scott's poem 'The Vision of Don Roderick' in the de luxe edition illustrated by Westall, marked her departure from school, Miss Wooler writing in the fly-leaf: 'Presented to Miss Brontë with the love and best wishes of a Sincere Friend. Heald's House, May 23rd 1838.'

ZAMORNA AGAINST ALL COMERS

HER return on 23 May coincided with a new departure on Branwell's side, a circumstance that may have had its share in deciding her to follow her own inclinations for once. After two and a half years' indecision at home Branwell was making a fresh start and setting up in Bradford as a professional portrait-painter, with a studio of his own and some three or four portrait-commissions among his father's old friends in the town awaiting him. The prospects of his making a living by art were not unpropitious, as the careers of his friends Thompson, Wilson Anderson, Geller, Cousens, Leyland, etc., at the time went to show. For months he had been working again at portraiture with his former master, William Robinson, riding over each week to his studio at Leeds and working directly from the model. For this second chance he was much indebted to his aunt, who not only paid his fees but his expenses for weekly lodging at a Leeds hotel. That his venture was encouraged by family and friends alike is evident from the fact that it was his father's old friend, William Morgan, Vicar of Christ Church, Bradford, who found him lodgings in his own street, Fountain St., off Manningham Lane, where he engaged a room and a studio for Branwell at No. 3 with the family of Mr. Isaac Kirby, a 'Porter & Ale Merchant' in the town. From Bradford Branwell could—and did— come home each week-end, a circumstance which heightened the family's general optimism about the outcome of events.

The proximity of Branwell and the hope that his many disappointments would at last be compensated by fulfilment and success in a profession so close to her heart were a major factor that spring in restoring Charlotte to health and spirits. For Branwell was still, inescapably, her *alter ego*, the person with whom she had most in life to share.

A glimpse of their closeness whenever holidays brought them together is afforded by Emily's and Anne's diary-paper written the previous June on Branwell's birthday (26 June), when all four young people were at home once again for a time.

Monday evening June 26th 1837

A bit past 4 o'clock, Charlotte working in Aunt's room, Branwell reading

Eugene Aram to her—Anne and I writing in the drawing-room—All tight and right in which condition it is to be hoped we shall all be on this day 4 years at which time Charlotte will be 25 and 2 months—Branwell just 24 it being his birthday—myself 22 and 10 months and a piece [*sic*] Anne 21 and nearly a half I wonder where we shall be and how we shall be and what kind of a day it will be then let us hope for the best—

Emily Jane Brontë—Anne Brontë[1]

One senses that Branwell's birthday treat of sharing a new book with Charlotte was heightened not exactly by the *exclusion* of Emily and Anne but by their preoccupation with other things. The old division into partnerships was as strong as ever.

Relieved for the time being of the intolerable burden of teaching that summer of 1838, Charlotte could resume with her own identity the precious liberty of thought from which she had been debarred for nearly three years past.

With Branwell safely established in his own studio, with all at home in good health, with no sister left in need of education, with a little money saved to secure her own independence, there were no immediate calls upon her conscience. The spring that had been so tightly wound up could now unwind. She could enter upon a period of calm that proved, in effect, to be the most propitious to her genius.

In the last holidays spent at home she had written a narrative of 18,000 words which, for atmosphere, for descriptive power, for penetration and sympathy, marked an important advance upon all her previous writings. The speed with which she must have written it in the limited leisure at her disposal (it was the Christmas when Anne still needed care) must have proved to herself, if nothing else did, that the only thing she needed now in order to become a writer was time to write.

The story, left without a title, is generally referred to as 'Mina Laury', from the main character in it, once the nurse of Zamorna's illegitimate son the Marquis of Almeida and, after his tragic death, Zamorna's mistress and the mother of his son Ernest, cruelly murdered in the Civil Wars.

'Mina Laury' is an almost faultless tale, imbued with a delicacy of feeling, an elegiac sweetness which she had not attained before. The fact is that with 'Mina Laury' Charlotte has done with juvenilia and emerges as an adult writer for the first time.[2] That Charlotte herself

---

[1] Diary Paper, 26 June 1837: BPM.
[2] 'Mina Laury', published in *Tales of Angria*: Collins, 1954.

recognized the change and felt the upsurge of irresistible forces within her cannot be doubted. Cut to the heart at being obliged to drop her work and return once more to school, 'again engaged in the old business—teach, teach, teach', she wrote in pathetic postscript to her tale on 17 January 1838: 'For a long space of time, good-bye, reader! I have done my best to please you; and though I know that through feebleness, dullness and iteration my work terminates rather in failure than triumph, yet you are sure to forgive, for I have done my best.'

With the recognition of new powers came the pain of their frustration. The collapse at Miss Wooler's had, in the final analysis, little of a medical origin (as her prompt restoration proved) but every symptom of an emotional repression, of an anguish of the soul that sees freedom within reach and is prepared to risk death to attain it.

In the course of the next year at home Charlotte wrote a number of novelettes and two major narratives that have been preserved. On her own showing in the Preface to the 'Professor', she wrote many more still, but with a newfound self-criticism 'destroyed almost as soon as composed'. The change from unselfconscious and un-adult dreaming to critical and artistic composition began in this year—all-important to her development—1838–9. The stories of this period are deeply revealing of the woman Charlotte was fast becoming. They also explain two decisions she took, which will be examined in due course.

Recaptured tranquillity infuses her drawings of the period, too, the landscapes to those later Angrian tales—'Mina Laury', 'Caroline Vernon'—which are recognizably inspired by the sketches of William Gilpin, sylvan, manorial, and riverain. Several examples are still preserved in Charlotte's old home. So connected were all subjects of artistic expression to her one overriding theme—the world of Angria—that she did not hesitate to use Gilpin's 'Cross of Rivaulx' for Zamorna's Hunting Lodge, where he secreted Mina Laury, and suit the description of the place in her story exactly to the sketch.

The new freedom of home palpitates in a letter to Ellen of 9 June 1838 in reply to news brought by Mary and Martha Taylor on their first visit to Haworth. It was a Saturday and Branwell was home for the week-end.

. . . They are making such a noise about me I cannot write any more. Mary is playing on the piano; Martha is chattering as fast as her little tongue can run; and Branwell is standing before her, laughing at her vivacity. My dear Ellen, good-bye. Aunt and my sisters unite in best love. . . . [The allusion to 'sisters' in the plural confirms that Emily was home for the holidays.][1]

Evidently there were visits to Branwell in his studio at Bradford. Spending her birthday with him, Emily copied out for him his long autobiographical poem 'The Wanderer' there on 31 July 1838. Charlotte's presence in Fountain Street is recorded in the recollections of the Kirbys' little niece, Margaret Hartley. She told a Dewsbury reporter many years later:

. . . From my girlhood for several years I resided with my uncle and aunt, Mr. & Mrs. Kirby, of Fountain St. Manningham Lane, Bradford. At that time when Patrick Branwell Brontë was about 22 or 23 he came to lodge with us and had one room as his studio, and there painted many portraits. . . . I recollect his sister Charlotte coming and I remember her sisterly ways. She stayed a day, and I believe that was her only visit. They left the house together, and he saw her off by the Keighley Coach. . . . It was young Mr. Brontë's practice to go home at each week-end, and I remember that while sometimes he took the coach for Keighley, he on other occasions walked to Haworth across the moors. . . .[2]

That Branwell, who had already tried after his London failure what drink and gambling could do, was steering a clear course at Bradford to start with, would appear from Margaret Hartley's further recollection of him: 'He was a very steady young gentleman, his conduct was exemplary, and we liked him very much. . . .'

Traces of the direct influence of Branwell on Charlotte's writings that summer abound in the tales loosely connected under the title 'The Duke of Zamorna', with which she returned to full-time writing. Masculine in theme and interest, racy in language, cynical in tone, they revert to earlier incidents and dead characters in the Angrian saga, as though to make up for certain gaps in Branwell's chronicles, which, under the new pseudonym of 'Captain Henry Hastings of the 9th—' he had been writing for the past two years.

As a sign of the brother and sister's continuing close collaboration, the stories have their importance; in particular they celebrate the emergence of Henry Hastings as the new emanation of Branwell in Charlotte's eyes, the direct successor to 'Wiggins'. With equal dispassion she shows him the perfect rake, permanently out of fortune in all his

[1] CB to EN. The correct date for the letter is 9 June 1838 and not 7 June (as in *SLL* No. 46): *W. & S.*
[2] Recollections of Margaret Hartley: *BST*, 1895.

enterprises, the horribly vulnerable parvenu wincing under each fresh social slight, the butt of every cruel beauty's wit; yet holding his own erratic course with a certain flourish—the poor man's Byron born with a conviction of his genius. 'Don't ye see, Henry my lad,' says his good-natured Commander, General Thornton, 'the women are trying to fool ye?' Remembering the ultimate degradation to which the fooling of a woman brought poor Branwell, the sister's penetration at this early stage has both its pathos and importance.

There is also evidence of a new similarity of outlook between brother and sister on the subject of religious cant. For years past religion, and the ministers of religion, had met with nothing but scathing comment from the pen of Branwell—particularly in a narrative of 1837 known as 'Percy'—but on Charlotte's part the subject had always been avoided in her imaginative writing. Now, however, lately emerged from the long illness that was her adolescent crisis of faith and fear, it was as though she felt the need to vent her sufferings. In a satiric vein not unworthy of Swift she did so forcibly in several narratives of 1838–9. But that *cant* and the expression of genuine faith were never confounded in Charlotte's mind—as in Branwell's—the whole body of her writings attests.

Nevertheless, even to Ellen Nussey, the keeper of her conscience, she had, at the height of her religious crisis at school, confessed to '. . . a dread lest, if I made the slightest profession I should sink at once into Phariseeism . . . an irksome disgust at the idea of using a single phrase that sounds like religious cant . . .'.[1] Under Branwell's influence again and in a revulsion of feeling against her recent tribulations, she seemed to fix upon their cause and origin in something as concrete and precise as the teachings of her aunt and—indiscriminately—in the practice of Methodism in general. Later in life her condemnation of *all* exaggerations of piety, of all exhibitionism in religious observance whether of one sect or another, was general and would be met with an equal and stern contempt. '. . . My conscience', she wrote to Ellen Nussey in 1840, 'will not let me be either a Puseyite or a Hookist . . .', but for the Dissenters she had no liking either. 'I consider Methodism, Quakerism and the extremes of High and Low Churchism foolish, but Roman Catholicism beats them all', she wrote from Brussels in 1842. That this condemnation of cant implied no criticism of religion as she understood it, her whole conduct sufficiently proved. Through the ordeals of a life which would be remarkable for domestic tragedies, her

[1] See *supra*, p. 101.

strong undemonstrative faith bore her through as no weaker rule of life could have done.

In a narration begun in 1837 and continued this summer, usually known as 'Julia' from one of its principal characters, and which is made up of unconnected episodes about Angrian society, there is one story whose style is directly borrowed from the *Methodist Magazine*, so intimately known to her in childhood. It describes the tribulations endured by certain preachers, or, as she puts it: 'the day of conflicts' imposed on 'the labourers in the field' superintending the Verdopolitan Methodist 'circuits'. The landlord of a warehouse required by the itinerant preachers for a meeting met their request with a flat refusal. They therefore set out to argue the matter with him at his private house. Told that he was at dinner and could not receive them, they answered:

'We can wait' ... and each of us taking a chair we sat in a circle round the hall. It was the servants hall, and they were arranging dinner upon the table. As I watched them bringing in first a tureen of soup, and then a leg of pork, and then a pie, vegetables etc., a voice came unto me: 'Arise and eat!'

'Thy will be done', I answered aloud and, getting up, I went towards the table.

'With your leave,' said I to a maid who was standing by, 'I will take a basin of that broth.'

She made no attempt to help me, so I took the ladle and served myself. I had no sooner finished this than the voice I had heard before came again, and I felt I stood in the situation of Elijah who, as he lay under the juniper tree, was again and again bidden to arise and eat. Obeying the supernatural impulse, I cut into the pork, and helping myself to greens, took such sustenance as the body needed. Then whispered my inward monitor: 'Give unto the men that are with thee.'

So, shaving a few slices of the leg of pork, and adding turnips, I passed it round. The maid, who was the only person who stood in the hall, looked greedily at us and said 'she should have to cook another dinner for the servants'. I made her no answer but, falling on my knees, went to prayer.

It was a time of peculiar freedom. I felt privileged to wrestle with God and to cry out importunately and insist upon the acceptance of my petitions.

'O Lord' said I, 'I will have what I want. I will take the gates of Thy favour by storm. The great cause shall prosper. It must! ... I spoke loud, and my words were fervent. So were the groans and responses of my friends. We drank of the living waters flowing from above as we had (which I forgot to mention) a few minutes before drunk two gallons of mellow old ale which stood on the table. Whilst we strove with God, in the midst of the footmen and maids who now flocked in from the kitchen, and stood staring at us as if we were wild beasts, a bell rang violently just above us. A footman ran to answer it. As he opened the door, we heard a rough and angry voice exclaim:

'What the devil is that damned noise?'

'The Methodist preachers,' answered the man. 'They've eat up all the dinner and drunk eight quarts of ale and now they're praying.'

'Praying! Be hanged to them', was the answer, 'kick them . . . out this minute, James. . . .'

Set on by the servants the preachers were soon out of doors, but the narrator managed to reach the dining-room where he found a comfortable party at table.

'Taking out my pocket-bible and holding it forth in my right hand, I commenced' he reported. 'Go to, ye rich men. Howl and cry for your miseries that are come upon you. . . .

'William Rhodes' he said, addressing the master of the house, 'you will not live long. I know you will not. You have nearly filled the measure of your iniquity. Repent then, while it is yet day. Even at the eleventh hour there may be hope. I exhort you in all brotherly kindness. My bowels yearn toward you. The crimes you have committed are black, are double-dyed, but the Lord's mercy knoweth no limits. . . .'

Borne out by the servants and dragged through a horse-pond, the preacher was given short shrift.

'But I survived all and, by the blessing of God, was that night able to make a hearty supper and to sleep as soundly as ever in my life. My Master avenged me in His own good time. About a fortnight after, I saw the body of Rhodes dragged out of his house, and, with the rope that he had been hung with still round his neck, I beheld him flung into that very horsepond where, by his orders, I had been nearly murdered. . . .'[1]

For the opening of their new white chapel, 'with its painted front turned towards the road', the Methodist preachers see to it that 'a hamper of wine, spirits, cold meat and bread and cheese, etc are conveyed into the vestry for our preachers proposed to work hard the next day and it was necessary that support should be provided for the flesh . . .'.[2]

Better than most Charlotte knew the formula, reiterated over the years in the *Methodist Magazine*, for the relation of edifying examples of judgement and repentance. 'For the full detail of all [the preachers] persecutions, trials, temptations, etc, I refer the reader to the last 7 numbers of our magazine, from December to June inclusive. . . . I

[1] Julia': 29 June 1837, Wrenn Library, Univ. of Texas.   [2] Idem.

would particularly direct the reader's attention to the last letter received from him by our superintendent. In the case of William Rhodes, Esq of Orchard Gate, it gives an awful instance of God's judgement upon the wicked. . . .'[1]

The value to Charlotte, at such a time, of the short sketch, the gossip-column, the item of reportage, is evident; pending the discovery of a worth-while subject, she wrote largely at random. 'I made a solemn resolve', she noted in the July of the following year, 'that I would write no more till I had somewhat to write about. . . .'

The subject, when it appeared, would oust almost all others, and never release her again. Upon the vicissitudes of love Charlotte Brontë was brooding already, with almost a sorcerer's insight and power, before the least experience of love had come her way. Familiar to her in name since childhood, in conception constantly changing before her awakened eyes like one of her own landscapes focused in strong light, and already treated with a sure touch in 'Mina Laury', the subject was suddenly forced upon her in a form very different from her dreams.

In the autumn of 1838 Ellen Nussey, after almost two years' residence in London and Bath with her doctor brother, returned to Birstall and claimed the company of her closest friend. Charlotte's visit, which no doubt gave much pleasure on both sides after the long separation, was repeated in the December at Ellen's urgent request. When, in January 1839, she wrote inviting Charlotte to come yet again, she was met by an amused though resolute refusal. '. . . I can hardly help laughing when I reckon up the number of urgent invitations I have received from you', wrote Charlotte on 20 January, 'during the last three months. Had I accepted all or even half of them the Birstallians would certainly have concluded that I had come to make Brookroyd my permanent home. . . .' (Since the previous year Mrs. Nussey had made Brookroyd, one of the family's several properties in the district, her permanent home in place of the larger and more expensive Rydings.) 'Frankly Ellen,' continued Charlotte, 'I *cannot come*. . . . Do you see nothing absurd in the idea of a person coming again into a neighbourhood within a month after they have taken a solemn and formal leave of all their acquaintance? . . . You must invite me no more, my dear Ellen, until next Midsummer, at the nearest . . .'[2] and Charlotte concluded by inviting Ellen shortly to visit Haworth. Neither the

---

[1] The MS. catalogued as 'Julia' signed and dated 29 June 1837. Text quoted from photostat copy of original MS. in Wrenn Library, Univ. of Texas.
[2] CB to EN, 12 Jan. 1839: *SLL* i. 152.

invitation to Haworth nor the refusal to revisit Brookroyd suited Ellen because she was bent on forwarding a scheme which she fondly hoped would contribute to the happiness of at least three persons very near to her: herself, her friend Charlotte, and her brother Henry.

Henry Nussey, the sixth son and ninth child of his parents, was Ellen's senior by five years. A former scholar of Magdalene College, Cambridge, and a graduate of that university, he had only just left Birstall to take up a post as curate-in-charge of the parish of Earnley near Chichester in Sussex. It is to be supposed that, during Charlotte's recent visits, Henry had met her. He had, undoubtedly, met her in previous years, during a long convalescence following a riding accident in 1835 when, acting as curate to the Vicar of Birstall, the Rev. William Margetson Heald (a close friend of the Nusseys and, by extension, of Charlotte's), he was continually in Charlotte's neighbourhood during her teaching years at Roe Head.

He had then gone as curate to a small parish in the East Riding near Bridlington—Harpham with Burton Agnes—his posting there corresponding with Charlotte's return to Haworth in the spring of 1838. Henry's vicar, the incumbent of Easton, the Rev. Mr. Lutwidge, for reasons that would appear later, but giving Henry's continued poor health as an excuse, asked for another curate in his place and was given one. So that by the end of 1838 Henry was obliged to look further afield. Through the good offices of his first vicar, Margetson Heald, he was recommended to the post in Sussex in November 1838.

Because of the non-residence of his new vicar he lived for the most part in the near-by Rectory of Donnington, a large and 'commodious' place where Ellen and then his sister Mercy were soon required to go and keep house for him. This was a state of things which Ellen interpreted after her own designs and resolved on utilizing to benefit her friend Charlotte Brontë. To this end she again invited her friend to Birstall in the January of 1839.

Charlotte's refusal, possibly understood by Ellen to mean more than it did, was doubtless transmitted to Henry Nussey in far-away Donnington. He was beginning to get settled in. Despite finding himself in 'a very low and flat neighbourhood near the sea', both his health and prospects were improved and, finding Donnington Rectory larger than a bachelor curate needed, he lost no time in seeking to remedy the situation by looking out for pupils and a wife. Charlotte was not the first candidate on his list, as Henry's own diary—kept since boyhood for the edification of posterity—betrays. His previous vicar at Burton

Agnes, Mr. Lutwidge, had a daughter Mary to whom—again the diary reveals—Henry had been paying some attention and who was, in short, the reason for Mr. Lutwidge's request for Henry's removal. The attractions of Miss Lutwidge and possibly the prospect of some little fortune with her, had decided Henry to return to the attack despite the parental embargo.

In mid February 1839 he therefore wrote to his former vicar, repeating the proposal for his daughter's hand. The entry in his diary on this occasion was made perhaps for his own personal reassurance: he noted that the young lady was 'a sedate, intelligent, sensible and, I trust, good girl, named Mary . . .'.

On 16 February he entered in the diary: 'Received a letter from Mr. L— senr. with a negative to my wishes. Thy Will, O Lord, be done.'[1] To make sure that no ambiguity had crept into his proposals, Henry repeated them by return of post, addressing them this time directly to the young lady herself. Noting in his diary on Monday 18 February that he had done so he added the significant entry: 'Wrote to sister Ellen. . . .' If Miss Lutwidge replied discouragingly it would be time to be planning the second stage of the campaign with an approach to his sister and, through her, to the next candidate on his list.

It would look as though Miss Lutwidge kept him waiting, for it was not until ten days later—26 February—that the reply from Easton came. Noting this on Thursday, 28 February, Henry wrote: 'On Tuesday last received a decisive reply from M.A.L's papa; a loss, but I trust a providential one. Believe not her will, but her father's. All right, but God knows best what is good for us, for His church, and for His own glory. . . .'[2]

Being happily prepared for the eventuality and having expressed suitable resignation to his fate, Henry was in a strong enough position to add, in the manner of Mr. Collins turning to Charlotte Lucas after rejection by Elizabeth Bennett: 'Write to a Yorks friend: C.B.'

The fact that it was his birthday and that he had turned 27 that day may have added to the sense of its being an auspicious occasion. He wrote to Charlotte Brontë a letter (not preserved) which, for one quality at least, she found praiseworthy: the 'good sense—and absence of flattery and cant' which it displayed.

That her answer, written on 5 March, was 'a decided negative' left him with very little to say. A repetition of the experience within ten

---

[1] Henry Nussey's diary: Chadwick. *W & S* i. **172 note.**
[2] Idem.

days might perhaps shake even the most self-possessed of lovers. In his diary for 8 March he merely entered: 'Received an unfavourable reply from C.B. The Will of the Lord be done.'

Ellen, awaiting the results of her innocent machinations and hearing neither from brother Henry nor her friend, wrote to Charlotte urging a fresh visit to Birstall and, confident that all must have gone well, came out into the open with the question: had Charlotte heard from Henry? Charlotte answered her on 12 March:

> . . . You ask me, my dear Ellen, whether I have received a letter from Henry. I have, about a week since. The contents, I confess, did a little surprise me, but I kept them to myself, and unless you had questioned me on the subject, I would never have adverted to it. Henry says he is comfortably settled at Donnington, that his health is much improved, and that it is his intention to take pupils after Easter. . . . [Easter fell on 31 March that year.]

> He then intimates that in due time he should want a wife to take care of his pupils, and frankly asks me to be that wife. Altogether the letter is written without cant or flattery, and in a common-sense style, which does credit to his judgement. . . .[2]

The almost insuperable difficulty of explaining her feelings to Ellen without either wounding her or revealing too much of herself charges each word in the ensuing passage with a double meaning for the reader of to-day who, unlike Ellen, has an insight into the heart and fiery imagination of the writer. Charlotte revealed to no one—except possibly her sisters and brother—the passion and poetry with which the whole realm of sentiment was invested for her, as her secret writings of the time attest. Only in comparison with their eloquence, completeness, and abandonment can the inadequacy of Henry Nussey's proposal be assessed.

> Now, my dear Ellen, there were in this proposal some things which might have proved a strong temptation. I thought if I were to marry Henry Nussey, his sister could live with me, and how happy I should be. But again I asked myself two questions: Do I love him as much as a woman ought to love the man she marries? Am I the person best qualified to make him happy? Alas! Ellen, my conscience answered *no* to both these questions. I felt that though I esteemed, though I had a kindly leaning towards him, because he is an amiable and well-disposed man, yet I had not, and could not have, that intense attachment which would make me willing to die for him; and, if ever I marry, it must be in that light of adoration that I will regard my husband. . . .[2]

[1] CB to EN, 12 Mar. 1839: *SLL* i. 153–5.   [2] Idem.

In the context of that letter, such an expression as 'that light of adoration' might pass unremarked, especially by such a reader as Ellen; doubtless Charlotte judged she could risk the expression having once set it down. How exactly it expressed the truth of her most sacred belief in the capacity of her own heart, Ellen would never guess.

'Ten to one I shall never have the chance again', continued Charlotte, with little thought that the chance *would* be repeated, and within the next five months. To Ellen, in this instance, more freely than to Henry, she could go on to explain the second major reason for her rejection of his proposal: her love of mental freedom *without* which any close relationship would lay an intolerable constraint.

. . . I was aware that Henry knew so little of me, he could hardly be conscious to whom he was writing. Why, it would startle him to see me in my natural home character; he would think I was a wild, romantic enthusiast indeed. I could not sit all day long making a grave face before my husband. I would laugh, and satirise, and say whatever came into my head first. And if he were a clever man, and loved me, the whole world weighed in the balance against his smallest wish should be light as air. Could I, knowing my mind to be such as that, conscientiously say that I would take a grave, quiet, young man like Henry? No, it would have been deceiving him, and deception of that sort is beneath me. So I wrote a long letter back, in which I expressed my refusal as gently as I could. . . .[1]

The whole tone of her letter to Henry surprises, indeed, by its gentleness. It is an answer singularly devoid of one wounding reflection, and yet it is generally believed Charlotte knew of Henry's previous proposal to Miss Lutwidge. In that case, her only comment bearing the slightest sting was in the reminder that she possessed no capital at all— not even enough to set up school. For the rest, her sense of obligation to the Nussey family and her fondness for Ellen, and even apparently some considerable regard for Henry himself, since she remained on good terms with him for many years, were enough to outweigh the feelings roused in her by the total *want* of all feeling on his part. She wrote to him on 5 March 1839:

My dear Sir,
    Before answering your letter I might have spent a long time in consideration of its subject; but as from the first moment of its reception and perusal I determined on what course to pursue, it seemed to me that delay was wholly unnecessary. You are aware that I have many reasons to feel

[1] Idem.

grateful to your family, that I have peculiar reasons for affection towards one at least of your sisters, and also that I highly esteem yourself—do not therefore accuse me of wrong motives when I saw that my answer to your proposal must be a *decided negative*. In forming this decision, I trust I have listened to dictates of conscience more than to those of inclination. I have no personal repugnance at the idea of a union with you; but I feel convinced that mine is not the sort of disposition calculated to form the happiness of a man like you. It has always been my habit to study the characters of those amongst whom I chance to be thrown, and I think I know yours and can imagine what description of woman would suit you for a wife. The character should not be too marked, ardent and original, her temper should be mild, her piety undoubted, her spirits even and cheerful, and her *personal attractions* sufficient to please your eyes and gratify your just pride. As for me, you do not know me; I am not the serious, grave, cool-headed individual you suppose; you would think me romantic and eccentric; you would say I was satirical and severe. However, I scorn deceit, and I will never, for the sake of attaining the distinction of matrimony and escaping the stigma of an old maid, take a worthy man whom I am conscious I cannot render happy. Before I conclude, let me thank you warmly for your other proposal regarding the school near Donnington. It is kind in you to take so much interest about me; but the fact is, I could not at present enter upon such a project because I have not the capital necessary to insure success. It is a pleasure to me to hear that you are comfortably settled and that your health is so much improved. I trust God will continue His kindness towards you. Let me say also that I admire the good sense and absence of flattery and cant which your letter displayed. Farewell. I shall always be glad to hear from you as a *friend*. Believe me, yours truly,

C. Brontë.[1]

Henry's reactions to the description of the qualities considered suitable by Charlotte in his wife and to her confession of her own opposite qualities are not known. Perhaps Charlotte herself feared that unless she spoke very plainly he would return to the attack, as he had done with Mary Lutwidge.

Henry Nussey has been identified by successive Brontë commentators as the prototype of St. John Rivers in *Jane Eyre*. In many respects the likeness holds—especially in the dispassionate nature of his proposals to two successive young ladies (showing that Charlotte knew all about Mary Lutwidge). But in the finer qualities of the portrait he could not compare with that other much more likely prototype about whom Charlotte had heard so much from her father—his Cambridge

---

[1] CB to Henry Nussey, 5 Mar. 1839: *SLL* i. 152–3.

friend the inspired missionary Henry Martyn. It was Martyn's heroic
and certainly not Nussey's pedestrian destiny she had in mind when
writing of Rivers. Charlotte's later contacts with Henry Nussey had
an obvious influence on the topography of *Jane Eyre*, but from there
to identifying the fictional with the real character is a far cry.

It was six years before Henry Nussey, newly appointed Vicar of
Hathersage in Derbyshire, found a bride. She was a Miss Emily Prescott, of Eversley in Hampshire, and they were married on 22 May
1845, at Everton near Lymington. (See *The Gentleman's Magazine* for
August 1845, p. 189.) Their installation at Hathersage was the occasion
for renewed contacts with Charlotte Brontë. Miss Prescott brought
her husband 'a handsome fortune', but it did not conduce to the
couple's happiness and by mutual consent they separated, Henry re-
signing from the Church and going to live in the south of France,
where he died in 1867.

Charlotte's second proposal of marriage in the same year was a less
calculated matter. She related it briefly in a letter to Ellen. Her friend
having no connexion with the principal actor on this occasion, it
allowed of a light-hearted treatment on Charlotte's part. She wrote on
4 August 1839.

. . . I have an odd circumstance to relate to you, prepare for a hearty laugh!
The other day Mr. Hodgson, papa's former curate, now a vicar [of Colne in
Lancashire] came over to spend the day with us, bringing with him his own
curate. The latter gentleman, by name, Mr. Bryce, is a young Irish curate,
fresh from Dublin University. It was the first time we had any of us seen
him, but however, after the manner of his countrymen, he soon made himself at home. His character quickly appeared in his conversation; witty,
lively, ardent, clever too, but deficient in the dignity and discretion of an
Englishman. At home, you know, Ellen, I talk with ease and am never shy,
never weighed down and oppressed by the miserable 'mauvaise honte'
which torments and constrains me elsewhere. So I conversed with this
Irishman and laughed at his jests, and though I saw faults in his character,
excused them because of the amusement his originality afforded. I cooled a
little, indeed, and drew in towards the latter part of the evening, because he
began to season his conversation with something of Hibernian flattery which
I did not quite relish. However, they went away, and no more was thought
about them. A few days after I got a letter, the direction of which puzzled me,
it being in a hand I was not accustomed to see. Evidently, it was neither from
you nor Mary Taylor, my only correspondents. Having opened and read it,
it proved to be a declaration of attachment and proposal of matrimony,
expressed in the ardent language of the sapient young Irishman! Well!

thought I, I have heard of love at first sight, but this beats all. I leave you to guess what my answer would be, convinced that you will not do me the injustice of guessing wrong. This is not like one of my adventures, is it? It more resembles Martha Taylor's. I am certainly doomed to be an old maid. Never mind, I made up my mind to that fate ever since I was twelve years old. . . .'[1]

There was a sad postscript to the tale. Poor Mr. Bryce—'a strong, athletic-looking man when I saw him and that . . . scarcely six months ago', wrote Charlotte the following 24 January, died suddenly 'of the rupture of a blood vessel' on 17 January 1840. '. . . Though I knew so little of him and of course could not be deeply or permanently interested in what concerned him,' she commented, 'I confess, when I suddenly heard he was dead I felt both shocked and saddened; it was no shame to feel so, was it?'

'Ten to one I shall never have the chance again—' 'I am certainly doomed to be an old maid. Never mind, I made up my mind to that fate ever since I was twelve years old. . . .' Such pronouncements on the part of romantic women are not rare. The rarity in Charlotte Brontë's case was not the extravagance of her dreams of love—far from it—but in their *reality*. Before ever Henry Nussey or poor Mr. Bryce had spoken, Charlotte knew the language of love, she had felt its fires, she had judged of its sufferings, she had experienced its loss, she had questioned its joy. Mina Laury already in a very profound analysis of her feelings for Zamorna, reached a truth that no actual experience would surpass. '. . . She had but one idea—Zamorna! It had grown up with her, become a part of her nature. Absence, coldness, total neglect for long periods together went for nothing. She could no more feel alienation from him than she could from herself. . . .'[2]

And again, in another passage, reviewing those same feelings, she had to confess that '. . . they were so fervid, so glowing in their colour that they effaced everything else. I lost the power of appreciating the value of the world's opinion, of discerning the difference between right and wrong.' Zamorna was 'something more to me than a human being. He superseded all things—all affections, all interests, all fears or hopes or principles. Unconnected with him my mind would be a blank. . . . I know the extent of my own infatuation. . . .'[3]

At 22 Charlotte was perfectly aware that to women like Mina

[1] CB to EN, 4 Aug. 1839: *SLL* i. 164.
[2] 'Mina Laury', 1836–8: *Tales of Angria*, Collins, 1954.
[3] Ibid. 143.

Laury—and herself—no lesser dedication of herself was honourable. If, as she said, she had already at the age of 12 renounced all prospect of marriage, it was because, seeing herself as even plainer than she was, she doubted whether there were in all the world about her one man capable of responding to her exalted conception of what the passion of love should be. How right she had been the proposals of Henry Nussey and Mr. Bryce appeared to prove. In rejecting them she was satisfied by her own prevision, which spared her any qualm of regret in losing something so immeasurably below her standards.

The motives behind Charlotte's rejection of her two suitors—both falling so far short, one might be tempted to say, of the Byronic ideal set once for ever upon her romantic girlhood—lay not, however, in her extravagant conceptions of what the Ideal Lover should be, nor in her exalted notions of what Love should be, but in what she knew love could be for her. It was not the perfection—or imperfection—of the Lover, but the completeness of the feelings he evoked that she judged by. Her certainty of this was based on feelings which, though imaginatively engendered, were actual and sharp, which experience would not alter, only confirm and intensify.

The originality of Charlotte's conception of the Ideal Lover—so opposite to that of her early Victorian contemporaries—lay in her acceptance of his imperfections. Superb as she had always pictured Zamorna in all the brilliance of his Regency regimentals, it was above all in his defects that he lived for her. These she had come to accept to the extent of preferring them to other men's virtues.

How the same almost eccentric characteristics would remain for her the embodiments of love can be seen in comparing her descriptions of Zamorna and Paul Emmanuel. The latter's impetuosity will be remembered by all readers of *Villette*. Mina Laury, restored after long separation to Zamorna (the former Marquis of Douro), says of him: '. . . he met me as Lord Douro used to meet me, with impassioned tenderness, dashed with his own blessed exacting impetuosity. I adored him. . . .'[1]

This preference for the man with imperfections influenced both her choice of hero in her novels—Rochester and Paul Emmanuel in particular—and her rejection of the conventional male for her companion. Henry Nussey, could he but have guessed it, was ruled out of court not only for his lack of ardour or of charm, but for his unexceptionable character. A man so negative could have no lasting hold upon her heart.

[1] 'Mina Laury', op. cit.

Born of the Satanic heritage transmitted through the Byronic heroes, Charlotte's acceptance of the fatal flaw in the heroic character had been increased with the passage of the years, rather than diminished; for was not the dearest being to her still her brother Branwell? How the need to fit *him* into the scheme of accepted morality and conventional conduct constantly exercised Charlotte's mind can be seen often enough in her fiction; in such an incident, for instance, as the following in her tale 'Julia', in which she describes the sinister Macara, 'taking a diminutive gold box from his pocket and administering to himself a grain of opium . . .'. His hand, she added, was 'wasted and colourless'. He confessed to 'his frame of mind not being like most men's, it is perverse, I own it . . .'.[1] When it is remembered that Branwell had started taking opium at about this time, such an incident assumes new meaning.

A man's love, possessive and tyrannical, was no mystery to Charlotte's imaginings; she believed in it as profoundly as she believed in the disinterestedness and adoration of a woman's love. Describing Zamorna at war, examining the medallion containing his wife's portrait—to whom he was constantly unfaithful—she makes him exclaim: ' ". . . One comfort remains to me, the consciousness that I can by one hour's ardour compensate for a year's neglect . . . I wish that hour were come, I wish you were beside me, sitting there within the grasp of this hand—utterly in my power . . .".'[2]

. . . Fury was the feeling at his heart, he desired something that he could not have . . . he imagined the bliss but could not attain it. . . . Recollection . . . showed him her image as he had seen it a hundred times—young, pallid, seldom smiling, waiting his approach in a Saloon of gorgeous state. . . . The Duke thought he at that hour looked down on her fair cheek resting on his shoulder, met the adoration of her eyes, felt the beating of her heart against his circling arm, saw the pulse flutter on her heaving breast, beheld the folds of satin disclosing her exquisite form. With his whole enthusiastic soul he loved her. . . . It had been to him the delight of his life at times to satisfy and soothe her intense idolatry—he was in the mood for that benevolent office now. . . .[3]

The hatred of all cant, social as well as religious, which had become of recent months so predominant a feature of Charlotte's character, made it impossible perhaps for her to see any action, any motive, any emotion, even that of love, except in the naked light of truth. This it is that makes her penetration—even into the passion that sways her

---

[1] 'Julia', MS. dated 29 June 1837: Wrenn Lib., Univ. of Texas.   [2] Idem.   [3] Idem.

characters—so little 'romantic', and so profoundly, so psychologically right.

Describing an interview between Zamorna and Louisa Vernon, the mistress of his enemy Percy who is under 'house arrest' in Zamorna's country home—a slightly comical though wholly credible vulgar little woman, whose daughter Caroline is to be one of Zamorna's victims —Charlotte has this to say:

> She felt that his eye, expressing in its large orb such paramount treachery and yet such youthful fire, such reckless devotion to the sport of the hour, thrilled her with inexpressible feelings when she met its glance—she hated him still, she would have been glad to see him stretched a corpse at her feet, but yet there was an enchanting interest in this moonlight conference. I speak according to nature; it could not be otherwise....[1]

In the novelettes of passion, as one may call the tales of 1837–9 —'Julia', 'Mina Laury', 'Caroline Vernon', 'Henry Hastings'—are features that already relate them to Charlotte's mature work. In them appears the master–pupil relationship developed in all four of her published novels, though strangely enough it has no scholastic connotation here. When Mina Laury calls Zamorna 'Master' it means she acknowledges he is the master of her heart. No ambiguity exists in Charlotte's description: '... Zamorna's cold lip pressed to her forehead and his colder hand clasping hers brought the sensation which it was her custom of weeks and months to wait for, and to consider, when attained, as the ample recompense for all delay, all toil, all suffering.... Her master's eye was insupportable. It burnt absolutely with infernal fire....'[2]

Together with the heroines' tragic abandonment to their passion goes a precocious preparedness for love that makes them inevitable victims. In spite of this, their guileless infatuation is so truthfully presented as not to make them contemptible. At a period when the revelations of Caroline Lamb's and Claire Claremont's pursuit of Byron disgusted society, Charlotte's heroines stand out as frank and touching. Zamorna's ward, Caroline Vernon (Louisa's illegitimate child), passes from gawkish girlhood to impassioned maturity in swift yet entirely credible stages; she is first shown, a noisy hoyden, dressed far too young for her age by her silly mother in a

> short-sleeved frock, worked trousers and streaming sash that would better have suited the age of 9 or 10 than that of 15 ... fresh naive romantic,

---

[1] Idem.
[2] 'Mina Laury': op. cit., pp. 150–3.

really romantic, throwing her heart and soul into her dream, longing only for the opportunity ... to die for somebody she loves ... to give up heart, soul and sensation to one loved hero, to lose independent existence in the perfect adoption of her lover's being. . . .[1]

She reads Lord Byron and thinks 'Lord Byron and Bonaparte and the Duke of Wellington and Lord Edward Fitzgerald the four best men that ever lived ...'.[2] She suffers early at the scant response her guardian gives her first tentative expressions of love, confessing to: '. . . the anguish of discovering that her strongest and most genuine feelings were not appreciated, that a person whom she was disposed to care for intensely would not condescend to let her tell him how much she regarded him, would not stoop to understand her emotion . . .'.[3]

It is the work of a few months, the influence of a few corrupting minds in Paris where she is sent to acquire 'the tone, the fashion', that exposes her vulnerability to revelations of her guardian's life of vice:

the young lady's feelings were not exactly painful, they were strange, new, and startling. She was getting at the bottom of an unsounded sea and lighting on rocks she had not guessed at. . . . Thus did Zamorna cease to be an abstract principle in her mind. Thus did she discover that he was a man, vicious like other men, with passions that sometimes controlled him, with propensities that were often stronger than his reason, with feelings that could be reached by beauty, with a corruption that could be roused by opposition. . . .[4]

From there to pursuing Zamorna and declaring her own love for him, is but a step that Caroline covers in frenzied haste: 'She had only one thought, one wish, one aim, one object ... to reach Freetown. That done, Hell was escaped, Heaven attained. She could not see the blind folly of her undertaking. She had no sense of the erroneous nature of the step. . . .'[5]

On introducing herself into Zamorna's house she learns the depth of his obliquity and the price of her folly. Her reaction to the shock of his conduct is a confession of the attractiveness of evil.

His deep voice as he uttered this, his high featured face, and dark large eye burning bright with a spark from the depths of Gehenna, struck Caroline Vernon with a thrill of nameless dread. Here he was, the man Montmorenci

[1] 'Caroline Vernon', July 1839, quoted from microfilm of original text by courtesy of the Curator, Elkins Widener Memorial Lib., Harvard.
[2] Idem.   [3] Idem.   [4] Idem.   [5] Idem.

had described to her. All at once she knew him. Her guardian was gone, something terrible sat in his place. . . .[1]

Even so, the power of the senses dominates all.

Caroline began to feel a new impression. She no longer wished to leave him, she clung to his side, infatuation was stealing over her. . . . She feared, she loved. Passion tempted, conscience warned her. But in a mind like Miss Vernon's conscience was feeble . . . and when Zamorna kissed her and said in a voice of fatal sweetness which has instilled venom into many an ear 'Will you go with me to-morrow, Caroline?' she looked up in his face with a kind of wild devoted enthusiasm and answered 'Yes'.[2]

At the end of a week, when Caroline's father braves Zamorna in his palace to demand his daughter, Zamorna defies him ever to find her: 'I placed her where she is safe and happy', he said, '. . . you had better leave the matter where it is, for you cannot undo what is done. . . .'[3] The author herself seems to feel that more commentary is superfluous.

In the great novels that were to come, the themes already set—the passionate master–pupil relationship in particular—would again be exploited, but to very different ends: what would constitute the whole difference between Jane Eyre and Caroline Vernon, between Lucy Snowe and Mina Laury, would precisely lie in the later heroines' power of conscience to reject temptation. This it would be that would invest mere fiction with the pathos and intensity of poetry—of dramatic poetry one might venture to add. But before such rarefied heights could be attained Charlotte herself had a long way to struggle up the thorny path of life. Harriet Martineau, who would complain of her exclusive concern with the one passion of love in *Villette*, would miss the whole nature of Charlotte's purpose, lacking the key which the earlier novelettes could supply.

By the lights of her youthful and imaginary experience, Charlotte was already worlds apart from such conventional men as Henry Nussey. What common ground could he or Mr. Bryce, genial as he seems to have been, or any but the highest intellects and most responsive natures find on which to meet a woman like Charlotte Brontë at 23?

For the time being the lack of any such equals was not felt by her; the world without and the world within was peopled for her by prodigious presences. The beloved sisters and brother alone understood and shared the rarefied atmosphere they breathed. None need hope to touch a heart that had for so long been Zamorna's. And where Zamorna reigned, no lesser men need aspire even to serve.

[1] 'Caroline Vernon', July 1839, op. cit.   [2] Idem.   [3] Idem.

'UNDER A STRANGE ROOF-TREE'

AT the actual time of Henry Nussey's proposal and of her rejection of him—between 21 February and 26 March—Charlotte was engaged in writing a narrative of fifty tight-packed pages of minute italic script about 'Henry Hastings' which, in its intense preoccupation with a brother-and-sister theme, shows something of her deep concern at the moment with Branwell.

After a propitious outset the Bradford experiment was ending in failure, no more portrait commissions coming Branwell's way. This was not entirely his fault; the town contained several better painters than he (his friends Geller, Thompson, and the brothers Cousen among them) and the new fashion in daguerrotypes was rapidly reducing the numbers of his potential 'sitters' among the professional classes. By the spring of 1839, therefore, he had very little alternative to returning home once again, no better off than he had left it a year ago.

That each successive failure in his chosen professions, whether as painter or writer, embittered and unsettled Branwell is obvious. The once high hopes of his family and his own vanity only further envenomed the situation and drove him into violent opposition against the 'establishment', as his own writings of the time and Charlotte's plainly show. He was fast conforming to the standard image, dear to his childhood, of the romantic rebel, and doing his best to achieve the status of a man at war with society and with his own soul, an outcast even from his own family—and not entirely succeeding in doing even that—as Charlotte's strangely disillusioned yet percipient study of just such a man in 'Henry Hastings' reveals.

Henry Hastings might be in revolt against all authority to the extent of shooting his superior officer through the head, but he has not the courage to face the firing-squad. Offered life in exchange for the names of his confederates, he chooses life. A coward and a weakling, Charlotte's only plea in submitting the portrait of such a being is that he is not wholly bad; something remains in him that his sister at least can

love. In making the confession, she does not shrink before the implication: that the truth about anything does not correspond to the ideal
one may have formed of it, but it is the truth that matters. To this profound conclusion not only Elizabeth Hastings but young Charlotte
Brontë had been brought at the age of 23 by the bitter and illuminating
lessons of life. Elizabeth Hastings could reflect:

It was very odd that his sister did not think a pin the worse of him for
all his dishonour: it is private moments not public infamy that degrade a
man in the opinion of his relations. Miss Hastings had heard him cursed by
every mouth, saw him denounced in every newspaper, still he was the same
brother to her he had always been—still she beheld his actions through, saw
him go away with a triumphant Hope—that his future actions would nobly
blot out the calumny of his enemies. Yet after all she knew he was an un-
redeemed villain—human nature is full of inconsistencies—natural affection
is a thing never rooted out where it has once existed. . . .[1]

What the passage equally reveals respecting the sister's plight as well
as the brother's is that, inevitably, the bitterness of the lowering of a
standard—in this instance hers by acceptance of his—forces her also
into an attitude of revolt, whether she wishes it or no. From then on,
Elizabeth Hastings—and Charlotte Brontë her interpreter—is committed to a position of antagonism towards the accepted fabric of
society because of that society's repudiation of her brother.

It will not only be poverty and the need to earn a living that will
drive Elizabeth Hastings—and Charlotte Brontë—firstly into herself
and then out into an alien world, but a sense of vicarious frustration for
the genius of her brother which, for some years longer, at least, she
will believe to have been balked of its legitimate recognition.

That the theme of failure should dominate her writing at a time
when she herself was conscious of powers just fully expanding, sufficiently shows how Branwell's fortunes obsessed her mind. The
lifelong fusion of feeling and interests in brother and sister meant
that it was *she* who suffered in *his* place. 'There is no bitterness
the human heart knows', she wrote in 'Henry Hastings', 'like that of
being alone and despised, whilst around it hundreds are loved and
idolized. . . .'[2]

Deeply committed to her brother's destiny, Elizabeth Hastings

[1] 'Henry Hastings.' Text quoted from microfilm of original MS., finished 26 Mar. 1839,
now in Harvard Univ.
[2] Idem.

loses, in the hour of Henry's shame, both her home and the means of livelihood. (She had been lady-companion to a young society beauty.) She had made her protest as her father crossed out Henry's name from his will and disowned him for ever. 'You have done wrong and un-naturally', she had the resolution to tell her father. 'My father was then scarcely himself and he was always quite as passionate as his son—he knocked me down in Mr. Warner's presence. I got up and said the words again. . . . I cared nothing. . . .'[1]

Without comment the daughter leaves home for ever. Henry's dis-grace makes even her post as lady-companion untenable. She is daily exposed to the taunts of the women and the solicitations of dis-honourable men. She resolves to set up a private school in a remote part of the town and within a fortnight has achieved her purpose. Charlotte had often thought on similar lines, and knew what she would do. 'She summoned all her address and lady-like manners to her aid—called on the wealthy manufacturers of the city and the aristocracy of the seats around' in pursuit of pupils. How she felt towards them and the life to which she was self-condemned, she told in a few trenchant words: '. . . she spent her mornings in her drawing-room, not wearily toiling to impart knowledge into yawning, obstinate children—a thing she hated and for which her sharp irritable temper rendered her wholly unfit—but instructing those who had already mastered the elements of education. . . .'[2]

So Charlotte, actuated by the strongest motives—pity and indigna-tion for the ill-luck of her brother—would immolate her own barely controllable longings for freedom and fulfilment in the next few years, to redeem his unfortunate beginnings.

Elizabeth Hastings's school is a success and earns its principal every-one's respect. Charlotte, measuring the gulf that separates such a ful-filment from the one her spirit cried out for, faced the cruel issue: '. . . she was one who scorned respect. She was always burning for warmer, closer attachment. She couldn't live without it, but the feeling never woke and never was reciprocated. . . .'[3]

Of 'warmer, closer attachments' Elizabeth Hastings, like her foster-sister Jane Eyre years after, was to experience only the bitterness of illicit proposals. Pursued by Sir William Percy, a brother of the Duchess of Zamorna, she is offered love on unacceptable terms. She has for long cherished a deep romantic feeling for him. Together they take an evening stroll across fields and enter an old country churchyard.

[1] 'Henry Hastings', op. cit.   [2] Idem.   [3] Idem.

She sits down on a tomb that bears one word only—'Resurgam'—a word which again links Elizabeth Hastings with Jane Eyre.

. . . . Miss Hastings was silent but she was not going to yield. Only the hard conflict of passionate love, with feelings that shrank horror-struck from the remotest shadow of infamy, compelled her for a moment of silent agony. . . . Henry, though a wild wanderer himself, would blow his brains out if he heard of his sister's adding to the disgrace that has heaped so thickly on the name of Hastings. . . .[1]

The thought of Henry, like the thought of Branwell, haunted the sister through the months of separation and the alien life to which his disgrace had condemned her. A strange foresight of sterner separations yet—separations of the spirit to come—infuses the passage in 'Henry Hastings' in which Charlotte sums up the sister's losses through the brother's fault.

. . . Sometimes when she was alone of an evening, walking through her handsome drawing-room by twilight, she would think of home—long for home, till she cried passionately at the conviction that she would see it no more. So wild was her longing that where she looked out on the dusky sky, between the curtains of her bay-window, fancy seemed to trace on the horizon, the blue outline of the moors. . . .[2]

Then, grieving over her brother's disgrace, vivid recollections of what he had been, of his presence in the home, would press on her mind, with images strangely reminiscent of Branwell's tastes and habits. Though essentially an artist by temperament, Branwell loved to follow the guns and range the moors with the dogs at his heels.

. . . Something would recall the whine and bark of Hector and Juno, Henry's pointers. Again the step of Henry himself would seem to tread in the passage, and she would distinctly hear his gun deposited in the house corner. . . . Henry was changed, she was changed, those times were departed for ever. She had been her brother's and father's favourite. She had lost one and forsaken the other. . . .[3]

'Henry Hastings' is a profoundly disillusioned tale; but it is also nearer experience and probability than anything Charlotte had written yet. Already at 23 she traced the pattern that would, with rich variations of invention, become the hallmark of her tales: whatever the drama in which her heroines would become involved, the issues would be fought out on the plane of conscience.

[1] Idem.   [2] Idem.   [3] Idem.

Following closely on the rejection of Henry Nussey's proposal, and set against the evidence of such a story as 'Henry Hastings', Charlotte's decision in the spring of 1839 to go out as a private governess takes on a far wider significance. Branwell had returned from Bradford for good. At the moment no other prospect of employment appeared either to him or his patient family. Though Charlotte had little choice, the motives behind her decision are all-important; not independence, but the desire to serve Branwell was the deciding factor with her.

It was not only Charlotte who saw the inevitable corollary to Branwell's failure to establish himself in a profession: Anne also startled the family by her determination that spring to earn her living, and in the event it was she who was the first to leave home.

In the teeth of the family's united opposition (delightfully described in the opening pages of *Agnes Grey*) Anne persistently overruled every tender persuasion and alarm raised—on the score of her delicate health and inexperience—and left home for a post as governess with the Ingham family of Blake Hall, Mirfield, on 8 April.

'. . . Poor child! she left us last Monday', Charlotte wrote Ellen on the 15th, torn between dismay, admiration, and dread of the ill consequence of Anne's resolute conduct. '. . . no one went with her; it was her own wish that she might be allowed to go alone, as she thought she could manage better and summon more courage if thrown entirely on her own resources. . . .'[1]

Accustomed for so long to consider Anne as a child, and uncertain of her capacities (of which Emily knew far more), Charlotte greatly doubted her ability to rise to the formidable challenge of a dependant's life among strangers. '. . . I hope she'll do', Charlotte wrote Ellen. 'You would be astonished what a sensible, clever letter she writes; it is only the talking part that I fear. But I do seriously apprehend that Mrs. Ingham will sometimes conclude that she has a natural impediment of speech. . . .'[2]

Though Anne might on occasion stammer when exceedingly shy, she showed unanswerable good sense and resolution in dealing with her savage young charges. That she also brought a sense of humour to bear on the situation at Blake Hall, the pages of *Agnes Grey* attest. She remained in her post in spite of the uncongenial circumstances until the following Christmas.

'. . . I am as yet "wanting a situation", like a housemaid out of place', Charlotte told Ellen in the same letter in which she announced

[1] CB to EN, 15 Apr. 1839: *SLL* i. 155.   [2] Idem.

Anne's departure from home. In the event it was another month before she was 'suited'. The wrily humorous declarations contained in the same letter that she would not be a cook ('I hate cooking') or a nursery-maid, or a lady's-maid, or a lady's-companion, or a mantua-maker, or a straw-bonnet maker, or a taker in of plain-work ('I won't be anything but a housemaid') show well enough how bitter the prospect was to her.

No coercion was brought to bear on the girls to go out, as is plainly seen by Charlotte's comment to Ellen: '... Papa wishes me to remain at home a little longer, but I begin to be anxious to set to work again....'[1]

Anne's situation had certainly been secured, via the Miss Woolers, through the recommendation of their brother-in-law, the Rev. Edward Nicoll Carter, who had been curate of Mirfield over irregular periods for 10 years, and was, indeed, the clergyman who had christened all the little Inghams of Blake Hall, Anne's prospective pupils. Mr. Carter it was now who, in all probability, intervened to help Charlotte find a post as governess, for since leaving Mirfield for good in 1838 he had been appointed curate-in-charge to the new church (consecrated 22 October 1838) at Lothersdale, four miles from Skipton. The first patron and churchwarden of the new church was Mr. John Benson Sidgwick, the owner of Stonegappe, a considerable property situated barely a mile above the village of Lothersdale, and there Charlotte went as governess to the Sidgwick children in May 1839. The connexion is sufficiently apparent. Mr. Carter it was who had prepared Charlotte for Confirmation while she was a pupil at Roe Head, in 1832, and who, through her long connexion with the school and its headmistress, knew her character and circumstances better than most. He and his wife, the former Susanna Wooler (married at Mirfield, 30 December 1830) had three children; during Charlotte's residence at Stonegappe they had a fourth, Catherine Elizabeth, baptized at Lothersdale on 28 July 1839. To the Carters Charlotte was to owe what little happiness she found in her new situation.

In her letter of 8 June addressed to Emily, she wrote: '... I am getting quite to have a regard for the Carter family. At home I should not care for them, but here they are friends. Mr. Carter was at Mirfield yesterday, and saw Anne. He says she was looking uncommonly well....'[2]

The Carters, pending the building of a regular parsonage house, lived in a farmhouse on the Stonegappe estate—Lower Leys Farm (sometimes spelt 'Lays')—which was at an easy distance from the

---

[1] Idem.   [2] CB to EJB, 8 June 1839: *SLL* i. 158–60.

Sidgwicks' home. Charlotte, exercising her young pupils, had repeated occasion for calling on them, and receiving their moral support.

Mrs. Sidgwick, by repute if not by personal acquaintance, was not a total stranger to Charlotte, being the daughter of a wealthy Keighley manufacturer, John Greenwood of The Knowle and Knowle Mills, one of the foremost properties in the town. Sarah Hannah Greenwood, as she had been, married Mr. Sidgwick at Keighley Parish Church on 10 January 1827, the ceremony being conducted by a very old friend of Mr. Brontë's, the Rev. Hammond Roberson.[1] In any case the Greenwoods of Keighley[2] were no strangers to the Brontë family, for Sarah Hannah's elder sister Anne had married the Rector of Keighley, the Rev. Theodore Dury, a close colleague of Mr. Brontë's, after the loss of his first wife in 1821. With the Dury family and Mr. Dury's children by both marriages, the Brontës were on visiting terms, and especially so during the forthcoming curacy at Haworth of William Weightman, Mr. Brontë's 'sunny-tempered' curate, from 1839–42.

Charlotte had, therefore, more than one connexion with the family of her new employers before taking up the post at Stonegappe; she was destined, however, to be none the happier for that. The very fact of knowing Mrs. Sidgwick, if only through the gentlemen of their respective families, perhaps aroused expectations that Mrs. Sidgwick had no inclination to satisfy. In two letters Charlotte complained, rather unreasonably when viewed in the light of contemporary usage, that Mrs. Sidgwick 'did not intend to know me' and regarded her purely in the light of an employee out of whom 'the greatest possible quantity of labour' may be squeezed. Mrs. Sidgwick, according to her governess, made no attempt to consider her feelings, overwhelmed her with needlework and what Charlotte considered menial tasks, and gave her no support in attempting to discipline her children.

Charlotte's position was clearly that of 'nursery governess', only the youngest children being in her care. There were, as yet, four children in the family: Margaret, born 14 November 1827; William, born 25 April 1829; Mathilda, born 3 August 1832; John Benson, born 2 August 1835. On 18 August 1839, only a month after Charlotte left the family, Mrs. Sidgwick had a son, christened Edward. The family was completed in 1845 by the birth of a last son, Charles.[3]

Charlotte's pupils were Mathilda (aged 6½) and John Benson (aged 4).

[1] Registers of Keighley Parish Church.
[2] William Keighley, *Keighley Past & Present*, 1879.
[3] Registers of St. Andrew's Church, Kildwick.

When Mrs. Gaskell recorded Charlotte's tribulations with 'a little boy, three or four years old' and his 'elder brother, a lad of eight or nine' who threw stones at her for attempting to prevent their playing in a stable-yard (a pleasure expressly forbidden by their mother), she was speaking of John Benson and his elder brother William. The incident, arising from the mother's prohibition and the elder boy's tempting of the little one to disobey it, and leading to Charlotte's intervention and resultant cut forehead, epitomizes her uneasy situation with the Sidgwicks. Expected to enforce the mother's authority, but given no support with which to do so, she was an obvious victim of her pupils' indiscipline. Her pluck, however, in not betraying them when they stoned her, gained her some respect at least, and from John Benson that now famous declaration: 'I love 'ou, Miss Brontë', which called down on him his mother's equally famous rebuke: 'Love the *governess* my dear!'

At all times hopelessly at a disadvantage among strangers, Charlotte was especially so when the strangers were her employers. Mrs. Sidgwick, beloved by her own family circle and appreciated in society, could not, even if she had wished, penetrate the reserve of the awkward and unhappy girl to whom she had committed the care of her children that summer. Intensely resenting the position of subservience to which her employment relegated her, Charlotte was constantly on the look-out for affronts. Bewildered by numbers, she was, as she wrote to Emily, afflicted by the entirely novel scene and the strange and constantly changing faces of the visitors filling the large house. How differently the gay ladies occupying the sofas and large settees of the Stonegappe drawing-room behaved, looked, and spoke compared with the Angrian beauties among whom she had spent her girlhood! Life was proving very unpleasant now it had to be lived in actual surroundings; nothing of an exhilarating nature happened, though the heart's hunger for excitement and adventure was just as acute. Only in the observation of the truth was there food for a fermenting intelligence. To Emily she could empty her heart with the caution not to let 'papa or aunt' see her letter, for fear they should think she was never satisfied. The text of her first letter to be preserved reads:

Stonegappe June 8th 1839

Dearest Lavinia—I am most exceedingly obliged to you for the trouble you have taken in seeking up my things and sending them all right. The box and its contents were most acceptable. I only wish I had asked you to send me some letter-paper. This is my last sheet but two. When you can send the other articles of raiment now manufacturing, I shall be right down glad of them.

I have striven hard to be pleased with my new situation. The country, the house, and the grounds are, as I have said, divine. But alack-a-day! there is such a thing as seeing all beautiful around you—pleasant woods, winding white paths, green lawns, and blue sunshiny sky—and not having a free moment or a free thought left to enjoy them in. The children are constantly with me, and more riotous, perverse, unmanageable cubs never grew. As for correcting them, I soon quickly found that was entirely out of the question: they are to do as they like. A complaint to Mrs. Sidgwick brings only black looks upon oneself, and unjust, partial excuses to screen the children. I have tried that plan once. It succeeded so notably that I shall try it no more. I said in my last letter that Mrs. Sidgwick did not know me. I now begin to find that she does not intend to know me, that she cares nothing in the world about me except to contrive how the greatest possible quantity of labour may be squeezed out of me, and to that end she overwhelms me with oceans of needlework, yards of cambric to hem, muslin nightcaps to make, and, above all things, dolls to dress. I do not think she likes me at all, because I can't help being shy in such an entirely novel scene, surrounded as I have hitherto been by strange and constantly changing faces. I *used* to think I should like to be in the stir of grand folks' society but I have had enough of it—it is dreary work to look on and listen, I see now more clearly than I have ever done before that a private governess has no existence, is not considered as a living and rational being except as connected with the wearisome duties she has to fulfil. While she is teaching the children, working for them, amusing them, it is all right. If she steals a moment for herself she is a nuisance. Nevertheless, Mrs. Sidgwick is universally considered an amiable woman. Her manners are fussily affable. She talks a great deal, but as it seems to me not much to the purpose. Perhaps I may like her better after a while. At present I have no call to like her. Mr. Sidgwick is in my opinion a hundred times better—less profession, less bustling condescension, but a far kinder heart. It is very seldom that he speaks to me, but when he does I always feel happier and more settled for some minutes after. He never asks me to wipe the children's smutty noses or tie their shoes or fetch their pinafores or set them a chair. One of the pleasantest afternoons I have spent here—indeed, the only one at all pleasant—was when Mr. Sidgwick walked out with his children, and I had orders to follow a little behind. As he strolled on through his fields, with his magnificent Newfoundland dog at his side, he looked very like what a frank, wealthy, Conservative gentleman ought to be. He spoke freely and unaffectedly to the people he met, and though he indulged his children and allowed them to tease himself far too much, he would not suffer them grossly to insult others. . . . As to Mrs. Collins' report that Mrs. Sidgwick intended to keep me permanently, I do not think that such was ever her design. Moreover, I would not stay without some alterations. For instance, this burden of sewing would have to be removed. It is too bad for anything. I never in my whole life had my time so fully taken up. Next week we are going to Swarcliffe, Mr. Greenwood's place near Harrogate, to stay three weeks or a month. After that time I hope Miss Hoby [doubtless a former governess] will return. Don't show this letter to papa or aunt, only to Branwell. They will think I am never satisfied, wherever I am. I complain to you because it is a relief, and really I have had some unexpected mortifications to put up with. However, things may mend, but Mrs. Sidgwick expects me to do things that I cannot do—to love her children and be entirely devoted to them. I am really very well. I am so sleepy that I can write no more. I must leave off. Love to all.—Good-bye.

Direct your next despatch—J. Greenwood, Esq, Swarcliffe, near Harrogate.

C. Brontë.[1]

The exception in favour of Mr. Sidgwick is notable as foreshadowing a situation that was to recur with each one of her posts: at odds as she invariably found herself with the ladies, the gentlemen—Mr. Sidgwick, Mr. White, Monsieur Heger—found a varying degree of favour in her sight. This, it must be remembered, arose as much from the quality of her mind, that craved intelligent communications (and never found it in the uneducated female of the day) as from mere prejudice in favour of the stronger sex.

Mr. Sidgwick was, in all probability, a more interesting person than his wife. Born in 1800, son of a wealthy cotton-spinner, William Sidgwick, of Leeds origin, whose mills were at Skipton, he was typical of his time and district, in which new fortunes were rapidly made and landed property passing out of the hands of the old families into those of the rising manufacturers. The acquisition of Stonegappe in 1798 by William Sidgwick from the Bawdwen family—landowners in the district since Tudor times—was symptomatic of this changing society.

Mention of a dwelling at 'Stone Gap' goes back to 1300, and Lothersdale itself was named in Domesday Book. The house Charlotte Brontë knew was rebuilt in 1725 on the site of a far older structure, but as the eighteenth century advanced the fortunes of the Bawdwen family declined, and by 1798, after various unsatisfactory tenancies (to the Chippendale family among others) the old owners were glad to sell, and parted with the estate for £4,691 to William Sidgwick.[2]

A glimpse at the origins of his fortune is afforded by the report of a

[1] CB to EJB, 8 June 1839: *SLL*, No. 51.
[2] John Stell, Memoir of Stone Gappe.

Royal Commission investigating 'The State of Children Employed in Manufactures' held in 1816, at which Sir Robert Peel's father was in the chair. Asked the numbers employed by him, William Sidgwick said he believed—'at a mere guess'—that he employed something like 100 or 120 children in his Skipton Mills. In reply to queries about their health, he said he considered it very good: '. . . as a matter of opinion', he said, 'I think the health of children employed much better than the health of children roaming at large.' Asked the number of hours worked daily in his mills, he said: 'We work from 5 o'clock in the morning till 12 o'clock and we work from 1 o'clock to 7, making 13 hours.'

> Q. 'Is there any refreshment during that time?'
> A. 'The breakfast is brought to the people at the mill, generally by the parents of the children. . . .'
> Q. '. . . should you suppose, in the morning and afternoon together, half an hour or three-quarters of an hour is occupied in taking refreshment?'
> A. 'As to myself, I view it this way, that there is no remittance of labour; the labour at the Mills is not perpetual labour it is attention; and the child may be half an hour together and have no labour to perform; so that the child takes refreshment at his convenience and there is no interruption to the child. . . .'

Asked whether he imagined 'that children confined 14 or 15 hours a day in cotton mills would be so healthy as those who are only confined 10 or 12 hours', Mr. Sidgwick could see no reason 'to apprehend a diminution in health'. Asked outright if he knew any manufactory in fact that worked 14 or 15 hours, he owned that he did not.[1]

Marriage into the Benson family of York (the family had been tenants of Fountains Abbey in 1348) yet further advanced Mr. Sidgwick's social status; so that while his elder son succeeded him in the mills and at Stonegappe, his second son, William, was able to go to Cambridge, take Holy Orders, and become Headmaster of Skipton Grammar School. It was *his* daughter, Mary, who married her cousin three times removed, Edward White Benson, the future Archbishop of Canterbury, who called on Mr. Brontë in his old age.

Sidgwicks, Bensons, and Greenwoods, Charlotte Brontë found that Stonegappe, a pleasant house indeed in summer, was continually open to the many and various ramifications of the families of her

[1] Report on 'The State of Children Employed in Manufacture', 1816, by courtesy of Mrs. Greenwood of Swarcliffe.

employers—a going and coming of callers and of long-term visitors that bewildered the shy governess, though seen for the most part from the distance of her second-floor schoolroom. (Edward White Benson, though a frequent visitor at his uncle's house, regretted in after years that he had *not* been there at the same time as Charlotte Brontë. In 1839 he was 10.)[1]

Stonegappe was built in a commanding position overlooking the valley of the Lother and slightly below the crest of the high road running from Kildwick (three miles distant) to the village of Lothersdale. From this it was both sheltered from the north, and beautifully exposed to the south, with its terraces and sloping lawns embracing the whole vista of the dales. These lawns, with their enclosing shrubberies on either hand, were the setting of Charlotte's main walks abroad. In the second field below the house, stood Lower Leys Farm where the Carters lived.

With the drawing- and dining-rooms and the library and the elegant three-arched passage linking them on the ground floor, the governess's life was little concerned. She lived for the greater part of each day in the large schoolroom on the second floor, the central room with three bays overlooking the south, from whose deep window-seats the radiant scene without lay temptingly spread to her view, but from which she had often to turn her envious eyes. Beautiful as all nature was about Stonegappe, the freedom to enjoy it, as she said, was denied her. The task she hated, like Elizabeth Hastings, of 'wearily toiling to impart knowledge into yawning and obstinate children', was hers in this room throughout each day, and even when the children were consigned to their beds of an evening they were still not beyond her care (their bedrooms adjoined the schoolroom) and their slumbers demanded her supervision.

During the long summer evenings when she sat alone, her lap filled with Mrs. Sidgwick's 'oceans of needlework'—in place of the writing or the book in which she longed to lose herself—no one from the noisy self-absorbed house-party below came to share her solitude. Even in summer weather the winds about Stonegappe keep up a wuthering sound—especially in the high schoolroom where Charlotte sat—and this was her best companion, for in the wind there was word of home.

At the end of the top-floor corridor, otherwise occupied by the women-servants, and in a corner-room facing east overlooking the entrance hall and the sweeping gravel-drive to the house-door, was

[1] Benson, A. C., *Life of Edward White Benson, Archbishop of Canterbury.*

Charlotte's bedroom. It, too, had deep window seats and Georgian panes to its window-frames, and through them a lonely girl could look down unobserved on the arrivals and departures, the gentlemen on their horses and the ladies in their carriages, that animated the summer scene. Almost filling the view was a noble copper-beech at a bend in the drive that tradition has it was a favourite of Charlotte's.

The north aspect of the house, backing on to the cliff-face of the highway, was filled with offices and the coach-stables forbidden the Sidgwick children.

Mrs. Sidgwick's father, John Greenwood of Keighley, had acquired in 1805 an extensive property near Harrogate, Swarcliffe, and there he liked to assemble his family—the married sons and daughters and their partners and children—during every summer. Swarcliffe, embowered in its woods, was yet another beauty-spot, but the change there could be fraught with little pleasure for the governess. Writing to Ellen from there on 30 June, she described her utter inability to react to the strain of yet another fresh environment.

My dearest Ellen, I am writing a letter to you with pencil because I cannot just now procure ink without going into the drawing-room—where I do not wish to go. I only received your letter yesterday, for we are not now residing at Stonegappe, but at Swarcliffe a summer residence of Mr. Greenwood's, Mrs. Sidgwick's father. It is near Harrogate and Ripon; a beautiful place in a beautiful country—rich and agricultural. I should have written to you long since, and told you of every detail of the utterly new scene into which I have lately been cast, had I not been daily expecting a letter from yourself, and wondering and lamenting that you did not write, for you will remember it was your turn. I must not bother you too much with my sorrows, Ellen, of which I fear you have heard an exaggerated account, if you were near me, perhaps I might be tempted to tell you all—to grow egotistical and pour out the long history of a Private Governess's trials and crosses in her first situation. As it is, I will only ask you to imagine the miseries of a reserved wretch like me, thrown at once into the midst of a large family—proud as peacocks and wealthy as Jews—at a time when they were particularly gay, when the house was full of company—all strangers, people whose faces I had never seen before—in this state of things having the charge given me of a set of pampered, spoilt, and turbulent children, whom I was expected constantly to amuse as well as instruct. I soon found that the constant demand on my stock of animal spirits reduced them to the lowest state of exhaustion; at times I felt and I supposed seemed depressed. To my astonishment I was taken to task on the subject by Mrs. Sidgwick with a stress of manner and a harshness of language scarcely credible. Like a fool, I cried most bitterly;

I could not help it—my spirits failed me at first. I thought I had done my best—strained every nerve to please her—and to be treated in that way merely because I was shy and sometimes melancholy was too bad. At first I was for giving all up and going home, but after a little reflection I determined to summon what energy I had and to weather the storm. I said to myself I have never yet quitted a place without gaining a friend. Adversity is a good school—the Poor are born to labour, and the Dependent to endure. I resolved to be patient—to command my feelings and to take what came; the ordeal, I reflected, would not last many weeks, and I trusted it would do me good. I recollected the fable of the Willow and the Oak; I bent quietly, and I trust now the storm is blowing over me. Mrs. Sidgwick is generally considered an agreeable woman; so she is, I dare say, in general Society. Her health is sound, her animal spirits are good; consequently she is cheerful in company. But, oh! Ellen, does this compensate for the absence of every fine feeling, of every gentle and delicate sentiment?

She behaves somewhat more civilly to me now than she did at first, and the children are a little more manageable; but she does not know my character, and she does not wish to know it. I have never had five minutes' conversation with her since I came—except while she was scolding me. Do not communicate the contents of this letter to any one—I have no wish to be *pitied*, except by yourself—do not even clatter with Martha Taylor about it. If I were talking to you I would tell you much more; but I hope my term of bondage will soon be expired and then I can go home and you can come and see me; and I hope we shall be happy. Good-bye, *dear, dear* Ellen.

Write to me again very soon and tell me how you are; direct J. Greenwood, Esquire, Swarcliffe, Nr. Harrogate. Perhaps, though, I may be at home before you write again. I don't intend to stay long after they leave Swarcliffe, which they expect shortly to do.[1]

The Greenwood family consisted at that time of Mrs. Sidgwick's father, her eldest brother Frederick (born 1797), and second brother Edwin (born 1798) who later inherited the Swarcliffe estate and rebuilt the house; their wives and children. Frederick Greenwood, as the eldest son, inherited the Keighley property on the death of his father in 1846, but in 1848 he bought Norton Conyers, near Ripon, the house which has repeatedly been identified as the original of Thornfield Hall in *Jane Eyre*.

This is due to various points of resemblance, although the main feature of Thornfield, its battlemented roof, was absent. In the absence of direct evidence of Charlotte's having visited the place, the belief rests on the recollection of Ellen Nussey, who said in later years that

---

[1] CB to EN, 1 July 1839: *W & S*, No. 76.

Charlotte had told her she had visited it with her employers during the stay at Swarcliffe. She had been much impressed by the story of a mad-woman confined there in an upper room in the eighteenth century. The attic rooms at Norton Conyers, panelled, and dark and low, had been, on the occasion of her visit, filled with old furniture and furnishings from another abandoned house belonging to the then owner, Sir Reginald Henry Graham. These, and the oak staircase, and the armour in the panelled entrance hall, were sufficiently striking for Charlotte to mention to Ellen. Ellen, always inclined to associate places and persons in Charlotte's novels with herself, was the more disinterested witness in this case, in that her own old home, Rydings, at Birstall, had both the battlemented roof and the rookery so vividly described in *Jane Eyre*, and was the more obvious original for Mr. Rochester's home. If Charlotte visited Norton Conyers, especially if the story of the madwoman was told her, she probably absorbed as much of the one house as of the other, and evolved an amalgam of both from her memory, with no bias towards either, when the time for creation came.[1]

With the exception of such possible excursions, life at Swarcliffe was not very different to life at Stonegappe for the governess; the same tasks had to be performed, the same 'pampered, spoilt, turbulent children' controlled and occupied, if not actually taught during the holiday season. Thrown back upon her own resources even more completely because of her isolation among a host of strangers, the best outlet for Charlotte's faculties was in a concentrated observation of the world about her. In this context it must be remembered that when the scenes in *Jane Eyre* describing the house-party at Mr. Rochester's are dismissed as grotesque exaggerations, due to the inexperience of the author, just such experience of country-house social life fell to Charlotte's lot at Stonegappe and at Swarcliffe during her employment as the Sidgwicks' governess.

A hurried little note to Emily gives the measure of her longing for home and the love of her own people.

Mine bonnie love, I was as glad of your letter as tongue can express: it is a real, genuine pleasure to hear from home; a thing to be saved till bed-time, when one has a moment's quiet and rest to enjoy it thoroughly. Write whenever you can. I could like to be at home. I could like to work in a mill. I could like to feel mental liberty. I could like this weight of restraint to be taken off. But the holidays will come. *Corragio.*[2]

---

[1] Wroot, Herbert, 'Persons & Places in the Brontë Novels': *BST*, 1906.
[2] CB to EJB: *SLL* (No. 53), 162, July 1839.

By the third week in July, probably the 19th, Charlotte's longings were fulfilled and the painful experiment brought to an end. Writing on the 26th to Ellen from home she said: '. . . I left Stonegappe a week since. I never was so glad to get out of a house in my life. . . .'[1]

Mrs. Sidgwick, confined of her fifth child on 18 August, might possibly also have exclaimed that she was never so glad to be rid of a governess, seeing in her late employee no single quality corresponding to the requirements of such a post, except integrity. She would be unlikely to reflect that women of her time in need of earning a living had no choice of employment or of fitting their capacities to the task, as their modern counterparts can have; and that genius is a cruel handicap in dealing with the exigencies of the nursery.

[1] CB to EN, 26 July 1839: *W & S*, No. 78.

FIRST FLIGHT

THE 'mental liberty' for which she groaned in her letter to Emily, the relief from 'restraint', loomed even larger than love of home on quitting the Sidgwicks; for the moment, to escape was all her longing.

As by a miracle, a means of escape was offered her at that very time. Ellen Nussey was ordered to the sea for her health and she wrote to Charlotte asking her to accompany her. 'Your proposal has almost driven me "clean daft"', Charlotte answered her on 26 July. '...I should indeed like to go—but I can't get leave of absence for longer than a week and I'm afraid that wouldn't suit you—must I then give it up entirely? I feel as if I could not—I never had such a chance of enjoyment before. ...'[1] A week later she was writing rapturously: '...The idea of seeing the *sea*—of being near it—watching its changes by sunrise, sunset, moonlight, and noonday—in calm, perhaps in storm—fills and satisfies my mind. ...'[2]

Ellen had been ordered away for several weeks and from this stemmed a host of petty and distracting impediments that harassed Charlotte inexpressibly during a month of preparations. She could neither afford so long a holiday ('I happen to be very low in cash', she confided to Ellen) nor could she persuade her father and aunt to consent to it (the 'utmost stretch' they would concede was for a fortnight). The caution of the elders of the family—alarmed at two young ladies embarking without escort on a holiday to the sea—was not unkindly meant; a plan had indeed been broached at that very time by Miss Branwell for Mr. Brontë and herself to take all the young people to Liverpool for a fortnight's holiday, but it had not materialized. Meanwhile, as Charlotte's successive plans for flight proved abortive, Mr. Brontë and Miss Branwell raised increasing objections to it. In their sober judgements, the whole escapade was ill advised. The girls had not even made up their minds where they were going,

---

[1] *W & S*, No. 78.   [2] CB to EN, 4 Aug. 1839: *SLL* 164.

hesitating between Cleethorpes and Burlington (as Bridlington was known at that time). Eventually they decided on Burlington. This led to further complications and delays. Henry Nussey, when curate of Burton Agnes, had lived within six miles of Burlington, and still had good friends there; he wrote to them for advice and particulars respecting lodgings, etc., and meanwhile the girls could not set out.

Charlotte felt all the bitterness of frustration and by 14 August was for giving up all hope of accompanying Ellen.

I have in vain packed my box and prepared everything for our anticipated journey. It so happens that I can get no conveyance this week or the next. The only gig let out on hire in Haworth is at Harrogate, and likely to remain there, for aught I can hear. Papa decidedly objects to my going by the coach, and walking to Birstall, though I am sure I could manage it. Aunt exclaims against the weather, and the roads, and the four winds of heaven; so I am in a fix, and, what is worse, so are *you*. . . . I grieve that I should have so inconvenienced you; but I need not talk of either Friday or Saturday now, for I rather imagine there is small chance of my ever going at all. The elders of the house have never cordially acquiesced in the measure; and now that impediments seem to start up at every step opposition grows more and more. Papa, indeed, would willingly indulge me, but this very kindness of his makes me doubt whether I ought to draw upon it; so, though I could battle out aunt's discontent, I yield to papa's indulgence. He does not say so, but I know he would rather I stayed at home. . . . Reckon on me no more; leave me out in your calculations; perhaps I ought, in the beginning, to have had prudence sufficient to shut my eyes against such a prospect of pleasure, so as to deny myself the hope of it. . . .[1]

Ellen recalled in after years realizing that 'Charlotte was sinking into despair', and that there 'seemed only one chance of securing her the pleasure', which was to go and fetch her. This she did, in her brother's carriage; took the parsonage party by surprise ('everybody rose into high good humours, Branwell was grandiloquent, he declared it was a brave defeat, the doubters were fairly taken aback')[2] and bore Charlotte off to Leeds, where they took the train for Selby. The line went no further at that time, and the rest of the journey, via York and Driffield, was by coach.

It was unthinkable that on a journey undertaken in the true spirit of Catherine Moreland no adventures should befall them and, happily for their enjoyment, this was soon the case. At York there were no seats

[1] *SLL* i. 166–7.
[2] EN, 'Reminiscences of CB': *Scribner's Magazine*, May 1871.

left on the coach, and they were sent on by open 'fly'. The weather was lovely, as Ellen remembered, and they immensely enjoyed their drive. Naturally, the coach got to Driffield before them, and here their second adventure awaited them. Henry Nussey had done more than advise his friends, the Hudsons, of his sister's coming; he had obviously asked them to keep an eye on her and Charlotte; and to meet their coach, there was Mr. Hudson in his gig, on the look out—and on the pounce —for the travellers. Mr. and Mrs. Hudson had no intention of allowing two unchaperoned young ladies—and one of them their late curate's sister—to stray among the marine dangers of Burlington Quay, and were firmly resolved on abducting them to their own pleasant farm-house at Easton.

When the coach arrived without the travellers, Mr. Hudson left orders with the innkeeper to intercept them and send them on by post-chaise to Easton. And thus, Charlotte, craning her neck at every rise in the road as they neared the coast for a first sight of the sea, was sicken-ingly disappointed at the journey's end by finding herself virtually a prisoner and as far from the sight and sound and smell of it as ever.

The Hudsons were obdurate. Miss Nussey and her friend must by no means venture down among the lobster-pot alleys and crowded wharves of the Quay. It was not a place, they opined, for unaccom-panied young ladies. For as long as they liked to make Easton House Farm their holiday-home, Mr. and Mrs. Hudson were delighted to entertain them; and from this decision there was no shaking them, and the girls had perforce to comply.

At first Charlotte felt crushing disappointment; as Ellen remembered, 'Whenever the sound of the sea reached her ears in the grounds around the house wherein she was a captive guest, her spirit longed to rush away and be close to it.'[1]

Easton House lay two miles inland to the west of Burlington, and as the lie of the land all along that coast drops in level below the high ridge of the cliffs, no sight of the sea can be had until close upon it. The month was early September, and while the harvest was being carried in fields all round the farm, in others the ploughs were out, and all day flocks of seagulls followed the freshly turned furrows. Their cries were the only intimation to reach Charlotte of the proximity of the sea.

On the second day after their arrival, she could bear her impatience no longer, and set out with Ellen to walk to the coast. They followed the course of the Gypsy Race—the stream that bordered the Hudsons'

[1] EN, 'Reminiscences of CB', op. cit.

ground, and flows out to sea at the little harbour by the Quay. So over-wrought was Charlotte by then that as soon as they were near enough to see the sea, 'she was quite overpowered', said Ellen, 'she could not speak till she had shed some tears'. She signed to her friend to leave her and walk on. This she did for a few steps, knowing full well what Charlotte was passing through, and the stern efforts she was making to subdue her emotion. Ellen turned to her as soon as she thought she might without inflicting pain; 'her eyes were red and swollen, she was still trembling . . . for the remainder of the day she was very quiet, subdued and exhausted . . .'.[1]

Since the wood-cuts of Bewick had stirred her childish mind to conceive of the wonder of the sea, since her girlhood's reading of Byron—she had felt a foreknowledge of the kind of power it would exercise over her spirit could she but find it in reality for herself. The discovery was every bit as momentous as she had imagined; and she responded to it with all the ardour of her nature, so singularly receptive to every influence of physical and spiritual beauty in the world.

Burlington was a very different place then to what it has become now. The two parts of the town were yet distinct; the Quay, with its old inns and gabled houses clustering closely round the little harbour where the fishing fleets came and went; and Old Burlington, the digni-fied Georgian streets with their pillared doorways and bow-windows, converging on the medieval Bayle Gate and the Priory Church of St. Mary's. Here, in all probability, Charlotte situated in after years 'the clean and ancient town of Bretton'—the place 'where Sundays and holidays seemed always to abide—so quiet was its atmosphere, so clean its pavement . . .'.[2]

The traveller who today follows in Charlotte's steps, and walks the length of St. John's Street and High Street to the town's end by West-gate, and so out upon the tree-bordered highway to Easton (where Mr. Hudson's house still stood till 1961) will find the description holds. The house-fronts are still unaltered Georgian; the bow-windows of the old inns and shops alternate with the flat fronts and Regency sash-bars of the windows and the flat-pillared deep-set doorways painted in pastel shades. The decorum and the cleanliness are still entire, as is the silence, chiefly broken in those narrow streets, where few vehicles pass, by the quarters striking at St. Mary's clock. Charlotte, who would return to Burlington when she was already brooding on *Villette*, was clearly enough attracted to the place to choose it for the part-setting of her tale.

[1] EN RCB, op. cit.   [2] *Villette*, ch. 1.

The proximity of the sea being once ocularly demonstrated, and a return there established as a daily possibility, Charlotte settled down to enjoy the many pleasures her stay at Easton House afforded her. Mr. and Mrs. Hudson were as pleasant as their surroundings, people of forthright and cheerful character who knew how to cut through Charlotte's diffidence and shyness and make her feel at home. That she quickly felt so appears from a sketch she made of her hosts in the garden of their house. The house, built *c.* 1810, was long and low, of red-brick but whitewashed as is general in the district, and it had the red-tiled roof characteristic of the East Riding. The porch and trellised walls were covered with honeysuckle and wild roses, and for the rest it wore a mantle of ivy. At the back of the house was a pleasant garden bordered with laurel, which formed into an arch above the little gate. There were only two farmhouses in the place—the Hudson's and Robert Ryecroft's—and indeed the total number of inhabitants at the time, according to White's *Directory*, was nineteen. The whole estate of 720 acres belonged to Sir George Strickland.

John and Sophia Hudson, who had been married in 1830, were a childless couple, and had staying with them at the time of Charlotte's visit a little seven-year-old niece of Mrs. Hudson's—Fanny Whipp, whom they later adopted. She was a sagacious and original child whose winning ways completely captivated Charlotte and Ellen. The conquest, where Charlotte was concerned, was all the more notable in that she had had little experience of likeable children, the young Sidgwicks having done nothing to predispose her in their favour. Fanny—little 'Hancheon'—as they called her in their then pro-German studious temper—afforded them keen amusement. Their days at the farm were ordered by the strictest—yet most benevolent—time-table, established by Mrs. Hudson, who was described by one who knew her as 'a model of primness and old-world sweetness'. They were up at 6.30, breakfasted at 7.30, dined at noon, had 'tea'—that essentially North-country comprehensive meal—at 4.30, and were in bed by 9.30— barring those evenings when the Hudsons entertained 'company'.[1]

After her recent trials of that summer, nothing could have suited Charlotte better than the wholesome round of Easton House, where in reality the girls enjoyed an unaccustomed liberty. They visited Henry Nussey's former parish at Burton Agnes, one of the most picturesque

[1] For particulars concerning Easton, see P. F. Lee, 'CB and the East Ridings': *BST* 1896; W. Scruton, 'Reminiscences of EN': *BST*, 1898; F. R. Pearson, *CB on the E. Yorkshire Coast*, 1957.

EASTON HOUSE, drawing by Charlotte Brontë 1839

villages in the East Riding; called on his friends; spent their days wandering in the woods at Boynton, and in following the Gypsy Race upstream. But always the sea lured Charlotte as no other attraction could. At last, after a stay at Easton of two to three weeks, Mr. and Mrs. Hudson were sufficiently convinced that there was no flightiness in their young guests to give their consent to their going into lodgings down at the Quay for the last week of their holiday.

They stayed at a house on the cliff, opposite the pierhead, on what has since been called the Esplanade. Its vicinity to the new Methodist Chapel—the 'Ranters Chapel' as it was called—places it fairly conclusively: closer to the sea they could not have gone.[1]

Their rapture was complete; although, even then, they were not out of tutelage. Every day they were visited by Mr. and Mrs. Hudson who brought them provisions from the farm, a gesture whose value they only fully appreciated at the week's end when they called for their bill. They had intended providing their own board, but were thankful indeed for the generosity of Mrs. Hudson in supplying them with most things, for they found that their little stock of money would not have been enough to pay all.

To watch the sea from the cliff edge and to walk on the sands—that phenomenal stretch of sands that makes the fame of Bridlington—was Charlotte's only desire. Of an evening, however, the human spectacle afforded the girls their chief entertainment. Ellen recorded how 'the conventionality of most of the seaside visitors amused Charlotte immensely. The evening parade on the pier struck her as the greatest absurdity. It was an old pier in those days, and of short dimensions, but thither all the visitors seemed to assemble in such numbers, it was like a packed ballroom; people had to march round and round in regular file to secure any movement whatever. Charlotte and her friend thought they would go away from this after making one essay to do as others did; they took themselves off to the cliffs to enjoy the moonlight, but they had not done this long, ere some instinct as to safety warned them to return; on entering their lodgings another novelty impressed itself upon them, they encountered sounds which came from a Ranters' meeting-house across the street, there was violent excitement within its walls, and Charlotte was wild to go in amongst the congregation and see as she said, "What they were up to"; but was restrained by the reflection that those people who were making such awful noises were

[1] See F. R. Pearson, *Charlotte Brontë's Holiday at Bridlington*: Bridlington Public Library publications, Spring 1949.

acting as they believed on religious impulses, and "ought neither to be criticised nor ridiculed in their midst . . ."'.[1]

When at last the time for returning home was come, the girls bore away with them nothing but happy memories. 'Charlotte's impressions of the sea never wore off,' wrote Ellen Nussey, 'she would often recall her views of it, and wonder what its aspect would be at the time she was speaking of it. . . .'

Charlotte wrote Ellen on 24 October:

. . . Have you forgot the sea by this time? Is it grown dim in your mind? Or still can you see it,—dark blue, and green, and foam-white; and hear it roaring roughly when the wind is high, or rushing softly when it is calm? . . . I think of Easton very often, and of worthy Mr. Hudson, and his kind-hearted helpmate, and of our pleasant walks to Harlequin Wood, to Boynton; our merry evenings, our romps with little Hancheon, etc., etc. If we both live, this period of our lives will long be a theme of pleasant recollection. . . .[2]

To Henry Nussey, she wrote on 28 October:

. . . I enjoyed my late excursion with Ellen with the greater zest because such pleasures have not often chanced to fall in my way. I will not tell you what I thought of the sea, because I should fall into my besetting sin of enthusiasm. I may, however, say that its glories, changes, its ebbs and flow, the sound of its restless waves, formed a subject for contemplation that never wearied either the eye, the ear, or the mind. Our visit to Easton was extremely pleasant; I shall always feel grateful to Mr. & Mrs. Hudson for their kindness. . . .

That 'enthusiasm' was still, at that time, the 'besetting sin' with her which it always remained with Branwell, is a sad commentary on the course of her life, for the experience of the next immediate years effectually cured her of it.

The impression created by the sea, however, did not wear off. Years later, in 1845, when Ellen returned to Burlington in charge of her invalid brother George, Charlotte wrote to her:

. . . Remember me very kindly to Mrs. Hudson, to whom I shall direct this letter—not knowing your address at the Quay. Tell her that our stay at Easton is one of the pleasant recollections of my life—one of the green spots

1 EN, 'Reminiscences of CB': *Scribner's Magazine*, May 1871, op. cit.
2 CB to EN, 24 Oct. 1839: *SLL* i. 167–8.

that I look back on with real pleasure. I often think it was singularly good of her to receive me, a total stranger, so kindly as she did . . .[1]

To Easton and the Hudsons Charlotte would return yet again, but under very different circumstances. The sea by then would hold another meaning for her, and the place be seen through eyes that were dimmed with tears. Life seldom held for her a repetition of joys; it was enough to have possessed them once.

[1] CB to EN, 4 Mar. 1845: *W & S* ii. 26–27.

CHAPTER XI

THE PATH OF DUTY

FOR the eighteen months following her holiday at the sea Charlotte remained at home and had the leisure to take stock of her prospects and to crystallize her views on life.

Several circumstances contributed to making this as happy and care-free a period as any she would know. The reprieve from 'exile' among strangers was sufficiently justified and excused even to her conscience by the illness and retirement of Tabby, which threw on Emily and herself the entire work of the house—'except for a little girl to run errands', as she told Ellen on 21 December. The 'little girl' was Martha, the second of John Brown's six daughters, barely 11 at the time. '. . . I manage the ironing and keep the rooms clean,' Charlotte told Ellen, 'Emily does the baking and attends to the kitchen. . . . I excited Aunt's wrath very much by burning the clothes the first time I attempted to iron but I do better now. Human beings are queer things. I am much happier—blackleading the stoves—making the beds and sweeping the floors at home, than I should be living like a fine lady anywhere else. . . .'[1]

While 'happiness' must not be allowed to be her objective, and the search for a fresh place must never wholly fall into abeyance, Charlotte did not hide her dismay at the prospect of resuming the servitude of Stonegappe. '. . . I intend to force myself to take another situation when I can get one,' she told Ellen in the same letter, 'though I *hate* and *abhor* the very thoughts of governesship. But I must do it and therefore I heartily wish I could hear of a Family where they want such a Com-modity as a Governess. . . .'[2]

The dismissal of Anne that Christmas from her post with the Ing-hams of Blake Hall brought nearer home yet the realities of the gover-nesses' life—the injustices and hardships to which it exposed even such scrupulously conscientious girls as Anne. Knowing how much *less* amenable to her employers' whims she herself was, Anne's ill-success gave Charlotte further pause for reflection. '. . . You would never live

[1] CB to EN, 21 Dec. 1839: *SLL* i. 172–3.   [2] Idem.

in an unruly violent family of modern children, such, for instance, as those at Blake Hall', she warned Ellen (in a letter of 24 January 1840), who was toying with the idea of taking a post: '. . . as for the children, it was one struggle of life-wearing exertion to keep them in anything like decent order . . .'.

The ordeal of 19-year-old Anne Brontë, faithfully related in after years by the fictional Agnes Grey, appeared so incredible to the book's first readers that Mrs. Gaskell had to vouch for its veracity on the evidence of Charlotte, who said that 'none but those who had been in the position of a governess could ever realise the dark side of "respectable" human nature . . .'.[1]

At the time of writing the letter to Ellen, Charlotte was declining a post with 'a certain Mrs. H—' and realizing to the full her misery at the necessity of finding another better place—or indeed *any* place of the kind. '. . . I am miserable when I allow myself to dwell on the necessity of spending my life as governess', she wrote Ellen. 'The chief requisite for that station seems to me to be the power of taking things easily as they come and of making oueself comfortable and at home wherever we may chance to be—qualities in which all our family are singularly deficient. . . .'[2]

The fresh realization of their oneness as a family—in temperament, outlook, and sensibility—was brought home to Charlotte at that time by Branwell's new departure on 1 January 1840 as tutor in the family of Mr. Postlethwaite of Broughton-in-Furness. It was his first attempt at earning a living since giving up his studio at Bradford, and Charlotte saw him go with inevitable misgivings. '. . . I who know his variable nature', she wrote Ellen on 28 December [1839], 'and his strong turn for active life, dare not be too sanguine. We are as busy as possible preparing for his departure, and shirt-making and collar-stitching fully occupy our time. . . .'[3]

Both Charlotte and Anne began scanning the advertisement-columns for private posts as governess from then on, and let no likely chances escape them. How little the eventual Currer Bell considered professional authorship as a means to independence is sufficiently obvious from her pursuit of the one career. A further indication of her resignation is the total absence of manuscripts for the period under review. With as much time on her hands as she had ever enjoyed, it is unthinkable that she had given up writing. But it is a sign of growing self-criticism and

[1] Gaskell 114.   [2] CB to EN, 24 Jan. 1840: *SLL* i. 174–5.
[3] CB to EN, 28 Dec. 1839.

of loss of faith in the ends of authorship that nothing remains. In the eventual preface to *The Professor* she confessed to destroying as much as she wrote, in the period immediately preceding her first attempt at professional writing. She wrote there:

... This little book was written before either 'Jane Eyre' or 'Shirley', and yet no indulgence can be solicited for it on the plea of a first attempt. A first attempt it certainly was not, as the pen which wrote it had been previously worn a good deal in a practice of years. I had not, indeed, published anything before I commenced 'The Professor', but in many a crude effort, destroyed as soon as composed, I had got over any such taste as I might once have had for ornamented and redundant composition, and come to prefer what was plain and homely. . . .[1]

(She was not speaking of 'Caroline Vernon', of 'Henry Hastings', and other stories of 1839, since she preserved those, but of the output of the time when she was attempting to put into practice the precepts to which she had declared her fresh allegiance in her 'Farewell to Angria', in which the curtain had been rung down on the romantic scenario of her youth.)[2]

Obviously her attempts at the 'plain and homely' themes dissatisfied her and she destroyed them, showing none of the passionate indulgence she had hitherto extended to her juvenilia. The fact was that the experience of life, without which the realistic treatment is sham and hollow, was lacking as yet. This she recognized and wisely waited her time.

Experience of a sort came to her and her sisters during those months at home. For the first time in their lives they made intimate acquaintance with a young man, with whom they suddenly found themselves on a footing of perfect equality—a circumstance not only rare in their lives, but in that of their female contemporaries. The young man was their father's new curate, the Revd. William Weightman, who took up his functions at Haworth on 19 August 1839. He was the son of an Appleby brewer and was christened in the church of St. Lawrence there on 29 May 1814.[3] He was therefore 25 on reaching Haworth, his first curacy, and had just come down from Durham after taking his M.A. in classics. He was not only a 'first-class scholar', for which Mr. Brontë prized him, but a 'handsome—clean—prepossessing—good-humoured young man', as Charlotte shortly described him. Added to

---

[1] Author's Preface to *The Professor*—posthumous edition by Smith, Elder, 1857.
[2] 'Farewell to Angria': Bonnell Collection No. 125. BPM.
[3] Registers of St. Lawrence Church, Appleby, Westmorland.

the 'advantages of his looks', his bright complexion, merry eyes, and auburn locks, Willie Weightman possessed charm, sanguine spirits, and imperturbable temper. He was also extremely susceptible to female company.

His remarkable achievement where Haworth parsonage was concerned was in gaining the goodwill of all its inhabitants. In a household of diffident geniuses his self-assured good humour was a passport to success with one and all. To Mr. Brontë and Miss Branwell his bearing was filial, and while his learning and Arminian views secured for him the liking of his minister, his repartee subjugated the lady. Towards the girls he at once adopted the best method of cutting through their reserve, by completely ignoring it, and taking them so frankly into his confidence as to disarm them. He came to Haworth reputedly engaged to a young lady of Appleby, Miss Agnes Walton, which made his admittance into the family circle all the easier. That a condition of amorousness was habitual with Willie Weightman they only gradually perceived.

The period of their happiest intercourse was certainly during three weeks in February and March 1840 when Ellen Nussey stayed at the parsonage. By then Mr. Weightman was sufficiently intimate to be a constant attendant on their simple pleasures, their moorland walks and fireside gatherings. It needed only the addition of a strange and not unattractive young woman to the home circle to complete his good-humour. By then it was apparent that no firm engagement bound him to far-away Agnes Walton, and Charlotte, who had constituted herself his chief confidante, was pleased to perceive the dawn of romance breaking between him and her favourite friend. Willie Weightman was certainly prodigal of attentions towards Ellen, and Emily, whether in good horse-sense (in which she excelled) or in banter, insisted on acting chaperon to Ellen on their walks across the moors; thus earning from Weightman the nickname of 'The Major'.

It was a time for nicknames in that usually sober circle. Weightman himself, because of his ready blushes and tight curls, was dubbed 'Celia-Amelia' by Charlotte, and for some months was only spoken of thus. The highlight of Ellen's visit was the excitement created over the Valentines posted to the girls by Weightman in Bradford, so as to put Mr. Brontë and Miss Branwell effectually off the scent. Valentines[1] were not objects that had ever found their way into Haworth parsonage, and the individual verses, nicely calculated to suit each girl by the

[1] See below, Additional Notes for CB's reply to W. W.'s Valentines.

quick-witted curate, touched them more deeply than he ever guessed. The titles of three of the Valentines, 'Fair Ellen, Fair Ellen', 'Away fond Love', and 'Soul Divine', were remembered by Ellen Nussey in old age, and she also recalled Willie Weightman sitting for his portrait in cap and gown for Charlotte. He was vain and eager to show off the silk and velvet, and insisted on Ellen trying them on.[1]

Then there was the plotting and counter-plotting in order to secure Miss Branwell's consent to the girls going down to Keighley one stark February night to hear Mr. Weightman lecture on the classics to the Mechanics' Institute. Circumventing the old lady's doubts of the proprieties of such a proceeding was further cause for merriment, and they walked home the four miles escorted by Mr. Weightman and the Rector of Keighley at past midnight to a late cup of coffee and a scolding.[2] These were happy, care-free times, though in them lay the germ of lasting tragedy for Anne, and disillusionment for Charlotte.

By her own avowal Charlotte took a genuine liking to Mr. Weightman and had a 'great pleasure in cheering and amusing him' when he 'was lonely and rather melancholy'. Whether she avowed it or not, however, her interest was not entirely disinterested and this Ellen herself saw, much to Charlotte's surprise.[3]

Susceptible though Ellen was to all the clergy, she did not appear to have been overpowered by Mr. Weightman (perhaps because she was much occupied at the time over the proposal of a Mr. Vincent whom she could not make up her mind to accept). But she perceived in her admired friend Charlotte a weakness where he was concerned, and did not hesitate to communicate to the irrepressible Martha Taylor what she had discovered. The communication was made all the more piquant by her declaring herself under an embargo from Charlotte to reveal any of the details. This brought the inevitable heckling from Martha, and the swift retort from Charlotte.[4] She wrote her on 17 March 1840:

My dear Mrs. Eleanor, I wish to scold you with a forty horse power for having told Martha Taylor that I had requested you 'not to tell her every-

[1] The present author came temptingly near to finding the portrait recently, whose existence in the possession of an old lady evacuated to Wales during the last war was reported to her; too late unfortunately to be traced. The old lady had died and her effects been dispersed.

[2] EN, op. cit., 'Reminiscences of CB'.   [3] CB's letter to EN, 3 March 1841.

[4] It is significant, as Mrs. Chadwick remarked, of the place William Weightman took in Charlotte's mind that Mrs. Gaskell, who saw all her letters to EN and must have been the best-informed on the subject, never mentioned him in the 'Life'. See below.

thing' which piece of information of course has thrown Martha into a tremendous ill-humour besides setting the teeth of her curiosity on edge with the action, that there is something very important in the wind which you and I are especially desirous to conceal from her. Such being the state of matters I desire to take off any embargo I may have laid on your tongue which I plainly see will not be restrained and to enjoin you to walk up to Gomersal and tell her forthwith every individual occurrence you can recollect, including Valentines, 'Fair Ellen, Fair Ellen—'Away fond Love', 'Soul Divine' and all—likewise if you please the painting of Miss Celia Amelia Weightman's portrait and that young lady's frequent and agreeable visits—By the bye I inquired into the opinion of that intelligent and interesting young person respecting you—it was a favourable one. She thought you a fine-looking girl and a very good girl into the bargain.—Have you received the newspaper which has been dispatched containing a notice of her lecture at Keighley? . . .[1]

For a while the merriment provoked by Mr. Weightman's flirtations was allowed to prevail, and acknowledged in the same letter to Ellen: 'We feel very dull without you, I wish those three weeks were to come over again. . . .'

Three weeks later she was still indulging Mr. Weightman's whims, 'painting a portrait of Agnes Walton for our friend Miss Celia Amelia' and sufficiently pleased with him to note 'how his eyes sparkle with delight when he looks at it like a pretty child pleased with a new plaything . . .'.[2]

Ellen having yet again thrown the ball into Charlotte's court, Charlotte returned it promptly with a: 'Good-bye to you—let me have no more of your humbug about Cupid etc. you know as well as I do it is all groundless trash. . . .'[3]

Time, which would involve Willie Weightman in a score of flirtations—some of which he attempted to cover up—would lose him Charlotte's good graces, and her good offices with Ellen. '. . . don't set your heart on him', Charlotte wrote after a short visit to Brookroyd in June. 'I'm afraid he is very fickle—not to you in particular but to half a dozen other ladies . . . his present object of devotion is Caroline Dury [daughter of the rector of Keighley] to whom he has just despatched a most passionate copy of verses, poor lad, his sanguine temperament bothers him grievously. . . .'[4] Then she wrote to Ellen

[1] CB to EN, 17 Mar. 1840: *SLL* i. 175.
[2] CB to EN, 9 Apr. 1840: *SLL* i. 177-8.
[3] CB to EN, 9 Apr. 1840: Idem.   [4] CB to EN, June 1840: *W & S.*

on 14 July: '. . . I am glad you continue so heart-whole, I rather feared our mutual nonsense might have made a deeper impression on you than was safe. . . .'[1]

Willie Weightman was off to Ripon for several weeks on the occasion of his Ordination, and Charlotte commented further:

I am fully convinced, Ellen, that he is a thorough maleflirt, his sighs are deeper than ever and his treading on toes more assiduous.—I find he has scattered his impressions far and wide—Keighley has yielded him a fruitful field of conquest, Sarah Sugden is quite smitten so is Caroline Dury—she however has left—and his Reverence has not yet ceased to idolize her memory—I find he is perfectly conscious of his irresistibleness and is as vain as a peacock on the subject—I am not at all surprised at this—it is perfectly natural—a handsome—clean—prepossessing—good-humoured young man —will never want troops of victims amongst young ladies—So long as you are not among the number it is all right—He has not mentioned you to me, and I have not mentioned you to him—I believe we fully understand each other on the subject. I have seen little of him lately and talked precious little to him— . . . now that he has got his spirits up and found plenty of acquaintances I don't care and he does not care either.

There is no doubt he will get nobly through his examination, he is a *clever* lad.[2]

The comedy was ended, and if the principal performers in it remained unscathed (for no one noticed Anne's silent love, not even Willie Weightman) the lesson to be learnt from it was not without its bitterness, at least for Charlotte. The experience had brought home to her afresh the cruel revelation received at Roe Head when Mary Taylor told her how ugly she was. With little else being talked of but flirtations and love-affairs and proposals of marriage that summer, Charlotte observed her own prospects with characteristic clear-sightedness. Advising Ellen on the laggard proposals of Mr. Vincent, she wrote to her on 15 May: '. . . I am tolerably well convinced that I shall never marry at all. Reason tells me so, and I am not so utterly the slave of feeling but that I can *occasionally hear* her voice. . . .'[3]

Far in advance of her day as the author of *Jane Eyre* proved herself to be in her claim for equality of the sexes, before love, Charlotte was much divided in her mind about the wisdom of a woman laying her feelings bare, even to the beloved object. The bias of society was all

[1] CB to EN, 14 July 1840: *SLL* i. 188–9.   [2] Idem.
[3] CB to EN, 15 May 1840: *SLL* i. 185–6.

against her, and suffering was her only certain fate. She was evidently thinking a great deal that year about a woman's prospects of happiness in marriage and, well aware of her own intense sensibility, wondered whether marriage did not hold more pain than pleasure for such as she. Writing to Ellen 'like her own grandmother', as she claimed her superior wisdom entitled her to speak, she advocated a line of conduct with which she knew her own temperament was wholly out of tune.

... no young lady should fall in love, till the offer has been made, accepted —the marriage ceremony performed and the first half year of wedded life has passed away—a woman may then begin to love, but with great precaution—very coolly—very moderately—very rationally—if she ever love so much that a harsh word or cold look from her husband cuts her to the heart— she is a fool....[1]

That same summer brought her yet further food for reflection on the subject with the case of her own brother and her admired friend Mary Taylor. Dismissed by Mr. Postlethwaite on 1 June Branwell came home, in no penitent mood for yet another failure, but full of excitement and optimism following a meeting with Hartley Coleridge at Ambleside on 1 May. He had strongly advised him to stick to literature and praised the translation he was then engaged on of Horace's Odes. Mary Taylor stayed at the parsonage that June (and got on famously with Mr. Weightman over the chessboard) and the visit afforded Charlotte an eloquent—and tragic—commentary on the folly of a woman's betraying her feelings to a man, even where she knew them reciprocated.

Branwell, who had been immensely taken with Mary on their first meeting two years before, no sooner saw that she returned his feelings than he withdrew, and fled her. Advising Ellen to consider an honest proposal of marriage without necessarily indulging in what the French call 'Une Grande Passion', and to adopt as precept in marriage 'Mediocrity is wisdom—mediocrity in the sensations is superlative wisdom', Charlotte went on to comment on Mary's tale:

Did I not once tell you of an instance of a Relative of mine who cared for a young lady till he began to suspect that she cared more for him and then instantly conceived a sort of contempt for her? You know to what I allude— never as you value your ears mention the circumstance—but I have two studies—*you* are my study for the success the credit, and the respectability of a quiet, tranquil character. Mary is my study—for the contempt, the remorse

[1] CB to EN, 20 Nov. 1840: *SLL* i. 197.

—the misconstruction which follow the development of feelings in themselves noble, warm—generous—devoted and profound—but which being too freely revealed—too frankly bestowed—are not estimated at their real value. God bless her—I never hope to see in this world a character more truly noble—she would *die* willingly for one she loved—her intellect and her attainments are of the very highest standard yet I doubt whether Mary will ever marry. . . .[1]

To Ellen's brother Henry, who corresponded with Charlotte all that year on Mr. Vincent's affair, Charlotte again made use of the term 'the folly that the French call "Une Grande Passion",' against which she had warned Ellen. Charlotte's knowledge of what the French said and felt on the subject was derived at second hand from the latest French novels which Joshua Taylor made a habit of lending her—forty volumes at a time—he being constantly in touch with Brussels and Paris over his business contacts. Mentioning the novels to Ellen in a letter of 20 August Charlotte said: '. . . I have read about half—they are like the rest—clever wicked sophistical and immoral—the best of it is they give one a thorough idea of France and Paris, and are the best substitute for French conversation I have met with. . . .'[2]

If Charlotte were hurt by the want of sensibility in William Weightman's response to her friendship, she had far too much common sense and charity to allow it to warp either her sense of justice or of humour. She could still write in bantering mood about him to Ellen in September: '. . . I know Mrs. Ellen is burning with eagerness to hear something about Wm. Weightman,' she wrote on the 29th, 'whom she adores in her heart, and whose image she cannot efface from her memory. . . . To speak Heaven's truth, I have precious little to say, inasmuch as I seldom see him except on Sunday when he looks as handsome, cheery, and good-tempered as usual. . . .'[3]

That there was a 'better side to his character' (the side which won Anne's love and that she portrayed in Edward Weston in *Agnes Grey*), the charitable and compassionate side that made him beloved by the poor of Haworth, Charlotte in all fairness presented to Ellen, and summed up with a view of Willie Weightman that was as penetrating as it was generous. '. . . This proves that he is not all selfishness and vanity. No doubt there are defects in his character, but there are also

[1] C. W. Hatfield was among those who identified the reference here as relating to Branwell Brontë. See CB to EN, 20 Nov. 1840: *SLL* i. 197.

[2] CB to EN, 20 Aug. 1840: *SLL* i. 191.

[3] CB to EN, 29 Sept. 1840: *SLL* i. 191-5.

good qualities. God bless him! I wonder who, with his advantages would be without his faults. I know many of his faulty actions, many of his weak points, yet, where I am, he shall always find rather a defender than an accuser. . . .'[1]

By that time Charlotte had rather gained than lost by the acquaintance. The tolerance and penetration she applied to studying his variable nature was remarkable. The future novelist and profound analyst of character was already speaking when she said: '. . . I find he is perfectly conscious of his irresistibleness. . . . I am not at all surprised at this . . . it is perfectly natural. . . .'[2]

As she weighed his advantages against his faults, Willie Weightman presented her with the opportunity for her first close study of a man— though it must not be forgotten that tolerance towards essentially male foibles had characterized her Angrian heroes. It is notable that in some of his weaknesses—though not in his flirtatiousness—Weightman appeared to resemble Charlotte's eventual publisher, George Smith, who unmistakably furnished the spoilt and pampered aspects of Dr. John Graham Bretton in *Villette*.

But due to Charlotte's understanding, no discordant note was allowed to enter into the family's relations with the 'bonny-faced curate of Haworth' and he remained a favourite with all, Branwell included, with whom he beat the grouse-moors during those autumn days.

On 1 October Branwell left home again, this time on a wholly novel venture. With the opening of the Manchester–Leeds railway, personnel were needed for the new stations on the line, and on application Branwell was accepted for the post of 'Assistant Clerk' at the new station at Sowerby Bridge, at a starting salary of £75 per annum.[3] His departure was the prelude for a fresh family break-up, Charlotte and Anne setting themselves resolutely to finding new situations as the winter advanced. Charlotte, however, told Ellen two or three times that she was 'severely baffled', and it was March before they were 'suited'.

Charlotte left home on 2 March to go into the family of a Bradford merchant called White, at Rawdon; and Anne towards the end of the month to Thorp Green Hall, Little Ouseburn, 12 miles from York and all of 70 miles from home.

[1] CB to EN, idem.
[2] CB to EN, 14 July 1840: *SLL* i. 188–9.
[3] For the details relating to Branwell's engagement with the railways, see Gérin, *Branwell Brontë*, 179–84.

Giving Ellen her early impression of her place on the day after her arrival Charlotte wrote:

. . . I am fairly established in my new place. It is in the family of Mr. White of Upperwood House, Rawdon. The house is not very large but exceedingly comfortable and well regulated; the grounds are fine and extensive. In taking the place I have made a large sacrifice in the way of salary, in the hope of securing comfort by which word I do not mean to express good eating and drinking, or warm fire, or soft bed, but the society of cheerful faces, and minds and hearts not dug out of a lead mine, or cut from a marble quarry. My salary is not really more than £16 p.a., though it is nominally £20, but the expense of washing will be deducted therefrom. My pupils are two in number, a girl of eight [Sarah Louisa] and a boy of six.

As to my employers, you will not expect me to say much respecting their characters when I tell you that I only arrived here yesterday. I have not the faculty of telling an individual's disposition at first sight. Before I venture to pronounce on a character I must see it first under various lights and from various points of view. All I can say, therefore, is, both Mr. & Mrs. White seem to me good sort of people. I have as yet had no cause to complain of want of consideration or civility. My pupils are wild and unbroken, but apparently well disposed. I wish I may be able to say as much next time I write to you. My earnest wish and endeavour will be to please them. . . . [1]

Without some frictions, and without homesickness, it was not possible for Charlotte to settle among strangers. Even so the acceptable features of Upperwood House far outweighed its inconveniences from the outset. She wrote Ellen at the end of the first three weeks:

. . . This place is far better than Stonegappe, but, God knows, I have enough to do to keep a good heart in the matter. . . . Home-sickness afflicts me sorely. I like Mr. White extremely. Respecting Mrs. White I am for the present silent. I am trying hard to like her. The children are not such little devils incarnate as the Sidgwicks, but they are over-indulged, and at times hard to manage. *Do, do, do* come to see me; if it be a breach of etiquette, never mind. If you can only stop an hour, come. . . .[2]

Some skirmishes with Mrs. White who had not reckoned on the governess receiving visitors in her employer's time, nor claiming half-holidays, led to a hardening in Charlotte's attitude; and indeed by early May the prospect did not look too hopeful, with Charlotte falling back on social snobbery against her 'nouveaux riches' employers. '. . . Well can I believe that Mrs. White has been an excise-

[1] CB to EN, 3 Mar. 1841: *SLL* i. 203–5.
[2] CB to EN, 21 Mar. 1841: *SLL* i. 206–7.

man's daughter,' she wrote Ellen on 4 May, commenting on an exhibition of that lady's 'very coarse unlady-like' temper, 'and I am convinced also that Mr. White's extraction is very low—Mrs. White when put out of her way is highly offensive—She must not give me any more of the same sort—or I shall ask for my wages and go. . . .'[1]

Charlotte was finding that the experience of life was of all sorts, and when her readers still to-day doubt the truth of her delineation of the ladies in *Jane Eyre* in their conduct towards their servants and governesses, it should be remembered that she had first-hand knowledge of them and knew how they spoke and acted.

In the event she did not call for her wages and go, but adapted herself surprisingly to the new environment, and stayed. She even suspected herself of 'growing rather fond of the fat baby' of the family, and nursing it with surreptitious joy. When released for the summer holidays (offered one week she stood out for three) she was resolved to return, well realizing that she was not likely to find a much better place.

Submission to the call of duty was made the easier since on her return home she heard from her father and aunt of a project that would benefit her whole future and bring independence—and even liberty—within her grasp. Upon the hope of that fulfilment she lived for the next half-year at the Whites, parting from them only at Christmas, and with real regret on both sides.

When it came to it, she told Ellen:

the parting scene between me and my late employers was such as to efface the memory of much that annoyed me while I was there, but indeed, during the whole of the last six months they only made too much of me. . . .[2]

[1] 4 May 1841: *SLL* i. 209–10.
[2] CB to EN, 10 Jan. 1842: *SLL* i. 226.

CHAPTER XII

THE WISH FOR WINGS

THE project mooted by the elders of the family during the holidays that brought Charlotte and Anne home (though not together) was nothing less than the suggestion that the three girls set up a school of their own. Towards its initial expenses, moreover, their aunt was prepared to advance a small capital. '. . . I have often, you know, said how much I wished for such a thing,' Charlotte wrote Ellen in great excitement on 19 July, 'but I never could conceive where the capital was to come from. . . .'[1]

There is no doubt that the suggestion, far from glamorous though it might appear to other girls, caused Charlotte the keenest pleasure. What is still more remarkable, it equally delighted Emily and Anne. In their secret diary-letters written for each other on 30 July (Emily's birthday) they both recorded the hopes such a plan held out for them. It is interesting how much more optimistic Emily sounded about the venture than either Charlotte or Anne. Emily wrote:

. . . A scheme is at present in agitation for setting us up in a school of our own; as yet nothing is determined, but I hope and trust it may go on and prosper and answer our highest expectations. This day 4 years I wonder whether we shall still be dragging on in our present condition or established to our heart's content. Time will show.

I guess that at the time appointed for the opening of this paper [four years hence] Charlotte, Anne, and I, shall be all merrily seated in our own sitting-room in some pleasant and flourishing seminary, having just gathered in for the midsummer holyday. Our debts will be paid off, and we shall have cash in hand to a considerable amount. Papa, aunt, and Branwell will either have been or be coming to visit us. It will be a fine warm summer evening, very different from this bleak look-out, and Anne and I will perchance slip out into the garden for a few minutes to peruse our papers. I hope either this or something better will be the case. . . .[2]

---

[1] CB to EN, 19 July 1841: *SLL* i. 213–14.
[2] EJB, Diary Paper, 30 July 1841, quoted from text in Ratchford, *Gondal's Queen* (1955), 189.

Anne, contenting herself with moderate expectations wrote:

... We are thinking of setting up a school of our own but nothing definite is settled about it yet, and we do not know whether we shall be able to or not. I hope we shall. ...[1]

Charlotte, though deeply excited, was practical enough to see the difficulties. She wrote Ellen further on 19 July:

... There are matters to be considered which throw something of a damp upon the scheme. I do not expect that aunt will risk more than £150 on such a venture; and would it be possible to establish a respectable (not by any means a *showy*) school and to commence housekeeping with a capital of only that amount? ... We do not care how modest, how humble a commencement be, so it be made on sure ground, and have a safe foundation. ...[2]

The mere thought of liberty was kindling to her mind. She instantly thought of 'all possible and impossible places where we could establish a school', and harked back in imagination to Burlington, scene of her previous flight, where she had experienced such rare happiness and where, her practical spirit argued, a school might do well. She recalled seeing only one girls' school at Burlington and thought it might offer little rivalry to a new venture. '... I have thought of Burlington', she confided to Ellen. 'Do you remember whether there was any other school there besides that of Miss J—? ...'[3]

To confide in Miss Wooler and canvas her views was a natural gesture on Charlotte's part in seeking for her sisters and herself an establishment on the model of her former teacher's. Miss Wooler brought the scheme a stage nearer realization by offering Charlotte the reversion of Dewsbury Moor, which was frankly failing under her sister Eliza's direction. She believed it could yet be built up again under energetic management like Charlotte's and offered her, with the school's goodwill, its furniture and equipment for a start. It was, as Charlotte said, 'a decent, friendly proposal on Miss W's part, and cancels all or most of her little foibles in my estimation ...'.[4] Miss Wooler, whom Charlotte was greatly to value as they both grew older, was not yet fully forgiven for her composure on the occasion of Anne's illness at Roe Head.

[1] AB's Diary Paper. Idem.   [2] CB to EN, 19 July 1841.
[3] Miss C. S. Jack's Academy, King Street Quay. See White's *Directory* for Burlington, 1840. The proximity of King Street Quay to CB's lodgings on the Cliff will have brought the school daily to C's notice.
[4] CB to EN, 17 Oct. 1841, 2 Nov. 1841: *SLL* i. 221–3.

If events had been allowed to take their course the Miss Brontës would, in all likelihood, have set up school either at Dewsbury Moor or somewhere else—made a moderate success and earned a modest livelihood by their pains—and never been heard of more. But in that month of August, while Charlotte was priming the little Whites, and corresponding on ways and means of acquiring Dewsbury Moor, a clarion-call reached her from quite another direction. It came from Mary Taylor, who was in Brussels, where Martha had gone to school since the previous May, and where they were then spending the holidays together under the escort of their brother Joe.

The whole Taylor family had suffered dispersal that year in consequence of the death of their father the previous Christmas. None of the young people, except Joshua the eldest son who inherited his father's cloth manufacture at Hunsworth Mills, would stay with their cantankerous mother any longer, and Mary, though preferring to work for a living rather than live at home, was firmly resolved never to be 'a governess, a teacher, a milliner, a bonnet-maker nor a housemaid'. . . . She had come to the startling decision (startling when viewed by the conventions of her time) to emigrate to New Zealand with her youngest brother Waring, and set up a business or shop there. Meanwhile (and Mary had to wait till 1845 before realizing her plan) she travelled as much as she could with her brothers John and Joe and her Birmingham cousins the Dixons, whose business at that time took them frequently to Brussels. On their advice Martha was placed in a boarding-school in the environs, where they befriended her and where Mary herself joined her later to perfect her music and languages.

From Brussels Mary wrote to Charlotte one of those stirring, disruptive epistles at which she and Martha were adepts; sweeping aside complacency of sentiment and their native syntax to proffer in elliptical language a challenge to the tyranny of convention.

Mary had no great difficulty in rousing her imprisoned friend. What she spoke of—the culture and beauty of a foreign city—found a ready echo in a heart hungry since childhood for aesthetic joys and intellectual stimulus. She opened a vista of such radiant delight for the space of time it took Charlotte to read her letter that it left her in a trance-like state. Charlotte told Ellen on 7 August:

. . . Mary's letter spoke of some of the pictures and cathedrals she had seen—pictures the most exquisite—and cathedrals the most venerable—I hardly know what swelled to my throat as I read her letter—such a vehement impatience of restraint and steady work. Such a strong wish for wings—

wings such as wealth can furnish—such an urgent thirst to see—to know—to learn—something internal seemed to expand boldly for a minute—I was tantalized with the consciousness of faculties unexercised—then all collapsed and I despaired. My dear Nell—I would hardly make that confession to any one but yourself—and to you rather in a letter than 'viva voce'—these rebellious and absurd emotions were only momentary I quelled them in five minutes—I hope they will not revive—for they were acutely painful. . . .[1]

Though to Ellen she spoke of crushing the upsurge of such mad desires, and described her own and Emily's and Anne's deep interest in finding a school ('it is our polar-star and we look to it under all circumstances of despondency'),[2] to Mary Taylor she wrote in very different terms. Mary wrote again firmly urging Charlotte to do like herself and get abroad, into a foreign school and, while perfecting herself in the 'accomplishments' needed for conducting a successful boarding-school, enjoy the stimulus foreign residence brings.

When Charlotte hesitated for a brief moment to follow the siren voices—doubting as always whether life were intended to hold joys for her—Mary wrote again with practical good advice, pointing out how greatly Charlotte's chances of making a success of a school depended on a further period of training for herself. The more she thought of it, the less Mary's promptings seemed to be sheer self-indulgence and the more they appeared as hard-headed business sense.

She broached the subject with the Whites who, instead of damping her ardour, encouraged her. 'In extreme excitement' as she later confessed, she wrote home, laying her altered and so much more ambitious plan before her aunt, to whom she directly appealed to lay out £50 or £100 in allowing herself and Emily to go abroad to a good finishing school. She wrote on 29 September 1841 in the most diplomatically worded document of her life:

Dear Aunt, I have heard nothing of Miss Wooler yet since I wrote to her intimating that I would accept her offer. I cannot conjecture the reason of this long silence unless some unforeseen impediment has occurred in concluding the bargain. Meantime, a plan has been suggested and approved by Mr. & Mrs. White, and others, which I wish now to impart to you. My friends recommend me, if I desire to secure permanent success, to delay commencing the school for six months longer, and by all means to contrive, by hook or by crook, to spend the intervening time in some school on the Continent.

[1] CB to EN, 7 Aug. 1841: *SLL* i. 218.
[2] Idem.

They say schools in England are so numerous, competition so great, that without some such step towards attaining superiority we shall probably have a very hard struggle, and may fail in the end. They say, moreover, that the loan of £100, which you have been so kind as to offer us, will, perhaps, not be all required now, as Miss Wooler will lend us the furniture; and that, if the speculation is intended to be a good and successful one, half the sum, at least, ought to be laid out in the manner I have mentioned, thereby, insuring a more speedy repayment both of interest and principal.

I would not go to France or to Paris. I would go to Brussels, in Belgium. The cost of the journey there, at the dearest rate of travelling, would be £5; living is there little more than half as dear as in England, and the facilities for education are equal or superior to any other place in Europe. In half a year, I could acquire a thorough familiarity with French. I could improve greatly in Italian, and even get a dash of German, i.e. providing my health continued as good as it is now. Martha Taylor is now staying in Brussels, at a first-rate establishment there. I should not think of going to the Chateau de Koekelberg, where she is resident, as the terms are much too high; but if I wrote to her, she, with the assistance of Mrs. Jenkins, the wife of the British Consul[1] would be able to secure me a cheap and decent residence and respectable protection. I should have the opportunity of seeing her frequently, she would make me acquainted with the city; and, with the assistance of her cousins, I should probably in time be introduced to connections far more improving, polished and cultivated, than any I have yet known.

These are advantages which would turn to vast account, when we actually commenced a school—and, if Emily could share them with me, only for a single half-year, we could take a footing in the world afterwards which we can never do now. I say Emily instead of Anne; for Anne might take her turn at some future period, if our school answered. I feel certain, while I am writing, that you will see the propriety of what I say; you always like to use your money to the best advantage, you are not fond of making shabby purchases; when you do confer a favour, it is often done in style; and depend on it £50, or £100, thus laid out, would be well employed. Of course, I know no other friend in the world to whom I could apply on this subject except yourself. I feel an absolute conviction that, if this advantage were allowed us, it would be the making of us for life. Papa will perhaps think it a wild and ambitious scheme; but who ever rose in the world without ambition? When he left Ireland to go to Cambridge University, he was as ambitious as I am now. I want us all to go on. I know we have talents, and I want them to be turned to account. I look to you, aunt, to help us. I think you will not refuse. I know, if you consent, it shall not be my fault if you ever repent your kindness. . . .[2]

---

[1] The British chaplain, in fact.
[2] CB to Elizabeth Branwell, 29 Sept. 1841: *SLL* i. 219–21.

Every argument that could be adduced against the plan had been foreseen by Charlotte; not only Miss Branwell but Mr. Brontë was persuaded by the letter. Knowing Charlotte's deeply serious mind, they
accepted her judgement and gave their consent to a six-month absence
abroad for herself and Emily—providing always that a suitable
arrangement could be made.

Expense ruled out Martha's school, otherwise Charlotte and Emily
would have set off long before they actually did, at the beginning of
February. The interval was filled with active negotiations, in which
Mary Taylor spared no pains.

How intensely Charlotte felt about the whole plan can be judged by
the very language she used in expressing her hopes, her frustrations,
her undeviating purpose to get to Belgium. She had not time to tell
Ellen in detail the complicated course of events that changed her whole
horizon that autumn. Impatiently she wrote her on 17 October: 'The
humour I am in is worse than words can describe. . . . Don't expect me
to write a long letter. I am not going to Dewsbury Moor, as far as I
can see at present. . . . I burn to go somewhere else. I think, Nell, I see
a chance of getting to Brussels. Mary Taylor advises me to this step. My
own mind and feelings urge me on—I can't write a word more. . . .'[1]

She wrote again on 2 November (Ellen had been hurt by hearing
from others of her change of plan).

. . . Now let us begin to quarrel. . . . You heard from others of Miss
Wooler's overtures before I communicated them to you myself . . . most true
—I cannot give you my *excuse* for this behaviour the word *excuse* implies
confession of a fault and I do not feel that I have been in fault. The plain fact
is I was not, I am not now, certain of my destiny. . . . Miss Wooler did most
kindly propose that I should come to Dewsbury Moor and attempt to revive
the school—at first I received the proposal cordially and proposed to do my
utmost to bring about success—but a fire was kindled in my very heart which
I could not quench—I so longed to increase my attainments to become
something better than I am—. . . . Mary Taylor cast oil on the flames—encouraged me and in her own strong energetic language heartened me on—
I longed to go to Brussels—. . .[2]

On 10 December she wrote once more: '. . . My plans advance
slowly, and I am not yet certain where I shall go . . . Brussels is still my
promised land, but there is still the wilderness of time and space to
cross before I reach it. . . .'[3]

[1] CB to EN, 17 Oct. 1841: *SLL* i. 221.
[2] CB to EN, 2 Nov. 1841: *SLL* i. 222–3.
[3] CB to EN, 10 Dec. 1841: *SLL* i. 224–5.

The 'wilderness of time and space' made dreary crossing in Charlotte's then wrought-up mind. The impediments were so many, the
chances so unforeseen. Problems on the domestic plane harassed her in
addition: what was to become of Anne in her sisters' absence? Emily
was not happy at a plan which excluded Anne. Charlotte consoled her
as best she could: '. . . Anne seems omitted in the present plan,' she
agreed, 'but if all goes well I trust she will derive her full share of
benefit from it in the end. . . .'[1] In confiding her full objectives to Emily
at so early a stage, she was little likely to reassure her on Anne's account;
for what Charlotte already aimed at was to stay at least a year in
Brussels. '. . . Before our half-year in Brussels is completed', she wrote
Emily on 7 November, 'you and I will have to seek employment abroad.
It is not my intention to retrace my steps home till twelve months, if all
continues well and we and those at home retain good health. . . .'[2]

It speaks volumes for her influence on Emily, and for Emily's life-
long confidence in Charlotte's direction, that she could speak so openly
about a long-term plan that meant separation from Anne and from the
home that mattered more to her than the finest cities in the world.
Charlotte reckoned on Anne giving up her post at Thorp Green and
taking Emily's place as housekeeper at home. She anxiously sought
domestic help for Anne, wondering how she would get on with
Martha Brown. In the event Anne returned to Thorp Green, having
as Charlotte put it, 'rendered herself so valuable in her difficult situation
that they have entreated her to return to them, if it be but for a short
time . . .'.[3]

There was Branwell who had not been home for months and whom
she wanted to see before going abroad; but Branwell had his own
reasons for avoiding a meeting. In April he had been transferred from
Sowerby Bridge to the new station along the line at Luddenden Foot,
with an increased salary of £130 per annum. There he was 'Clerk in
Charge', a first promotion that had looked like 'getting on at any rate',[4]
as his sisters had hoped on hearing the news. But appearances were
misleading and after a few months of wretched living conditions and
worse company, Branwell was in very bad shape indeed—so shattered
by 'the cold debauchery of his life' as he himself spoke of it later, as to
shrink from facing the loving glances of those at home.[5]

[1] CB to EJB, 7 Nov. 1841: *SLL* i. 223–4.
[2] Idem.
[3] CB to EN, 10 Jan. 1842: *SLL* i. 226–7.
[4] CB to EJB, 2 Apr. 1841: from original text.
[5] PBB to Grundy, 22 May 1842: *W & S*.

Ellen, who had been in Sussex all the autumn looking after her brother Henry's rectory while Charlotte was planning her Brussels campaign, was still difficult of access even after she returned home, and unable to fall in with Charlotte's invitations. Urging her to come to Haworth before her own departure, Charlotte held out as chief inducement: 'Mr. Weightman is still here just the same as ever. I have a curiosity to see a meeting between you and him. . . .'[1]

Ellen could not come and Charlotte could not go to her, lamenting that it would be many a long day in all probability before they could exchange confidences again 'by the fireside or between the blankets'.[2] On 20 January (1842) she sent Ellen a last image of Mr. Weightman, however, which on two counts has its importance. It showed him concerned at last with Anne, whose unacknowledged love was the one deep sentiment he inspired and the theme in the ensuing years of her major novel and of her finest poetry. It showed something else as well: how completely unaware Charlotte was of Anne's feelings, else could she never have urged on Ellen to make him 'a comfortable wife'.

. . . Your darling 'his young reverence' as you tenderly call him—is looking delicate and pale—poor thing, don't you pity him? I do from my heart—when he is well and fat and jovial I never think of him—but when anything ails him I am always sorry—He sits opposite to Anne at Church sighing softly and looking out of the corners of his eyes to win her attention—and Anne is so quiet, her look so downcast—they are a picture—He would be the better for a comfortable wife like you to settle him, you would settle him I believe—nobody else would— . . .[3]

It was through Ellen that the contact with Brussels was supplied in the end, by which Charlotte's choice of school was made. It happened that among her clerical acquaintances was the Revd. David Jenkins, whose brother was the Revd. Evan Jenkins, British Chaplain (not Consul) in Brussels. Once the connexion was made, Mr. Brontë wrote to Belgium asking for suitable addresses for his daughters. The connexion was no new one, as it happened, for David Jenkins had succeeded Mr. Brontë as curate of Dewsbury thirty years before.

Even so, there were fluctuations of fortune up to the last minute. Mrs. Jenkins had no good report to send on French schools in Brussels (of the price Charlotte and Emily could afford) and as late as the third week in January (1842) Charlotte feared their destination must be

---

[1] CB to EN, 10 Jan. 1842: *SLL* i. 226–7.
[2] CB to EN, 20 Jan. 1842: *W & S*, No. 129.
[3] Idem.

changed for Lille, where the Haworth Baptist minister Noel 'and other clergymen' recommended a school to Mr. Brontë. Lille was not Brussels, and Charlotte suffered a cruel disappointment at the proposed change, which meant the loss of Martha Taylor's companionship as well.

At the eleventh hour, however, Mrs. Jenkins wrote to recommend yet another school with which she put Charlotte in immediate touch. It was the Pensionnat Heger, kept by a married lady, whose prompt replies to Charlotte's inquiries were so satisfactory as to warrant instant acceptance. With no more time to be lost, the day of departure was fixed. Only then, when Brussels and not Lille became again their destination, could Charlotte feel that the Promised Land was with any certainty in sight.

CHAPTER XIII

THE PROMISED LAND: BRUSSELS, 1842

CHARLOTTE and Emily set out from home on the first lap of their journey to Brussels on Tuesday, 8 February 1842.[1] They were accompanied by their father and piloted by Mary and Joe Taylor, who had already made the crossing to Belgium several times and, after their recent trips through the Low Countries and the Rhineland, bore in the Brontës' eyes all the glamour of experienced continental travellers.

The train left Leeds at 9 a.m. and was scheduled to reach Euston Square at 8 p.m.—though a subsequent experience of Charlotte's showed that delays of anything up to two hours were not uncommon. Mr. Brontë knew London only from his rare visits from College and for his Ordination over 40 years before. To the same old-fashioned, respectable, and essentially masculine hostelry—the Chapter Coffee House in Paternoster Row, that he had then frequented—he conducted his daughters now. The aura of the men of Letters who had been habitués there—Chatterton, Johnson, Goldsmith—still hung about the low-ceilinged panelled rooms, the dark oak staircases, the warren-like bedrooms of the upper stories, from whose latticed windows Charlotte and Emily received their first sight of London the following morning.

Branwell had stayed there on his disastrous trip in 1835, and in his description of the place in his 'History of Angria' had paid tribute to its literary associations by calling it 'Johnson's Hotel'.[2] To Charlotte now, the great adventure on which she was embarked in the pursuit of learning, of culture, of art, was already begun by these first tangible links with the illustrious figures of the past. Every sight and sound was stimulating to her eager observant senses. How alien the speech of the Londoners sounded to her northern hearing she related afterwards in *Villette*: '. . . The strange speech of the cabmen and others waiting round, seemed to me odd as a foreign tongue. I had never before heard the English language chopped up in that way. . . .'[3]

---

[1] Emily Brontë's Diary Paper, 30 July 1845: *Gondal's Queen*, op. cit.
[2] 'Adventures of Charles Wentworth', Hist. of Angria, vol. vi, 1836: Brotherton Coll., Univ. of Leeds.   [3] *Villette*, ch. 5.

The Ostend 'Packet' ('La Malle Anglaise' as it was inversely called) left London Bridge Wharf only twice a week, on Wednesdays and Saturdays. As the party did not arrive in London till late on the Tuesday evening, there could be no question of attempting to catch the morning's boat; the more so that, according to the movements of the tides, the packets often weighed anchor before dawn. In any case, there was both business and pleasure to keep them in London before they engaged on the next lap of their journey. Their crossing was therefore fixed for Saturday, 12 February, which gave them three full days in which to see the sights of London.

Mr. Brontë recorded in the notebook of his travelling expenses and movements that he went to the Belgian Consul's Office in London to get his own and his daughters' passports. They cost him 5s. each, and he noted that had he gone to the French Consul's Office instead, he would have had to pay 10s. apiece.[1]

Mary Taylor, always an infidel where conventional judgements and established criteria were concerned, remembered with amusement years later Charlotte's decided choice of Galleries and Museums to visit during their crowded and exciting three days in London. ' . . . She seemed to think our business was and ought to be, to see all the pictures & statues we could. She knew the artists and knew where other productions of theirs were to be found. I don't remember what we saw except St. Paul's. Emily was like her in these habits of mind, but certainly never took her opinion, but always had one to offer. . . .'[2]

The permanent exhibition of the Royal Academy (only since 1837 established at Burlington House), the Suffolk Street Galleries, and the Royal Institute Galleries (where so much of Martin's work had first been shown) were certain to have been among Charlotte's objectives; as well as the more obvious exhibitions at the National Gallery, and the Elgin Marbles. The latter, as well as the Egyptian Room at the British Museum, had stirred Branwell to rapturous comment on his previous visit. Though the time was past when every experience to be savoured to the full had to be shared with Branwell, a one-sided correspondence between sister and brother still continued, and what she saw then and the impressions she received were laid by in Charlotte's mind for future reappraisal with Branwell.

In the pages of *Villette* are preserved the impressions of her first confrontation with great art and noble buildings during the three days

[1] Mr. Brontë's notebook of travelling expenses, impressions, itinerary: BPM.
[2] MT to Mrs. Gaskell, published in third edition of the *Life of CB*, 146.

in London: '. . . Prodigious was the amount of life I lived that morning. Finding myself before St. Paul's, I went in; I mounted to the dome; I saw thence London, with its river, and its bridges, and its churches; I saw antique Westminster, and the green Temple Gardens, with sun upon them, and a glad, blue sky, of early spring above; and, between them & it, not too dense a cloud of haze. . . .'[1]

For Charlotte it was a time of hope, if ever there was such a period in her life. The longing for wider horizons, for a more stimulating life, for freedom in exchange for her recent bondage—that 'wish for wings' that had gripped her as with a physical ache months ago when Mary Taylor first wrote from Belgium—was at long last being fulfilled in those few crowded days in London. There she tasted joys of which she had hitherto only read and to which, more than most of the sightseers filling London, she was so ready to respond. She described the feeling of that time in *Villette*: 'I went wandering whither chance might lead, in a still ecstasy of freedom and enjoyment. . . .'[2]

On the Saturday morning while it was still dusk, the party drove down to the Steamship Company's wharf at London Bridge and went on board the packet. The passage, under normal good weather conditions, took 14 hours, but might take considerably longer. A seat in the First Class Cabin cost 38 francs (30s. at the current rate of exchange of 25 Belgian francs to the £) and 32 francs for a seat in the Second Class Cabin. The cost of the whole journey from London to Brussels was between £5 and £6, according to the class travelled.

The ship coasted down the Thames for several hours before striking the open sea ' . . . I was not sick till long after we passed Margate,' Charlotte recalled in *Villette* of that first passage, 'and deep was the pleasure I drank in with the sea breeze; divine the delight I drew from the heaving Channel waves, from the sea-birds on their ridges, from the white sails on their dark distance, from the quiet, yet beclouded sky, overhanging all. . . .'[3]

In both accounts of her journeys to Belgium she confesses to becoming extremely sick in the end and having to 'falter down into

[1] *Villette*, ch. 6.
[2] Idem. Nearly ten years later, CB, commenting on Joe Taylor's wedding trip during which he ran his bride off her feet, recalled his manner of showing them London on that first visit en route for Belgium (CB to EN, 14 Oct. 1850): ' . . . Is this the usual way of spending the honeymoon? . . . it all reminds me too sharply of the few days I spent with Joe in London nearly 10 years since, when I was many a time fit to drop with the fever & faintness resulting from long fasting & excessive fatigue. . . .'
[3] *Villette*, ch. 6.

the cabin. . . .'. It may be some reflection on the 14 hours of the Ostend crossing in those days that Mr. Brontë returned home via Calais.

Thackeray, who made the journey in the same year as the Brontës, recorded some lively scenes upon the crossing of which he was witness. He took the longer sea-route to Antwerp, crossing on the Belgian packet the 'Antwerpen', that sailed alternately with the English packet the 'Wilberforce', on Tuesdays and Fridays from London.

What a merry place a steamer is on a calm sunny summer forenoon, and what an appetite every one seems to have! . . . We are, I assure you, no less than 170 noblemen and gentlemen together pacing up and down under the awning, or lolling on the sofas in the cabin, and hardly have we passed Greenwich than the feeding begins. . . . The forepart of the vessel is crowded to the full as much as the genteeler quarter. There are four carriages, each with piles of imperials and aristocratic gimcracks of travel, under the wheel of which those personnages have to clamber who have a mind to look at the bowsprit, and perhaps to smoke a cigar at ease. The carriages overcome you find yourself confronted by a huge penful of Durham oxen, lying on hay and surrounded by a barricade of oars. . . . Beyond the cows come a heap of cotton-bags, beyond the cotton-bags more carriages, more pyramids of travelling trunks, and valets and courriers bustling and swearing round about them. . . . At one, dinner begins in the after-cabin—boiled salmon, boiled beef, boiled mutton, boiled cabbage, boiled potatoes, and parboiled wine for any gentlemen who like it, and two roast ducks between 70. After this knobs of cheese are handed round on a plate, and there is a talk of a tart somewhere at some end of the table . . . somehow at half-past three o'clock we had dropped a long way down the river. The air was delightfully fresh, and the sky a faultless cobalt. . . . After dinner (of which the second service was at three) we ascend upon deck, and after eyeing each other for a brief space . . . we begin anon to converse about the weather and . . . confide to each other our respective opinions of the ladies round about us. . . . Yonder is . . . an English gentleman and his family. Children, mother, grandmother, grown-up daughters, father and domestics, twenty-one in all. They have a table to themselves on the deck, and the consumption of eatables among them is really endless. . . . There is, as you may fancy, a number of such groups on the deck, and a pleasant occupation it is for a lonely man to watch them and build theories upon them. . . . Now the sun is gone, and the steward is already threading the deck, asking the passengers, right and left, if they take a little supper. . . . Lo! the horned moon shines pale over Margate, and the red beacon is gleaming from distant Ramsgate pier. . . . A great rush is speedily made for the mattresses that lie in the boat at the ship's side; and, as the night is delightfully calm, many fair ladies and worthy men determine to couch on deck for the night. The proceedings of the former, especially if they be young and pretty, the philosopher watches with indescribable emotion and interest. What a number of pretty coquetries do the ladies perform, and into what pretty attitudes do they take care to fall. All the little children have been gathered up by the nursery-maids, and are taken down to roost below. . . .[1]

It was midnight before the Ostend packet reached port, and the Brontës and Taylors went straight to an hotel for the remainder of the night. How her trunk was made away with to the Customs and how a 'rough individual' walked into her room next morning demanding her keys, Charlotte has written in *Villette*.

As can be seen from the Police Registers recording the party's arrival, they spent all Sunday and Sunday night again at Ostend, only travelling to Brussels on the Monday morning. They took the 'Diligence', an already out-moded means of conveyance, rather than the recently opened railway from Ostend to Brussels, as appears from Charlotte's accounts of the journey both in *The Professor* and *Villette*. (The new Gare du Nord in Brussels serving the Ostend line, whose foundation-stone was laid by Leopold I and his sister the Duchess of Kent on 28 September 1841, was not yet completed in February 1842.)

The countryside is still today very much as Charlotte described it. There is, indeed, a permanence about the character of the Flanders countryside, deriving as much from the way of life of its rural population as from the nature of the terrain itself, that allows the traveller of today to recognize the precision of her observations made over 120 years ago. ' . . . I enjoyed that day,' she wrote in *Villette*, 'though we travelled slowly, though it was cold, though it rained. Somewhat bare, flat, and treeless was the route along which our journey lay; and slimy canals crept, like half-torpid green snakes, beside the road; and formal pollard willows edged level fields, tilled like kitchen-garden beds. . . .'[2] The straight lines of canal, the unbending highways bordered by pollard trees, the apple-orchards and market-gardens laid out in neat oblongs of cabbage and turnips, have not changed, nor the white windmills and white Flemish mares, whose patient stance evokes the countless canvases of Wouvermans. Charlotte summed up its impression in *The Professor*.

. . . Don't call the picture a flat or a dull one, it was neither flat nor dull to me when first I beheld it. When I left Ostend on a mild February morning,

[1] Thackeray, 'Little Travels & Roadside Sketches': *Fraser's Magazine*, May 1844.
[2] *Villette*, ch. 7.

and found myself on the road to Brussels, nothing could look vapid to me. My sense of enjoyment possessed an edge whetted to the finest, untouched, keen, exquisite. . . . I gazed often, and always with delight, from the window of the diligence . . . not a beautiful, scarcely a picturesque object met my eye along the whole route; yet to me, all was beautiful, all more than picturesque. . . .[1]

In the early 1840's, before the expanding prosperity of the relatively new régime had thrown out a whole new ring of suburbs around the old city, the landmarks of medieval Brussels literally towered above the flat surrounding scene; the pointed spires of St. Nicholas and of the Hôtel de Ville, and the square grey towers of Ste Gudule on its eminence could still at that time be seen from miles away.

It was not till darkness had fallen, however, 'a darkness that might almost be felt', as Charlotte described it, that the Ostend Diligence entered the city by the Porte de Flandre, reduced—like all the city gates—by Napoleon to a mere customs guard-post by then, and through which they passed after a cursory inspection, to drive to the coach-terminus in the Rue de la Madeleine. Here, before the bureau of the Diligence Co. of Van Gend et Cie, they drew up and were finally released after a journey lasting the whole day. (Even the trains at that time took four and a half hours to cover the distance.) Mary Taylor recalled nothing more than that they 'arrived in the dark', but Charlotte, on whom nothing was lost of those first impressions, said that 'It was through streaming and starless darkness my eye caught the first gleam of Brussels. . . .'[2]

Thanks to the Police Register recording the arrivals of foreign visitors, the Brontës' movements can be followed that night: they put up at the Hôtel d'Hollande[3] (No. 1 Rue de la Putterie), whose situation in a street neighbouring the Diligence terminus was the most convenient to the travellers. Advertising in the 'Indicateur de Bruxelles' and other 'Almanachs' of the time, the Hôtel d'Hollande claimed that it 'was distinguished by the persons of rank who sojourned there'. More modest were the claims made for it by Charlotte in an obvious reference in *Villette*: for Lucy Snowe, seeking 'a quiet inn' in which to stay a couple of nights pending the arrival of her lost trunk, Dr. John wrote an address on a leaf torn from his pocket-book, assuring her that it was just such a place as she wanted and 'not far off'. Its proximity

[1] *The Professor*, ch. 7.   [2] Idem., ch. 7.
[3] Registre des Etrangers, 1842—Archives de l'Hôtel de Ville.

to the Rue d'Isabelle, where she and Emily had to present themselves at school the following morning, was indeed a chief consideration for the strangers that they were.

In the morning Joe Taylor and Mary took their leave of the Brontës. '... We went next morning to our respective schools', recorded Mary. 'We were, of course, much preoccupied and our prospects were gloomy.'[1] It may be doubted whether Mary, speaking as much for herself as for Emily Brontë in their equal detestation of confinement and subjection to authority, interpreted Charlotte's feelings aright on this occasion, since the return to school life, even to its discipline, began by wholly delighting her.

The Brontës were fetched from their hotel next morning by Mr. and Mrs. Jenkins (whose home outside the city walls on the Chaussée d'Ixelles was too far out to be reached the previous night) and together they walked the short distance to the Pensionnat Heger. It was Mrs. Jenkins, we are told, who effected the introduction to Madame Heger.[2] Of M. Heger the party saw nothing—for the good reason that he was teaching in his own boys' school at that hour. Mr. Brontë therefore lost the one opportunity he ever had of meeting the man whose influence would be paramount in Charlotte's life.

Having safely deposited his daughters at their new school, Mr. Brontë departed in the company of Mr. and Mrs. Jenkins. It was Tuesday, 15 February, exactly a week since they had set out from home. For the next few days Mr. Brontë stayed with the Jenkins, visited the battlefield of Waterloo, and saw the main sights of Brussels. He also saw his daughters again and was able to introduce them into the Jenkins's home. From Mrs. Jenkins they received a standing invitation to visit there on Sundays or on half-holidays.[3] Of their wellbeing Mr. Brontë could have no doubt before he finally left Brussels to return home via Dunkerque and Calais.

The Pensionnat Heger was situated in a narrow street dating from the period of the Spanish occupation and called after the last Spanish Governor of the Netherlands, the Infanta Isabella. The street was built in 1625, to provide a short-cut for the general public to the Collegiate Church of S. Michael and Ste Gudule through property that had long been privately held by the powerful Guild of the Arbelétriers. The proximity of the Rue d'Isabelle to the church was one of its outstanding

[1] MT to Gaskell: 'Life', third ed., 146.
[2] Chadwick: evidence derived from Mrs. Jenkins herself, ch. 15.
[3] Idem.

characteristics for Charlotte, upon whom the deep tone of the great bell punctuating the hours and ringing to Matins, Vespers, and to 'Salut' throughout the catholic year, took on a special meaning for her in her loneliest hours. The presence of this chronicler in the Brussels sky, seeming to comment upon the drama of her days, assumed in *Villette* a role similar to that of the Chorus in Greek tragedy.

To an onlooker standing at the main gate of the pensionnat, or looking out of its windows towards the north-west, the towers of Ste Gudule might indeed appear to fill the sky. The low level of the Rue d'Isabelle, set among overhanging buildings, largely contributed to this impression. Parts of the original city walls dating from the ninth century skirted the street for a great part of its length; in the Middle Ages its emplacement had been used as kennels for the reigning duke's hounds—as its original name 'Fossé aux Chiens' confirmed. Readers of *Villette* will remember Charlotte's conversion of this name into the 'Rue Fossette'.

It was some time, however, before Charlotte and Emily could explore the quarter of the town in which they had come to live. The Rue d'Isabelle and its adjoining blocks of houses could be said to con-stitute a half-way halt between the higher level of the town—the fashionable eighteenth-century quarter with its colonnaded Place Royale, Parc, and Palace, and the long Rue Royale with its aristo-cratic houses and hotels, to which the Rue d'Isabelle ran parallel and to which it was connected by a steep flight of stone steps—and the lower, medieval level of the town, still predominantly Spanish in character, with its huddle of narrow streets, steep roofs, and ornate chimney-stacks. Above resided the rich idle and courtly circles of the town; below the busy prosperous traders and shopkeepers. Immediately next to the Pensionnat Heger were the solid houses of bankers, merchants, and the straggling buildings of other schools. Everywhere, at every level of the town, squeezed in be-tween the dwelling-houses and the shops, the signorial palaces and the convents, were churches dating from every period of the city's history.

In contrast again to these divergent elements still living side by side in the rapidly changing aspect of nineteenth-century society was the large pauper population hidden away in the very heart of the city, in timbered tenements that had escaped the bombardment of Louis XIV in 1695. It would take the town-planners another 70 years after Char-lotte Brontë's day to bring them down. The demolition of old Brussels

BRUSSELS: RUE ROYALE IN THE 1840's, showing the entry to the
Parc, and Ste Gudule

BRUSSELS: THE PARC, showing the statue of General Belliard;
lithograph of 1840

has, indeed, altered the sharply contrasting character it formerly presented of a citadel upon three levels. In the names of the narrow streets immediately neighbouring the Pensionnat Heger, however, and linking the higher and lower quarters of the city—in the 'Montagne du Parc' and 'Montagne de la Cour'—the hilly nature of its foundations was still sufficiently stressed.

The pensionnat itself, and the other houses in the Rue d'Isabelle, dated from the turn of the century, probably from 1800 itself, and were constructions in the French style, reflecting the taste of the French emigrés flocking into Brussels. Only the gateway to the garden of the pensionnat, still bearing a Latin inscription of the seventeenth century, told of the original building of the Infanta Isabella. Madame Heger acquired the house in 1830 immediately after the Belgian Revolution. The long façade of the school, with its high walls and barred windows looking out upon the street, entirely hid the interior quadrangle of buildings, the playground and garden that stretched behind. These covered a considerable area, reaching to the buildings in the adjoining Rue Terarken on the south and the Rue des Douze Apôtres on the west, which belonged to the premier boys' school in Brussels, the Athénée Royal. Of this proximity Charlotte was to make the fullest use in her two novels of Brussels life. From the solitary window piercing the blank wall of the Athénée dormitory buildings, William Crimsworth spied into Mlle Reuter's enclosed garden, and love-letters were showered down for Ginevra Fanshawe. Because of this window's position of vantage over the garden of her 'demoiselles' pensionnat', Madame Heger had had to make that part of it 'out of bounds', and hence the name Charlotte soon learnt to know it by: 'l'Allée défendue.' The proximity of the Athénée buildings had another and more direct bearing on the family fortunes of the Hegers, for Monsieur was one of the professors at the Athénée and Madame could call upon his services to teach in her school.

When Charlotte and Emily entered the Pensionnat in February 1842 the Hegers had been married six years (since 3 September 1836) and were still at that time a young couple. Monsieur, born 10 July 1809, was not yet 33; Madame was his senior by five years, having been born on 13 July 1804. There were as yet three children of the marriage: Marie Pauline, the eldest, aged four, born 20 September 1837, Louise Florence, born 14 July 1839, and Claire Zoë Marie, born 27 July 1840. Within six weeks of the Brontës' arrival Madame Heger gave birth to her first son, Prospère, and in the course of the next four years two more children, Victorine (15 November 1843) and Paul, (14 December 1846) were born.

It was, therefore, into a young household that Charlotte and Emily came, and it was perhaps the predominantly domestic atmosphere of the place that made its most striking difference from any educational establishment they had previously known. The fact that the Hegers lived in the midst of the school with a growing family and their own domestic staff, emphasized the difference between such an establishment and those of the Miss Woolers or the Miss Patchetts. Part of the 'foreignness' of the pensionnat, indeed, was due to the permanent presence at all hours of a man, and of a staff of visiting male teachers, and in the fact that the school's principal was a married and not a maiden lady (as Charlotte was quick to note), with a constant increase in family to attest to the fact.

The paternalist atmosphere reigning over the pensionnat was not only made apparent in the wording of the Prospectus, where the healthy district was adduced as its chief attraction, but was apparent in all the details regulating the school's routine, in which the health and welfare of the pupils were made a primary object. The easy hours, the excellent food, the benign supervision, early struck Charlotte as exceptional in her experiences of boarding-school life. That nothing was left to chance, and no child abandoned to its own devices—or even *vices*—was a corollary she did not at first reckon on. Her later condemnation of Madame Heger's system of supervision, which Charlotte did not hesitate to call spying, arose from her ignorance of foreign school-life in general, and from personal resentment when she suspected this system was applied to herself in particular. But it was evident from the start that the school was centred on the family life of its directors, and the two outsiders from England, whose ages debarred them from the friendship and confidence of their fellow pupils, found it at first full of interest and variety.

Madame Heger still had her mother living with her. Her parents' story had not been without its drama, her father being an emigré from the French Revolution who had fled to Brussels in the wake of the Comte d'Artois in 1789. Monsieur Parent, as he was called, had preserved in exile—and even in comparative poverty—the style and appearance of his former mode of life. To the end of his days he wore his hair powdered and in a 'queue'. He was of an original and philosophic turn of mind and sought consolation for his losses in the new manner of life forced upon him by circumstances. He acquired a house in the

Rue du Bois Sauvage that skirted Ste Gudule, in the garden of which were several natural springs (the site of the subsequent Bains de S. Sauveur built over the property). There he cultivated not only the proverbial cabbage garden, but flowers, and harboured a great variety of wild birds which became his peculiar delight.

Two events came to modify his misfortunes: he was, firstly, joined by his sister, Anne-Marie Parent,[1] a nun in a convent at Charleville disestablished by the Revolution; and shortly afterwards he wooed and won the hand of a young lady, Charlotte Legrand, who brought him some money as well as her own not inconsiderable charm. She was noted for her good looks, wore her hair 'à la Titus'—according to the Napoleonic mode—and had served as model for several fashionable painters.

Thus early in the story of the Heger family there figured a nun; not the immured nun whose ghost haunted the garden shades and attic recesses of *Villette*, but an authentic nun with an important part to play in the establishment of the family's scholastic fortunes. Something of her force of character is discerned in the story of her initial escape from Charleville when Dumouriez's armies were besieging the town. The nuns were all arrested and lived in daily expectation of the guillotine. The officer in charge of them, picking upon Anne-Marie Parent to confer a chance of life, sent her a note inside a loaf of bread saying he would have a peasant's costume ready for her escape. Her answer was a refusal unless he could procure *two* costumes—for one of her companions in misfortune as well as for herself. The costumes were procured, the two girls smuggled away to walk the distance from the French frontier at Givet to Brussels in their wooden clogs, where they finally arrived with crippled feet.

Anne-Marie went straight to her brother's house and, as events decreed, never left it again. Her Order being permanently disestablished she sought—and obtained after the restoration of peace—official sanction to re-enter 'the world' and, beginning on a small scale with the rising family of her brother, set up school in the commodious house in the Rue du Bois Sauvage—work for which she showed singular aptitude and in which she speedily prospered. Monsieur and Madame Parent had five children; four girls, called Anne-Marie, Charlotte, Claire Zoë, Clara, and one boy, Gustave. Of these, Claire Zoë, born on 13 July 1804, was to become the future Madame Heger.

The Pensionnat Parent was conducted upon the strictest lines.

[1] Depage, Henri, 'Les Origines du Pensionnat Heger', *Revue Edelweiss*, Juin 1956.

A black silk dress with a long train was the uniform worn by the pupils; soon the school's emphasis on pre-revolution deportment and manners secured it the patronage of aristocratic circles. Family tradition has it that at the time of the battle of Waterloo the intrepid Directrice converted the schoolrooms into hospital wards for the English wounded, and herself with her elder pupils undertook the nursing.

In all her activities her example was closely followed by her niece Zoë, and eventually when Anne-Marie died and two of her nieces entered convents, it was Zoë who decided to succeed her aunt and set up school. This was immediately after the 1830 revolution when the house in the Rue d'Isabelle fell vacant. It was No. 32 in the street and there she moved in with her mother. At No. 54 in the street directory for 1840 there also lived a Monsieur Parent—no doubt her brother Gustave whose status was given as 'of independent means'.

A great friend of Zoë Parent's was a girl with the same christian name—Zoë de Gamond, who, at about the same time, also set up as schoolmistress. She was intensely concerned over the inequality of women's position in society, and was resolved to better it by bringing a higher standard of education within their range. Already in 1833 Zoë de Gamond was publishing in the *Revue Encyclopédique* articles on the social position of women in the nineteenth century, and on their scant opportunities for either private or public education. Her pioneer work, actively pursued after she became Madame Gatti de Gamond, was continued by her daughter Isabelle, who was one of the prime movers in the campaign for secondary education for women in Belgium.

It was at the home of her friends the Gatti de Gamonds, in the Rue de la Montagne, that Zoë Parent first met Constantin Heger in 1834. Like her, he was a teacher—a teacher with a sense of mission—and she soon came to respect his forceful ideas and opinions and to wish to engage him as an auxiliary teacher in her school.

His own story, which she gradually learnt (seated, perhaps, like Mlle Reuter with William Crimsworth, in the shade of her pleasant garden) was a tragic one. He was born 10 July 1809 in Brussels, and named Constantin Georges Romain. His great-grandfather had emigrated from the Rhineland, but for three generations before Constantin's birth, the family had been established in Belgium. Only the absence of an acute accent in spelling their name now indicated their Germanic origin.[1]

---

[1] While it is correct to pronounce the name as though it had an accent, it must not be written so.

Constantin's father, Joseph Antoine Heger,[1] was a wealthy jeweller in business at the corner of the Rue Royale and the Treurenberg (on the site of the actual No. 78). The boy's early prospects were rosy and he was brought up to expect an easy affluent life. His mother was Marie-Thérèse *née* Maré. In a gesture that was singularly typical of the son who succeeded him, M. Heger 'père' lent a large sum of money to a friend in distress and lost it all. Overnight Constantin's prospects were reversed. From the spoilt darling of a well-to-do family he found himself in his teens without a profession and ill-equipped for life. Unable to bear the comments of his fellow townsmen, M. Heger sent his son to Paris in 1825, there to seek his fortune, or at least a decent livelihood.

He found a post as secretary to a solicitor, an initiation into the legal world which greatly attracted him and into which, had he had money, he would have liked to qualify for admittance. This he later confessed to Charlotte Brontë. But he had neither the time nor the money to consider such a career. The only pleasures he could allow himself were to go to the Comédie Française as a paid *claqueur* and to study declamation in this manner at second-hand. In later years, when he became so notable a teacher, this close study of the classic actors stood him in good stead. In his readings aloud to his pupils, as Charlotte recorded in *Villette*, he would make some tragedy 'grand by grand reading, ardent by fiery action—some drama, whereof, for my part, I rarely studied the intrinsic merit; for he made it a vessel for an outpouring, and filled it with his native verve and passion like a cup with a vital brewage. . . .'[2]

In 1829 he returned to Brussels (apparently on the death of his father) and sought out his remaining brothers: Vital Heger was a carpet manufacturer, and Jules a printer and stationer. In the same year Constantin obtained a post as teacher at the Athénée Royal, at an initial salary of 500 francs per annum.[3] The scale of salaries was calculated upon a complicated system of bonuses and premiums, and within the same year the school registers record him as receiving a supplementary sum of 480 francs. For the year 1830–1 he is entered as a teacher of French and mathematics with a salary of 800 francs per annum.[4]

Such as it was it allowed him to marry, and this he very shortly did. His bride was Marie-Josephine Noyer (whose memory Charlotte

[1] Louis Quiévreux, 'Bruxelles, les Brontës et la famille Heger', *La Lanterne*, avril 1953.
[2] *Villette*, ch. 28.
[3] Dorchy, Henri, *L'Athénée Royal de Bruxelles: son histoire*, 1950.
[4] Idem. Records of the Athénée Royal de Bruxelles—Organization and Rules up to 1850.

Brontë evoked as Justine-Marie of *Villette*). He was barely married when the Belgian revolution broke out. During the fighting (23–27 September 1830) M. Heger joined the Nationalists at the barricades and his wife's young brother was killed at his side, one of the 445 'martyrs' who fell in the cause of Belgian liberty.

The perfect happiness which his marriage brought was of short duration. On 26 September 1833 he lost both his wife and child in a cholera epidemic that killed 864 people in Brussels alone. The man of ardent feelings and profound affections that he proved himself all his life to be did not emerge from the experience unaltered. Thereafter, towards strangers he bore a morose exterior, his temper became explosive, he could be tyrannical, unreasonable, petty ('he fumed like a bottled storm...' as Charlotte felicitously described him).[1] He could be, and also frequently was, immensely generous, patient, and tender-hearted. He was, moreover, a profoundly religious man. He had it in him to have found his vocation in the priesthood but he became, instead, one of the most notable teachers of his century. When he died at a great age, the national press was unanimous in paying tribute to his remarkable gifts not only as a teacher, but as a moral influence over the children he taught. 'He possessed a very precious gift,' one newspaper said of him; 'a kind of intellectual magnetism with children. . . .'[2]

It was during the first years of his widowerhood that he met Zoë Parent at the Gatti de Gammonds and began giving literature lessons at her school.[3] The similarity of their tastes, the high seriousness they both brought to their profession, made the outcome almost inevitable: they married on 3 September 1836.

While Madame Heger remained the titular—and business—head of the pensionnat, M. Heger continued professor at the Athénée, which for the first five years of their marriage was still housed in its old buildings in the Rue de Namur, and only moved into the Rue des Douze Apôtres, flanking the pensionnat in the Rue d'Isabelle, in 1838, shortly before the Brontës arrived at the school.

The Hegers' course, thereafter, was one of unchecked progress and united effort; as teachers they established a high reputation. In 1886, when they celebrated their golden wedding, the press of the day said of them: '. . . Here is a couple that has taught hundreds of our families, that has, in fact, brought up a whole society. The country owes them much. . . .'[4]

---

1 *Villette*, ch. 15.   2 *L'Indépendance Belge*, 9 May 1896.
3 Quiévreux, op. cit.   4 *L'Indépendance Belge*, 4 Sept. 1886.

Small wonder then that when Charlotte wrote her preliminary inquiries, setting out her own and Emily's objectives in seeking to enter
a continental school, confessing frankly to their limited means and
equally unlimited ambitions, she was met with sympathetic—and
generous—understanding. From what M. Heger later told Mrs. Gaskell,
he and his wife were so struck by 'the simple earnest tone' of Charlotte's
letter that they decided at once on giving her and her sister advantageous conditions.[1] The full fees for boarders were 650 francs per annum
(£26) but there were extras for music, drawing, and dancing. The
Brontë girls were to be charged no extras at all. Whatever the outcome,
on their arrival Charlotte and Emily were given the kindest welcome
as representing the very type of cultured girl without money whom
the Hegers wished to help.

The long dormitory, lighted by five french windows, was capable of
sleeping 20 boarders, but was occupied at the time by only 12 other
girls. They were given curtained beds and extra bed-space, and each
boarder had an individual washstand. Curtained off in what amounted
to their own corner at the far end of the immense room, the Brontës
enjoyed as much privacy as though upon their own. As it was a predominantly Catholic establishment (although there were at one time
as many as eight other English girls) they were excused attendance at
prayers, divinity-lessons, and the evening 'lecture pieuse' upon which
the day's duties closed, if they so wished. If, however, as proved to be
the case, they wanted to attend in order to improve their French they
were equally free to do so.

At the time the Brontës arrived at the pensionnat there were some
40 day-girls. Among the boarders was one English girl, Maria Miller,
the undoubted prototype of Ginevra Fanshawe. Madame Heger had
also at the time an English 'gouvernante' for her children, 'in rank
something between a lady's maid and a nursery-governess' Charlotte
explained to Ellen, called Martha Trotman.

With the exception of these compatriots and the visiting English
master (most probably the same Mr. Brown who taught English at the
Athénée and ran the English bookshop in Brussels and published a
newsletter, 'The British and Continental Mercury', taken by all the
English colony), and whose name Charlotte made use of in *The Professor*, the girls found themselves among foreigners speaking no word
of their language. The effort required of them in following the day's

[1] Gaskell, ch. xi, p. 161.

lessons was therefore considerable and put an added strain on all they did.

Their knowledge of French on reaching Brussels was, in the recollection of M. Heger, negligible. Charlotte, however, would not acknowledge this, telling Ellen Nussey that Emily had had 'greater difficulties to contend with' than she had. 'Indeed,' she added, 'those who come to a French school for instruction ought previously to have acquired a considerable knowledge of the French language, otherwise they will lose a great deal of time, for the course of instruction is adapted to natives and not to foreigners. . . .'[1] Strangely enough, the surviving examples of Charlotte's and Emily's earliest French *devoirs* show Emily to have been considerably the better linguist. A comparison of her *devoirs* with Charlotte's shows, moreover, fewer corrections in the hand of M. Heger.[2]

There were three resident women teachers, called according to the custom of the time by their christian names: Mesdemoiselles Blanche, Sophie, and Marie; and seven visiting masters. Upon these devolved the teaching of advanced subjects—science and mathematics, for example—and the accomplishments—music, dancing, and foreign languages other than French. One or two of these taught at the Athénée also; Kint, de Hamel, Vanderlinden among them, names used by Charlotte in *Villette*, suggesting that she had personal knowledge of them in school.

Charlotte's descriptions of the actual premises of the pensionnat in both her novels have been acknowledged to be accurate by those most competent to judge: the family Heger itself, and succeeding pupils. Now that the house and street are gone, buried beneath a whole complex of new buildings, it is well so acute an observer left a description of them on record; for she knew the pensionnat from its attics to the portress's lodge, from the Hegers' private apartments to the kitchens, and succeeded in making them as familiar to her readers.

Entered by the main door in the Rue d'Isabelle through its black and white flagged hall—the 'Carré' as it was called—the school buildings fell into two distinct halves: the Hegers' quarters on the left, the classrooms and refectory on the right. Facing the street door was the glass-covered 'Galerie' giving access to the garden behind, which it divided off from the stone-flagged playground proper, with its 'Pas de Géant' (Giant-stride) on the right half of the inner quadrangle.

---

[1] CB to EN, 5 May 1842: *SLL* i. 237–8.
[2] For the list of CB's preserved French *devoirs*, see below, Additional Notes.

Squaring off the quadrangle on the further side of the garden and playground were the main classroom on the ground floor and the long dormitory above. Connecting the front and back quarters of the house was the long refectory, at the narrow tables of which, each lighted by an oil-lamp from above, the girls assembled of an evening to hear the 'lecture pieuse'. In the little first-floor oratory, forming the angle between the front and back buildings of the school, a permanently lighted lamp burned before the image of the Virgin.

Of the high-walled garden, with its double row of fruit-trees down the centre, its trellised arbours and hidden walks, Charlotte has given more than a visual description. She made it a dramatic, almost a living element in her tales; never did she write of it with less than gratitude. She wrote in *Villette*:

> . . . Behind the house at the Rue Fossette there was a garden—large considering that it lay in the heart of a city, and to my recollection at this day it seems pleasant. . . . Independently of romantic rubbish . . . that old garden had its charms. On summer mornings I used to rise early, to enjoy them alone; on summer evenings to linger solitary, to keep tryst with the rising moon, or taste one kiss of the evening breeze. . . . The turf was verdant, the gravelled walks were white; sun-bright nasturtiums clustered beautiful about the roots of the doddered orchard giants. There was a large berceau [arbour] above which spread the shade of an acacia; there was a smaller, more sequestered bower, nestled in the vines which ran all along a high and gray wall. . . . Doubtless at high noon . . . when Madame's . . . large school turned out rampant . . . doubtless *then* the garden was a trite, down-trodden place enough. But at sunset or the hour of 'Salut', when the externes were gone home, and the boarders quiet at their studies, pleasant was it then to stray down the peaceful alleys, and hear the bells of St. Jean Baptiste [Ste Gudule] peal out with their sweet, soft exalted sound. . . .[1]

Apart from the self-imposed necessity of making good use of every leisure-hour, the curriculum to which Charlotte and Emily were subjected—like the youngest girl in the school—was not an exacting one. Lessons were from 9 to 12 and 2 to 4, and after the boarders had dined at 5 there was an evening study-hour, followed by the 'lecture pieuse' and bed.

. . . Nothing could be better than all Madame's arrangements for the physical well-being of her scholars. No minds were overtasked; the lessons were well-distributed and made incomparably easy to the learner; there was

---

[1] *Villette*, ch. 12.

a liberty of amusement, and a provision of exercise which kept the girls healthy; the food was abundant and good; neither pale nor puny faces were anywhere to be seen in the Rue Fossette. She never grudged a holiday; she allowed plenty of time for sleeping, dressing, washing, eating; her method in all these matters was easy, liberal, salutary, and rational: many an austere English school-mistress would do vastly well to imitate her—and,—I believe many would be glad to do so, if exacting English parents would let them....[1]

It was not for fully six weeks after their arrival in Brussels that the Brontës and the Taylor girls first met and could exchange their views on life in foreign schools. Meantime, if Charlotte and Emily denied themselves the indulgence of the Thursday half-holidays, their only outings were to church on Sundays.

There was as yet no Anglican church established in Brussels (the Belgian Protestants themselves had only received official recognition some 30 years before) and the Anglican services were held in the 'Temple du Musée', or 'Chapel Royal' as it was more generally called, both from the character of its origin and from the fact that the newly elected Belgian king, Leopold I—a Coburg by birth and a Protestant—had his regular stall there and frequently attended the Sunday services. The little chapel lay at no great distance from the Pensionnat Heger, in the Place du Musée, part of Charles of Lorraine's former splendid rococo palace. This, built on the model of Versailles and Schonbrünn, consisted of two main buildings linked by a central semi-circular crescent wing. It was in this wing that Charles's little chapel had unobtrusively been tucked, and which had served as his private chapel from 1771, when it was finished, to the French Revolution, when the Austrian governors were permanently driven out of Brussels. Disestablished after the revolution, the little chapel remained unused till 1803 when Napoleon stayed in Brussels and, recognizing the fair claims of the growing Protestant community in the town, offered it to them for their own place of worship—the first in nearly three centuries of persecution they could legally call their own. It was solemnly dedicated to the purpose on 1 January 1805.

The former furtive life of the Belgian Protestants can best be realized by the fact that they had no legal burial-ground for their dead. Up to the period when Napoleon took their case in hand, they were buried clandestinely in ground situated in the Rue des Alexiens, in the heart of the old city. Napoleon showed his practical sympathy for them by

[1] *Villette*, ch. 8.

putting two sites at their disposal: one for paupers outside the Porte de Hal and the other in a beautiful situation outside the Porte de Louvain. It was with this one that Charlotte and Emily Brontë would later make melancholy contact.

A new and unexpected addition to the Protestant community of Brussels resulted from the battle of Waterloo, with the influx of English nationals who crossed the channel to stay with their wounded husbands, brothers, and sweethearts. Many of these, finding life both pleasant and cheap in the Belgian capital, resolved to stay, and formed the nucleus of a new and thriving English colony, whose businesses became gradually integrated into the country's industry. In the 1840's the English colony numbered some 2,000 persons.

For these 'residents by adoption' an English chaplain was provided. The first one so to officiate was the Duke of Kent's chaplain, for the Duke, until the expected birth of his daughter,[1] was a Brussels resident for several years after Waterloo. (He married a sister of King Leopold.) Their place of worship was the little 'Chapel Royal' where, alternating with Belgian Protestant and German Lutheran services, each Sunday an Anglican service was celebrated morning and afternoon. It was here that Charlotte and Emily went most Sundays to the 2 p.m. service to hear the resident chaplain, the Revd. Evan Jenkins, M.A. He had held the post since 1826 and because of the King's attendance at his chapel was able to style himself 'Chaplain to H.M. King Leopold'.

Other Anglican services were also celebrated in St. George's Chapel, the converted chapel of the House of Nassau, where the Revd. William Drury officiated till 1876, only two years before his death. Though the Wheelwright family whom Charlotte and Emily would shortly know attended Mr. Drury's services rather than Mr. Jenkins's, the latter's connexion through his brother with the West Riding influenced the Brontës to prefer the Chapel Royal. A charming little chapel it was, an islet of eighteenth-century taste and elegance as it still is today in its twentieth-century complex of concrete, glass, and steel. Indeed, it is impossible not to wonder if the highly ornate character of its interior decoration—reflecting its Hapsburg origin—did not somewhat startle the congregations of nineteenth-century Protestants who worshipped there. What did Charlotte and Emily make of its bas-reliefs of stucco cherubs floating on clouds, its gilt and wrought-iron galleries, its painted ceiling (the work of Heilbroeck) representing Carlo Borromeo carrying extreme unction to the victims of the plague? Charlotte did

[1] The future Queen Victoria, whose birth had necessarily to occur on English ground.

record her reactions to the congregation of fellow countrymen and women: scanning them with her usual sharpness, she noted the shabbiness and inelegance of their dress. Readers of *The Professor* will remember Crimsworth's pursuit of the lost Frances Henri and how he 'sought her in the two Protestant chapels; I attended these latter at the German, French and English services, not doubting that I should meet her at one of them . . .', adding the piquant description:

> . . . on the afternoon of the 4th Sunday I turned from the door of the Chapel-royal which the door-keeper had just closed and locked, and followed in the wake of the last of the congregation, now dispersed and dispersing over the square. I had soon outwalked the couples of English gentlemen and ladies. (Gracious goodness! why don't they dress better? My eye is yet filled with visions of the high-flounced, slovenly, and tumbled dresses in costly silk and satin, of the large unbecoming collars in expensive lace; of the ill-cut coats and strangely fashioned pantaloons which every Sunday, at the English service, filled the choirs of the chapel-royal, and after it, issuing forth into the square, came into disadvantageous contrast with freshly and trimly attired foreign figures, hastening to attend 'salut' at the church of Coburg.) I had passed these pairs of Britons, and the groups of pretty British children, and the British footmen and waiting-maids. . . . I had crossed the Place Royale and got into the Rue Royale, then I had diverged into the Rue de Louvain—an old and quiet street— . . .[1]

The itinerary of some of Charlotte's Sunday walks is certainly contained here.

The visits to Mrs. Jenkins, by which many such a Sunday walk ended, were fraught with as much discomfort to the hosts as to the guests, so unable in their shyness were the Brontës to sustain the slightest small-talk with strangers. In the recollection of the Jenkins's sons, John and Edward (later, in succession to their father, chaplain and assistant chaplain to the Chapel Royal), who were sent to escort the Brontë girls from the pensionnat—or from church—to the other end of the Chaussée d'Ixelles (No. 304) where they lived, there was opposed to them a wall of silence which no tentative conversation on their part could breach. After several such frustrating attempts to make themselves agreeable, the brothers told their mother they had had enough, and she, seeing how patently unhappy Emily Brontë was in particular, herself put an end to the situation. What was the use, she later asked Mrs. Chadwick, if no one derived any pleasure, and if what was intended as a kindness was regarded in the light of an imposition?[2]

[1] *The Professor*, ch. 19.
[2] Chadwick, E: *In the Footsteps of the Brontës*, 1914, ch. 15–20.

Of the 'Bright City' of which Charlotte had formed such yearning anticipations, she saw enough to tell Ellen Nussey in her very first letter: '. . . there are a hundred things which I want to tell you, but I have not time. Brussels is a beautiful city. . . .'[1]

Easter Sunday that year fell on 27 March, and on the previous day Charlotte and Emily went out to Koekelberg to spend the day with Mary and Martha Taylor in their pensionnat. The Taylors put part of the time to good use by sending a joint news-letter to Ellen Nussey, from which their first reactions to life in a foreign school can be gleaned. The pleasure at meeting true friends of over 10 years' standing was intense and, contrasted with their recent experiences among strangers, made their value appear even greater than before.

'. . . Just now we are at Koekelberg', wrote Charlotte on the back of Mary's long letter, describing the idiosyncrasies of the teachers at her pensionnat, her very full days, Martha's considerable improvement, and the cheerful noisy world into which they had been plunged, ' . . . spending the day with Mary and Martha Taylor—to us such a happy day—for one's blood requires a little warming, it gets cold with living amongst strangers. You are not forgotten as you feared you would be. I will write another letter sometime and tell you how we are placed and amongst what sort of people. Mary and Martha are not changed; I have a catholic faith in them that they cannot change. . . .'[2]

From Martha Taylor's addition to the news-sheet it appeared that the girls were given 10 days' holiday at Easter and very unwilling, Martha expressed herself at the end of that time, 'to begin lessons again. I am tired of this everlasting German. . . . Would you like', she apostrophized Ellen, 'to be here cracking your head with French and German? By the way you must excuse me if I send you some unintelligible English, for in attempting to acquire other languages I have almost forgotten the little I knew of my own. . . .'[3] With her own individual approach to most subjects, Martha declared furthermore that 'our dragon' (her sister Mary sitting at that moment on the other side of her), 'staring into a German dictionary and looking as fierce as a tiger', was benefiting by the experience. 'There is a very sweet, lady-like elegant girl here', Martha added, 'who has undertaken to civilise our dragon, and she is actually improving a little under her hands. . . .' How she herself was profiting by the civilizing atmosphere of a foreign school may be seen from the postscript to her letter: '. . . It is all the fashion

---

[1] CB to EN, 5 May 1842: *SLL* i (No. 103), 237–8.
[2] CB to EN, 26 Mar. 1842: *SLL* i. 235–6.   [3] Idem.

for gentlemen to paint themselves. Shall I send you some paint for George? When you see my brother Joe, have the kindness to pull his hair right well for me and give John a good pinch. . . .'[1] Martha at 23 was still as Charlotte described her as a child, gay, chattering, arch; 'with her little piquant face, engaging prattle, and winning ways she was made', as Charlotte testified, 'to be a pet', and everybody's pet she continued to the end.

All traces of the Taylors' school at Koekelberg have vanished. Only by piecing together scattered clues and relating them to certain statements of Charlotte's can its location, even perhaps the old building itself, be identified. In her references to the school Charlotte always called it the 'Château' of Koekelberg, 'château' being a term loosely employed in Brabant to describe anything between a gentleman's country seat and a manor-farm, the latter especially if of any antiquity. Lying to the north-west of Brussels Koekelberg was open country in the Brontës' day, and was reached via the Porte de Flandre and following the long Chaussée de Gand for some two miles. Cab-hire for places outside the city boundaries was doubled, and though Charlotte describes Mme Beck driving out to the Bretton's 'château'—la Terrasse—in a 'neat little fiacre'—it is unlikely Charlotte and Emily themselves were so free with their money. That they walked it is not only more in keeping with their financial position and their tastes, but would also explain Charlotte's familiarity with a route she covered only a few times in all.

On the terrain of Koekelberg, in a turning off the Chaussée de Gand and reached by a long avenue of limes, there stood until recent years the manor-farm of Careveld (or Karreveld as it is also spelt) set among lush meadows, watered by numerous springs, threaded by its own stream and overlooking and reflected in the waters of its own pond. It was considered the most original-looking manor in all the Brussels countryside, being composed of two distinct buildings, the one a fortified farm and the other a sixteenth-century château, complete with round tower, stepped gables, and stone mullions. That Charlotte had it in mind when describing 'La Terrasse' appears extremely likely; the exact site and the salient features being so similar. Its further identification with the Taylors' school would then appear to follow, for in her few outings from Brussels Charlotte would hardly know in the same locality two distinct 'châteaus' so thoroughly well.[2] '. . . This is a

[1] Op. cit.

[2] Arthur Costyn, *Sites Brabançonnes*, 47. See also *Lippencott's Monthly Magazine*, Dec. 1885. Theo. Wolfe, *Scenes of CB's Life in Brussels*, in which the comparison between La Terrasse and the Château de Koekelberg is made.

quaint little château', she wrote of 'La Terrasse' in *Villette*: 'I don't know if you may have noticed it in your walk—in the old style of the Basse Ville [i.e. sixteenth century]. It is rather a manor than a château. . . .'[1] It is a description which exactly fits the Château de Careveld.

One direct reference to the 'Château de Koekelberg' as once a school for boys is in an account of 1815, when the author of a guide-book described meeting the 'pupils of Koekelberg' on one of their weekly walks to the ponds of the neighbouring village, accompanied by their headmaster and assistant master, who were both, he assured his readers, 'fully qualified to instruct young people of good family'.[2]

By the Taylors' time it was a big and expensive boarding-school for girls, with an English headmistress, a Miss Evans mentioned by Mary Taylor in her letter to Ellen, and a predominance of English and German pupils which led to very little French being spoken ('and that little . . . bad', as Mary complained). The school appears to have been locally known as 'le Pensionnat des Dames Anglaises'. Charlotte later borrowed the name of Miss Evans for the half-English, half-Swiss heroine of *The Professor*, Frances Evans Henri.

On Easter Monday, 28 March, Madame Heger gave birth to her first son, christened Prospère Édouard Augustin. This accounts for the fact that, in the first weeks, even months, of Charlotte's sojourn in Brussels, she had fewer direct contacts with Madame, who was taken up with her nursery duties, than with Monsieur. The six lines devoted to Madame Heger, and the whole page to Monsieur in her first long letter to Ellen is perhaps a consequence of this: '. . . Madame Heger, the head, is a lady of precisely the same cast of mind, degree of cultivation and quality of intellect as Miss Catherine Wooler. I think the severe points are a little softened, because she has not been disappointed, and consequently soured. In a word, she is a married instead of a maiden lady. . . .'[3]

Charlotte's knowledge and understanding of Madame Heger's character were not formed until much later. So far she had seen her mainly at a distance, a maternal figure taken up with her children, seated in the garden on summer mornings with her little brood and the youngest class of the school ranged about her to hear them read, simplifying their earliest lessons for them. Madame Heger, as outside evidence shows, was a woman of great dignity and reserve, who

---

[1] *Villette*, ch. 17.   [2] Guide du Touring Club de Belgique.
[3] CB to EN, 5 May 1842: *SLL* i. 237–8.

did not wear her heart upon her sleeve or facilitate familiarity with strangers. Her manner was universally benevolent to all, as later English pupils, Frederika Macdonald among them, testified; but because it was studied and not spontaneous, Charlotte found her far more difficult to fathom than the extrovert M. Heger.[1]

M. Heger she saw at close quarters every day—tempestuous, vehement, unreasonable, humorous, quite the opposite of his wife. At once amused and outraged by his complete lack of inhibitions, Charlotte studied him as though he were some rare species at a fair, his foreignness being something completely beyond her reckoning. She wrote to Ellen in May:

> ... There is an individual of whom I have not yet spoken, M. Heger the husband of Madame. He is professor of rhetoric, a man of power as to mind, but very choleric and irritable in temperament; a little black being, with a face that varies in expression. Sometimes he borrows the lineaments of an insane tom-cat, sometimes those of a delirious hyena; occasionally, but very seldom, he discards these perilous attractions and assumes an air not above 100 degrees removed from mild and gentlemanlike. ...[2]

Gathering up what nervous resistance she had to meet his outbursts of impatience, constantly watchful of his changing moods, often waiting a week in vain for one syllable of approbation, she realized nevertheless that, exhausting as he might be, she had never at any moment of her previous schooling had a teacher like him. The trouble he took to give her the knowledge she craved was, of itself, his highest commendation in her eyes. The amplitude of his comments and corrections of her work, filling the margin of her exercise-books with fresh food for thought, witnessed more eloquently to his generosity of character than sweet words could. And sweet words were not always wanting; surprisingly, at some sign of progress or understanding on her part, his face would break into a childlike beam of delight, and he would proffer a 'bon-bon' or a piece of sweet cake with which his pockets were stuffed (for he seldom had time for regular meals) with the same simple gesture as he would recompense one of the children in the baby class. Because so rare, his commendation would become for her a thing to covet.

M. Heger's methods, developed over fifty years of teaching, gained him in the end almost national recognition. That 'intellectual magnet-

---

[1] Frederika Macdonald, *The Secret of CB*: Edinburgh, 1914; 'The Brontës at Brussels' (*Woman at Home*, July 1894).

[2] CB to EN, 5 May 1842: op. cit.

CONSTANTIN HEGER

THE HEGER FAMILY, portrait group by
Ange François 1847

ism' on which the press commented in his old age made his lessons not only memorable, but unforgettable. It was said of him that 'il égayait la grammaire, il faisait vivre le syntaxe...'. Of this magnetism, Charlotte Brontë, more susceptible to such influences than most, felt the full force.

What clearly emerges from her first accounts of life at the pensionnat is her general satisfaction with everything. In the joint letter written from Koekelberg, she summed up her own and Emily's situation thus: '... You will have heard that we have settled at Brussels instead of Lille. I think we have done well—we have got into a very good school —and are considerably comfortable....'[1]

And again, in the letter of May: '... I think I am never unhappy; my present life is so delightful, so congenial to my own nature, compared with that of a governess. My time, constantly occupied, passes too rapidly. Hitherto both Emily and I have had good health, and therefore we have been able to work well....'

Emily's surprising readiness to adapt herself to the strange conditions of a foreign school was a matter of profound thankfulness to Charlotte, who had not counted on it. Since it was so, it made it possible for her to consider a prolongation of their time abroad, which in her heart she desired. Writing to Ellen in July she told her of a proposal just made by Madame Heger which would give her and Emily another half-year at school.

... I consider it doubtful whether I shall come home in September or not. Madame Heger has made a proposal for both me and Emily to stay another half-year, offering to dismiss her English master, and take me as English teacher; also to employ Emily some part of each day in teaching music to a certain number of the pupils. For these services we are to be allowed to continue our studies in French and German, and to have board, etc., without paying for it; no salaries, however, are offered. The proposal is kind, and in a great selfish city like Brussels, and a great selfish school, containing nearly ninety pupils, (boarders and day-pupils included) implies a degree of interest which demands gratitude in return. I am inclined to accept it.... I don't deny I sometimes wish to be in England, or that I have brief attacks of home-sickness; but, on the whole, I have borne a very valiant heart so far; and I have been happy in Brussels, because I have always been fully occupied with the employments I like. Emily is making rapid progress in French, German, music and drawing. Monsieur and Madame Heger begin to recognise the valuable parts of her character under her singularities....[2]

[1] CB to EN, 27 Mar. 1842: op. cit.
[2] CB to EN, July 1842: *SLL* i. 239–40.

Mary Taylor, already resolved so far as her own movements were concerned to stay abroad at all costs (though planning to leave Belgium for Germany), applauded Charlotte's decision to stay in Brussels. 'You will see by Charlotte's letter', she wrote Ellen after another Sunday reunion with the Brontës, 'that you are not likely to have your heart rejoiced by her presence. I am sorry for your sake, but not for any other reason. I intend to follow her example myself as speedily as possible. . . .'[1]

Charlotte's one reservation was over the antipathetic character of the Belgians, which she attributed without discrimination to their religion. Mrs. Gaskell, finding herself in an inextricable predicament years later when she got to this period in Charlotte's life, thankfully fixed on this as the main reason for Charlotte's eventual dislike of Madame Heger and of the widening gulf that grew up between them. The true reason, however, was the increasing distance developing between *Monsieur* Heger and herself. '. . . The difference in country and religion makes a broad line of demarcation between us and the rest', Charlotte wrote Ellen in May; 'we are completely isolated in the midst of numbers. . . .'[2] And a little later:

If the national character of the Belgians is to be measured by the character of most of the girls in this school, it is a character singularly cold, selfish, animal and inferior . . . their principles are rotten to the core. We avoid them, which is not difficult to do, as we have the brand of Protestantism and Anglicism upon use. People talk of the danger which Protestants expose themselves to in going to reside in Catholic countries. . . . My advice to all Protestants who are tempted to do anything so besotted as to turn Catholics is, to walk over the sea on to the Continent; to attend Mass sedulously for a time; to note well the mummeries thereof; also the idiotic, mercenary aspect of all the priests; and *then*, if they are still disposed to consider Papistry . . . let them turn Papists at once—that 's all. I consider Methodism, Quakerism and the extremes of High and Low Churchism foolish, but Roman Catholicism beats them all. . . .[3]

It is in the next phrase of this vehement attack that its true importance lies for an understanding of Charlotte's feelings at the time: Catholicism moved her chiefly in so far as it concerned Monsieur Heger. '. . . At the same time,' she continued, 'allow me to tell you that there are some Catholics who are as good as any Christians can be to whom the

[1] MT to EN, July 1842: *W & S.*
[2] CB to EN, 5 May 1842: op. cit.
[3] CB to EN, July 1842: *SLL* i. 239–40.

Bible is a sealed book, and much better than many Protestants. . . .'
M. Heger, she had daily proof, was one who attended Mass sedulously,
who listened to the 'idiotic priests', who shared in 'the mummeries' as
she neither could nor would. It was *this* that aroused her vehement
anger. She already had no doubts about his singular goodness and
integrity, and to oppose him on so vital an issue was wormwood.

In July there arrived at the pensionnat as day-boarders five little
English girls, the daughters of Dr. Thomas Wheelwright, of No. 1
South Place, Finsbury, who, for reasons of failing eyesight and loss of
fortune had taken up his abode in Brussels. Ranging from 14 years of
age to six and a half, the children were Laetitia Elizabeth (born 23 May
1828), Emily (born 10 September 1829), Frances (born 2 May 1831),
Sarah Ann (born 7 October 1834), and Julia (born 30 October 1835).

From the moment of their arrival Charlotte took a great liking to
them, especially to Laetitia the eldest, whose truculent nationalism in
the midst of foreigners aroused her amused admiration and friendship.
The friendship begun abroad and, as far as the Wheelwrights were
concerned, in childhood, lasted Charlotte's lifetime, and many recollections of her the Wheelwrights bore into old age.[1]

Of Emily their memories were unanimous, and as unsympathetic as
those of Charlotte were fond: 'I am afraid my recollections of Emily
Brontë will not aid you much', Laetitia wrote Clement Shorter in 1896.
'I simply disliked her from the first, her tallish, ungainly, ill-dressed
figure contrasting so strongly with Charlotte's small, neat, trim person,
although their dresses were alike; always answering our jokes with 'I
wish to be as God made me'.[2] Emily's unpopularity with the young
Wheelwrights sprang in part from the circumstance that she gave
piano-lessons to the three youngest, Frances, Sarah Ann, and Julia,
and insisted on teaching them during recreation so as not to lose her
own study hours. The young persons, however, far more disposed to
hang from the knotted ropes of the 'Pas de Géant' in the playground
than to learn their scales, took this imposition very hard and met her
severity with rebellion and tears. To their chagrin Emily taught them
the piano for four months but, as Laetitia commented in after years,
'fortunately she was summoned home in November and did not return
to Brussels'.

[1] J. J. Green: 'The Brontë–Wheelwright Friendship' (*Friends Quarterly Examiner*,
Nov. 1915); 'Two Brussels Schoolfellows', *BST*, 1913 (Chadwick, chs. 15–20).
[2] Obituary notice of Miss Fanny Wheelwright, *Hastings and St. Leonards Observer*,
22 Mar. 1913.

That the Wheelwrights were not always the best judges of character is shown by their infatuation for Maria Miller, the other English girl at the pensionnat. Maria, fashionable, dashing, and worldly, was supposed to be well-off and was in the habit of giving 'good presents' to the Wheelwright girls and even expensive jewellery. Fanny Wheelwright, more perspicacious perhaps than the rest, noted the great difference in Maria's treatment of the very little girls, whom she openly despised, and Charlotte Brontë's, who 'always noticed us youngest ones very kindly. I liked her, but not Emily Brontë'. Of Maria Miller the Wheelwright girls told a tale that could well be credited of Ginevra Fanshawe. She gave Laetitia a ring allegedly containing a lock of her hair, but in truth it was fur from the hearth-rug.[1]

That Emily was not equally disliked by all her young pupils appeared from the evidence of Louise de Bassompierre, a 16-year-old pupil, who retained into old age a cult for her former piano-teacher and preserved as a cherished souvenir a drawing of a tree Emily gave her before leaving Brussels. She preferred Emily to Charlotte: Miss Emily 'était beaucoup moins brillante que sa sœur, mais bien plus sympathique. Elle voulait se perfectionner dans l'étude du dessin et y avait acquis un véritable talent. Elle m'a donné un joli paysage signé de son nom et que je garde avec soin. . . .'[2] Louise de Bassompierre won a measure of Charlotte's esteem by bringing her fellow pupils to order one day when Napoleon was the subject of their study. The whole class had rounded on Charlotte as being in some way— by reason of her nationality—responsible for his fall, until Louise demonstrated to them how stupidly they argued, and secured for Charlotte a grudging recognition from the class of a right to her own opinions.

Even before the *grandes vacances* began on 15 August (Feast of the Assumption of the Virgin Mary and the official breaking-up date in all Catholic schools) Martha Taylor went home to England in charge to her brother John, where she was later joined by Mary. Writing to Ellen Nussey from Leeds on 22 June Martha promised to tell her 'all about Miss Brontës and my sister when I see you'. Again on 19 August, from her brother's house at Hunsworth Mills, Martha wrote inviting Ellen in the vein that was peculiarly hers: 'Now will you come? or will you be as stupid as you were about going to Brier Hall, and if you refuse you will make me seriously angry with you, and you had better

---

[1] J. J. Green, op. cit.
[2] Two Brussels schoolfellows of the Brontës: *BST*, 1913.

not, or I will tell all kinds of things of you to Miss Brontë. . . .'[1] 'Miss
Brontë' and Emily, staying throughout the *grandes vacances* in a pensionnat empty save for six or eight other boarders, experienced for
the first time what 'Asiatically hot' weather a continental summer could
bring in.

Of the art galleries, churches, and museums, which had made
Brussels appear in anticipation like the 'bright city' of her childhood's
dreams, Charlotte saw something now. In particular, she saw the trien-
nial exhibition of paintings in that year's 'Salon', as her descriptions of
particular paintings in *Villette* show. The painting she stigmatized as
the 'Cleopatra' existed in fact, as a comparison with the catalogue description of a painting of a similar subject and style has revealed, as well
as several other paintings described by her and exhibited in that year's
'Salon'.[2] The late Professor Charlier was the first to identify the pictures
described by Charlotte with certain paintings of which detailed and
analytical critiques, with illustrative lithographs, appeared in the contemporary Brussels press.[3]

Loving pictures as she did from childhood, she was fortunate in the
fact that her stay in Belgium coincided with a 'Salon', for unlike Paris
the Brussels exhibition was held only once in three years. It was an
innovation dating from 1830 and sponsored by the new King Leopold
I, with the object of 'encouraging a taste for the Arts' in the Belgian
people. Prior to Charlotte's visit there had only been four other
'Salons'.

The standard of painting, as the generally carping tone of the
Brussels press conveys, was low; but nevertheless the exhibition gave
Charlotte a chance of seeing some 388 paintings by contemporary
continental artists. With her usual regard to detail and penetrating observation, she memorized the minutiae of certain of the exhibits so well
that she was able to write of them recognizably ten years later. This is
particularly the case with the 'Cleopatra'—a painting of a lascivious
Egyptian dancer 'lounging away the noon on a sofa' and clad in 'in-
efficient raiment'—which appeared in the catalogue of the exhibition
as 'Une Almée', No. 102. It was the work of the painter Defiefve, in
which the drapery, the décor, and the general disorder, so condemned
by Charlotte, very exactly figure. Articles in *La Renaissance* and

---

[1] Martha Taylor to EN: *SLL* i. 240.
[2] Landoy, Eugène, Le Salon de 1842: *Revue Complète et analyse critique de tous les
tableaux*'. Chez l'éditeur.
[3] Gustave Charlier, 'Paysages', *Renaissance du Livre*, 1947; Gustave Charlier, 'The
Brussels of CB': *BST*, 1955.

L'Émancipation of the day so far echoed Charlotte's strictures as to find that 'The head has a somewhat vulgar character, the face of a woman of low degree', and to take exception to the form and pose of the figure for suggesting 'something of the voluptuous indolence of the harem'.

Eugène Landoy, the art critic, however, writing in the *Revue Complète et analyse critique de tous les tableaux de l'Exposition de Bruxelles*, found the 'Almée's' voluptuous pose very attractive. '. . . What delicious promise in those black and fiery eyes, in that sultry complexion, in that sweet abandon. . . . I could almost declare I am in love with that Almée—she's devilish beautiful!'[1]

A triptych representing scenes of a woman's life—'La Vie d'Une Femme' (Nos. 233–42)—and remembered by Charlotte as four distinct panels representing A Young Girl, A Married Woman, A Mother, and Widowhood, were in reality the work of a woman painter called Fanny Geefs, who had shown considerable promise in her earlier work 'in the style of Reynolds and Lawrence', so the critic said, but who here greatly disappointed her followers. 'Instead of advancing . . . she has lamentably gone backwards', Eugène Landoy considered. 'The poetry one had recognised in her earlier work was only one of form, not of thought . . .', he sadly concluded, and implored her, before it was too late, 'to study more closely the manner of our great painters, especially in the treatment of shadows'[2]—advice which gives appositeness to Charlotte's descriptions of the series as painted in a 'flat, dead, pale and formal' manner.

Portraits, seascapes, historical subjects abounded in that exhibition, but what Charlotte preferred to all were certain 'exquisite little pictures of still life: wild flowers, wild fruit, mossy wood-nests, casketing eggs that looked like pearls seen through clear green sea water'.[3] These received eulogistic notices from the art critic of *La Renaissance*, who picked on the 'Fruits and Flowers of Autumn' by the Parisian painter Chazal, the 'Fruits and Flowers' of Charrette-Duval, and the 'Flowers and Fruits' of Van Os, for his particular commendation. 'It seemed to me', Charlotte summarized her impressions of the exhibition, 'that an original and good picture was just as scarce as an original and good book; nor did I, in the end, tremble to say to myself, standing before certain "chefs-d'œuvres" bearing great names, "Those are not a whit like Nature. . . ."'[4]

Mary Taylor, back at school in September, found the Brontë girls

[1] Eugène Landoy, op. cit.   [2] Idem.   [3] *Villette*, ch. 19.   [4] Idem.

contented enough, as she wrote to Ellen on the 24th: '. . . Charlotte & Emily are well; not only in health but in mind and hope. They are content with their present position and even gay and I think they do right not to return to England though one of them at least could earn more at the Beautiful town of Bradford than she is now doing. . . .'[1]

When Mary Taylor spoke of Charlotte and Emily being 'even gay' in humour, she had either not seen them for several days or else the news from home that month was very late in reaching them. For on 6 September William Weightman had died of cholera, after a fortnight's sufferings. His 'bright but brief course' was run. Mr. Brontë, delivering his funeral sermon in Haworth Church on 2 October, could not speak of him without great emotion; he had, as he said, loved him as a son. Mr. Brontë said something more, that remains as a corrective to the accusation of fickleness Charlotte had levelled at Weightman on more than one occasion: '. . . His character wore well,' said Mr. Brontë, 'the surest proof of real worth. He had, it is true, some peculiar advantages. Agreeable in person and manners, and constitutionally cheerful, his first introduction was prepossessing. But what he gained at first, he did not lose afterwards. . . .'[2]

Poor Willie Weightman was 28. He had charmed the whole family, the elders, and the susceptible young hearts alike, and his loss wrung such sobs from Branwell (the only member of the family in the parsonage pew at the funeral) that the congregation heard him.[3] Anne, the one who had loved him best, endured the heartbreak of his loss alone in distant Thorp Green, with none to witness her suffering.

Even as Mary was writing to Ellen on that 24 September, Martha fell ill. The symptoms, so general at that time of bad water-supplies— and so generally wrongly diagnosed as dysentery—were only recognized as those of cholera when it was too late. Charlotte first heard of her illness on 12 October and hurried out to Koekelberg on the morning of the 13th (a Thursday half-holiday) only to hear that she had died in the night.

She had, in fact, died at 10 o'clock the previous evening. Incredulity mingled with shock. It was impossible to believe Martha Taylor could die. Charlotte had never known a gayer or more carefree companion. The spoilt Martha, the darling of her indulgent father, had never

[1] MT to EN: *W & S* i.
[2] 'Funeral Sermon of the Revd. William Weightman, M.A., preached in Haworth Church on 2 Oct. 1842.' J. U. Walker, Halifax, 1842.
[3] Chadwick 169.

needed to mind her words, defying the grave Miss Woolers with ineffable grace. She had ordered about her friends with perfect assurance because she was confident of their tireless indulgence. Now she had died in her youth and brilliance, to the stupefaction of her family and friends, at the age of 23.[1]

As dissenters the Taylors did not seek burial for her by a clergyman of the Established Church. Applying to the Belgian Protestant community, her funeral service was conducted by a Protestant Pastor of the Reformed Church—Chrétien-Henri Vent—at the Chapel Royal on 14 October. From there the cortège passed through the Porte de Louvain and out to the Protestant Cemetery on the Chaussée de Louvain some two miles away. There she was buried in the first square on the right, opposite grave No. 91.[2] The closing down of the cemetery and redevelopment of the whole area in recent years make it no longer possible for English tourists to visit Martha's grave—a circumstance that would particularly have hurt Charlotte, for what weighed most heavily on her heart both at the time and years afterwards was the fact that Martha had to lie in foreign soil. The sense of abandonment that her funeral left with her over the years found its eloquent expression in *Shirley* where, evoking that bitter scene, she wrote:

... This evening reminds me too forcibly of another evening some years ago; a howling, rainy autumn evening too—when certain who had that day performed a pilgrimage to a grave new-made in a heretic cemetery, sat near a woodfire on the hearth of a foreign dwelling. They knew they had lost something whose absence could never be quite atoned for so long as they lived: and they knew that heavy falling rain was soaking into the wet earth which covered their lost darling: and that the sad, sighing gale was mourning above her buried head ...[3]

Mary, as Charlotte later told Ellen, 'was taken away to Brussels. I have seen Mary frequently since. She is in no ways crushed by the event; but while Martha was ill she was to her more than a mother—more than a sister: watching, nursing, cherishing her so tenderly, so unweariedly. I have seen Martha's grave—the place where her ashes lie in a foreign country. . . .'[4]

---

[1] Martha Taylor's death-certificate delivered by the Commune de Koekelberg, 13 Oct. 1842, stated that she had died at 10 o'clock the previous evening 'au Pensionnat des dames anglaises en cette commune...'.

[2] Entry in register of the Temple du Musée, 14 Oct. 1842.

[3] *Shirley*, ch. 23.   [4] CB to EN, 10 Nov. 1842: *SLL* i. 246.

Happily for Mary her cousins, the Dixons, were then living in Brussels in a furnished house, 11 rue de la Régence (not far from the Pensionnat Heger). There Mary was welcomed into a family atmosphere whose harmony and affection struck her agreeably by contrast to her own parents' strangely unequal union. Writing to Ellen on 30 October she said: 'I am now staying with the Dixons in Brussels. I find them very different to what I expected. They are the most united, affectionate family I ever met with. They have taken me as one of themselves and have made me such a comfortable happy home that I should like to live here all my life. . . .'[1]

On that very day, a Sunday, Mary was expecting Charlotte and Emily to go with her to visit Martha's grave. Continuing her account on the following day, she wrote: 'Well, I have seen her and Emily. We have walked about six miles to see the cemetery and the country round it. We then spent a pleasant evening with my cousins, and in presence of my uncle and Emily, one not speaking at all, and the other once or twice. . . .'[2]

On this walk to the Protestant Cemetery Charlotte based the memorable scene in *The Professor* in which William Crimsworth finds the lost Frances Henri at the grave of her aunt. The place was of considerable beauty, set in a valley well wooded with limes, surrounded by high walls and entered by wrought-iron gates. On either side of these were inscribed the texts:

Jésus-Christ a détruit la mort et a mis en évidence la vie et l'immortalité par son évangile (2 Timothy i. 10)

on the left hand, and upon the right:

Heureux ceux qui meurent au seigneur; désormais ils se reposent de leurs travaux et leurs œuvres les suivent (Acts xiv. 13).[3]

On 2 November, only two days after their visit to Martha's grave, Charlotte and Emily received news from home that their aunt was seriously ill. They did not hesitate in making up their minds to go back at once, Branwell being the only one there to deal with the situation. By the next day's post, however, on the Thursday morning, they heard that Miss Branwell was dead. (She died on 29 October.) Too late now to reach home in time for the funeral, they waited for Sunday's

[1] MT to EN, 30 Oct. 1842: *SLL* i. 243–4.
[2] Idem.   [3] Costyn, op. cit.

steam-packet from Antwerp, rather than rush their departure by taking Friday's boat from Ostend.

Stunned by the rapid succession of mournful events, they packed up for the return to England and made their farewells. For Emily it was, indeed, her last farewell to Brussels. But Charlotte had reason to hope that it might not be for her. She carried with her a letter from M. Heger to her father. Over and above the customary expressions of condolence for the death of their aunt, she knew that it contained a eulogy of her own and Emily's conduct and progress during the nine months of their schooling in Brussels, and an eloquent appeal to Mr. Brontë to allow *one* of them if not both to return for a final year's study on a more profitable footing even than before, i.e. with a salary as well as free lessons in exchange for their services. M. Heger wrote more as a friend than as a teacher; he spoke of the girls' departure as 'grieving' him and his wife greatly. With an insight into the structure of Brontë family life that was remarkable, he judged the father after the conduct and character of the daughters, laying to *his* credit their energy in learning and devotion to duty. Towards two such dear pupils, M. Heger said, he and his wife had grown to have feelings of affection that were almost paternal. On the question of his daughters' return he left the decision, naturally, to Mr. Brontë.[1]

This letter was followed by one from Madame Heger addressed to Charlotte after she reached home, the affectionate terms of which left her in no doubt whatever that both Monsieur and Madame genuinely wished her to go back to them.[2] And not only that: it left her in no doubt either of their *equal* kindness and affectionate regard for her.

The point is important and has not sufficiently been stressed in considering Charlotte's eventual remorse for the step she took. Diffident all her life, not of her mental powers but of her powers to please, the effect of feeling herself liked and valued was always decisive. As she had written years before, after the patched-up quarrel with Miss Wooler, 'If anybody likes me I can't help liking them.'[3]

She had no sooner left Brussels than she yearned to be back there. Though a complete reorganization of the domestic arrangements of the parsonage was necessary after the death of Miss Branwell, Charlotte was quite sure that she did not want to remain as her father's housekeeper. Little given to hope as she was by temperament—'the mixed

[1] M. Heger to Revd. P. Brontë, 6 Nov. 1842: *SLL* i. 248–50.
[2] CB to EN, 15 Nov. 1843, *W & S*; *SLL* i. 273–4. See below, page 249.
[3] CB to EN, 4 Jan. 1838: *SLL* i. 145.

cup' as opposed to the 'bitter brewage' of unrelieved sorrow was the most she asked of life—she hoped now with all her heart that her duty might square with her inclination and that she might be allowed to return to her friends in Belgium. To earn her living honourably among them appeared to her now all she wanted. In furtherance of this hope, the letters of Monsieur and Madame Heger seemed indeed to bring the guarantee of her return.

CHAPTER XIV

THE BLACK SWAN: BRUSSELS, 1843

By a strange continuance of the calamities that had darkened that autumn, barely a fortnight after Charlotte and Emily left Brussels, Julia, the youngest of the Wheelwright girls, who was just turned seven, died of cholera on 19 November. A letter from Madame Heger on the occasion written to the bereaved parents, preserved by the family, is of interest as revealing a side of her nature little in accordance with Charlotte's picture of her. Those who knew Madame Heger intimately could never, indeed, recognize the elements of that portrait as in any way resembling her. Of her unobtrusive charities and genuine piety many have given evidence. Writing of her in 1846 the Baronne de Willmar had this to say: 'Madame Heger, une femme d'élite, vraiment pieuse, mais de cette dévotion qui ne blesse pas, au contraire. J'ai vu obliger et soulager bien des infortunes sa physiognomie semble refléter un rayon de bonheur autour des personnes qui l'approchent. . . .'[1]

Madame Heger wrote on Monday 21 November 1842 to the eldest of the Wheelwright girls:

Ma chère Létitia, I intended visiting your mamma yesterday morning, but being unwell I had to stay indoors. To-day I am better but still being unable to go out, I want at least to have news of you. How is your mamma? I greatly fear that the nights of watching, of fatigue and grief will have affected her health. Happily for her all her children are so good, so well brought up, that she will find a consolation for the cruel loss she has suffered in their loving care.

When I can get to see your parents I will tell them how much I appreciate the very great kindness of your papa's letter. I am truly grateful to him for having thought of us at such a tragic time, one that will leave lasting traces among us here as with you. The little angel for whom we weep deserved all our tears, though we must try to say to ourselves that she has escaped from the trials and griefs that we still have to bear.

Good-bye, my dear Létitia; please kiss your little sisters for me and present to your parents, whom I daily learn to value more, my respectful affection.   Your devoted

Z. Heger[2]

[1] Willmar, Baronne de, *Souvenirs de Bruxelles*, 260: E. Devroye, 1862.
[2] Translation of original letter in the author's possession.

Julia Wheelwright[1] died at the Hotel Cluysenaar and was buried in the Protestant Cemetery of Brussels on 22 November. The funeral service was taken by the Revd. William Drury, M.A., chaplain of St. George's.[2] Another sombre touch had been added to the Brussels scenes of Charlotte's memories, and the alien ground now held two hostages of her affections.

At home in Haworth, some weighty problems confronted Charlotte. There was not only the pressing one of the domestic reorganization of the house and her father's comfort, but Anne's health and Branwell's latest disaster. Little more than a month after their departure for Brussels, Branwell had been dismissed from his post with the railways for a default in his accounts. The actual misappropriation could not be fixed on him—it was his porter who was the real culprit—but Branwell, as chief clerk at Luddenden Foot, had been made responsible and the missing sum—£11. 1s. 7d.—deducted from his salary.[3] Since April he had been at home in a virtual state of collapse and with no prospect of further decent work.

It is surprising with what ease—as by the magic intervention of the genii of her childhood—all these problems resolved themselves without Charlotte's having to take any part in them. Emily declared it her intention to stay at home and keep house for her father; a decision which met with his cordial assent. Anne solved the seemingly insoluble problem of Branwell's unemployable state by securing for him the post of tutor with the Robinsons, where she herself was governess, while at the same time reassuring the family about her own precarious health. Even Ellen Nussey, who was pressing to see Charlotte, was placated by a prompt visit to Brookroyd and a return visit to Haworth in the short space of a month. By mid-January there appeared no longer any doubts of Charlotte's freedom to return to Brussels. Breathlessly, as she did everything in those days, she wrote Ellen on the 15th to say: 'I cannot tell precisely what day I leave home, but it will be the last week in this month', adding, with all the relief of assured victory: 'My address—Miss Brontë, Chez Mme Heger-Parent, No 32 Rue d'Isabelle, Bruxelles, Belgium. Write to me again; that's a good girl. Very soon—in a fortnight, you know—there will be no more scribbling. . . .'[4]

Her return bore all the traces of the somnambulist's compulsion. So

---

[1] Julia's obituary appeared in the *Journal de Bruxelles*, 21 Nov. 1842.
[2] Register of the United Anglican Churches, Brussels: by courtesy of the Revd. H. Isherwood.   [3] British Transport Commission Records.
[4] CB to EN, 15 Jan. 1843: *SLL* i. 253.

little was it in character to scamp the needs of others and to put her own interests first that one senses in her haste the fear that, after all, conscience might prevail.

Only *she* knew for what reason she was rushing back to Brussels. The family's very encouragement of her to go laid a further burden on her mind, but she could not have explained her qualms to them. She was driven by a force beyond her control, as she recognized when she told Ellen later: '. . . I returned to Brussels after aunt's death against my conscience, prompted by what then seemed an irresistible impulse. I was punished for my selfish folly by a total withdrawal for more than two years of happiness and peace of mind . . . .'[1]

Charlotte had reached the turning-point in her life. Without the experience of her second year in Brussels the full potentialities of her nature and genius would not have been explored. It was to be her fulfilment—not instant but gradual—without which she would not have become the woman she did nor have produced the books by which she is known.

She left home on Friday, 27 January 1843. Writing to Ellen on the following Tuesday she gave a succinct account of her journey, which she elaborated in the pages of *Villette*.

Brussels, January 30th 1843

Dear Ellen—I left Leeds for London last Friday at nine o'clock; owing to delay we did not reach London till ten at night—two hours after time. I took a cab the moment I arrived at Euston Square, and went forthwith to London Bridge Wharf. The packet lay off that wharf, and I went on board the same night. Next morning we sailed. We had a prosperous and speedy voyage, and landed at Ostend at seven o'clock next morning. I took the train at twelve and reached Rue d'Isabelle at seven in the evening. Madame Heger received me with great kindness. I am still tired with the continued excitement of three days' travelling. I had no accident, but of course some anxiety. Miss Dixon called this afternoon. Mary Taylor had told her I should be in Brussels the last week in January. You can tell Joe Taylor she looks very elegant and ladylike. I am going there on Sunday D.V. . . . Good-bye, dear. C.B.[2]

Though she returned to Brussels without Emily and without the Taylors, two factors heartened her from the outset: the kindness of Madame Heger's welcome and the friendship extended her by Mary Dixon. A letter addressed by Charlotte to Mary Dixon at this time, and hitherto unpublished, reveals her relative contentment and the bright prospects of happiness during her second year in Brussels. It confirms

[1] CB to EN, 14 Oct. 1846: *SLL* i. 339.
[2] CB to EN, 30 Jan. 1843: *SLL* i. 260.

the Hegers' kindness to her, and the interest she took in the English lessons she was giving M. Heger. It is evident that she found Mary Dixon congenial. On the envelope she wrote: 'Lest you should think that this comes from some handsome mustachioed young gent, I beg to inform you that it is from Miss Brontë, may be forwarded with propriety. C.B.'

The text reads:

My dear Miss Dixon,

I find I cannot come on Thursday; when I asked Mde Heger's leave, she said she had formed a prior engagement for me to go with herself and Mr. Heger. However I will come on Friday afternoon at two p.m. if that hour will suit you—I must be back by four as M. Heger will want his English lesson after dinner.

I surrender my unfortunate head to you with resignation—the features thereof may yield good practice as they never yet submitted to any line of regularity—but have manifested such a spirit of independence, unedifying to behold—You are mistaken however in your benevolent idea that my portrait will yield pleasure to Mary Taylor—do not give it to her, or if you do—do not expect thanks in return—she likes me well enough—but my face she can dispense with—and would tell you so in her own sincere and truthful language if you asked her.

Do not think I am quite disinterested in so readily consenting to serve you for a model—I shall have pleasure in coming and sitting with you for a little while, even though according to the custom of artists, you may not allow me to speak, or turn my head.

> I am dear Miss Dixon
> Yours sincerely,
> C. Brontë

Tuesday morning.

Do send a letter for Mary to be enclosed in your packet.[1]

At the Dixons Charlotte spent several Sundays and occasional half-holidays. In a letter of 6 March she told Ellen that the Dixons were very kind to her. 'This letter will probably go by Mr. Tom', she explained. 'Miss Dixon is certainly an elegant and accomplished person. When she leaves Brussels I shall have nowhere to go. I shall be very sorry to lose her society. . . .'[2] (This did not in fact occur till the end of June when Mary Dixon went on a trip to Germany with her brothers.)

The Dixon family, of whom Mary Taylor had written the previous autumn that they were 'the most united, affectionate family I ever met', consisted at the time of her widower uncle, Mr. Abraham Dixon, and

---

[1] Text quoted from photostat copy of original letter in Berg Coll., N.Y. Public Lib.
[2] CB to EN, 6 Mar. 1843: *SLL* i. 262.

his six children, four of whom—Abraham, Mary, George, and Tom—frequently joined him during his residences in Belgium. Born in 1779, he had married Laetitia Taylor in 1808, and was thus Mary Taylor's uncle by marriage. An inventor, he was living in Brussels and renting a house in the Rue de la Régence, in the hopes of selling his patents to the Belgian government and to the Belgian woollen manufacturers; projects that, incidentally, did not always prosper. Having recently lost his wife, his daughter Mary joined him in Brussels in the summer of 1842. She was 32 at the time, five years older than Charlotte Brontë. Tom Dixon was still studying, 'hard at work with his German' as his father reported, for which he took lessons from King Leopold's librarian in the royal palace itself.[1] George Dixon, with his elder brother Abraham, was already working for the Birmingham firm of Rabone & Company, export merchants, of which he eventually became the head, travelling to and from Belgium on the firm's behalf, which allowed both him and Tom to become the bearers of Charlotte's letters home. '. . . Mr. George Dixon will take this letter to England', Charlotte wrote Ellen on 13 October, adding: 'He is a pretty-looking and pretty-behaved young man, apparently constructed without a backbone; by which I don't allude to his corporal spine, which is all right enough, but to his character. . . .'[2] George Dixon, 23 at the time, lived to become an educational reformer and Liberal M.P., first for Birmingham, from 1867 to 1876, and later for the Edgbaston Division from 1885 until 1898, in which year he died at the age of 78.

Mary Dixon's health, always delicate, became a great cause of anxiety to Charlotte in later years, for the friendship begun in Brussels lasted undiminished. Unfortunately Mary did not keep Charlotte's letters.

From Mary Taylor, who had gone to Germany at the end of December, Charlotte heard often. She was living with a Madame Schmidt whose daughter had been at Koekelberg, and after a few months took the 'intrepid' course of teaching in a boys' school at Iserlohn in Westphalia—a step that startled Charlotte considerably. She predicted that 'opinions and custom would run strongly against what she did . . .'. But genius like Mary's, she wrote to Ellen, often 'triumphs over every obstacle without the aid of prudence . . .'. She was anxious on Mary's account, sensing that her letters 'are not the letters of a person in the enjoyment of great happiness . . .', adding the significant comparison with her own situation: '. . . She has nobody to be

1 Dixon Letters: Leeds City Museum.
2 CB to EN, 13 Oct. 1843: *W & S*, No. 165.

as good to her as M. Heger is to me; to lend her books, to converse with her sometimes, etc. . . .'.

The Wheelwrights she now saw much more often than in the previous year; as they frankly admitted to Clement Shorter later, it had been too high a price to pay to see Charlotte to have to invite Emily as well! Dr. Wheelwright lived, like Mr. Home de Bassompierre in *Villette*, in a furnished apartment in the Hotel Cluysenaar (the Hotel Crecy of the novel), the fashionable residence that accommodated scores of foreign visitors and which Charlotte, through her frequent visits to the Wheelwrights, got to know very well. It was built in 1838 by the fashionable architect Cluysenaar at the further end of the Rue Royale, in the new district growing up around the lately opened Gare du Nord. The Hotel Cluysenaar was connected by a covered way with the old Rue Notre Dame aux Neiges, where in *The Professor* Frances Henri lodged in secret penury. Charlotte's specific mention of the street and knowledge of the old decaying quarter, surprising perhaps in itself, is thus explained by her visits to the Wheelwrights living in the new quarter growing up out of the old.

The Wheelwrights[1] were people after her own heart, cultured, spiritual, and at that period far from prosperous. The bankruptcy of Mrs. Wheelwright's family bank (Ridge, Murray & Co. of Chichester), coinciding with Dr. Wheelwright's declining eyesight in 1842, had decided the family to sell up their home in South Place and, like many another English family of the time, recoup their fortunes by living on the Continent. Mrs. Wheelwright, the daughter of a Unitarian banker, William Ridge, had been brought up as a Unitarian, but after marriage with Mr. Wheelwright (whose mother had been a Quaker) the whole family was 'converted' to the Church of England. Her 'sweet disposition and saintly character' impressed all those who knew her, Charlotte Brontë among them. With people of such integrity she could be at ease, reading or sewing with Mrs. Wheelwright and the girls, listening intently to Dr. Wheelwright's liberal conversation and feeling herself free to take part in it. Even more self-effacing in company than Lucy Snowe, Charlotte's role in the Wheelwright circle can well be pictured from the comparable scenes in *Villette*.

Their views on the Belgians were identical. They detested all their ways with insular ferocity though, to do Charlotte justice, she admitted their cleanliness (which the Wheelwrights denied), remarking on the sparkling brightness of their window-panes, the complexion of the

[1] For the Wheelwright family see J. J. Green, op. cit.; *BST*, 1913; Chadwick.

women, the crisp freshness of their frocks. 'They are very dirty here,' declared young Fanny Wheelwright, 'they never wash themselves, they are disgusting and I do not like them, they are like pigs, they are greedy!' The travelling English of the nineteenth century, of whom Thackeray was one, took with them an unshakeable sense of their own superiority in every walk of life. It seemed to prevent them casting more than a superficial glance on the surface of life abroad. Of its depths and meaning they remained wholly incurious and ignorant.

Visiting Brussels at the very time Charlotte was there, Thackeray wrote:

Early the next morning we walked through a number of streets in the place, and saw certain sights. The park is very pretty, and all the buildings round about it have an air of neatness—almost of stateliness. The houses are tall, the streets spacious, and the roads extremely clean. In the park is a little theatre, a cafe somewhat ruinous, a little palace for the king of this little kingdom, some smart public buildings (with S.P.Q.B. emblazoned on them, at which pompous inscription we cannot help laughing) and other rows of houses somewhat resembling a little Rue de Rivoli. Whether from my own natural greatness and magnanimity, or from that handsome share of national conceit that every Englishman possesses, my impressions of this city are certainly anything but respectful. It has an absurd kind of Lilliput look with it....[1]

In considering Charlotte's antipathy to the Belgians the general Anglo-Saxon attitude of the time must be kept in mind; the point is of importance when judging the rights and wrongs of some of her accounts of life at the Pensionnat Heger. In her case, however, the prejudice was not the effect of a too superficial view of the foreign life around her, but of the depth and intensity of feelings roused by her first experience of love. This is nowhere more apparent than in the lyrical invocation to Belgium with which she prefaced the Brussels chapters in *The Professor*, and which are in no way a tribute to the country but rather a tribute to one of that country's sons!

. . . Belgium ! name unromantic and unpoetic, yet name that whenever uttered has in my ear a sound, in my heart an echo, such as no other assemblage of syllables, however sweet or classic, can produce. Belgium!...It stirs my world of the past like a summons to resurrection; the graves unclose, the dead are raised; thoughts, feelings, memories that slept, are seen by me ascending from the clod—haloed most of them—.[2]

---

[1] Thackeray, 'Little Travels and Roadside Sketches': *Fraser's Magazine*, May, 1844.
[2] *The Professor*, ch. 7.

On her return to the pensionnat her new status in the school as its English teacher was marked by her being called 'Mlle Charlotte'. This was enforced by M. Heger not only because it was a rule of the school, but because it gave her a needed authority with the girls who had so recently been her fellow pupils. Her salary was fixed at £16 per annum. The modesty of this figure has been instanced by various biographers as an example of the way Charlotte was exploited by her foreign employers; but the truth is that teachers' salaries were generally low at the time. M. Heger himself had begun at the Athénée at a basic salary of £20 per annum. It must also be remembered that Charlotte was not a full-time teacher and that she received lessons in French in return for her services. Admittedly she had to pay for her German coaching and found it expensive, the German teacher, Mlle Mühl, charging her as much singly per hour as she had Charlotte and Emily together in the previous year: 10 francs a month. Charlotte had, furthermore, to pay her own laundry (5 francs a month). Writing home for money at the end of May she had to explain the request and added that these various outlays 'made havoc in £16 per annum'.[1]

By the terms of her aunt's will, proved in the prerogative court of York on 28 December 1842, Charlotte benefited by a fourth part of her aunt's total estate, valued at under £1,500. She had, therefore, for the first time in her life a little capital to draw upon.

However modest her salary it allowed her to have several dresses made during her stay abroad, of which the bills are preserved. Both the cheapness and the perfection of cut of foreign dressmakers much impressed Charlotte; she unreservedly admired the girls' school uniform on all occasions, whether on fête-days or ordinary working days. '. . . The clean fresh print dress, and the light straw bonnet,' she wrote of their summer attire, 'each made and trimmed, as the French workwoman alone can make and trim, so as to unite the utterly unpretending with the perfectly becoming. . . . Nobody flaunted in faded silk; nobody wore a second-hand best article. . . .'[2]

Realizing her new isolation among strangers now that Emily was gone, the Hegers offered Charlotte the free run of their own sitting-room, urging her to join them there of an evening when the day's work was done and they could relax 'en famille'. The offer touched her and presumably she availed herself of it once or twice, but it irked her to encroach on their intimacy and she quickly gave up going.

[1] CB to EJB, 29 May 1843: *SLL* i. 267–8.
[2] *Villette*, ch. 33. See also Frederika Macdonald, *The Secret of Charlotte Brontë*.

She told Ellen on 6 March:

... As I told you before, M. & Madame Heger are the only two persons in the house for whom I really experience regard and esteem and, of course, I cannot always be with them, nor even often. They told me, when I first returned, that I was to consider their sitting-room my sitting-room also, and to go there whenever I was not engaged in the school-room. This, however, I cannot do. In the day-time it is a public room, where music masters and mistresses are constantly passing in and out; and in the evening I will not and ought not to intrude on M. and Madame Heger and their children. Thus I am a good deal by myself out of school-hours; but that does not signify ...[1]

The cause of the unmistakable note of sadness here, the first to creep into her accounts of life in this second year abroad, was not yet even suspected by herself. She attributed it to her solitude among strangers for whom, with the declared exception of two, she had no liking. But it arose just as much from the few happy contacts she had among them, the rare pleasures whose very intensity made the *absence* of them pain.

Ever since her return to the pensionnat one of her duties was to give English lessons to M. Heger and the brother-in-law of his late wife M. Chapelle, a duty which brought her into a totally different relationship with the man whom hitherto she had only known as a master. In the reversed roles he could allow himself full outlet for his natural ebullience, the vivacity and cheerfulness that was as much a part of his nature as the ferocity and gloom; he could in fact be charming. Charlotte, on the other hand, in the role of teacher, could give the full measure of her mind which, as the shy scholar struggling to express herself in a foreign tongue, she had never yet been able to do in his presence. Both enjoyed the exchange. The company of the two brothers-in-law, moreover, brought Charlotte into a closer understanding of M. Heger's personal life. M. Chapelle was married to a sister of M. Heger's first wife, the Marie-Josephine he had lost so tragically as a young man, and undoubtedly it was at this period that Charlotte learnt to know his feelings on this and many other subjects, not only relating to his life but to his tastes and opinions. It was now that he began regularly to lend her books, those surprising loans that she often only found on opening her desk after dark in the deserted schoolroom, accompanied sometimes by cryptic little notes, and always by the tell-tale whiff of his cigar. Then, for a little while, she was happy, moved to her heart's core by his kindness.

Utterly unselfconscious as he was in all his actions and beliefs he was

[1] CB to EN, 6 Mar. 1843: op. cit.

not embarrassed to discuss with her quite openly the tenets of the Catholic religion, to which, she gradually learnt, he held not in bigotry but in genuine love of God and his fellow men. Not from his own lips certainly, but perhaps from M. Chapelle's (he was a pianist, a man of fine and sensitive feelings), she learnt of his many charitable activities, inquiring into needy cases and distributing charitable trusts. To read M. Heger's personal correspondence with certain wealthy and charitable patrons who relied on him to bring cases of genuine desert to their knowledge is to realize a side of his character that must have appealed intensely to Charlotte Brontë. The picture she had formed of him at the beginning became strangely modified. He was not an easy man to know; his passions and prejudices were mostly beyond his control. But in the long run his single-mindedness and truth had to prevail. There was no suppressing them.

That she was not the only one to be mistaken by first appearances emerges from the accounts of many of his pupils. Charlotte knew better than they how to describe what she saw, however, as a comparison of the following passages shows.

. . . A little dark man he certainly was, pungent and austere. Even to me he seemed a harsh apparition, with his close-shorn, black head, his broad, sallow brow, his thin cheek, his wide and quivering nostril, his thorough glance and hurried bearing. Irritable he was; one heard that, as he apostrophised with vehemence the awkward squad under his orders. . . .[1]

. . . M. Heger is a very serious-minded man; on first impressions one would think him very hard, cold and uncommunicative, wrote a former intimate of the household, the Baronne de Willmar in 1846; that would be a mistake; M. Heger, like all learned men has a preoccupied air; nevertheless, he is more than ready to do kindnesses. . . . He has very great qualities under that rather cold exterior; he has a will of iron and a really creative genius; he writes admirably and has as much talent as he has modesty. . . .[2]

Of the other facets of his nature, the childlike simplicity and gaiety that Charlotte noted among the storms and thunders of the daily round, there is abundant evidence from other sources. 'He had a naturally gay and enthusiastic character and a remarkably alert intelligence. His generosity was inexhaustible and discreet.'[3]

Charlotte wrote to Ellen Nussey of the new stimulus of the English lessons: '. . . I now regularly give English lessons to M. Heger and his

[1] *Villette*, ch. 14.   [2] Willmar, *Souvenirs de Bruxelles*, 1846: op. cit.
[3] Auguste Slosse, *Paul Heger*, Éditions de l'Université.

brother-in-law, M. Chapelle. They get on with wonderful rapidity, especially the first. He already begins to speak English very decently. If you could see and hear the efforts I make to teach them to pronounce like Englishmen, and their unavailing attempts, you would laugh to all eternity. . . .'[1]

Delightful as the fresh intimacy was, the lessons were also frustrating. For the more she fed upon the pleasure of his company and friendship, the more she realized what little claim she had to either. Never, outside her own family, had she known a mind like his; probing, daring, disputing, ranging through history with a zest for knowledge equal to her own, and with gifts of eloquence and memory that left her envious whilst full of admiration.

> . . . I have said that, for myself, I had no impromptu faculty, and perhaps that very deficiency made me marvel the more at one who possessed it in perfection. M. Emanuel was not a man to write books; but I have heard him lavish, with careless, unconscious prodigality, such mental wealth as books seldom boast; his mind was indeed my library, and whenever it was opened to me, I entered bliss. . . .[2]

The bliss was Janus-faced, like the old masks of Comedy and Tragedy. The more she tasted it the more she craved, and soon *not* to be in his company was torment. To be relegated to the secondary role of employee, when at times she could be the confidante of his expansive moods, was almost too bitter to be borne—however absurd the claim. But she knew that it was absurd. It was this that made her forgo the Heger's sitting-room in the evening, rather than any feeling of delicacy about encroaching on the family privacy.

The sight of his absorption in family-life could rouse feelings so rebellious and searing that she would rather endure loneliness than provoke them. Unable for many months to diagnose them for what they were—a jealousy such as Madame Heger never knew—their suppression almost unhinged her. How little guarded she was against the consequences of such propinquity is best understood perhaps by the realization that M. Heger in no way corresponded to Charlotte's ideal man. He was no Zamorna, as her first descriptions of him attest, though with time he acquired the essential characteristics of her youthful hero. And had he not been the 'small spare man in spectacles' of her first encounter, she might have been more upon her guard against the perils of their daily intercourse.

[1] CB to EN, 6 Mar. 1843: op. cit.   [2] *Villette*, ch. 33.

It was only too probable that a girl like Charlotte, bred on the most extravagant romantic poetry, should one day come to dedicate her whole heart and imagination to the service of just such an unrequited and unrecognized love—however she was guarded against it by all the principles and precepts in which she had been reared. But though unrecognized by her, and still more so by its object, it was not long unrecognized by Madame Heger. A great part of Charlotte's bewilderment and ultimate rancour was to come from the subtle change this recognition occasioned in Madame Heger's attitude to her. Not that Madame Heger felt jealousy, either then or later. She had confidence in her husband. But she was genuinely shocked by the intensity of feeling that Charlotte only partially succeeded in hiding, and she was concerned too at the threat to her domestic calm and to the good conduct of her school. No betrayal of romantic feeling for any of the masters in this convent-like establishment could be tolerated: and it would have to lead to the departure of one or other of the parties immediately. That the romantic feeling should be entertained for the Principal's husband was unthinkable. But the complicating factor for Madame Heger was that the young woman was an employee and a stranger, and could not be dismissed without scandal. To avoid that—and to avoid undue hardship—became Madame Heger's principal problem that spring and summer of 1843.

While the happiness lasted (just so long as no inkling of its origin had touched Madame Heger's mind) all was well for Charlotte. Writing to Ellen of Mary Taylor's loneliness in her German school, she said: '. . . her letters are not the letters of a person in the enjoyment of great happiness. She has nobody to be as good to her as M. Heger is to me; to lend her books, to converse with her sometimes, etc. . . .'[1] Among the etceteras must be numbered his taking her and one of the pupils into town to see the Carnival, which she mentioned in the same letter. Ash Wednesday, the end of Carnival, fell that year on 1 March, and writing on the 6th she said:

The Carnival is just over, and we have entered into the gloom and abstinence of Lent. The first day of Lent we had coffee without milk for breakfast; vinegar and vegetables, with a very little salt fish, for dinner; and bread for supper. The Carnival was nothing but masking and mummery. M. Heger took me and one of the pupils into town to see the masks. It was amusing to see the immense crowds, and the general gaiety, but the masks were nothing. . . .[1]

[1] CB to EN, 6 Mar. 1843: op. cit.

March 11th was the feast of St. Constantin, M. Heger's patronal day. Charlotte delightfully described in *Villette* how such a fête was kept in a large Catholic school. The incident of the watch-guard may very well be pure fiction, but the presentation of bouquets of flowers by the whole school, from the youngest to the eldest, was a general custom it needed no invention to describe.[1]

M. Heger's whole career would attest to his love of young children. Charlotte noted as a point in his favour his discrimination between the pretentious ignorance of grown girls and the genuine ignorance of children, for which he had untiring patience. His 'heart *did* speak sometimes,' she wrote in *Villette*, 'though an irritable, it was not an ossified organ; in its core was a place, tender beyond man's tenderness; a place that humbled him with little children, that bound him to girls and women . . . on the whole he was better with them than with his own sex . . .'.[2]

In 1853, just ten years after Charlotte's schooldays in Brussels, M. Heger, who had begun as master of the lowest form at the Athénée— the 7th Class as it is in continental schools—and who had gradually climbed the academic ladder through the 4th to the 3rd Classes as French master and master of mathematics, was at last appointed Principal of the school—'Préfet des Etudes', as the title went. After only two years he resigned the much-coveted position because he disliked the directives imposed by a new minister of education, and the loss of contact with his pupils which the predominantly administrative role of principal required of him. But above all because he realized that his main value as a teacher was in teaching the very young. Towards them his patience was infinite, his kindness inexhaustible, his technique infallible. Not only did he resign as Principal, but he asked to return to his infants in the 7th Class. Answering the amazed comments of his colleagues and friends at such a decision in the very moment of success, he said laughingly: 'Si je suis supérieur, c'est dans les classes inférieures.' (If I am superior [as a teacher] it is in the lowest forms.)[3]

The comment of a friend on this occasion is illuminating. 'I think', he wrote to a mutual friend, 'that our friend has done wisely—He excels in interesting and stimulating children . . . he has too much warmth of heart and too much zest not to be discouraged in the daily contacts

---

[1] *Villette*, ch. 29.
[2] Idem.
[3] *L'Indépendance Belge*, 9 mai 1896.

with sceptics who only look for utility in education, with a lot of ambitious climbers who are only out for money. . . .[1]

Charlotte's letters written between the 1 April and 29 May hide as much as they reveal of the causes of the gradual deterioration in her relationships with the Hegers. She told Emily in the last of the letters that she was quite unable to guess at Mme Heger's reasons for no longer liking her, which shows the degree of her self-deception even at so advanced a date.

Yet the first letter of the series written to Ellen on 1 April, dealing squarely with the theme of love and marriage, shows sufficiently in what direction her thoughts had recently been forced. She advocates the repression of all facile hopes of happiness for women 'who have neither fortune nor beauty', who would 'make marriage the principal object of their wishes': this is too bitter not to proceed from personal sentiment. Something more than Ellen Nussey's foolish repetition of gossip had roused Charlotte. She was reviewing her own position and her own un-lovely prospects.

. . . There was an observation in your last letter [she wrote], which excited, for a moment, my wrath. At first I thought it would be folly to reply to it, and I would let it die. Afterwards I determined to give one answer, once for all. 'Three or four people' it seems, 'have the idea that the future époux of Mademoiselle Brontë is on the Continent'. These people are wiser than I am. They could not believe that I crossed the sea merely to return as teacher to Madame Heger's. I must have some more powerful motive than respect for my master and mistress, gratitude for their kindnesses, etc., to induce me to refuse a salary of £50 in England and accept one of £16 in Belgium. I must, forsooth, have some remote hope of entrapping a husband somehow, or somewhere. If these charitable people knew the total seclusion of the life I lead—that I never exchange a word with any other man than Monsieur Heger, and seldom indeed with him—they would perhaps cease to suppose that any such chimerical and groundless notion had influenced my proceedings. Have I said enough to clear myself of so silly an imputation? Not that it is a crime to marry, or a crime to wish to be married; but it is an imbecility, which I reject with contempt, for women, who have neither fortune nor beauty, to make marriage the principal object of their wishes . . . not to be able to convince themselves that they are unattractive, and that they had better be quiet, and think of other things than wedlock. . . .[2]

Mary Taylor, supplying Mrs. Gaskell with what recollections she

[1] Papiers Villermont II. A 38, by courtesy of the comte de Villermont.
[2] CB to EN, 1 Apr. 1843: *W & S*, No. 155, quoted from photostat of original in Henry Huntington Lib., San Marino.

could of Charlotte's schooldays in Brussels, had this to say of Charlotte's preoccupation with her future:

> ... The first part of her time at Brussels was not uninteresting. She spoke of new people and characters, and foreign ways of the pupils and teachers. She knew the hopes and prospects of the teachers, and mentioned one who was very anxious to marry, 'she was getting so old'. She used to get her father or brother (I forget which) to be the bearer of letters to different single men, who she thought might be persuaded to do her the favour, saying that her only recourse was to become a sister of charity if her present employment failed, and that she hated the idea. Charlotte naturally looked with curiosity to people of her own condition. This woman almost frightened her. 'She declares there is nothing she can turn to, and laughs at the idea of delicacy—and she is only ten years older than I am! . . . Well, Polly, I should hate being a sister of charity' '. . . She said she did not know how people could bear the constant pressure of misery. . . .' I promised her a better destiny than to go begging anyone to marry her, or to lose her natural feelings as a sister of charity. She said, 'My youth is leaving me; I can never do better than I have done, and I have done nothing yet. . . .'[1]

Deeply stirred as Charlotte would increasingly be at the lot of the unmarried and impecunious woman—rejoicing with those like Miss Wooler who achieved a competence and could afford to enjoy their retirement—it was in Brussels, in the constant presence of the complacent married woman, and that woman the wife of the man she loved and the mother of his children, that Charlotte's first rebellious feelings were aroused. Still, even now, comparing her position with what it had been at Mrs. Sidgwick's or Mrs. White's, she could write to Ellen that she 'was thankful'.

August 15th, the end of the school year, would normally have brought Charlotte home again. For Madame Heger it was the hoped-for solution; but as time passed, Charlotte found any such decision increasingly difficult to make. This is shown by a comment from Emily. Profiting by an opportunity to send a letter free to Charlotte through Ellen, Emily wrote to her on 22 May: '. . . Charlotte has never entioned a word about coming home. If you would go over for half a year, perhaps you might be able to bring her back with you, otherwise she might vegetate there till the age of Methusalah for mere lack of courage to face the voyage. . . .'[2]

---

[1] MT to Mrs. G, *SLL*: op. cit.
[2] EJB to EN, 22 May 1843: *SLL* i. 265.

The first avowal of a changing and deteriorating relationship with the Hegers as distinct from the rest of the household was contained in a letter to Branwell written on 1 May. Branwell's carelessness over correspondence, his increasing loss of interest in the home-circle, made it in some ways easier for Charlotte to be frank with him than with either Emily or Ellen. There is a disillusioned tone throughout the letter that shows Charlotte with her guard down. The letter, with its sad evocation of their former partnership in creation, of the Angrian ghosts that had haunted their childhood, is doubly sad when it is realized that it marked the end, not only of their joint creative urge, but of the love that had bound them in their brilliant childhood. Already the sense of Branwell's growing indifference was adding to her bitterness of heart.

Brussels. May 1st 1843

Dear B—I hear you have written a letter to me; this letter however as usual, I have never received, which I am exceedingly sorry for, as I have wished very much to hear from you. Are you sure that you put the right address and that you paid the English postage, 1s. 6d.? Without that, letters are never forwarded. I heard from papa a day or two since—all appears to be going on reasonably well at home—I grieve only that Emily is so solitary but however you and Anne will soon be returning for the holidays which will cheer the house for a time.

Are you in better health and spirits, and does Anne continue to be pretty well? I understand papa has been to see you. Did he seem cheerful and well? Mind when you write to me you answer these questions, as I wish to know. Also give me a detailed account as to how you get on with your pupil and the rest of the family. I have received a general assurance that you do well and are in good odour, but I want to know particulars.

As for me, I am very well and wag on as usual. I perceive, however, that I grow exceedingly misanthropic and sour—You will say that this is no news, and that you never knew me possessed of the contrary qualities—philanthropy and sugarinesss. 'Das ist wahr' (which being translated means, that is true); but the fact is, the people here are no go whatsoever. Amongst 120 persons who compose the daily population of this house, I can discern only one or two who deserve anything like regard. This is not owing to foolish fastidiousness on my part, but to the absence of decent qualities on theirs. They have not intellect or politeness or good-nature or good-feeling. They are nothing. I don't hate them—hatred would be too warm a feeling. They have no sensations themselves and they excite none. But one wearies from day to day of caring nothing, doing nothing—yes, I teach and sometimes get red in the face with impatience at their stupidity. But don't think I ever scold or fly into a passion. If I spoke warmly, as warmly as I sometimes used to do at Roe Head, they would think me mad. Nobody ever gets into a passion here. Such a thing is not known. The phlegm that thickens their blood is too gluey to boil. They are very false in their relations with each other, but they rarely quarrel, and friendship is folly they are unacquainted with. The black Swan, M. Heger, is the only sole veritable exception to this rule (for Madame, always cool, and always reasoning, is not quite an exception). But I rarely speak to Monsieur now, for not being a pupil I have little or nothing to do with him. From time to time he shows his kind-heartedness by loading me with books, so that I am still indebted to him for all the pleasure or amusement I have. Except for the total want of companionship I have nothing to complain of. I have not too much to do, sufficient liberty, and I am rarely interfered with. I lead an easeful, stagnant, silent life, for which, when I think of Mrs. Sidgwick, I ought to be very thankful. Be sure you write to me soon, and beg Anne to inclose a small billet in the same letter; it will be a real charity to do me this kindness. Tell me everything you can think of.

It is a curious metaphysical fact that always in the evening when I am in the great dormitory alone, having no other company than a number of beds with white curtains, I always recur as fanatically as ever to the old ideas, the old faces, and the old scenes in the world below. Give my love to Anne, and believe me

YOURN!

Dear Anne,—Write to me,—Your affectionate Schwester,

C.B.

Mr. Heger has just been in and given me a little German Testament as a present. I was surprised, for since a good many days he has hardly spoken to me.[1]

How her feelings were made to fluctuate between disillusionment and delight, appears in the postscript to this letter; after the bitterness of the confession of the loss of M. Heger's goodwill, she could not forbear adding it. In the flyleaf of the little German Testament—now in the Brontë Parsonage Museum—she wrote in gothic script: 'Herr Heger hat mir dieses Buch gegeben, Brüssel, Mai 1843. C.B.'

To Branwell she had referred to M. Heger as 'the black swan', Juvenal's groping definition of the rarest of rare birds. To analyse him more closely was already beyond her capacity: he was as he was, different to anyone she had ever met.

The English lessons with M. Heger had evidently already ceased. They could not have been discontinued because of the proficiency of the pupils, however rapid the learning she had ascribed to them.

[1] CB to PBB, 1 May 1843: Ashley Lib. B.M.

The most likely reason was an intervention by Madame Heger herself, and because this could not be done openly Charlotte would be all the more likely to suspect her of it. The course of events from now until Charlotte's departure at the end of the year suggest that Madame Heger had one policy in mind, a policy in perfect keeping with her known management of the school—the avoidance of scandal. There was to be no visible or vocal clash of wills, no open rupture. No suspicion of the English teacher's feelings for her master must reach the other teachers and the 90-odd children that composed the busy cheerful little world of the pensionnat; above all, no suspicion must reach M. Heger himself. To avoid this, all direct intercourse between M. Heger and Miss Brontë had to be prevented. For fiercely as Miss Brontë repressed her feelings, she was a woman whose soul glowed in her eyes and whose suffering cried out even through tight-shut lips. Knowing her husband's dislike of tears, and his direct searching way with anyone unhappy around him, Madame had everything to fear from opportunities for *éclaircissements* between the two. The only certain way of stopping such a thing was by keeping them apart. That in achieving her aim of keeping Charlotte's uncontrollable misery out of M. Heger's sight, Madame resorted to some of those devious ways of which Charlotte accused her in the end, can neither be proved nor wholly discredited. The situation was not an easy one for Madame Heger. By all accounts —from family, friends, pupils—she was an upright and charitable woman accustomed to dealing with a large school with no harsher measures than a grave reproof. Miss Brontë, however, was no child to be reproved, or recompensed with a 'bon-bon' or an extra good mark for her work. She was a woman of 27, with exceptionally complex feelings and sensibilities, vulnerable to pain as few adults are vulnerable, secretive and proud. Even if Madame Heger had felt so inclined she could not have spoken to Charlotte without outraging her pride and bringing upon herself the odium of harbouring thoughts unworthy of a lady. The very frankness Charlotte accused Madame Heger of *not* possessing was made impossible by the very nature of the case: for, of the three principals involved, only *one* was fully awake to what was going on. Madame Heger cannot be blamed for having greater insight than Charlotte or her husband; her nature was simply different from theirs. Nor can she be blamed for hesitating to rouse them to a consciousness of the danger lying ahead. She was obliged therefore to use methods that very likely appeared underhand to Charlotte, in order to isolate Charlotte both from her master and from her fellow teachers. She was prepared to watch over her privacy, and Charlotte did not hesitate to call this spying.

By 29 May, when Charlotte partially opened her heart in a letter to Emily, she was convinced that Madame Heger was employing the French teacher, Mlle Blanche, as a spy; that Madame disliked her and had succeeded in turning Monsieur against her. But *for what reason* all this suspicion was directed against her, she declared herself unable to guess, so little were her own feelings clear to her.

> . . . Things wag on much as usual here. Only Mlle Blanche and Madlle Haussé are at present on a system of war without quarter. They hate each other like cats. Mdlle Blanche frightens Mdlle Haussé by her white passions (for they quarrel venomously). Mdlle Haussé complains that when Mdlle Blanche is in a fury 'elle n'a pas de lèvres'. I find also that Mdlle Sophie dislikes Mdlle Blanche extremely. She says she is heartless, insincere, and vindictive, which epithets, I assure you, are richly deserved. Also I find she is the regular spy of Mme Heger, to whom she reports everything. Also she invents—which I should not have thought. I have now the entire charge of the English lessons. I have given two lessons to the first class... I am richly off for companionship in these parts. Of late days, M. and Mme Heger rarely speak to me, and I really don't pretend to care a fig for any body else in the establishment. You are not to suppose by that expression that I am under the influence of *warm* affection for Mde. Heger. I am convinced she does not like me—why, I can't tell, nor do I think she herself has any definite reason for the aversion; but for one thing, she cannot comprehend why I do not make friends of Mesdames Blanche, Sophie, and Haussé. M. Heger is wondrously influenced by Madame, and I should not wonder if he disapproves very much of my unamiable want of sociability. He has already given me a brief lecture on universal 'bienveillance' and, perceiving that I don't improve in consequence, I fancy he has taken to considering me as a person to be let alone—left to the error of her ways; and consequently he has in a great measure withdrawn the light of his countenance, and I get on from day to day in a Robinson-Crusoe-like condition—very lonely. That does not signify. In other respects I have nothing substantial to complain of, nor is even this a cause for complaint. Except the loss of M. Heger's goodwill (if I have lost it) I care for none of 'em. . . .[1]

Within a few days of writing this letter, however, in which for the first time she recognized hostility in Madame Heger's attitude to her, she was writing a little note to Ellen in German in which, recapitulating her reasons for returning to Brussels and the inevitable heartache of

[1] CB to EJB, 29 May 1843: *SLL* i. 267–8.

living among strangers, she added: '. . . I have, however, the great good fortune, to live with a lady who is very good to me. . . .'[1]

Charlotte was perhaps showing more self-control, was even perhaps a little less unhappy and hence less dangerous in Madame Heger's sight. It was Whitsun, and on Whit Sunday Charlotte went for a walk into the country with Mlle Haussé and three of the pupils, an obvious effort at sociability on her part. She did not, in any case, dislike or distrust Mlle Haussé as she did Mlle Blanche. She was, rather, an object of humorous observation. The portrait of her as Hortense Moore in 'Shirley' was so lifelike that the Wheelwright girls, reading the book years later, exclaimed at the resemblance. It was, indeed, this clue in the book that made them guess the identity of Currer Bell and renew their contact with Charlotte Brontë.[2] Mlle Haussé's self-satisfied complacency, delightfully portrayed in Hortense Moore, would be vastly gratified, one suspects, at 'Mees Charlotte' being willing to accompany her upon an outing. What better opportunity for exhibiting her own superior knowledge of the Brussels countryside than by acting guide to this somewhat truculent foreigner? Especially as the object of their walk, outlined in Charlotte's letter, was probably the summer Palace of Laeken, a building of historic and architectural beauty upon whose vicissitudes of fortune under the French Revolution and Napoleon Mlle Haussé could expatiate at length. They subscribed to the agreeable Belgian custom of taking 'gouter' out of doors and strolled home along the banks of the canal and down the fashionable 'Allée Verte', watching the elegant world ride by in its splendid carriages. In many a reference in *Villette* and *The Professor*, Charlotte confessed to the pleasure she had experienced in such outings into the Brussels countryside.

Unaccustomed as she was to the heat, she paid for the pleasure by catching cold, and had to remain indoors on the Whit Monday holiday.

Bruxel 5 Juin (1843)

Meine Liebe Freundinn — Du hast ohne Zweifel gehört dasz ich nach Belgium wieder gekehert bin. Es machte mir schmerz mein Vaterland zu verlassen, aber, wie du wohl weiszt, wenn mann nicht reich iszt, kann man nicht immer zu Haus bleiben, man musz in die Welt gehen und trachten mit Arbeitsamkeit und Erwerbsamkeit zu verdienen diese Unabhängigkeit, die dasz Glück ausgeschlagen hat. Oftmals, wenn man von seinen Aeltern entfernt ist, hat man viel Kummer und Leiden, weil man nicht die selbe Gunst und das selbe Vergnugen unter Fremden finden kann, wie in der einzigen

[1] CB to EN, draft letter in German dated 5 June 1843: Berg Coll., N.Y. Pub. Lib.
[2] J. J. Green, op. cit.

Familie; allein ich habe das grosse Glück, bei einer Dame die mir sehr gut ist zu wohnen.

Sonntag und Montag waren-zwei Tage Ferien. An Sonntag bin ich spazieren gewesen, mit Fräulein Haussé und drei der Schülerinnen; wir haben auf dem Lande gespeiszt, und des Abends sind wir durch die grüne Allee nach Haus gegangen. Da sahen wir viele Wagen und eine Menge Herren und Damen sehr geputz. Montag bin ich nicht ausgegangen, denn ich hatte den Schnupfen bekommen. Heute iszt es wieder classe und, weil wir unsere beschäftigungen anfangen mussen, so habe ich nicht viel Zeit dir zu schreiben. Ich bin deine Freundinn, C. Bronte.[1]

From Branwell there was no answer to her letter—as she told Emily on 29 May—and the dearth of news from home added further to her low spirits. She wrote to her father on 2 June:

. . . I was very glad to hear from home. I had begun to get low-spirited at not receiving any news, and to entertaining indefinite fears that something was wrong—You do not say anything about your health, but I hope you are well, and Emily also. I am afraid she will have a good deal of hard work to do now that Hannah is gone. [Hannah Brown then aged 10 and engaged at the parsonage.] I am exceedingly glad to hear that you still keep Tabby—It is an act of great charity to her, and do not think it will be unrewarded, for she is very faithful, and will always serve you, when she has occasion, to the best of her abilities; besides, she will be company for Emily, who, without her —would be very lonely—[2]

From then on a steady decline in cheerfulness and health marks her correspondence. Necessarily rare, because of their expense, her letters became rarer still with the departure of the Dixons and Taylors who had been her regular intermediaries. She withdrew more and more into herself as summer advanced, concentrating the whole force of her analytical mind on her personal predicament. The more she suffered, the more she saw nothing but enemies about her.

The resolution to put an end to her misery was still, however, beyond her capacity; she stayed on, although everything that had made the pensionnat pleasant was now withdrawn from her. She was no longer M. Heger's pupil, and he was no longer hers. More bitter still, the trust and friendship that had sprung up between them was undermined. Whatever the cause, he no longer freely sought her in her rare moments of leisure. The fact that he was 'wondrously influenced' by his wife

---

[1] CB's letter in German to EN dated 5 June 1843: Berg. Coll., N.Y. Public Lib.
[2] CB to Mr. Brontë: *W & S* i.

only added gall to the wormwood. For Charlotte, since she no longer enjoyed his open friendship and esteem, the rest of the world was turned to dust and ashes. Of the 120 persons who composed 'the daily population of this house', as she told Branwell, not one was worth anything to her—lacking the confidence of M. Heger.

It was in a state of mind bordering on panic that she saw the *grandes vacances* approach. Neither capable of breaking away, nor hopeful of any improvement in her relations with the only person who now mattered to her, she viewed the inevitable loneliness and dearth of occupation which the holidays must bring with dismay.

She wrote Ellen on 6 August reproaching her with not answering her last letter:

. . . I forewarn you I am in low spirits, earth and heaven are dreary and empty to me at this moment. In a few days our vacation will begin; everybody is joyous and animated at the prospect, because everybody is to go home. I know that I am to stay here during the five weeks that the holidays last, and that I shall be much alone . . . and consequently get downcast, and find both days and nights of a weary length. It is the first time in my life that I have really dreaded the vacation . . . Alas! I can hardly write, I have such a dreary weight at my heart; and I do so wish to go home. Is this not childish? Pardon me, for I cannot help it. . . . Would that the vacation were well over! it will pass so slowly. Do have the Christian charity to write me a long, long letter. . . . Do not think it is because people are unkind to me that I wish to leave Belgium; nothing of the sort. Everybody is abundantly civil, but homesickness keeps creeping over me. I cannot shake it off. . . .[1]

On the very day that school broke up, on 15 August that customarily ushered in the holidays in Catholic schools, two things happened to bring Charlotte a revival of happiness. She received proof that M. Heger had not forgotten her. He gave her as a personal present, to occupy the lonely days ahead, the works of Bernardin de S. Pierre in a two-volume edition. As with the little German Testament, she recorded the fact by writing on the fly-leaf of the first volume: 'The Gift of Monsieur Heger, Brussels, August 15th 1843.'

For M. Heger 15 August that year was a particularly busy day, as it fell to him to give the Speech-day Address at the Athénée Royal, a duty—and an honour—that occurred twice in his career. The burgomaster of Brussels and one of the Echevins (aldermen) always attended the function and distributed the palms to the prize-winners.

[1] CB to EN, 6 Aug. 1843: *SLL* i. 268–9.

M. Heger's speech on the occasion, later printed, was another of the personal gifts made to Charlotte.[1]

On the same day, a holiday not only in the schools but an annual public holiday as well, marking the Assumption of the Virgin, a concert was given in the park at 10 o'clock in the evening which it seems likely Charlotte attended. In chapter 38 of *Villette*, where Lucy Snowe under the strong opiate administered by Madame Beck, wanders out into the streets of the city at night, and finds herself in the midst of a great throng of holiday-makers, Charlotte recorded very exactly the scene that took place in the royal park of Brussels on 15 August 1843. The scene, one of the most vividly presented in the whole book, for all its dream-like quality of vision, is full of precise details and topographical indications, which show not only Charlotte's general familiarity with the broad walks, alleys, groves, and shrubberies of the Parc but also, by certain additional touches, that she had visited the Parc on that particular evening.

In the *Journal de Bruxelles* of 14 August appeared the advance notice of the Serenade Concert to be given in the 'Wauxhall' enclosure of the Parc on the following evening, when the chief attraction in the programme would be the performance by a German mixed choir—the 'Liedertafel' under the direction of its conductor, M. Girschner, then on a visit to Brussels. Among the five items advertised to be sung was a 'Jagd Chor' (a 'Chœur de Chasseurs' as the paper explained), which was precisely the feature of the evening's programme that Charlotte remembered in *Villette*.

. . . That festal night would have been safe for a very child. Half the peasantry had come in from the outlying environs of Villette, and the decent burghers were all abroad and around, dressed in their best. My straw hat passed amidst cap and jacket, short petticoat and long calico mantle, without, perhaps, attracting a glance. . . .

Safe I passed down the avenues—safe I mixed with the crowd where it was deepest. . . .

My vague aim, as I went, was to find the stone basin, with its clear depth and green lining; of that coolness and verdure I thought, with the passionate thirst of unconscious fever. Amidst the glare, and hurry, and throng, and noise, I still secretly and chiefly longed to come on that circular mirror of crystal, and surprise the moon glassing therein her pearly front.

I knew my route, yet it seemed as if I was hindered from pursuing it direct; now a sight, and now a sound, called me aside, luring me down this alley and

---

[1] 'Discours prononcé à la distribution de prix le 15 aout 1843', H. Remy, 20 pp.

down that. Already I saw the thick-planted trees which framed this tremulous and rippled glass, when, choiring out of a glade to the right, broke such a sound as I thought might be heard if heaven were to open— . . . The song, and sweet music, rose afar, but rushing swiftly on fast-strengthening pinions —there swept through these shades so full a storm of harmonies that, had no tree been near against which to lean, I think I must have dropped. Voices were there, it seemed to me, unnumbered; instruments varied and count-less—bugle, horn and trumpet I knew. The effect was, as a sea breaking into song with all its waves.

The swaying tide kept this way. . . . It led me towards a Byzantine build-ing—a sort of kiosk near the park's centre. Round about stood crowded thousands, gathered to a grand concert in the open air. What I heard was, I think, a wild Jager chorus; the night, the space, the scene, and my own mood, had but enhanced the sounds and their impression . . . here were ladies assembled, looking by this light, most beautiful; some of their dresses were gauzy, and some had the sheen of satin; the flowers and the blond trembled, and the veils waved about their decorated bonnets, as that host-like chorus, with its greatly-gathering sound sundered the air above them. Most of these ladies occupied the little light park-chairs; and behind and beside them stood guardian gentlemen. The outer ranks of the crowd were made up of citizens, plebeians, and police. . . .[1]

There could be no question, of course, of her going out alone like Lucy Snowe; whether accompanied by the other teachers or, not im-possibly even, by the Hegers, she was with a party. The strength of the impression created on her by the unaccustomed scene was heightened by an unaccustomed happiness. She was for once herself part of an animated crowd.

The importance of tracing her true experiences, as opposed to the fictional ones integrated into her novels, lies in their influence on her creative powers. The very intensity of her feelings during that period succeeded in sharpening even her exceptional powers of observation. All her perceptions, as though under the influence of a drug, were heightened to their fullest capacity by the struggle going on in her soul. What she saw and heard during those months of acute mental and emotional suffering were indelible impressions, colouring the texture of her mind so deeply as to supply in retrospect, not only the emotional content of two entire novels, but the smallest details on which their plots were made to hinge. *Villette* and *The Professor* represent half of her total output of published work; but the two years' experience of

[1] *Villette*, ch. 38.

which they are the product was by far the fullest and richest of her life. What had gone before was a necessary preparation, perhaps, for just such a conflagration of feeling; but what she became, afterwards, could never have been at all but for Brussels.

Within a day or two of that animating evening in the park, her Brussels world disintegrated about her. Monsieur and Madame Heger and their children went to Blankenberg as was their wont; the pupils dispersed to their several homes, even the foreign ones receiving invitations to join friends; the teachers too went home, the Parisienne Mlle Blanche going as far as Paris. Only Charlotte remained.

The domestic staff of the pensionnat was reduced to the cook, who combined the role of caretaker with that of feeding Charlotte. Unlike the previous year, there was not even one pupil left. Outside the pensionnat, it was almost as bad. The Wheelwrights, with whom she could have found solace, were due to leave Brussels at the end of the month; Mary Dixon, too, was out of town. There was no Emily now to share the long dormitory at night; the two rows of white-curtained beds stood empty on either side. For all the freedom she now possessed to open the high French windows as she pleased, the accumulated heat of the sultry day was not to be banished. Sleep abandoned her and left her the prey to hallucinating visions. The dreaded necessity of going to bed, much as she craved the oblivion that would not come, became a nightly ordeal. As once before at Dewsbury Moor she experienced all the horrors of hypochondria.

Had things been otherwise, the Hegers might have considered it their duty to invite her to join them at the sea. The fact that no such proposition was or could be made by Madame Heger only added to the sense of exclusion from all natural pleasures that caused Charlotte's acutest suffering then. The consciousness that what she asked was so little, and the bitter resentment at that little being denied her, acted like a goad to her wounded spirit.

The fiercest of her accusations levelled later at the low minds and still lower morals of the generality of Belgians proceeded essentially from this wound to her pride; her feelings were not only misunderstood, but shamefully misinterpreted. That others, Madame Heger in particular, could see further than she did, and recognized the signs of romantic love for what they were, was an affront she never forgave.

The fact remains that much of Charlotte's suffering could have been avoided if Madame Heger had not been quite so far-seeing. Had Charlotte been allowed to continue to enjoy the frank friendship of her master, an altogether saner attitude of mind might have been preserved. It was the sense of frustration and injury that turned her feelings to poison, and made her suspect intentional malevolence in every incident that ensued. Such treatment of a highly nervous subject like Charlotte did not, moreover, have the effect Madame Heger reckoned on. Far from driving Charlotte away, it rooted her to the spot. Like a seer who has once had a supernatural visitation, Charlotte stayed on the haunted ground of Brussels, waiting for the return of her ghost of happiness.

Within a fortnight of the breaking-up of school she was close to despair. Almost before she had been put to any test of endurance, she reached the end of her resistance. On 1 September, in a gesture that was as alien to her upbringing as to her previous rule of conduct, she confessed herself to a Roman Catholic priest at Ste Gudule.

That she also felt the necessity of confiding this act to Emily betrays her terrible need of sympathy. From Emily she was unlikely to receive sympathy for this particular gesture, and even to her she found it very difficult to explain. When it came to making a clean breast of it, she faltered on the threshold of the truth; she attributed the sudden impulse to the effect of loneliness, whereas by now, even if not *before* unveiling her suffering to the priest, she realized that what tortured her was a love that could neither be expressed, returned, or understood by any living soul. The conviction of its absolute innocence only heightened the sense of injury at the contemptible suspicions harboured by Madame Heger, and the equally contemptible withdrawal of Monsieur Heger's friendship. She wrote Emily on 2 September:

... I should inevitably fall into the gulf of low spirits if I stayed always by myself here without a human being to speak to, so I go out and traverse the Boulevards and streets of Brussels sometimes for hours together.

Yesterday I went on a pilgrimage to the cemetery, and far beyond it on to a hill where there was nothing but fields as far as the horizon. When I came back it was evening; but I had such a repugnance to return to the house, ... I still kept threading the streets in the neighbourhood of the Rue d'Isabelle and avoiding it. I found myself opposite to Ste Gudule, and the bell, whose voice you know, began to toll for evening 'salut'. I went in quite alone (which procedure you will say is not much like me) wandering about the aisles where a few old women were saying their prayers, till vespers begun. I stayed till they were over. Still I could not leave the church or force myself to go home—to school I mean. An odd whim came into my head. In a solitary part of the Cathedral six or seven people still remained kneeling by the confessionals. In two confessionals I saw a priest. I felt as if I did not care what I did, provided it was not absolutely wrong, and that it served to vary my life and yield a moment's interest. I took a fancy to change myself into a Catholic and go and make a real confession to see what it was like. Knowing me as you do, you will think this odd, but when people are by themselves they have singular fancies. A penitent was occupied in confessing. They do not go into the sort of pew or cloister which the priest occupies, but kneel down on the steps and confess through a grating. Both the confessor and the penitent whisper very low, you can hardly hear their voices. After I had watched two or three penitents go and return, I approached at last and knelt down in a niche which was just vacated. I had to kneel there ten minutes waiting, for on the other side was another penitent invisible to me. At last that went away and a little wooden door inside the grating opened, and I saw the priest leaning his ear towards me. I was obliged to begin, and yet I did not know a word of the formula with which they always commence their confessions. It was a funny position. I felt precisely as I did when alone on the Thames at midnight. I commenced with saying I was a foreigner and had been brought up a Protestant. The priest asked if I was a Protestant then. I somehow could not tell a lie, and said 'yes'. He replied that in that case I could not 'jouir du bonheur de la confesse'; but I was determined to confess, and at last he said he would allow me because it might be the first step towards returning to the true church. I actually did confess—a real confession. When I had done he told me his address, and said that every morning I was to go to the rue du Parc—to his house—and he would reason with me and try to convince me of the error and enormity of being a Protestant ! ! ! I promised faithfully to go. Of course, however, the adventure stops there, and I hope I shall never see the priest again. I think you had better not tell papa of this. He will not understand that it was only a freak, and will perhaps think I am going to turn Catholic. . . .[1]

No doubt the priest enjoined her to be strong, and to prepare for a rupture with the object of her inadmissible love, and flee temptation. Though he gave her his address (in a street uncomfortably near the pensionnat) and she 'promised faithfully to go', she made the somewhat un-Brontë-like mental reservation of doing nothing of the sort, because the only course he *could* advocate was the one she knew herself incapable of following.[2]

A slight diversion from the absorbing melancholy of her thoughts was the visit of Queen Victoria to Brussels in the middle of September.

[1] CB to EJB, 2 Sept. 1843: *SLL* i. 270.

[2] It is significant of the importance Mrs. Gaskell gave this letter that she omitted it and the incident from the 'Life', though paraphrasing sufficient of its passages—those referring to CB's lonely rambles out of the city—to show that she had seen the original letter.

The papers were full of it and the programme of events, informal and lively by modern standards, as well as the curiosity of those at home, spurred Charlotte on to make an effort to see her pass. The Queen, accompanied by the Prince Consort, landed at Ostend on Friday, 15 September, and from the outset her visit was a source of good humour and amusement to all concerned. Landing considerably before the scheduled time, because of an unforeseen movement of the tide, she arrived to find the workmen, engaged in setting up an arc de triomphe in her honour, still struggling with the wreaths and bunting that should adorn it. The *Journal de Bruxelles* of the day, commenting on the incident, said the Queen laughed heartily at seeing their discomfiture and the flurry of all concerned, and won golden opinions by her informal demeanour. While making Ostend her headquarters her visit was to include all the principal towns of Belgium—Bruges, Ghent, Antwerp, and Brussels—and everywhere illuminations and fireworks by night, parades, *redoutes*, and concerts by day, greeted her passage. At Ghent she heard the celebrated violinist, Vieuxtemps, perform at a 'Grand Concert' on the Saturday evening. On Monday, 18 September, her arrival in Brussels was fixed for one o'clock in the afternoon. The burgomaster, wishing to ensure a hearty welcome for her, had put out a proclamation which Charlotte with everyone else in town would have seen posted on the public buildings. It read: 'Fellow Citizens! I have the great pleasure of informing you that H.M. the Queen of England will visit the capital of Belgium where she will make her entry by the Porte de Cologne on Monday at 1 p.m. and will drive to the Palace by the boulevard du Jardin Botanique and the Rue Royale.'

Flagpoles were set up along the whole route, connected by garlands of flowers.[1] It was at a point nearest the pensionnat, in the Rue Royale, that Charlotte saw the Queen. Answering Emily's query, she wrote on 1 October:

. . . You ask about Queen Victoria's visit to Brussels. I saw her for an instant flashing through the Rue Royale in a carriage and six, surrounded by soldiers. She was laughing and talking gaily. She looked a little stout, vivacious lady, very plainly dressed, not much dignity or pretension about her. The Belgians liked her very well on the whole. They said she enlivened the sombre court of King Leopold, which is usually as gloomy as a conventicle. . . .[2]

[1] *Journal de Bruxelles* for 15, 16, 18, and 20 Sept. 1843.
[2] CB to EJB, 1 Oct. 1843: *W & S* i.

The Queen, as Charlotte saw her, was in an open carriage with Queen Louise of the Belgians beside her and King Leopold (her 'dear uncle Leopold') and Prince Albert with their backs to the horses. Part of the enlivening programme consisted of a concert given at 5 p.m. in the Parc by the Société Royale de la Grande Harmonie, at which the royal party were accommodated in a raised pavilion opposite the kiosk (mentioned in *Villette*) where the musicians performed. After the concert there was a banquet at the Palace to which 63 guests were invited and afterwards the royal party drove out into the city to see the illuminations, which the newspapers declared were the finest since the Independence celebrations of 1830.

Queen Victoria had hardly sailed away from Antwerp on 20 September when the annual celebrations to commemorate the revolution of 1830 began. They were always fixed to begin on the first Sunday following, or immediately preceding, 23 September, the day on which the revolution had broken out. The culmination of the festivities in 1843 fell on Tuesday, 26 September, when the official programme included 'races, balloon ascensions, and, to crown all, Illuminations in the Parc at 7 o'clock in the evening during which the Société Royale de la Grande Harmonie would be heard in the Kiosque'.

A passage in *Villette* evokes just such a night when the sounds of festivity, if not the sights, reached Charlotte in the solitude of the pensionnat.

In the summer it was never quite dark and then I went upstairs to my quarter of the long dormitory, opened my own casement (that chamber was lit by five casements large as great doors) and, leaning out, looked forth upon the city beyond the gardens and listened to band-music from the park or the palace-square, thinking meantime my own thoughts, living my own life, in my own still, shadow world. . . .[1]

By the end of that week the household were reassembled and the boarders returned, though full school did not start until the Monday, 2 October. The ordeal of loneliness was over; had it been the authentic cause of Charlotte's misery, her spirits would have revived at the return of the vivacious noisy crowds that filled the old house again. That nothing but bitterness and depression resulted from the reunion with the Hegers is made apparent by the letter she wrote Emily that week-end.

Brussels, 1st October 1843

Dear E. J.—This is Sunday morning. They are at their idolatrous 'messe', and I am here—i.e.—in the réfectoire—I should like uncommonly to be in

---

[1] *Villette*, ch. 13.

the dining-room at home, or in the kitchen or in the back-kitchen—I should like, even, to be cutting up the hash, with the Clerk and some registry people at the other table, and you standing by, watching that I put enough flour and not too much pepper, and, above all, that I save the best piece of the leg of mutton for Tiger and Keeper, the first of which personages would be jumping about the dish and carving knife, and the latter standing like a devouring flame on the kitchen floor. To complete the picture, Tabby blowing the fire, in order to boil the potatoes to a sort of vegetable glue! Yet I have no thought of coming home just now. I lack a real pretext for doing so; it is true this place is dismal to me; but I cannot go home without a fixed prospect when I get there; and this prospect must not be a situation; that would be jumping out of the frying-pan into the fire. *You* call yourself idle! absurd! absurd! Is Papa well? Are you well? and Tabby? . . . Tell me whether Papa really wants me very much to come home, and whether you do likewise. I have an idea that I should be of no use there—a sort of aged person upon the parish. I pray, with heart and soul, that all may continue well at Haworth; above all in our grey, half-inhabited house. God bless the walls thereof! Safety, health, happiness, and prosperity to you, Papa and Tabby. Amen—[1]

Evidently no healing words had been spoken by either Monsieur or Madame Heger, though we can be sure that no unkind ones had been spoken either. Charlotte had passed beyond accepting ordinary treatment from them, and received each omission of a distinguishing mark of interest and friendship as an affront. They could do no right now. The material reminder even of their religion was an added irritant, and to know that they were upstairs in the little Oratory, or gone to S. Jacques sur Coudenberg (their parish church), was only a bitter reminder of the gulf between them. To take the irrevocable step of quitting Monsieur Heger was still beyond her powers; the hope that a happier relationship might be restored, that she might yet regain his confidence and interest, held her prisoner of her own suffering and prevented the liberating gesture that only she was in a position to make.

Some incident, more hurtful than any before, must have occurred within the next fortnight to have provoked an *éclaircissement* with Madame Heger, and the yet more decisive step of giving her notice. The temper, of which she had reminded Branwell in her letter of that spring, and of which Miss Wooler had had more than one example, must have got the better of her usual iron self-command. She did not

[1] *W & S* i.

care what she said to Madame Heger, or how much she betrayed her wounded feelings. But Madame Heger's response was enough to sober Charlotte at once; she quietly accepted the notice flung at her. That she added no wounding comments plainly appears from the worst Charlotte could find to say of her then: '. . . Madame Heger is a politic, plausible, and interested person. I no longer trust her. . . .' Madame Heger had no need to confound Charlotte with further reproaches. She had achieved what she had been waiting for so patiently for months: Charlotte's notice to quit.

Madame Heger's peace of mind was short-lived. No sooner did Monsieur hear of what had been decided between them than he took control of the situation. He violently disapproved of what he took to be merely a headstrong gesture on Charlotte's part. His wife successfully concealed that she was deeply concerned in the issue, and to this extent Charlotte's accusation of duplicity may be said to be justified: Madame Heger sedulously sought to hide the truth from her husband. Her motives, which Charlotte was the last person to interpret impartially, may not have been so interested as Charlotte declared. By her continental standards, Charlotte's conduct was wholly incorrect, and the kindest attitude to adopt towards it was an apparent ignorance of all that it implied.

Commenting on her loss of companionship since the departure of the Wheelwrights and of Mary Dixon, Charlotte wrote to Ellen of the crisis in her affairs on 13 October.

> Brussels is indeed desolate to me now. Since Mary Dixon left I have had no friend. . . . I cannot count the Belgians as anything. . . . Madame Heger is a politic, plausible, and interested person. I no longer trust her. It is a curious position to be so utterly solitary in the midst of numbers. Sometimes the solitude oppresses me to an excess. One day, lately, I felt as if I could bear it no longer, and I went to Madame Heger and gave her notice. If it had depended on her I should certainly have soon been at liberty; but M. Heger having heard of what was in agitation, sent for me the day after, and pronounced with vehemence his decision that I should not leave. I could not, at that time, have persevered in my intention without exciting him to passion; so I promised to stay a little while longer. How long that will be I do not know. I should not like to return to England to do nothing.[1]

Her decision to stay was not due to the fear of provoking Monsieur Heger's explosive temper but to his renewed interest in her affairs.

[1] CB to EN, 13 Oct. 1843: *SLL* i. 271–3.

Charlotte described too frequently in *Villette* what his probing kindness, his benevolent bullying were like not to have experienced them in reality. However ready in reply, however dignified in evasion, the girl she had been and reincarnated in Lucy Snowe was not armed to resist such odd, such violent manifestations of sympathy. Her heart melted before human kindness. Readers of *Villette* will remember the incident of Lucy crying alone in the refectory and M. Paul spying at her through a glass panel in the wall and the subsequent dialogue:

It was very much his habit to wear eyes before, behind, and on each side of him; he had seen me through the little window—he now opened the refectory door, and there he stood.

'Mademoiselle, vous êtes triste.'

'Monsieur, j'en ai bien le droit.'

'Vous êtes malade de cœur et d'humeur,' he pursued. 'You are at once mournful and mutinous. I see on your cheek two tears which I know are hot as two sparks, and salt as two crystals of the sea. While I speak you eye me strangely. Shall I tell you what I am reminded while I am watching you?'[1]

The opening is followed by a page of acrimonious inquisition and evasion, the master attempting in vain to extort the secret of her sorrows. The expressions, however, here placed in the mouth of M. Paul are strangely similar to expressions used in reality by M. Heger. '. . . Vous êtes malade de cœur et d'humeur', M. Paul accused her. Ten years after the death of Charlotte Brontë, M. Heger, in a correspondence opened by Ellen Nussey, spoke of Charlotte's 'pauvre cœur blessé', an adjective he erased in favour of 'pauvre cœur malade'.[2] Both expressions are important as revealing how much M. Heger understood of Charlotte. For *that*, when all has been said and done, remains the enigma of the story.

A note written in the fly-leaf of her geography book—'Russell's General Atlas of Modern Geography' (still preserved in the Brontë Parsonage Museum) dated 14 October—betrays the state of her mind after the recent encounter with Madame and Monsieur Heger. Her equanimity, too shaken by her increasing insight into her own feelings, is not restored; her only comfort is in a renewal of trust and liking for her master.

14th October '43. Brussels, Sat. morning.

First class—I am very cold—There is no fire—I wish I were at home—it is a dreary life—especially as there is only *one* person in this house worthy of being liked—also another, who seems a rosy sugar plum, but I know her to be coloured chalk—

[1] *Villette*, ch. 21.   [2] M. Heger to EN: *W & S* iv. 248.

On 15 November Madame Heger gave birth to her fifth child (and fourth daughter, christened Julie Marie Victorine, eventually the only daughter to marry), an event affording both women some respite from daily contacts and a suspension of hostilities. It also gave Charlotte some hint of M. Heger's absorbing love for his children. She remembered him afterwards as tirelessly patient and tender towards them. 'You never frowned or looked severe when Louise, Claire or Prospère approached you', she wrote to him later.[1]

Charlotte attended one concert in the recently opened and much publicized Salle de la Grande Harmonie, as is shown by her knowledge of its interior and her description of a concert given there in chapter 20 of *Villette*. The concert of which she gave so minute an account took place on 10 December. Its distinguishing features were the presence of the King and Queen of the Belgians, with the young Duc de Brabant, and the drawing of a lottery afterwards for the benefit of a charity, features peculiar to this one only concert during 1842 and 1843. Charlotte's presence at this particular concert is, therefore, certain. The point is of interest in reading the last letters she wrote from Brussels that autumn, with their emphasis on her loneliness and the neglect she suffered at Madame Heger's hands. She could not have attended the concert without an escort, and the possibility that the Hegers took her cannot be excluded. The presence of the pianist M. Chapelle in charge of the choir can be inferred from *Villette*.

On 15 November Charlotte wrote to Ellen:

To-day the weather is gloomy, and I am stupefied with a bad cold and headache. I have nothing to tell you, my dear Ellen. One day is like another in this place. I know you, living in the country, can hardly believe it possible life can be monotonous in the centre of a brilliant capital like Brussels; but so it is. I feel it most on holidays, when all the girls and teachers go out to visit, and it sometimes happens that I am left, during several hours, quite alone, with four great desolate schoolrooms at my disposition. I try to read, I try to write; but in vain. I then wander about from room to room, but the silence and loneliness of all the house weighs down one's spirit like lead. You will hardly believe that Madame Heger (good and kind as I have described her) never comes near me on these occasions. I own, I was astonished the first time I was left alone thus; when everybody else was enjoying the pleasures of a fête-day with their friends, and she knew I was quite by myself, and never took the least notice of me. Yet, I understand, she praises me very much to everybody, and says what excellent lessons I give. She is not colder

[1] CB to M. Heger, 18 Nov. 1845: BM.

to me than she is to the other teachers; but they are less dependent on her than I am. They have relations and acquaintances in Brussels. You remember the letter she wrote me, when I was in England? How kind and affectionate that was? Is it not odd? I fancy I begin to perceive the reason of this mighty distance and reserve; it sometimes makes me laugh, and at other times nearly cry. When I am sure of it, I will tell you. In the meantime, the complaints I make at present are for your ear only.[1]

The presence of the King and Queen gave the concert Charlotte attended on 10 December unusual publicity. The full programme, announced in the press, showed a preponderance of vocal and choral items, to allow of as many stars contributing to it as possible. Given in 'benefit of the Society in aid of Working Class Mothers, and the Mothers of the Poor, under the patronage of Their Majesties', it was announced to commence at 7.45 and to consist of:

Part I

1. A Fantasia for Orchestra by M. Snel.
2. A Hymn to Friendship by M. Limnander. Sung by the choir of the 'Réunion Lyrique' of Malines.
3. Air from Bellini's 'Roméo' sung by Madame Bron de Heusch.
4. The Sailor's Farewell, lyrical drama for chorus and orchestra. Words by M. Oppelt, music composed and arranged by M. Snel.
5. Air from the 'Don Juan' of Mozart, sung by M. W.-P. de Chavonnes Vrught.
6. Children of the Night, Valse fantasque by M. Limnander, sung by the choir of the 'Réunion Lyrique' of Malines.
7. Overture to 'Faust' by L. Spohr, arranged for 8 hands on 2 pianos. The Soloists being Mlles Chapine, Delibe, Margaillon et M. Debrauwer. 'Premiers Prix' of the Brussels Royal Conservatoire.
8. A Hymn to Harmony, chorus by M. Limnander, sung by the 'Réunion Lyrique' of Malines.
9. Grand Fantasia for Flute on the Airs of 'Norma', performed by M. Botgorschak, solo-flautist of H.M. King William II of the Netherlands.
10. Bolero, by M. Limnander, sung by the 'Réunion Lyrique' of Malines.[2]

---

[1] CB to EN, 15 Nov. 1843: *W & S*, also *SLL* i. 273–4. Cf. *Villette*, ch. 13, where an almost identical passage occurs. '. . . The spectacle of a suspicious nature so far misled by its own inventions, tickled me much. . . .'

[2] *Journal de Bruxelles*, 8 Dec. 1843; advertisement of concert.

The concert was to be followed by 'A magnificent Lottery, consisting of 90–100 prizes in gold, gold-plate & silver articles, clocks, crystal pendants and vases, etc., etc.' The doors to be open at 6.30. Price of admission 3 francs which includes 'a ticket for the Lottery'.[1]

Charlotte described in *Villette*[2] how she responded to the pleasure of the night; it was far less the music than the novelty of the festive scene that absorbed her. '... I suppose people who go every night to places of public amusement, can hardly enter into the fresh gala feeling with which an opera or a concert is enjoyed by those for whom it is a rarity', she wrote. 'I am not sure that I expected great pleasure from the concert, having but a very vague notion of its nature . . .', she added, confessing that her impressions would 'not be worth while . . . as they were the impressions of an "ignorance crasse" '. But it would be enough to be going out at an hour when normally her day was done and to be mixing with a gay fashionable crowd in place of the solitude of an unheated classroom.

The Salle de la Grande Harmonie, only opened to the public the previous March, was the work of the same fashionable architect, Cluysenaar, who had built the hotel where the Wheelwrights lived. It was situated at the top of the Rue de la Madeleine, in the quarter of the town lying just below the Place Royale, hence not far from the King's Palace, nor, for that matter, from the Pensionnat Heger.

In the statutes laid down by the Société de la Grande Harmonie, as far back as 1812, evening dress was obligatory for all concert-goers, a detail which explains why Lucy Snowe was obliged to accept the pink silk dress forced on her by her godmother for the occasion.[3]

The hall was very exactly described by Charlotte as

grand, wide and high, whose sweeping circular walls, and domed hollow ceiling, seemed to me all dead gold. Pendant from the dome, flamed a mass that dazzled me—a mass, I thought, of rock-crystal, sparkling with facets, streaming with drops, ablaze with stars, and gorgeously tinged with dews of gems dissolved, or fragments of rainbow shivered. It was only the chandelier, reader, but for me it seemed the work of eastern genii.[4]

In a setting that for once realized the exorbitant visions of her girlhood, surrounded by a society whose clothes and jewels corresponded to her earliest sketches of Angrian beaux and belles, how appropriate

[1] *Journal de Bruxelles*, 8 Dec.: op. cit.
[2] *Villette*, ch. 20.
[3] Statuts de la Société Royale de la Grande Harmonie — Bruxelles, 1890.
[4] *Villette*, ch. 20.

and how inevitable, one feels, that her comparisons should revert to the origin of all her creative output, the eastern genii of her childish reading. For intensity of experience, Angria had been the right prelude to Brussels.

The entry of the royal party upon a packed parterre was described by the *Journal de Bruxelles*—as well as by Charlotte Brontë: 'A little before 8 o'clock,' the paper reported, 'the King, the Queen, and the Duke of Brabant made their entry to the cries of "Long Live the King! Long Live the Queen! Long Live the Prince Royal!" ', a moment which Charlotte recorded in a passage of *Villette*: '. . . A signal was given, the doors rolled back, the assembly stood up, the orchestra burst out, and, to the welcome of a choral burst, enter the King, the Queen, the Court of Labassecour. . . .'

The one-time widower of the Princess Charlotte, Leopold the First elected King of the Belgians, was 53 at the time; his second wife, Louise, daughter of Louis Philippe, was only just 30. Their three children, the heir apparent, then present and later Leopold the Second was eight years old; his younger brother Philippe Comte de Flandre was five and a half, and the Princess Marie Charlotte Amélie was three.

Charlotte saw behind the glitter and the polished surface of that court into something of the heartache of its Queen, of the 'rooted melancholy' of its King:

Well do I recall that King, a man of fifty, a little bowed, a little grey; there was no face in all that assembly which resembled his. I had never read, never been told anything of his nature or his habits; and at first the strong hieroglyphics graven as with iron stylet on his brow, round his eyes, beside his mouth, puzzled and baffled instinct. Ere long, however, if I did not *know* at least I *felt*, the meaning. . . . There sat a silent sufferer—a nervous melancholy man . . . The queen, his wife, knew this . . . the reflection of her husband's grief lay, a subduing shadow, on her own benignant face. A mild, thoughtful, graceful woman, that princess seemed . . . Her little son . . . accompanied her; he leaned on his mother's knee . . . she often bent her head to listen to the boy's remarks, and would then smilingly repeat them to his sire.[1]

Of the singers and instrumentalists performing that night, Charlotte left identifiable thumbnail sketches in *Villette*. The young laureates from the Conservatoire played Spohr's duets for eight hands; she wrote of them: 'The young ladies of the Conservatoire, being very

[1] *Villette*, ch. 20.

much frightened, made rather a tremulous exhibition on the two grand pianos. . . .' Of Mme Bron de Heusch in the Bellini air, she said: 'Following the white muslin pianists, came a fine, full-grown, sulky lady in white satin. She sang. Her singing just affected me like the tricks of a conjuror: I wondered how she did it. . . .' Monsieur de Chavonnes Vrught in his air from 'Don Juan' did not meet with any more favour in her eyes.

Afterwards stepped forth a gentleman, who, bending his body a good deal in the direction of the king and queen, and frequently approaching his white-gloved hand to the region of his heart, vented a bitter outcry against a certain 'fausse Isabelle', his state of mind was very harrowing, and I was glad when he wound up his musical exposition of the same.

The 'Réunion Lyrique' of Malines pleased her better: '. . . Some rousing choruses struck me as the best part of the evening's entertainment. There were present deputies from all the best provincial choral-societies . . . their hearty exertions had at least this good result—the ear drank thence a satisfying sense of power. . . .'

The concert on 10 December occurred only a few days before Charlotte's sudden decision to go home. In after years she thanked Mary Taylor for making the decision for her, and it was as a result of a letter from Mary in Germany—so Mary later told Mrs. Gaskell—urging Charlotte to go home or elsewhere before she sank into deeper gloom and lost the energy to move, that Charlotte finally acted. To Mary, who destroyed all her letters, she may have opened her heart more than to others, and have confessed the impasse in which she found herself; certainly the brisk, energetic advice shook her out of her lethargy. A poem written later suggests that she knew her decision to be a flight from temptation.[1]

By 17 December it was officially known throughout the school that she was leaving at the end of the year, as a hitherto unpublished letter from Mlle Sophie to Charlotte proves, and on 19 December Charlotte wrote home to announce her decision to Emily.

Of her three fellow-teachers at the pensionnat Charlotte loathed Mlle Blanche, tolerated Mlle Haussé (the prototype of Hortense Moore),

---

[1] The poem 'Reason', of which the last verse runs:

> Have I not fled that I may conquer?
> Crost the dark sea in firmest faith
> That I at last might plant my anchor
> Where love cannot prevail to death?
>
> *W & S PCBBB*

and tolerably liked Mlle Sophie. That their relations had been unspoilt and even friendly, Mlle Sophie's little farewell note reveals. She wrote in a covering letter with a parting gift addressed to 'Mademoiselle Charlotte Brunté' [*sic*].

Ma Chère Charlotte,
    Please do me the pleasure of accepting this little box as a keepsake. I have far too good an opinion of your heart to suppose that it needs the sight of any object to recall me to your indulgent memory. No, I am convinced that the friendship you have always shown me has its source in the finest feelings. All the same, you would grieve me if you refused me this mark of your affection. Goodbye, my good kind Charlotte; I like to think that I shall not be losing you for ever in a couple of weeks' time and that you will deign from time to time, when you have seen your homeland again to turn your thoughts towards dreary Belgium, where more than one person will be thinking of you.

Devotedly,
Your friend Sophie

Brussels, 17th December 1843[1]

The letter home, announcing her decision, is naturally short, entering into no reasons and as though complying with an injunction from the family to take this very course:

Brussels, December 19th, 1843
    Dear E. J.—I have taken my determination. I hope to be at home the day after New Year's Day. I have told Mme. Heger. But in order to come home I shall be obliged to draw on my cash for another £5. I have only £3. at present, and as there are several little things I should like to buy before I leave Brussels—which you know cannot be got as well in England—£3. would not suffice. Low spirits have afflicted me much lately but I hope all will be well when I get home,—above all, if I find papa and you and B. and A. well. I am not ill in body. It is only the mind which is a trifle shaken—for want of comfort.
    I shall try to cheer up now.—Good-bye.   C.B.[2]

From the moment that her decision was taken, the chilling atmosphere about her changed; at least it appeared so to her. Expressions of kindness came not only from the teachers, but from her pupils also. '. . . I was surprised', she wrote to Ellen Nussey after her return home, 'at the degree of regret expressed by my Belgian pupils, when they

[1] Translation of the original letter of Mlle Sophie: BPM.
[2] CB to EJB, 19 Dec. 1843: *SLL* i. 274.

knew I was going to leave. I did not think it had been in their phleg-matic nature. . . .'[1] A letter from one of her pupils received in the fol-lowing year (and to be quoted in due course) bears testimony to the affection Charlotte had aroused, and to the moral influence she exercised over some of her girls.

One of her last engagements in Brussels was to dine with Mr. and Mrs. Jenkins on Christmas Day where she met, among other members of the English colony, Abraham Dixon, who mentioned the fact in a letter to his daughter Mary (in England again), a letter which Charlotte posted in England for him. 'Miss Bronté [sic] leaves on Sunday for her home and does not mean to return . . .' he wrote.[2]

The contacts with M. Heger during the last days would appear to have been of the serenest, and if one fact emerges more clearly than another at this stage it is that a rupture was so little intended, either by Monsieur or by Madame, that they planned sending one of their little girls to Charlotte as a pupil when her school should be established.

The emphasis in that final phase of her schooldays in Brussels was all upon the career for which she had been fitting herself; she had come to study foreign languages with a view to opening a school of her own, and, not forgetting this, M. Heger gave her a diploma testifying to her qualifications, which he sealed with the official seal of the Athénée Royal. He dated it 29 December 1843.

Of his interest in her welfare and of his personal kindness, his con-duct during those last days left her in no doubt whatever. It was the only comfort she was capable of receiving, and it reached her stricken heart. Very significant is the wording of her account of the parting be-tween them, written to Ellen shortly afterwards: it has not the finality of despair, but reveals an element of hope. '. . . I suffered much before I left Brussels. I think, however long I live, I shall not forget what parting with M. Heger cost me; it grieved me so much to grieve him, who has been so true, kind, and disinterested a friend. . . .'[3]

The separation was a different suffering from what she had endured for the past year. Though she had to go, she was allowed to feel that it was a friend she was leaving. She was called into the Hegers' private sitting-room and a parting gift was put into her hand, a recent an-thology of French poetry—*Les Fleurs de la Poésie Française depuis le commencement du XVIe Siècle*, published at Tours in 1841. According

[1] CB to EN, 23 Jan. 1844: *SLL* i. 276–7.
[2] Abraham Dixon to Mary Dixon, 30 Dec. 1843: Leeds City Museum.
[3] CB to EN, 23 Jan. 1844 (see above note 1).

to continental habit it was not inscribed, but when she reached home she wrote in the fly-leaf: 'Given to me by Monsieur Heger on the 1st January 1844, the morning I left Brussels.'[1]

Quite certainly no note of finality was struck in that last interview. The prospect of future communication, the invitation to correspond, the plan for sending one of the little girls over to England, the likelihood even of a future return on her part to the Continent, and of re-union with her Brussels friends, were all held out to her in alleviation of the pang of parting. So much the sequel showed. Only so can the eventual heartbreak be explained; because the rupture when it came was wholly unexpected.

That Charlotte's own attitude was primarily responsible for this only heightened the agony; and it was only human that she should lay the full burden of the blame on Madame Heger. Just because she was *not* bereft of hope on leaving Brussels, it took two years of protracted torture to stifle it finally. Only then would she know the extent of what she had lost. It would take her the rest of her life to discover what she had gained.

She left Brussels on Monday, 1 January 1844, Madame Heger accompanying her to the boat at Ostend, which left on the morning's tide of Tuesday, 2 January. The biggest single experience of her life was over.

---

[1] In the poem 'Master and Pupil' (*W & S PCPBB* 231–5) the parting scene is dramatized to resemble the cruelty of a separation imposed upon two devoted friends, like that in *Villette.*

A SLAVE TO SORROW

In one of her letters to M. Heger written during the two years following her return from Brussels Charlotte used a term in describing her
feelings that contains the whole kernel of her suffering: she confessed
to having become 'the slave to a sorrow . . . the slave to a dominant
and fixed idea . . .',[1] and in the same sentence recognized how humiliating such a condition was.

From this awareness of the causes and nature of her own suffering—
of the loss of mental freedom and independence of spirit—came her
sharpest pain. No longer mistress of her mind or of her emotions, she
fell into a condition of servitude which was far worse than the yoke
laid on her formerly by such employers as Mrs. Sidgwick and Mrs.
White. That had been a physical servitude; now she was to suffer the
imprisonment of the spirit. Charlotte, who had written of dungeons as
a child with a peculiar horror, and throughout adolescence cherished
adventurous deeds as alone worthy of a heroine's life, was now self-
immured in the cruellest of confinements, of which she appeared to
have had a nightmare foreknowledge. Similarly the betrayal of love,
with the agonies of which her heroines—Mary Percy, Mina Laury,
Caroline Vernon, Elizabeth Hastings—were so familiar, she now knew
herself. Though M. Heger was no Zamorna her previous imaginings
were preparation for the degree of suffering she was to experience now.

The stages by which she reached this extremity appear, from the
evidence of her remaining letters, to have been gradual. When she returned from Brussels in January 1844 she was not broken-hearted. She
was convinced that M. Heger's friendship was a treasure for life, something that could not be taken away from her. The sorrow she felt then,
though keen, was one of separation rather than of total loss. For most
of 1844, indeed, she acted energetically, throwing herself into the scheme
for setting up a private school with her sisters, and showing herself
capable of taking important decisions. It was not till January 1845—a

[1] CB to M. Heger, 18 Nov. 1845: BM.

full year after leaving Brussels—that, with the virtual cessation of M. Heger's letters, the irremediable nature of her loss was borne in upon her. Then hope died, and but for the indestructible nature of her creative impulse she herself would in all probability have died too.

She arrived home on 3 January, to find Anne and Branwell on holiday from Thorp Green. For the moment she could submerge her own interests in those of the family. Correspondence, expensive and erratic, had left much unsaid and unexplained over the past year; Charlotte found Mr. Brontë's eyesight greatly worse than she had expected, and Branwell's prospects, to her no small amazement, greatly better. He was, as she shortly reported to Ellen, 'wondrously valued' in his situation. Ellen she was eager to see, and was keenly disappointed at finding no welcoming letter to greet her.

> . . . I cannot tell what occupies your thoughts and time. [she wrote her] Are you ill? Is some one of your family ill? Are you married? Are you dead? If it be so, you may as well write a word and let me know—for my part, I am again in old England—I shall tell you nothing further till you write to me. . . .[1]

Ellen was in Sussex with Henry Nussey (still unsuccessful in finding a wife) and looking after his Rectory near Chichester. Charlotte was genuinely disappointed. 'It was a great disappointment to me to hear that you were in the South of England. I had counted upon seeing *you soon*, as one of the great pleasures of my return; now, I fear, our meeting will be postponed for an indefinite time. . . .'[2]

The main subjects broached in the letter—her immediate plans for turning her new qualifications to practical use—and her unselfconscious account of her parting from M. Heger, show how much importance she attached to the one, and how secure she felt in the friendship of the other. Her pain at parting from him was an *avowable* pain, natural under the circumstances, and in no way envenomed by a sense of neglect and frustration:

> Every one asks me what I am going to do, now that I am returned home, and every one seems to expect that I should immediately commence a school. In truth, it is what I should wish to do. I desire it above all things. I have sufficient money for the undertaking, and I hope now sufficient qualifications to give me a fair chance of success; yet I cannot yet permit myself to enter upon life—to touch the object which seems now within my reach, and which

---

[1] CB to EN, Jan. (undated) 1844: *SLL* i 276.
[2] CB to EN, 23 Jan. 1844: *SLL*, No. 131.

I have been so long straining to attain. You will ask me why. It is on Papa's account; he is now, as you know, getting old, and it grieves me to tell you that he is losing his sight. I have felt for some months that I ought not to be away from him; and I feel now that it would be too selfish to leave him (at least as long as Branwell and Anne are absent) in order to pursue selfish interests of my own. With the help of God I will try to deny myself in this matter, and to wait.

I suffered much before I left Brussels. I think, however long I live, I shall not forget what the parting with M. Heger cost me; it grieved me so much to grieve him, who has been so true, kind, and disinterested a friend. At parting he gave me a kind of diploma certifying my abilities as a teacher, sealed with the seal of the Athénée Royal, of which he is a professor. I was surprised also at the degree of regret expressed by my Belgian pupils, when they knew I was going to leave. I did not think it had been in their phlegmatic nature. When do you think I shall see you? I have, of course, much to tell you, and I dare say you have much also to tell me, of things which we should neither of us wish to commit to paper.[1]

The realization of a change in herself, of the disillusioning effects of experience and passing youth, was still sufficiently rational to be confided to her friend; she was not yet aware of the causes of the chief change in her, and even supposed they could be shared by Ellen. She continued:

I do not know whether you feel as I do, [she wrote on] but there are times now when it appears to me as if all my ideas and feelings, except a few friendships & affections, are changed from what they used to be; something in me which used to be enthusiasm, is tamed down and broken. I have few illusions; what I wish for now is activer exertion—a stake in life.

The one essential at that moment—a fully occupied life—was denied her. The school, which had always been envisaged by herself and her sisters as being away from Haworth, had become an impossibility because of Mr. Brontë's increasing dependence on them. Charlotte, realizing fully now for the first time that she ought not to be away from him, was also confronted by a fresh dilemma: how to bear the inaction of home-life after the noise and animation of Brussels. 'Haworth seems such a lonely, quiet spot, buried away from the world', she wrote in the same letter to Ellen. How, above all, to fill the void created by the separation from M. Heger?

The school project, while it had been maturing in her mind, had clearly become emotionally related to M. Heger. Besides being a

[1] CB to EN, 23 Jan. 1844: *SLL*, No. 131

practical measure which would bring her financial independence, it had always been the object of her studies abroad; it was in a direct manner the fulfilment of M. Heger's training. He had fully approved the plan, and had, indeed, personally sponsored it by giving her the diploma of the Athénée Royal; it was so much a subject of common interest between them that it was a way of keeping in touch with him, of continuing to seek his advice. As the successful headmistress of a school Charlotte need not feel herself cut off from him. Within a year or so he would confide his little girls to her—she would yet prove her gratitude to him.

Upon the realization of this dream Charlotte had built high hopes. The necessity to abandon it was the first sharp reversal she suffered on reaching home.

When Anne and Branwell had returned to their posts at Thorp Green the expanse of each day's unemployed time loomed large ahead. It was winter, and the shortness of the days, the sparse light, the iron hardness of the cold shutting her within the parsonage, only accentuated her sense of imprisonment. She saw her home, as she later confessed, for the first time in her life, with unloving eyes. The inability to readapt herself was complete. Never before had she lacked congenial employment for her leisure (her adolescent writing always coincided with returns home) and a sign of the radical change in her now was the disinclination to write. It was the most alarming symptom not only of her present unhappiness but of that subservience to the spirit of another that was sapping her life-force.

She had sacrificed, under M. Heger's influence, her ambition to become a writer; she was self-condemned to the teaching profession, and if she had opened a school now her dedication to it would have been complete. That she had confided to M. Heger her youthful ambitions to become an author, and had, moreover, on returning to Brussels in 1843, taken back with her a sample of her juvenilia, has come to light by the devious processes of chance and time. The manuscripts preserved apparently by M. Heger, and even bound together by him, found their way after his death on to the stall of a second-hand bookshop in Brussels, where they were picked up in 1892 by a professor of the University, Professor Ernest Nys. He, in his turn, sold them to the British Museum. Consisting of Angrian fragments dating mostly from 1834-5, the manuscripts were a cross-section of Charlotte's narrative, verse, journalese, and drama of the time, written as ever under the *nom de plume* of Lord Charles Florian Wellesley. The volume had been given the title

'Manuscrits / De / Miss Charlotte Brontë / (Currer Bell)' / showing that the binding was done after Charlotte's reputation had been established.[1]

M. Heger's views on these productions, and his general advice on the wisdom of authorship and the security it offered, can be judged from a passage in Charlotte's letter to him written in the July after her return home:

There is nothing I fear so much as idleness, the want of occupation ... the lethargy of the faculties. ... I should not know this lethargy if I could write. Formerly I spent whole days and weeks and months in writing. ... But that cannot be—it is not to be thought of. The career of letters is closed to me—only that of teaching is open. It does not offer the same attractions, never mind, I shall enter it.[2]

The only writing for which she felt any inclination was the writing of letters to her former master. As the life of inaction bore her down, the vital interest of the past couple of years rushed back to obsess her and she realized all that she had lost. It began to assume a giant importance, and was regretted with an uncontrollable longing. Then was the time of those first foolish letters written when the heart was full.

The correspondence, authorized originally by the Hegers, got off to a bad start. Charlotte wrote a letter, if not more than one, that she was constrained to acknowledge later to have been unwise: '... Ah! Monsieur!' she wrote him on 24 July, 'je vous ai ecrit une fois une lettre peu raisonnable, par ce que le chagrin me serrait le coeur, mais je ne le ferai plus....'[3]

The letter brought an answer, which was in effect a startled and covert rebuke. From the evidence of the subsequent correspondence it plainly appears that she was reprimanded for her expressions of extravagant feelings and morbid outlook, and bidden to confine her letters to news of her health and activities, and of her family—not, in other words, to write out of turn.

This was precisely what Charlotte found it so difficult to do. While bowing to the Hegers' wishes in principle, she did not, or would not, grasp the nature of the embargo laid upon her. By every opportunity that offered, by Mrs. Wheelwright, by Joe Taylor, by the Dixons, she

---

[1] 'The Spell and other MSS. by Charlotte Brontë': Add. MSS. BM. No. 34255.

[2] CB to M. Heger, 24 July 1844: BM.

[3] Idem. Mlle Louise Heger, the professor's daughter, believed that Charlotte wrote many more letters than the four preserved: *BST* (1949), 260.

sent letters to Brussels couched in a language which, being foreign, might say more than it was meant to say, but which to the Hegers appeared crystal clear as the language of passion.

For the first time, the farouche and inarticulate girl they had sought to humanize by the influence of their family life spoke with eloquence; more, she spoke with an authority which entirely reversed their roles. It was *she* who was speaking from full knowledge, it was they who were the neophytes. Unaware that they were corresponding with one of the great writers of English prose, they were concerned only with one thing: to check Charlotte before she had either in writing or action committed a regrettable folly. The state of mind revealed in her letter of 24 July could not preclude the possibility of her making a sudden reappearance in Brussels, which would be fraught with great awkwardness for all parties.

M. Heger had, therefore, very little choice but to discourage her correspondence and ignore the revelation of her feelings. Such an obligation was, without doubt, genuinely painful to him. He wrote to her on several occasions. When Mrs. Gaskell visited Brussels in 1856 for data for her life of Charlotte, M. Heger received her very kindly. Relating the interview in a letter to Ellen Nussey on 9 July 1856, Mrs. Gaskell said:

> I want to write you a long letter, and tell you all my adventures. Brussels, where Madame Heger, understanding that I was a friend of Miss Brontë's refused to see me; but I made M. Heger's acquaintance, and very much indeed I both like and respect him . . . I promised M. Heger to ask to see his letters to her; he is sure she would keep them, as they contained advice about her character, studies, mode of life.[1]

The letters have not come to light. How delightful they could have been, had no fear of Charlotte's misunderstanding their kindness existed in the writer's mind, can be judged by reading other letters written by him over many years to former pupils, English girls also, Marion Douglas and her sister Kate, who later sent her own daughter Meta Mossman to the pensionnat. It is understandable that a letter from him was Charlotte's 'stay and prop' for months.

He wrote to Meta on 21 November, 1887:

> I have just re-read your nice letters of 18th May and 2nd November last. I often give myself this pleasure at the end of my day's work, at the hour when between 'chien et loup' I like to talk with my dead or absent friends.

[1] Mrs. Gaskell to EN, 9 July 1856: *W & S* iv. 201–3.

I say your *nice* letters because they are not only sincere but frank and open, showing you just as you are, my dear—neither more nor less reasonable than in reality. This is the way I like you to behave to me, treating me as a friend, thus greatly flattering and pleasing me as being a proof of both affection and confidence.

You are sorry that I did not write your name in the books I have sent you. This omission was not due to forgetfulness; the volumes were paper-backed when I bought them, and the bookshop undertook to have them bound and sent. There is my excuse.

How could you write that having received no letter from me you said to yourself that it was impertinence on your part to imagine that M.H. would have time to write to anyone so unimportant as yourself!

I beg you never to write to me nor to anyone else that which you do not think. It is sufficient to say everything we think! That is prudent and dis-creet, but what can one call that which you have done in saying the opposite to what you think! I hope it will not happen again between us, dear Meta, on your side or on mine.

I heartily approve your good idea of translating some pretty tales for children from English into French, and if it suits you, send me your work— I promise not to delay over reading it or giving you my frank opinion.[1]

In a further letter to the same, he wrote:

At the end of your nice letter, which is in front of me, you say, 'I remain your *little* friend—' Allow me to disapprove of a phrase too humble to be sincere; you are not little in my eyes, neither in size nor age nor reason; nor by the affection which you have inspired in me and in my family. We feel this as strongly as ever though you are far from us. 'If that is true', you will say to me, 'why have you been so slow in answering me?' Why? It will be easy for me to show that although it is true that I have not written, I have nevertheless answered you frequently and at length, and this is how. Letters and the post are not, luckily, the only means of communication, or the best, between people who are really fond of one another: I am not referring to the telephone, which allows one to speak, to have conversations, from a distance. I have something better than that. I only have to think of you to see you.

[1] Translation of original letter from M. Heger to Meta Mossman, 21 Nov. 1887: by courtesy of Walter Cunliffe, Esq. Meta's mother was Kate Douglas, whose home was near Ilkley; together with her sisters Marion and Lucy she went to the pensionnat in the 1860's. Kate married William Mossman, a friend of the Taylors, and it was his sister, the red-haired Violet, who visited Haworth with Joe and Henry Taylor in June 1848 for particulars about the pensionnat—the incident related by CB to EN in her letter of 26 June 1848. In her turn Kate Mossman sent her daughters to the Pensionnat Heger in the 1880's (Meta and May). Like Charlotte and Emily Brontë, they differed in their views about M. Heger: Meta adored him, May did not; but both agreed in saying Mme was 'a sweet old lady', 'not a bit like Mme Beck'. They also declared that the name 'Brontë' was taboo in the school.

I often give myself the pleasure when my duties are over, when the light fades. I postpone lighting the gas lamp in my library, I sit down, smoking my cigar, and with a hearty will I evoke your image—and you come (without wishing to, I dare say) but I see you, I talk with you—you, with that little air, affectionate undoubtedly, but independent and resolute, firmly determined not to allow any opinion without being previously convinced, demanding to be convinced before allowing yourself to submit—in fact, just as I knew you, my dear M—— and as I have esteemed and loved you.

In thinking it over you will have no difficulty in admitting that you yourself have experienced a hundred times that which I tell you about communication between two distant hearts, instantaneous, without paper, without pen, or words, or messenger, etc., a hundred times without noticing it, without its having attracted your attention, without anything extraordinary.

I end by saying that if it is true that I have not written, you cannot thereby conclude that I have neglected to answer you. I have often done so, and with all my heart, but I realise that it was very wrong of me to allow appearances to be against me. I ask your forgiveness. From now on you shall have your fill of paper, words, sentences—but—do not ask me to give up my precious and more convenient methods of communication, spiritual, magnetic, or by suggestion, for as much as the last word has become *French*.

Please deign to accept from your old friend a little remembrance sent to you, my dear Meta (by post) with my best wishes and sincere affection to you, to your excellent mother, to Monsieur your father, and all your family.

Your very devoted

C. Heger.[1]

The evidence of Mrs. Gaskell, and of references in Charlotte's own letters, show that M. Heger not only answered some of hers, but that he did so in his own hand. This is implicit in Charlotte's letter of 24 July, in which she wrote that she considered 'his letters as one of the greatest joys known to me'; and, again, in her letter of 18 November 1845, she acknowledged receiving one from him six months before, and spoke of the bitter disappointment when the post did not bring her 'the joy of seeing his writing'. The fact that he wrote to her at all is proof of his genuine interest in her welfare, for he hated letter-writing of all things. In his family it came to be considered an idiosyncrasy, and when his wife was not immediately available as amanuensis his daughters as they grew up were always called upon to write to his dictation. Any letter, therefore, addressed to him, was subject to more than his personal scrutiny, and well Charlotte knew this. Nevertheless, she addressed every one of her letters personally to him. That the style

[1] Translation of original letter from M. Heger to Meta Mossman: by courtesy of Walter Cunliffe, Esq.

of her letters placed him in a most difficult predicament she never seems to have realized. Only when his answers became more rare, and when they ceased altogether, did she attribute his silence to the intervention of Madame. She, as Charlotte well knew, had entertained suspicions of her since the previous year, suspicions at which Charlotte had sometimes laughed—and also sometimes cried; and on Madame she now laid the blame for every disappointment she suffered when the post-hour passed and no letter came from Brussels. Madame, she did not hesitate to believe, was not only the first to open the incoming mail from England, but to ensure that it did not reach Monsieur's hands. How unjustified she was in this suspicion the sequel showed.

As time passed she no longer entrusted her letters to the post but committed them to a friend with specific instructions to hand them personally to M. Heger. Repeatedly she put the question to him: had he received her previous letters, and specified their dates.

Nothing demonstrates more plainly the absence of all secrecy in her correspondence than this confiding of her letters to outsiders. She also asked them to be the bearers of M. Heger's replies. Of her right to correspond as her heart dictated, she made no scruple. Feeling it to be her right, she could not understand the painfully difficult situation she was creating for Monsieur and Madame Heger. She forced upon them the response most calculated to cause her suffering, to drive her to desperation. The more they ignored her appeals, the more frantic she became. The last letter of the series, that of November 1845, contains the most poignant declarations of love. In it she said: '. . . To forbid me to write to you, to refuse to answer me, would be to tear from me my only joy on earth . . .'.

Contrary to what she then believed M. Heger received her letters; that he set no great store by them appears from the fact that sooner or later he tore them up. How mistaken Charlotte was respecting Madame's part in the affair came to light many years after, when it was discovered that the letters owed their ultimate preservation to her. Fearing some blame might attach to her husband in the correspondence with a by then famous author, she diligently collected the torn-up pieces from his basket, stitched, gummed, pasted, and glued them together again. She put them aside till her death, as evidence of her husband's complete innocence.[1] Whatever happened the integrity of M. Heger as a teacher of young girls must never be called in doubt. He had always been, as

[1] M. H. Spielmann, *The Inner History of the Brontë–Heger Letters*: Chapman & Hall, 1919.

Charlotte wrote of Paul Emanuel, 'of spotless fame. Innocent childhood, beautiful youth were safe at his side. . . .'¹ The only charge that can possibly be made against M. Heger is that he showed too much caution in his determination not to appear to be encouraging Charlotte.

The absence of Ellen Nussey in the south, and the frustration of her school plans concerned her after her return, and the oppression of the time was deepened by her father's increasing blindness.

It was with immense relief that she at last received an invitation from Ellen Nussey early in March. Answering it on the 4th, she wrote: 'Monday Morning—My dear Ellen I received your note this morning. I shall have great pleasure in accepting the kind invitation which it conveys from your mother. I know nothing which can prevent me from coming on the day you fix, viz Thursday next—'²

She stayed away nearly three weeks, her poor health and spirits now a recognized fact as can be seen from her letter of 25 March written after returning home. 'Dear Nell—I got home safely, and was not too much tired on arriving at Haworth. I am rather better to-day, than I have been, and in time hope to regain more strength. . . .'³ Writing again on 7 April, in answer to Ellen's queries, she said: '. . . You ask me how I am. I really have felt much better the last week—I think my visit to Brookroyd did me good. What delightful weather we have had lately. I wish we had had such while I was with you. Emily and I walk out a good deal on the moors, to the great damage of our shoes, but I hope to the benefit of our health. . . .'⁴

With Emily, who had shared some of her Brussels experiences, she could talk of what wholly occupied her mind and heart. She found great solace in this, as appears from the last letter she wrote to M. Heger in November 1845,⁵ in which she told him that she had tried to forget him, and to that end had even deprived herself of the pleasure of speaking of him to Emily. Emily's comments, unlikely to be encouraging (she had 'not pulled well' with M. Heger), would contain wholesome good sense at least.

The unexpected return from Germany of Mary Taylor in April was a piece of 'good news' that aroused Charlotte's curiosity. She wrote to Ellen on the 7th:

. . . Can you tell me what caused the change in Mary's plans, and brought her so suddenly back to England? Is it on account of Mary Dixon? Is it the

¹ *Villette*, ch. 33.   ² CB to EN, 4 Mar. 1844: *SLL*, No. 144.
³ CB to EN; 25 Mar. 1844: *SLL*, No. 132.
⁴ CB to EN, 7 Apr. 1844: *SLL*, No. 134.   ⁵ See below, pp. 291–3.

wish of her brother, or is it her own determination? I hope, whatever the reason be, it is nothing which can give her uneasiness or do her harm. Do you know how long she is likely to stay in England, or when she arrives at Hunsworth?[1]

Hunsworth Mills, Cleckheaton, situated in the pleasant Spen Valley, and powered by its waters, was Mary's home in England since the death of her father in 1841, and the centre of Joe Taylor's business operations. Though their widowed mother continued to live at the Red House, Gomersal, none of her children, save her eldest son Joshua, was prepared to stay with her, and even he left when he got married. Referring to this in November 1845, Charlotte wrote to Ellen: 'I am not surprised to hear that Mr. & Mrs. T. are about to leave the old lady; her unhappy disposition is preparing for her a most desolate old age.'[2]

The house at Hunsworth was still very much as the young people's grandfather had built it in 1804 after a fire had destroyed the original building of 1785. 'I am going to stretch the house at Hunsworth,' Mary wrote to Ellen from the Dixons' home in Birmingham, 'and make it hold three or more people to stay, whereas I understand that now it only holds two (strangers).'[3]

Thanking Ellen for a note of welcome, Mary planned an early reunion with her friends. 'How did you smell out so speedily that I was come? I shall see you and ask you this and a thousand other questions in about a fortnight, and then I hope to see C.B. also.'

Of that meeting, which took place in May, Ellen wrote an unusually lively account to her friend Mary Gorham.

Miss Brontë has been a few days with Mary. I set off with my youngest brother [George] at nine o'clock at night to see her and there I found Charlotte also; both were walking and talking with all their might in the garden. It was so dark when I joined them that we could distinguish nothing but figures, and so afraid were we each of saluting a wrong individual that we cautiously peered into each other's faces; then all at once a 'Bless you' burst forth in all the power of friendship and affection.[4]

Greatly unlike herself, Charlotte was clinging to any spar thrown out by others; she was living at second-hand, dependent on the interest

1 CB to EN, 7 Apr. 1844: *SLL*, No. 134.
2 CB to EN, 20 Nov. 1845: *SLL* i. 312.
3 MT to EN, Apr. 1844: *SLL*, No. 136.
4 EN to Mary Gorham, 1845: *W & S*.

afforded her by others' lives. She found that she could not rest, could not sleep. Later she described to M. Heger how, even in her dreams, she saw him perpetually irritated with her.[1] At night she could weep unseen, and it is a sad commentary on this time that she writes repeatedly of her failing sight and the need to spare her eyes. Sorrow was blinding her surely. In later life she never mentioned defective sight, however hard pressed by work.

The early and fine spring, the freedom both physical and mental that escape on to the moors afforded her after the confinement of winter, helped to revive her spirits, and the return of Anne and Branwell for the summer holidays heralded happier days. She wrote to Ellen on Sunday, 23 June:

My dear Ellen—Anne & Branwell are now at home, and they and Emily join their request to mine, that you will join us at the beginning of next week. Write and let us know what day you will come, and how—if by coach, we will meet you at Keighley. Do not let your visit be later than the beginning of next week, or you will see little of Anne & Branwell, as their holidays are very short. They will soon have to join the family at Scarborough.[2]

The invitation extended on behalf, not only of herself, but of all the family, read like old times: after the forced separation of recent years the family entity was once more established, their singleness of purpose once more declared. It was an illusory entity, as Charlotte afterwards found, for already Branwell was far away from them in spirit. Recalling his behaviour that summer, she wrote of him in the following January to Ellen: '. . . Branwell has been quieter and less irritable on the whole this time than he was in summer. . . .' But no inkling of the special cause of his excitement and irritability had yet reached her, or the rest of the family—with the exception of Anne who was with him at Thorp Green—and nothing at the time really warranted Mrs. Gaskell's careful antedating of his ruin from the following year to this one, anxious as she was to suppress the real cause of Charlotte's growing unhappiness. That Branwell was eluding them all may have been the inescapable and saddening conclusion of those holidays, but one irrefutable proof that he was *not* the scandalous incubus he later became—and that Mrs. Gaskell supposed he already *was*—is shown in the sudden change Charlotte made in her school-plans that July.

[1] CB to M. Heger, 9 Jan. 1845: BM.
[2] CB to EN, 23 June 1844: *SLL*, No. 138; *W & S* ii. 6.

During Ellen's visit to Haworth the decision was reached by the three girls—and sanctioned by Mr. Brontë—that instead of setting up school away from home, they would, with a minimum of alteration, adapt the parsonage to the purposes of a school—or rather to accommodating 'a limited number of pupils . . .'. Since Branwell's moral and physical collapse in the following year was the reason why Charlotte abandoned the plan, it is evident that he presented no particular obstacle to it in the summer of 1844. Charlotte wrote to Ellen on 20 July, almost immediately after the latter's departure from Haworth:

I have seriously entered into the enterprise of keeping a school, that is I have begun to seek in good earnest for pupils—I wrote to Mrs. White, not asking her for her daughter, I cannot do that, but informing her of my intentions. I received an answer from Mr. White expressive of, I believe, sincere regret that I had not informed them a month sooner, in which case, he said, they would gladly have sent me their own daughter, and also Colonel Stott's, but that now both were promised to Miss Cockhill. I was partly disappointed by this answer, and partly gratified; indeed, I derived quite an impulse of encouragement from the warm assurance that if I had but applied a little sooner they would certainly have sent me Sarah Louisa. I own, I had misgivings that nobody would be willing to send a child for education at Haworth. These misgivings are partly done away with. I have written also to Mrs. Busfield of Keighley, and have enclosed the diploma which M. Heger gave me before I left Brussels.[1]

The opportunity to make use of M. Heger's diploma at last, and to be actively pursuing the object in which he had shown so much interest, raised her spirits. Her hope and confidence in the project are shown by the letter she wrote to M. Heger on 24 July, only a few days after writing to Ellen. The return of Mrs. Wheelwright to Brussels afforded her a further excuse. She wrote on 24 July:

Monsieur, I am well aware that it is not my turn to write to you, but as Mrs. Wheelwright is going to Brussels and is kind enough to take charge of a letter—it appears to me that I ought not to neglect so favourable an opportunity of writing to you.

I am very pleased that the school-year is nearly over and that the holidays are approaching—I am pleased on your account, Monsieur—for I am told that you are working too hard and that your health has suffered somewhat in consequence. For that reason I refrain from uttering a single complaint for your long silence—I would rather remain six months without receiving news from you than add one grain to the weight, already too heavy, which

---

[1] CB to EN, 20 July 1844: *W & S* ii. 9.

overwhelms you. I know well that it is now the period of compositions, that it will soon be that of examinations and later on of prizes—and during all that time you are condemned to breathe the stifling atmosphere of the class-rooms—to spend yourself—to explain, to question, to talk all day, and then in the evening you have all those wretched compositions to read, to correct, almost to rewrite—Ah, Monsieur! I once wrote you a letter that was less than reasonable, because sorrow was at my heart; but I shall do so no more—I shall try to be selfish no longer; and even while I look upon your letters as one of the greatest felicities known to me I shall await the receipt of them in patience until it pleases you and suits you to send me any. Meanwhile I may well send you a little letter from time to time:—you have authorised me to do so.

I greatly fear that I shall forget French, for I am firmly convinced that I shall see you again some day—I know not how or when—but it must be for I wish it so much, and then I should not wish to remain dumb before you—it would be too sad to see you and not be able to speak to you. To avoid such a misfortune I learn every day by heart a half a page of French from a book written in familiar style: and I take pleasure in learning this lesson, Monsieur; as I pronounce the French words it seems to me as if I were chatting with you.

I have just been offered a situation as first governess in a large school in Manchester, with a salary of £100 (i.e. 2,500 francs) per annum. I cannot accept it, for in accepting it I should have to leave my father, and that I can-not do. Nevertheless I have a plan—(when one lives retired the brain goes on working; there is the desire of occupation, the wish to embark on an active career). Our parsonage is rather a large house—with a few alterations there will be room for five or six boarders. If I could find this number of children of good family I should devote myself to their education. Emily does not care much for teaching but she would look after the housekeeping and, although something of a recluse, she is too good-hearted not to do all she could for the well-being of the children. Moreover she is very generous, and as for order, economy, strictness—and diligent work—all of them things very essential in a school—I willingly take that upon myself.

That, Monsieur, is my plan, which I have already explained to my father and which he approves. It only remains to find the pupils—rather a difficult thing—for we live rather far from towns and one does not greatly care about crossing the hills which form as it were a barrier around us. But the task that is without difficulty is almost without merit; there is great interest in triumphing over obstacles. I do not say I shall succeed but I shall *try* to suc-ceed—the effort alone will do me good. There is nothing I fear so much as idleness, the want of occupation, inactivity, the lethargy of the faculties: when the body is idle the spirit suffers painfully.

I should not know this lethargy if I could write. Formerly I passed whole days and weeks and months in writing, not wholly without result, for Southey and Coleridge[1] two of our best authors, to whom I sent certain manuscripts—were good enough to express their approval; but now my sight is too weak to write.—Were I to write much I should become blind. This weakness of sight is a terrible hindrance to me. Otherwise do you know what I should do, Monsieur?—I should write a book and I should dedicate it to my literature-master—to the only master I ever had—to you, Monsieur. I have often told you in French how much I respect you—how much I am indebted to your goodness, to your advice; I should like to say it once in English. But that cannot be—it is not to be thought of. The career of letters is closed to me—only that of teaching is open. It does not offer the same attractions; never mind, I shall enter it and if I do not go far it will not be from want of industry. You too, Monsieur—you wished to be a barrister —destiny or Providence made you a professor; you are happy in spite of it.

Please convey to Madame the assurance of my esteem. I fear that Marie, Louise, Claire have already forgotten me. Prospère and Victorine never knew me well; I remember well all five of them, especially Louise. She had so much character—so much naiveté in her little face.—Goodbye, Monsieur, your grateful pupil,   C. Brontë

I have not begged you to write to me soon as I fear to importune you— but you are too kind to forget that I wish it all the same—yes, I wish it greatly. Enough: after all, do as you wish, Monsieur. If, then, I received a letter and if I thought that you had written it *out of pity*—I should feel deeply wounded.

It seems that Mrs. Wheelwright is going to Paris before going to Brussels —but she will post my letter at Boulogne. Once more goodbye, Monsieur; it hurts to say goodbye even in a letter. Oh, it is certain that I shall see you again one day—it must be so—for as soon as I shall have earned enough money to go to Brussels I shall go there—and I shall see you again if only for a moment.[2]

It would appear from this letter ('I am told that you are working too hard and that your health has suffered somewhat in consequence') that some direct news of the pensionnat and of M. Heger was reaching her. A hitherto unpublished letter from a former pupil found in her desk after death shows that some information was available to her. There were no doubt other letters. The naïve and touching one signed 'Mathilde', though concerned only with an adolescent's feelings, con- firms not only that Charlotte had awakened some devotion among her

---

[1] Southey had written to Charlotte in Mar. 1837, see above, p. 110. It was Hartley Cole- ridge to whom she wrote in 1840, following his kindness to Branwell. See Gérin, *Branwell Brontë*, 176.

[2] B.M. Add. MSS. 38732/A, English translation by M. H. Spielmann, *SBC*. For original French text see Appendixes.

pupils (as she herself was surprised to find on leaving Brussels) but that she was sufficiently interested in one of them at least to correspond with her.

There could be no question of using Mathilde to gain news of M. Heger, but the letters were a reminder of the pensionnat in summer, and acted on her like a reviving draught. Though undated—the letter was written in July of this year.[1] It reads:

Ma chère Demoiselle,
Had I been able I would long ago have made use of the address you sent me and whose receipt gave me such pleasure.

With the approach of the month of August we have more work on our hands than ever, but that would be nothing if I had not visiting masters at home as well, and on top of that I have to practise my piano for all I am worth, for in consequence of the illness of several of our pianistes at school we are short, and for want of a better they have had to choose me to play at Madame's fête.[2] I cannot imagine how I shall get through it; unhappily for me the very idea of someone listening to me makes me lose my head, however hard I try, and I greatly fear my début will be a failure. All the same, I do so want to succeed. One of my cousins, who has had every sort of family misfortune, is now my piano-teacher, she has a number of pupils among Mme H's girls, but in the kingdom of the blind a one-eyed man is king, so it happens that I am the best of a bad lot. We are very fond of our dear teacher as she deserves, and that's a very great deal. You can imagine how much I could disappoint her and injure her prospects if I didn't come up to her expectations—So Courage, I must hope that God will help me in a matter so small in itself, but which can have good or evil consequences for my cousin.

There is a word in your letter, Mlle Charlotte, which has given me great pleasure. I may be mistaken, for you probably used it without giving it so particular a meaning as I have done: do you remember saying to me, I shall not cease to think of you with affection and even with estim. [sic] Well! You can't imagine what pleasure that word estime [sic] has given me! I would even say it has made me happy. It seemed to me up to now that I could hope for the friendship of certain people whom I greatly esteemed, but to receive their esteem seemed to me so much more than their friendship, though I don't think I have ever up to this time done anything, in spite of my faults, that made me contemptible. That word, used by you, my kind teacher, has done me more good—Well! you just can't imagine how much.

If you only knew how short a time ago I had the blackest of black thoughts! I was certain, for one thing, that no one would ever love me, although one of

[1] The original letter addressed 'Mademoiselle Charlotte Brontë, Angleterre' must have been remitted by hand through an intermediary. The letter-paper is stamped with initials in Gothic lettering—'G.W.' at the top left-hand corner. It is at the BPM.
[2] Ste Claire, 12 Aug.

my old friends cured me of that; I had real bouts of melancholia, so that Mamma thought I must be ill. Happily, though it hasn't quite gone, it is much better now.

Ma chère demoiselle, I must scold you, for you have given me no news of your health! I hope you will say something about it at the first opportunity you have of writing to me, and to show you the way, I will tell you that I am so well at the moment that I hope it is the same with you. Good-bye, Mlle Charlotte, good-bye, I embrace you with all my heart, since I cannot even do it in anticipation.

Your very devoted
Mathilde

Mlle Charlotte, please forgive my folly, but when I write to you it seems to me the door of my heart opens wide and only the want of time and of letter-paper forces me to close it.

Apologizing for the shy avowal that the mere act of writing to her beloved teacher opened the door of her heart, Mathilde could have little suspicion that such language was all too understandable to her correspondent.

Meanwhile, having set her mind on the establishment of a school Charlotte did not draw back. On 29 July she reported further progress to Ellen: '. . . I am driving on with my small affair as well as I can. I have written to all the friends on whom I have the slightest claim, and to some on whom I have no claim—Mrs. Busfield for example. On her, also, I have actually made bold to call. . . .'

Elizabeth Hastings,[1] as long ago as 1839, had traced Charlotte's path for her, doing exactly what she was doing now, summoning 'all her address and lady-like manners to her aid' to call 'on the wealthy manu-facturers of the city and the aristocracy of the seats around' in pursuit of pupils. The wings she had so desired had brought her back to her exact starting-point; Mrs. Busfield, receiving her most politely and regretting that her own children 'were already at school at Liverpool', could not guess on what a wonderful and circuitous flight they had taken her meanwhile.

Mrs. Busfield remarked that she thought the terms very moderate—but that, as it is, not having house rent to pay, we can offer the same privileges of education that are to be had in expensive seminaries, at little more than half their price. . . . Thank you for the very pretty little purse you have sent me. I make you a curious return in the shape of half a dozen cards of terms.

[1] 'Henry Hastings', fragment of a tale, written Feb.–Mar. 1839: Harvard University.

Make use of them as your judgement shall dictate. You will see that I have fixed the sum at £35.[1]

Modelled on the prospectus of the Pensionnat Heger, Charlotte had drawn up a circular for the projected school; it read:

The Misses Brontë's Establishment

For

THE BOARD AND EDUCATION

of a limited number of
Young Ladies
The Parsonage, Haworth,
Near Bradford.

Terms

	£	s.	d.
Board and Education, including Writing, Arithmetic, History, Grammar, Geography, and Needle Work, per Annum	35	0	0
French German Latin each per Quarter		1 1	0
Music Drawing each per Quarter		1 1	0
Use of Piano Forte, per Quarter		5	0
Washing, per Quarter		15	0

Each young Lady to be provided with One Pair of Sheets, Pillow Cases, Four Towels, a Dessert and Tea Spoon.

A Quarter's Notice, or a Quarter's Board, is required previous to the Removal of a Pupil.

She sent Ellen a further couple of circulars for distribution in a note of 15 August, and again on 16 September. By then the complete lack of response from parents had made it apparent that no pupils would be forthcoming. On 2 October Charlotte wrote to Ellen accepting defeat:

Dear Ellen,—I, Emily, and Anne are truly obliged to you for the efforts you have made on our behalf, and if you have not been successful, you are only like ourselves. Every one wishes us well, but there are no pupils to be

1 CB to EN, 29 July 1844: *SLL*, No. 139; *W & S* ii. 15.

had. We have no present intention, however, of breaking our hearts on the subject, still less of feeling mortified at defeat. The effort must be beneficial whatever the result may be, because it teaches us experience and an additional knowledge of the world.[1]

In spite of brave words, the failure was a blow to her; it deprived her of an objective at a time when one was essential. There was nothing now to divert her thoughts from the other—and profounder cause—of her depression. No answer had come from Brussels to her letter of 24 July.

Mary Taylor had returned there for half a year, teaching and studying music until something better offered. Her brother's business, and the Dixons' presence, was still an incentive for keeping her there, but by 16 September she had communicated to Charlotte the completion of her great plan, projected as long ago as 1841: 'Mary Taylor is going to leave our hemisphere', Charlotte wrote Ellen on that day. 'To me it is something as if a great planet fell out of the sky. Yet, unless she marries in New Zealand, she will not stay there long. . . .'[2]

In the same letter Charlotte excused herself for not writing sooner on the grounds that she had had a letter from Mary Taylor 'and had to reply to her, and to write sundry letters to Brussels to send by opportunity. My sight will not allow me to write several letters per day, so I was obliged to do it gradually. . . .'

The 'opportunity' to write yet again to Brussels occurred on 24 October when Charlotte confided a letter for M. Heger to Joe Taylor, whose return at the end of the year without bringing a reply struck the death-blow to her friendship:

Monsieur,—I am in high glee this morning—and that has rarely happened to me these last two years. It is because a gentleman of my acquaintance is going to Brussels and has offered to take charge of a letter for you—which letter he will deliver to you himself, or else, his sister, so that I shall be certain that you have received it.

I am not going to write a long letter; in the first place, I have not the time —it must leave at once; and then, I am afraid of worrying you. I would only ask if you heard from me at the beginning of May and again in the month of August? For six months I have been awaiting a letter from Monsieur— six months' waiting is very long, you know! However, I do not complain and I shall be richly rewarded for a little sorrow if you will now write a letter and give it to this gentleman—or to his sister—who will hand it to me without fail.

[1] CB to EN, 2 Oct. 1844: *SLL*, No. 142; *W & S*, ii. 17.
[2] CB to EN, 16 Sept. 1844: *SLL*, No. 141; *W & S* ii. 16–17.

I shall be satisfied with the letter however brief it be—only do not forget to tell me of your health, Monsieur, and how Madame and the children are, and the governesses and pupils.

My father and my sister send you their respects. My father's infirmity increases little by little. Nevertheless he is not yet entirely blind. My sisters are well, but my poor brother is always ill.

Farewell, Monsieur; I am depending on soon having your news. The idea delights me for the remembrance of your kindnesses will never fade from my memory, and as long as that remembrance endures the respect with which it has inspired me will endure likewise.—

Your very devoted pupil,
C. Brontë.

I have just had bound all the books you gave me when I was at Brussels. I take delight in contemplating them; they make quite a little library. To begin with, there are the complete works of Bernardin de St. Pierre—the Pensées de Pascal—a book of poetry, two German books—and (worth all the rest) two discourses of Monsieur le Professeur Heger, delivered at the distribution of prizes of the Athénée Royal.[1]

In prosecuting her plans for the school, Charlotte received every support and encouragement from Emily and Anne, especially from the latter, who would no longer have to go away to earn her living. In two letters to Ellen, Charlotte expressed their joint gratitude to her for her efforts to publicize the school. 'I hope', she wrote on 16 September, 'that if a time should come when Emily, Anne, or I shall be able to serve you, we shall not forget that you have done your best to serve us.'

And again, on 2 October in the letter already quoted, she joined Emily's and Anne's thanks to her own. That the plan was not wholly abandoned, her letter of 14 November showed; in it she wrote: '... We have made no alteration yet in our house. It would be folly to do so while there is so little likelihood of our ever getting pupils. ...' Ellen herself, by her continued exertions on her friends' behalf, would appear to have been one of the reasons why the plan had not already been completely given up. '. . . I fear you are giving yourself too much trouble on our account,' Charlotte went on. 'Depend on it, if you were to persuade a Mamma to bring her child to Haworth, the aspect of the place would frighten her, and she would probably take the dear girl

---

[1] CB to M. Heger, 24 Oct. 1844: B.M. Add. MSS. 38732/B, English translation by M. H. Spielmann, *SBC*. For original French text, see Appendixes.

back with her instanter. We are glad we have made the attempt, and we will not be cast down because it has not succeeded. . . .'[1]

As the autumn advanced, a fresh preoccupation filled Charlotte's mind; Mary Taylor, who had written from Brussels in September definitely announcing her departure for New Zealand in the early spring, was expected back in England before the end of the year to take farewell of her family and friends. Together with her concern for Mary's own welfare and the hope of a few last times together, Charlotte hoped too that Mary, coming from Brussels, would be the bearer of a letter for her. '. . . I wonder when Mary Taylor is expected in England,' Charlotte asked in her letter of 14 November of Ellen; 'it surprises me to hear of Joe being in Switzerland—probably she is with him there also—in that case it may yet be some weeks before they return . . . '.[2]

Hope deferred acted like a perpetual irritant to her nerves. As she shortly told M. Heger, it was nearly eight months since she had heard from him, and the strain of keeping up outward appearances caused an inner conflict that had become well-nigh unbearable. She knew of no other recourse to alleviate her suffering than by a direct appeal to him. Every day she waited for the post, hoping for the miracle to happen and for that white square of paper—of which she wrote so eloquently in *Villette*—to be delivered into her hand.

My hour of torment was the post-hour. Unfortunately, I knew it too well, and tried as vainly as assiduously to cheat myself of that knowledge; dreading the rack of expectation, and the sick collapse of disappointment which daily preceded and followed upon that well-recognised ring. . . . The letter—the well-beloved letter—would not come; and it was all of sweetness in life I had to look for.[3]

Meantime, Joe Taylor began sending her French newspapers—a habit he continued for years and which, for the chance they brought her of keeping up her French and for their intrinsic interest—above all, for the spiritual link she felt them to constitute with M. Heger—afforded her keen pleasure. The Hegers had sufficiently wide contacts with academic, charitable, and religious circles for occasional echoes of their activities to reach the press. It may indeed be from an announcement in the newspapers of the birth of their second son, Paul, on 14

[1] CB to EN, 14 Nov. 1844: *SLL*, No. 143; *W & S* ii. 19–21.
[2] CB to EN, 14 Nov. 1844: *SLL*, No. 143; op. cit.
[3] *Villette*, ch. 24.

December 1846, that Charlotte heard of it, and conceived the name for the hero of *Villette*; for by then the news was unlikely to reach her by a more personal channel.

The year drew to its close. Refusing an invitation from Ellen for herself and Anne to spend Christmas at Brookroyd, ostensibly on Anne's account ('her vacations are so short she would grudge spending any part of them from home')[1] she waited for news of Mary Taylor's return. At last it came. Instantly, Charlotte invited her to Haworth, where she went at the beginning of January. There was no letter for Charlotte from M. Heger.

This was the turning-point in her relations with him. A sense of outrage entered now into her feelings; there was anger mixed with the desolation. Though she still might exonerate him from the worst cruelties—because she was convinced he was not wholly free to act as he would—she no longer hesitated to point the finger at the enemy working through him: she scornfully challenged those 'reasonable', 'cold-headed' persons who charged her with losing her senses, and it was plain that she meant Madame Heger. The idea that an enemy was bent on her destruction—however wrong it may have been—was implanted for ever. 'Madame Beck' was born in that January of the suffering caused by M. Heger's silence.

Yet from the depths of her own misery she could hold out a saving hand to a friend in distress. Mary Taylor had come with news that Ellen's only likeable brother, George, had had a severe mental breakdown—a disaster that would darken the Nusseys' home for years, as Branwell's would shortly darken the Brontës'. Instantly Charlotte wrote to Ellen: '. . . Poor Mr. George! I am very sorry for him, very sorry; he did not deserve this suffering. I know, too, what a calamity his severe illness will be to all the family, and most especially for you. . . . When you do write, inform me how you all bear the fatigue of body and anxiety of mind you have had to go through. . . . Good-bye, dear Ellen.'[2] For the next few months, at the height of her own crisis, her letters to Ellen were filled with encouraging reflections on George's case, tender inquiries, soothing advice.

Having written immediately to Ellen, on 6 January, she wrote to M. Heger two days later. No one of her acquaintance going over to Belgium at the time, she posted the letter. Now preserved at the British Museum, it bears the Haworth and also the Bradford postmarks for

[1] 14 Nov. 1844: op. cit.
[2] CB to EN, 6 Jan. 1845: *W & S* ii. 21.

9 January 1845, and was delivered in Brussels on 12 January. She wrote
without preamble:

Mr. Taylor has returned. I asked him if he had a letter for me. 'No;
nothing.' 'Patience,' said I—'his sister will be here soon.' Miss Taylor has
returned. 'I have nothing for you from Monsieur Heger,' says she; 'neither
letter nor message.'

Having realised the meaning of these words, I said to myself what I
should say to another similarly placed: 'You must be resigned, and above
all do not grieve at a misfortune which you have not deserved.' I strove to
restrain my tears, to utter no complaint.

But when one does not complain, when one seeks to dominate oneself
with a tyrant's grip, the faculties start into rebellion and one pays for external
calm with an internal struggle that is almost unbearable.

Day and night I find neither rest nor peace. If I sleep I am disturbed by
tormenting dreams in which I see you, always severe, always grave, always
incensed against me.

Forgive me then, Monsieur, if I adopt the course of writing to you again.
How can I endure life if I make no effort to ease its sufferings?

I know that you will be irritated when you read this letter. You will say
once more that I am hysterical (or neurotic)—that I have black thoughts,
etc. So be it, Monsieur, I do not seek to justify myself; I submit to every sort
of reproach. All I know is, that I cannot, that I will not, resign myself to lose
wholly the friendship of my master. I would rather suffer the greatest physical
pain than always have my heart lacerated by smarting regrets. If my master
withdraws his friendship from me entirely I shall be altogether without hope;
if he gives me a little—just a little—I shall be satisfied—happy; I shall have
a reason for living on, for working.

Monsieur, the poor have not need of much to sustain them—they ask
only for the crumbs that fall from the rich man's table. But if they are refused
the crumbs they die of hunger. Nor do I, either, need much affection from
those I love. I should not know what to do with a friendship entire and
complete—I am not used to it. But you showed me of yore a *little* interest,
when I was your pupil in Brussels, and I hold on to the maintenance of that
little interest—I hold on to it as I would hold on to life.

You will tell me perhaps—'I take not the slightest interest in you, Mademoiselle Charlotte. You are no longer an inmate of my House; I have forgotten you.'

Well, Monsieur, tell me so frankly. It will be a shock to me. It matters not.
It would be less dreadful than uncertainty.

I shall not re-read this letter. I send it as I have written it. Nevertheless, I
have a hidden consciousness that some people, cold and common-sense, in
reading it would say—'She is talking nonsense.' I would avenge myself on
such persons in no other way than by wishing them one single day of the

torments which I have suffered for eight months. We should then see if they would not talk nonsense too.

One suffers in silence so long as one has the strength so to do, and when that strength gives out one speaks without too carefully measuring one's words.

I wish Monsieur happiness and prosperity.

C. B.[1]

The very echoes of certain expressions in that letter—written in French though they are—can be found in the key-poem 'Frances'—to which on that account an approximate date can be given.

> Who can for ever crush the heart,
> Restrain its throbbing, curb its life?
> Dissemble truth with ceaseless art,
> *With outward calm mask inward strife?*[2]

However incapable she felt herself at the time of prolonged composition, she could and did unburden her heart in verse in which, unequal and pedestrian as much of it was, the full revelation of her grief is to be found. The poems reflect the new sense of outrage and anger first betrayed in the letter of 9 January.

> Unloved—I love; unwept—I weep;
> Grief I restrain—hope I repress:
> Vain is the anguish—fixed and deep;
> Vainer, desires and dreams of bliss—
>
> My love awakes no love again,
> My tears collect, and fall unfelt;
> My sorrow touches none with pain,
> My humble hopes to nothing melt.
>
> For me the universe is dumb,
> Stone-deaf, and blank, and wholly blind;
> Life I must bound, existence sum
> In the strait limits of one mind;
>
> That mind my own. Oh! narrow cell;
> Dark—imageless—a living tomb!
> There must I sleep, there wake and dwell
> Content, with palsy, pain, and gloom.[3]

---

[1] CB to M. Heger, 9 Jan. 1845: B.M. Add. MSS. 38732/D, English translation by M. H. Spielmann, *SBC*. For original French text, see Appendixes.

[2] 'Frances': *W & S, PCPBB*, 20–28.

[3] 'Reason': Idem, 239–40.

The rambling poem, echoing many moods, was an attempt to clarify what remained inexplicable to herself, the cause of the change in her master.

> Oh! Love was all a thin illusion;
> Joy, but the desert's flying stream;
> And glancing back on long delusion,
> My memory grasps a hollow dream.
>
> Yet whence that wondrous change of feeling,
> I never knew, and cannot learn;
> Nor why my lover's eye, congealing,
> Grew cold and clouded, proud and stern.—
>
> Nor wherefore, friendship's forms forgetting,
> He careless left, and cool withdrew;
> Nor spoke of grief, nor fond regretting,
> Nor e'en one glance of comfort threw.
>
> And neither word nor token sending,
> Of Kindness, since the parting day,
> His course, for distant regions bending,
> Went, self-contained and calm, away.[1]

The poem 'Frances', published in 1846 in the collected *Poems by Currer, Ellis and Acton Bell*, was much modified from the original draft which, under the title 'Reason', was far more revealing of its author's sentiments. In that original version she did not hesitate to acknowledge both her physical inadequacy and her flight from temptation. As it stood, the poem formed only part of the later 'Frances'.

> Unloved—I love; unwept—I weep;
> Grief I restrain—hope I repress:
> Vain is the anguish—fixed and deep;
> Vainer, desires and dream of bliss.
>
> My life is cold, love's fire being dead;
> That fire self-kindled, self-consumed;
> What living warmth erewhile it shed,
> Now to how drear extinction doomed!
>
> Devoid of charm how could I dream
> My unasked love would e'er return?
> What fate, what influence lit the flame
> I still feel inly, deeply burn?

[1] 'Reason': *W & S*, PCPBB, 239–40.

Alas! there are those who should not love;
I to this dreary band belong;
This knowing let me henceforth prove
Too wise to list delusion's song;

No, Syren! Beauty is not mine;
Affection's joy I ne'er shall know;
Lonely will be my life's decline,
E'en as my youth is lonely now.

Come Reason—Science—Learning—Thought—
To you my heart I dedicate;
I have a faithful subject brought:
Faithful because most desolate.

Fear not a wandering, feeble mind:
Stern Sovereign, it is all your own
To crush, to cheer, to loose, to bind;
Unclaimed, unshared, it seeks your throne.

Soft may the breeze of summer blow,
Sweetly its sun in valleys shine—
All earth around with love may glow,
No warmth shall reach this heart of mine.

Vain boast and false! Even now the fire
Though smothered, slacked, repelled, is burning
At my life's source; and stronger, higher,
Waxes the spirit's trampled yearning.

It wakes but to be crushed again:
Faint I will not, nor yield to sorrow;
Conflict and force will quell the brain;
Doubt not I shall be strong to-morrow.

Have I not fled that I may conquer?
Crost the dark sea in firmest faith
That I at last might plant my anchor
Where love cannot prevail to death?[1]

Though belonging to a later period (December 1847) the poem of
harshest accusation, 'He saw my heart's woe', with its image of her
suffering seen in retrospect, speaks nevertheless of what she underwent
in 1845, and has therefore its place here.

[1] 'Reason': *W & S*, *PCPBB*, 239–40.

He saw my heart's woe, discerned my soul's anguish,
How in fever, in thirst, in atrophy it pined;
Knew he could heal, yet looked and let it languish,
To its moans spirit-deaf, to its pangs spirit-blind.

But once a year he heard a whisper low and dreary,
Appealing for aid, entreating some reply;
Only when sick, soul-worn and torture-weary,
Breathed I that prayer—heaved I that sigh.

He was mute as is the grave, he stood stirless as a tower;
At last I looked up, and saw I prayed to stone;
I asked help of that which to help had no power,
I sought love where love was utterly unknown.

Idolator I kneeled to an idol cut in rock,
I might have slashed my flesh and drawn my heart's best blood,
The Granite God had felt no tenderness, no shock;
My Baal had not seen nor heard nor understood.

In dark remorse I rose—I rose in darker shame,
Self-condemned I withdrew to an exile from my kind;
A solitude I sought where mortal never came,
Hoping in its wilds forgetfulness to find.

Now Heaven heal the wound which I still deeply feel;
Thy glorious hosts look not in scorn on our poor race;
Thy King eternal doth no iron judgment deal
On suffering worms who seek forgiveness, comfort, grace.

He gave our hearts to love, he will not love despise,
E'en if the gift be lost as mine was long ago,
He will forgive the fault—will bid the offender rise,
Wash out with dews of bliss the fiery brand of woe;

And give a sheltered place beneath the unsullied throne,
Whence the soul redeemed may mark Time's fleeting course round earth;
And know its trial o'erpast, its sufferings o'er gone
And feel the peril past of Death's immortal birth.[1]

Her Brussels experience still dominated her vision and much of the
poetry written at that time re-creates the Brussels scene. The poems
inserted in *The Professor*—and undoubtedly written before the novel

[1] *W & S, PCPBB*, 240–1.

—show this; as does, for example, the poem 'Gilbert' published in the *Poems by Currer, Ellis and Acton Bell* in 1846. Evoking an incident— imagined or real—when she had been ill at the pensionnat and her master had shown concern, she described how, on her return to the classroom, he had ordered her out into the garden; and in every descriptive touch evoked the garden of the Rue d'Isabelle.

. . .

Jane, till to-morrow you are free
From tedious task-rule;
This afternoon I must not see
That yet pale face in school.

Seek in the garden-shades a seat,
Far from the play-ground din;
The sun is warm, the air is sweet:
Stay till I call you in:

A long and pleasant afternoon
I passed in those green bowers;
All silent, tranquil, and alone
With birds, and bees, and flowers.[1]

In the setting of the opening verses of 'Gilbert' occurs a still more recognizable evocation of the pensionnat garden.

Above the city hung the moon,
Right o'er a plot of ground
Where flowers and orchard-trees are fenced
With lofty walls around:

'Twas Gilbert's garden—there to-night
Awhile he walked alone;
And, tired, with sedentary toil,
Mused where the moonlight shone.

This garden, in a city-heart,
Lay still as houseless wild,
Though many-windowed mansion fronts
Were round it closely piled . . .

The city's many-mingled sounds
Rose like the hum of ocean.[2]

[1] 'Master and Pupil': *W & S, PCPBB*, 231–5.
[2] 'Gilbert': Idem, 29–32.

The same garden became one of the focal spots of the action in *Villette*:

Behind the house at the Rue Fossette there was a garden, large, considering that it lay in the heart of a city. . . . The windowless backs of houses built in this garden, and in particular the whole of one side, was skirted by the rear of a long line of premises—being the boarding-houses of the neighbouring college. . . . On the night in question, I was sitting on the hidden seat . . . listening to what seemed the far-off sounds of the city. Far off, in truth, they were not: this school was in the city's centre.[1]

If memory clung to the places connected with her love, how much more was it haunted by the beloved image itself! In the poem 'The Letter', the girl bent over her writing was described as glancing up at the portrait of the husband to whom the letter is addressed, and of him she said:

> A stalwart form, a massive head,
> A firm determined face,
> Black Spanish locks, a sunburnt cheek,
> A brow high, broad, and white,
> Where every furrow seems to speak
> Of mind and moral might.[2]

the prototype already of Paul Emanuel—with his 'Spanish face', his 'swart, sallow, southern darkness which spoke of his Spanish blood'.[3]

Before the letters of Charlotte Brontë to M. Heger were bequeathed to the British Museum by his son in 1913, there existed students of her work (May Sinclair notably among them)[4] who denied the existence of any deeper feeling in Charlotte's relations with her master than those of a grateful and devoted pupil. The theorists had inevitably to change their views when those letters were published. And yet, even now, they defy interpretation.

The *idée fixe*, to which Charlotte herself confessed, was a consuming passion that dominated everything, finally inspiring her acknowledged masterpiece *Villette*, as it had prompted the meagre and uninspired writings of this difficult period. It was a rare passion, transcending anything purely material. What, after all, was Charlotte hoping for? She certainly had no thought of seducing M. Heger from his marital duties—hence her scorn for his wife's suspicions. She explained in *Villette* what his friendship meant to her:

While he spoke, the tone of his voice, the light of his now affectionate eye, gave me such pleasure as, certainly, I had never felt. I envied no girl her

[1] *Villette*, ch. 12. [2] 'The Letter': *W & S, PCPBB.*
[3] *Villette*, ch. 27. [4] May Sinclair, *The Three Brontës*, London, 1912.

lover, no bride her bridegroom, no wife her husband; I was content with this my voluntary, self-offering friend. If he would prove reliable, and he *looked* reliable, what, beyond his friendship, could I ever covet?[1]

How little she asked, indeed, few—certainly not the Hegers—could credit. When she wrote 'je n'ai pas besoin de beaucoup d'affection de la part de ceux que j'aime je ne saurais que faire d'une amitié entière et complète . . .' (I do not need much affection from those I love. I should not know what to do with a friendship entire and complete . . .)[2] she was not being disingenuous. Her imagination needed little to build on, and out of little she could make much.

Her sensibility responded to the limited experience of her life with exceptional intensity. Her feelings were never stirred but *to their depths*; she was incapable of a superficial response to any stimulus, if she were moved it was to 'the finest fibre of her being'. To such a woman the degree of feeling roused for any object was sure to be in excess of the conventional limit. Since childhood she had lived in an emotional 'climate' where feeling reigned supreme—and where feeling *was extreme*—where friendship was like love, and love like worship. What she now asked of her friend was a transcendental, God-like love, present though unseen, felt though intangible, enfolding though removed.

It is significant that the imagery she used on several occasions to describe the beloved object was directly derived from the divine conception. Jane Eyre, for instance, would say: 'My future husband was becoming to me my whole world and, more than the world: almost my hope of heaven. He stood between me and every thought of religion, as an eclipse intervenes between man and the broad sun. I could not, in those days, see God for his creature: of whom I had made an idol.'[3] 'Idolator I kneeled to an idol cut in rock', she had written directly of her worship of M. Heger.

> I might have slashed my flesh and drawn my heart's best blood,
> The Granite God had felt no tenderness, no shock;
> My Baal had not seen nor heard nor understood.[4]

A passage in *Villette*, written, it must be remembered, some seven or eight years later, carries the same concept a stage further: the beloved idol has become identified with Fate, an impersonal power her pleadings glance off like arrows off chain-mail. 'That evening more firmly than

[1] *Villette*, ch. 36.   [2] CB to M. Heger, 9 Jan. 1845: BM.: op. cit.
[3] *Jane Eyre*, ch. 24.   [4] 'He saw my heart's woe...': *W & S, PCPBB*, 240–1: op. cit.

ever fastened into my soul the conviction that Fate was of stone, and Hope a false idol—blind, bloodless, and of granite core. . . .'[1] For all the Brontës the dedication of their hearts contained an element of religion: for them, it is true to say that worship and love were one.

Not to be loved had been Charlotte's ultimate dread since childhood. The nightmare of her schooldays, as Mary Taylor recalled, was the vision of her beloved dead sisters, returned, but changed towards her; unloving and censorious. The impression lasted all her life, and in *Villette* it haunted her again with a recurrent horror. '. . . Methought the well-beloved dead, who had loved *me* well in life, met me elsewhere, alienated: galled was my inmost spirit with an unutterable sense of despair. . .'[2] Summing up Lucy Snowe's anguish, Charlotte had nothing more to say than that it was contained in the 'insufferable thought of being no more loved. . . .'[3]

By the beginning of 1845 she had received overwhelming confirmation that this was indeed her own case. The departure of Mary Taylor, fixed for early spring, and the continuing illness of George Nussey, helped to take her mind off herself but could hardly do much to revive her in the weeks immediately following her letter of 9 January to M. Heger. She arranged to visit Mary, as she wrote to Ellen on 13 January: '. . . Shortly after Branwell and Anne leave [for Thorp Green] I shall go to Hunsworth for a week, if all be well. . . .'

Arriving there at the beginning of February Charlotte found a house full of Taylors—cousins and connexions—and their friends, all come to bid Mary god-speed before her great venture. Undaunted as the Taylors always were by family upheavals, Charlotte found that she was alone oppressed by the pending separation—and by her private sorrows. The occasion was her last meeting with Mary Taylor, who returned to England fifteen years later, only after Charlotte's death.

She wrote Ellen on 20 February, after returning home:

I spent a week at Hunsworth, not very pleasantly. Headache, sickliness, and flatness of spirits made me a poor companion, a sad drag on the vivacious and loquacious gaiety of all the other inmates of the house. I never was fortunate enough to be able to rally, for so much as a single hour, while I was there. I am sure all, with the exception perhaps of Mary, were very glad when I took my departure. I begin to perceive that I have too little life in me, nowadays, to be fit company for any except very quiet people. Is it age, or what else, that changes one so?[4]

[1] *Villette*, ch. 15.   [2] Idem.
[3] Idem.   [4] CB to EN, 20 Feb. 1845: *W & S* ii. 25–26.

Mary, who had made up her mind on her father's death to be neither 'a governess, a teacher, a milliner, a bonnet-maker or a housemaid', in Charlotte's words, and seeing 'no means of obtaining employment she would like in England', had decided as long ago as April 1841 to emigrate to New Zealand. She realized her ambition at last in March 1845. Her youngest brother Waring accompanied her. '. . . I should like to hear whether Mary is actually gone', Charlotte inquired of Ellen on 2 March. By 24 March, knowing she had sailed, Charlotte asked for fuller details.

Have you any particulars of Mary Taylor's departure—what day she sailed—what passengers were in the ship—in what sort of health and spirits she set off—Glean what intelligence you can and transmit it to me—Yesterday I was much surprised to receive a newspaper directed in Mary's hand—its date was the 9th of March—the Post-Mark I could not make out—it was a Weekly Despatch—.[1]

The contrast between her own and Mary's destiny absorbed her thoughts at this time. Charlotte wrote to Ellen on 2 April:

Mary Taylor finds herself free, and on that path to adventure and exertion to which she had so long been seeking admission. Sickness, hardship, danger are her fellow-travellers—her inseparable companions. She may have been out of the reach of these S.W.N.W. gales before they began to blow, or they may have spent their fury on land and not ruffled the sea much. If it has been otherwise she has been sorely tossed, while we have been sleeping in our beds, or lying awake thinking about her.[2]

Charlotte's portion was certainly to lie awake and listen to those equinoctial gales, thinking not only of Mary Taylor, but of the other friend she had lost. Thinking to what a narrow compass her own life was now reduced, and remembering the last argument with Mary on the course she should rouse herself to take, she could but turn her face to the wall and bewail the wasted opportunities of her life. Years later Mary Taylor told Mrs. Gaskell of that last argument between the friends in the final days at Hunsworth.

When I last saw Charlotte . . . she told me she had quite decided to stay at home. She owned she did not like it. Her health was weak. She said she should like any change at first, as she had liked Brussels at first, and she thought that there must be some possibility for some people of having a life

[1] CB to EN, 24 Mar. 1845: *W & S* ii. 28.
[2] CB to EN, 2 Apr. 1845: *W & S* ii. 30.

of more variety and more communion with human kind, but she saw none
for her. I told her very warmly, that she ought not to stay at home; that to
spend the next five years at home, in solitude, and weak health, would ruin
her; that she would never recover it. Such a dark shadow came over her face
when I said, 'Think of what you'll be in five years hence!' that I stopped, and
said, 'Don't cry, Charlotte!' She did not cry, but went on walking up and
down the room, and said in a little while, 'But I intend to stay, Polly.'[1]

Anne's diary-paper written only three months later (on 31 July)
shows, however, that Charlotte *did* allow herself to dream of an escape
from her self-imposed retirement. Commenting on the abandonment
of the school-plan, Anne noted: '. . . Charlotte is thinking about getting another situation. She wishes to go to Paris. Will she go? . . .'[2]
The 'wish for wings' was not wholly crushed by her Brussels experience, and Anne's resignation in June from her post at Thorp Green and
consequent return home gave Charlotte a fresh excuse for taking flight.
How short-lived the temptation was, events would decide.

A philosophy of suffering was gradually shaping itself in Charlotte's
mind. Comparing her own passive part in life to Mary's active one,
she reflected to Ellen: 'these real, material dangers, when once past,
leave in the mind the satisfaction of having struggled with difficulty
and overcome it. Strength, courage, and experience are their invariable
results; whereas I doubt whether suffering purely mental has any good
result, unless it be to make us by comparison less sensitive to physical
suffering'. Admiration of Mary for being so different from herself was a
constant stimulus and dominated even her sense of loss. '. . . I repeat
then, Mary Taylor has done well to go to New Zealand,' she wrote,
'but I wish we could soon have another letter from her. I hope she may
write soon from Madeira. . . .'[3]

When letters were received from Mary at the end of May, they
afforded Charlotte intense interest. '. . . the first part of the letter contained an account of their landing at Santiago', Charlotte told Ellen on
1 June. 'Her health at that time was very good, and her spirits seemed
excellent. They had had contrary winds at first setting out . . . but still
she was well, and freer from headache and other ailments than any
other person on board. . . .'[4]

Charlotte tried equally to absorb herself in Ellen Nussey's domestic
trials. George's prolonged illness called from her constant encourage-

---

[1] MT to Mrs. Gaskell, Jan. 1856: *W & S* ii. 26.
[2] AB Diary Paper, 31 July 1845—quoted from text in Ratchford, 'Gondal's Queen'
1958.   [3] 2 Apr. 1845: *W & S* ii. 30.   [4] 1 June 1845: *W & S* ii. 36.

ment and concern, and in April she was interested to learn of Henry Nussey's engagement. The marriage, projected the previous summer and postponed several times, did at last take place on 22 May. The bride was a Miss Emily Prescott of Eversley in Hampshire, and was not without worldly goods. Charlotte was naturally interested in the event, concerning as it did a former suitor.

I see by the cards you sent also by the newspaper that Henry is at last married. How did you like your office of bridesmaid? and how do you like your new sister and her family? You must write to me as soon as you can, and give me an *observant* account of everything. It seems strange that after all Henry should be married, and well married, before George. Who would have thought that such would have been the case ten years ago?[1]

Ellen, left in charge of Henry's vicarage at Hathersage during the honeymoon, wrote to suggest that Charlotte should join her there. '. . . As to my going to see you there,' Charlotte answered her on 13 June, 'it is quite out of the question. It is hardly worth while to take so long a journey for a week or a fortnight, and longer I could not stay . . . I feel reluctant indeed to leave Papa for a single day—his sight diminishes weekly . . . he now has the greatest difficulty in either reading or writing. . . .'[2]

By 18 June, however, a change had unexpectedly occurred in the domestic arrangements of the parsonage: Anne and Branwell had come home for the holidays and Anne, to the surprise and pleasure of the family, had announced that she had given notice to Mrs. Robinson and had left Thorp Green for good. As a result, Charlotte was able to write to Ellen: '. . . her presence at home certainly makes me feel more at liberty. Then, dear Ellen, if all be well, I will come and see you at Hathersage . . .'.[3]

She went there on Thursday, 26 June, for a fortnight's visit, and enjoyed herself enough to authorize Ellen to write to Emily suggesting a prolongation of the visit. In characteristic vein Emily replied:

Dear Miss Nussey—If you have set your heart on Charlotte staying another week, she has our united consent. I, for one, will take everything easy on Sunday. I am glad she is enjoying herself; let her make the most of the next seven days to return stout and hearty. Love to her and you from Anne and myself and tell her all are well at home.—

Yours

Emily Brontë[4]

[1] Idem.   [2] CB to EN, 13 June 1845: *W & S* ii. 37–39.
[3] CB to EN, 18 June 1845: *W & S* ii. 39–40.   [4] EJB to EN, *W & S* ii. 41.

Emily and Anne, reunited after the long separation of the last four years, had themselves enjoyed a little excursion during Charlotte's absence—the 'first long journey by ourselves together', as Emily described it. Intending at first to go to Scarborough—a plan which they abandoned for special reasons—they went to York (both places were peculiarly dear to Anne who had visited them repeatedly while with the Robinsons), spending a day and night there, and another night at Keighley, and walking home from there on the third day. Emily recorded the incident in her diary-paper for Anne on 30 July, and added: '. . . though the weather was broken, we enjoyed ourselves very much, except during a few hours at Bradford . . .'.[1]

Charlotte returned home on Saturday, 19 July. An incident on the journey was magnified by her into a matter of importance because it bore some connexion in her mind with M. Heger. She told Ellen about it in her letter of thanks:

I got home very well. There was a gentleman in the railroad carriage whom I recognised by his features immediately as a foreigner and Frenchman. So sure was I of it, that I ventured to say to him in French: 'Monsieur est français, n'est-ce pas?' He gave a start of surprise and answered immediately in his own tongue; he appeared still more astonished, and even puzzled, when after a few minutes' further conversation, I inquired if he had not passed the greater part of his life in Germany. He said the surmise was correct. I had guessed it from his speaking French with a German accent.[2]

What Charlotte really meant and hesitated to admit even to Ellen, was that the gentleman spoke with a Belgian accent, and brought M. Heger vividly to mind. That this was so, and that the encounter left a deep impression, is shown by her mentioning it as long afterwards as November, when she wrote once again to M. Heger.

On her return from Hathersage a new and unforeseen disaster overtook the Brontë family and changed the current of Charlotte's life once more. Branwell, who for two and a half years had appeared to have made a success of his engagement as tutor, was suddenly suspected by Mr. Robinson of conducting an intrigue with his wife. The discovery, made at Scarborough where the Robinsons were spending their customary holidays, led to Branwell's instant dismissal. The disgrace of its cause and the despair into which the separation from the woman he loved now threw Branwell, caused an upheaval at the parsonage such as

---

[1] EJB Diary-Paper, 30 July 1845; quoted from text in 'Gondal's Queen': op. cit.
[2] CB to EN, 31 July 1845: *W & S* ii. 42–43.

the much-tried family had never yet experienced. Charlotte, entering the house at 10 o'clock at night on her return from Hathersage, was met with the calamitous news, as she related in her letter to Ellen of 31 July:

It was ten o'clock when I got home. I found Branwell ill. He is so often owing to his own fault. I was not therefore shocked at first, but when Anne informed me of the immediate cause of his present illness I was greatly shocked. He had last Thursday received a note from Mr. Robinson sternly dismissing him, intimating that he had discovered his proceedings, which he characterised as bad beyond expression, and charging him on pain of exposure to break off instantly and for ever all communication with every member of his family. We have had sad work with Branwell since. He thought of nothing but stunning or drowning his distress of mind. No one in the house could have rest.[1]

From that evening onwards, it was not only M. Heger but the spectre of Branwell's ruin that haunted Charlotte. The impact of this fresh sorrow was too much for her; she met it with a stunned impatience, frayed nerves, and a shaken mind. Small wonder that to M. Heger she wrote like one who had reached the end of her endurance; the letter of 18 November has a tone of desolate finality:

Monsieur,—The six months of silence have run their course. It is now the 18th of Novr.; my last letter was dated (I think) the 18th of May. I may therefore write to you without failing in my promise.

The summer and autumn seemed very long to me; truth to tell, it has needed painful efforts on my part to bear hitherto the self-denial which I have imposed on myself. You, Monsieur, you cannot conceive what it means; but suppose for a moment that one of your children was separated from you 160 leagues away, and that you had to remain six months without writing to him, without receiving news of him, without hearing him spoken of, without knowing aught of his health, then you would understand easily all the harshness of such an obligation. I tell you frankly that I have tried meanwhile to forget you, for the remembrance of a person whom one thinks never to see again and whom, nevertheless, one greatly esteems, frets too much the mind; and when one has suffered that kind of anxiety for a year or two, one is ready to do anything to find peace once more. I have done everything; I have sought occupations; I have denied myself absolutely the pleasure of speaking about you—even to Emily; but I have been able to conquer neither my regrets nor my impatience. That, indeed, is humiliating— to be unable to control one's own thoughts, to be the slave of a regret, of a memory, the slave of a fixed and dominant idea which lords it over the

[1] CB to EN, 31 July 1845: op. cit.

mind. Why cannot I have just as much friendship for you, as you for me—neither more nor less? Then should I be so tranquil, so free—I could keep silence then for ten years without an effort.

My father is well but his sight is almost gone. He can neither read nor write. Yet the doctors advise waiting a few months more before attempting an operation. The winter will be a long night for him. He rarely complains; I admire his patience. If Providence wills the same calamity for me, may He at least vouchsafe me as much patience with which to bear it! It seems to me, Monsieur, that there is nothing more galling in great physical misfortunes than to be compelled to make all those about us share in our sufferings. The ills of the soul one can hide, but those which attack the body and destroy the faculties cannot be concealed. My father allows me now to read to him and write for him; he shows me, too, more confidence than he has ever shown before, and that is a great consolation.

Monsieur, I have a favour to ask of you; when you reply to this letter, speak to me a little of yourself, not of me; for I know that if you speak of me it will be to scold me, and this time I would see your kindly side. Speak to me therefore of your children. Never was your brow severe when Louise and Claire and Prosper were by your side. Tell me also something of the School, of the pupils, of the Governesses. Are Mesdemoiselles Blanche, Sophie and Justine still at Brussels? Tell me where you travelled during the holidays—did you go to the Rhine? Did you not visit Cologne or Coblentz? Tell me, in short, *mon maître*, what you will, but tell me something. To write to an ex-assistant-governess (No! I refuse to remember my employment as assistant-governess—I repudiate it)—anyhow, to write to an old pupil cannot be a very interesting occupation for you, I know; but for me it is life. Your last letter was stay and prop to me—nourishment to me for half a year. Now I need another and you will give it me; not because you bear me friendship—you cannot have much—but because you are compassionate of soul and you would condemn no one to prolonged suffering to save yourself a few moments' trouble. To forbid me to write to you, to refuse to answer me would be to tear from me my only joy on earth, to deprive me of my last privilege—a privilege I never shall consent willingly to surrender. Believe me, *mon maître*, in writing to me it is a good deed that you will do. So long as I believe you are pleased with me, so long as I have hope of receiving news from you, I can be at rest and not too sad. But when a prolonged and gloomy silence seems to threaten me with the estrangement of my master—when day by day I await a letter and when day by day disappointment comes to fling me back into overwhelming sorrow, and the sweet delight of seeing your handwriting and reading your counsel escapes me as a vision that is vain, then fever claims me—I lose appetite and sleep—I pine away.

May I write to you again next May? I would rather wait a year, but it is impossible—it is too long.

C. Brontë.

I must say one word to you in English—I wish I could write to you more cheerful letters, for when I read this over, I find it to be somewhat gloomy— but forgive me my dear master—do not be irritated at my sadness—according to the words of the Bible: 'Out of the fulness of the heart, the mouth speaketh' and truly I find it difficult to be cheerful so long as I think I shall never see you more. You will perceive by the defects in this letter that I am forgetting the French language—yet I read all the French books I can get, and learn daily a portion by heart—but I have never heard French spoken but once since I left Brussels—and then it sounded like music in my ears— every word was most precious to me because it reminded me of you—I love French for your sake with all my heart and soul.

Farewell my dear Master—may God protect you with special care and crown you with peculiar blessings.

C.B.

Novr. 18th,
Haworth, Bradford, Yorkshire.[1]

If the words of Charlotte's poem 'He saw my heart's woe . . .' are to be taken literally—'. . . once a year he heard a whisper lone and dreary . . .'—then it may be assumed that she still wrote to M. Heger, if only at yearly intervals, after 1845. But the correspondence was virtually over with the letter of 18 November, to which, as to its immediate predecessors, no answer came.

[1] CB to M. Heger, 18 Nov. 1845: B.M. Add. MSS. 38732/C, English translation by M. H. Spielmann, SBC. For original French text, see Appendixes.

THE *ALTER EGO*

IN the absence of all previous letters intimating a suspicion on Charlotte's part of Branwell's conduct at Thorp Green, the account given of his dismissal in her letter to Ellen is perplexing.[1] Without further explanation of the circumstances, Charlotte would seem to be referring to a subject not wholly unsuspected by herself or her friend, with whom she had just been staying; as though Branwell's 'proceedings' and the fear of their 'exposure' had recently been discussed between them. The letter is difficult to interpret otherwise.

One recalls Charlotte's reference in a letter of 13 January of that year to Ellen, in which she contrasted Branwell's behaviour during the Christmas holidays with that of the previous summer: '. . . Branwell has been quieter and less irritable on the whole this time than he was in the summer . . .' she had written. The 'irritability' and the 'excitement' caused, on his own subsequent admission, by his passion for Mrs. Robinson, may have aroused in Charlotte some suspicion of the true state of affairs at Thorp Green, without in any way defining them. Branwell loved to speak in riddles, by innuendo, and with bravado; behind the fact that he was highly in favour with his employers—with Mrs. Robinson in particular—his family had little to go on.

A passage in one of Charlotte's letters to M. Heger—dated clearly 24 October 1844 in the original—may be charged with more meaning than the date would suggest when set in the context of the 1845 catastrophe: '. . . mes sœurs se portent bien', Charlotte had written, 'mais mon pauvre frère est toujours malade. . . .'[2]

'Malade', as the exact translation of 'ill', the term always used by Charlotte to describe Branwell's drunkenness, might here again mean nothing more; though why Branwell at Thorp Green, in the company of the woman he loved, should have resorted to the old bad ways, *unless* distracted by some new check upon his love, is not clear.

The reticence of Anne about a situation that so deeply wounded her

---

[1] See above, p. 291.   [2] See above, p. 275.

feelings made the truth even more difficult to penetrate for those at home. She had not hidden how much she hated the atmosphere of Thorp Green, or with what scant respect she regarded Mrs. Robinson; yet she stayed at her post even against the wishes and advice of her family. A strong sense of service she certainly had towards her pupils, the three Robinson girls; but stronger still would appear her devotion to Branwell, when the whole truth was discovered. She had undoubtedly remained at Thorp Green in the hope of averting the worst from him.

It was not Anne, therefore, who was the most stunned when Mr. Robinson's letter came; she had long had reason to fear just such a catastrophe. The judgements of Emily on the conduct of mortals were seldom harsh; the most she was ever reported as saying of Branwell was that he 'was a hopeless being'. It was not Emily's tongue that Branwell had to fear.

His father's anger, disappointment, and shame, converted into pity and protective care as the physical decay of his once beautiful son became a daily and hideous spectacle, was of a silent sort. From Charlotte, chiefly, Branwell had to suffer, and it was to Charlotte and not to his father that he wrote in the first flush of his disgrace, to beg pardon and promise amendment. The importance of this gesture on Branwell's part cannot be overrated, for it sets the seal, as it were, upon the long devotion of brother to sister, and inaugurates the new tragic relationship that followed his ruin.

As Branwell 'thought of nothing but stunning or drowning his distress of mind', as Charlotte wrote to Ellen, and 'no one in the house could have rest', Mr. Brontë sent him away for a week in the care of John Brown—from 27 July to 3 August—first to Liverpool and then to North Wales. It was from there that he wrote to Charlotte. 'He has written to me this morning,' she told Ellen on 31 July, 'and expressed some sense of contrition for his frantic folly; he promises amendment on his return, but', she added with the disillusion that marked her whole approach to Branwell's disaster from the outset, 'so long as he remains at home I scarce dare hope for peace in the house. . . .'[1]

This was to become the leitmotiv of her attitude to her brother's tragedy. 'Hope, in his case,' she wrote on 18 August, barely a month after the event, 'seems a fallacy, . . . My hopes ebb low indeed about Branwell. I sometimes fear he will never be fit for much. His bad habits seem more deeply rooted than I thought. . . .'[2]

[1] CB to EN, 31 July 1845: *W & S* ii. 42–43.
[2] CB to EN, 18 Aug. 1845: *SLL* i. 307.

The sad fact soon becomes apparent that, for Charlotte, Branwell's course had been run; in her eyes, from the first, he was not only guilty, but irredeemable. Her condemnation, never lightened throughout the two and a half years of Branwell's decline, was immediate, certain, and complete. Not once in any preserved statement of hers did she express doubt of the justice of the accusations made, or faith in Branwell's repentance or ability to reform, or incline to sympathize with his sufferings. On the contrary, as they were self-inflicted, she had scant pity for them. '. . . You say well in speaking of Branwell', she wrote Ellen some five months after the event, 'that no sufferings are so awful as those brought on by dissipation. Alas! I see the truth of this observation daily proved. . . .'[1]

Such lack of hope might, it could be argued, spring from the closest knowledge. If anyone knew Branwell, it was Charlotte. But it would, and without a shadow of doubt *did*, spring from the very degree and depth of her former love for him. The disillusionment was commensurate with the adulation, and her first great expectations made the shattering of her hopes all the more complete.

There was something else which must not be forgotten in considering her judgement of her brother. In many of her pronouncements on his conduct she did not hesitate to apply the word 'vice', showing how she regarded his connexion with Mrs. Robinson. From the first breaking of the news, she accepted without protest or incredulity Mr. Robinson's estimate of her brother's conduct. In her eyes Branwell had been guilty of a sin which, of all sins at that particular time, appeared the most dastardly to Charlotte. He had committed adultery. Whether he had *in fact* done so or not (and the proof would never appear) Charlotte believed it to be so. Had Branwell committed any other cardinal sin at that time Charlotte might have found it in her heart to forgive him. But he had ignominiously yielded, so she judged, to the very temptation it had been her Purgatory to resist. She had come through the purifying flame too recently herself to have much pity left for those who, like her brother, had fallen by the wayside.

Branwell's *kind* of love moreover—vainglorious, weak, and cowardly —was the very kind to rouse her bitterest scorn. Far from softening her towards him, her own love for M. Heger (which the impartial might say was also love of an illicit sort) only hardened her heart; for she had fled her temptation, and Branwell had succumbed to his.

How she felt towards their relative situations she shortly afterwards

[1] CB to EN, 31 Dec. 1845: *SSL* i. 313.

described in *The Professor*: William Crimsworth, deciding to leave his employer's house on learning that he was to marry Mlle Reuter—who had plainly shown her preference for himself—had this to say:

I was no pope—I could not boast infallibility: in short, if I stayed, the probability was that, in three month's time, a practical modern French novel would be in full process of concoction under the roof of the unsuspecting Pelet. Now, modern French novels are not to my taste, either practically, or theoretically. Limited as had yet been my experience of life, I had once had the opportunity of contemplating, near at hand, an example of the results produced by a course of interesting and romantic domestic treachery. No golden halo of fiction was about this example, I saw it bare and real, and it was very loathesome. I saw a mind degraded by the practice of mean subterfuge, by the habit of perfidious deception, and a body depraved by the infectious influence of the vice-polluted soul. I had suffered much from the forced and prolonged view of this spectacle; those sufferings I did not now regret, for their simple recollection acted as a most wholesome antidote to temptation. They had inscribed on my reason the conviction that unlawful pleasure, trenching on another's rights, is delusive and envenomed pleasure— its hollowness disappoints at the time, its poison cruelly tortures afterwards, its effects deprave for ever.[1]

As the weeks passed, and the family had to adjust itself to the new burden of Branwell's presence in the house—a partial invalid already and a permanent charge upon the charity and patience of his father— Charlotte would not soften her verdict nor allow herself to be deluded by even the slightest appearances of improvement. If for a time he seemed to control himself better, she did not attribute it to will-power or moral energy, but purely to lack of funds with which to buy opium and spirits. '. . . It is only absolute want of means', she wrote to Ellen on 18 August, 'that acts as any check to him. . . .'[2] Later the same month she added: '. . . his health and consequently his temper have been somewhat better this last day or two, because he is now *forced* to abstain...'.[3]

She would give him no credit, either, for attempting to find fresh work—although in fact he did so, as his letters to Grundy that autumn prove.[4] '. . . Branwell makes no effort to seek a situation', Charlotte wrote on 8 September, postponing a promised visit from her friend, 'and while he is at home I will invite no one. . . .'[5] The

---

[1] *The Professor*, ch. 20.   [2] *W & S* ii. 57–58.   [3] *W & S* ii. 59.
[4] PBB to Grundy, Oct. 1845: BPM.   [5] *W & S* ii. 60.

visit, deferred to the autumn, had again to be cancelled. She wrote on
4 November:

I had hoped to ask you to Haworth. Branwell seemed to have a prospect
of employment . . . but the place [a secretaryship to a railroad committee]
is given to another person. Branwell still remains at home and while he is
here, you shall not come. I am more confirmed in that resolution the more
I know him. I wish I could say one word in his favour, but I cannot, therefore I will hold my tongue.[1]

'Branwell offers no prospect of hope,' she again wrote on 23 January
(1846), 'he professes to be too ill to think of seeking employment, he
makes comfort scant at home. . . .'

Her pessimism regarding Branwell was so complete that she made
no attempt to hide the family disgrace even from Miss Wooler, who
had not then, though she did later, reached the degree of intimacy
warranting such confidence at the time. '. . . You ask about Branwell',
she wrote in reply to Miss Wooler's inquiries, on 30 January: 'He never
thinks of seeking employment, and I begin to fear he has rendered
himself incapable of filling any respectable station in life; besides, if
money were at his disposal he would use it only to his own injury; the
faculty of self-government is, I fear, almost destroyed in him. . . .'[2]

Such condemnation, coming from Charlotte, constitutes, it must not
be forgotten, a two-edged sword; for while Branwell's misery was,
doubtless, made the greater by her hardness, how great must also have
been her own misery in the realization of his ruin. He was lost to her,
and life was permanently embittered by the fact. Only six years had
passed since, considering just such a contingency, she had written of
Elizabeth Hastings's reactions to her brother's disgrace; then she had
thought '. . . It was very odd that his sister did not think a pin the
worse for him for all his dishonour', and added the significant words:
'it is private moments not public infamy that degrade a man in the
opinion of his relations . . .'.[3]

It was not Branwell who had changed so much, but Charlotte's
knowledge of him. It was the experience of her own 'private moments'
that had altered life for her, hardening her heart against her brother's
lack of moral fibre and courage. The cowardice of his collapse, seen at
close quarters—his self-pity, his self-indulgence, the wild recourse to

---

[1] *SBC* 122. For fuller data concerning Branwell's ruin, see Gérin, *Branwell Brontë*,
(London, 1961), 245–301.

[2] CB to Miss Wooler, 30 Jan. 1846: Fitzwilliam Museum, Cambridge.

[3] 'Henry Hastings', Feb.–Mar. 1839: Harry Elkins Widener Memorial Lib., Harvard
Univ., Cambridge, Mass.: op. cit.

palliatives—estranged her from him as much as his actual sin. He was no longer a Henry Hastings. Nothing of the Byronic ideal remained in this weak, nerveless wreck of a man, wholly unable as he now was to defy his fate. (That the Byronic ideal still remained a yardstick with Charlotte with which to measure a man's moral stature Mr. Rochester would shortly confirm.)

The harshness of her judgement on the once-idolized brother can be compared with her attitude to other and similar cases. In the same year as Branwell's tragedy, Ellen Nussey also underwent great domestic trials; her brother George went mad and had to be confined to York Asylum. The blow, falling upon an innocent man, was viewed by Charlotte with deep sympathy and patience. Her many letters to Ellen on the subject are full of kindness and encouragement. 'Do not dear Ellen be disheartened because his improvement in health is slow,' she wrote her friend on 24 March 1845; 'it cannot all at once regain its healthy state—it must have time—but with time I do believe a complete cure will yet be effected. I should not hope it, if George were a man of irregular habits—but as it is—I think there is the best ground for confident hope.'[1]

Commenting later on the burden George's illness threw on his sisters, she wrote on 31 December 1845: 'Ann and Mercy [Nussey] must have a weary and burdensome life of it, in waiting upon their unhappy brother. It seems grievous, indeed, that those who have not sinned should suffer so largely....'[2]

Only a few years would alter her own position cruelly and radically; but at the time of Branwell's disaster she was firmly convinced that suffering was merited if it had its origin in sin. There was the case of another of Ellen's brothers, Joseph Nussey—her senior by 18 years and the successor to his father in the management of the cloth-manufacturing firm that had founded the family's fortunes. He had led a dissipated life and brought virtual ruin on the family and himself. Of his death in June 1846 Charlotte wrote:

I hope all the mournful contingencies of death are by this time removed from Brookroyd, and that some little sense of relief is beginning to be experienced by its wearied inmates. Joseph suffered greatly. I trust and even believe that his long sufferings on earth will be taken as sufficient expiation. I wish you all may get a little repose, and enjoyment now.[3]

Joseph, like Branwell, had brought calamity on himself.

---

[1] CB to EN, 24 Mar. 1845: *W & S* ii. 27–28.
[2] *SLL* i. 313, 31 Dec. 1845; *W & S* ii. 74–75.   [3] *W & S* ii. 95.

The question naturally poses itself, how far did Branwell's family share Charlotte's views? It is obvious that at the beginning Emily and Anne harboured almost childish hopes of his regeneration. Writing on the same day, Emily's birthday, 30 July 1845, in their four-year diary of family events, they spoke in almost identical language of Branwell's misfortune: '. . . Branwell has left Luddenden Foot', noted Anne, 'and been a tutor at Thorp Green and had much tribulation and ill-health. He was very ill on Thursday [Tuesday] but he went with John Brown to Liverpool, where he now is, I suppose; and we hope he will be better and do better in future. . . .' Typical of Anne is the use of the word 'tribulation' showing more pity than blame for her unfortunate brother. '. . . We are all in decent health,' wrote Emily, 'only that papa has a complaint in his eyes, and with the exception of Branwell, who, I hope, will be better and do better hereafter. . . .'[1]

Mr. Brontë's role, during his son's moral and physical decline, was to be all important. He took him to sleep in his own room, so as to keep guard over him night and day—the threat of suicide, of murder, of fire being all too real during the hours of frenzy that followed on enforced abstinence from opium and drink. Upon him, as the only man in the household of women, fell the constant burden of Branwell's care. '. . . To papa he allows rest neither day nor night,' Charlotte wrote a few months later, 'he is continually screwing money out of him, some-times threatening that he will kill himself if it is withheld from him . . . he will do nothing except drink and make us all wretchèd. . . .'[2]

The incident, related by the Haworth stationer John Greenwood,[3] of Branwell setting the curtains of his bed on fire during a drunken sleep, shows the need of Mr. Brontë's vigilance. Whatever he may have said to Branwell's face, he spoke *of* him with pity rather than condemna-tion. In this connexion it must not be overlooked that Mr. Brontë shared bedrooms with his son for the last two years of his life and was better informed than anyone in the family of Branwell's version of the Thorp Green story. Such as it was it left Mr. Brontë in no doubt of Mrs. Robinson's guilt in the affair. Writing to Mrs. Gaskell years after, upon the publication of her 'Life' of Charlotte, he said: '. . . The pictures of my brilliant and unhappy son, and of his diabolical seducer, are master-pieces. . . .'[4]

---

[1] Diary Papers of E. and A. Brontë, 30 July 1845. 'Gondal's Queen': op. cit., pp. 189–94.

[2] 17 June 1848: *SLL* i. 332.

[3] A. Preston, 'John Greenwood and the Brontës': *BST*, 1951.

[4] Mr. Brontë to Mrs. Gaskell, 2 Apr. 1857: *BST*, 1934.

Mr. Robinson's injunction on Branwell to 'break off instantly and for ever all communication with every member of his family' left Branwell a spineless wreck. He had neither plan nor prospect with which to combat his despair or defend his love. He built such hopes as he had upon the anticipation of Mr. Robinson's death and the resulting liberation of his Lydia from the bonds that united her to an old and dying husband—so Branwell liked best to represent Mr. Robinson, although the truth was that he and his wife were both 45 and Mr. Robinson's health had only recently declined. Badly as Branwell behaved in the first flush of his grief he was still upheld by the hope that Mr. Robinson's death would follow before long, and that Lydia would keep faith with him and bestow both her person and her fortune upon him. These extravagant hopes were proved wholly unfounded. The death of Mr. Robinson did in fact occur on 26 May following. But Mrs. Robinson's double-dealing had not been foreseen. She simulated sickness and despair, whilst leading a giddy social round and preparing advantageous marriages for her daughters. She further engineered her own remarriage, with an old and wealthy kinsman. Only then did Branwell give full measure to his frantic grief, and the much-tried family realized how relatively rational he had been until then. From then on his conduct became truly abject; his craving for drink and drugs drove him even to the expedient of 'screwing' money out of Mrs. Robinson to keep him in funds. Knowledge of his degradation was not spared the family, and Charlotte in particular referred on several occasions to the money Branwell extorted from Mrs. Robinson through the mediation of the Thorp Green doctor, Dr. Crosby. In after years she told Mrs. Gaskell of it, who mentioned it in the first edition of her 'Life' of Charlotte.[1]

Mrs. Robinson's refusal ever to see him again completed Branwell's heart-break. He made no more effort to brace himself. The cheapness and availability of opium, sold openly at all druggists (Branwell had only to cross the street from his father's church to buy sixpence-worth of oblivion at Betty Hardacre's drug-shop), completed the ruin begun with drink. When he came to die—in September 1848, at the age of 31 —he was a skeleton, and his death-certificate bore no more specific cause of death than 'Chronic bronchitis—Marasmus'—a wasting of the flesh from no identifiable disease. The course of his destruction almost exactly confirmed Charlotte's gloomiest forebodings, and proved how right she had been. It would have been far better for both of them if she could have preserved some illusions.

[1] Gaskell, 196.

It was inevitable that the wreck of the family's hopes concerning Branwell brought about a subtle change in the sisters' relationships. The partnerships lasting since childhood were forcibly dissolved; Charlotte, bereft of her brother's confidence, turned as never before to her sisters for comfort and companionship. Of Anne, only just returned home after an absence of four and a half years, she had little close knowledge since both had grown up. The short holidays that had restored Anne to the twin-like relationship with Emily had seldom coincided with Charlotte's presence at home. She had to get to know Anne afresh. With Emily, Charlotte had, of course, gone to Brussels for the first year; their shared experience had become a new bond between them, from which she had derived the only comfort to be found on her return home in 1844. With Emily, in 'the delightful weather' of that spring—as she told Ellen—she had walked a good deal on the moors, to the 'great damage of our shoes'. To Emily, undoubtedly, she had unburdened her heart. The proof of this lies in her last letter to M. Heger (of 18 November 1845) where she confessed to having latterly deprived herself even of the pleasure of *speaking of him to Emily*.

Though she had confided in Emily, the sequel would show that Emily, the silent repository of her sister's secrets, had shared none of hers with Charlotte. What had befallen Charlotte during the last year in Brussels became known to Emily, but what had befallen Emily within the fastness of her soul, only a chance accident would reveal to Charlotte, and then the discovery was fiercely resented by Emily.

In that summer of 1845 the lives of Emily and Anne were as intertwined as ever; nothing had broken the magic ring of their union, despite Anne's absence and the experience of Thorp Green. In their joint birthday-letters of 30 July they still spoke the same language and inhabited the same world of their childhood: 'The Gondals still flourish as bright as ever.' Emily noted barely ten days after Branwell's dismissal by Mr. Robinson. 'I am at present writing a work on the First War. Anne has been writing some articles on this, and a book on Henry Sophona. We intend sticking firm by the rascals as long as they delight us, which I am glad to say they do at present.'[1] 'Emily is engaged in writing the Emperor Julius' life', wrote Anne on the same day. 'She has read some of it and I want very much to hear the rest. She is writing some poetry too. I wonder what it is about?'[2] 'I am

[1] EJB's Diary Paper: 'Gondal's Queen', 191–3: op. cit.
[2] AB's Diary Paper: idem 193–4.

quite contented for myself,' wrote Emily, 'seldom or never troubled with nothing to do, and merely desiring that everybody could be as comfortable as myself, and as undesponding, and then we should have a very tolerable world of it.'[1] 'This afternoon I began to set about making my grey silk frock that was dyed at Keighley. What sort of a hand shall I make of it? E. and I have a great deal of work to do,' commented Anne, 'when shall we sensibly diminish it?' Their gentle serenity and unworldliness, their candid incompetence over such feminine avocations as turning dyed silk dresses, brought sweetness into the home, and Charlotte, embittered by her sorrows, was grateful for it.

Her sisters now became the focal point of her life. How she saw them at that time, she set down in *Jane Eyre* in the picture she painted of Diana and Mary Rivers.

Two young, graceful women—ladies in every point—sat, one on a low rocking chair, the other on a lower stool . . . a large old pointer dog rested its massive head on the knee of one girl—in the lap of the other was cushioned a black cat. . . . I cannot call them handsome—they were too pale and grave for the word: as they each bent over a book, they looked thoughtful almost to severity. . . . Both were fair complexioned and slenderly made; both possessed faces full of distinction and intelligence.[2]

A tigress in defending their feeble strength (as she had assessed it in years gone by), Charlotte had taught them, protected them, nursed them in illness, and supported them in exile with ambition and energy enough for three, but never before, perhaps, had she seen them as beings from whom *she* could derive life and purpose, as now happened in the months following on Branwell's misfortune.

Of the priceless boon of sisterly love she wrote at that time to Miss Wooler. As the only woman of their acquaintance who had succeeded in making a school pay and who showed ability in conducting her own business-affairs, Miss Wooler had been consulted by the Brontë girls about how best to invest their legacies from Miss Branwell; and with her blessing had taken up shares in the new railroad companies. Over the fluctuation in railway fortunes they had all suffered some shocks, especially during Charlotte's absence abroad, during which time she had perforce to leave the care of her investments in Emily's hands. She wrote Miss Wooler on 30 January, 1846:

I thought you would wonder how we were getting on when you heard of the Railway Panic, and you may be sure I am very glad to be able to answer your kind enquiries by an assurance that our small capital is as yet undiminished.

---

[1] Idem: op cit.   [2] *Jane Eyre*, ch. 28.

The York and Midland is, as you say, a very good line—yet I confess to you I should wish for my part, to be wise in time. I cannot think that even the very best line will continue for many years at their present premiums, and I have been most anxious to sell our shares ere it be too late. . . . I cannot, however, persuade my sisters to regard the affair precisely from my point of view, and I feel as if I would rather run the risk of loss than hurt Emily's feelings by acting in direct opposition to her opinion. She managed in a most handsome and able manner for me when I was in Brussels, and prevented by distance from looking after my own interests; therefore, I will let her manage still, and take the consequences. Disinterested and energetic she certainly is, and if she be not quite so tractable or open to conviction as I would wish, I must remember perfection is not the lot of humanity; and as long as we can regard those we love and to whom we are closely allied, with profound and never-shaken esteem, it is a small thing that they should vex us occasion-ally by what appear to us unreasonable and headstrong notions. You my dear Miss Wooler know fully as well as I do the value of sisters' affection to each other; there is nothing like it in this world, I believe, when they are nearly equal in age and similar in education, tastes and sentiments.[1]

From these cherished sisters Charlotte now received another great blessing: they rekindled the creative impulse in her. She has recounted in her own words the discovery she made in the late autumn of 1845 of the notebooks in which Emily copied out her poetry. Anne knew of these poems (though even she had not been shown them as her July diary-paper showed), but on Charlotte their impact was all the more forcible because she was unprepared, and because her need at that time was so great for just such a summons to resurrection.

One day in the autumn of 1845, I accidentally lighted on a MS volume of verse in my sister Emily's handwriting. Of course I was not surprised, knowing that she could and did write verse; I looked it over, and something more than surprise seized me,—a deep conviction that these were not com-mon effusions, nor at all like the poetry women generally write. I thought them condensed and terse, vigorous and genuine. To my ear, they had also a peculiar music—wild, melancholy, and elevating.[2]

What she read as she feverishly turned the pages were lines like these:

> How clear she shines! How quietly
> I lie beneath her silver light
> While Heaven and Earth are whispering me,
> 'To-morrow wake, but dream to-night'.

[1] Allbutt Bequest: Wooler letters, Fitzwilliam Museum, Cambridge.
[2] Memoir of Ellis Bell prefixed to the Smith, Elder posthumous edition of her *Works*, 1850.

Yes, Fancy, come, my Fairy love!
These throbbing temples softly kiss;
And bend my lonely couch above
And bring me rest and bring me bliss.

The world is going—Dark world, adieu!
Grim world, go hide thee till the day;
The heart thou canst not all subdue
Must still resist if thou delay!

Thy love I will not, will not share; . . .

While gazing on the stars that glow
Above me in the stormless sea,
I long to hope that all the woe
Creation knows, is held in thee!

And this shall be my dream to-night—
I'll think the heaven of glorious spheres
Is rolling on its course of light
In endless bliss through endless years;[1]

While Charlotte had been torn between delight and torment in
Brussels, Emily, lying on the little camp bed in the tiny nursery at
home, had reached out beyond the visible world towards unbounded
space where her liberated soul had lost itself in the source of being.

    . . . Let Grief distract the sufferer's breast,
        And Night obscure his way;
    They hasten him to endless rest,
        And everlasting day.
    To Thee the world is like a tomb,
        A desert's naked shore;
    To us, in unimagined bloom
        It brightens more and more.

    And could we lift the veil and give
        One brief glimpse to thine eye
    Thou woulds't rejoice for those that live,
        Because they live to die.[2]

    . . . Three Gods within this little frame
        Are warring night and day.

---

[1] *The Complete Poems of Emily Jane Brontë*, edited by C. W. Hatfield: Oxford (1941),
184–5.   [2] Idem 200.

> Heaven could not hold them all, and yet
> They all are held in me
> And must be mine till I forget
> My present entity.
>
> O for the time when in my breast
> Their struggles will be o'er;
> O for the day when I shall rest,
> And never suffer more![1]

The impact of Emily's poems was so overwhelming that not even Emily's rage at Charlotte's indiscretion could quell the tumult of hope, ambition, and resolve that stirred in her. Writing of the incident two years later to her publisher, Mr. Williams, she said of the poems:

> Of their startling excellence I am convinced, and have been from the first moment the MS fell by chance into my hands. . . . They stirred my breast like the sound of a trumpet when I read them alone and in secret. The deep excitement I felt forced from me the confession of the discovery I had made. I was sternly rated at first for having taken an unwarrantable liberty. This I expected ... But by dint of entreaty and reason I at last wrung out a reluctant consent to have the 'rhymes' as they were contemptuously called, published. The author never alludes to them, or, when she does, it is with scorn. But I know no woman that ever lived that ever wrote such poetry before.[2]

Never for a moment hesitating over their excellence or doubting their ability to stand the test of publication, Charlotte did not rest until she had turned Emily's grudging consent to the practical purpose of finding a publisher. 'We had very early cherished the dream of one day becoming authors', she wrote in the collected edition of her sisters' works. 'This dream, never relinquished even when distance divided and absorbing tasks occupied us, now suddenly acquired strength and consistency; it took the character of a resolve. We agreed to arrange a small selection of our poems, and, if possible, get them printed.'[3]

The resolve, no sooner taken, was instantly acted upon. Pooling the resources of their poetic output over the recent years, the girls read to each other, argued, rejected, selected the hitherto hidden contents of their respective notebooks; copied them fair, counted the probable pages the choice would make in print; and decided on sending them

---

[1] *The Complete Poems of Emily Jane Brontë*, op. cit., 220.
[2] CB to W. S. Williams, September 1848, *W & S* ii. 256.
[3] 'Memoir of Ellis Bell', 1850: op. cit.

out to a publisher. Here they encountered their first obstacle; they had read poetry all their lives, but it was the best poetry by established authors, and they did not realize that by approaching Moxon, Wordsworth's publisher, or Murray who published Byron, that they—mere beginners as they were—were exposing themselves to a rebuff.

The bringing out of our little book was hard work . . . neither we nor our poems were at all wanted. . . . The great puzzle lay in the difficulty of getting answers of any kind from the publishers to whom we applied. Being greatly harassed by this obstacle, I ventured to apply to Messrs Chambers of Edinburgh for a word of advice; *they* may have forgotten the circumstances, but *I* have not, for from them I received a brief and business-like, but civil and sensible reply, on which we acted, and at last made way.[1]

Chambers's advice was to try a small firm of publishers who specialized in religious poetry, Messrs. Aylott & Jones of Paternoster Row. To Aylott & Jones Charlotte wrote on 28 January 1846 and by return of post received an encouraging reply. On the 31st, acknowledging their letter, she entered into details of format, type, and cost and on 7 February dispatched the completed manuscript of the poems. Her career as a professional writer had begun.

Lines from the poem chosen to open the volume, Charlotte's early 'Pilate's Wife's Dream', echo the expectation roused by that day's enterprise:

> This day, time travails with a mighty birth,
> This day, Truth stoops from heaven and visits earth,
> Ere night descends, I shall more surely know
> What guide to follow, in what path to go;
> I wait in hope—I wait in solemn fear,
> The oracle of God—the sole—true God—to hear.[2]

---

[1] Idem.
[2] *Poems by Currer, Ellis and Acton Bell*, 1846.

RESURGAM

THE alternation between the destructive and creative principles, so constantly apparent in the Brontës' lives—the same that in childhood had raised 'Glasstown' from the graves of Maria and Elizabeth—now operated in the months immediately following Branwell's disgrace to even greater purpose. In that dark time, when his presence in the house, a disreputable figure shuffling between home and village in quest of drink and drugs, brought to nothing the carefully laid plan of the preceding years; when the 'pleasant and flourishing seminary' of Emily's imagination, that was to have brought them in cash 'to a considerable amount', had to be abandoned as an impossibility because of his compromising presence; at that very time Charlotte's discovery of Emily's poems led to a magical flowering of their genius. By such a chance—as it appeared—were the Brontës' masterpieces engendered, and their creators set firmly back upon the road pursued in childhood, from which they should never have turned. In single-minded childhood they had known themselves for 'genii'; the painful lessons of life had driven them to accept the humbler status of governess as a duty.

Even now, in the fresh recognition of their powers as writers, their fear was to fail financially. They were prepared to risk a fraction of their aunt's precious legacies in order to get their poems launched, but they still looked to the *practical* ends of authorship. This appeared in all Charlotte's dealings with the publishers, with whom she adopted a very businesslike tone. Anticipating rewarding royalties she instructed Aylott & Jones in a letter of 11 May (1846) to spend more than the agreed £2 on advertising, 'especially as the estimate is increased by nearly £5, in consequence, it appears of a mistake. If you do not object, the additional amount of the estimate can be remitted when you send in your account at the end of the first six months.'[1]

It was agreed that the authors should contribute £31. 10s. od. towards costs of publication (to which was later added a further £5); Charlotte, acting as agent for the authors (as 'C. Brontë, Esq.'), sent

[1] CB's correspondence with Aylott & Jones is preserved in the BPM.

this sum on 3 March. The authors were furthermore to pay £2 towards advertising the book in the literary journals.

Before Emily's consent to publication had been gained she had insisted on their assuming a *nom de plume*. Disliking complete anonymity and too honest to adopt 'positively masculine names' they compromised by making what Charlotte later described as 'an ambiguous choice' of names neither masculine nor feminine, but bearing their own initials: Currer, Ellis and Acton—adding to them the surname Bell. Though they never explained this choice, its origin is not far to seek in the context of that particular year, 1845, which brought to Haworth a stranger from Ireland, Mr. Brontë's new curate, Arthur Bell Nicholls. Unknown as he was, and held at distance by the Brontë girls, no suspicion of the subterfuge was likely to reach him or the outer world. Time would divulge the truth in the end, when ironically enough Mr. Nicholls legitimately conferred his name on Currer Bell.

Charlotte's own choice of pseudonym is the least difficult of the three to trace to a recognizable origin: she had on two distinct occasions, at Cowan Bridge and at Stonegappe, contacts with Miss Currer of Eshton Hall, one of the first patrons and subscribers to the school and the owner of one of the most considerable libraries in the north —from which she made donations, incidentally, to the Mechanics' Institute Library of Keighley. The Currers were lords of the manor of Kildwick, and while at Stonegappe attending services at Kildwick Church Charlotte must have sat under the memorial tablet to the family, even if she never accompanied the Sidgwicks when they called at Kildwick Hall.

The proofs of *Poems by Currer, Ellis and Acton Bell* began to come in on 11 March and continued throughout the month, at a speed refreshingly brisker than present-day methods allow, and by the third week in May the book was out. It sold at 4*s.*, numbered 165 pages, and was bound in dark green ribbed cloth with gilt lettering and decorated with a geometric design. (When Smith, Elder reissued the unsold first edition, the design was replaced with one representing a lyre.)

The poems by the three authors were presented in rotation, one by 'Currer' being followed by one of 'Ellis's' and by one of 'Acton's'. The volume contained 61 poems, Emily and Anne contributing 21 poems each and Charlotte 19. Of her own Charlotte became swiftly critical, her meteoric rise to fame within the next two years as a best-selling writer of fiction making her very conscious of her imperfections as a poet. Writing to Mr. Williams in September 1848, she said: 'I am glad the little volume of the Bell's poems is likely to get into Mr. Smith's hands. I should feel unmixed pleasure in the chance of its being brought under respectable auspices before the public, were Currer Bell's share in its contents absent. Of that portion I am by no means proud. Much of it was written in early youth; I feel it now to be crude and rhapsodical.'[1]

The adjectives are judiciously chosen, for the majority of her poems were marred by declamatory passages. They were not quite so much the product of 'early youth' as she gave Mr.Williams to suppose, but included verse written in her later schooldays at Roe Head and during and after her Brussels period; and earlier poems revised in the light of that experience.

The poems which Charlotte knew to have failed, failed by their want of individual fire. The fear of revealing experience of a personal nature robbed even those that had been written under genuine emotion of their original impulse. The poem 'Frances' (examined in a previous chapter) affords eloquent example of this; comparison between the original poem, called 'Reason' in the manuscript, and the printed version shows how destructive had been the editorial pencil.

Charlotte's contribution to the volume of 'Poems' was not only less interesting than her sisters'—who allowed much of the personal element to remain in their selection—but it did less than credit even to her gift as poet; for she could do, and had done, better. The trouble with her was that at that precise time all her faculties were concentrated on a theme about which she felt herself in honour—and discretion—bound to silence. How it obsessed her was plainly shown in the weeks following immediately on the publication of the poems. Their production had, undoubtedly, unlocked the flood-gates of invention and memory and carried all away. The resolve to appear before the public to better purpose than as the part-author of a slight volume of verse seemed to inform all three sisters at once. Certainly they were more agreed over the publication of their first novels than they had been over the poems. The fact was that each one of them had already to hand, in a fairly advanced state, the manuscript of a work of fiction, before ever the *Poems by Currer, Ellis and Acton Bell* came from the press.

This is shown by Charlotte's letter of 6 April to Aylott & Jones, in which she made the following inquiry:

Gentlemen—C, E and A. Bell are now preparing for the press a work of fiction, consisting of three distinct and unconnected tales, which may

[1] CB to WSW, Sept. 1848: *W & S* ii. 256.

be published either together, as a work of three volumes, of the ordinary novel size, or separately as single volumes, as shall be deemed most advisable—

It is not their intention to publish these tales on their own account. They direct me to ask you whether you would be disposed to undertake the work after having, of course, by due inspection of the MS, ascertained that its contents are such as to warrant an expectation of success.

An early answer will oblige, as, in case of your negativing the proposal, enquiry must be made of other publishers—[1]

Aylott & Jones did not publish fiction, but were willing to advise the Bells about other firms which did so, an offer which Charlotte accepted gratefully in a letter of 11 April.

I beg to thank you for your obliging offer of advice. I will avail myself of it to request information on two or three points. It is evident that unknown authors have great difficulties to contend with. . . . Can you give me any hint as to the way in which these difficulties are best met ? . . . in the present case, where a work of fiction is in question, in what form would a publisher be most likely to accept the MS, whether offered as a work of 3 vols, or as tales which might be published as numbers, or as contributions to a periodical ?

What publishers would be most likely to receive favourably a proposal of this nature ?

Aylott & Jones immediately supplying the answers to these queries, together with a list of likely publishers, Charlotte wrote to them on 15 April: 'I have to thank you for your obliging answer to my last. The information you give is of value to us, and when the MS is completed your suggestion shall be acted on.'

The manuscripts were not two months being completed, the fair copy of *The Professor* is dated 27 June—and on 4 July the three novels were offered to Henry Colburn. The accompanying letter read:

Sir—

I request permission to send for your inspection the M.S. of a work of fiction in 3 vols—It consists of 3 tales each occupying a volume and capable of being published together or separately, as thought most advisable.

The Authors of these tales have already appeared before the public.

Should you consent to examine the work, would you, in your reply,

---

[1] The correspondence with Aylott & Jones over the publication of the *Poems* is at the BPM.

state at what period, after transmission of the M.S. to you, the authors may expect to receive your decision upon its merits.

I am, Sir,

Address Mr. Currer Bell   Yours respectfully,
            Parsonage   C. Bell
            Haworth
            Bradford
            Yorkshire

Whereas the whole correspondence with Aylott & Jones over the publication of the *Poems* had been conducted by Charlotte in her own name—C. Brontë—acting on behalf of Messrs. C., E., & A. Bell, the letter accompanying the manuscript of the novels was signed by her author's name, boldly prefixed by 'Mr.'. The 'conscientious scruple' regarding the assumption of a name 'positively masculine' had evidently been waived by then. The resolution to abide by the pseudonym might also denote a strengthening of the intention to make a career in letters.

The manuscript of the novels went the rounds of six successive publishers—as Charlotte later recalled—'for the space of a year and a half' before any of them found acceptance. *Wuthering Heights* and *Agnes Grey* were accepted in July 1847 (and published in December), but Charlotte's own contribution to the 'three distinct and unconnected tales'—*The Professor*—never did find a publisher in her lifetime.

The reasons for this were complicated. Besides its own intrinsic demerit caused by the masculine first-person narrator, *The Professor* suffered as much by its successors' triumphs, as from its own short-comings. Charlotte's eventual publishers, expecting ever greater excellences from her, deferred from year to year the consideration of her earliest work. The loss to literature was made good, for had *The Professor* been published early Charlotte would not, in all probability, have written *Villette*. Once she was dead and no more masterpieces could be looked for, her publishers were thankful to fall back on *The Professor*.

Discussing the book with W. S. Williams in later years, Charlotte said:

all that relates to Brussels, the Belgian school, etc, is as good as I can write; it contains more pith, more substance, more reality, in my judgement, than much of 'Jane Eyre'. It gives, I think, a new view of a grade, an occupation, and a class of characters—all very commonplace, very insignificant in themselves, but not more so than . . . that portion of 'Jane Eyre' which seems to please most generally.[1]

[1] CB to WSW, 14 Dec. 1847: *W & S* ii. 161–2.

The treatment of *The Professor* by the publishers has long since been judged unmerited, and the book accepted as a considerable, if not a major, achievement. The publishers who rejected it did so even while recognizing that it was 'original' and 'faithful to nature', because they had no confidence in its sales-potential; they said 'it was deficient in startling incident' and 'thrilling excitement' and therefore 'would never suit the circulating libraries'. Judged subsequently by other standards than those of the circulating libraries, it still suffered because it was for a long time regarded as an earlier version of *Villette*.

That it was nothing of the kind was instantly—and thankfully—recognized by Mrs. Gaskell who, knowing that it dealt with Charlotte's schooldays in Brussels, had 'dreaded lest it should involve anything with M. Heger'. Mrs. Gaskell's important evidence should long ago have dispelled the belief that *The Professor* and *Villette* had identical subjects; she clearly stated that, though *The Professor* did relate to the school, it did not relate to M. Heger.[1]

For this reason, as will appear later, *The Professor* is of considerable importance to Charlotte's biographer. Finished by the spring of 1846, it bears witness to the author's state of mind during the last year of her correspondence with M. Heger. Her mind was obsessed with the recollection of her Brussels experience; like all people in love, her only pleasure was to speak (and if not to speak, to write) about everything that surrounded the beloved object, even if, as in her case, she could not bring herself as yet to speak of the beloved object himself. On the outward circumstances of his life she could fix her gaze and evoke even 'the sparkling clearness of the air' in Brussels, the 'gay clean aspect of the white-washed or painted houses'—testing the accuracy of her memory of the scenes that surrounded him.

Here, for the first time, with topographical precision, she could place the streets, the churches, the houses that had served as setting to her own unhappy adventure. In *The Professor* she could give their real names to the Rue d'Isabelle, the Rue Royale, the statue of General Belliard, the Parc, Ste Gudule, Rue N.D. aux Neiges, etc., which, in the later *Villette*, she camouflaged under fictitious names. The need to do so in the later book is evidence of how much more of the psychological and emotional truth of her own story she revealed in its pages. She did not do so in *The Professor*. With unselfconscious precision she described the Pensionnat itself, the black and white marble 'carré' of its entrance

[1] See Appendixes B and D below. Also letter of Mrs. Gaskell to Emily Shaen, 8 Sept. 1856: *W & S* iv. 209.

hall, the glass doors leading to the playground, the pleasant garden, the refectory, the communicating classrooms. The need to linger about the places where she had lived in daily contact with the man she loved was assuaged in this way, even if all other consolations were denied her.

She had first seen Brussels with all the zest of the traveller noting fresh sights; in recollection the stimulus of her original mood outweighs the late depression. It is notable that much of *The Professor* (as opposed to *Villette*) is written in a comic vein. The portraits of the Belgian characters are brightly satirical. The old ladies—Mesdames Pelet and Reuter—dressed in frowsy camisoles and downtrodden slippers by day, but resplendent by tea-time in bright coloured silk gowns and flower-bordered caps, reflect Charlotte's good-humoured enjoyment. These are new types to her, and as a novelist she cherishes them. More important still, the Belgian protagonists, Zoraïde Reuter and M. Pelet, as opposed to the English protagonists William Crimsworth and Frances Henri, are observed with light irony of the kind she would later apply to the portrait of Paul Emanuel himself. But the important point about M. Pelet is that he does not, like Paul Emanuel, embody M. Heger, he was only confounded with the latter by critics unaware of the identities of the two originals. The lack of scruple, of plain morality even, in M. Pelet, should have been enough to show that he was not M. Heger. His identity was, in any case, clearly defined by Charlotte; he was not attached to the pensionnat de demoiselles in any capacity, as M. Emanuel was, but was the director of the adjacent boarding-house of the boys' Athénée Royal, which occupied the north side of the Rue Terarken and whose rear wall (pierced in fact as in fiction by one small bedroom window) overlooked the garden of the Pensionnat Heger. In successive Brussels directories and almanacs of the time, M. Joachim-Joseph Lebel figures as the Director of the establishment. He was a Frenchman (as Charlotte described) born at St. Pol in the Pas de Calais, 24 December 1807, and educated in Paris, emigrating to Belgium as a refugee from the Revolution of July; a man 'distinguished in air, quiet in method, Parisian in characteristics, suave and silky in manner' (as acquaintances remembered him), and so resembling Charlotte's portrait of him as 'M. Pelet' (note the similarity of names) as to be recognized by the first Brussels readers of *The Professor* as a 'startling likeness'.

M. Lebel[1] was a well-known figure in the Heger household; his

[1] For M. Lebel's identification with M. Pelet see M. H. Spielmann, *Charlotte Brontë in Brussels*, Centenary Memorial: Fisher Unwin (1917), 96–99.

intimacy with M. Heger would appear to have been fairly close, not only as a neighbour but as a colleague, both men being teachers on the staff of the Athénée Royal; and Charlotte must have had plenty of occasions for observing him. Her links with him acquired an even closer character, for he had received as a memento of St. Helena a piece of the coffin of Napoleon which he gave to M. Heger and which M. Heger, in his turn, gave to Charlotte.

'M. Pelet' was a secondary character in Charlotte's own experience. And in the character of 'Mlle Reuter' she did not attempt a full-length portrait of Madame Heger either. To do this, while still so close to the experience of her Brussels schooldays, was emotionally beyond her.

In this avoidance of the major issues, this shrinking from unveiling the heart of her mystery in *The Professor*, Charlotte betrayed how close she still was to its suffering. It is this that makes *The Professor* not a rough draft of *Villette*, but a book on its own, containing the surface image of her Brussels experience but little of its depths.

Apart from the name 'Zoraïde', which contained an echo of the 'Zoë' of Madame Heger, Mlle Reuter is a separate creation, and her complete success is one of the earliest intimations of Charlotte's genius as a novelist. She is wholly credible, a character complete in all parts, borrowing here and there, admittedly, from Madame Heger (especially as a capable headmistress, 'sensible sagacious and affable') but moving between her old mother, her pupils, and her lover with admirable duplicity and ease, with no trace of the 'dumpy little woman' Charlotte perceived in Madame Heger, and essentially seductive. It is as though, in emphasizing this aspect of her, Charlotte were deliberately obscuring the resemblance to Madame Heger. *The Professor*, written from the viewpoint of a man, could the more easily allow of such a reversal of the facts. What Charlotte had experienced had been the seductive quality of the husband, not of the wife.

With William Crimsworth, the real protagonist, and Frances Henri, the incomparable heroine of *The Professor*, Charlotte was upon native ground and among old acquaintants. William Crimsworth, indeed, was but another incarnation of the juvenile Charles Townsend, bearing with him into adult life the old hate-theme between rival brothers of which Charlotte had written in childhood concerning Douro and his brother Lord Charles Florian Wellesley, and would still be writing in the last draft of a tale on her death-bed about the Ellin brothers. Even the names Edward and William, so often used in Charlotte's 'brother' dramas, were brought into *The Professor*. William Crimsworth, moreover, had many of the characteristics of Charlotte's juvenile heroes; his cool incivility of manner, suspicious outlook, and fundamental despondency, belonged to the earliest heroes.

In Frances Henri, though drawn with some of the early pathos that coloured the portraits of Marian Hume, Charlotte made her first great advance in characterization. Having decided to exclude herself from the story (as she did not in *Villette*) she could afford to endow her heroine with qualities very different from her own. Frances Henri has a sweetness of disposition absent in all Charlotte's other heroines—*all* of whom were self-portraits in varying degrees. Yet, as Frances Henri had to be the vehicle for the sentiment of the tale, Charlotte had to imbue her with feelings whose strength she herself had tried. Her situation was Charlotte's; she suffered from the enmity and intrigue of a jealous woman; she was forcibly separated from the man she loved. But, resolved as Charlotte was not to attempt the relation of her own complex and all-but inexplicable predicament, she allowed to Frances Henri a freedom of destiny that was wholly unlike her own. No insurmountable obstacle prevented the marriage of Frances and William; they could marry and live happily ever after. The last parts of *The Professor*, when the happy ending is assured, are, however, particularly uninteresting. For the author the essential truth of the tale went out of it when the anguish was appeased.

Nevertheless, writing *The Professor* in the last year of her correspondence with M. Heger, when her instinct told her they were moving towards a permanent rift, kept Charlotte sane. The urge to write had not entirely deserted her even in her darkest hour (witness her first letter to M. Heger in which she admits as much); but it had been a question of what to write at that obsessive time, when the pensionnat filled her horizon and one single figure haunted her memory. She knew that she was not yet ready to write about him (her crude poems about him are proof of this), but she could try to see the world in which he moved in an objective light. One thing is certain: she could not have written a novel at that time which excluded Brussels. But having done so the way was clear for the totally different setting of *Jane Eyre*.

How true this is appears from the scheme for a novel she had jotted down in May 1843, while still in Brussels. After the period of strict self-suppression that had lasted from her period as governess with the Whites, the compulsion to write had returned; she considered in detail the framework of a novel and noted down its essentials inside the front cover of one of her Brussels exercise-books, under the heading: 'Scheme for a May Tale'.[1] The particulars are listed thus:

Time	— from 30–50 years ago
Country	— England
Scene	— Rural
Rank	— Middle
Person	— First
Subject	— Certain remarkable occurrences
Sex of Writer	— At discretion
No of Characters	— Limited
Plot	— Domestic—the romantic not excluded
Opening	— Cheerful or Gloomy
Occurrences	— 1st Reverses of Fortune— 2nd New arrival 3rd Loss of Relations 4th Crosses in the Affections 5. Going abroad Return 6th
Characters	— Hero—Heroine—Family of dº—Rival or Rivalness—Villain N.B. Moderation to be observed here—Friends Avoid Richardsonian Multiplication
P.S.	As much compression—as little explanation as may be.
Mem	— To be set about with proper spirit— To be carried on with the same— To be concluded idem
Observe	— No grumbling allowed.

Inside the back cover of the same exercise-book were written some more notes.

Uncle	— R.C. Priest—Atonement
Eliza	— some food—like Mr. R—Georgiana
School	— L—e not for 1st person—2nd character
Sympathy	— Keep 1st person for Spectator—Narrator Commentator

As an insight into her literary ideals—the checks on extravagance, the avoidance of 'multiplication', the use of 'compression', of 'as little explanation as may be', the notes are interesting and show how close, in the achievement of *Villette*, Charlotte came to realizing her own

[1] The original MS. is in the BPM.

standards of excellence. Except in the circumstances of 'Going abroad' and 'Crosses in the Affections', *The Professor* cannot be fitted into the 'Scheme for a May Tale'—but it may have marked Charlotte's first step on the road to recovery. Even before the chance discovery of Emily's manuscript poems, Charlotte had dragged herself some way out of her despondency. How far Branwell's disaster might have thrust her deep down again had it not been for the incentive given her by her sisters, cannot now be judged. But from Emily and Anne came the new resolve to make something of all their lives.

The discovery that they had been writing (and furthermore in secret) works good enough for publication had an electrical effect on Charlotte. That they, who had seemed to lack literary ambition, should in the event have outdistanced her, was the keenest incentive to action. She set herself to catch up with them. The revelation of what they had been doing while she had almost succumbed to lethargy was among the great surprises of her life.

From then on the evening sessions spent in the quiet dining-room when the household had retired to bed (and, with luck, even Branwell was safely shut in his father's room) became the focal point of each day's activity. Then could the works in hand be advanced, and when certain points in the narration were reached, read aloud, debated and challenged, appraised and censured in a spirit of absolute frankness and equality. Mutual admiration was by no means the overruling sentiment in these discussions. Charlotte never hesitated, even after her sisters' deaths rendered their memories exquisitely tender, to criticize what she considered the crudities of *Wuthering Heights*, the incongruous plot of *Wildfell Hall*. She recalled vividly the heated arguments that had raged at the time of their writing: '. . . If the auditor of her work read in MS', she wrote in the Preface to the posthumous edition of Emily's novel, 'shuddered under the grinding influence of natures so relentless and implacable, of spirits so lost and fallen; if it was complained that the mere hearing of certain vivid and fearful scenes banished sleep by night, and disturbed mental peace by day, Ellis Bell would wonder what was meant, and suspect the complainant of affectation. . . .'[1]

In her attempts to dissuade Anne from making *Wildfell Hall* the close study of drunkenness and moral degradation she had set out to achieve, she succeeded no better. Anne stuck to her original intention and carried it through. Charlotte wrote of her in the joint Memoir to her sisters:

[1] 'Memoir of Ellis Bell': Smith, Elder, 1850.

She had been called on to contemplate, near at hand, and for a long time, the terrible effects of talents misused and faculties abused. . . . What she saw sank deeply into her mind; it did her harm. She brooded over it till she believed it to be a duty to reproduce every detail . . . as a warning to others. . . . When reasoned with on the subject, she regarded such reasonings as a temptation to self-indulgence. She must be honest; she must not varnish soften, or conceal.[1]

Even when the moral and artistic intentions of the writers were at stake, as these excerpts show, Charlotte did not hesitate to question and oppose her sisters' judgements. *Wuthering Heights* and *Wildfell Hall*, however, show how unshakeable those judgements were. Fortunately for English literature the Bells knew their own minds, and even when not united in methods pursued each their own appointed course. Charlotte herself consistently refused to make radical changes in her plots and only met her father's objections to the tragic ending of *Villette* to the extent of leaving it ambiguous. Yet the free communication with kindred minds became not only one of the greatest pleasures in writing, it became a necessity to her. Writing *Villette* alone when her sisters were dead, she realized with a pang how she had come to depend on their sympathy and judgement. '. . . I can hardly tell you', she wrote to her publisher regarding *Villette* on 30 October 1852, 'how I hunger to hear some opinion beside my own, and how I have sometimes desponded and almost despaired, because there was no one to whom to read a line, or of whom to ask a counsel. "Jane Eyre" was not written under such circumstances, nor were two-thirds of "Shirley". . . .'[2]

Their mutual dependence was all the greater because, having once entered into a common secret and a common purpose, they agreed to keep it strictly to themselves. Neither success nor fame would ever have altered Emily's fierce resolve to confine the knowledge of her writings to the family circle. Dread of disappointing their father if they failed was a further inducement to silence. As women, handicapped by the prejudices of the age, they were determined not to expose themselves to ridicule. Hidden behind their pseudonyms, Currer, Ellis, and Acton Bell felt safe to pursue their chosen way.

They were not even suspected by Ellen Nussey, from whom significantly they sedulously hid the truth. This was not always easy, as Ellen from time to time complained of Charlotte's neglect, or suggested a

[1] 'Memoir of Ellis and Acton Bell': Smith, Elder, 1850.
[2] CB to GMS, 30 Oct. 1852: *W & S* iv. 13.

visit that had, with no very sufficient excuse sometimes, to be deferred.

This was the case in the winter and early spring of 1846 when the 'Poems' were being prepared for the press. On 23 January Charlotte wrote to Ellen: 'I must write to you to-day whether I have anything to write or not, or else you will begin to think that I have forgotten you. . . . I have no news whatever to communicate. No changes take place here. Branwell offers no prospect of hope. . . . I hold my intention of going to Birstall as soon as I can, that is, provided you will have me.'[1] Not till 13 February (the manuscript of the 'Poems' having been dispatched to Aylott & Jones on the 7th) did Charlotte write again: 'Will it suit you if I come to Brookroyd next Wednesday, February 18th, and stay till the Wednesday after; if convenient tell me so at once and fix your own time.'[2]

The visit was timed not to interfere with the business correspondence over the 'Poems' (Charlotte acted as agent for them all) and allowed her to exchange two further letters with the publishers—on 15 and 16 February—about the safe arrival of the manuscript, format and type, before leaving home.

Once in possession of her friend, Ellen was loath to part with her so soon, and begged for an extension of her stay. In reply she received one of Emily's rare letters.

Haworth, Feb 25th 1846

Dear Miss Nussey—I fancy this note will be too late to decide one way or other with respect to Charlotte's stay. Yours only came this morning (Wednesday), and unless mine travels faster you will not receive it till Friday. Papa, of course, misses Charlotte, and will be glad to have her back. Anne and I ditto; but as she goes from home so seldom, you may keep her a day or two longer, if your eloquence is equal to the task of persuading her—that is, if she still be with you when you get this permission.
Love from Anne.—Yours truly,

Emily J. Brontë[3]

Charlotte returned home on 2 March, and sent Aylott & Jones the estimated £31. 10s. 0d. for costs on the 3rd. Writing to Ellen on the same day to announce her safe return, she gave the family news—omitting, of course, all mention of the publishing venture.

---

[1] CB to EN, 23 Jan. 1846: *W & S* ii. 75.
[2] CB to EN, 13 Feb. 1846: *W & S* ii. 78.
[3] EJB to EN, 25 Feb. 1846: *W & S* ii. 78.

The news of Branwell was sufficiently bad to warrant filling the
greater part of her letter with it:

I went into the room where Branwell was, to speak to him, about an hour
after I got home; it was very forced work to address him. I might have
spared myself the trouble, as he took no notice, and made no reply; he
was stupefied. My fears were not in vain. I hear that he had got a sovereign
from papa while I have been away, under pretence of paying a pressing debt;
he went immediately and changed it at a public-house, and has employed it
as was to be expected. Emily concluded her account by saying he was a hopeless being; it is too true. In his present state it is scarcely possible to stay in
the room where he is. What the future has in store I do not know.[1]

On the subject of Branwell Charlotte confided fully to Ellen. Ellen's
comparable trials over the madness of her brother George and the ruin
of her brother Joseph made her understanding.

'You ask if we are more comfortable,' Charlotte wrote on 14 April
(three days after writing to Aylott & Jones for the names of publishers
likely to consider fiction), 'I wish I could say anything favourable, but
how can we be more comfortable so long as Branwell stays at home and
degenerates instead of improving? . . . he refuses to make an effort;
he will not work—and at home he is a drain on every resource—an
impediment to all happiness. But there is no use in complaining. . . .'[2]

On 26 May Mr. Robinson, on whose death Branwell had been
counting, died at Thorp Green. The event, far from fulfilling his hopes,
blighted them for ever, and drove him several degrees further down the
road to death. Writing to Ellen on 17 June Charlotte had a sorry tale
to tell.

The death of Mr. Robinson which occurred about 3 weeks or a month
ago, served Branwell for a pretext to throw all about him into hubbub and
confusion with his emotions, etc, etc . . . Shortly after, came news from all
hands that Mr. Robinson had altered his will before he died and effectually
prevented all chance of a marriage between his widow and Branwell, by
stipulating that she should not have a shilling if she ever ventured to reopen
any communication with him. Of course, he then became intolerable. . . .
Branwell declares that he neither can nor will do anything for himself;
good situations have been offered him more than once, for which, by a
fortnight's work, he might have qualified himself, but he will do nothing,
except drink and make us all wretched.[3]

---

[1] CB to EN, 3 Mar. 1846: *W & S* ii. 83–84.
[2] CB to EN, 14 April 1846: *W & S* ii. 88.
[3] CB to EN, 17 June 1846: *SLL* i. 331; *W & S* ii. 96–97.

News of the death of Mr. Robinson was reported in the Yorkshire press of the day and could not, therefore, have been hidden from Branwell, even had he not received the visit at Haworth of the Robinson coachman, sent to prevent his attempting a return to Thorp Green. The shock, coming in the hour of his anticipated reunion with Mrs. Robinson, caused him to have a fit at the 'Black Bull', where the barmaid found him long after the coachman's departure lying on the floor 'bleating like a calf'.[1]

These were the circumstances accompanying the publication, in the third week of May, of the *Poems by Currer, Ellis and Acton Bell*; small wonder that no expressions of pleasure on the authors' part have been recorded. With Branwell the secret was never shared; he died without knowing that his sisters had 'ever published a line', as Charlotte later told her publishers.

Of the book's reception no echo reached the authors till July; then they received from Aylott & Jones copies of the first two journals to give it a notice—*The Critic* and *The Athenaeum*. Heart-warming to the authors were the few words devoted to it by *The Critic*, which said: 'They in whose hearts are chords strung by Nature to sympathise with the beautiful and true, will recognise in these compositions the presence of more genius than it was supposed this utilitarian age had devoted to the loftier exercise of the intellect. . . .'[2]

The Athenaeum for 4 July, reviewing the book in company with others in an article called 'Poetry for the Million', had the discernment to pick out the work of Ellis as possessing 'a fine quaint spirit and an evident power of wing that may reach heights not here attempted . . .'.[3]

Thus encouraged, the Bells thought it worth while to invest a further £10 in advertising the book. Charlotte's instructions to this effect were sent on 10 July. On the 15th, having heard nothing more, she wrote asking: 'Whether *any*, or how many copies have yet been sold? . . .' The answer came by return of post: two copies had been sold.

Using the same formula of courtesy as though it had been 2,000, Charlotte wrote back on 18 July: 'The Messrs Bell are obliged to you for the information respecting the number of copies sold.'

One of their two readers, Mr. F. Enoch of Leamington, the song writer, wrote through the medium of the publishers asking for their autographs. In returning these—the three signatures on one sheet of paper—Charlotte wrote on 23 July: 'I think I before intimated that

¹ Duclaux 145; Gaskell 197.   ² *W & S* ii. 102.
³ Idem.

the Messrs Bell are desirous for the present of remaining unknown, for which reason they prefer having the note posted in London to sending it direct. . . .'

With the exception of a few more reviews—that in the *Dublin University Magazine* rousing their particular gratitude—no more stir was created by the publication of the 'Poems'. 'Ill-success failed to crush us', wrote Charlotte in after years; 'the mere effort to succeed had given a wonderful zest to existence; it must be pursued. . . .'[1]

Before the news of the 'Poems' failure had reached the authors, the completed manuscripts of *The Professor*, *Wuthering Heights*, and *Agnes Grey* had been posted to Henry Colburn on 4 July. The will to survive had triumphed. Neither heart-break, nor daily domestic tribulation, nor apparent failure were strong enough to repress the resurgent spirit once fairly launched in flight.

[1] *Memoir of Ellis and Acton Bell*: Smith, Elder, 1850.

CHAPTER XVIII

THE ACHIEVEMENT OF *JANE EYRE*

O N the domestic front the tribulations showed no signs of slackening, and with advancing summer a crisis could no longer be averted. Mr. Brontë, whose failing sight Charlotte had mentioned as long ago as her return from Brussels in January 1844, had now to face the operation for cataract. As Charlotte's later accounts show, the initiative for such a step had to come entirely from herself. Mr. Brontë very much dreaded, and doubted the success of, such an extreme course. On her return from Brookroyd in March Charlotte wrote to Ellen: '. . . I found Papa very well; his sight very much the same . . . He was much cheered by my report of Mr. Carr's opinion [the Nussey's doctor] and of old Mrs. Carr's experience; but I could perceive he caught gladly at the idea of deferring the operations a few months longer. . . .'[1]

By early August Mr. Brontë was advised to lose no more time in consulting a specialist. Charlotte and Emily went to Manchester to seek one out at the Manchester Institution for Curing the Diseases of the Eye, and there described Mr. Brontë's case to a Dr. Wilson. '. . . He could not tell from the description whether the eyes were ready for an operation', Charlotte wrote Ellen on 9 August. 'Papa must therefore necessarily take a journey to Manchester to consult him; if he judges the cataract ripe, we shall remain—if, on the contrary, he thinks it not yet sufficiently hardened, we shall have to return—and papa must remain in darkness a while longer. . . .'[2]

On Wednesday, 19 August, Charlotte accompanied her father to Manchester where an appointment had been arranged with Dr. Wilson. On examination the doctor found that the eye was quite ready for the operation, which was accordingly fixed for the following Monday. (In the event, it did not take place till the Tuesday, 25 August.)

Their stay in Manchester being now decided, and likely to last several weeks, they needed to find suitable lodgings. In this, as in everything

[1] CB to EN, 3 Mar. 1846: *W & S* ii. 83–84.
[2] CB to EN, 9 Aug. 1846: *W & S* ii. 105–6.

else, they found Dr. Wilson both kind and helpful. He recommended them to a retired servant of his, a Mrs. Thomas Ball, who with her husband let rooms in their house at No. 83, Mount Pleasant, Boundary Street, a turning off the Oxford Road. Mount Pleasant (destroyed in the blitz) was a quiet terrace of brick houses, removed from the noise of the centre yet easily accessible from Dr. Wilson's house in Mosley Street (he lived at No. 72) and the Royal Infirmary in Piccadilly. 'We got into our lodgings yesterday,' Charlotte wrote Ellen on 21 August, 'I think we shall be comfortable; at least, our rooms are very good, but there is no mistress of the house (she is very ill, and gone out into the country) and I am somewhat puzzled in managing about provisions; we board ourselves . . . there will be a nurse coming in a day or two, and I am afraid of not having things good enough for her.'[1] In the event, Mr. Ball (whose profession was given as 'agent' in the street-directories of the time) proved himself a capable substitute for his wife, and Mr. Brontë noted in his expense-account for the trip that the nurse 'boarded at Mr. Ball's' at a cost of 15s. a week. For the rooms Mr. Brontë paid 25s.

Whether on advice or by good fortune, Mr. Brontë had come to one of the foremost eye-specialists of the day. William James Wilson[2] was a Leeds man. He had been early apprenticed to surgeons at Lancaster and Chester before proceeding to London where he studied at Bart's and gained experience at the Infirmary for Diseases of the Eye in Charterhouse Square. In 1813 he settled in Manchester where he was mainly responsible in the next year for the founding of the Manchester Institution for Curing the Diseases of the Eye. As surgeon at that hospital his reputation was early established and by 1826 he was appointed surgeon on the staff of Manchester Infirmary, where he remained 29 years. He was a man of liberal and charitable principles, with an immense capacity for work, and a pleasing personality. 'Easy and graceful in movement, witty and polished in conversation,' according to the terms of his obituary notice, 'his face lit up with intelligence and the most agreeable courtesy of expression in conversation. Probably no person in any walk of life was, during 40 years, more generally known and esteemed in Manchester.'[3]

The ordeal, made worse by Mr. Brontë's age (he was nearly 70 at

---

[1] CB to EN, 21 Aug. 1846: *W & S* ii. 106–7.
[2] For Dr. Wilson's career see Edward Mansfield Brockbank's 'Sketches of the Lives and Work of the Honorary Medical Staff of the Manchester Infirmary'; M.U.P., 1904.
[3] Idem.

the time) and the absence of any anaesthetic, had to be endured by Charlotte as well as by the patient, since he wanted her by him in the room. She wrote of it next day to Ellen:

Manchester, August 26th 1846

Dear Ellen—The operation is over; it took place yesterday. Mr. Wilson performed it; two other surgeons assisted. Mr. Wilson says he considers it quite successful; but papa cannot yet see anything. The affair lasted precisely a quarter of an hour; it was not the simple operation of couching Mr. Carr described, but the more complicated one of extracting the cataract. Mr. Wilson entirely disapproves of couching. Papa displayed extraordinary patience and firmness; the surgeons seemed surprised. I was in the room all the time, as it was his wish that I should be there; of course, I neither spoke nor moved till the thing was done, and then I felt that the less I said, either to papa or to the surgeons, the better. Papa is now confined to his bed in a dark room, and is not to be stirred for four days; he is to speak and be spoken to as little as possible. I am greatly obliged to you for your letter and your kind advice—I had arranged most things in accordance with it. . . . I hope Mr. Wilson will soon allow me to dispense with the nurse; she is well enough, no doubt, but somewhat too obsequious, and not, I should think, to be trusted much; yet I am obliged to trust her in some things.[1]

On the 31st she reported: 'Papa is still lying in bed. . . . Mr. Wilson seemed perfectly satisfied and said all was right. . . .'

It was a matter of time and how best to drag through the weary days. As Mr. Brontë was not allowed to speak, Charlotte spent most of the time in the sitting-room, or if the nurse sat there she took refuge in her bedroom. It does not appear that she was tempted to stray far out of doors and inspect Manchester.

At that time, in a house in Upper Rumford Street—a long artery that almost reached to Boundary Street at one end—Mrs. Gaskell was living, no more known to the literary world as yet than Charlotte Brontë. 'Our house', Mrs. Gaskell wrote her friend Tottie Fox a few years later, 'is a mile and a half from the very middle of Manchester; the last house *countrywards* of an interminably long street the other end of which touches the town, while we look into fields from some of our windows; not very pretty our rural fields it must be owned, but in which the children can see cows being milked and hay being made in summer.'[2]

Mrs. Gaskell, who in the August of the previous year had suffered

---

[1] CB to EN, 26 Aug. 1846: *W & S* ii. 107–8.
[2] Mrs. Gaskell to Mrs. Fox, 29 May 1849: *Letters of Mrs. Gaskell*, ed. Chapple and Pollard, M.U.P. 1966, p. 81.

the great grief of her life in the death of her baby son from scarlet fever, gave birth during Mr. Brontë's stay in Manchester to the last and perhaps the most brilliant of her daughters, Julia, who so successfully 'possessed herself of a minute fraction' of Charlotte's heart in later years.

As yet, in that hot August and September of 1846, the comfort of Mrs. Gaskell's friendship was not accorded Charlotte, though both women were moving almost simultaneously towards the high literary position they were shortly to attain. Like Charlotte, Mrs. Gaskell had written some verse—'Sketches among the Poor', published in *Black-wood's Magazine* for January 1837. She had also written some short stories of Manchester life, to be published in the following June in *Howitt's Journal*, William Howitt and his wife Mary having met the Gaskells on a trip up the Rhine and having encouraged Mrs. Gaskell to take up writing seriously (or, as he put it, 'for the public benefit'). But the chief incentive to Mrs. Gaskell's writing had come from her husband (the Unitarian minister of Cross St. Chapel) who, after the death of their little boy, had urged her to write in the hope of healing her sorrow. The book undertaken at his instance was *Mary Barton*, whose anonymous publication in October 1848 almost rivalled the sensation caused by the also anonymous publication of *Jane Eyre* in October 1847. Thus, without any knowledge of each other's destiny, or of the eventual crossing of their paths, Mrs. Gaskell and Charlotte Brontë were near neighbours in the late summer of 1846.[1]

Even then Charlotte was taking the first steps towards their mutual fame and friendship. On the very morning of Mr. Brontë's operation, she received back from the publishers—presumably forwarded by Emily—the manuscript of *The Professor* accompanied by a few curt words of rejection.[2] These were presumably from Henry Colburn, the publisher to whom the manuscript had been sent on 4 July. Whether she communicated with her sisters then and there to decide on the second publisher to be approached, the manuscript was sent out again, as she later told, and submitted to six firms in succession.

The rejection, coming at the time of her father's operation, instead of crushing her, had the contrary effect. It drove her to take up her pen and begin a new book. The enforced seclusion, the long unoccupied days—the very insecurity and anxiety of her circumstances—provided

[1] For data concerning Mrs. Gaskell in Manchester see W. H. Brown, 'Mrs. Gaskell: A Manchester Influence', *Manchester Quarterly; British Weekly*, 29 Oct. 1908; *Manchester Guardian*, 22 Feb. 1910.   [2] Gaskell 213.

an incentive to creation that happier surroundings might never have supplied. If her father's operation failed and his blindness became total, it was unlikely he could continue as incumbent of Haworth. Their home and very livelihood were in danger; and with the rapid deterioration in Branwell's condition—the son of the house from whom in other families help would have come—the worst threat of all faced Charlotte at that time: the break-up of family life. Whatever hopes she and her sisters had cherished of earning a living by their writing received a severe check by that morning's post.

By every standard, other than the Brontë standard, her circumstances were overwhelmingly against her. She was suffering, in addition, from intolerable toothache that kept her awake at night. With the stoicism common to her family she had suffered from it for weeks without considering going to a dentist. As long ago as 24 July she had written to Ellen: 'A series of tooth-aches prolonged and severe, bothering me both day and night, have kept me very stupid . . . to-day, after a fierce night of pain, I am better—much better, and I take the advantage of the interval of ease to discharge my debt.'[1] At the end of the letter she had had to confess: 'Holding down my head does not suit my tooth-ache.'

Now, in Manchester, she wrote to Ellen: 'I have had bad nights from the tooth-ache since I came to Manchester.' Even so, she made no apparent effort to obtain relief. In the 'intervals of ease' from raging toothache *Jane Eyre* was begun.

Begun almost as a gesture of despair, she was soon completely under its spell. As she remembered afterwards, she wrote for three weeks without ever stopping. Ellen Nussey, inquiring how she managed to kill the time, was told: 'You ask if I have any enjoyment here; in truth, I can't say I have—and I long to get home, though, unhappily, home is not now a place of complete rest. It is sad to think how it is disquieted by a constant phantom, or rather two—sin and suffering; they seem to obscure the cheerfulness of day, and to disturb the comfort of evening.'[2] The thought of her sisters' ordeal, left to manage as best they might with Branwell, added to her anxiety for her father. '. . . I wonder how poor Emily and Anne will get on at home with Branwell', had been her immediate cry on hearing that Dr. Wilson meant to operate at once.

The sojourn at Manchester lasted, in the event, for over five weeks,

[1] CB to EN, 24 July 1846: *W & S* ii. 104–5.
[2] CB to EN, 13 Sept. 1846: *W & S* ii. 109–10.

from 19 August to 28 September, by which date Charlotte wrote to Ellen to announce their return home—rather earlier than it had been thought. Dr. Wilson's obligatory departure for Scotland had 'set them at liberty'. In fact, the operation had promised complete success almost from the outset. Dr. Wilson 'seemed perfectly satisfied and said all was right' within five days; only the absolute necessity of immobility and darkness for the patient kept Mr. Brontë in bed and in a shuttered room for so long. The success, upon which Mr. Brontë's livelihood and continuance of family life depended, was not only complete but lasting. Writing six years after the event to her Brussels friend, Laetitia Wheelwright, whose father was similarly afflicted, Charlotte could say:

> Let me not forget to answer your question about the cataract. Tell your papa my father was seventy at the time he underwent an operation; he was most reluctant to try the experiment—could not believe that at his age and with his want of robust strength it would succeed. I was obliged to be very decided in the matter, to act entirely on my own responsibility. Nearly six years have now elapsed since the cataract was extracted (it was not merely depressed). He has never since, during that time, regretted the step, or a day seldom passes that he does not express gratitude and pleasure at the restoration of that inestimable privilege of vision whose loss he once knew.[1]

By 17 November Mr. Brontë's sight and his shocked constitution were so completely restored as to permit him to resume in full his pastoral duties. Writing on that day to Ellen, Charlotte said: 'Papa continues to do very well. He read prayers twice in Church last Sunday. Next Sunday he will have to take the whole duty of the three services himself, as Mr. Nicholls is in Ireland.'[2]

Without Mr. Nicholls, Mr. Brontë's curate since May of the previous year (he took his first service on Sunday, 25 May 1845), the progressive failure in Mr. Brontë's sight and his inability to perform his duties might have had more serious consequences. Though the incumbency of Haworth was a life-appointment, the accident of blindness could have terminated it.

Mr. Nicholls's arrival at Haworth barely two months before Branwell's disgrace had thus coincided with a double crisis in the family's

---

[1] CB to LW, *W & S* iii. 331.

[2] For Mr. Brontë's dependence on Mr. Nicholls, see CB's letter to EN of 29 June 1847 (*W & S* ii. 137): '. . . When can you come to Haworth? Another period of fine weather is passing without you—I fear now your visit will be dull indeed—for it is doubtful whether there will be a curate to enliven you—Mr. Nicholls is likely to get a district ere long and then Papa will be left without assistance. . . . This rather troubles me—the whole duty is too much for him at his age. . . .'

affairs. Mr. Brontë's dependence on him, and the daily spectacle of Branwell's mental and physical collapse, initiated him early into the darkest corners of their lives—a major reason in all probability why Charlotte from the start kept him at arm's length. Anything like pity, or obtrusive sympathy, was harder to bear than the burden of family suffering itself. The curate was, at best, a painful necessity. '. . . Papa has got a new curate lately,' she had written on 26 May 1845 to a national school teacher with whom she was not at all intimate, 'a Mr. Nicholls from Ireland. He did duty for the first time on Sunday—he appears a respectable young man, reads well, and I hope will give satisfaction.' But to Ellen, before a month was out (on the eve of her visit to Hathersage) she spoke without reserve.

I have no desire to see your medical-clerical curate. I think he must be like most other curates I have seen; and they seem to me a self-seeking vain, empty race. At this blessed moment we have no less than three of them in Haworth parish, and God knows, there is not one to mend another. The other day, they all three, accompanied by Mr. Smidt . . . dropped, or rather rushed, in unexpectedly to tea. It was Monday (baking day) and I was hot and tired; still, if they had behaved quietly and decently I would have served them out their tea in peace; but they began glorifying themselves and abusing Dissenters in such a manner, that my temper lost its balance, and I pronounced a few sentences sharply and rapidly, which struck them all dumb. Papa was greatly horrified also. I don't regret it.[1]

By the summer of 1846, shortly before Mr. Brontë's operation, Charlotte had occasion to silence gossip linking her name with Mr. Nicholls. She did so with contempt. She wrote Ellen on 10 July:

Who gravely asked you whether Miss Brontë was not going to be married to her Papa's curate? I scarcely need say that never was rumour more unfounded. A cold far-away sort of civility are the only terms on which I have ever been with Mr. Nicholls. I could by no means think of mentioning such a rumour to him even as a joke. It would make me the laughing-stock of himself and his fellow curates for half a year to come. They regard me as an old maid, and I regard them, one and all, as highly uninteresting, narrow and unattractive specimens of the coarser sex.[2]

Her attitude towards Mr. Nicholls suffered at the outset from her contempt for curates in general; she judged them ignorant, narrow-minded, vain. Her few allusions to Mr. Nicholls in the years immediately

[1] CB to EN, 18 June 1845: *SLL* i. 301; *W & S* ii. 39.
[2] CB to EN, 10 July 1846: *SLL* i. 333; *W & S* ii. 100–1.

following his arrival vary little from the strictures heaped on the proto-types of the tribe in *Shirley*. If, as would appear later, Mr. Nicholls possessed certain qualities of heart and mind that distinguished him from the others, his narrow principles and sectarian outlook made him appear, in her eyes, no different from them. It was his misfortune to be tarred with the same brush as his selfish and vainglorious fellows at the very time when, it is evident, he was trying to shoulder some of the family's worst burdens in an attempt to please Charlotte. Never unjust where genuine kindness was meant, the fact that Charlotte misjudged Mr. Nicholls for so long shows that she simply failed to notice his good deeds. Absorbed as she was in her writing during the first years of his curacy, she seldom gave him a thought. When catastrophe overtook the family, she had eyes only for those she loved; and little did she suspect or care how she herself had become an object of solicitude to the curate.

With Mr. Brontë sufficiently restored to take full duty in his own church again, there was little to disturb the daily round at the parsonage as autumn advanced—save occasional outbursts from Branwell and unpleasant contingencies arising from his running up debts in the pubs he frequented as far away as Halifax. Writing to Ellen at the beginning of the winter, Charlotte had such a tale to tell:

> You say I am to tell you plenty. What would you have me say? Nothing happens at Haworth; nothing, at least, of a pleasant kind. One little incident occurred about a week ago to sting us to life; but if it gives no more pleasure for you to hear than it did for us to witness, you will scarcely thank me for adverting to it. It was merely the arrival of a Sheriff's officer on a visit to Branwell inviting him either to pay his debts or take a trip to York [where was the County Jail]. Of course his debts had to be paid. It is not agreeable to lose money time after time, in this way; but it is ten times worse to witness the shabbiness of his behaviour on these occasions; but where is the use of dwelling on such subjects? It will make him no better.[1]

Despite her absorption in *Jane Eyre* and Emily and Anne's equal absorption in new writing—verse and prose—they derived no sense of security or fulfilment from the pursuit of their life's dream. As the 'Poems' proved themselves a 'drug on the market', the sales-figures remaining at two, and the manuscript of the 'three distinct and uncon-nected tales' were returned with sickening regularity, the hope of making money by writing appeared increasingly a mockery and a delusion.

[1] CB to EN, 15 Dec. 1846: *SLL* i. 341; *W & S* ii. 118–19.

And money was a matter of great concern to them, as Branwell's progressive ruin told more and more heavily on the family's limited resources, and no attempt was made to earn money as they had in the past. The writing of novels, much as they had yearned all their lives for the leisure to indulge that delight, showed no signs of leading towards independence during the year that *Wuthering Heights*, *Agnes Grey*, and *The Professor* were going the rounds.

Nor was the 'wish for wings' wholly stilled in Charlotte. Home under existing circumstances was not the haven she had hoped for on abandoning the teacher's life, and though she resisted the temptation the urge yet remained to get out into the world before it was too late. Answering a suggestion from Ellen to go out again in pursuit of independence, she wrote on 14 October 1846:

I read your letter with attention, not on my own account, for any project which infers the necessity of my leaving home is impracticable to me. If I could leave home I should not be at Haworth now—I know life is passing away and I am doing nothing, earning nothing—a very bitter knowledge it is at moments—but I see no way out of the mist. More than one favourable opportunity has now offered which I have been obliged to put aside; probably when I am free to leave home I shall neither be able to find a place nor employment; perhaps, too, I shall be quite past the prime of life, my faculties will be rusted, and my few acquirements in a great measure forgotten. These ideas sting me keenly sometimes; but when I consult my conscience, it affirms that I am doing right in staying at home, and bitter are its upbraidings when I yield to an eager desire for release. I returned to Brussels after aunt's death against my conscience, prompted by what then seemed an irresistible impulse. I was punished for my selfish folly by a total withdrawal for more than two years of happiness and peace of mind. I could hardly expect success if I were to err again in the same way.[1]

In the admission, both of her 'selfish folly' and of the 'total withdrawal' of happiness, lies the proof, if any were needed after the writing of *The Professor*, that the suffering of Brussels was now exorcized and could be spoken of with detachment.

Jane Eyre was a direct result of this 'catharsis'. It was conceived as a whole and perfectly fused experience and invention: her childhood suffering at Cowan Bridge and the death of her sisters, her ordeals as a governesss, and the testing experience of love, all found their place in it. Nothing that had deeply affected Charlotte was absent from the

[1] See above, p. 218: *SLL* i. 260; *W & S* ii. 114–15.

emotional content of *Jane Eyre*. Because feeling was experienced by her on two levels at the same time—the actual and the re-created—her vision was not always recognized or accepted by others as true to experience. The range, depth, and acuteness of her sensibilities imparted a dream-like quality on occasions to the most ordinary circumstances. How many writers, after twenty years, could have retained just that blend of the unearthly and the real that re-created in Helen Burns her dead sister Maria? Mr. Williams, the reader for Charlotte's firm of publishers, was exceptional in his acceptance of the reality of Helen Burns. Charlotte wrote to him on 28 October 1847, barely a fortnight after the book's publication:

You are right in having faith in the reality of Helen Burns; she was real enough. I have exaggerated nothing there. I abstained from recording much that I remember respecting her, lest the narrative should sound incredible. Knowing this, I could not but smile at the quiet self-complacent dogmatism with which one of the journals lays it down that 'such creations as Helen Burns are very beautiful but very untrue'.[1]

Cowan Bridge, once it was evoked in the Manchester lodgings during Mr. Brontë's convalescence, rushed back in scene upon scene, in sights and sounds, none of them clearly ever far from her thoughts. Helen's headstone, with its single word for epitaph—*Resurgam*—was a memory indelibly printed on her mind by the headstone in Tunstall churchyard, raised to one of the girls of Cowan Bridge School who died of the typhus epidemic. The friendship with Melaney Hayne supplied further material. She was the girl from the West Indies whose brother was her guardian and paid her school-bills, and whose thrilling appearances, a sallow man doubtless suffering from the English cold, provided exotic touches in *Jane Eyre*. He was the direct prototype of Mr. Mason.

The surprising thing about Rochester was that he was not M. Heger. He had no other antecedents but Zamorna, Charlotte's first and most enduring creation. Zamorna's mistresses and illegitimate daughters had supplied the heroines of Charlotte's early tales from Mina Laury to Louisa Vernon. The reality of Zamorna was irrefutable and had preceded the reality of M. Heger; indeed, without it, the living man would never have gained so complete an ascendancy over Charlotte, for he was in great measure a projection of her imaginary hero. Rochester, rising from the ashes of this love, was none the less individual and

<hr>

[1] *W & S* ii. 150.

unique; his moral image had taken shape in childhood, and he bore the physical likeness of a Belgian schoolmaster. In him more than in any of her creations, the dual nature of Charlotte's imagination shows itself, the real and the invented blending to form the pattern of his character, as it does the pattern of the novel itself. The marriage was impossible for the reason that had separated Charlotte from M. Heger: the existence of a wife.

Even her childhood story 'The Fairy Gift', written in 1830 when she was 14, contributed to *Jane Eyre*. In that story the hero who is given four wishes (and, characteristically, 'found the desire for beauty was uppermost in my mind . . .') receives as his second wish a horrible wife, huge, brawny, and villainously strong, who attempts to strangle him and haunts the corridors and stairways of a great mansion in the true Bertha Mason style. Whether St. John Rivers was the evocation of her father's early hero, Henry Martyn, or of her rejected suitor Henry Nussey, is not certain. But the need to debate religious doubts and beliefs had been a reality throughout most of Charlotte's life, and it was natural that such debates should occur in her novel. What makes *Jane Eyre* of such compelling interest is the biographical basis of its component parts. Had Mrs. Gaskell never written Charlotte's 'Life', the major experiences of it could be surmised from the contents of this novel.

Allusions to the great frost of the winter of 1846—the frost that killed the destitute Irish in their thousands after the year of famine, even those escaping to Liverpool who died of exposure on the quays—recur frequently in Charlotte's letters to Ellen. It was a safe subject with which to deflect curiosity, but the cold itself was sapping her vitality. '. . . The cold here is dreadful', she wrote on 13 December. 'I do not remember such a series of North-Pole days— England might really have taken a slide up into the Arctic Zone; the sky looks like ice; the earth is frozen; the wind is as keen as a two-edged blade. I cannot keep myself warm. . . .'[1] '. . . I hope this excessively cold weather has not harmed you and yours much . . .', she wrote two months later. 'It has nipped me severely, taken away my appetite . . . and given me toothache. . . . The consequence is that at this present speaking I look almost old enough to be your mother—grey, sunk, and withered. . . .'[2]

The sense of time passing to no purpose oppressed her greatly: '. . . I shall be thirty-one next birthday', she wrote on 24 March 1847.

[1] 13 Dec. 1846: *W & S.* ii. 118–19.   [2] 14 Feb. 1847: *W & S* ii. 126–9.

'My youth is gone like a dream; and very little use have I ever made of it. What have I done these last thirty years? Precious little. . . .'[1]

Though she never told Ellen how she occupied her time, the sense of the futility of her life appears genuine enough, a sad commentary upon the creation of a masterpiece—on which she was at that very time engaged.

The total lack of encouragement with which the 'Poems' had been received was understandably responsible for much of her dejection. When the volume had been in circulation for a year the authors decided to save what could be saved from the wreck; it was not money but honour they sought to retrieve when they sent complimentary copies to the great literary figures of the day, accompanied by the same wryly humorous little note, dated 16 June 1847. The writers so distinguished were: Wordsworth, Tennyson, Hartley Coleridge, De Quincey, Lockhart. The latter's has been preserved, as has De Quincey's.

To J. G. Lockhart, Esq

Sir—My relatives, Ellis and Acton Bell, and myself, heedless of the repeated warnings of various respectable publishers, have committed the rash act of printing a volume of poems.

The consequences predicted have, of course, overtaken us; our book is found to be a drug; no man needs it or heeds it. In the space of a year our publisher has disposed but of two copies, and by what painful efforts he succeeded in getting rid of these two, himself only knows.

Before transferring the edition to the trunkmakers, we have decided on distributing as presents a few copies of what we cannot sell; and we beg to offer you one in acknowledgement of the pleasure and profit we have often and long derived from your works.

> I am, sir, yours very respectfully,
> Currer Bell.[2]

Lockhart was editor of the *Quarterly Review*, which published in December 1848 the notice of *Jane Eyre* that so deeply wounded Charlotte. He did not himself write the review, but asked Miss Rigby to do it. Recalling the earlier incident of the 'Poems', he wrote to Miss Rigby on 13 November 1848:

About three years ago [*sic*] I received a small volume of 'Poems by Currer, Acton, and Ellis Bell', and a queer little note by Currer, who said the book had been published a year, and just two copies sold, so they were to burn the rest, but distributed a few copies, mine being one. . . .

[1] 24 Mar. 1847: *W & S* ii. 129–30.   [2] 16 June 1847: *W & S* ii. 136.

I think the poems of Currer much better than those of Acton and Ellis, and believe his novel is vastly better than those which they have more recently put forth.

I know nothing of the writers, but the common rumour is that they are brothers of the weaving order in some Lancashire town. . . . If you have any friend about Manchester, it would, I suppose, be easy to learn accurately as to the position of these men.[1]

In such a light were the Bells and their works considered by the literary establishment. Encouragement, however, so long delayed, came at length in an unexpected form from the fifth publisher to whom the manuscript of the 'three distinct and unconnected tales' had been submitted. He was Thomas Cautley Newby, head of a small new firm with premises in Mortimer Street, Cavendish Square, who wrote in the July of 1847 to say that he was prepared to consider *Wuthering Heights* and *Agnes Grey*, but *not* disposed to take *The Professor*. A heart-searching predicament was thus thrust upon the three authors—whether or not to accept Newby's offer. If they did, Charlotte's book would suffer and would be likely to be rejected as below standard length. Charlotte, understandably, never had much of an opinion of Newby, a view his subsequent behaviour fully justified.[2] She feared too the adverse conditions offered her sisters: they were to bear the costs of production to the amount of £50. The edition was to be of 350 copies, and if the work were successful and had to be reprinted, Newby undertook to refund a part of the sum. Bad as the conditions were, even Charlotte could not urge her sisters to decline them—acceptance under *any* conditions was a necessity. Emily and Anne had, in fact, no intention of refusing Newby's offer, and lost no time in concluding with him. By mid-August they received the first proof-sheets. Yet the books themselves did not appear till mid-December. By then, Charlotte could freely express her regret at her sisters' haste, for as it turned out she was after all to be the first in print.

The rejection of *The Professor* and the acceptance of the novels that would have made it up to the standard length certainly lessened its chances of success. Sent out once again on 15 July to the relatively unknown firm of Smith, Elder & Co. of Cornhill, Charlotte received no acknowledgement of her parcel. Her anxiety, heightened by the fact that the manuscript was now alone, made her write again on 2 August

---

[1] *Letters & Journals of Lady Eastlake* (Rigby), i. 221–2, quoted in *SBC* 321.
[2] For Newby's 'defence' of himself, see below, Additional Notes.

to inquire if it had arrived safely. She received an answer by return of post. Describing that incident in after years, she said:

There came a letter which he opened in the dreary anticipation of finding two hard, hopeless lines, intimating that 'Messrs Smith, Elder & Co were not disposed to publish the MS', and instead, he took out of the envelope a letter of two pages. He read it trembling. It declined, indeed, to publish that tale for business reasons, but it discussed its merits and demerits so courteously, so considerately, in a spirit so rational, with a discrimination so enlightened, that this very refusal cheered the author better than a vulgarly expressed acceptance would have done. It was added that a work in three volumes would meet with careful attention.[1]

The 'work in three volumes'—*Jane Eyre*, begun the previous August—was then nearing completion. Writing to Smith, Elder on 6 August Charlotte could happily say: 'I have a 2nd narrative in 3 volumes now in progress and nearly completed, to which I have endeavoured to impart a more vivid interest than belongs to "The Professor". In about a month I hope to finish it. . . .'[2]

'Currer Bell' was better than his word. The finished manuscript of *Jane Eyre* was sent to Cornhill on 24 August 1847 with the accompanying letter:

I now send you per rail a MS entitled 'Jane Eyre', a novel in three volumes by Currer Bell. I find I cannot prepay the carriage of the parcel, as money for that purpose is not received at the small station-house where it is left. If, when you acknowledge the receipt of the MS, you would have the goodness to mention the amount charged on delivery, I will immediately transmit it in postage-stamps. It is better in future to address Mr. Currer Bell, under cover to Miss Brontë, Haworth, Bradford, Yorkshire, as there is a risk of letters otherwise directed not reaching me at present. To save trouble, I enclose an envelope.

Currer Bell.[3]

George Smith, the firm's young director, recalled in after years those first transactions with 'Currer Bell', and the *naïveté* of his business proceedings. 'In July 1847', said Mr. Smith, 'a parcel containing a MS—The Professor—reached our office . . . bearing the scored out addresses of 3 or 4 other publishing houses; showing that the parcel had been previously submitted to other publishers. This was not calculated to

[1] *Memoir of Ellis and Acton Bell*: Smith, Elder, 1850.
[2] Gaskell 223.   [3] *W & S* ii. 141.

prepossess in favour of the MS. . . .'[1] Charlotte had, further, omitted to enclose a stamped addressed envelope for the reply, and on receiving none and realizing her oversight, wrote in great perturbation again on 6 August, enclosing a stamp and saying that 'it had been intimated to the writer by an "experienced friend" that publishers often refrained from answering communications unless a postage-stamp was furnished for the purpose . . .'. Both the omission, and the *admission*, were naïve enough and, though not positively betraying the sex and inexperience of the author, led George Smith to realize that he was dealing with a rather unusual writer.

Francis Leyland,[2] Branwell's friend and first biographer, did not hesitate to assert that the 'experienced friend' Charlotte mentioned in her letter to George Smith was none other than Branwell. What other friend 'experienced' in corresponding with publishers or magazine editors had she indeed? The incident is of interest mainly because of Charlotte's subsequent statement that her brother never knew that the sisters had published a line. This is not inconsistent, however, with the knowledge that they corresponded with publishers.

Jane Eyre was no sooner read by the firm's reader, William Smith Williams, than the rarity of its quality was recognized; it was devoured on his recommendation by Mr. Smith in the course of a Sunday. Beginning it after breakfast, he interrupted his reading merely by a sandwich and a glass of wine for lunch, cancelled an afternoon engagement with a friend to go riding into the country, bolted his dinner, and did not go to bed till he had finished the book. The whole operation between acceptance and publication took only six weeks; the book was out on 16 October 1847. Writing to acknowledge her six complimentary copies on 19 October, Charlotte said:

Gentlemen—The six copies of 'Jane Eyre' reached me this morning. You have given the work every advantage which good paper, clear type, and a seemly outside can supply; if it fails the fault will lie with the author; you are exempt.

I now await the judgement of the press and the public.—

I am, gentlemen, yours respectfully
C. Bell[3]

Her pleasure in at last holding in her hand a published work of her

---

[1] *Cornhill Magazine*, Dec. 1900.
[2] Francis Leyland, *The Brontë Family, with Special Reference to Patrick Branwell Brontë*, 2 vols., London, 1885.
[3] 19 Oct. 1847: *W & S* ii. 149.

own was not only derived from the fulfilment of a lifetime's dream, but from the contacts it gave her with men of intellectual standing—the first since her severance from M. Heger. Mr. Smith and Mr. Williams, personally unknown to her as they yet were, had treated her with a courtesy and kindness, a recognition of her powers, which affected her personal happiness as much as her susceptibilities as an author. Very quickly, with Mr. Williams in particular, she established a degree of confidence which allowed her to debate in her letters not merely points of literature, but general philosophical matters. The habit, soon formed, brought her a veritable resurgence of life and interest. Before three months were out she was writing to Mr. Williams: '. . . I cannot thank you sufficiently for your letters, and I can give you but a faint idea of the pleasure they afford me; they seem to introduce such light and life to the torpid retirement where we live like dormice. . . .'[1]

The firm's honest dealings with her from the first made her instantly want to benefit her sisters by her own good fortune. On 10 November she wrote to Mr. Williams:

A prose work by Ellis and Acton Bell will soon appear: it should have been out, indeed, long since; for the first proof-sheets were already in the press at the commencement of last August, before Currer Bell had placed the MS of 'Jane Eyre' in your hands. Mr. Newby, however, does not do business like Messrs Smith & Elder; a different spirit seems to preside at 172, Mortimer Street to that which guides the helm at 65, Cornhill. Mr. Newby shuffles, gives his word and breaks it. My relations have suffered from exhausting delay and procrastination, while I have to acknowledge the benefits of a management at once businesslike and gentlemanlike, energetic and considerate. . . .

I should like to know if Mr. Newby often acts as he has done to my relations. . . . Do you know, and can you tell me anything about him? You must excuse me for going to the point at once, when I want to learn anything; if my questions are impertinent you are, of course, at liberty to decline answering them.[2]

The astute Newby, watching the soaring sales of *Jane Eyre* and listening to the chorus of praise poured from the whole literary press, reckoned he had little to lose in publishing the works of the 'relatives' (if 'relatives they were') of the author of the hour; and accordingly hurried through the publication of *Wuthering Heights* and *Agnes Grey*. On 17 November, in reply to Mr. Williams's offer to intervene with Newby, Charlotte wrote: '. . . Ellis and Acton beg to thank you for the

---

[1] CB to WSW, Dec. 1847: *W & S* ii.
[2] CB to WSW, 10 Nov. 1847: *W & S* ii. 154.

kind offer of your services with Mr. Newby, but as the last of the proof-sheets has at length been sent down for correction they deem it useless to trouble you on the subject, trusting that the publication of the work cannot now be delayed much longer. . . .'[1]

By 14 December Charlotte could in effect write: ' "Wuthering Heights" is, I suppose, at length published, at least Mr. Newby has sent the authors their six copies.' But still regretting the bad bargain her sisters had struck, she had many reservations to make on the quality of Newby's productions: 'The books are not well got up—they abound in errors of the press. On a former occasion I expressed myself with perhaps too little reserve regarding Mr. Newby, yet I cannot but feel painfully, that Ellis and Acton have not had the justice at his hands that I have had at those of Messrs Smith & Elder.'[2]

The dream of authorship had come true, and by the Christmas of 1847 all three sisters had a published work to their credit.

Anne, furthermore, was already well advanced with a second work —*Wildfell Hall*—and Emily, as a letter from Newby of the following February shows, was also planning a second work. Messrs. Smith, Elder were not long in urging Charlotte to write a successor to the best-selling *Jane Eyre*, which was already being reprinted. '. . . I have just received your kind and welcome letter', she wrote Mr. Williams on 14 December. '. . . Of course a second work has occupied my thoughts much . . . My wish is to recast "The Professor," add as well as I can what is deficient, retrench some parts, develop others, and make of it a three-volume work. . . .'[3] The suggestion did not meet with the approbation of Smith, Elder, and Charlotte, recognizing the sound-ness of the advice, agreed to wait. The text of the original manuscript shows, however, that Charlotte revised *The Professor* on several occa-sions; probably after the publication of *Jane Eyre* and certainly after that of *Shirley*.

Meanwhile she derived untold happiness from the stimulus of the reviews, personal letters, and literary contacts that the triumph of *Jane Eyre* brought in its wake. In a period when critics were noted for their savagery, Charlotte was fortunate with the major literary journals, as even a cursory glance through their long, detailed, and attentive notices can show.

' "Jane Eyre" is a remarkable production', wrote *The Times*. 'Fresh-ness and originality, truth and passion, singular felicity in the descrip-

[1] CB to WSW, 17 Nov. 1847: *W & S* ii. 155.
[2] CB to WSW, 14 Dec. 1847: *SLL* i. 375; *W & S* ii. 162.   [3] Idem.

tion of natural scenery and in the analysis of human thought, enable this tale to stand boldly out from the mass. . . .'

'. . . A very pathetic tale,' pronounced *Blackwood's*, '. . . so like truth that it is difficult to avoid believing that much of the characters and incidents are taken from life. . . .'

'. . . From out the depths of a sorrowing experience here is a voice speaking to the experience of thousands. It is a book of singular fascination . . .' said the *Edinburgh Review*.

'. . . Reality—deep, significant reality—is the characteristic of this book . . .' was the summing up of *Fraser's*.

In almost a hundred and twenty years of academic comment and analysis, the peculiar qualities of *Jane Eyre* have not been more surely recognized than by the first reviewers of the book. The one-time chronicler of Glass Town had come far: neither extravagant wealth, unflawed beauty, nor illustrious names entered into the composition of the tale that now so impressed the literary establishment. *Fraser's* reviewer, in calling attention to its 'Reality—deep, significant reality', had penetrated into the secret of its conception and of the author's evolution from the infatuated seer to the sober recorder of the everyday scene. What had always been there, however, and what now informed even the quietest passages with an inward fire, was the writer's intensity of participation in her creature's destiny. The heart of her heroine was still at the book's centre, and it was this that infused even the most ordinary incidents affecting her with poetry.

The year 1848 opened auspiciously for the Bells. A sense of fulfilment, gratitude, and hope coloured Charlotte's reply to Mr. Williams's New Year wishes: '. . . I wish you, too, *many, many*, happy new years, and prosperity and success to you and yours. . . .'[1] she wrote him on 4 January 1848, for the first time in adult life looking with some confidence towards the future.

---

[1] CB to WSW, 4 Jan. 1848: *W & S* ii. 170.

CHAPTER XIX

RECOGNITION

AMONG the complimentary copies of *Jane Eyre* sent out by the publishers was one to Thackeray—who at that time was issuing *Vanity Fair* in monthly parts. His letter of acknowledgement to Mr. Williams written on 23 October 1847 read:

I wish you had not sent me 'Jane Eyre'. It interested me so much that I have lost (or won if you like) a whole day in reading it at the busiest period with the printers I know waiting for copy. Who the author can be I can't guess, if a woman she knows her language better than most ladies do, or has had a 'classical' education. It is a fine book though, the man and woman capital, the style very generous and upright so to speak. I thought it was Kinglake for some time. The plot of the story is one with which I am familiar. Some of the love passages made me cry, to the astonishment of John who came in with the coals. St. John the Missionary is a failure I think but a good failure, there are parts excellent. I don't know why I tell you this but that I have been exceedingly moved and pleased by 'Jane Eyre'. It is a woman's writing, but whose? Give my respects and thanks to the author, whose novel is the first English one (and the French are only romances now) that I've been able to read for many a day.[1]

Mr. Williams did not delay in forwarding Thackeray's views—and extracts of Thackeray's letter—to Charlotte, in whom it aroused more pride and delight than did any other appreciation. 'There are moments when I can hardly credit that anything I have done should be found worthy to give even transitory pleasure to such men as Mr. Thackeray... that my humble efforts should have had such a result is a noble reward,'[2] she wrote on 11 December.

The receipt of her first royalty, pleasurable as it was, still could not equal the delight 'which cheered me when I received your letter containing an extract from a note by Mr. Thackeray in which he expressed himself gratified with the perusal of "Jane Eyre"....'[3]

---

[1] *The Letters and Private Papers of W. M. Thackeray*, ed. Gordon N. Ray, 4 vols.: O.U.P. (1943), ii. 318–19.
[2] CB to WSW, 11 Dec. 1847: *W & S* ii. 159.   [3] Idem.

Thackeray had for long been her most admired author. 'I have long recognized in his writings genuine talent, such as I admired, such as I wondered at and delighted in. . . . One good word from such a man is worth pages of praise from ordinary judges.'[1]

The value to Charlotte of Thackeray's discernment lay in his indifference to the sex of the writer and his recognition of her intellectual powers. He judged her as a writer only, by her use of language, and incidentally paid a pretty tribute to her father's teaching. For if the Brontë girls wrote better English than their female contemporaries it was, as Thackeray expertly diagnosed, due to the 'classical' education their father had given them.

On 5 November Mr. Williams forwarded a letter to Charlotte from G. H. Lewes, who had also received a complimentary copy of *Jane Eyre*. Charlotte so little knew his literary standing as to have to ask Mr. Williams for information about him, and so little trusted the effect of her novel on such a critic as to await nothing but condemnation at his hands.

Nothing, indeed, better reveals the genuine modesty of her own assessment of her powers and expectations of success than her repeated warnings to her publishers not to expect too much, either from *Jane Eyre* or from any subsequent work of hers. In her scrupulous view, to allow them such expectation was an act of dishonesty. She wrote Mr. Williams as early as 4 October:

Permit me, Sir, to caution you against forming too favourable an idea of my powers, or too sanguine an expectation of what they can achieve. I am myself sensible both of deficiencies of capacity and disadvantages of circumstance which will, I fear, render it somewhat difficult for me to attain popularity as an author. The eminent writers you mention—Mr. Thackeray, Mr. Dickens, Mrs. Marsh, etc, doubtless enjoyed facilities for observation such as I have not; certainly they possess a knowledge of the world, whether intuitive or acquired, such as I can lay no claim to, and this gives their writings an importance and a variety greatly beyond what I can offer the public.[2]

Even when the first reaction of her readers promised success, she wrote, more in concern for her publishers' profits than for her own, to Mr. Williams on 28 October:

I would still endeavour to keep my expectations low respecting the ultimate success of 'Jane Eyre'. But my desire that it should succeed augments,

[1] CB to WSW, 28 Oct. 1847: *SBC* 377–8.
[2] CB to WSW, 4 Oct. 1847: *W & S* ii. 145–6.

for you have taken much trouble about the work, and it would grieve me seriously if your active efforts should be baffled and your sanguine hopes disappointed. Excuse me if I again remark that I fear they are rather *too* sanguine: it would be better to moderate them.[1]

It is traits of character such as these that made Charlotte—and her sisters as well—so much respected and regarded by the few who ever came in contact with them. Absolute integrity, allied to unworldliness in their case, was a distinguishing Brontë trait. It was this strength of honesty, moreover, that allowed Charlotte to deal so fearlessly with people—people like Lewes, from whom she had much to fear. Writing to him after reading his novel *Ranthorpe*, and before his review of *Jane Eyre* was written for *Fraser's*, she said:

You were a stranger to me—I did not particularly respect you. I did not feel that your praise or blame would have any special weight. I knew little of your right to condemn or approve. *Now* I am informed on these points. You will be severe.... Well! I shall try to extract good out of your severity; and besides, though I am now sure you are a just, discriminating man, yet being mortal, you must be fallible; and if any part of your censure galls me too keenly to the quick ... I shall for the present disbelieve it, and put it quite aside, till such time as I feel able to receive it without torture.[2]

(A reply singularly in character with her own Jane Eyre!)

The reviews which came in thick and fast and were forwarded regularly to Charlotte by Mr. Williams might have turned another woman's head, but not hers. Her sound judgement and modest assessment of her merits were unshakeable. '... I have received the newspapers', she wrote her publishers on 26 October. 'They speak quite as favourably of "Jane Eyre" as I expected them to do.' 'I duly received your letter containing the notices from the "Critic" and the two magazines and also the Morning Post', she wrote on 6 November. 'I hope all these notices will work together for good; they must, at any rate, give the book a certain publicity.'[3]

The near unanimity of praise did not make her flinch from censure. Expecting a severe notice in the *Spectator* she rather reproached the firm for keeping it from her. 'Dear Sir,' she wrote Mr. Williams on 10 November, 'I have received the "Britannia" and the "Sun", but not the "Spectator", which I rather regret, as censure, though not pleasant,

[1] CB to WSW, 28 Oct. 1847: *SBC* 378–9.
[2] CB to G. H. Lewes, 22 Nov. 1847: *W & S* ii. 156.
[3] CB to Smith, Elder & Co., 26 Oct. 1847: *W & S* ii. 149–50.

is often wholesome. . . .'¹ When the paper was sent her, she accepted the review calmly enough. Writing on 13 November she commented:

The critique . . . gives that view of the book which will naturally be taken by a certain class of mind. I shall expect it to be followed by other notices of a similar nature. The way to detraction has been pointed out, and will probably be pursued. Most future notices will in all likelihood have a reflection of the 'Spectator' in them. I fear this turn of opinion will not improve the demand for the book. . . .²

Within three days, however, further encomiums reached her. Her reactions to these latest reviews were typical of an attitude which would harden and obtain a more powerful hold on her as she gained experience and a widening public. The criterion she really cared about was the *moral* estimation in which her book was held. The deepest wounds she received were those directed against the purity of her intentions, as from the December *Quarterly* review by Miss Rigby (later Lady Eastlake), who said among other hurtful things that if the book were written by a woman it must be by one 'who had forfeited the society of her sex . . .'; and from the equally hurtful opinion of Harriet Martineau when reviewing *Villette*, that the author saw everything through the medium of one passion only—the passion of love. Charlotte wrote Mr. Williams on 17 November 1847:

The perusal of the 'Era' gave me great pleasure, as did that of the 'People's Journal'. An author feels peculiarly gratified by the recognition of a right tendency in his works; for if what he writes does no good to the reader, he feels he has missed his aim, wasted, in a great measure, his time and his labour. The 'Spectator' seemed to have found more harm than good in 'Jane Eyre', and I acknowledge that distressed me a little.³

Only when Mr. Williams gave her some assurance that he was not by nature of a sanguine temperament, and did not generally indulge in optimistic prognostications about new authors, did Charlotte feel sufficiently at ease to discuss *Jane Eyre*'s prospects with him.

I am glad to be told you are not habitually over-sanguine. I shall now permit myself to encourage a little more freely the hopeful sentiment which your letters usually impart, and which hitherto I have always tried to distrust. Still I am persuaded every nameless writer should 'rejoice with trembling' over

    ¹ CB to WSW, 10 Nov. 1847: *W & S* ii. 153–4.
    ² CB to Smith, Elder & Co., 13 Nov. 1847: *W & S* ii. 155.
    ³ CB to WSW, 17 Nov. 1847: *W & S* ii. 155–6.

the first doubtful dawn of popular goodwill; and that he should hold himself prepared for change and disappointment; critics are capricious and the public is fickle; besides one work gives so slight a claim to favour.[1]

She received her first payment for *Jane Eyre* on 10 December and a further £100 on 17 February. At no time in her life had she received so large a sum at once, and though well-wishers and friends subsequently urged her to ask for better conditions from her publishers she never did so, remaining deeply grateful both for what she considered their generosity and their friendship. She received altogether £500 for *Jane Eyre* (and the same sum for her subsequent works). Ellen Nussey recorded Charlotte as saying in after years that Smith, Elder had been pleased to accept her manuscripts after they were rejected by other publishers and 'unless they forsook her she certainly would never forsake them'.[2] She wrote the firm on 10 December:

Having already expressed my sense of your kind and upright conduct, I can now only say that I trust you will always have reason to be as well content with me as I am with you. If the result of any future exertion I may be able to make should prove agreeable and advantageous to you, I shall be well satisfied; and it would be a serious source of regret to me if I thought you ever had reason to repent being my publishers.[3]

Aware that business men seldom wrote in such style, she added: 'Excuse the informality of my letter. . . .'

Concern for her sisters' very different fortunes made her write to George Smith, in acknowledging the £100, on 17 February 1848:

Your conduct to me has been such that you cannot doubt my relatives would have been most happy, had it been in their power to avail themselves of your proposal respecting the publication of their future works, but their present engagements to Mr. Newby are such as to prevent their consulting freely their own inclinations and interests, and I need not tell you, who have so clearly proved the weight honour has with you as a principal [*sic*] of action, that engagements must be respected whether they are irksome or not. For my own part I peculiarly regret this circumstance.[4]

In speaking of her sisters' future publishing commitments Charlotte was voicing her own rather than their sentiments. Much as she urged them now and later to come to Smith, Elder, she met, as in the case of

[1] CB to WSW, 17 Nov. 1847: *W & S* ii. 155–6.
[2] W. Scruton, 'Reminiscences of EN': *BST*, 1898.
[3] CB to Smith, Elder & Co., 10 Dec. 1847: *W & S* ii. 159.
[4] CB to George Smith, 17 Feb. 1848: *W & S* ii. 190.

their railway investments, with a steady opposition to her views that nothing could dislodge—not even Newby's flagrant dishonesty over the American rights of *Wildfell Hall.*

The fact that the three Bells had appeared together as authors of the 'Poems' had early given rise to speculation over their identity. The critic on the *Dublin University Magazine* had 'conjectured' (as Charlotte wrote to Mr. Williams on 10 November) 'that the soi-disant three personages were in reality but one . . .'. Lockhart, as has been seen, reported as common rumour that they were 'brothers of the weaving order in some Lancashire town' and asked Miss Rigby 'If you have any friend about Manchester . . . to learn accurately as to the position of these men. . . .'[1]

Charlotte had no objection to curiosity, provided it strayed wide of the mark. 'Your account of the various surmises respecting the identity of the brothers Bell amused me much; were the enigma solved it would probably be found not worth the trouble of solution; but I will let it alone: it suits ourselves to remain quiet, and certainly injures no one else. . . .'[2]

Commenting on the speculations of the *Dublin University Magazine,* she added: '. . . This is an ingenious thought in the reviewer—very original and striking, but not accurate. We are three. . . .'

Lockhart had himself first believed them to be women, as he told Miss Rigby in his letter of 13 November 1848. At first it was generally said that Currer was a lady, and Mayfair circumstantialized by making her 'the "chère amie" of Thackeray'.[3] The circles in which Miss Rigby moved further 'circumstantialized' the evidence by making her the discarded mistress of Thackeray, who revenged herself by creating Rochester in Thackeray's image! Whereupon Thackeray was reported to have gone one better and portrayed 'Currer Bell' in Becky Sharp! It needed not many additions to the gossip to endow the 'chère amie' of Thackeray with the status of governess to his daughters—a position perfectly in keeping with the novel's ambience. This was a form of entertainment in which Mayfair and the literary coteries were particularly adept.[4]

Charlotte, protected alike by her distance from Mayfair and the discretion of her publishers, received no echo of these rumours, which, in

[1] J. G. Lockhart to Elizabeth Rigby, 13 Nov. 1848: *SBC* 320.
[2] CB to WSW, 10 Nov. 1847: *W & S* ii. 153–4.
[3] Elizabeth Rigby, 'Vanity Fair, Jane Eyre and the Report for 1847 of the Governesses Benevolent Institution': *Quarterly Review* (Dec. 1848), 174–5.
[4] See Additional Notes for the terms of Miss Rigby's article in the *Quarterly.*

the event, proved a source of injury to her. *Jane Eyre*, first published
on 16 October, was reprinting by early December. Moved by a purely
spontaneous feeling of gratitude for his generous tributes to the book,
and his own works that had long been the object of her ardent admiration, Charlotte dedicated the second edition of *Jane Eyre* to Thackeray.

   The terms are well known. As might have been foretold, the dedication was dynamite. Thackeray, living at the heart of literary London,
knew not only what was thought in the coteries, but suffered cruelly from
the wholly fortuitous resemblance between his own domestic circumstances and those of Rochester; for Thackeray, like Charlotte's hero,
had a mad wife whom he had been obliged to put away. But there the
resemblance ended. Thackeray had married at 25, on 20 August 1836,
Isabella, daughter of Lt.-Colonel Shawe, and in four years his happiness
was ended. The couple had three little girls (the second died in infancy)
and it was in consequence of the birth of the third in May 1840 that
Mrs. Thackeray became insane. After two years' vain pursuit of cures,
she had to be sent away for good, in the keeping of a couple called
Thompson, to Leigh in Essex. There she lived till her death in 1894,
outliving her famous husband by 31 years. Of this tragedy Charlotte
was wholly ignorant, and Thackeray knew her guiltless. Torn between
the natural kindness of his heart and the pain her gesture had given
him, he did not know how to answer the compliment contained in her
dedication. At last he wrote to Mr. Williams:

   I am quite vexed that by some blundering of mine I should have delayed
answering Currer Bell's enormous compliment so long. I didn't know what
to say in reply; it quite flustered and upset me. Is it true, I wonder? I'm—But
a truce to egotism.
   Thank you for your kindness in sending the volumes, and (indirectly) for
the greatest compliment I have ever received in my life—[1]

To postpone yet longer acknowledging the compliment to the author
served no purpose; with great candour, he wrote at last to Charlotte
telling her the truth.

   It pained her deeply, all the more so because he allowed no pain of
his own to appear. He reproached her with nothing. With an honesty
equal to his own, Charlotte recognized how valueless in such a case
were all regrets. She wrote to Mr. Williams on 28 January 1848:

   My dear Sir—I need not tell you that when I saw Mr. Thackeray's letter
enclosed under your cover, the sight made me very happy. It was some time

[1] *The Letters and Private Papers of W. M. Thackeray*: op. cit. ii. 340–1.

before I dared open it, lest my pleasure . . . should be mixed with pain on learning its contents—lest, in short, the dedication should have been . . . unacceptable to him.

And, to tell you the truth, I fear this must have been the case; he does not say so, his letter is most friendly in its noble simplicity, but he apprises me . . . of a circumstance which both surprised and dismayed me.

I suppose it is no indiscretion to tell you this circumstance, for you doubtless know it already. It appears that his private position is in some points similar to that I have ascribed to Mr. Rochester, that thence arose a report that 'Jane Eyre' had been written by a governess in his family, and that the dedication coming now has confirmed everybody in the surmise.

Well may it be said that fact is often stranger than fiction! The coincidence struck me as equally unfortunate and extraordinary. Of course I knew nothing whatever of Mr. Thackeray's domestic concerns. . . . Of all regarding his personality, station, connections, private history, I was, and am still in a great measure, totally in the dark; but I am *very sorry* that my inadvertent blunder should have made his name and affairs a subject for common gossip.

The very fact of his not complaining at all and addressing me with such kindness . . . increases my chagrin. I could not half express my regret to him in my answer, for I was constrained by the consciousness that that regret was just worth nothing at all—quite valueless for healing the mischief I had done.[1]

The incident, which would give a further handle to gossip, provoked a quite uncalled-for comment from Miss Rigby in her *Quarterly* article, which wrung from Charlotte the angry retort:

The critic would certainly be a little ashamed of herself if she knew what foolish blunders she had committed, if she were aware how completely Mr. Thackeray and Currer Bell are strangers to each other. . . . If Currer Bell had known that there existed in Mr. Thackeray's private circumstances the shadow of a reason for fancying personal allusion, so far from dedicating the book to that gentleman, he would have regarded such a step as ill-judged, insolent, and indefensible, and would have shunned it accordingly.[2]

The reprint of *Jane Eyre* brought yet further confusions of identity upon the Bells. This time they were intentional—even maliciously so. They were fostered by Newby who, following the successes of Charlotte's book, 'framed' his advertisements for *Wuthering Heights* and *Agnes Grey* so as to favour the impression that Ellis Bell was the author

[1] CB to WSW, 28 Jan. 1848: *W & S* ii. 183–4.
[2] CB to WSW, 2 Mar. 1849: *W & S* ii. 314.

of *Jane Eyre*. The substitution of Ellis for Currer in the role of successful author took Charlotte somewhat aback. She had supposed the
contrary was the case; that Currer—by far the most publicized of the
Bells—had been given the benefit of the triple authorship of the Bell's
novels. Her love for Emily was disinterested enough, however, to accept
the implied tribute, and to add further to it herself. She wrote Mr.
Williams on 22 January 1848:

> I see I was mistaken in my idea that the 'Athenaeum' and others wished to
> ascribe the authorship of 'Wuthering Heights' to Currer Bell; the contrary
> is the case, 'Jane Eyre' is given to Ellis Bell: . . . if Mr. Newby had much
> sagacity he would see that Ellis Bell is strong enough to stand without being
> propped by Currer Bell, and would have disdained what Ellis himself of all
> things disdains—recourse to trickery. However, Ellis, Acton and Currer
> care nothing for the matter personally; the public and the critics are welcome
> to confuse our identities as much as they choose; my only fear is lest Messrs
> Smith & Elder should in some way be annoyed by it.[1]

If she felt vexation it was chiefly at Newby's dishonesty and at
her sisters' continuing obstinacy in sticking to him. She knew both of
them to be engaged on new books—Anne had been so since the previous summer—and feared they would persist in giving them to Newby.
In the event, when *Wildfell Hall* was finished Anne did so, but secured
tolerably good conditions from him. She was to receive £25 on publication and a further £25 on the sale of 250 copies; £50 more when
400 copies were sold, and another £50 when sales reached 500. This was
much better than the terms she and Emily had agreed to for *Wuthering
Heights* and *Agnes Grey*, when they had shared the risks with the publishers and advanced £50 towards the costs. The sum was to be refunded directly sales had covered expenses; they were, indeed, to be paid
£100 upon the sale of 250 copies.[2] As Charlotte had occasion in after
years to record, no portion of that sum was ever refunded, though both
Wuthering Heights and *Agnes Grey* went into second impressions.

Charlotte's own long delay in settling down to a new book appears,
from her correspondence that winter and spring with Mr. Williams,
to have arisen from her inability to settle on a choice of subject. The

---

[1] CB to WSW, 22 Jan. 1848: *W & S* ii. 181–2.
[2] When Anthony Trollope consulted his mother, the successful novelist Frances
Trollope, over his first MS., *The Macdermots of Ballycloran*, she offered it to Newby
(in the same year 1847 that Ellis and Acton Bell offered him their first novels). Like
them, young AT fared ill at Newby's hands, but characteristically bore him no ill will.
See *Autobiography of AT*, 64 (World's Classics).

many suggestions put forward by Mr. Williams only increased her indecision. '. . . Of course a second book has occupied my thoughts much', she wrote him as early as 14 December. Discarding his suggestion to adopt instalment technique—followed by both Dickens and Thackeray at the time—she said: 'I decidedly feel that ere I change my ground I had better make another venture in the three-volume novel form. . . . Respecting the plan of such a work, I have pondered it, but as yet with very unsatisfactory results. Three commencements have I essayed but all three displease me.'[1] She wrote to him again on 15 February: 'As to my next book, I suppose it will grow to maturity in time, as grass grows or corn ripens; but I cannot force it. It makes slow progress thus far: it is not every day, nor even every week, that I can write what is worth reading . . . in due time I hope to see such a result as I shall not be ashamed to offer you, my publishers, and the public.'[2]

On 11 March she wrote again on the question of an illustrated edition of *Jane Eyre*, to be executed by herself, the suggestion having obviously arisen through the example of Thackeray:

As to your second suggestion, it is . . . a very judicious and happy one: but I cannot adopt it, because I have not the skill you attribute to me. . . . I have, in my day wasted a certain quantity of Bristol board and drawing-paper, crayons, and cakes of colour, but when I examine the contents of my portfolio now it seems as if during the years it has been lying closed some fairy had changed what I once thought sterling coin into dry leaves, and I feel much inclined to consign the whole collection . . . to the fire; I see they have no value now. If, then, 'Jane Eyre' is ever to be illustrated, it must be by some other hand than that of its author.[3]

The hesitation to commit herself to the new book was due not only to the question of subject (her real trouble was that she had too many subjects to blend into an organic whole) but to her fear of failing to repeat the success of *Jane Eyre*. 'I *do* trust I may have the power so to write in future as not to disappoint those who have been kind enough to think and speak well of "Jane Eyre"; at any rate, I will take pains. But still, whenever I hear my one book praised, the pleasure I feel is chastened by a mixture of doubt and fear . . . it is much too early for me to feel safe' she wrote on 12 May 1848, referring to yet another tribute to *Jane Eyre* in the *Morning Chronicle*.[4] Her perception and

[1] CB to WSW, 14 Dec. 1847: *W & S* ii. 161–2.
[2] CB to WSW, 15 Feb. 1848: *W & S* ii. 188–9.
[3] CB to WSW, 11 Mar. 1848: *W & S* ii. 197–8.   [4] Idem. 212–13.

acceptance of her own limitations saved her from attempting what she could not do. Never did she mistake her gifts for those of a Thackeray or a Dickens—penetrating though she also was in detecting *their* shortcomings.

Her strength as a writer derived, in great part, from her strength as critic. She had severe criteria which she applied not only to others, but to herself. How this operated is admirably seen in her judgement of Thackeray—then publishing *Vanity Fair* in serial parts—which she wrote to Mr. Williams on 29 March 1848. By implication it contrasted what Thackeray *was*, with everything she herself was *not*.

You mention Thackeray and the last number of 'Vanity Fair.' The more I read Thackeray's works the more certain I am that he stands alone—alone in his sagacity, alone in his truth, alone in his feeling (his feeling, though he makes no noise about it, is about the most genuine that ever lived on a printed page), alone in his power, alone in his simplicity, alone in his self-control. Thackeray is a Titan, so strong that he can afford to perform with calm the most herculean feats; there is the charm and majesty of repose in his greatest efforts; *he* borrows nothing from fever, his is never the energy of delirium—his energy is sane energy, deliberate energy, thoughtful energy. The last number of 'Vanity Fair' proves this peculiarly. Forcible, exciting in its force ... carrying on the interest of the narrative in a flow, deep, full, resistless, it is still quiet—as quiet as reflection, as quiet as memory; Thackeray is never borne away by his own ardour—he has it under control. His genius obeys him—it is his servant, it works no fantastic changes at its own wild will ... Thackeray is unique. I *can* say no more, I *will* say no less.[1]

In the postscript of her letter to Mr. Williams of 12 May, she touched on one of the themes which she would treat in her new book —'the condition of women', showing the trend her thoughts were taking at the time.

I find in glancing over yours, that I have forgotten to answer a question you ask respecting my next work. I have not therein so far treated of governesses, as I do not wish it to resemble its predecessor. I often wish to say something about the 'condition of women' question, but it is one respecting which so much 'cant' has been talked, that one feels a sort of repugnance to approach it. It is true enough that the present market for female labour is quite overstocked, but where or how could another be opened. ... One can see where the evil lies, but who can point out the remedy?[2]

---

[1] CB to WSW, 29 Mar. 1848: *W & S* ii. 200-1.
[2] CB to WSW, 12 May 1848: *W & S* ii. 215-16.

She pursued the same subject in the next letter to Mr. Williams, moved to consider it afresh by the situation of Mr. Williams's grown-up daughters, just about to go out into the world and concerning whose careers he had consulted her.

I have always been accustomed to think that the necessity of earning one's subsistence is not in itself an evil, but I feel it may become a heavy evil if health fails, if employment lacks, if the demand upon our efforts made by the weakness of others dependent upon us becomes greater than our strength suffices to answer. . . . Most desirable then is it that all, both men and women, should have the power and the will to work for themselves—most advisable that both sons and daughters should early be inured to habits of independence and industry. It seems to me that your kind heart is pained by the thought of what your daughter may suffer if transplanted . . . among strangers. Suffer she probably will. . . . A governess's experience is frequently indeed bitter, but its results are precious; the mind, feeling, temper are there subjected to a discipline equally painful and priceless. I have known many who were unhappy as governesses, but not one who regretted having undergone the ordeal, and scarcely one whose character was not improved—at once strengthened and purified, fortified and softened, made more enduring for her own afflictions, more considerate for the afflictions of others.[1]

The place in society of the unmarried and unendowed woman was constantly and increasingly in Charlotte's mind. The observation of her own sisters' inward-looking, wholly studious, and unpractical lives, with their scant opportunities for social intercourse or experience of any kind, was theme enough for any book, and was certainly one— if not the first—that moved her to the writing of *Shirley*. The second, and not wholly unrelated subject of local curates, whose society for all its blatant disadvantages was almost their only intercourse, followed naturally from the first. The contrast between the curates of the new era, mostly Puseyites, with Oxford accents, High Church vestments, and loud, ignorant self-assertive manners, and the sombre ways, speech, and dignity of the old Yorkshire Evangelical clergy in whose parishes they were sent to serve—while bent on ridiculing and displacing them —appeared to Charlotte full of potential comedy and drama. It was these domestic issues, rather than the political upheaval, of the 1840's (which she had been very much tempted to deal with), that were, after many a false start, to be the material for her new novel. *Shirley* was not the integrated masterpiece Charlotte had achieved with *Jane Eyre*;

---

[1] CB to WSW, 15 June 1848: *W & S* ii. 219–20.

her initial uncertainties left their mark on the finished work, and were detected by such astute critics as George Lewes: 'In "Shirley" all unity is wanting', he wrote in his review of the book in the *Edinburgh Review* of January 1850. 'There is no passionate link; nor is there any artistic fusion, or intergrowth by which one part evolves itself from another. . . . The various scenes are gathered up into three volumes, they have not grown into a work.'[1]

The judgement was sound. *Shirley* suffered not only from the irresolution at the beginning, but from the many and tragic interruptions over the next two years. More than any of Charlotte's books, it is the barometer of the Brontë family fortunes. These, at the very time of the triumph of *Jane Eyre*, were darkening.

The happiness perceptible in Charlotte's letters to Mr. Williams, her absorption in literary projects and pursuits, her contacts with some of the leading literary figures of the day, were of course only a part of her life at the time. The enduring objects of her love and care—home and her sisters and brother—were as present as ever. To Ellen Nussey she wrote as exclusively of these as to Mr. Williams she wrote of her preoccupations as an author. The two only very occasionally overlapped, as when Anne[2] had to write in her place to Ellen, because Charlotte had an urgent business communication to get off to Mr. Williams.

Charlotte's letters to Ellen and Miss Wooler during the first half of 1848 report no improvement in Branwell, whilst revealing an increasing concern over Anne's persistent ill health. Without betraying the cause of Anne's overwork (engaged as she was since the previous summer on *Wildfell Hall*) Charlotte had confided to Ellen on 7 October 1847:

I would fain hope that her health is a little stronger than it was and her spirits a little better, but she leads much too sedentary a life, and is continually sitting stooping either over a book or over her desk. It is with difficulty we can prevail on her to take a walk or induce her to converse. I look forward to next summer with the confident intention that we shall—if possible—make at least a brief sojourn at the seaside.[3]

Midwinter brought its inevitable train of illness for the whole household. Anne wrote to Ellen as Charlotte's deputy on 4 January:

We are all cut up by this cruel east wind, most of us i.e. Charlotte, Emily and I have had the influenza or a bad cold instead, twice over in the space

[1] *Edinburgh Review*, Jan. 1850. [2] AB to EN, 4 Jan. 1848: BPM.
[3] CB to EN, 7 Oct. 1847: *W & S* ii. 146–7.

of two weeks. Papa has had it once—Tabby has escaped it altogether. I have
no more news to tell you, for we have been nowhere, seen no one, and done
nothing (to speak of) since you were here—and yet we contrive to be busy
from morning to night.[1]

(The scrupulous Anne found it hard even to skirt round the truth—
hence the parenthesis.)

Mentioning their winter influenza in a letter of 31 March to Miss
Wooler, Charlotte had to report that its worst effects had been left on
Anne. 'My sisters and myself have each had a visit from it,' she said,
'but Anne is the only one with whom it stayed long or did much mischief; in her case it was attended with distressing cough and fever;
but she is now better, though it has left her chest weak.'[2]

Anne's 'weak chest' was decidedly the only weak thing about
her, as Charlotte had previously recognized. Writing to Ellen on
13 December (1846) she had said:

We have all had severe colds and coughs in consequence of the severe
weather. Poor Anne has suffered greatly from asthma. . . . She had two nights
last week when her cough and difficulty of breathing were painful indeed to
hear and witness, and must have been most distressing to suffer; she bore it,
as she does all affliction, without one complaint, only sighing now and then
when nearly worn out. She has an extraordinary heroism of endurance. I
admire it, but I certainly could not imitate her.[3]

One Brontë estimating another's stoical acceptance of pain makes
impressive reading. Charlotte herself, enduring toothache for months
on end, still put pride before the alleviation of suffering. 'What you say
about the effects of ether on Catherine Swaine', she wrote Ellen on
29 November 1847, 'rather startled me. I had always consoled myself with the idea of having my front teeth extracted and rearranged
some day under its soothing influence—but now I should think twice
before consenting to inhale; one would not like to make a fool of oneself.'[4]

The news of Branwell sent to Ellen on 11 January 1848 was an
epitome of his state and conduct for the remainder of his life. Charlotte wrote on that day:

We have not been very comfortable here at home lately, far from it, indeed.
Branwell has, by some means, contrived to get more money from the old

[1] AB to EN, 4 Jan. 1848: BPM.
[2] CB to MW, 31 Mar. 1848: W & S ii. 202.
[3] CB to EN, 13 Dec. 1846: W & S ii. 118.   [4] CB to EN, W & S ii. 157.

quarter, and has led us a sad life with his absurd and often intolerable conduct. Papa is harassed day and night; we have little peace; he is always sick; has two or three times fallen down in fits; what will be the ultimate end, God knows. But who is without their drawback, their scourge, their skeleton behind the curtain? It remains only to do one's best, and endure with patience.[1]

The embargo on confiding their literary activity to Ellen—an embargo imposed principally by Emily, as the sequel would show—prevented Charlotte from sharing with her friend the source of her new contentment and heightened courage. Ellen claimed in after years that she had perfectly divined the meaning of Charlotte's proof-correcting while staying at Brookroyd in September of 1847, when *Jane Eyre* was going through the press. '*Specially* informed I was not,' she recorded, 'but I had seen proof-sheets corrected at Brookroyd, and passed them to the house letter-bag without glancing at the address. Perceiving that confidence was not volunteered, it was not sought. Charlotte confessed afterwards what a struggle it cost her to retain silence.'[2]

With Ellen, therefore, only the family news could be shared, yet from Ellen she could not entirely hide her altered and more optimistic outlook on life when her birthday came round again in April 1848:

I had quite forgotten, till your letter reminded me, that it was the anniversary of your birthday and mine. [Ellen's was the day after Charlotte's—22 April.] I am now thirty-two. Youth is gone—gone—and will never come back: can't help it. I wish you many happy returns of your birthday and increase of happiness with increase of years. It seems to me that sorrow must come sometime to everybody, and those who scarcely taste it in youth, often have a more brimming and bitter cup to drain in after life; whereas those who exhaust the dregs early, who drink the lees before the wine, may reasonably expect a purer and more palatable draught to succeed. So, at least, one fain would hope.[3]

The year 1848 would cruelly belie Charlotte's rare moments of optimism, and teach her how illusory, in the lives of certain apparently predestined people, are the appearances of hope.

Meanwhile the spring and summer advanced, with no visible portents of what was to come. Ellen went to London in June to stay with her brother in Cleveland Row and there she found 'there was quite a furore about the authorship of the new novel'. *Jane Eyre* had gone

---

[1] CB to EN, *W & S* ii. 178.   [2] Reminiscences of EN, *W & S* ii. 228.
[3] CB to EN, 22 Apr. 1848: *W & S* ii. 205.

into a third printing in April. 'The work was quickly obtained, and as soon as arrived, seized on and the first half-page read aloud. It was as though Charlotte herself was present in every word.'[1] Not daring to declare her recognition of Currer Bell's identity to Charlotte, Ellen wrote her nevertheless in the hope of eliciting something, and received a tart reply. 'Your naïveté in gravely enquiring my opinion of "the last new novel" amuses me,' Charlotte wrote her on 26 June. 'We do not subscribe to a circulating library in Haworth, and consequently "new novels" rarely indeed come in our way, and, consequently again, we are not qualified to give opinions thereon.'[2]

'New novels' by the Bells were once again the talk of the town. Anne, having finished *Wildfell Hall*, gave it to Newby. It was published that June, when Ellen was in London. It was an instant success, though admittedly something of a *succès de scandale* because of the controversial character of its subject-matter. It challenged not only the accepted views on the married woman's status but on Divine Judgement as well, the author vehemently proclaiming her faith in salvation for all at least ten years before Dean Farrar defended so heretical a notion.

Wildfell Hall promised instantly to become a best-seller and Newby lost no time in cashing-in once again on the identity puzzle presented by the Bells. In advertising the book under the heading:

'Opinions of the Press
On Mr. Bell's First Novel'

he quoted indiscriminately from reviews of *Wuthering Heights*, *Jane Eyre*, and *Agnes Grey*, allowing it to be inferred that the new work was by the author of them all. What had been said of *Wuthering Heights* in *Britannia* for instance was quoted as applying to the author of *Wildfell Hall*. ('The work is strangely original. It reminds us of "Jane Eyre". The author is a Salvator Rosa with his pen.') In this intentional confusion of authors, *Agnes Grey* was passed off as 'A Colossal Performance' (the pronouncement of 'Atlas' on *Wuthering Heights*) and in the words of Douglas Jerrold those readers 'who love novelty' were strongly recommended to get this story, 'for we can promise them they never read anything like it before. It is like *Jane Eyre.*'

Newby's trickery did not end there. In offering *Wildfell Hall* to the New York firm of Harper Brothers, which had taken *Wuthering*

---

[1] EN, Reminiscences of CB: Op. cit.
[2] CB to EN, 26 June 1848: *W & S* ii. 227.

Heights but *not Agnes Grey*, he did not hesitate to say that the new work was by the author of the already world-famed *Jane Eyre*, adding that, to the best of his belief, all the Bell novels were by one and the same author.

It so happened that Harpers had already entered into an agreement with Smith, Elder for the next novel by Currer Bell, whose *Jane Eyre* was as sensational a success in the States as in England. As recently as 22 June Charlotte had written to Mr. Williams: 'I am amused to hear that the American printers have got hold of "Jane Eyre". It is a pity that no benefit can accrue to English publishers from the circulation of their books in America. . . .'[1] Though no law of copyright operated as yet to protect English authors and publishers in America, the advantages of getting their books published in the States were sufficient (between honourable firms) to make the loss of such an agreement considerable to Smith, Elder. Newby's boast to Harpers of New York raised further questions: was *Wildfell Hall* by Currer Bell, and had he gone behind Smith, Elder's back and given his new book to another publisher?

George Smith wrote at once to Haworth. 'We wrote to Currer Bell', he related afterwards, 'to say that we should be glad to be in a position to contradict the statement, adding at the same time we were quite sure Mr. Newby's statement was untrue.'[2]

This diplomatic letter reached Charlotte on Friday, 7 July. Its effect was electrical. Within the hour she and Anne had decided to go up to London as living proof of their separate identities. While re-assuring Mr. Smith they could confound Mr. Newby with his own duplicity.

Emily, whose presence was ideally required in order to quash all future rumours regarding the identity of the Bells, was not prepared to go. As Charlotte explained later about this very journey, Emily 'would never go into any sort of Society *herself*. . . . When pressed to go, she would sometimes say, "What is the use? Charlotte will bring it all home to me . . .".'[3] So now, where a confrontation with publishers was required, there was no question of Emily's going to London with her sisters. What is more, she roundly charged Charlotte to keep *her* name out of it. Meanwhile, she would keep house for all, and enjoy the report of their adventures on their return. 'I could on my return', Charlotte later recorded, 'communicate to her a pleasure that suited

[1] CB to WSW, 22 June 1848: *W & S* ii. 226.
[2] *Cornhill Magazine*, Dec. 1900: Op. cit.
[3] CB to WSW, 19 Nov. 1849: *W & S* iii. 38.

her, by giving the distinct faithful impression of each scene I had witnessed. . . . I delighted to please her thus. . . .'[1]

What reason, if any, was given Branwell for his sisters' absence, or
whether he even noticed it, is not known. Charlotte clearly stated
after his death that he was not aware 'his sisters had ever published a
line', adding the significant comment: 'we could not tell him of our
efforts for fear of causing him too deep a pang for his own talents . . .
misapplied . . .'.[2] For the same reason they would conceal from him
now the object of their London journey. Indeed, to spare him pain the
whole family had for over a year hidden from him the fact that the
Robinson girls corresponded frequently with Anne,[3] their letters
speaking openly of their mother's affairs. At the same time as their
London journey Charlotte wrote to Ellen of Branwell's 'shattered
constitution', and how '. . . Papa, and sometimes all of us, have sad
nights with him, he sleeps most of the day, and consequently will lie
awake at night . . .'.[4] The departure of his sisters for London may well
have coincided with some such day of drugged sleep.

Mr. Brontë obviously knew of his daughters' literary activities, and
put no difficulties in their way. Ever since the publication of *Jane Eyre*
and his classic pronouncement on first reading it that 'it was better than
likely', he had, Ellen Nussey later witnessed, taken the intensest interest
in their successes, reading every review as it came in and never tiring
'of walking to and fro between his study and the parlour as an outlet
for his feelings . . .'.[5]

Mr. Brontë had always known about his children's writing; they
had been at it since infancy, and nothing surprised him in their inheriting to so marked a degree his own life-long delight in putting pen
to paper. He told Mrs. Gaskell in after years (letter of 20 June 1855):

When my daughters were at home they read their MSS to each other and
gave their candid opinions of what was written. I never interfered with them
at such times—I judged it best to throw them upon their own responsibility.
Besides, a clergyman bordering upon the age of 80 years [*sic*] was likely to
be too cold and severe a critic for the efforts of buoyant and youthful genius!
Hence it came to pass that I never saw their works till they appeared in print.[6]

1 Idem.
2 CB to WSW, 2 Oct. 1848: *W & S* ii. 261–2.
3 CB to EN, 1 Mar. 1847: *W & S* ii. 128.
4 CB to EN, 28 July 1848: *W & S* ii. 239–40.
5 EN, Reminiscences of CB: Op. cit.; *W & S* ii. 228.
6 *BST*, 1933.

To Mary Taylor,[1] on the other side of the world, Charlotte later wrote a very detailed account of that departure and journey. 'On the very day I received Smith and Elder's letter, Anne and I packed up a small box, sent it down to Keighley, set out ourselves after tea, walked through a snow-storm to the station, got to Leeds, and whirled up by the night train to London. . . .'

Born in the West Riding, a snowstorm in July would not have surprised Mary unduly. It was but the culmination of a summer of ceaseless rain (frequently referred to by Charlotte in her letters) which at those altitudes has an unseasonable habit of falling as snow. The girls were very wet before reaching the station and had no opportunity of changing clothes till the next morning in London (a circumstance for which Anne suffered later). To ensure a maximum of privacy and comfort (ladies did not generally travel unaccompanied by gentlemen), they took First Class tickets, an extravagance that cost each of them £2. 5s. 6d.[2] Despite Charlotte's concern over the misunderstanding with her publishers, the journey was probably the most carefree she had undertaken in her life. To Mary Taylor, writing two months later, she confessed that she and Anne were both pleasurably excited.

She knew of only one place to stay at in London, the old Chapter Coffee House to which her father had taken her. She does not seem to have realized how exclusively masculine, both in staff and clientele, it was. How two such shy, inexperienced ladies would strike the old waiters and the older clerics, the boots and the black-coated clerks who ate their mutton-chops in the oak-panelled dining-room, she never considered, though to Mrs. Gaskell following in her footsteps ten years later it presented touching evidence of the Brontë's unworldliness. Charlotte told Mary:[3]

We arrived at the Chapter Coffee House (our old place, Polly, we did not well know where else to go) about eight o'clock in the morning. We washed ourselves, had some breakfast, sat a few minutes, and then set off in queer inward excitement to 65, Cornhill. Neither Mr. Smith nor Mr. Williams knew we were coming—they had never seen us.

Charlotte did not, in fact, know much more about her publishers than they did of her—neither about the firm nor the two men whose 'gentlemanly conduct' towards herself had so impressed her from the start.

---

[1] CB to MT, 4 Sept. 1848: *W & S* ii. 250-4—q.o.t. Manchester Univ. Lib.
[2] The little notebook of Charlotte's expenses for the London journey is still preserved at the BPM.   [3] Op. cit.

META, FLOSSY, AND MARIANNE GASKELL (left to right), by A. C. Duval 1845

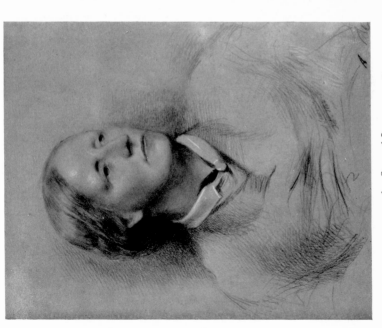

MRS. GASKELL, by Samuel Lawrence 1854

The firm's[1] origins went back to 1816 when two young Scotsmen, George Smith a native of Elgin and Alexander Elder a native of Banff-shire, went down to London to set up a bookseller's and stationer's shop in premises at 158, Fenchurch Street. They sold everything from slate-pencils to schoolbooks, and prospered. In 1820 (on 12 October, when he was 31) George Smith married Elizabeth Murray, daughter of another Scots emigré, also from Elgin, the glassware manufacturer Alexander Murray. Late in 1824, the year Charlotte's Mr. Smith was born (over the shop in Fenchurch Street), the partners moved business premises, and the Smiths their home, to 65 Cornhill, enlarging their business to include a publishing department and, as so many firms did at the time, a banking-house. At the same time a third partner was taken into the firm so as to open an East Indian Agency, and the firm became Smith, Elder and Co. 65 Cornhill in White Lion Court was not more than 100 years old, that part of Cornhill having twice been des-troyed by fire, in 1666 and again in 1748.

Between the years 1828 and 1843 the firm owed its greatest success to the publication of *Friendship's Offering*, the 'Annual' that had given Charlotte so much pleasure in adolescence. Mr. Elder, whose main interest was in the artistic side of book-production, was respon-sible for the fine series of art-albums issued by the firm—among them a 'Byron Gallery' with 36 engravings on subjects from Byron's poems, the 'Annuals', and a very successful series of scientific 'Voyages', which included Darwin's *Voyage of the Beagle* and Sir John Herschel's ac-count of his five years' mapping the stars of the Southern Hemis-phere.

In 1844 ill health obliged Mr. Smith senior to retire and he took his family to live at Box Hill, Surrey, leaving young George, who had entered the firm at 14 and was then just 20, in charge of the business. George lived in lodgings in town, riding out to Box Hill on Sundays.

The whole weight of the firm's responsibilities fell on his shoulders with the retirement of Mr. Elder in 1845, and the death of his father, on 21 August 1846. The house at Box Hill had, of course, to be aban-doned, and the Smith family, consisting of George's widowed mother, his three sisters, Eliza, Sarah, and Isabella, and young brother Alex-ander ('Alick') went to live in Bayswater, at 4 Westbourne Place; the house which Charlotte described as 'splendid' on her first visit. It was

---

[1] *George Smith: A Memoir by his Widow*, 1902: privately printed. *The House of Smith, Elder 1816–1916*, by Dr. Leonard Huxley: privately printed, 1923.

then that the strength, resilience, and cheerfulness of his mother—
the remarkable woman portrayed by Charlotte as 'Mrs. Bretton' in
Villette—proved such a blessing to young George Smith. At the end
of his successful career he spoke of the 'cheerful spirit' that never forsook her ('No stroke of disaster ever shook her serene courage') even
in the anxious months following her husband's death. Not only had the
whole of her husband's assets been sunk in the firm, but her own
jointure as well—and she had a young family to bring up. 'In looking back,' wrote George Smith, 'I can see that she devoted herself to
sustaining my courage . . . She had some gift of mimicry, and on one
occasion drew such a humorous picture of the result of our utter ruin,
when she expressed her intention . . . of having a Berlin Wool Shop in
the Edgware Road . . .',[1] that she changed his whole outlook from
despondency to buoyant confidence.

Mr. Williams's beginnings had been directed towards the graphic
arts rather than towards publishing, and throughout his long life he
sought the company of artists and wrote in appreciation of their
works in art journals, *The Spectator* in particular. He was considerably
older than George Smith. Born in 1800, he was apprenticed as a young
man to Taylor & Hessey of Fleet Street, Keats's publishers, and got to
know the firm's authors well—Leigh-Hunt, Lamb, and Keats himself.
When Keats left England for Rome it was Mr. Williams who saw
him off at London Docks, on 18 September 1820.

His nature was far more attuned to the arts and artists than to business and businessmen. George Smith recalled how he first met him
when he was employed as accountant in a firm of lithographers who did
business with Smith, Elder—Messrs. Hullmandel and Walter. It was
'a job at which he was extremely bad', Smith said. 'He was a most agreeable and most intelligent man with literary gifts wasted in uncongenial
work. . . .'[2] Sensing the value to him of such an assistant George
Smith offered him a post as literary adviser, and soon found he could
rely on him as a reader. It was Williams who spotted 'the great literary
power' in *The Professor* and thereby secured *Jane Eyre* for the firm.

Such were the backgrounds of the two men Charlotte was now about
to meet; the practical genial businessman, and the idealist. In the
tragedy that would soon bereave her of her family, the friendship of
these two proved a sustaining force and helped to keep the creative
artist in her alive.

[1] *Cornhill Magazine*, Dec. 1900: Op. cit.
[2] *House of Smith, Elder*: Op. cit., ii.

Pursuing her account to Mary Taylor, Charlotte wrote:

We found 65 Cornhill to be a large bookseller's shop, in a street almost as bustling as the Strand. We went in, walked up to the counter. . . . There were a great many young men and lads here and there; I said to the first I could accost: 'May I see Mr. Smith?' He hesitated, looked a little surprised. We sat down and waited awhile, looking at some of the books on the counter. . . . At last we were shown up to Mr. Smith.[1]

George Smith himself published in after years an account of that first meeting with Currer Bell. Later he published for a host of 'eminent Victorians'—Thackeray, Mrs. Gaskell, Matthew Arnold, Ruskin, Browning—but they came to him *after* Currer Bell, and in two instances at least (Mrs. Gaskell and Thackeray) through her intermediary. Up till then his only successful novelist was G. P. R. James.

'That particular Saturday', wrote Mr. Smith, 'I was at work in my room when a clerk reported that two ladies wished to see me. I was very busy and sent out to ask their names. The clerk returned to say the ladies declined to give their names but wished to see me on a private matter. After a moment's hesitation I told him to show them in. . . .'[2]

George Smith, aged 24 at the time, and an extremely good-looking tall young man—except for an early tendency to stoutness—was working under pressure, as was very often the case. He was dictating to one clerk while two others were engaged in copying other correspondence. This was his custom, even on a Saturday. ('There were no Saturday half-holidays in those days', he recorded later.) Often his day's work kept him at the office till 3 or 4 in the morning, especially when the India Mail was going, and as often he would work two days and a night without going home. The intruders, it may be supposed, were hardly welcome. Like his prototype Dr. John in *Villette*, however, he was something of a philanthropist, and the sight of them as they came in instantly melted his heart. He saw them as 'two rather quaintly dressed little ladies, pale faced and anxious looking', and divined that some genuine matter was afoot. 'One of them came forward and presented me with a letter—addressed to "Currer Bell, Esq.". I noticed that the letter had been opened, and said with some sharpness: "Where did you get this from?" "From the post-office," was the reply, "it was addressed to me. We have both come that you might have ocular proof that there are at least two of us."'[3]

[1] CB to MT: Op. cit.
[2] *Cornhill Magazine*, Dec. 1900.   [3] Op. cit.

Charlotte, reporting the same scene to Mary Taylor, confessed that Mr. Smith looked so perplexed that she had to laugh.

Then

a recognition took place—I gave my real name: Miss Brontë. We were in a small room—ceiled with a great skylight—and there explanations were rapidly gone into: Mr. Newby being anathematised, I fear, with undue vehemence. Mr. Smith hurried out and returned quickly with one whom he introduced as Mr. Williams, a pale, mild, stooping man of fifty [Mr. Williams was actually 48 at the time] very much like a faded Tom Dixon. Another recognition and a long, nervous shaking of hands. Then followed talk—talk—talk Mr. Williams being silent, Mr. Smith loquacious.[1]

While Charlotte had taken the first hurried survey of her publishers, they had done no less by her and Anne. Mr. Smith observed Anne with a benevolent eye. '. . . Her manner was curiously expressive of a wish for protection and encouragement . . .', he noted, 'a kind of constant appeal, which invited sympathy . . . She was . . . by no means pretty, yet, of a pleasing appearance. . . .'[2] The publishers had had the advantage over Currer Bell's other early readers, in that they alone had read *Jane Eyre* in manuscript; by the handwriting they had unhesitatingly judged the author to be a woman. Hence the sex of Currer Bell caused George Smith little surprise; her appearance was another thing. '. . . I must confess,' he recorded later, 'my first impression of Charlotte Brontë's appearance was that it was interesting rather than attractive. She was very small and had a quaint old-fashioned look. . . .'[3]

So much he may have taken in at a first glance. His subsequent observations of Charlotte, whether made during the course of that day or over the next seven years, were among the most penetrating of any of Charlotte's acquaintances, apart from Thackeray. Neither Mrs. Gaskell, nor Harriet Martineau, nor G. H. Lewes, nor James Kay-Shuttleworth, nor even James Taylor, recognized the predominant need for love, and the longing for physical beauty that had blasted her life. George Smith discovered not only Currer's identity on this occasion but also began to realize something of the true nature of her sensibility.

She had fine eyes, but her face was marred by the shape of the mouth and by the complexion. There was but little feminine charm about her; and of this fact she was herself uneasily and perpetually conscious. . . . I believe she would have given all her genius and all her fame to have been beautiful. Perhaps few women ever existed more anxious to be pretty than she, or more angrily conscious of the circumstance that she was not pretty.[1]

He offered Charlotte and Anne the hospitality of his mother's house, which they firmly declined, excusing themselves on the score of the shortness of their visit. The very idea horrified them and made them hurry back to Paternoster Row, but not before George Smith had extracted a promise to await his sisters and himself that evening when an invitation to dinner at his mother's next day would be arranged.

On the way back to the Chapter Coffee House the realization of their extreme inadequacy of dress for such an occasion—and perhaps the fine London weather—made them buy parasols and a new pair of gloves each. The cost of these, carefully entered by Charlotte in her accounts for the journey, were 8s. each for the parasols and eighteen pence a pair for the gloves. 'We returned to our inn,' Charlotte carried on the tale for the benefit of Mary Taylor, 'and I paid for the excitement of the interview by a thundering headache and harassing sickness. Towards evening, as I got no better and expected the Smiths to call, I took a dose of salvolatile. It roused me a little; still, I was in grievous bodily case when they were announced.'[2]

Mr. Williams had also urged on them an invitation to dine at his house during their stay, and in spite of the sickness and headache, Charlotte sat down to write to him in the course of the afternoon.

> Chapter Coffee House,
> Ivy Lane,
> July 8th 1848

My dear Sir—Your invitation is too welcome not to be at once accepted—I should much like to see Mrs. Williams and her children, and very much like to have a quiet chat with yourself—Would it suit you if we came to-morrow after dinner—say about 7 o'clock, and spent Sunday evening with you?

We shall be truly glad to see you whenever it is convenient to you to call.[3]

George Smith swept aside these arrangements and replaced them with others of his own, the first of which took effect that evening on his reaching the Chapter Coffee House with his sisters, Eliza and Sarah—'two elegant young ladies in full dress, prepared for the Opera—Mr. Smith himself in evening costume, white gloves etc.', as Charlotte wrote to Mary. 'We had by no means understood that it was settled we

---

[1] Op. cit.
[2] Op. cit.   [3] *W & S* ii. 230.

were to go to the Opera, and were not ready', she confessed.[1] But to the Opera they were hurried away, their hesitancy and the unsuitability of their high-necked frocks equally overruled. Charlotte 'put her headache in her pocket', and allowed herself to be taken in control by her highly efficient host and publisher. In the Smiths' carriage outside Mr. Williams was waiting.

Charlotte was acutely conscious of her appearance in their sophisticated company. She told Mary:

> They must have thought us queer quizzical-looking beings, especially me in my spectacles. I smiled inwardly at the contrast which must have been apparent, between me and Mr. Smith, as I walked with him up the crimson-carpeted staircase of the Opera House and stood, amongst a brilliant throng at the box door, which was not yet open. Fine ladies and gentlemen glanced at us with a slight, graceful superciliousness quite warranted by the circumstances. Still, I felt pleasantly excited in spite of headache & sickness and conscious clownishness, and I saw Anne was calm and gentle, which she always is.[2]

The Opera that night was Rossini's *Il Barbiere di Siviglia*, performed by the Royal Italian Company.[3]

Charlotte told Mary that the Opera was very brilliant, but she fancied 'there are things I should like better', adding that they only 'got home after one o'clock,' from which it must be inferred they stayed to see the whole programme through. 'We had never been in bed the night before, and had been in constant excitement for twenty-four hours. You may imagine we were tired', concluded Charlotte.

It had been decided with their hosts that they would be introduced as the 'Miss Browns',[4] should the necessity arise. As London was seething with rumours about the *real* Currer Bell another pseudonym was needed, and Charlotte and Anne were equally anxious to avoid the name of Brontë, the more so because Ellen Nussey was then in town. (She remained in the south of England for several months, going on to stay with friends in Sussex after London.) Their crowded days of sightseeing were spent in places where such a meeting was only too likely.

To Mr. Williams had been confided during the evening Anne's great desire to hear the famous preacher Dr. Croly, Rector of St. Stephen, Walbrook, and there Mr. Williams took Charlotte and Anne on the Sunday morning, after picking them up at the Chapter Coffee

---

[1] CB to MT: Op. cit.   [2] Idem.
[3] See Additional Notes.   [4] Gaskell 275.

House. The church, one of Wren's masterpieces and the parish church of the Lord Mayor, has a baroque splendour and spaciousness very different from the crowded and dark North country churches to which the Brontë girls were accustomed. Even when the vast centre floor-space was filled with box-pews the great effect of light produced by the dome and the rounded marble columns could not be dimmed. But Anne was disappointed, for Dr. Croly was not preaching that day. She and her sister were interested in him not only because of his eloquence and philanthropy but because he was an Irishman, educated at Trinity College, Dublin, and had published several literary works—much like their father.

After church, Mr. Smith arrived at Paternoster Row with his mother to fetch Charlotte and Anne to 'dinner' at Westbourne Place, showing them Kensington Gardens on the way. Charlotte told Mary:

Mr. Smith's residence is at Bayswater. The rooms, the drawing-room especially, looked splendid to us. There was no company—only his mother, his two grown-up sisters [Eliza and Sarah], and his brother, a lad of 12 or 13, and a little sister—['good, quiet, studious little Bell' as Charlotte later called her]—the youngest of the family, very like himself. They are all dark-eyed, dark-haired, and have clear, pale faces. The mother is a portly, handsome woman of her age [51 at the time] and all the children more or less good-looking. . . . We had a fine dinner, which neither Anne nor I had appetite to eat, and were very glad when it was over.[1]

It was in this house at 4 Westbourne Place that the fate of *Jane Eyre* had been decided on one Sunday the previous August, when George Smith had brought the manuscript home. The dining-room, as in most London houses at the time, was the ground-floor front room, and George Smith's study was behind it at the back of the house. Here he had entrenched himself until late evening when he had finished reading. The drawing-room that Charlotte found so 'splendid' was on the first floor, over the dining-room. Here the afternoon was spent.

'Mr. Smith made himself very pleasant', Charlotte told Mary. 'He is a *practical* man. I wish Mr. Williams were more so, but he is altogether of the contemplative, theorising order. . . .'[2]

Charlotte and Anne were able to see Mr. Williams at his ease in his own home the next day, Monday, when they took tea with him and met his eight children. Mrs. Williams was too ill to see them and, as

[1] CB to MT: Op. cit.   [2] Idem.

Charlotte's correspondence shows, her health continued a source of anxiety for the following year.

In the course of the Monday they visited the Royal Academy and the National Gallery, dined again at Mr. Smith's, and, in a hurried interval, did some shopping for those at home, buying the new volume of Tennyson's poems for Emily (*The Princess*, published 1847), and a book each for Tabby and Martha.[1]

Charlotte wrote Mary Taylor:

On Tuesday morning we left London laden with books which Mr. Smith had given us, and got safely home. A more jaded wretch than I looked when I returned it would be difficult to conceive. I was thin when I went, but was meagre indeed when I returned; my face looked grey and very old, with strange deep lines ploughed in it; my eyes stared unnaturally. I was weak and yet restless. In a while . . . the bad effects of excitement went off.[2]

Mr. Smith would not have been surprised at the instant recourse to her mirror on reaching home, and the bitter realization it brought. It was almost as an afterthought that she added to her letter: '. . . We saw Mr. Newby, but of him more another time. . . .'[3]

The encounter with Mr. Newby, almost the chief objective of the journey, had sunk into the shade beside the sunshine that had poured upon her from Cornhill. Her publishers were no longer impersonal and remote. They had families; they had homes, no detail of which had escaped the observation of Currer Bell; they had shown a benevolent interest in her. She was immeasurably enriched by the encounter and brought back from her London journey a store of nourishing memories. To one as starved of intellectual intercourse as she had been since the severance from M. Heger, to meet them had been a most rewarding experience. She was grateful for their personal kindness as well as their business acumen. And it was of course of immense importance too that Mr. Smith and Mr. Williams had so obviously *liked* her. In the glow of that unaccustomed feeling, she wrote to thank Mr. Williams:

Haworth, July 13th, 1848

My dear Sir—We reached home safely yesterday, and in a day or two I doubt not we shall get the better of the fatigues of our journey.

It was a somewhat hasty step to hurry up to town as we did, but I do not regret having taken it. In the first place mystery is irksome, and I was glad to

---

[1] CB's notebook of expenses on London journey: BPM.
[2] CB to MT: Op. cit.   [3] Idem.

shake it off with you and Mr. Smith, and to show myself to you for what I am, neither more nor less—thus removing any false expectations that may have arisen under the idea that Currer Bell had a just claim to the masculine cognomen he, perhaps somewhat presumptuously, adopted—that he was, in short, of the nobler sex.

I was glad also to see you and Mr. Smith, and am very happy now to have such pleasant recollections of you both, and of your respective families. My satisfaction would have been complete could I have seen Mrs. Williams. The appearance of your children tallied on the whole accurately with the description you had given of them. Fanny was the one I saw least distinctly; I tried to get a clear view of her countenance, but her position in the room did not favour my efforts.

I have just read your article in the 'John Bull'; it very clearly and fully explains the cause of the difference obvious between ancient and modern paintings. I wish you had been with us when we went over the Exhibition and the National Gallery: a little explanation from a judge of art would doubtless have enabled us to understand better what we saw; perhaps, one day, we may have this pleasure.

Accept my own thanks and my sister's for your kind attention to us while in town, and—Believe me, yours sincerely,

Charlotte Brontë

Itrust Mrs. Williams is quite recovered from her indisposition.[1]

For the first time Currer Bell was writing in her own name to her publishers. Their friendship was a new vital influence on her as a creative writer.

[1] CB to WSW, *W & S* ii. 230–1.

CROSSING THE ABYSS[1]

ANNE'S worsening cough in consequence of the drenching on the journey out, and Branwell's 'shattered constitution', were the realities Charlotte faced on her return home. But it was sweetened for her by Emily's keen interest in everything that had befallen them on their journey. Remembering that time on subsequent visits to London when both dear sisters were gone, she tenderly recalled 'the last time I went and with whom, and to whom I came home, and in what dear companionship I again and again narrated all that had been seen, heard, and uttered in that visit.'[2]

One thing had been said at Cornhill that Charlotte had hurriedly to withdraw: it was the disclosure of Ellis Bell's identity as well as Anne's and her own. Hoping to avert the consequences of this indiscretion, she wrote to Mr. Williams on 31 July:

> Permit me to caution you not to speak of my sisters when you write to me. I mean, do not use the word in the plural. Ellis Bell will not endure to be alluded to under any other appellation than the 'nom de plume'. I committed a grand error in betraying his identity to you and Mr. Smith. It was inadvertent—the words 'we are three sisters' escaped me before I was aware. I regretted the avowal the moment I had made it; I regret it bitterly now, for I find it is against every feeling and intention of Ellis Bell.[3]

The identity puzzle was still as baffling as ever, despite the hard words to Newby and the confidence reposed in Mr. Smith. In the Preface to the second edition of *Wildfell Hall*, written on 22 July shortly after the London journey, Anne made yet another categorical denial of the single authorship of the four Bell novels: 'Respecting the author's identity, I would have it to be distinctly understood that Acton Bell is neither Currer nor Ellis Bell and therefore let not his faults be attributed to them. As to whether his name be real or fictitious, it cannot greatly signify to those who know him only by his works.'

---

[1] Chapter-title quoted from letter of CB to WSW, 18 Jan. 1849. See below, p. 381.
[2] CB to WSW, 19 Nov. 1849: *SBC* 160–1; *W & S* iii. 38.
[3] CB to WSW, 31 July 1848: *W & S* ii. 240–3.

The reprint was already in circulation by the 31st of the month when Charlotte commented on it in her letter to Mr. Williams. Her judgement of Anne's achievement is important mainly because it reflects her judgement of Anne herself. The limitations she would have imposed on her sister's choice of subject were conditioned by the very limitations of her knowledge of Anne. Charlotte always saw her as a child, a frail child in need of defence, and Anne's reticence added to the impression. (It was because Emily accepted her as an absolute equal that with her Anne had no reserves.) Emily's power Charlotte had felt all her life—and Emily did not allow herself to be led; but Charlotte was wrong in thinking Anne pliant because she seldom contested a point. She was particularly wrong in assessing Anne's mental powers by her physical condition; the former were unimpaired long after the other was broken. This Charlotte discovered too late, when her sister's posthumous papers fell into her hands.

It is of interest to note, in passing, that Charlotte's low estimate of *Wildfell Hall* never altered. When Mr. Smith asked her eventually to edit a posthumous edition of her sisters' works—which she made a true labour of love—she still wrote to Mr. Williams: ' "Wildfell Hall" it hardly appears to me desirable to preserve. The choice of subject in that work is a mistake: it was too little consonant with the character, tastes, and ideas, of the gentle, retiring, inexperienced writer';[1] a judgement, incidentally, which provoked George Moore to say that it was 'Charlotte who first started the critics on their depreciation of Anne...'.[2]

Other subjects besides the identity of the Bells had been discussed at Cornhill between authors and publishers: among them the failure of the volume of 'Poems'. Convinced of his own ability to sell the book, George Smith secured the authors' consent to buy up the unsold copies from Aylott & Jones. 'I am glad the little volume of the Bell's poems is likely to get into Mr. Smith's hands', Charlotte wrote Mr. Williams early in September; 'I should feel unmixed pleasure in the chance of its being brought under respectable auspices before the public, were Currer Bell's shares in its contents absent. Of that portion I am by no means proud.'[3]

Published in October under the imprint of Smith, Elder, in olive green cloth with a cover design of Apollo's lyre, the book was freshly reviewed in the major literary journals. Acknowledging some of these in a letter to Mr. Williams of 2 November, Charlotte wrote: 'As

[1] CB to WSW, 5 Sept. 1850: *W & S* iii. 156.
[2] *Conversations in Ebury Street*, pp. 214–23 (London, 1930).
[3] CB to WSW: *W & S* ii. 256.

critiques, I should have thought more of them had they more fully recognised Ellis Bell's merit; but lovers of abstract poetry are few in number.' Writing again on 16 November on the same subject, she was still incensed at the treatment Ellis Bell received. '"The Spectator" consistently maintains the tone it first assumed regarding the Bells. I have little to object to its opinion as far as Currer Bell's portion of the volume is concerned. . . . Blind is he as any bat, insensate as any stone, to the merits of Ellis Bell.'[1]

By 7 December the Bells received what in effect amounted to their first payment for the 'Poems'. Writing to George Smith on that day Charlotte said: 'I have received today the sum of £24. 0. 6. paid by you to Messrs. Aylott & Jones for Bells' Poems.' Even then, her chief concern was that the transaction 'may not in the end prove disadvantageous to you . . .'.[2]

By 7 December so much had happened, and was happening in the Bells' home, that payment for a former financial loss appeared of little importance.

With less commotion than had accompanied any other act in his life, Branwell suddenly died on Sunday, 24 September. Failing as he was throughout the summer, he went out into the village two days before the end. The fever and exhaustion that at last cast him on his bed were little different from the symptoms with which the family were all too familiar by then: after every drunken bout he was prostrated. This time, however, the will to bestir himself was gone; and together with the resignation came another and startling change: a reversion to the feelings and affections of his youth. Charlotte told Ellen: 'His mind had undergone the peculiar change which frequently precedes death two days previously. The calm of better feelings filled it; a return of natural affection marked his last moments.'[3] And she told Mr. Williams:

all at once he seemed to open his heart. . . . The remembrance of this strange change now comforts my poor father greatly. I myself, with painful, mournful joy, heard him praying softly in his dying moments; and to the last prayer which my father offered up at his bedside he added 'Amen'. How unusual that word appeared from his lips, of course you, who did not know him, cannot conceive. Akin to this alteration was that in his feelings towards his relations—all the bitterness seemed gone.[4]

[1] CB to WSW: *W & S* ii. 269.
[2] CB to George Smith, 7 Dec. 1848: *W & S* ii. 291.
[3] CB to EN, 9 Oct. 1848: *W & S* ii. 264.
[4] CB to WSW, 6 Oct. 1848: *W & S* ii. 262.

Branwell's death shook Charlotte in a manner that her subsequent bereavements did not. From Branwell she had been divided for over three years; after the closeness of their early ties, this severance had been deeply unnatural and wounding. When he was gone she felt it as a physical ill. For the fortnight following his funeral she was ill with jaundice. She was surprised at the violence of her feelings and sought to excuse them on the score of his death being the first she had witnessed (this was not quite exact) and to rationalize her sorrow by reflecting on the miserable failure of his life and on the happy release death brought him. But it would not do. 'The final separation, the spectacle of his pale corpse, gave more acute, bitter pain than I could have imagined. Till the last hour comes, we never know how much we can forgive, pity, regret a near relation.'[1]

The memory of what he had been once, above all what he had been *to her*, crushed her heart. It was not the poor wreck of a man who had just died that she lamented, but the golden boy—the Branny of her girlhood—whose eager mind had made her universe for whom she wept now. She wrote Mr. Williams on 2 October:

I do not weep from a sense of bereavement, there is no prop withdrawn, no consolation torn away, no dear companion lost—but for the wreck of talent, the ruin of promise, the untimely dreary extinction of what might have been a burning and a shining light. My brother was a year my junior. I had aspirations and ambitions for him once, long ago—they have perished mournfully. Nothing remains of him but a memory of errors and sufferings. There is such a bitterness of pity for his life and death, such a yearning for the emptiness of his whole existence as I cannot describe. I trust time will allay these feelings.[2]

Nothing but the bitterness of the pity for Branwell's life, not the sorrow of his death, tormented her. 'When I looked on the noble face and forehead of my dead brother', she wrote four days later, 'and asked myself what had made him go ever wrong, tend ever downwards, and he had so many gifts to induce to, and aid in, an upward course, I seemed to receive an oppressive revelation of the feebleness of humanity—of the inadequacy of even genius to lead to true greatness if unaided by religion and principle . . .'[3]

The sense of desolation for such a life overwhelmed her even as she

[1] CB to EN, 9 Oct. 1848: *W & S* ii. 264.
[2] CB to WSW, 2 Oct. 1848: *W & S* ii. 261.
[3] CB to WSW, 6 Oct. 1848: *W & S* ii. 262.

wrote; she could *not* refuse the comfort her father and sisters pressed upon her—the assurance that Branwell was at peace.

When the struggle was over, and a marble calm began to succeed the last agony, I felt, as I have never felt before, that there was peace and forgiveness for him in Heaven. All his errors—to speak plainly, all his vices—seemed nothing to me in that moment; every wrong he had done, every pain he had caused, vanished; his sufferings only were remembered; the wrench to the natural affections only was left. . . . The doctor has told me I must not expect too rapid a restoration to health; but to-day I certainly feel better. I am thankful to say my father has hitherto stood the storm well; and so have my *dear* sisters, to whose untiring care and kindness I am chiefly indebted for my present state of convalescence.[1]

In the emphasis she laid on her *dear* sisters can be felt her complete reliance on them to restore her mental as well as bodily health. Branwell had been an incubus since the summer of 1845, and well might his removal—however cruel—be looked upon in the light of a deliverance. Domestic peace might now confidently be hoped to be restored. Mr. Brontë had survived the shock; and though he called on Charlotte not to fail him now, it was he who sustained her. As she told Mr. Williams: 'My poor father naturally thought more of his *only* son than of his daughters, and, much and long as he had suffered on his account, he cried out for his loss like David for that of Absalom—my son! my son! and refused at first to be comforted.'[2]

But he weathered the storm and Charlotte could say of him after three weeks that he had 'in a great measure recovered his mental composure . . .'.

Physically prostrated as she herself had been and dependent on her sisters' nursing, she was not at once conscious of their reaction to the event. 'Emily and Anne are pretty well', she wrote Ellen on 9 October,' though Anne is always delicate, and Emily has a cold and cough at present . . .'. These symptoms, 'regarded as things of course', as Charlotte later confessed to Mr. Williams,[3] were thought little of by the family, particularly by Anne and Emily themselves. Emily's cold, caught at Branwell's funeral, was taken for nothing more than a seasonal ill scarcely to be avoided at the fall of the year. By 29 October, however, when Charlotte could report that she herself was almost restored to her 'normal condition of health', she reported:

[1] CB to WSW, 6 Oct. 1848: *W & S* ii. 262.
[2] CB to WSW, 2 Oct. 1848: *W & S* ii. 261.
[3] CB to WSW, 18 Jan. 1849: *W & S* ii. 301.

I feel much more uneasy about my sisters. . . . Emily's cold and cough are very obstinate. I fear she has a pain in the chest, and I sometimes catch a shortness in her breathing, when she has moved at all quickly. She looks very, very thin and pale. Her reserved nature occasions me great uneasiness of mind. It is useless to question her, you get no answers. It is still more useless to recommend remedies; they are never adopted. Nor can I shut my eyes to the fact of Anne's great delicacy of constitution. The late sad event has, I feel, made me more apprehensive than common.[1]

The experience of the next few weeks would bring the fearful realization that ill health had been undermining the whole family for a long time. She wrote in the New Year to Mr. Williams:

All the days of this winter have gone by darkly and heavily like a funeral train. Since September sickness has not quitted the house. It is strange it did not use to be so, but I suspect now all this has been coming on for years. Unused, any of us, to the possession of robust health, we have not noticed the gradual approaches of decay; we did not know its symptoms: the little cough, the small appetite, the tendency to take cold at every variation of atmosphere have been regarded as things of course. I see them in another light now.[2]

Five weeks had not elapsed since Branwell's death and already the peace which had so ardently been prayed for was as far away as ever. The speed with which Emily's condition deteriorated was a fearful feature of the ordeal which suddenly overwhelmed the home. Charlotte wrote on 2 November to Mr. Williams:

I would fain hope that Emily is a little better this evening, but it is difficult to ascertain this. She is a real stoic in illness: she neither seeks nor will accept sympathy. To put any questions, to offer any aid, is to annoy; she will not yield a step before pain or sickness till forced; not one of her ordinary avocations will she voluntarily renounce. You must look on and see her do what she is unfit to do, and dare not say a word—a painful necessity for those to whom her health and existence are as precious as the life in their veins. When she is ill there seems to be no sunshine in the world for me. The tie of sister is near and dear indeed, and I think a certain harshness in her powerful and peculiar character only makes me cling to her more.[3]

To Ellen she spoke more openly. On her return from her long stay in the south of England (where she still was when Branwell died)

[1] CB to EN, 29 Oct. 1848: *W & S* ii. 267–8.
[2] CB to WSW, 18 Jan. 1849: *W & S* ii. 300–1.
[3] CB to WSW, 2 Nov. 1848: *W & S* ii. 269.

Ellen offered to visit the bereaved family at Haworth. Charlotte answered her on 27 November:

I mentioned your coming here to Emily with the faint hope that the prospect might cheer her, as she really esteems you perhaps more than any other person out of this house. I found, however, it would not do; any, the slightest excitement or putting out of the way is not to be thought of.... Yet I should have liked to see you, and so would Anne. Emily continues much the same ... to-day she is not so well. I hope still—for I *must* hope—she is dear to me as life.[1]

Already Charlotte had realized the impending disaster and cried out to avert the horror. Yet neither for her love, nor for any other pleading, did Emily linger. She held straight on her course until, within sight of her goal, she could 'dare the final bound'.[2] 'Never in all her life had she lingered over any task that lay before her,' Charlotte wrote in the memoir of her two sisters, 'and she did not linger now. She sank rapidly. She made haste to leave us. Yet, while physically she perished, mentally she grew stronger than we had yet known her. Day by day, when I saw with what a front she met suffering, I looked on her with an anguish of wonder and love. I have seen nothing like it.'[3]

On 16 November Charlotte wrote to Mr. Williams: 'Her symptoms continue to be those of slow inflammation of the lungs, tight cough, difficulty of breathing, pain in the chest and fever. We watch anxiously for a change for the better—may it come soon—'.[4]

Mr. Williams, a fervent advocate of homeopathy, wrote urging Charlotte to call in a homeopathic doctor for Ellis Bell. 'After reading your letter,' she told him, 'she said "Mr. Williams's intention was kind and good, but he was under a delusion. Homeopathy was only another form of quackery." '[5]

By the beginning of December Mr. Brontë was 'very despondent about her', remembering the similar symptoms in Maria and Elizabeth. 'Anne and I cherish hope as we can,' wrote Charlotte, 'I must cling to the expectation of her recovery, I cannot renounce it.'[6]

In her heart, already, she knew that the hope was illusory. Like the recurrence of a dreaded nightmare, her childish anguish for Maria was being lived through all over again. 'Moments as dark as these I have

[1] CB to EN, 27 Nov. 1848: *W & S* ii. 289.
[2] See *Complete Poems of Emily Jane Brontë*, ed. Hatfield (1941), 239.
[3] *Memoir of Ellis and Acton Bell*, 1850: Op. cit.
[4] CB to WSW, 16 Nov. 1848: *W & S* ii. 272.
[5] CB to WSW, 22 Nov. 1848: *W & S* ii. 287.
[6] CB to WSW, 7 Dec. 1848: *W & S* ii. 290.

never known. I pray for God's support to us all.'[1] Even as she wrote those words on the morning of 19 December in a hurried note to Ellen, Emily was dying. By two o'clock in the afternoon she was dead.

The death of Emily Brontë has puzzled three generations of readers. Why did she refuse all medical help? Why did she refuse to go to bed and even deny she was ill until the moment of dying? Why did she pursue her household tasks, even to the last night when she insisted on feeding the dogs? Such extreme stoicism is not understood. It has been variously interpreted to argue a will to die, heart-break for the death of Branwell, the bitter disillusionment of the unrecognized genius (though this claim cannot be substantiated), or the physical collapse of an over-taxed frame.

The evidence does not support these theories. There was in Emily Brontë a simple, primitive streak that might better explain her motives. Like the gipsies and the hill-folk she so resembled and the animals she championed and loved, she clung to her natural habitat and instinctive ways with great tenacity, distrusting the unknown methods and manners of 'civilized' society. Like a sick animal she would rather drag herself into a corner she knew—to recover or not—than be handled by strangers and removed to an alien place. The fear of being sent from home to a mild climate, if medical aid were called in, may have been foremost among her fears. The treatment was general at the time; Charlotte's own first impulse when Anne was pronounced incurable 'was to hasten her away to a warmer climate...'.[2] All her life Emily had been, as Ellen Nussey testified, 'a law unto herself—and a heroine in keeping to her law...',[3] and she resented nothing so much as what she considered prying into her affairs. She held all doctors in equal contempt, and judged their prescriptions as so much 'quackery'. She could less endure their interference than face death on her northern hills. She had, in an overpowering measure, a superstitious belief in natural forces, and to *them* she committed her life. Only in the last hour when she realized that they had abandoned her, did she submit to the will of others; knowing herself to be dying even then, she said to her sisters: 'You can send for a doctor if you like'—and was gone before any force could detain her. There is nothing in Charlotte's evidence to suggest a desire to die on Emily's part. On the contrary, in a rending evocation of her death she spoke of Emily 'turning her dying eyes reluctantly from the pleasant sun...'.[4]

[1] CB to EN, 19 Dec. 1848: *W & S* ii. 293.   [2] CB to EN, 18 Jan. 1849: *W & S* ii. 300-1.
[3] *SBC* 162.   [4] CB to WSW, 13 June 1849: BM. Ashley Lib.

So far as material causes are reckoned, Emily died of galloping consumption. Never known to ail before, once the illness was declared she was dead in three months.

For those who feel that there is an enigma to be explained, there remains *Wuthering Heights*; and if anyone doubts how Emily felt about the liberation of death, the longing of the imprisoned spirit to cast its chains, and of the lonely soul for reunion with the universal fount from which it came, they had better re-read the death of Heathcliff.

Two images of Charlotte remain from this time of her darkest sorrow that stamp her likeness on our memory more surely than Richmond's portrait can do; images showing her in the struggle with death and using almost supernatural aids to lure back Emily to life. It was as though she challenged her spirit to spirit not to forsake this earth which could hold such things as these—to remind her in her own words:

> Few hearts to mortals given
> On earth so wildly pine;
> Yet none would ask a Heaven
> More like this Earth than thine.[1]

Mrs. Gaskell has beautifully told of that quest on Emily's last morning for a sprig of heather.[2] Charlotte went far over the stiff and frozen moors in the December sunrise to find it; but when she returned Emily's eyes were already glazed to the things of earth. On the evening before, she read aloud to Emily from the Essays of Emerson that her publishers had sent to beguile the invalid's long day. 'The opening of the parcel and examination of the books cheered her', Charlotte wrote later. 'The very evening before her last morning dawned I read to her one of Emerson's essays. I read on, till I found she was not listening— I thought to recommence the next day. Next day, the first glance at her face told me what would happen before nightfall.'[3]

Emily died on Tuesday, 19 December, and was buried on Friday, 22 December, Mr. Nicholls conducting the service. Writing to Ellen the next day, Charlotte said: 'She died on *Tuesday*, the very day I wrote to you. I thought it very possible she might be with us for weeks; and a few hours afterwards she was in eternity.... We are very

---

[1] *The Complete Poems of EJB*, ed. Hatfield, 164.
[2] Gaskell 257.
[3] CB to WSW, 3 Mar. 1849: *SBC* 160.

calm at present. Why should we be otherwise? The anguish of seeing her suffer is over.'[1]

Charlotte wrote Mr. Williams on Christmas Day:

Emily is nowhere here now. Her wasted mortal remains are taken out of the house. We have laid her cherished head under the church aisle beside my mother's, my two sisters'—dead long ago—and my poor, hapless brother's. . . . Well, the loss is ours, not hers, and some sad comfort I take, as I hear the wind blow and feel the cutting keenness of the frost, in knowing that the elements bring her no more suffering; their severity cannot reach her grave; her fever is quieted, her restlessness soothed, her deep, hollow cough is hushed for ever; we do not hear it in the night nor listen for it in the morning; we have not the conflict of the strangely strong spirit and the fragile frame before us—relentless conflict—once seen, never to be forgotten.[2]

The storm had not passed, only receded; already the crack of its return was in her ears:

My father says to me almost hourly, 'Charlotte, you must bear up, I shall sink if you fail me'; these words, you can conceive, are a stimulus to nature. The sight, too, of my sister Anne's very still but deep sorrow wakens in me such fear for her that I dare not falter. Somebody *must* cheer the rest.

So I will not ask why Emily was torn from us in the fulness of our attachment, rooted up in the prime of her own days, in the promise of her powers; why her existence now lies like a field of green corn trodden down, like a tree in full bearing struck at the root. I will only say, sweet is rest after labour and calm after tempest, and repeat again and again that Emily knows that now.[3]

To Ellen Nussey, who had been absent in the south at the time of Branwell's death, Charlotte now wrote begging for her company. 'Could you now come to us for a few days? I would not ask you to stay long. Write and tell me if you could come next week, and by what train. I would try to send a gig for you to Keighley. You will, I trust, find us tranquil. Try to come. I never so much needed the consolation of a friend's presence.'[4]

Ellen came. Poles removed as she was temperamentally and spiritually from the Brontës, she had always been endowed with a strange prescience where Emily was concerned, seeing her with tenderly perceptive eyes. To Ellen is owed the description of Emily: 'Few people

---

[1] CB to EN, 23 Dec. 1848: *W & S* ii. 294.
[2] CB to WSW, 25 Dec. 1848: *W & S* ii. 294–5.
[3] CB to WSW, 25 Dec. 1848.
[4] CB to EN, 23 Dec. 1848: *W & S* ii. 294.

have the gift of looking and smiling as she could look and smile. One of her rare expressive looks was something to remember through life, there was such a depth of soul and feeling, and yet a shyness of revealing herself.'[1]

Ellen's visit, intended to console for the loss of one sister, coincided with sentence of death being passed upon the other. Dr. Teale, the lung-specialist called in from Leeds by Mr. Brontë to examine Anne, saw her on 5 January, while Ellen was there. He immediately diagnosed consumption in both lungs and frankly told the family that she had not long to live. From Anne herself, 'looking sweetly pretty and flushed', as Ellen recorded, the truth was not hidden. When the doctor had gone, Mr. Brontë came and sat on the couch beside her, drew her towards him, and merely said: 'My *dear* little Anne!'[2]

For Charlotte, the road to Calvary had again to be taken. The only difference in the death of her second sister was that every medical aid was employed to stave off the fatal hour. Anne was given the treatment prescribed by two specialists (Dr. Teale of Leeds and Dr. Forbes, the famous London specialist) and was under the care of the local Haworth doctor throughout. 'There is some feeble consolation in thinking we are doing the very best that can be done', wrote Charlotte to Ellen on 30 January. 'The agony of forced, total neglect, is not now felt, as during Emily's illness. Never may we be doomed to feel such agony again. It was terrible.'[3]

Anne, preparing her soul for death with the fortitude that her last verses reveal, still wanted to live. She complied with every one of the painful prescriptions in vogue at the time: the running blisters, kept open in her side, the cod-liver-oil 'that tasted and smelt of train oil' and made her perpetually sick—as Charlotte described—the vegetable balsam. None brought any alleviation, and there could be no question of a cure.

Her endurance impressed Charlotte with a new recognition of her spirit: 'Anne is very patient in her illness, as patient as Emily was unflinching. I recall one sister and look at the other with a sort of reverence as well as affection—under the test of suffering neither has faltered . . .', she wrote Mr. Williams on 18 January.

The repetition of the nightmare could only heighten the horror for Charlotte.

'When we lost Emily I thought we had drained the very dregs of our

[1] *SBC* 162.   [2] *BST* (1932), 21–22.
[3] CB to EN, 30 Jan. 1849: *W & S* ii. 304.

cup of trial, but now when I hear Anne cough as Emily coughed, I tremble lest there should be exquisite bitterness yet to taste. However, I must not look forwards, nor must I look backwards.'[1]

With her capacity for seeing through appearances, Charlotte suddenly saw her state, as though separated from it and outside of herself, and expressed it in the memorable phrase: '. . . Too often I feel like one crossing an abyss on a narrow plank—a glance round might quite unnerve. . . .'[2]

In the presence of death not only Emily and Anne gained in stature, but Charlotte also; she wholly submerged herself now in the care of Anne. Writing to Ellen on 15 January with the latest news, she added:

Do not fear that I shall relax in my care of her. She is too precious to me not to be cherished with all the fostering strength I have. I avoid looking forward or backward, and try to keep looking upward. This is not the time to regret, dread or weep. What I have and ought to do is very distinctly laid out for me; what I want, and pray for, is strength to perform it. The days pass in a slow, dark march; the nights are the test; the sudden wakings from restless sleep, the revived knowledge that one lies in her grave, and another not at my side, but in a separate sick bed.[3]

Anne's decline was both less violent and less rapid than Emily's; it was, however, as inevitable. She lived till the end of May. Her desire to die by the sea that she loved above all things added to the ordeal for Charlotte, since the journey to Scarborough had to be undertaken in almost impossible circumstances, Anne so weak as to have to be carried from platform to platform at each stage of the journey.

Ellen accompanied them.[4] Leaving home on 24 May, a Thursday, they broke the journey at York, where Anne was able to visit the Minster a last time. They arrived in Scarborough on Friday, having booked rooms at the Cliff lodgings where Anne had often stayed with the Robinsons in past years. The splendour of the weather and Anne's delight allowed Charlotte a momentary peace of mind. She wrote Mr. Williams on the Saturday:

It made her happy to see both York and its Minster, and Scarborough and its bay once more. Our lodgings are pleasant. As Anne sits at the window she can look down on the sea, which this morning is as calm as glass. She says

[1] CB to WSW, 18 Jan. 1849: *W & S* ii. 301. [2] Ibid.
[3] CB to EN, 15 Jan. 1849: *W & S* ii. 299.
[4] For AB's last journey see T. Wemyss-Reid, *Charlotte Brontë, A Monograph*, London (1877), pp. 95–97; EN's diary for May 1849, BPM; CB's account-book, BPM. For further details of AB's last journey and death see the present author's *Anne Brontë*, Nelson (1959), pp. 303–23.

if she could breathe more freely she would be comfortable at this moment—
but she cannot breathe freely. . . . Write to me. In this strange place your
letters will come like the visits of a friend.[1]

The request need not have been made. Before even Mr. Williams
could answer her letter, Anne had died. On Wednesday, 30 May, Charlotte wrote to tell him so: 'My dear Sir—My poor sister is taken home
quietly at last. She died on Monday. With almost her last breath she
said she was happy, and thanked God that death was come, and come
so gently. I did not think it would be so soon.'[2]

On Charlotte revolved the major decision whether to bury Anne at
Scarborough, or take her home. In response to Anne's known wishes—
and also to spare her father yet a third family funeral in six months—
she chose Scarborough, going with Ellen Nussey to choose a spot in the
churchyard on the Castle Hill overlooking the bay, where Anne had so
often walked in former years, and where she had placed the proposal
scene in *Agnes Grey*.

The funeral service, attended only by themselves (and a sympathetic
lady visitor from Birstall), took place at Christ Church, Scarborough,
on 30 May. Charlotte's long task was over.

Realizing her need for rest, her father wrote telling her not to
come home yet. Presumably because the lodgings had been engaged till
7 June, Charlotte stayed at Scarborough till that date, and then went
on to Filey, Ellen accompanying her. On 4 June she wrote to Mr.
Williams:

2, Cliff, Scarboro', June 4th 1849
My dear Sir—I hardly know what I said when I wrote last. I was then
feverish and exhausted. I am now better and, I believe, quite clear.

You have been informed of my dear sister Anne's death. Let me now add
that she died without severe struggle, resigned, trusting in God—thankful
for release from a suffering life—deeply assured that a better existence lay before her. She believed, she hoped—and declared her belief and hope with her
last breath. Her quiet, Christian death did not rend my heart as Emily's
stern, simple, undemonstrative end did. I let Anne go to God, and felt He had
a right to her. I could hardly let Emily go. I wanted to hold her back then,
and I want her back now. Anne, from her childhood, seemed preparing for an
early death. Emily's spirit seemed strong enough to bear her to fulness of
years. They are both gone, and so is poor Branwell, and Papa has now me

only—the weakest, puniest, least promising of his six children. Consumption has taken them all.

For the present Anne's ashes rest apart from the others. I have buried her here at Scarboro', to save Papa the anguish of the return and a third funeral.

I am ordered to remain at the sea-side awhile. I cannot rest here, but neither can I go home. Possibly I may not write again soon—attribute my silence neither to idleness nor negligence. No letters will find me at Scarboro' after the 7th. I do not know what my next address will be. I shall wander a week or two on the East Coast, and only stop at quiet lonely places. No one need be anxious about me as far as I know. Friends and acquaintance seem to think *this* the worst time of suffering. They are surely mistaken. Anne reposes now—what have the long desolate hours of her patient pain and fast decay been?

Why life is so blank, brief, and bitter I do not know. Why younger and far better than I are snatched from it with projects unfulfilled I cannot comprehend, but I believe God is wise—perfect—merciful.

I have heard from Papa. He and the servants knew when they parted from Anne they would see her no more. All tried to be resigned. I knew it likewise, and I wanted her to die where she would be happiest. She loved Scarboro'. A peaceful sun gilded her evening—

Yours sincerely,
C. Brontë.[1]

On 7 June Charlotte and Ellen went down the coast to stay at Filey, where they lodged at Cliff House[2] with Mrs. Smith, who was the widow of the man who had built it in 1824. He was land-agent to the Strickland family, and when he built his 'red-bricked house', it was, to quote a local guide-book of 1868, 'the farthest residence in a southerly direction in the whole resort and certainly one of the best frequented.' Mrs. Smith had no idea that her deeply afflicted lodger was a famous author, and never thought to keep her letters, though she regretted her error in after years.

The absolute seclusion of Filey was needful to Charlotte and, as her letters show, she would have preferred to stay there a second week rather than go to Easton to the Hudson's at Ellen's wish. This, however, they did, from 14 to 21 June.

The rooms at Filey and the Smith family were so pleasant that

---

[1] CB to WSW: *W & S* ii. 337–8.

[2] Cliff House, Filey. The house at Filey still stands. It is a solid, box-like Georgian house three-storeys high, with a flat-pillared portico and high first-floor windows—the former best parlours—where the select visitors would sit and view the sea, unobscured then by any intervening houses. Only the cliff-face, profusely wooded and overgrown with scrub, lay between the house and the shore below.

Charlotte returned there three years later. The daughter of the house waited on her and Ellen, and from the bow-windowed first-floor sitting-room of their lodgings she sat and looked out at the sea and was soothed by the beauty of the scene. In that regained tranquillity of spirit she wrote to Mr. Williams on 13 June:

Filey June 13th/49

My dear Sir—When I wrote to you last I thought it probable I might not address you again soon—but this evening I will write because I feel in the mood to do so without, I trust, paining you.

You have been kind enough to take a certain interest in my afflictions, and I feel it a sort of duty to tell you how I am enabled to sustain them. The burden is lightened far beyond what I could expect by more circumstances than one. Papa is resigned and his health is not shaken. Our immediate change of scene has done me good. All I meet are kind—my friend Ellen is affectionately so. You—on whom I have no claim—write to me in the strain best tending to consolation.

Then—my sister died happily; nothing dark, except the inevitable shadow of death overclouded her hour of dissolution—the doctor—a stranger—who was called in—wondered at her fixed tranquillity of spirit and settled longing to be gone. He said in all his experience he had seen no such deathbed, and that it gave evidence of no common mind. Yet to speak the truth—it but half consoles to remember this calm—there is piercing pain in it. Anne had had enough of life such as it was—in her twenty-eight years—she laid it down as a burden. I hardly know whether it is sadder to think of that than of Emily turning her dying eyes reluctantly from the pleasant sun. Had I never believed in a future life before, my sisters' fate would assure me of it. There must be Heaven or we must despair—for life seems bitter, brief—blank.

To me, these two have left in their memories a noble legacy. Were I quite solitary in the world—bereft even of Papa—there is something in the past I can love intensely and honour deeply—and it is something which cannot change—which cannot decay—which immortality guarantees from corruption.

They have died comparatively young—but their short lives were spotless—their brief career was honourable—their untimely death befell amidst all associations that can hallow, and not one that can desecrate.

A year ago—had a prophet warned me how I should stand in June 1849— how stripped and bereaved—had he foretold the autumn, the winter, the spring of sickness and suffering to be gone through—I should have thought —this can never be endured. It is over. Branwell—Emily—Anne are gone like dreams—gone as Maria and Elizabeth went twenty years ago. One by one I have watched them fall asleep on my arm—and closed their glazed eyes—I have seen them buried one by one—and—thus far—God has upheld me. From my heart I thank Him.

I thank too the friends whose sympathy has given me inexpressible comfort and strength—you, amongst the number.

Filey, where we have been for the last week—is a small place with a wild rocky coast—its sea is very blue—its cliffs are very white—its sands very solitary—it suits Ellen and myself better than Scarbro' which is too gay. I would stay here another week—but Ellen says I must go tomorrow to Bridlington—and after I have been a week there, I intend to return home to Papa. May I retain strength and cheerfulness enough to be a comfort to him and to bear up against the weight of the solitary life to come—it will be solitary— I cannot help dreading the first experience of it—the first aspect of the empty rooms which once were tenanted by those dearest to my heart—and where the shadow of their last days must now—I think—linger for ever. Ellen lives much too far off to see me often—her home is twenty miles distant from mine; but I trust in the power which has helped me hitherto.

I hope that your little invalid daughter is now quite well, and that her parents are relieved from anxiety on her account.

Should you write to me again soon—and I shall be glad to hear from you address

Miss Brontë
J. Hudson's Esq
Easton
Bridlington   CB.[1]

Much as Charlotte liked the Hudsons and retained the happiest memories of her previous holiday at Easton ten years before, she spoke of 'that dismal Easton' on her return home from this visit. She took cold[2] and was—understandably—alarmed at her own symptoms,

[1] Text quoted from original in Ashley Lib., BM.

[2] A special interest attaches to the fact of Charlotte's taking cold at Easton, and to the possibility of her calling in a doctor there, for she knew of the notable Burlington doctor whose name was to find an echo in *Villette*. He was Edward Samuel *Brett*, physician and surgeon, who set up practice at the Quay in 1834, and died there, a noted local figure, in 1870. White's *Directory* shows that he had a surgery at the Quay in 1839 at the time of Charlotte's first visit there, and his private residence in High Street, Burlington, that old street of Georgian houses believed to be described by Charlotte as 'Bretton' in the opening of *Villette*. Dr. Brett could well have been known to the Hudsons and to Henry Nussey and, by their recommendation, to Charlotte. In March 1845 Ellen Nussey took her sick brother George to stay at the Quay; writing to her on 4 Mar. Charlotte urged her to 'take the advice of the medical man you have consulted at Burlington . . .' (who recommended a change for George and isolation from his family). The foremost doctor in the town was Dr. Brett and, considering the gravity of George's case, he would be the likely one to be consulted. When Dr. Brett died in 1870 he was buried in the family vault in the north aisle of the Priory Church; the name may thus have become familiar to Charlotte on the occasions of her attending service at the Priory Church. No ordinary coincidence, certainly, dictated her choice in naming the *place* and the secondary hero—Dr. John Graham Bretton—in *Villette*.

and at great pains to hide them from her father. 'I dare communicate no ailment to papa,' she confessed later to Ellen; 'his anxiety harasses me inexpressibly.'[1]

The return home had at last to be made and, refusing the kind offer of Ellen to accompany her, she travelled to Haworth on 21 June. What it cost her she wrote to Mr. Williams on the 25th:

My dear Sir—I am now again at home, where I returned last Thursday. I call it *home* still—much as London would be called London if an earthquake should shake its streets to ruins. But let me not be ungrateful: Haworth parsonage is still a home for me, and not quite a ruined or desolate home either. Papa is there, and two most affectionate and faithful servants, and two old dogs, in their way as faithful and affectionate—Emily's large house-dog which lay at the side of her dying bed, and followed her funeral to the vault, lying in the pew couched at our feet while the burial service was being read— and Anne's little spaniel. The ecstasy of these poor animals when I came in was something singular. At former returns from brief absences they always welcomed me warmly—but not in that strange, heart-touching way. I am certain they thought that, as I was returned, my sisters were not far behind. But here my sisters will come no more. Keeper may visit Emily's little bedroom—as he still does day by day—and Flossy may still look wistfully round for Anne, they will never see them again—nor shall I—at least the human part of me. I must not write so sadly, but how can I help thinking and feeling sadly? In the daytime effort and occupation aid me, but when evening darkens, something in my heart revolts against the burden of solitude—the sense of loss and want grows almost too much for me. I am not good or amiable in such moments, I am rebellious, and it is only the thought of my dear father in the next room, or of the kind servants in the kitchen, or some caress from the poor dogs, which restores me to softer sentiments and more rational views. As to the night—could I do without bed, I would never seek it. Waking, I think, sleeping, I dream of them; and I cannot recall them as they were in health, still they appear to me in sickness and suffering. Still, my nights were worse after the first shock of Branwell's death—they were terrible then; and the impressions experienced on waking were at that time such as we do not put into language. Worse seemed at hand than was yet endured—in truth, worse awaited us.

All this bitterness must be tasted. Perhaps the palate will grow used to the draught in time, and find its flavour less acrid. This pain must be undergone; its poignancy, I trust, will be blunted one day. Ellen would have come back with me, but I would not let her. I knew it would be better to face the desolation at once—later or sooner the sharp pang must be experienced.[2]

[1] CB to EN, 14 July 1849: *W & S* iii. 8.
[2] CB to WSW, 25 June 1849: *W & S* ii. 348–9.

Happily, the one anodyne for grief such as hers was at hand; she need not seek it elsewhere, it was within her. 'Labour must be the cure not sympathy', she told Mr. Williams. 'Labour is the only radical cure for rooted sorrow. . . . Total change might do much; where that cannot be obtained, work is the best substitute.'[1]

Henceforward, her life would take its warmth and colour and much of its purpose from the imaginary world in which she worked. This had been so since childhood, but then she had lived in a world of wonder which she shared with others. They were all gone now and for the first time she found herself alone to explore the unknown regions of her mind. Her direst suffering would come from the realization that the imaginary world was not enough; she longed inexpressibly for kindred spirits—and sought them in vain. The world no longer contained beings like Emily, Branwell, Anne. The key to existence lay no more in a magic formula—'Open Sesame'—but in the bleak acceptance of Anne's last words to her at Scarborough: 'Courage, Charlotte, courage—'.

She was 33. For all companionship she must look now to her father, a man of 72 who, despite his once lively mind, followed a rigid routine of life that nothing would alter again. From him she could not expect the swift exchanges, the keen responses, the ardour of argument she had revelled in with her sisters and brother. Mr. Brontë was *there*, much as an extinct volcano is pointed out to wondering travellers, a presence in the room across the hall; for his love, undemonstrative as it was by now, she was deeply grateful. In the mere fact of her thankfulness, both for his affection, and for that of the servants and dogs— can be measured the magnitude of her loss; they were all that was left after the 'earthquake'.

To Ellen she also wrote of that return, on 23 June:

I intended to have written a line to you to-day, if I had not received yours. We did, indeed, part suddenly; it made my heart ache that we were severed without the time to exchange a word; and yet perhaps it was better. I got home a little before eight o'clock. All was clean and bright, waiting for me. Papa and the servants were well; and all received me with an affection which should have consoled. The dogs seemed in strange ecstasy. I am certain they regarded me as the harbinger of others. The dumb creatures thought that as I was returned, those who had been so long absent were not far behind.

I left Papa soon and went into the dining-room: I shut the door. I tried to be glad that I was come home. I have always been glad before—except once,

[1] Ibid.

even then I was cheered. But this time joy was not to be the sensation. I felt that the house was all silent, the rooms were all empty. I remembered where the three were laid—in what narrow dark dwellings—never more to reappear on earth. So the sense of desolation and bitterness took possession of me. The agony that *was to be undergone*, and *was not* to be avoided, came on. I underwent it, and passed a dreary evening and night, and a mournful morrow; to-day I am better.

I do not know how life will pass, but I certainly do feel confidence in Him who has upheld me hitherto. Solitude may be cheered, and made endurable beyond what I can believe. The great trial is when evening closes and night approaches. At that hour, we used to assemble in the dining-room; we used to talk. Now I sit by myself; necessarily I am silent. I cannot help thinking of their last days, remembering their sufferings, and what they said and did, and how they looked in mortal affliction. Perhaps all this will become less poignant in time.[1]

Time would not bring any mitigation of her sorrows—for she would be stinted even of time. From her genius alone would comfort come.

[1] CB to EN: *W & S* ii. 347–8.

CHAPTER XXI

THE MIRACLE OF *SHIRLEY*

Mrs. Hudson,[1] who lived till 1878, recalled that during the week at Easton after Anne's death Charlotte had been writing most of the day— some of the time in the seclusion of the summer-house in the garden. She believed that it was on the manuscript of *Shirley* that she was engaged. According to Mrs. Gaskell the first chapter to be written after Anne's death was chapter xxiv, called: 'The Valley of the Shadow of Death'. She presumably learnt the fact from Charlotte herself.

The need to hide her occupation from Ellen was gone; when Emily died Ellen was initiated into the secret of their authorship during her visit to Haworth in January, and was given a copy of *Wuthering Heights*[2] as a keepsake.

Up to the period of Anne's death Charlotte had, in effect, written two-thirds of her book; even such an achievement is remarkable when the background against which she worked is remembered. Abandoned in October, it had only very tentatively been taken out from time to time during the spring. Each volume of the finished *Shirley* (published as a three-volume novel in conformity with the fashion of the day) had been subjected to the same ruinous break in continuity; the first, 'laid aside' on 18 October; the second, resumed during the spring as Anne's condition allowed; the third, written entirely after her death. Thus the book was begun in high spirits on the wave of confidence inspired by the success of *Jane Eyre*, with the curates providing lively comic relief, and the Taylors (accurately portrayed in the Yorke family) holding the forefront of the stage with an unmistakable evocation of Joe Taylor as the mill-owner hero, Robert Moore. Then the tale took on a graver, more reflective tone with the introduction of its heroine Shirley who, as Emily's life ebbed away, became increasingly endowed with the characteristics of her sister. Finally there was the change in Caroline's character. Even the colour of her eyes and hair came to resemble Anne's in the

---

[1] 'CB and the East Riding', *BST*, 1896: Scruton, 'Reminiscences of EN', *BST* (1898), 36: Pearson, 'CB on the E. Yorkshire Coast', 1957.
[2] CB to EN, 10 Jan. 1849: *W & S* ii. 299.

end. An interesting thesis has appeared to show how, by the time Anne was dead and the third volume begun, Charlotte discarded her heroine's earlier traits—the superficial resemblances of colouring and feature to Ellen Nussey, and the strong emotional likeness to herself—to make of Caroline a tribute to her sister Anne, as Shirley was a tribute to Emily.[1]

Perhaps because it was so organically related to the circumstances of her life, *Shirley* achieved less artistic independence and wholeness than any of Charlotte's books. Its faults, however, are of construction, rather than content. For the same reasons that the plot was dislocated, the book contains some of the most philosophical thinking and the sheerest poetry of expression of all Charlotte's novels. The source of its inspiration—certainly as the tale progressed and death was the atmosphere it breathed—was more sustainedly spiritual than either *The Professor* or *Jane Eyre*.

For its author, it represented the life-line that brought her into harbour after shipwreck. For that reason, if for no other, *Shirley* will always have its devotees. Yet admirable as the writing is, it might well have been better for the book if Charlotte had had the courage to put it aside completely, and wait for the healing power of time to have its effect before resuming it. But this, she realized, would be tantamount to suicide; her will to live was almost dependent on the ability to work.

A constant spur too was the desire to please her publishers, anxiously waiting for a successor to *Jane Eyre*. To them she dared not confess total cessation of work, though she frankly confessed how painful the struggle was. 'I try to write now and then', she told them in the early spring. 'The effort was a hard one at first. It renewed the terrible loss of last December strangely. Worse than useless did it seem to attempt to write what there no longer lived an "Ellis Bell" to read; the whole book, with every hope founded on it, faded to vanity and vexation of spirit.'[2]

The want of Emily, as a critic as well as a sister, was a severe handicap—it left Charlotte incapable of judging her own work; and the difficulty of continuing without consultation drove her to the unusual procedure of begging advice from her publishers themselves. On 1 February she wrote to Mr. Williams:

I will tell you what I want to do; it is to show you the first volume of my

MS, which I have copied. In reading 'Mary Barton' . . . I was a little dismayed to find myself in some measure anticipated both in subject and incident. I should like to have your opinion on this point, and to know whether the resemblance appears as considerable to a stranger as to myself. I should wish also to have the benefit of such general strictures and advice as you choose to give.

But remember, if I show it to you it is on two conditions: the first, that you give me a faithful opinion . . . the second, that you show it and speak of it to *none* but Mr. Smith. I have always a great horror of premature announcements. . . . All human affairs are so uncertain, and my position especially is at present so peculiar, that I cannot count on the time, and would rather that no allusion should be made to a work of which great part is yet to create.[1]

Every urge to renewed activity coincided noticeably with some small improvement in Anne's condition; the very letter asking permission to send the manuscript to Cornhill had begun: 'Anne seems so tranquil this morning, so free from pain and fever, and looks and speaks so like herself in health, that I too feel relieved, and I take advantage of the respite to write to you, hoping that my letter may reflect something of the comparative peace I feel.'[2]

The suggestion was welcomed by the publishers and she was encouraged to submit the manuscript forthwith. 'I send the parcel up without delay, according to your request', she wrote on February 4. 'The MS has all its errors upon it, not having been read through since copying.'[3] The interest shown at once reanimated her; she felt the friendliness of the gesture and hastened to meet its implications half-way by including in her confidence the firm's manager, James Taylor, whom she had not met on her visit to London. 'Your mention of Mr. Taylor[4] suggests to me that possibly you and Mr. Smith might wish him to share the little secret of the MS. . . . If so, admit him to the confidence by all means. I shall be glad of another censor. . . . I court the keenest criticism. Far rather would I never publish more, than publish anything inferior to my first effort.' James Taylor[5] was to exercise considerable influence over Charlotte in the future, though it was less as a publisher than as a man. He came very near to making her his wife.

He was a year younger than Charlotte—Branwell's age—and had,

---

[1] CB to WSW, 1 Feb. 1849: *W & S* ii. 305–6.   [2] Ibid.
[3] CB to WSW, 4 Feb. 1849: *W & S* ii. 306.
[4] Ibid.
[5] *SBC* 287.

moreover, a remarkable physical resemblance to Branwell. He had the same small stature and the same red hair, which affected Charlotte strangely at every meeting, but there the resemblance ended; for Taylor was a forceful, vigorous man, master of his own mind and with surplus energy to domineer over others as well. He was in charge of the clerical staff at Cornhill, numbering at the time no fewer than 40 young men and boys, and showed both an adventurous spirit and a purposeful character throughout his career—so purposeful, indeed, that it is impossible not to believe that he would have won Charlotte's hand had time been in his favour.

The very act of sending her manuscript to Cornhill gave Charlotte courage. In the letter that accompanied the parcel she wrote: 'Anne continues a little better—the mild weather suits her—surely we may hope a little. . . .' The hope was delusory, as we have seen, but the stimulus derived from London helped to support her through the constant set-backs of those days, and any sign of improvement in Anne would send her thoughts back to her novel with renewed confidence. On 2 March she wrote to Mr. Williams:

> My sister still continues better: she has less languor and weakness; her spirits are improved. This change gives cause, I think, both for gratitude and hope.
> I am glad you and Mr. Smith like the commencement of my present work. I wish it were *more than a commencement*; for how it will be reunited after the long break, or how it can gather force of flow when the current has been checked or rather drawn off so long, I know not.

To Mr. Taylor, who had also written his views of the manuscript, and who, moreover, had chosen and made up a selection of new books for herself and Anne to read, she had written on 1 March:

> The parcel arrived on Saturday evening. Permit me to express my sense of the judgement and kindness which have dictated the selection of its contents. . . . Thank you for your remarks on 'Shirley'. Some of your strictures tally with some of Mr. Williams. You both complain of the want of distinctness and impressiveness in my heroes . . . In delineating male character I labour under disadvantages. . . . When I write about women I am on sure ground.[1]

It was the first letter of a fairly well-sustained correspondence over the next three years.

---

[1] CB to James Taylor, 1 March 1849: *W & S* ii. 312-13.

All three readers in the firm had some reservations to add to their wholesale praise of the work; Charlotte's reactions to these give considerable insight into her views on writing.

My critics truly deserve and have my genuine thanks for the friendly candour with which they have declared their opinions on my book [she wrote on 2nd April]. Both Mr. Williams and Mr. Taylor express and support their opinions in a manner calculated to command careful consideration. In my turn I have a word to say. *You both of you dwell too much on what* you regard as the *artistic* treatment of a subject. Say what you will, gentlemen, say it as ably as you will—truth is better than art. Burns's Songs are better than Bulwer's Epics. Thackeray's rude, careless sketches are preferable to thousands of carefully finished paintings. Ignorant as I am, I dare to hold and maintain that doctrine.[1]

By the same post that brought her publishers' opinions on her new work, a letter was forwarded to her from Mary Howitt,[2] who with her husband William edited a literary journal and was, consequently, on the look out for new talent. She offered Charlotte to become a regular contributor to an American periodical. 'Of course I have negatived it', Charlotte answered. 'When I *can* write, the book I have on hand must claim all my attention.' The flattering offer made her realize for a moment, however, what her life as an author might be if *only* her domestic circumstances were different. 'Oh! if Anne were well, if the void Death has left were a little closed up, if the dreary word "nevermore" would cease sounding in my ears, I think I could yet do something.'[3]

By the beginning of May the illusory improvement in Anne had given place to alarming symptoms, '. . . the very same symptoms which were apparent in Emily only a few days before she died', and the trip to Scarborough was planned for the end of the month. Over-scrupulous as ever where her publishers' interests were concerned, Charlotte wrote in anxiety to urge them not to risk a cheap reprint yet of *Jane Eyre*.

He had better wait awhile—the public will be sick of the name of that one book. I can make no promise as to when another will be ready—neither my time nor my efforts are my own. That absorption in my employment to which I gave myself up without fear of doing wrong when I wrote 'Jane

---

[1] CB to WSW, 2 Apr. 1849: *W & S* ii. 319–20.
[2] For data concerning William and Mary Howitt see Amice Lee, *Laurels and Rosemary* (O.U.P., 1955).
[3] CB to WSW, 2 Apr. 1849: *W & S* ii. 319–20.

Eyre', would now be alike impossible and blamable; but I do what I can, and have made some little progress. We must all be patient.[1]

In the following weeks *Shirley* was laid aside once more during the last phases of Anne's illness. The manuscript was not opened again until Charlotte was at Easton.

How necessary was the discipline of work, Charlotte explained to Mr. Williams shortly after her return to Haworth. Writing to him on 3 July about careers for his daughters, she added the significant comment:

Lonely as I am, how should I be if Providence had never given me courage to adopt a career—perseverance to plead through two long, weary years with publishers till they admitted me? How should I be with youth past, sisters lost, a resident in a moorland parish where there is not a single educated family? In that case I should have no world at all: the raven, weary of surveying the deluge, and without an ark to return to, would be my type. As it is, something like a hope and motive sustains me still. I wish all your daughters—I wish every woman in England, had also a hope and a motive. Alas! there are many old maids who have neither.[2]

There, in a sentence, lay the kernel of the plot of *Shirley*—a book about the predicament of women—women in love, women suffering from unrequited love, women who have never, and never will be, loved. Two of these conditions had been experienced by Charlotte: the lot of the woman whose love was unrequited (and none knew better than she the bitterness of the post-hour when the longed-for letter did not come), and she was learning, even then, the loneliness of the bereaved woman. Life was not to condemn her to the lot of the third category of women, of those who would never be loved, but it was her fate to kindle loves she could not return. 'I get on as well as I can', she reassured Ellen on 4 July. 'Home is not the home it used to be—that you may well conceive; but so far, I get on.' To Mr. Williams, who had suggested she engage a young lady companion to share her solitude, she frankly owned she would not like to see a young creature immured to such a miserable life. 'The fact is,' she told him on 26 July, 'my work is my best companion; hereafter I look for no great earthly comfort except what congenial occupation can give. For society, long seclusion has in a great measure unfitted me, I doubt whether I should enjoy it if I might have it. . . . The prisoner in solitary confinement,

[1] CB to WSW, 8 May 1849: *W & S* ii. 328–9.
[2] 3 July 1849: *W & S* iii. 4.

the toad in the block of marble, all in time shape themselves to their lot.'[1]

By 16 August she was able to report to her publishers: 'Since I last wrote to you I have been getting on with my book as well as I can, and I think I may venture to say that in a few weeks I hope to have the pleasure of placing the manuscript in the hands of Mr. Smith.' And sooner than they dared to expect came the news, in a letter of the 29th: 'The book is now finished (thank God).'[2]

The inability to judge her own achievement still harassed her. 'I thought I should be able to tell whether it was equal to "Jane Eyre" or not, but I find I cannot—it may be better, it may be worse—I shall be curious to have your opinion, my own is of no value.'[3]

Now that it was finished, the realization of the support it had been to her was intensified: 'Whatever now becomes of the work, the occupation of writing it has been a boon to me: it took me out of dark and desolate reality into an unreal but happier region. . . . You can write nothing of value unless you give yourself wholly to the theme, and when you so give yourself you lose appetite and sleep—it cannot be helped.'[4]

Cornhill's first reaction to the news was to suggest that some allusion be made in the preface to the loss the author had sustained by the deaths of Ellis and Acton Bell. With such publicity, if that is what it was, Charlotte would have no truck; she wrote at once to Mr. Williams on 31 August:

My dear Sir—I cannot change my preface. I can shed no tears before the public, nor utter any groan in the public ear. The *deep*, real tragedy of our domestic experience is yet terribly fresh in my mind and memory. It is not a time to be talked about to the indifferent. . . . What we deeply feel is our own. . . . Ellis and Acton Bell were, for me, Emily and Anne; my sisters— to me intimately near, tenderly dear—to the public they were nothing.[5]

Before ever the manuscript was finished, it had been agreed, on a suggestion of Mr. Williams', that instead of committing it to the post, it should be picked up by James Taylor on his way south from a holiday in Scotland. The suggestion did not displease Charlotte, though it put her in some perplexity. 'Did I see Mr. Taylor when I was in London; I cannot remember him,'[6] she frankly owned to Mr. Williams.

1 CB to WSW, 26 July 1849: *W & S* iii. 9.
2 CB to WSW, 29 Aug. 1849: *W & S* iii. 15.   3 Ibid.
4 Ibid.   5 CB to WSW, 31 Aug. 1849: *W & S* iii. 15.
6 CB to WSW, 24 Aug. 1849: *W & S* iii. 14.

And she was by no means certain how best to entertain a gentleman visitor. She wrote to Mr. Williams on 24 August:

I would with pleasure offer him the home hospitalities of the Parsonage for a few days, if I could at the same time offer him the company of a brother, or if my father were young enough and strong enough to walk with him on the moors. . . . Without being in the least misanthropical or sour-natured, papa habitually prefers solitude to society. . . . Were it not for difficulties of this sort, I believe I should ere this have asked you to come down to Yorkshire. . . . You will see the force of these considerations, and understand why I only ask Mr. Taylor to come for a day instead of requesting the pleasure of his company for a longer period; you will believe me also . . . when I say I shall be most happy to see him.[1]

Mr. Taylor was not daunted, though further warned by Charlotte that he would 'find Haworth a strange, uncivilised little place, such as, I dare say, he never saw before,' and made an appointment for Saturday, 8 September.

The visit certainly had repercussions, though Charlotte allowed little trace of them to appear in her immediate letters. All she cared for at the moment was the impression *Shirley* would make at Cornhill. Inevitably a week passed before she could hear of them, and then the pronouncement was favourable.

Charlotte wrote Mr. Williams on 17 September:

Your letter gave me great pleasure. An author who has showed his book to none, held no consultation about plan, subject, characters, or incidents, asked and had no opinion from one living being, but fabricated it darkly in the silent workshop of his own brain—such an author awaits with a singular feeling the report of the first impression . . . and truly glad is he when that report proves favourable.[2]

Now that the long effort was over, she wanted change and companionship, and wrote urging Ellen to visit her. Family affairs (including the belated marriage of Ann Nussey—aged 53—to Mr. Robert Clapham) prevented Ellen accepting for the time being, but instead it was agreed that Charlotte should go to Brookroyd for a week—from 24 to 31 October.

Her visit coincided with the publication of *Shirley* on 26 October, and she was amazed to find herself famous in the quiet circles she had known since her schooldays at Roe Head. She had not counted on the effect of lifting the embargo of silence on Ellen. Only the previous month she had reassured Mr. Williams about this: 'You

[1] CB to WSW, 24 Aug. 1849: *W & S* iii. 13–14.
[2] CB to WSW, 17 Sept. 1849: *W & S* iii. 21.

asked me . . . whether I thought I should escape identification in York-shire. I am so little known that I think I shall. Besides, the book is far less founded on the Real than perhaps appears. It would be difficult to explain to you how little actual experience I have had of life, how few persons I have known, and how very few have known me.'[1]

Of these 'very few', however, several now revealed themselves as knowing her secret, and as having already read *Jane Eyre*. It was Charlotte's first experience of bridging the two worlds of Charlotte Brontë and Currer Bell, and she did not find it an entirely happy one.

There was her godmother, for instance, Mrs. Atkinson, wife of the Vicar of Hartshead, who considered *Jane Eyre* a wicked book, bold, irreligious, and unwomanly; and who desired to see her no more. There was Miss Wooler who, to Charlotte's amazement, far from feeling gratification at her brilliant pupil turning novelist, felt obliged to give her an assurance that nothing should be changed between them! Others there were, old school connexions like Amelia Walker of Lascelles Hall, who renewed acquaintance for the pleasure of patronizing her. For the most part, however, the Birstall circle—the Nusseys, the Taylors, the Vicar's family (the Rev. W. M. Heald who had his role in *Shirley* as the Rev. Cyril Hall)—showed their pride in her achievement. Charlotte wrote to Mr. Williams on 1 November:

During my late visit I have too often had reason, sometimes in a pleasant, sometimes in a painful form, to fear that I no longer walk invisible. 'Jane Eyre', it appears, has been read all over the district—a fact of which I never dreamt—I met sometimes with new deference, with augmented kindness: old schoolfellows and old teachers, too, greeted me with generous warmth. And, again, ecclesiastical brows lowered thunder at me.[2]

With Ellen, in the hour before bed-time when the friends sat with their feet on the fender and curled their hair, Charlotte no doubt spoke of James Taylor's visit, describing his appearance, his forceful manner, his evident interest in her. It was enough for the incorrigibly romantic Ellen to draw deductions that Charlotte had very shortly to snub.

Her complimentary copies of *Shirley* did not reach her till late (owing to a confusion of posts), and it was from home on 5 November that she acknowledged them to Mr. Williams: 'I was very much pleased with the appearance and getting up of the book; it looks well.'[3]

The first review to reach her, from the *Daily News*, filled her 'with

[1] CB to WSW, 21 Sept. 1849: *W & S* iii. 23.
[2] CB to WSW, 1 Nov. 1849: *W & S* iii. 29.
[3] CB to WSW, 5 Nov. 1849: *W & S* iii. 31.

indignation and grief'; she told Mr. Williams that it struck her 'as to the last degree incompetent, ignorant and flippant. A thrill of mutiny went all through me when I read his small effusion. To be judged by such a one revolted me.'[1] The reviewer had found the first chapter of *Shirley* 'disgusting and vulgar'.

'*It is not, it is real*', Charlotte retorted; the hurtful attack on her veracity and taste cruelly reviving her sense of isolation in an alien world. 'Were my sisters now alive they and I would laugh over this notice; but they sleep, they will wake no more for me, and I am a fool to be so moved by what is not worth a sigh.'[2]

The truth was, as she confessed, that her bereavement had made her ultra-sensitive to all harsh treatment; lacking the love and understanding of those dearest to her, she felt defenceless before the world. 'You must spare me if I seem hasty', she added in a postscript, 'I fear I really am not so firm as I used to be, nor so patient. Whenever any shock comes, I feel that almost all supports have been withdrawn.'[3]

Happily, the majority of the reviews that came in thick and fast, brought her comfort; they were very cordial.

The Morning Chronicle said:

'Shirley' is an admirable book, totally free from cant affectation, or conventional tinsel of any kind: genuine English in the independence and uprightness of the tone of thought, in the purity of heart and feeling, which pervade it; genuine English in the masculine vigour or rough originality of its conception of character; and genuine English in style and diction. It is a tale of passion and character rather than of incident; and, thus considered, it is a veritable triumph of psychology.

The Times said:

'Shirley' is very clever. It could not be otherwise. The faculty of graphic description, strong imagination, fervid and masculine diction, analytic skill, all are visible. . . . Gems of rare thought and glorious passion shine here and there.

The Morning Post said:

'Shirley' is a novel of remarkable power and brilliancy, it is calculated to rouse attention, excite the imagination, and keep the faculties in eager and impatient suspense. It will unquestionably add to the reputation of the author. Currer Bell's powers of description are displayed to greater advantage in this novel than in its predecessor.

[1] CB to WSW, 1 Nov. 1849: *W & S* iii. 29–33.
[2] CB to WSW, 1 Nov. 1849: *W & S* iii. 29–30.   [3] Ibid.

Many a pang did reference to Ellis and Acton Bell in the reviews occasion her. 'The "Critic", our old friend, is a friend still', Charlotte wrote to Mr. Williams on 19 November. 'Ellis and Acton Bell are referred to, and where are they? I will not repine. Faith whispers they are not in those graves to which imagination turns—the feeling, thinking, the inspired natures are beyond earth, in a region more glorious. I believe them blessed.'

With touching regard for her correspondent's patience, she added: 'Does it weary you that I refer to them? If so, forgive me. . . .'[1]

In such a mood, the letter she received next day from one of the recipients of her book—Mrs. Gaskell—was bound to move her deeply: 'The letter you forwarded me this morning', she wrote Mr. Williams on 20 November, 'was from Mrs. Gaskell, authoress of "Mary Barton"; she said I was not to answer it, but I cannot help doing so. The note brought the tears to my eyes. She is a good, she is a great woman. Proud am I that I can touch a chord of sympathy in souls so noble.'[2]

In the same letter Charlotte asked Mr. Williams to send Harriet Martineau a copy from herself. 'For her character—as revealed in her works—I have a lively admiration, a deep esteem. Will you enclose with the volume(s) the accompanying note?'[3]

Harriet Martineau kept this first communication from Currer Bell; it read: 'Currer Bell offers a copy of "Shirley" to Miss Martineau's acceptance, in acknowledgement of the pleasure and profit he has derived from her works. When Currer Bell first read "Deerbrook" he tasted a new and keen pleasure, and experienced a genuine benefit. In his mind "Deerbrook" ranks with the writings that have really done him good, added to his stock of ideas, and rectified his views of life.'

Miss Martineau's answer was heart-warming, as Mrs. Gaskell's had been. 'I ought to be thankful,' Charlotte wrote Mr. Williams on 24 November, 'and I trust I am for such testimonies of sympathy from the first order of minds. When Mrs. Gaskell tells me she shall keep my works as a treasure for her daughters, and when Harriet Martineau testifies affectionate approbation, I feel the sting taken from the strictures of another class of critics.'[4]

With these ladies, her fellow authors, she still strictly adhered to the *nom de plume*; she was more anxious than ever, she told Mr. Williams,

---

[1] CB to WSW, 19 Nov. 1849: *W & S* iii. 39.
[2] CB to WSW, 20 Nov. 1849: *W & S* iii. 40.
[3] Ibid.   [4] CB to WSW, 24 Nov. 1849: *W & S* iii. 45.

to preserve her secret—above all, to pass for a man in a world where the weight of opinion was so heavily charged against women. 'I wish you did not think me a woman—I wish all reviewers believed Currer Bell to be a man,' she wrote to G. H. Lewes on November 1st, 'they would be more just to him. You will, I know, keep measuring me by some standard of what you deem becoming to my sex; where I am not what you consider graceful you will condemn me.'[1]

To George Lewes she acknowledged her emotional need for a life of absorbing work. Recalling their earlier exchanges, she wrote: '. . . since then it has been my lot to pass some black milestones in the journey of life. Since then there have been intervals when I have ceased to care about literature and critics and fame; when I have lost sight of whatever was prominent in my thoughts at the first publication of "Jane Eyre"; but now I want these things to come back vividly, if possible. . . .'[2]

The yearning for a renewal of that earlier happy phase, when success came to her overnight with *Jane Eyre*, for the gift of intellectual stimulus, of human sympathy and friendship, made her accept in principle an invitation from her publishers to go up to London. She told Mr. Williams on 15 November:

I am trying by degrees to inure myself to the thought of some day stepping over to Keighley, taking the train to Leeds, thence to London, and once more venturing to set foot in the strange, busy whirl of the Strand and Cornhill. I want to talk to you a little and to hear by word of mouth how matters are progressing. Whenever I come, I must come quietly and but for a short time—I should be unhappy to leave papa longer than a fortnight.[3]

By the 19th the 'resolution of coming to London' was presenting itself to her 'under a pleasant aspect'. Possibly the welcome given her book by Harriet Martineau and Mrs. Gaskell heartened her to make a tentative—very tentative—appearance among her fellow writers.

To Ellen, in announcing her trip to London (to be followed by a visit from Ellen to Haworth), she reported having the dressmaker in the house, and at the end of a week expressed herself as satisfied with her work. 'The dress-maker has done my small matters pretty well, but I wish you could have looked over them, and given a dictum. I insisted on the dresses being made quite plainly.'

1 CB to G. H. Lewes, 1 Nov. 1849: *W & S* iii. 31.
2 Ibid.
3 CB to WSW, 15 Nov. 1849: *W & S* iii. 35–36.

There had been a slight demur on her part in accepting an invitation to stay with George Smith's mother, and she had suggested an alternative plan. Since the previous year she had renewed correspondence with her Brussels friends the Wheelwrights, who had settled again in London that autumn and given her a standing invitation to come whenever it suited her. She sensed (erroneously as it turned out) that her identity and activities as Currer Bell might not appeal to their earnest cast of mind, and submitted therefore with a good grace to staying with the Smiths.

On Thursday, 29 November, accordingly, she went up to London. The Smiths were still living in the house she had visited with Anne the previous year, 4 Westbourne Place; the house whose many floors and great array of room-doors made her 'stand in tribulation' which to open, as she later confessed to her hostess; from whom and from the whole family, Charlotte received the most genuine kindness.

She told Ellen in a first letter dated 4 December:

I found, when I mentioned to Mr. Smith my plan of going to Dr. Wheelwright's it would not do at all, he would have been seriously hurt; he made his mother write to me, and thus I was persuaded to make my principal stay at his house. I have found no reason to regret this decision. Mrs. Smith received me at first like one who had received the strictest orders to be scrupulously attentive. I had fires in my bedroom evening and morning, wax candles, etc, etc. Mrs. Smith and her daughters seemed to look upon me with a mixture of respect and alarm. But all this is now changed, that is to say, the attention and politeness continue as great as ever, but the alarm and estrangement are quite gone. She treats me as if she liked me, and I begin to like her much; kindness is a potent heartwinner. I had not judged too favourably of her son on a first impression; he pleases me much. I like him better even as a son and brother than as a man of business.[1]

Mr. Williams, too, she saw again with pleasure. But undeniably her chief scrutiny was directed on James Taylor, the third power in the firm, and, so far, the unknown quantity for Charlotte.

Mr. Taylor—the little man—has again shown his parts; of him I have not yet come to a clear decision; abilities he has, for he rules the firm (which Dr. Wheelwright told me the other day is considerably the largest publishing concern in London), he keeps 40 young men under strict control of his iron will. His young superior likes him, which, to speak truth is more than I do at present; in fact, I suspect he is of the Helstone order of men—rigid, despotic,

[1] Quoted from *W & S* (the text in *SLL*, No. 398, is incomplete and erroneous): *W & S* iii. 52.

and self-willed. He tries to be very kind and even to express sympathy sometimes, but he does not manage it. He has a determined, dreadful nose in the middle of his face which when poked into my countenance cuts into my soul like iron. Still he is horribly intelligent, quick, searching, sagacious, and with a memory of relentless tenacity. To turn to Williams after him, or to Smith himself, is to turn from granite to easy down or warm fur.[1]

The fact was that James Taylor was falling in love with Charlotte, in the masterful, domineering manner of her own heroes, and the resemblance, touching her in a weak spot, startled her not a little. The more he thought he recognized the method of winning her, the more she shrank within herself.

Ellen, immediately jumping to conclusions, received a cool douche on her ardour. 'You seem to suppose', Charlotte wrote to her on 9 December, 'I must be very happy, dear Nell, and I see you have twenty romantic notions in your head about me. These last you may dismiss at once.'[2] Ellen was recompensed, however, with a further allusion to the subject of her chief interest: 'An attack of rheumatic fever has kept poor Mr. Taylor out of the way since I wrote last', Charlotte added: 'I am sorry for his sake.' Though intending to convey her own relief in the circumstances, Charlotte could not prevent herself feeling sympathy with the victim of rheumatic fever provided he remained out of her sight. This attitude was to be typical of the whole course of her relations with him: she was drawn to him in absence, and repelled in his company.

Charlotte's wish to preserve her incognito, and, above all, to prevent any reference to her personal sorrows reaching her public, while respected by her publishers, could not entirely be achieved. This is shown by the partial truths concerning Currer Bell being rumoured about town after the publication of *Shirley*; a letter from Catherine Winkworth to her friend Eliza Paterson is typical: 'So you like "Shirley" better than "Jane Eyre",' she wrote from Gt. Ormond Street on 5 December, 'so do I, in some parts. . . . The book is infinitely more original and full of character than the ordinary run of novels—it belongs quite to a higher class—but it is also infinitely below such as "Mary Barton" and "Deerbrook".' (Catherine Winkworth was a close friend both of Mrs. Gaskell and of Harriet Martineau.)

Commenting on the 'unhappy tone of the book', Miss Winkworth

---

[1] Quoted from *W & S* (the text in *SLL*, No. 398, is incomplete and erroneous): *W & S* iii. 52.   [2] CB to EN, 9 Dec. 1849: *W & S* iii. 55.

said: 'That is not . . . so much to be wondered at, when one knows that the author is herself threatened with consumption at this time, and has lost her two sisters, Ellis and Acton Bell by it. Their real name is Brontë; they are of the Nelson family.'[1] Catherine Winkworth would in good time learn from Currer Bell herself the rights and wrongs of her assumptions.

One of Charlotte's first actions on reaching town was to call on Dr. and Mrs. Wheelwright whom she had not seen since Brussels. They were only just settled in a house in Lower Phillimore Place, Kensington (29, the third house from the corner of Argyll Road), which had formerly (from 1813 to 1824) belonged to the painter David Wilkie. It was an old house, one of a terrace facing the Kensington Road, and built in the 1780's by the then owner of the Phillimore estate, William Phillimore. On its first completion it had had the misfortune to arouse the ire of George III driving past on his way to Kensington Palace. The terrace and its pendant—Upper Phillimore Place—was decorated along the whole length of its front with one of the conventional 'linen' mouldings on the level of the drawing-room floors. 'Dishclout Row!' shouted the King, on the terrace being pointed out to him; 'nothing but a Dishclout Row!'

Uniform the houses were, but built of seasoned brick and lying back from the road behind railed-off gardens; wrought-iron balconies marked the drawing-room floors (as well as the offending 'dishclout' motif) and the Wheelwrights were lucky in that their house was covered by a creeper.

None of the Wheelwright girls had married since Charlotte had parted from them in Brussels (their ages now were: Laetitia 21, Emily 20, Frances 18, and Sarah-Ann 15). The friendship resumed on the same cordial and confidential level that it had reached when interrupted; with Dr. and Mrs. Wheelwright, Charlotte found herself in the same sincere, unaffected atmosphere that had pleased her so much before.

To her surprise, and no little trepidation, she found that the secret of her authorship was already known to the family. A review of *Shirley* in the current *Illustrated London News* had given away the identity of Currer Bell to their penetrating observation. They did not need to be told that the creator of 'Hortense Moore' had been at the Pensionnat Heger with them, for they instantly recognized in her the living likeness of Mademoiselle Haussé. No one but Charlotte Brontë,

---

[1] Catherine Winkworth to Eliza Paterson: *W & S* iii. 55.

they declared, could have drawn that portrait; it was executed to the life. Contrary to Charlotte's anxious anticipations, the Wheelwrights thought no less of her for being a successful novelist, and Dr. Wheelwright had nothing but praise to bestow on her publishers—as she reported in her letter to Ellen.[1]

Her visit to Kensington occurred on the day Thackeray was expected to dinner at the Smiths (Monday, 3 December), and the Wheelwright girls remembered in after years Charlotte's anticipatory agitation. She left them with the promise of spending a couple of days with them before leaving London.

In her excitement and hurry that day, Charlotte had eaten nothing since 'a very slight breakfast'; and confessed later to being 'thoroughly faint from inanition' by the time Thackeray was announced at 7 o'clock. 'Excitement and exhaustion together made savage work of me that evening', she told Ellen, adding ruefully: 'What he thought of me I cannot tell.'

Recalling that first encounter with an author she idolized, she later told Mr. Williams: 'When Mr. Thackeray was announced, and I saw him enter, looked up at his tall figure, heard his voice, the whole incident was truly dream-like.'[2]

Thackeray's conduct that evening did not, however, escape all censure on the part of his admirer. Crippled with shyness as Charlotte generally was in company, the dread of being 'lionized' as a successful author now imposed a further strain on her nerves, and on her hosts' diplomacy. George Smith related in after years how, in inviting Thackeray, he had impressed on him the need to avoid all mention of Currer Bell and 'his' works when conversing with Miss Brontë; and how mischievously the Titan failed him. Smith reported:

When the ladies had left the dining-room I offered Thackeray a cigar. The custom of smoking after dinner was not common then, but I had been told he liked a cigar, and so provided for his tastes. To my dismay, when we rejoined the ladies in the drawing-room, he approached Miss Brontë and quoted a . . . passage from 'Jane Eyre'. It was that in which she describes 'the warning fragrance' which told of the approach of Mr. Rochester. . . . The quotation . . . did credit to Thackeray's memory . . . but not to his memory of his agreement with me. Miss Brontë's face showed her discomposure, and in a chilly fashion she turned off the allusion. . . . She cast an accusing look at me.[3]

---

[1] For further data upon the Wheelwright family see J. J. Green, 'The Brontë–Wheelwright Friendship', *Friends Quarterly Examiner*, Nov. 1915. See also below, Additional Notes.　　　　　[2] CB to WSW, 19 Dec. 1849: *SBC* 390.

[3] *Cornhill Magazine*, Dec. 1900.

Reporting on the evening to her father next day, Charlotte mentioned none of its trials:

Yesterday I saw Mr. Thackeray. He dined here with some other gentlemen. [Sir John Forbes was of the party.] He is a very tall man—above six feet high—with a peculiar face—not handsome, very ugly indeed, generally somewhat stern and satirical in expression, but capable also of a kind look. He was not told who I was, he was not introduced to me, but I soon saw him looking at me through his spectacles; and when we all rose to go down to dinner he just stepped quietly up and said, 'Shake hands'; so I shook hands. He spoke very few words to me, but when he went away he shook hands again in a very kind way. It is better I should think, to have him for a friend than an enemy, for me he is a most formidable-looking personage. I listened to him as he conversed with the other gentlemen. All he says is most simple, but often cynical, harsh, and contradictory. I get on quietly. Most people know me, I think, but they are far too well bred to show that they know me, so that there is none of that bustle or that sense of publicity I dislike.[1]

Charlotte's inability to accept Thackeray on his own terms was the cause of her greatest social failure. He was irritated by the exalted standard she exacted from those she admired, even from such a man of whims and unreliable moods as himself. Hers was the loss, since in company she had little to give and he had much; but that much he withheld, retreating behind his defensive armour of cynical badinage, with which he sought protection against the 'bores' he so much execrated in society. The essential chivalry and sentimentality of his nature were veiled from her. She would have been astounded by his tribute to her after her death, in which he recalled that very first meeting at George Smith's:

I saw her first as I rose out of an illness from which I had never thought to recover. I remember the trembling little frame, the little hand, the great honest eyes. An impetuous honesty seemed to me to characterise the woman. . . . I fancied an austere little Joan of Arc marching in upon us, and rebuking our easy lives, our easy morals. She gave me the impression of being a very pure, and lofty, and high-minded person.[2]

[1] CB to Revd. PB, 4 Dec. 1849: *W & S* iii. 54, erroneously dated and quoted in *SLL*, No. 510. George Smith reported further of that evening: '. . . Thackeray however, had no sense of either awkwardness or guilt. From my house he went to the smoking-room of the Garrick Club and said: "Boys! I have been dining with 'Jane Eyre'." To have her identity expounded in the smoking-room of the Garrick Club was the last experience which the morbidly shy and sensitive little lady would have chosen.' Quoted in *Letters and Private Papers of W. M. Thackeray*, ii. 612, from *The House of Smith, Elder*, pp. 67–68.
[2] 'The Last Sketch': *Cornhill Magazine*, Apr. 1860.

Thackeray had occasion on subsequent meetings with Charlotte in other years to feel the full force of her tongue and the flash of those 'great honest eyes' turned in condemnation upon him and his 'easy life', but he also penetrated to the heart of her mystery as only one or two others in all her circle ever did; and in charity, as well as chivalry, abstained from open judgement.[1]

Currer Bell's peculiar brand of shyness was a trial not only to herself but to her hosts. George Smith related how her susceptibility and 'dislike of fuss' sometimes threatened to daunt even Mrs. Smith's generalship. 'My mother and sisters found her a somewhat difficult guest,' he wrote, 'and I am afraid she was not perfectly at her ease with them. Strangers used to say that they were afraid of her. She was very quiet and self-absorbed, and gave the impression that she was always engaged in observing and analysing the people she met.'[2] Charlotte herself was much concerned at her inability to come out of her shell; it was a physical as well as a psychological disability, which she deeply regretted since she saw it distressed those whose intentions were so kind. She wrote to Ellen on returning home:

I used to bear up as well and as long as I possibly could, for, whenever I flagged, I could see Mr. Smith become disturbed; he always thought that something had been said or done to annoy me, which never once happened. ... I explained to him over and over again that my occasional silence was only failure of the power to talk, never of the will, but still he always seemed to fear there was another cause underneath.[3]

Mr. Smith's concern for his author's pleasure and comfort was not lost on his mother. That lady, from his first assuming the control of the family fortunes, had but one purpose: to ensure his happiness and further his interests, among which had, inescapably, to be counted, sooner or later, the prospect of his marriage. That Mrs. Smith preferred to envisage her son's future partner as one endowed with health and some few graces of fortune and physique was only natural. Hence the unflagging vigilance with which she surrounded those within whose orbit he came—Currer Bell among the rest. Charlotte wrote to Ellen:

Mrs. Smith is rather stern, but she has sense and discrimination; she watched me very narrowly when surrounded by gentlemen, she never took

1 For Thackeray's estimate of CB see *Letters and Private Papers*, ed. G. N. Ray, ii. 318–19, 340–1, and iii. 12, 13, 15, 19, 67, 231, 233, 248, 252, 253.
2 *Cornhill Magazine*, Dec. 1900.
3 CB to EN, 18 Dec. 1849: *W & S* iii. 60.

her eye from me, I liked the surveillance, both when it kept guard over me amongst many, or only with her cherished one. She soon, I am convinced, saw in what light I received all, Thackeray included. Her 'George' is a very fine specimen of a young English man-of-business; so I regard him, and I am proud to be one of his props.[1]

While Mrs. Smith watched Charlotte and her son, Charlotte watched them. As she listened and looked, the story-teller in her, always on the alert, was already busily spinning the opening pages of *Villette*. 'Emptied' of her last tale, and already intellectually athirst for fresh material, Charlotte happened at that identical moment to be subjected to impressions and connexions which set her inventing furiously. The renewed intercourse with the Wheelwrights awakened vivid echoes of the Brussels scenes and experiences, and supplied the spark to a powder-magazine long stored away ready for just such an explosion. If the actual writing of *Villette* was not begun for months, the conception of it took place that winter in London. The long malady that had been her love for M. Heger had, in the past year of suffering from other causes, been shed, and was now something de-tached from herself, to be looked at and assessed for what it had been, without it affecting her personally any more. Fresh in her recollection, too, were 'the fine antique streets' and the order and cleanliness of Burlington, revisited that summer. No wonder George Smith was sometimes alarmed by her silences. Both he and Mr. Williams put themselves out to please their author by every means in their power. Charlotte was taken to the theatre to see Macready in *Macbeth* and in *Othello*, and astonished a dinner-party by saying she did not like him, judging his acting as much outdistanced by Shakespeare's *writing* as John Forster's 'loud swagger' was by Thackeray's 'simple port'.

She was taken to the National Gallery and to an exhibition of Turner's paintings which delighted her above all. 'Nothing charmed me more during my stay in town', she told Miss Wooler of his water-colours.[2] Mr. Williams took her to the new Houses of Parliament.

Perhaps the highlight of her visit was the meeting with Harriet Martineau. From the Smiths Charlotte learnt within a few days of arriving in town that Harriet Martineau was staying at her cousin's, Richard Martineau, in Westbourne Street, just round the corner from

[1] Ibid.
[2] CB to Margaret Wooler, 28 Jan 1850: Fitzwilliam Museum.

Westbourne Place. She sat down at once to write her a note. It was dated 8 December and was handed to Miss Martineau at dinner. It read:

My dear Madam, I happen to be staying in London for a few days; and having just heard that you likewise are in town, I could not help feeling a strong wish to see you. If you will permit me to call upon you, have the goodness to tell me when to come. . . . Do not think this request springs from mere curiosity. I hope it has its origins in better feelings. It would grieve me to lose this chance of seeing one whose works have so often made her the subject of my thoughts.

The note was signed 'Currer Bell'.[1]

Harriet Martineau has told in her *Autobiography* of the receipt of that note and of her instant reply. Her cousins, Richard Martineau and his wife, suggested Currer Bell should join them at tea the next evening, Sunday, at 6.0 p.m. To which Charlotte sent round a rather touching note of acceptance. 'My dear Madam,' she wrote, 'I hope to have the pleasure of seeing you at six o'clock to-day: and I shall try now to be patient till six o'clock comes.'[2]

The woman Charlotte so eagerly waited to see had a double claim on her interest: she was, indisputably, the leading woman writer of the day (neither Mrs. Gaskell's, Mrs. Browning's, nor Charlotte's own reputation as yet equalled hers), and she had for Charlotte the additional personal interest of being sister to the Revd. James Martineau who had encouraged and befriended Branwell. Though Charlotte did not know it at the time, the intense affection and intellectual partnership existing between Harriet and her brother had many resemblances to her own with Branwell; and like that it was to suffer the same tragic end. At the time of the meeting with Charlotte, Harriet Martineau was 47, having been born at Norwich on 12 June 1802.[3] Her reputation as a writer and social reformer had been established as long ago as 1832 when she had launched her series of tales bearing on aspects of political economy. Of a family of Huguenot refugees her forebears had been professional men, surgeons and lawyers, in the city; her father was the first 'manufacturer' in the family, as she liked to emphasize. Her background was thus dissenting and middle-class, her parents, because of their religious isolation (they were Unitarians), belonging to the shop-keeper class rather than the gentry of Norwich. Her education was nevertheless

---

[1] Harriet Martineau, *Autobiography* (3 vols., 1877), ii. 323 et seq.
[2] Idem.
[3] Wheatley, Vera, *The Life and Work of Harriet Martineau*, 1957.

remarkably thorough for a girl of her time and station, and though born with an unhappy temperament and living on a footing of constant disharmony with her family—with her mother and one sister in particular—her exceptional intelligence was acknowledged by them and her avid craving for knowledge not opposed. Her severe deafness at the age of sixteen (the result in great measure of the emotional stresses of family life) allowed her considerable liberty to lead the studious life she preferred. Though she had, earlier, attended two good schools, her education came chiefly through her own extensive reading.

The ruin of her father's business after the Napoleonic wars (he was a manufacturer of army cloth, like Mary Taylor's father), his subsequent death, and the virtual destitution of his widow and daughters gave Harriet her great chance to earn her own and her mother's keep by writing. She began by reviewing books for *The Repository* at a salary of £15 per annum and by good fortune won three prizes offered by the Unitarian Association for the best exposition of their tenets to be presented to the Catholics, the Jews, and the Mohammedans.

Her wide reading of the political news of the day as the country moved inevitably towards reform made her an ardent advocate of Reform, and not only within the framework of Parliament. She was oppressed by the countless injustices rife in the country, and conceived a plan on a really gigantic scale for bringing to the public notice the most blameworthy issues of the hour. She planned to write a series of tales bearing upon subjects like population problems, taxation, the Poor Laws, and education, presenting them as matters of general interest and importance. She was not a writer with a gift for creating plots and had to depend on personal experience and the reported experience of others.

It took her two and a half years to write the whole series of her tales, but she made £2,000 from them. A nation-wide interest was aroused in her project and she received letters from men in many walks of life, Cabinet Ministers, Manchester cotton operatives, Poor-law Guardians, and school-masters, who supplied her with hard facts and figures. These were what she wanted to prove her theses. The titles of the tales were as varied as their subjects, and were well chosen. 'The Hamlets' exemplified the proposed Poor-law reform; 'Berkeley the Banker' related the disasters of the years 1824–5, when private banks (her father's among them) were ruined; 'Sowers not Reapers' spoke against the Corn-laws; 'Cinnamon and Pearls' exposed the monopolies of the Ceylon trade. No sooner was this colossal task accomplished than she went to America, in August 1834, to see how their methods of 'applying justice and mercy' compared with the English. Wherever she went, she was hailed as the champion of the under-privileged.

Her only full-scale novel, *Deerbrook*, was written on her return to England, and barely finished before the inevitable breakdown interrupted her work. She became an invalid for six years, during which time, as she liked later to declare, she achieved her 'complete religious emancipation'—the first step towards the grievous rupture with her favourite brother James. The cure was due in the end, she firmly believed, to mesmerism; it was first used in June 1844, and she was restored to normal health by November. She went to recuperate at Windermere, taking a house for six months 'which stands precisely at the head of the lake and whose grassplat is washed by its waters...'.[1]

She found there not only health but her spiritual home, and decided to settle in Windermere for good. 'My ideal of an innocent and happy life', she wrote in her *Autobiography*, 'was a house by my own among poor improvable neighbours, with young servants whom I might train and attach to myself; with pure air, a garden, leisure, solitude at command, and freedom to work in peace and quietness. When to all this could be added fine natural scenery, the temptations were such as London could not rival.'

With the Wordsworths for neighbours, she built herself a house at Ambleside which, from its commanding position, she called 'The Knoll'. In her thirty years' tenure, it became famous for the illustrious guests she received. In due course, Charlotte Brontë would be among the number.

Harriet Martineau and Charlotte were not at all alike. The one had discarded not only the religion of her fathers, but all religion; she was a woman of wide and practical knowledge, commanding a standing in the society of men by her sheer ability; widely travelled and possessed of countless friends in two hemispheres. She did not know what it was to be afraid so long as a truth remained to be proclaimed or a wrong to be righted. Literature had been for her a means to an end, not an end in itself as for Charlotte Brontë. Today Harriet Martineau would have sat on the bench of magistrates, won a seat in parliament, presided on international conferences, addressed audiences on television and radio; in the mid-nineteenth century her only weapon was a pen, and she wielded it to good account.

---

[1] Martineau, *Autobiography*: op. cit.

The sincerity and humanity of her motives were what chiefly mattered in Charlotte's eyes. Mrs. Smith had the kindness to send Charlotte round in the carriage for the call in Westbourne Street.

Harriet and her cousins had, meanwhile, turned Charlotte's letter over in every possible direction and decided that 'it was a *woman's* note'. Currer Bell was still an enigma for Harriet; she was full of curiosity. She recorded in her *Autobiography*:

I had more reason for interest than even the deeply-interested public in knowing who wrote 'Jane Eyre', for, when it appeared, I was taxed with the authorship . . . or with knowing the author and having supplied some of the facts for the first volume from my own childhood. When I read it I was convinced that it was by some friend of my own, who had portions of my childish experience in his or her mind. 'Currer Bell' told me long after, that she had read with astonishment those parts of 'Household Education' which relate to my own experience. It was like meeting her own fetch—so precisely were the fears and miseries there described the same as her own.[1]

Of that first meeting between the two women Harriet Martineau left a very graphic account:

We were in a certain state of excitement all day, and especially towards evening. A little before six there was a thundering rap: the drawing-room door was thrown open, and in stalked a gentleman six feet high. It was not 'Currer', but a philanthropist who had an errand about a model lodging-house. Minute by minute I, for one, wished him away; and he did go before any body else came. Precisely as the time-piece struck six a carriage stopped at the door; and after a minute of suspense, the footman announced, 'Miss Brogden'; whereupon my cousin informed me that it was Miss Bronti [*sic*]; for we had heard the name before, among others, in the way of conjecture. I thought her the smallest creature I had ever seen (except at a fair) and her eyes blazed, as it seemed to me. She glanced quickly round; and my trumpet pointing me out, she held out her hand frankly and pleasantly; and then came a moment which I had not anticipated. When she was seated by me on the sofa, she cast up at me such a look—so loving, so appealing—that, in con-nexion with her deep mourning dress, and the knowledge that she was the sole survivor of her family, I could with the utmost difficulty return her smile, or keep my composure. I should have been heartily glad to cry. We soon got on very well; and she appeared more at her ease that evening than I ever saw her afterwards, except when we were alone together. My hostess was so con-siderate as to leave us together after tea, in case of Charlotte Brontë desiring to have private conversation with me. She was glad of the opportunity to

[1] Idem.

consult me about certain strictures of the reviewers which she did not understand, and had every desire to profit by. I did not approve the spirit of those strictures; but I thought them not entirely groundless.

The meeting was a memorable one for both women and gave Charlotte that rare experience—a pleasure without alloy. Harriet Martineau was kind without being condescending, helpful without being officious, as full of life and zest and energy as Charlotte was nervously exhausted, pessimistic, despondent. But to true sympathy she always reacted and felt stronger, morally and physically, for it. The recollection of that meeting was uppermost in her mind when writing to thank Mr. Williams for all his attentions after her return home. 'Brief as my visit to London was, it must for me be memorable. I sometimes fancied myself in a dream—I could scarcely credit the reality of what passed. For instance, when I walked into the room and put my hand in Miss Martineau's, the action of saluting her and the fact of her presence seemed visionary.'[1]

Before leaving London she spent a couple of days with the Wheelwrights in Kensington, returning to Westbourne Place to spend the last evening with the Smiths. 'The evening after I left you', she wrote Laetitia on 17 December from home, 'passed better than I expected. Thanks to my substantial lunch and cheerful cup of coffee, I was able to wait the eight o'clock dinner with complete resignation, and to endure its length quite courageously, nor was I too much exhausted to converse.'

The Smiths' guests that evening were seven men, five of them critics, 'men more dreaded in the world of letters than you can conceive. I did not know how much their presence and conversation had exhausted me till they were gone,' Charlotte had to own to Laetitia, 'and then reaction commenced. . . . Night passed, morning came, and I rose without having known a moment's slumber. So utterly worn out was I when I got to Derby, that I was obliged to stay there the night.'[2]

To Mrs. Smith she wrote with a simplicity of expression that spoke of the genuine gratitude she felt. 'It made me rather sad to leave you; regretful partings are the inevitable penalty of pleasant visits. I believe I made no special acknowledgement of your kindness when I took leave, but I thought you very kind. I am glad to have had the oppor-

[1] CB to WSW, 19 Dec. 1849: *W & S* iii. 61.
[2] CB to Laetitia Wheelwright, 17 Dec. 1849: *W & S* iii. 59.

tunity of knowing you, and, whether I ever see you again or not, I must always recall with grateful pleasure the fortnight I spent under your roof.'[1]

There was a special message for 'Miss Smith' whose 'little boots are a perfect treasure of comfort; they kept my feet warm the whole way', and a letter enclosed for George Smith. She wrote him:

> I should not feel content if I omitted writing to you as well as to your mother, for I must tell you as well as her how much the pleasure of my late visit was enhanced by her most considerate attention and goodness. As to yourself, what can I say? Nothing. And it is as well; words are not at all needed. Very easy it is to discover that with you to gratify others it is to gratify yourself; to serve others is to afford yourself a pleasure. I suppose you will experience your share of ingratitude and encroachment, but do not let them alter you. Happily, they are the less likely to do this because you are half a Scotchman, and therefore must have inherited a fair share of prudence to qualify your generosity, and of caution to protect your benevolence. Currer Bell bids you farewell for the present.
>
> C.B.

Charlotte reached home on Saturday, 15 December, thankful to find that 'papa was quite well', and wrote her various letters of thanks on the 17th. The return, just in time for the anniversary of Emily's death on the 19th, needed to be charged with pleasant recollections of her trip; for ahead of her lay an unchanged desolation of winter and loneliness. She had, however, brought back with her from London two lasting sources of support: the germ of a new book, and the friendship of people like Harriet Martineau.

[1] CB to Mrs. Smith, 17 Dec. 1849: *W & S* iii. 58.

CHAPTER XXII

THE 'BRIGHT-HAIRED SPRITE'[1]

WHEN the Bells published their novels almost simultaneously in the autumn of 1847, rumour had been busy with their origins and identities. But the triumph of *Shirley*, and the partial lifting of the mystery surrounding its author, led to a manifestation of curiosity and indiscretion that is, perhaps, unique in the publishing annals of the nineteenth century. (Fanny Burney had provoked an almost identical reaction in the London drawing-rooms of seventy years before.)

What seemed inexplicable about Currer Bell was not only the fact that she was a woman (and a woman who had written 'a naughty novel' as G. H. Lewes reminded Charlotte on their first meeting) but an obscure woman, with no literary 'sponsor' or social backing; a woman living in retirement and moving in none of the accepted circles in which lady novelists—even her contemporaries Mrs. Gore or Miss Jewsbury—were usually found. She was a woman, furthermore, who was neither beautiful, striking, nor masculine in appearance and character—neither a Mrs. Norton nor a George Sand—and whose physical aspect, described by the few who had met her, helped in no way to explain her phenomenal emergence on the literary scene. Charlotte's appearance presented, rather, a challenge to credulity, for in a world predominantly controlled by men the reputation of women writers had generally to be backed by something more than their literary gifts. In this regard, Charlotte Brontë had nothing to offer the sensation-mongers, neither in looks, nor dress, nor conversation. Had she been even ordinarily good-looking and at her ease in society, the interest she aroused would not have been nearly so unbridled; for the conviction remained with those who had glimpsed her that there *was* something to explain. This exposed Charlotte to a good deal of vulgar curiosity, and she was pursued even into the privacy of her own home.

The few who met her were subjected to the most intensive questioning, and even Mrs. Gaskell cannot be wholly exonerated from fanning

[1] Mrs. Gaskell thus described CB on first reports: see below, p. 415.

the flame of this sort of sensationalism, however genuine was her early admiration for the work of Currer Bell. '. . . Have you heard that Harriet Martineau has sworn an eternal friendship with the authoress of "Shirley"? If not I'll tell you', she wrote to her friend Ann Shaen on 21 December. Mrs. Gaskell, living in Manchester, had not as yet met Currer Bell, but the circle of her acquaintance in London was wide (it included her intimates the Winkworth sisters, the Shaens, the Howitts, the Carlyles, and Harriet Martineau herself) and little that was new in the world of books remained hidden from her.

She sent 'Shirley' to H.M. H.M. acknowledged it in a note directed to Currer Bell, Esq—but inside written to a *lady*. Then came an answer requesting a personal interview . . . the time appointed was 6 o'clock on Sunday evening and the place appointed was at Mr. Richard Martineau's (married a Miss Needham) . . . so Mr. & Mrs. Martineau and Harriet M. sat with early tea before them, awaiting 6 o'clock, and their mysterious visitor, when Lo! and behold, as the clock struck in walked a little, very little bright-haired sprite, looking not above 15, very unsophisticated neat and tidy. She sat down and had tea with them, her name being still unknown.[1]

Catherine Winkworth's letter of 5 December, previously quoted, shows Mrs. Gaskell misinformed here. Charlotte's name was announced when she entered the room, and was already giving rise to the current rumour of her relationship with Lord Nelson, which was typical of the unreflecting acceptance of any fable concerning Currer Bell. The gossips could hardly have given much thought to the matter, for Nelson's Sicilian title of Duke of Bronté was merely a recompense bestowed by the King of Naples for services rendered.

Typical, too, of Mrs. Gaskell's narration of the meeting of Harriet Martineau and Currer Bell is the choice of such terms as 'mysterious visitor' and 'sprite'; for they perfectly express the writer's belief in—or wish for—a fairy-tale foundation to the Currer Bell story. However sober the facts themselves, Mrs. Gaskell could not keep out of her narration the sense of having made 'a scoop'.

Her account continued:

She said to H.M. 'What did you really think of "Jane Eyre"? H.M. 'I thought it a first-rate book.' Whereupon the little sprite went red all over with pleasure. After tea Mr. & Mrs. Richard M. withdrew, and left sprite to

[1] Mrs. Gaskell to Ann Shaen, 20 Dec. 1849: *Letters of Mrs. Gaskell*, ed. Chapple and Pollard, M.U.P., 1966, pp. 96–97. Ann Shaen sister of William Shaen who married Emily Winkworth.

a 2-hours tete-a-tete with H.M. to whom she revealed her name and the history of her life. Her father a Yorkshire clergyman who has never slept out of his house for 26 years [*sic*] she has lived a most retired life . . . never been in society, and many other particulars which H.M. is not at liberty to divulge. . . . H.M. is charmed with her; she is full of life and power etc, etc. H.M. hopes to be of great use to her. There! That's all I know, but I think it's a pretty good deal!

The future biographer of Charlotte Brontë, however close she would come to the sober truth of her subject's life, would never wholly be able to conquer her novelist's tendency to romance about ordinary things. Her palette was several tones too bright for the low key of Charlotte's background.

While the London coteries hummed with the echoes of Currer Bell's visit, the provinces began to awake to the realization that they had a *rara avis* in their midst, and to wish to hunt it out. Ellen Nussey's deferred visit was now realized, and she arrived at Haworth on 28 December; she stayed till 19 January. Her presence in the silent house recalled for Charlotte not only the last time she had come, just after Emily's death and at the beginning of Anne's illness, but the many other visits of the last eighteen years. Seeing Ellen afresh both against the background of their long friendship, and against the recent setting of the London scene, gave Charlotte certain insights into their relationship which she expressed in a letter of 3 January 1850 to Mr. Williams.

Excusing her delay in answering him because of the presence in the house of her friend, she said:

. . . just now I am enjoying the treat of my friend Ellen's society, and she makes me indolent and negligent—I am too busy talking to her all day to do anything else. . . . True friendship is no gourd, springing in a night and withering in a day. When I first saw Ellen I did not care for her; we were schoolfellows. In course of time we learnt each other's faults and good points. We were contrasts—still, we suited. Affection was first a germ, then a sapling—then a strong tree—now, no new friend, however lofty and profound in intellect—not even Miss Martineau herself—could be to me what Ellen is.[1]

What Ellen could *never* be, the confidante of her inner life of writer, Charlotte also revealed in the following summary: 'Yet she is no more

---

[1] CB to WSW, 3 Jan. 1850: *W & S* iii. 63–64.

than a conscientious, observant, calm well-bred Yorkshire girl. She is without romance. If she attempts to read poetry, or poetic prose, aloud, I am irritated and deprive her of the book—if she talks it, I stop my ears; but she is good; she is true; she is faithful, and I love her.'[1]

Just before Ellen's visit an echo of another sort reached Charlotte from the past, reviving memories of her life in Brussels. She was barely returned home from London when Joe Taylor called on 21 December bringing her an invitation to spend Christmas with his cousins, the Dixons, then living at Hay Hall, Birmingham.

Mary Dixon, after her travels on the Continent, had at last settled down in Birmingham to keep house for her two bachelor brothers, Abraham and George (later M.P. for Birmingham and Edgbaston), who were working their way up to become directors of the firm of Rabone Brothers, for which they had originally left Yorkshire. Temporarily they rented Hay Hall, a fourteenth-century manor-house enlarged in Tudor times, where the whole family, including the Taylor branch, were reuniting for Christmas. The wish to befriend Charlotte on the first Christmas after her triple bereavement, points to a recent resumption in relations between the friends, who had not seen each other since 1843 in Brussels.

Charlotte corresponded with Mary for the rest of her life. Her letters expressed constant concern for Mary's health and movements. After the death of Mr. Dixon senior in 1850 and the marriage of her Birmingham brothers, Mary again became something of a rolling stone, tempted to regain her health in the sun of the West Indies and of Australia, where her family had property. It is doubtful, however, if the two friends actually met again, the invitation to Charlotte—following on three weeks' absence from home—being unacceptable. 'Of course I could not go', she told Ellen.

Local awareness of Charlotte's new status as a successful author, which she first began to notice while staying with Ellen at the end of October, was now further forced on her by some direct reactions from the 'originals' of her *Shirley* characters. The Birstall circle were not only recognizing themselves in the book, but taking the author to task, and what was even more disagreeable to her, trying to extract confidences respecting the other characters. This at no time would Charlotte allow. But it was the price she had to pay for introducing living characters into her tales.

[1] Idem.

From the Revd. William Margetson Heald, her vicar at Birstall, Ellen received the following letter while staying with Charlotte that January: dated Birstall, near Leeds, 8 January 1850, it ran:

Fame says you are on a visit with the renowned Currer Bell, the 'great unknown' of the present day. The celebrated 'Shirley' has just found its way hither. . . . The story goes that either I or my father [both gentlemen were vicars of Birstall in succession] . . . are part of 'Currer Bell's' stock-in-trade, under the title of Mr. Hall, in that Mr. Hall is represented as black, bilious, and of dismal aspect, stooping a trifle, and indulging a little now and then in the indigenous dialect. This seems to sit very well on your humble servant—other traits do better for my good father than myself. However, though I had no idea that I should be made a means to amuse the public, Currer Bell is perfectly welcome to what she can make of so unpromising a subject. *But I think I have a fair claim in return to be let into the secret of the company I have got into.* Some of them are good enough to tell. . . . I can tabulate for instance, the Yorke family for the Taylors, Mr. Moore—Mr. Cartwright, and Mr. Helstone is clearly meant for Mr. Roberson, though the authoress has obviously got her idea of his character through an unfavourable medium . . . Mary thinks she descries Cecilia Crowther and Miss Johnstone [afterwards Mrs. Westerman] in two old maids.

Now pray get us a full light on all other names and localities that are adumbrated in this said 'Shirley'. When some of the prominent characters will be recognized by every one who knows our quarters, there can be no harm in letting one know who may be intended for the rest.[1]

Birstall, Hartshead, Dewsbury, Gomersal—the parishes and places featuring in *Shirley*—awoke gradually to their new-found importance and became vociferous in their curiosity. 'All you tell me about the notoriety of "Shirley" in Dewsbury, etc.,' Charlotte wrote Ellen on 19 January, 'is almost as good as an emetic to me. I really should "go off at side" if I thought too much about it.'

But worse was to follow for Charlotte. The ripple of repercussions over her 'Yorkshire' novel had inevitably spread. But equally inevitably the centre of interest came to be fixed on the last place Charlotte wanted, on Haworth itself.

John Brown, her father's sexton, came home from Halifax one day at the beginning of February brimming over with the news. No sooner spilt in his house in Church Lane than Martha his daughter came bursting with it into her mistress's presence. Charlotte wrote to Ellen on 4 February:

Martha came in yesterday, puffing and blowing, and much excited. 'I've heard sich news', she began. 'What about?' 'Please ma'am, you've been and written two books, the grandest books that ever was seen. My father heard it at Halifax, and Mr. George Taylor and Mr. Greenwood, and Mr. Merrall at Bradford; and they are going to have a meeting at the Mechanics' Institute, and to settle about ordering them.' 'Hold your tongue, Martha, and be off.' I fell into a cold sweat. 'Jane Eyre' will be read by John Brown, by Mrs. Taylor, and Betty. God help, keep, and deliver me![1]

Jane Eyre was not only read by the locals Charlotte expected, but it was read by her father's curate, Mr. Nicholls, who lodged at the Browns'. Having devoured it, he cried out for the 'other book': 'he is to have it next week—much good may it do him . . .' Charlotte commented sourly to Ellen. But Mr. Nicholls surprised her; he was delighted with *Shirley*. John Brown's wife, his landlady, reported being seriously alarmed lest he should have 'gone wrong in his head' as she heard him 'giving vent to roars of laughter as he sat alone, clapping his hands and stamping on the floor'. 'He would read all the scenes about the curates aloud to papa', Charlotte wryly commented to Ellen, ending with the almost audible groan: 'What Mr. Grant will say is another thing.'[2] Mr. Grant figured in *Shirley* as the egregious Mr. Donne.

While Ellen was staying at Haworth in January Charlotte had received a letter from Sir James Kay-Shuttleworth of Gawthorpe Hall, near Burnley, containing the inevitable commendations of *Shirley* and also expressing a most flattering desire for her acquaintance and inviting her to stay with his wife and himself at Gawthorpe. Charlotte instantly disposed of this threat, as she supposed, 'thanking and declining as neatly as I knew how'. But she counted without Sir James's tenacity, of which she knew nothing as yet. He wrote again; a letter which, Charlotte told Ellen, 'did not make me laugh'. She again declined the pressing invitation, making the kind of excuses she was accustomed to make in such emergencies: her father's age, his need of her care, and her own precarious health and inability to travel at that time of year.

Charlotte may not then have been aware that Sir James, the former Dr. Kay, had counted among his multiple activities that of practising physician at the Manchester dispensary twenty years before, and that he retained throughout his long and varied career in public life an acute interest in his first profession. To know that Currer Bell added

[1] CB to EN, 4 Feb. 1850: *W & S* iii. 73.
[2] CB to EN, 28 Jan. 1850: *W & S* iii. 71.

indifferent health to her other sensational attractions as the season's most enigmatic novelist instantly doubled his interest in her. The misfortune from Charlotte's point of view lay in the fact that Gawthorpe Hall was a mere ten miles as the crow flies across the Lancashire border from Haworth. Since Currer Bell would not come to Gawthorpe, the owner of Gawthorpe would call on Currer Bell. This the purposeful gentleman announced his intention of doing in yet another courtly note, naming the day and hour for his call. In vain Charlotte replied to Lady Shuttleworth, expressing her 'scruple that it should be so little worth your while'. The call was made, with due state, on the morning of 1 March.

In Sir James Kay-Shuttleworth the 'curiosity' hunt in pursuit of the 'bright-haired sprite' reached its height; none of Currer Bell's readers pursued her quite so persistently or so unremittingly as he. Actuated by motives of true benevolence, as well as of business acumen, Sir James had but to see the frail form and experience the confining atmosphere of the parsonage to be convinced of his ability to lend health to the one and social status to the other. Currer Bell quite evidently needed a physician, and a sponsor in society—and Sir James was prepared to fill both roles at an instant's notice. Charlotte was vehemently urged to step into the waiting carriage and return forthwith with Sir James and Lady Shuttleworth to Gawthorpe Hall. She was only just able to defer the visit a few days to suit her convenience. She wrote to Ellen on 5 March:

I scribble a few lines in haste to tell you my proceedings. . . . Sir James K. Shuttleworth and Lady Shuttleworth have persisted in coming; they were here on Friday. The baronet looks in vigorous health, he scarcely appears more than 35, but he says he is forty-four; Lady Shuttleworth is rather handsome and still young. They were both quite unpretending, etc . . . they again urged me to visit them. Papa took their side at once, would not hear of my refusing; I must go—this left me without plea or defence. I consented to go for three days, they wanted me to return with them in the carriage, but I pleaded off till to-morrow. I wish it was well over . . . Sir James is very courtly, fine-looking; I wish he may be as sincere as he is polished. He shows his white teeth with too frequent a smile; but I will not prejudge him.[1]

Sir James's white teeth would also, in due course, give Mrs. Gaskell pause.[2]

[1] CB to EN, 5 Mar. 1850: W & S iii. 81.
[2] Hopkins 206. Mrs. Gaskell to George Smith: '. . . he generally has a double set of motives for all his actions . . . Meta says you are to watch those teeth! . . .'.

Charlotte paid her visit to Gawthorpe on 6 March, staying there three days. Glad, once the visit was over, that she had been (as she always was after new experiences) she told Ellen: '. . . I could not have endured to prolong it; a few days at once, in an utterly strange place amongst utterly strange faces, is quite enough for me.' To Mr. Williams she wrote, 'The house is very much to my taste, near 3 centuries old, grey, stately, and picturesque.'[1]

Gawthorpe, at the time of Charlotte's first visit, was still the Elizabethan hall built between 1600 and 1605 by the Revd. Lawrence Shuttleworth. Within the next twelve months, however, Sir James called in Sir Charles Barry, architect of the new Houses of Parliament, and effected several 'improvements', including the characteristic pierced stone parapet to the roof, the terraces, and the garden walks, which Charlotte knew later.

She found her host

. . . a man of polished manners, with clear intellect and highly cultivated mind. On the whole, I got on very well with him. His health is just now somewhat broken by his severe official labours; and the quiet drives to old ruins and old halls situate amongst older hills and woods, the dialogues (perhaps I should rather say monologues, for I listened far more than I talked) by the fireside in his antique oak-panelled drawing-room, while they suited him, did not too much oppress and exhaust me.[2]

Some of these 'monologues' must have acquainted Charlotte with the circumstances of Sir James's career, as well as given her insight into his character.

He had been owner of Gawthorpe only since February 1842, by virtue of his marriage with Janet, heiress of the Shuttleworths, when he assumed by Royal Licence the name of Kay-Shuttleworth. He had received his baronetcy the previous autumn (gazetted 25 December 1849) from Lord Russell in return for his services to the ministry. His long and useful career as Dr. Kay, the pioneer in national education, had also only quite recently been brought to a halt, following a complete breakdown in health in December 1848. Charlotte's acquaintance with him coincided therefore both with his changed social status, and with the first period of enforced leisure that he had known in his

[1] CB to WSW, 16 Mar. 1850: *W & S* iii. 82.
[2] Ibid.

hard-working life. He had all the more time to take an interest in his new protégée.[1]

He had been born at Rochdale in 1804, the eldest of six children, his father being a cotton-manufacturer. After schooling at Salford Grammar School, he entered his uncle Fenton's bank at Rochdale at the age of 15. The Kays were Nonconformists and James was a devout and enthusiastic teacher in the local Sunday-school, where his first ideas about education on a national scale were formed. In 1824 he entered Edinburgh University as a medical student and within two years was serving as assistant in Edinburgh New Town Dispensary. His hospital experience, like his experience as a teacher among the children of the poor, awakened not only his dissenting conscience but his enthusiasm for sanitary and social improvement. The twin evils of poverty and disease made an early pioneer of him in the cause of social reform. 'It was clearly something outside scientific skill or charity which was needed for the cure of this social disease', he wrote in later life. The cure, as he saw it, must come from public education.

In 1827 he took his degree of M.D. and decided on devoting himself to work among the poorest classes in Manchester. Like Dr. Wilson, whose philanthropic career much resembled his own, he worked for seven and a half years in the Ancoats district of Manchester as physician at the dispensary. But all the while his zeal was directed more towards sanitary reform than towards medicine. This was exemplified in his conduct during the cholera epidemic of 1832, when his devotion to his patients showed more of the common sense of the sanitary inspector than of the physician. He concerned himself less with the dying than with those liable to being infected. He insisted on the houses of the infected areas being whitewashed, and on isolating the sick. He was eloquent on the subject of dirt and poverty as the main causes of the disease.

He voted, naturally, in favour of the Reform Bill of 1832 (an action that lost him his post as medical officer) and set about consolidating his *own* programme for social reform, publishing pamphlets in support of free-libraries, free-education, and free-trade. He was the first president of the Manchester Statistical Society, formed to investigate social conditions, and he founded the Manchester Provident Society.

A longing for a wider outlet for his immense energies decided him to leave Manchester in 1835, when a quite new direction was given to

[1] For further facts relating to Sir James Kay-Shuttleworth see the biography of him by Frank Smith (Murray, 1923).

his career. He entered the administration as one of the first Poor Law Commissioners in Norfolk and Suffolk. His new contacts with the pauper class only confirmed his previous conviction of the crying need for public education, and Dr. Kay it was who initiated the scheme for opening schools in workhouses. Due to his drive and organization teachers, mostly brought down from Scotland, were introduced into the workhouses. For the children immured there Dr. Kay planned not only better chances than their parents had ever had, but positive practical instruction.

The fame of his achievements went before him, and in 1838 he was called to London as Poor Law Commissioner for the Metropolitan Area. Wherever he inspected the institutions where pauper children were housed he saw the confirmation of his theories. Convinced that children were perverted by their parents and the other adult paupers in the workhouses, he separated them from their families. Intent on his reforms, and achieving considerable successes by them, he was not the man to be deflected from his ends by considerations of individual hardships. The good parents who treasured their children could not be considered any more than the bad. The children's welfare was what he sought.

His first large-scale experiment for an institution housing 1,100 children was at Norwood in 1839. Here boys and girls alike were given the rudiments of education and taught a trade. It was as a result of Lord Russell's visit to the Institution at Norwood in 1839 that Dr. Kay was appointed First Secretary to the new Committee of Council on Education set up by the Privy Council, and thus became the first state official for elementary education in the country. He travelled much abroad to inspect foreign educational methods and introduced the best of them in Britain. As a promoter of the first Normal school for the training of teachers, he became an object of attack from the Tories and from the Established Church alike, who feared the education of the masses would pass out of Church control into that of the laity.

Dr. Kay was immensely hard-working and painstaking, an organizer who supervised the minutiae of every project, a man who did not know how to delegate authority. In 1840, when government inspectors for schools were established, he exchanged daily letters with his inspectors during their tours, controlling their smallest actions. At his own risk he founded—on the Swiss model—the first government training school for teachers at Battersea—the later St. John's College—

living there himself with his mother and sister, and directing all its activities.

It was at Battersea that he first met his future wife, Janet Shuttleworth (born 9 November 1817, hence 13 years younger than himself). She visited the school for new ideas in setting up a school of her own for the village children of Padiham on her Gawthorpe estate. The marriage, on 24 February 1842, again gave a fresh direction to Dr. Kay's energies. In going to live on his wife's estates, he by no means abandoned his reforming zeal or pedagogic principles. He immediately set about organizing education for the younger children in the factories rearing their high chimneys round Gawthorpe. He was busy with this enterprise, as well as with his own growing family of children, when he first met Charlotte. His later activities (he lived till 1877) were much taken up with the cotton-slump in Lancashire during the 60's, and he became high sheriff for the county. A national tribute was paid to his pioneer work when the Education Bill was passed in 1870. The Vice-President of the Committee of Council on Education then said that he had been 'the man to whom, probably more than any other, we owe national education in England'.

In Currer Bell Sir James believed there was to be found a subject for improvement after his own heart (he was an ardent advocate for higher education for women). He had not allowed his successes in many fields to prevent his energies breaking out in new directions, and when he sought Charlotte's acquaintance he had written a novel, *Scarsdale*, and was contemplating writing another, which was eventually published as *Ribblesdale*. As Mrs. Gaskell guessed, some of his intense interest in the publishing adventures of Currer Bell was due to the fact that he wanted an introduction to a publisher for himself.[1] Charlotte as yet knew nothing of this ambition. She was told that her host's first interest in her had been awakened by a Burnley resident, who mentioned to him the Bells' novels.

Of that visit to Gawthorpe Charlotte wrote to Ellen:[2]

When the train stopped at Burnley, I found Sir James waiting for me. A drive of about three miles brought us to the gates of Gawthorpe, and after passing up a somewhat desolate avenue, there towered the hall, grey, antique, castellated and stately before me. . . . The people, however, were of still more interest to me than the house. Lady Shuttleworth is a little woman

---

[1] Mrs. Gaskell to George Smith, 5 Apr. 1860: *Letters of Mrs. Gaskell*, ed. Chapple and Pollard, M.U.P., 1966, p. 611.
[2] CB to EN, 19 Mar. 1850: *W & S* iii. 86–88.

thirty-two years old, with a pretty, smooth, lively face. Of pretension to aristocratic airs, she may be entirely acquitted; of frankness, goodhumour, and activity she has enough; truth obliges me to add, that as it seems to me, grace, dignity, fine feeling were not in the inventory of her qualities. These last are precisely what her husband possesses; in manner he can be gracious and dignified, his tastes and his feelings are capable of elevation; frank he is not, but on the contrary, politic; he calls himself a man of the world and knows the world's ways. . . . In him high mental cultivation is combined with an extended range of observation, and thoroughly practical views and habits. His nerves are naturally acutely sensitive, and the present very critical state of his health has exaggerated sensitiveness into irritability. His wife is of a temperament precisely suited to nurse him and wait on him; if her sensations were more delicate and acute she would not do half so well. They get on perfectly together. The children, there are four of them, are all fine children in their way.[1]

Particularly noticed by Charlotte was the children's German governess: 'a quiet, well-instructed interesting girl, whom I took to at once, and, in my heart, liked better than anything else in the house. She also instinctively took to me. She was very well treated for a governess, but wore the usual pale, despondent look of her class. She told me she was home-sick, and she looked so.'[2]

Charlotte mentioned the German governess in letters after subsequent meetings with the Shuttleworths and evidently entertained no suspicion of the nefarious influence she would come to exercise over Lady Shuttleworth. In the memoir of his father written by the eldest son, he revealed a domestic drama as compelling as any incident imagined by the author of *Jane Eyre* or *Villette*.

The nervous ill health from which both Sir James and his wife increasingly suffered, and to which there are constant references in Charlotte's letters, led to the German governess acquiring an almost hypnotic influence over Lady Shuttleworth who, in consequence, made of her children's governess her almost inseparable companion. Together they travelled abroad, wandering from spa to spa in pursuit of health for Lady Shuttleworth, while Sir James stayed at home. A rift formed which the German had every interest in keeping open, and she used all her influence over the wife to prevent it healing again. 'Besides cherishing a love of power, she cherished a hatred of Sir

[1] CB to EN, 19 March 1850: *W & S* iii. 86–88. The Shuttleworth children Charlotte met on that occasion were: Jane Elizabeth, born 6 May 1843; Ughtred James, born 18 Dec. 1844; Robert, born 20 Oct. 1847; Lionel Edward, born 14 Feb. 1849. A fifth child, Stewart, was not born till 8 Nov. 1851.   [2] Ibid.

James', the latter's son testified.[1] How unnatural was the separation, and how united in one particular the couple remained, is shown in their mutual love of their children and in their continued correspondence. Sir James always consulted his absent wife on all questions relating to the children's welfare. The death of Lady Shuttleworth at the German spa of Soden in 1872 preceded by five years that of Sir James at his daughter's house in London.

In 1850 these events were far removed from the anticipations of Charlotte Brontë. She found, however, that Sir James was not a man to be satisfied with small concessions. He insisted that the acquaintance, once established, must continue, that further and fuller opportunities for serving his new-found celebrity must be made; he would listen to none of Charlotte's excuses for refusing the invitation he pressed on her to join him and his wife during the coming London season. It was as effectual to make excuses to Sir James as to stand in the path of a mountain torrent; he had a way of sweeping all remonstrances aside. Charlotte's own extreme depression that spring, the weight of loneliness oppressing her, and the utter lack of hope in her future prospects made her even less able than usual to withstand vigorous opposition forcibly expressed. The realization, also, that if she were to continue to find subject-matter for her writing she must widen her experience made her less rebellious to the plan. She envisaged the visit to London under such auspices as disagreeable, but probably salutary. To Mr. Williams she confided her fears:

She wrote him after her return from Gawthorpe on 16 March:

The worst of it is that there is now some menace hanging over my head of an invitation to go to them in London during the season—this, which would doubtless be a great enjoyment to some people, is a perfect terror to me. I should highly prize the advantages to be gained in an extended range of observation, but I tremble at the thought of the price I must necessarily pay.[2]

The project was not allowed to lapse. On 12 April she again wrote to Mr. Williams: 'that invitation I mentioned in a previous letter is still urged upon me. . . . My conscience tells me it would be the act of a moral poltroon to let the fear of suffering stand in the way of improvement.'[3]

A sharp attack of bronchitis confining Mr. Brontë to his bed at the end of April and greatly alarming Charlotte made it necessary to put

[1] Frank Smith: op. cit.
[2] CB to WSW, 16 Mar. 1850: *SBC* 421.
[3] CB to WSW, 12 Apr. 1850: *W & S* iii. 98–100.

the whole plan off for a time. Sir James was a model of patience; he would naturally await Mr. Brontë's complete restoration. By mid-May, presumably, Charlotte would be in a position to join him and Lady Shuttleworth at Gawthorpe and proceed together in a leisurely way to London. 'Last Friday was the day appointed for me to go to Lancashire', Charlotte wrote Ellen on 11 May. 'But I did not think papa well enough to be left and accordingly begged Sir James and Lady Shuttleworth to return to London without me. It was arranged we were to stay at several of their friends' and relatives' houses on the way. . . . I would as lief have walked among red-hot ploughshares.'[1]

This was lionizing the author of the hour with a vengeance. In gratitude for the escape Charlotte submitted to joining her self-appointed sponsors after their arrival in town. A further postponement, caused by the sudden illness of Sir James himself, left the whole question of Charlotte's journey to London that season in suspense. Sir James wrote Charlotte two notes, 'claiming a promise that I will wait till he is better, and not allow any one else to introduce me', she told Ellen, 'into the Oceanic life of London'.[2] Sincerely sorry as she admitted to being for him, Charlotte 'could not help smiling' at the expression; she pacified him with a promise. 'I know something of him,' she confided to Ellen, 'and like part at least of what I know. I do not feel in the least tempted to change him for another'[3] in the role of cicerone.

The London visit seemed precariously poised between two uncertainties: Mr. Brontë's health, and that of Sir James. Once more Charlotte was thrown back on the solitude and heartache of the long days and longer sleepless nights in the silent house.

The beauty of the May weather drove her out on to the moors, and there more than anywhere the void oppressed her. The sense of her sisters' presence overwhelmed her. She had not learnt, and she daily realized that she would never learn, how to bear their loss. The degree of her desolation can be seen in a letter she wrote to a comparative stranger—James Taylor. Pitying him for the heat and confinement of London during those hot days, she said:

For my part, I am free to walk on the moors; but when I go out there alone everything reminds me of the times when others were with me, and then the moors seem a wilderness, featureless, solitary, saddening. My sister Emily had a particular love for them, and there is not a knoll of heather, not

---

[1] CB to EN, 11 May 1850: *W & S* iii. 108–9.
[2] CB to EN, 21 May 1850: *SBC* 423.   [3] Idem.

a branch of fern, not a young bilberry leaf, not a fluttering lark or linnet, but reminds me of her. The distant prospects were Anne's delight, and when I look round she is in the blue tints, the pale mists, the waves and shadows of the horizon. In the hill-country silence their poetry comes by lines and stanzas into my mind; once I loved it; now I dare not read it, and am driven often to wish I could taste one draught of oblivion and forget much that, while mind remains, I never shall forget.[1]

The recipient of this letter, whose sentiments towards Charlotte were deeply sincere, was the last man to minimize the pulse of pain beating in every line. The loneliness it conveyed must have been mentioned to his partners in the firm, for almost by return Charlotte received an invitation from George Smith's mother to make of their house her headquarters for a London visit. On 25 May Charlotte replied to Mrs. Smith:

You shall hear exactly how I am situated. Yesterday's post brought me a note from Sir James K. Shuttleworth . . . reminding me that my visit is only postponed and requesting an assurance to the effect that I will keep myself disengaged. . . . I consider it, however, very doubtful whether he will be well enough to render my visit advisable; and even should I go, still my conviction is that a brief stay will . . . be best. In that case, after a few days with my 'fashionable friends' as you call them, I believe I should be excessively disposed, very probably profoundly thankful, to subside into any corner of your drawing-room where I might find a chair of suitable height.

I am sorry you have changed your residence, as I shall now again lose my way in going up and down stairs, and stand in great tribulation, contemplating several doors and not knowing which to open—I regret that my answer to your kind note must be so inconclusive; the lapse of a fortnight or 3 weeks will probably facilitate a decision.[2]

The 'decision', however, was hastened by Mr. Brontë, who showed himself extremely anxious for Charlotte to 'get over her London visit', and by 30 May 1850, a Thursday, she set off to stay at Mrs. Smith's.

The weather was glorious, the kindness of her hosts was undimmed, and she was given a few days' freedom for sight-seeing without having to encounter celebrities; even the threat from the Shuttleworths was reduced to a few morning calls. On 3 June she sent Ellen a first report: dated from the Smiths' new house, 76 (later 112) Gloucester Terrace, it read: 'Here I feel very comfortable. Mrs. Smith treats me with a

[1] CB to James Taylor, 22 May 1850: *W & S* iii. 111–12.
[2] CB to Mrs. Smith, 25 May 1850: *W & S* iii. 113.

serene equable kindness which just suits me. Her son is as before genial and kindly. I have seen very few persons, and am not likely to see many, as the agreement was I was to be very quiet. . . . I shall not stay longer than a fortnight in London.'[1]

In the event she stayed from 30 May to 25 June, the visit proving far less nervously exhausting, she told Ellen, than the previous one, and 'much surpassing' her expectations in the end. She found London, as she wrote to Martha Brown (keeping house in her absence), 'particularly gay and noisy, as this is what is called the height of the London season, and all the fine people are in town'.[2]

In her first day's freedom, she was taken to the opera, where she saw 'a good many lords and ladies . . . and except for their elegant dresses, do not think them either much better or much worse than other people'.[3]

An outing rather more after her own heart was a visit to the Summer Exhibition of the Royal Academy, where she inevitably fixed on two pictures, Landseer's portrait of the Duke of Wellington on the field of Waterloo, and a picture by her childhood's favourite John Martin (still alive and not to die for another four years), his 'Last Man' on the theme of Campbell's poem—'a grand, wonderful picture,' she wrote her father, 'showing the red sun fading out of the sky, and all the soil of the foreground made up of bones and skulls'.[4]

She was taken to the Zoo, for which she received an 'honorary ticket of admission' from the secretary, and entertained Mr. Brontë at great length with descriptions of the animals she saw. George Smith took her to the Houses of Parliament. She also achieved a life's ambition of another sort: she saw the Duke of Wellington. George Smith took her to the service at the Chapel Royal, St. James's (probably on her second Sunday in town), for the express purpose, knowing that Wellington generally attended service there when in town. 'He is a real grand old man', Charlotte told Ellen after seeing him.[5]

She notified the Wheelwrights of her presence in town immediately on her arrival and arranged to visit them. She was, in short, 'getting on very well' as she told Ellen after a fortnight had passed. By then she had been subjected to only two ordeals: a morning call from Thackeray

[1] CB to EN, 3 June 1850: *W & S* iii. 115.
[2] CB to Martha Brown, 12 June 1850: *W & S* iii. 119.
[3] Ibid.
[4] CB to Revd. PB, 4 June 1850: *W & S* iii. 116–17.
[5] See below, Additional Notes, for CB's attendance at Newman's lectures.

and a luncheon at the Smiths to which G. H. Lewes was invited to meet her.

Her last contact with him had been over his review of *Shirley* in the *Edinburgh Review* which had deeply hurt her and aroused a stinging retort of two lines: 'I can be on my guard against my enemies,' she wrote to him, 'but God deliver me from my friends.'¹ Lewes's offence, as she explained to him afterwards, was not because his criticism was 'keen or its blame sometimes severe', but because he insisted on judging her work as a woman's and attacked her 'roughly'—Charlotte even thought 'cruelly'—on the question of sex.

Lewes was not a man to be crestfallen for a dressing-down from a fellow-author: he met Currer Bell with perfect equanimity. Leaning across George Smith's dinner-table towards her, he said: 'There ought to be a bond of sympathy between us, Miss Brontë, for we have both written naughty books.' George Smith, recalling the incident years later, shuddered at the effect of Lewes's words. 'This fired a train with a vengeance and an explosion followed',² he remembered. Charlotte herself would never admit that *Jane Eyre* presented any sort of challenge to conventional religion or morality. The truth and sanity of her outlook on the position of women in love was such that she could not herself begin to understand the shock her outspokenness provoked at the time. George Smith quoted, in support of this conventional view, Lady Herschel's remark to his mother on finding *Jane Eyre* lying about Mrs. Smith's drawing-room: 'You surely do not leave such a book as *this* about, at the risk of your daughters reading it?'³

The meeting with Lewes had a strange ending. Looking at him across the Smiths' dining-table, Charlotte saw, not the face of an enemy, but features that she had loved more than any in life:

... were he almost a fiend in character, I would not feel otherwise to him than half sadly, half tenderly—a queer word that last, but I use it because the aspect of Lewes's face almost moved me to tears; it is so wonderfully like Emily, her eyes, her features, the very nose, the somewhat prominent mouth, the forehead, even, at moments, the expression; whatever Lewes does or says, I believe I cannot hate him.⁴

Charlotte was so particular in mentioning the features in Lewes's face that resembled Emily that her statement cannot be wholly discredited

¹ CB to G. H. Lewes: *W & S* iii. 67.
² *Cornhill Magazine*, Dec. 1900.
³ Idem.
⁴ CB to EN, 12 June 1850: *W & S* iii. 118.

or attributed to the aberration of a short-sighted woman in great grief.

Emily, it was all too evident, was never long out of her mind. Sitting to have her portrait sketched by George Richmond (a kind attention from Mr. Smith for Mr. Brontë), Charlotte was again overcome on being shown the finished work; she could not restrain her tears. Realizing how incomprehensible such conduct must seem to the artist, she explained that the face he had drawn most powerfully resembled her dead sister Emily. (George Smith, in his report of this incident, named 'Anne' as the sister mentioned.)

Charlotte's first real ordeal during those London days was a morning call from Thackeray—a call uniquely addressed to herself, at which apart from George Smith she alone was present. In later years George Smith tried to analyse the particular reasons why Charlotte and Thackeray—such genuine admirers of each other's work—never hit it off. 'The truth is,' he wrote, 'Charlotte Brontë's heroics roused Thackeray's antagonism. He declined to pose on a pedestal for her admiration. . . . She wanted to persuade him that he was a great man with a mission, and Thackeray with many wicked jests, declined to recognise the "mission".'[1]

Such must have been the theme of the two authors' converse at Gloucester Terrace, which George Smith rather surprised Charlotte afterwards by designating as 'a queer scene'. She admitted on reflexion to Ellen:

I suppose it was. The giant sat before me; I was moved to speak to him of some of his shortcomings (literary, of course); one by one the faults came into my mind, and one by one I brought them out, and sought some explanation or defence. He did defend himself, like a great Turk and heathen; that is to say, the excuses were often worse than the crime itself. The matter ended in decent amity.[2]

Thackeray was unsuspecting enough to invite 'the austere little Joan of Arc' to a dinner at his house on 12 June, when he assembled a company of persons, mostly literary ladies, beauties, and celebrities, who he hoped might please and entertain the lioness of the hour.

For the first time since the break-up of his home in 1842, follow-

[1] *Cornhill Magazine*, Dec. 1900.
[2] CB to EN, 12 June 1850: *W & S* iii. 118.

ing his wife's incurable illness, Thackeray (who had lived in bachelor quarters at 88 St. James's Street) set up housekeeping in 1846, when he took the house at 13 Young Street, Kensington. It was one of a small street of private houses, inns, and courts, leading into Kensington Square, which he immortalized in *Esmond* and *The Virginians* and which gave him the atmosphere he preferred above all, that of Queen Anne's London. Here he made a home for his two daughters and here he wrote a great part of *Vanity Fair*, *Esmond*, *Pendennis*, and some of *The Newcomes*. The house, which is still standing, had a distinctive character. Built of eighteenth-century brick it presented a double front of bow-windows to the street. It lay only across the park from Gloucester Terrace where Currer Bell was staying, but for her it might have been Mecca, so far removed from her own severely inartificial world did it appear.

She was the guest of honour. The others, the beautiful and celebrated women and men convened by Thackeray, were invited to meet *her*.[1] For this occasion Charlotte—more than one feminine eye-witness recorded—wore a 'little barège dress with a pattern of faint green moss' (it can still be seen in Charlotte's old home) and she wore her hair as always 'en bandeaux'. The elegant Mrs. Brookfield noted further: 'There was just then a fashion for wearing a plait of hair across the head, and Miss Brontë, a timid little woman with a firm mouth, did not possess a large enough quantity of hair to enable her to form a plait, so therefore wore a very obvious crown of brown silk.'[2]

A letter to Ellen dated 29 April lifts the veil upon this mystery. Ellen, always appealed to in matters of dress, had evidently been commissioned to buy a plait of artificial hair: 'I received the plait,' Charlotte wrote, 'it is very nice and I shall keep it—but I will thank you also to get me 3 yards of brown satin ribbon.'[3]

Thackeray's daughters, Anne and Harriet, were aged 13 and 10 at the time, but their indulgent father and kind governess, Miss Trulock, were agreed in allowing them to stay up for the rare treat of an evening spent with the author of *Jane Eyre*. Anne Isabella Thackeray (the eventual Lady Ritchie) never forgot that hot summer evening and

---

[1] Thackeray's note of invitation to Monckton Milnes (later Lord Houghton) has been preserved. Dated 11 June, it reads: My dear Milnes—Miss Brontë dines here tomorrow at 7. If you are by any wonder disengaged, do come too. Yours truly, W. M. Thackeray. *Letters and Private Papers of W. M. Thackeray*, ii. 673.

[2] C. and F. Brookfield: *Mrs. Brookfield and her Circle*, Pitman, 1905.

[3] CB to EN, 29 April 1850: *W & S* iii. 107.

her record of the occasion preserves some of her original girlish excitement.[1]

One of the most notable persons who ever came into our bow-windowed drawing-room in Young Street is a guest never to be forgotten by me—a tiny, delicate, little person, whose small hand nevertheless grasped a mighty lever which set all the literary world of that day vibrating. I can still see the scene quite plainly—the hot summer evening, the open windows, the carriage driving to the door as we all sat silent and expectant; my father, who rarely waited, waiting with us; our governess and my sister and I all in a row, and prepared for the great event. We saw the carriage stop, and out of it sprang the active, well-knit figure of Mr. George Smith, who was bringing Miss Brontë to see our father. My father, who had been walking up and down the room, goes out into the hall to meet his guests, and then, after a moment's delay, the door opens wide, and the two gentlemen come in, leading a tiny, delicate, serious, little lady, pale, with fair straight hair, and steady eyes. She may be a little over thirty; she is dressed in a little barège dress, with a pattern of faint green moss. She enters in mittens, in silence, in seriousness; our hearts are beating with wild excitement. This, then, is the authoress, the unknown power whose books have set all London talking, reading and speculating; some people even say our father wrote the books—the wonderful books. To say that we little girls had been given 'Jane Eyre' to read scarcely represents the facts of the case; to say that we had taken it without leave, read bits here and read bits there, been carried away by an undreamed-of and hitherto unimagined whirlwind into things, times and places, all utterly absorbing, and at the same time absolutely unintelligible to us, would more accurately describe our state of mind on that summer's evening as we look at Jane Eyre—the great Jane Eyre—the tiny little lady. The moment is so breathless that dinner comes as a relief to the solemnity of the occasion, and we all smile as my father stoops to offer his arm; for, though genius she may be, Miss Brontë can barely reach his elbow. My own personal impressions are that she is somewhat grave and stern, especially to forward little girls who wish to chatter. Mr. George Smith has since told me how she afterwards remarked on my father's wonderful forbearance and gentleness with our uncalled-for incursions into the conversation. She sat gazing at him with kindling eyes of interest, lighting up with a sort of illumination every now and then as she answered him. I can see her bending forward over the table, not eating, but listening to what he said as he carved the dish before him.

I think it must have been on this very occasion that my father invited some of his friends in the evening to meet Miss Brontë—for every body was interested and anxious to see her. Mrs. Crowe, the reciter of ghost-stories, was there. Mrs. Brookfield, Mrs. Carlyle, Mr. Carlyle himself was present, so I am told, railing at the appearance of cockneys upon Scotch mountain sides;

[1] Anne Thackeray-Ritchie, *Chapters from Some Memoirs*, 1894, pp. 60–65.

there were also too many Americans for his taste, 'but the Americans were as gods compared to the cockneys', says the philosopher. Besides the Carlyles, there were Mrs. Elliott and Miss Perry, Mrs. Procter and her daughter, most of my father's habitual friends and companions. In the recent life of Lord Houghton I was amused to see a note quoted in which Lord Houghton also was convened. Would that he had been present—perhaps the party would have gone off better. It was a gloomy and a silent evening. Every one waited for the brilliant conversation which never began at all. Miss Brontë retired to the sofa in the study, and murmured a low word now and then to our kind governess, Miss Trulock. The room looked very dark, the lamp began to smoke a little, the conversation grew dimmer and more dim, the ladies sat round still expectant, my father was too much perturbed by the gloom and the silence to be able to cope with it at all. Mrs. Brookfield, who was in the doorway by the study, near the corner in which Miss Brontë was sitting, leant forward with a little commonplace, since brilliance was not to be the order of the evening. 'Do you like London, Miss Brontë?' she said; another silence, a pause, then Miss Brontë answers, 'Yes and No', very gravely. Mrs. Brookfield has herself reported the conversation. My sister and I were much too young to be bored in those days; alarmed, impressed we might be, but not yet bored. A party was a party, a lioness was a lioness; and—shall I confess it?—at that time an extra dish of biscuits was enough to mark the evening. We felt all the importance of the occasion; tea spread in the dining-room, ladies in the drawing-room. We roamed about inconveniently, no doubt, and excitedly, and in one of my incursions crossing the hall, after Miss Brontë had left, I was surprised to see my father opening the front door with his hat on. He put his fingers to his lips, walked out into the darkness, and shut the door quietly behind him. When I went back to the drawing-room again, the ladies asked me where he was. I vaguely answered that I thought he was coming back. I was puzzled at the time nor was it all made clear to me till long afterwards, when one day Mrs. Procter asked me if I knew what had happened once when my father had invited a party to meet Jane Eyre at his house. It was one of the dullest evenings she had ever spent in her life, she said. And then with a good deal of humour she described the situation —the ladies who had all come expecting so much delightful conversation, and the gloom, and the constraint, and how, finally overwhelmed by the situation, my father had quietly left the room, left the house, and gone off to his club. The ladies waited, wondered, and finally departed also; and as we were going up to bed with our candles after everybody was gone, I remember two pretty Miss L——'s, in shiny silk dresses, arriving full of expectation. . . . We still said we thought our father would soon be back, but the Miss L——'s declined to wait upon the chance, and drove away again almost immediately.[1]

---

[1] *Chapters from Some Memories*: op. cit.

Mrs. Brookfield, the spoilt darling of society for forty years, told George Smith that Currer Bell was the most difficult woman to entertain she had ever met. Neither Harriet Martineau nor Mrs. Gaskell would have agreed with her. Mrs. Brookfield's explanation of Charlotte's deficiencies in society affords some commentary upon the deficiencies of society itself:

The probable reason of the failure of the first party was perhaps Miss Brontë's own inability to fall in with the easy badinage of the well-bred people with whom she found herself surrounded.

Alert minded and keen brained herself, she was accustomed only to the narrow literalness of her own circle, and could scarcely have understood the rapid give and take, or the easy conversational grace of these new friends. Also she may hardly have appreciated the charming conciseness with which they told their stories; for the members of this set were the first to break away from the pedantic ponderousness usual with all great talkers, even those of their own time; and Miss Brontë, a square peg in a round hole, was doubtless, too, dismayed at anecdotes that gained in elegance as they lost in accuracy.[1]

Thackeray's mistake had been to assemble so large a party. Currer Bell was crushed by sheer weight of numbers and the alien atmosphere, an atmosphere, she shrewdly suspected, made up of sensation-mongers. She might be a 'bright-haired sprite', but she was not disposed to perform in public. The refusal to do so inevitably made her enemies. Millais, the painter, one of the offended guests, described her to his daughter as looking 'tired with her own brains'. He recognized the rarity of her looks, all the same, and sought to paint her, but was informed that she was sitting to Richmond. In after years he admitted that she was his idea of a woman of genius.

George Smith, well aware of his own family's difficulties in entertaining Currer Bell, was himself perfectly at ease with her. 'For my own part,' he said, 'I found her conversation most interesting: her quick and clear intelligence was delightful. When she became excited on any subject, she was really eloquent and it was a pleasure to listen to her.'[2]

There is no doubt that George Smith liked something more in Currer Bell than her conversation, or even than her genius. There was something in his optimistic and healthily extroverted nature that

[1] *Mrs. Brookfield and her Circle*: op. cit.
[2] *Cornhill Magazine*, Dec. 1900: op. cit.

responded to the intensity of feeling, to the smouldering of banked-down fires, he sensed behind the lamp-like eyes of Currer Bell.[1]

Many biographers have speculated upon the exact relations reached by Charlotte and her agreeable publisher, and in particular over the causes that prolonged her visit to London that summer and rounded it off with so romantic a sequel.[2] On 21 June Charlotte wrote to Ellen to fix her return home, which was to be combined with a visit to Ellen first, for the following Tuesday, 25 June, when she would arrive at Batley station at 4 p.m. She added the further information:

My London visit has much surpassed my expectation this time; I have suffered less and enjoyed more than before; rather a trying termination yet remains to me. Mrs. Smith's youngest son is at school in Scotland, and George, her eldest, is going to fetch him home for the vacation; the other evening he announced his intention of taking one of his sisters with him, and proposed that Miss Brontë should go down to Edinburgh and join them there, and see that city and its suburbs. I concluded he was joking, laughed and declined: however, it seems he was in earnest. The thing appearing to me perfectly out of the question, I still refused. Mrs. Smith did not favour it; you may easily fancy how she helped me to sustain my opposition, but her worthy son only waxed more determined. His mother is master of the house, but he is master of his mother. This morning she came and entreated me to go. 'George wished it so much'; he had begged her to use her influence, etc., etc. Now I believe that George and I understand each other very well, and respect each other very sincerely. We both know the wide breach time has made between us; we do not embarrass each other, or very rarely, my six or eight years of seniority, to say nothing of lack of all pretension to beauty etc are a perfect safeguard. I should not in the least fear to go with him to China.

[1] Smith related the following incident on which the evening at Thackeray's closed. '. . . One of Mr. Thackeray's guests was Miss Adelaide Procter, and those who remember that lady's charming personality will not be surprised to learn that I was greatly attracted to her. During our drive home I was seated opposite to Miss Brontë, and I was startled by her leaning forward, putting her hands on my knees, and saying "She would make you a very nice wife." "Whom do you mean?" I replied. "Oh! you know whom I mean", she said, and we relapsed into silence . . .'—*George Smith: A Memoir.*

[2] In an unpublished letter to Mrs. Humphry Ward, written 18 Aug. 1898 (when he was 74) George Smith clearly stated what had been his feelings for Charlotte. '. . . No, I never was in the least bit in love with Charlotte Brontë. I am afraid that the confession will not raise me in your opinion, but the truth is, I never could have loved any woman who had not some charm or grace of person, and Charlotte Brontë had none—I liked her and was interested in her, and I admired her—especially when she was in Yorkshire and I was in London. I never was coxcomb enough to suppose that she was in love with me. But I believe that my mother was at one time rather alarmed. . . .' I am indebted to the kindness of Mrs. Humphry Ward's granddaughter, Mary Moorman, for the permission to quote this letter.

I like to see him pleased, I greatly dislike to ruffle and disappoint him, so he shall have his mind, and, if all be well, I mean to join him in Edinburgh after I shall have spent a few days with you. With his buoyant animal spirits and youthful vigour he will make severe demands on my muscles and nerves, but I dare say I shall get through somehow, and then perhaps come to rest a few days with you before I go home.[1]

To modern eyes there might seem to be too much said about the 'safeguards' in this account, if, as Charlotte claimed, no safeguards were required. Could George Smith himself have seen this letter he would not have been surprised by the emphasis laid on looks—or rather, the lack of them; he had long since recognized Charlotte's obsession with the subject.

Having carried his mother along with him—despite her rooted objection—George Smith was genuinely annoyed to find Currer Bell more difficult to master. He had planned for her to meet him and his sister Eliza at Tarbert, in Argyllshire, and to travel up the west coast to Oban, going on from there to Edinburgh where his young brother Alick was at school. All that Charlotte would accept was to meet him on the last stage of his journey, in Edinburgh itself. From Brookroyd she wrote him on 27 June:

My dear Sir—It is written that I should not meet you at Tarbet [sic], and at this perversity of the Fates I should be more concerned than I am if I did not feel very certain that the loss in the matter will be chiefly my own. Of your three plans the last is the only one found practicable; Edinburgh is the true Phillipi and there I hope (D.V.) to see you again next Wednesday.

I left Sarah much better, but I think your mother had decided against her going to Scotland, thinking the journey too long.

Before I left London I had the opportunity of bidding Mr. Thackeray good-bye without going to his house for the purpose, and of this I was very glad.

With kind regards to your sister, and hopes that she has thus far borne her journey well . . . etc.[2]

Knowing Mrs. Smith's true sentiments in the matter, Charlotte wrote to tell her of the much-reduced programme for the Scots tour, adding simply: 'I only hope he will not be at all disappointed—and, indeed, as he is now in the full excitement of his tour, the change of plan will probably appear of no consequence. With love to Sarah and Bell, believe me dear Mrs. Smith.'[3]

[1] CB to EN, 21 June 1850: *W & S* iii. 120–1.
[2] CB to George Smith, 27 June 1850: *W & S* iii. 121–2.
[3] CB to Mrs. Smith, 28 June 1850: *W & S* iii. 122.

In the event, Charlotte limited her Scots tour to barely three days' sight-seeing. Arriving there on the evening of 3 July, she spent the 4th and 5th in Edinburgh, returning to Brookroyd late in the evening of the 6th. Writing from Edinburgh on the 5th she gave Ellen the time-table for her return:

We shall leave Edinburgh to-morrow morning at a quarter to ten, arrive in York at 40 min. past three. From York I think there is no train to Leeds till about 6.30. If so, I shall not reach Leeds till 8 o'clock; too late for the train to Batley. If it is really too late I shall take a cab at Leeds, for I would rather do that than stay at an Inn all night. I got to Edinburgh very safely; it is a glorious city. I wish you were with us and could see all we saw yesterday. London seems a dreary place compared to it. Mr. Smith was a little bit angry at first about my not having come. Unless plans are again changed we shall travel all together as far as York. We are just going out, so good-bye, dear Nell.[1]

From the letters that remain of Charlotte's Edinburgh visit it is plain that it gave her unalloyed pleasure. The tone of enthusiasm she allowed herself in all her correspondence dealing with it is remarkable. 'I always liked Scotland as an idea,' she wrote Mr. Williams on 20 July, 'but now, as a reality, I like it far better; it furnished me with some hours as happy almost as any I ever spent.'[2]

This is an extreme statement for Charlotte to make. But the idea of Scotland itself went back to the Brontës' childhood; indissoluble from memories of Emily and Branwell were the names of certain Scottish heroes and places. Chosen 'Chief Men' for their Island games, Sir Walter himself, Lockhart, Christopher North, the Ettrick Shepherd, and the landscape for their tales was swathed in Ossianic mists and sunsets. 'Do not fear . . . that I am going to bore you with description', Charlotte assured Mr. Williams on 20 July; but who, indeed, she asked,

that has once seen Edinburgh, with its couchant crag lion, but must see it again in dreams, waking or sleeping? My dear Sir, do not think I blaspheme when I tell you that your great London, as compared to Dun-Edin (mine own romantic town), is as prose compared to poetry. . . . You have nothing like Scott's monument or if you had that and all the glories of architecture assembled together, you have nothing like Arthur's seat, and above all you have not the Scotch national character; and it is that grand character after all which gives the land its true charm, its true greatness.[3]

[1] CB to EN, 5 July 1850: *W & S* iii. 123.
[2] CB to WSW, 20 July 1850: *W & S* iii. 125.   [3] Ibid.

It must not be forgotten that George Smith, despite his name, was a true son of Caledonia.

To Laetitia Wheelwright Charlotte gave some further particulars of her trip in a letter of 30 July:

My stay in Scotland was short, and what I saw was chiefly comprised in Edinburgh and the neighbourhood, in Abbotsford and Melrose, for I was obliged to relinquish my first intention of going from Glasgow to Oban and thence through a portion of the Highlands. But though the time was brief, and the view of objects limited, I found such a charm of situation, association, and circumstances that I think the enjoyment experienced in that little space equalled in degree and excelled in kind all which London yielded during a month's sojourn. Edinburgh compared to London is like a vivid page of history compared to a huge dull treatise on political economy; and as to Melrose and Abbotsford, the very names possess music and magic.[1]

More than a month later she wrote to James Taylor, still under the spell of the experience:

Edinburgh, Melrose, Abbotsford, these three in themselves sufficed to stir feelings of such deep interest and admiration that, neither at the time did I regret, nor have I since regretted, the want of wider space to diffuse the sense of enjoyment. There was room and variety enough to be very happy.... The Queen was right indeed to climb Arthur's Seat with her husband and children; I shall not soon forget how I felt, when, having reached its summit, we all sat down and looked over the city, towards the sea and Leith, and the Pentland Hills.[2]

The evidence of future letters both to and about James Taylor, suggests that during her month in London Charlotte had snubbed him, not apparently because of anything of a personal nature he had said to her but because he had allowed symptoms of jealousy of his young chief to show themselves. Charlotte had been displeased on George Smith's account. The hurt to James Taylor's feelings, which she later regretted, led her to add now in her letter: 'No doubt you are proud to being a native of Scotland, proud of your country, her capital, her children, and her literature. You cannot be blamed.'[3]

Echoes, from sources unsuspected by Charlotte, reached Mr. Brontë—busily concerned with builders and decorators during his daughter's absence—ascribing reasons for the 'music and magic' to

---

[1] CB to Laetitia Wheelwright, 30 July 1850: *W & S* iii. 128.
[2] CB to James Taylor, 5 Sept. 1850: *W & S* iii. 154.
[3] CB to James Taylor: op. cit.

other causes than those given by her. He was, in short, convinced that she was being 'courted', and alarmed by the fact. His alarm was greatly increased on hearing from Ellen that Charlotte was unwell and unable to leave Brookroyd when planned. He felt impelled to write at once to Ellen, a touching letter instructing her not to hesitate to call in a doctor at his expense and give Charlotte every care. He feared instantly for her life.[1]

Charlotte, quite unaware of the 'nervous excitement and alarm' she had provoked, arrived home to find John Greenwood, 'staff in hand', at the bottom of the hill, sent post haste by Mr. Brontë to seek news of her. When Mr. Brontë's panic over her health was allayed, Charlotte was able to diagnose the real cause of the trouble: it had, in part, arisen from a clear conviction that she 'was receiving overtures'. In Mr. Brontë's mind, then and later, the rooted belief that his daughter's feeble health would never be equal to the demands of marriage, was at the origin of his opposition to all her suitors.

Charlotte's knowledge of her father's opinion was an added source of depression. To Ellen, who had obviously shown alarm at Charlotte's indisposition while staying with her, she wrote her mind:

It is the undisguised and most harassing anxiety of others that has fixed in my mind thoughts and expectations which must canker wherever they take root. . . . I have had to entreat papa's consideration on this point. My nervous system is soon wrought upon. I should wish to keep it in rational strength and coolness; but to do so I must determinedly resist the kindly-meant but too irksome expression of . . . apprehension.[2]

Charlotte had unadvisedly blurted out to Ellen that she did not 'calculate on a long life', and was subjected in consequence to indiscreet expressions of anxiety. For Charlotte these apprehensions could not have come at a worse time, after the partial escape into a happier life.

With each return to the home that no longer held those she loved, her depression was extreme. She found that she had 'little faith in the power of any temporary excitement to do real good'. The fresh incentive that her new connexions with London gave her contained also within themselves the seed of disappointment. She had not passed through the fires of Brussels without acquiring wisdom. She would check herself in time from placing a too great reliance on the pleasures the post could bring. 'I have put off day by day writing to London to

[1] Revd. PB to EN, 12 July 1850: BPM.
[2] CB to EN, 7 Aug. 1850: W & S iii. 133.

tell them I am come home,' she told Ellen on the 18th July, '—and till then it was agreed that I should not hear from them. It is painful to be dependent on the small stimulus letters give . . . and I cease to look forward at post time to any letters but yours.'[1]

George Smith, however, had something better to give her as a keepsake of her London visit than a mere letter: he sent her a portrait of Wellington framed and to her father her own portrait by Richmond. The two packing cases arrived at the parsonage together. 'When you first told me that you had had the Duke's picture framed and had given it to me,' Charlotte wrote him on 1 August, 'I felt half provoked with you for performing such a work of supererogation, but now, when I see it, again, I cannot but acknowledge that, in so doing, you were felicitously inspired. It is his very image, and, as papa said . . . scarcely in the least like the ordinary portraits.'[2]

Mr. Brontë's judgement of his daughter's portrait is of special interest to those who never saw her. While he agreed that the 'expression was wonderfully good and life-like' he considered that the features were far from flattered and that it made her look older than she did in reality. In this he was supported by old Tabby who tenaciously maintained 'that it is not like—that it is too old-looking'; but, Charlotte added, 'as she, with equal tenacity, asserts that the Duke of Wellington's picture is a portrait of "the Master" I am afraid not much weight is to be ascribed to her opinion.'[3]

Charlotte's difficulty in settling down at home once more appears in her acceptance, however reluctant, of an invitation to visit the Kay-Shuttleworths at Windermere that August. Barely a month after returning home she wrote to Ellen on 16 August: 'I am going on Monday (D.V.) a journey, whereof the prospect cheers me not at all, to Windermere in Westmorland, to spend a few days with Sir J. K. Shuttleworth, who has taken a house there for the autumn and winter. I consented to go with reluctance, chiefly to please papa, whom a refusal on my part would have much annoyed: but I dislike to leave him.'[3]

Charlotte travelled to Windermere on Sunday, 18 August, and wrote her father from Briery Close in the morning:

I reached this place yesterday at eight o'clock, after a safe though rather tedious journey. I had to change carriages three times and to wait an hour and a half at Lancaster. Sir James came to meet me at the station; both he and Lady

[1] CB to EN, 18 July 1850: *W & S* iii. 125.
[2] CB to George Smith, 1 Aug. 1850: *W & S* iii. 130.
[3] Ibid.

Shuttleworth gave me a very kind reception. This place is exquisitely beautiful, though the weather is cloudy, misty, and stormy; but the sun bursts out occasionally and shows the hills and the lake. Mrs. Gaskell is coming here this evening.[1]

It was an important meeting for Charlotte. She had met educated women, she had met intelligent women before, but she had not met the exact mixture of talent and unaffected homeliness, cheerfulness, culture, and charm that Mrs. Gaskell possessed. She was indeed a very complete woman, beautiful, deeply understanding, sincerely sympathetic, spontaneously generous. She was, moreover, a *contented* woman, able to bestow from her own superfluity of mental peace something upon others. It was the serenity of her mind—the source of her unquenchable humour—more than her talents, that infused Charlotte with a new vitality every time they met. In Mrs. Gaskell Charlotte found what she had lacked all her life—a woman friend whose life was fulfilled.

[1] CB to Revd. PB, 19 Aug. 1850: *W & S* iii. 139–40.

CHAPTER XXIII

FRIENDSHIP

BRIERY CLOSE stands high on the hill-side above Low Wood on Windermere, and commands a breath-taking panorama of the lake, the Langdale Pikes, Coniston Fell, and the hills above Esthwaite. Mrs. Gaskell gave a very correct description of its position directly after her visit there in a letter to Catherine Winkworth of 25 August:[1] 'Dark when I got to Windermere station; a drive along the level road to Low Wood, then a regular clamber up a steep lane; then a stoppage at a pretty house . . . I had the most lovely view from my bedroom window over Windermere on to Esthwaite, Langdale, etc.'

Charlotte also travelled by train as far as Windermere station, which was newly opened that year. The station and the line's projected extension through Ambleside to Grasmere and Keswick had provoked many vehement protests from nature lovers, including William Wordsworth. Writing to the *Morning Post* on 9 December 1844 and subsequently, he pointed out that the lack of manufactures in the Lake District, the absence of mines, and even of cultivatable land, made communications with the rest of the country of minor consideration. 'The staple of the district', he claimed, 'is, in fact, its beauty and its character of seclusion and retirement.' These very qualities, Wordsworth argued, were not exportable, nor, by the *mass* of people transported there as trippers or sightseers, comprehensible in the true aesthetic sense. He instanced the first visitor to build a house on Windermere, who showed how little he appreciated the character of the situation, by setting up a length of high wall 'as exclusive as it was ugly'. Romantic scenery, Wordsworth submitted, was comprehended by the *few*, but could, if abandoned to the speculators, be ruined by the many. Before an appreciation and comprehension of natural beauty— as distinct from the utilitarian processes by which Man benefits from Nature—could spread, 'long processes of culture and opportunities of observation' would be required. Meanwhile, he put in a plea for

---

[1] Mrs. G. to C. Winkworth, *Letters of Mrs. G.*, p. 123: op. cit.

the preservation of the one daily coach service to Keswick, which more than met the requirements of the genuine lakelanders.

Briery Close, one of the new properties built on Windermere in consequence of the coming of the railway, was rented for the year by Sir James Kay-Shuttleworth. Built of the local Westmorland stone, with gables and windows picked out in fretted wood, it presented the rather alpine aspect that characterizes the houses of that period in the district. Without beauties of its own, it commanded beauty in plenty by its position. Mrs. Gaskell's 'steep lane', which was wooded all the way up, abutted on to a broad carriage drive in front of 'the pretty house'.

Carriage-drives and also boating on the lake were pleasures that Sir James could daily offer his guests. Briery Close, indeed, possessed its own landing-stage in a private enclosure on the waterfront, which faced the highroad linking Bowness and Ambleside, and the 'steep lane' opposite.

The drawing-room in which Mrs. Gaskell met Charlotte for the first time commanded the whole panorama of the lake, though on this occasion she was first 'dazzled' by the oil-lamps, as she told Catherine Winkworth, and then discerned

> ... a little lady in a black silk gown, whom I could not see at first for the dazzle of the room: she came up and shook hands with me at once. I went up to unbonnet etc, came down to tea, the little lady worked away and hardly spoke; but I had time for a good look at her. She is (as she calls herself) *undeveloped*; thin and more than $\frac{1}{2}$ a head shorter than I, soft brown hair not so dark as mine; eyes (very good and expressive looking straight and open at you) of the same colour, a reddish face; large mouth and many teeth gone; altogether *plain*, the forehead square, broad, and *rather* overhanging. She has a very sweet voice, rather hesitates in choosing her expressions, but when chosen they seem without an effort, *admirable* and *just* befitting the occasion. There is nothing overstrained but perfectly simple.[1]

Summing up her subsequent impressions of Charlotte, Mrs. Gaskell added:

> We were only 3 days together; the greater part of which was spent in driving about, in order to show Miss Brontë the Westmorland scenery, as she had never been there before. We were both included in an invitation to drink tea quietly at Fox How;[2] and I then saw how severely her nerves were

---

[1] Mrs. G. to C. Winkworth, 25 Aug. 1850: *Letters*, op. cit.

[2] Fox How, the Arnolds' home, Chadwick 418. See Martineau, *Autobiography*; Rawnsley, *Literary Association of the English Lakes, Past & Present at the English Lakes.*

taxed by the effort of going amongst strangers. We knew beforehand that the number of the party would not exceed twelve but she suffered the whole day from an acute headache brought on by apprehension of the evening.

Of Charlotte's own reactions, both to the noble scenery and to the strangers, she wrote with eloquence to her friends. To Miss Wooler she confided later:

Sir J. K. Shuttleworth is residing near Windermere at a house called 'The Briery', [*sic*] and it was there I was staying for a little while in August. He very kindly showed me the scenery—*as it can be seen from a carriage*—and I discerned that the 'Lake Country' is a glorious region, of which I had only seen the similitude in dream—waking or sleeping. But, my dear Miss Wooler, I only half enjoyed it, because I was only half at my ease. Decidedly I find it does not agree with me to prosecute the search of the picturesque in a carriage; a waggon, a spring-cart, even a post-chaise might do, but the carriage upsets everything. I longed to slip out unseen, and to run away by myself in amongst the hills and dales. Erratic and vagrant instincts tormented me, and these I was obliged to control, or rather suppress, for fear of growing in any degree enthusiastic, and thus drawing attention to the 'lioness', the authoress, the artist. Sir J. K. Shuttleworth is a man of ability and intellect, but not a man in whose presence one willingly unbends.[1]

To Ellen Charlotte further confided how the constraint imposed by her host sorted ill with the grandeur and beauty of the scene.

The scenery is, of course, grand; could I have wandered about amongst those hills *alone*, I could have drunk in all their beauty; even in a carriage with company, it was very well. If I could only have dropped unseen out of the carriage and gone away by myself in amongst those grand hills, and sweet dales, I should have drunk in the full power of this glorious scenery. In company this can hardly be. Sometimes, while Sir James was warning me against the faults of the artist class, all the while vagrant artist instincts were busy in the mind of his listener.[2]

Sir James's possessive and didactic approach to the beauties of his region compared unfavourably with George Smith's genial companionship on the trip to Scotland. To Mr. Williams she did not hesitate to make the point:

I fear I seemed to you to speak coolly of the beauty of the Lake scenery. The truth is, it was, as scenery, exquisite—far beyond anything I saw in

---

[1] CB to Miss Wooler, 27 Sept. 1850: *W & S* iii. 163-4: Allbutt Bequest, Fitzwilliam Museum.
[2] CB to EN, 26 Aug. 1850: *W & S* iii. 147-9.

Scotland; but it did not give me half so much pleasure, because I saw it under less congenial auspices. Mr. Smith and Sir J. K. Shuttleworth are two different people with whom to travel. I need say nothing of the former—you know him. The latter offers me his friendship, and I do my best to be grateful for the gift.[1]

Mrs. Gaskell noticed how Charlotte, when she *could* escape the attentions of her host and lose herself in the contemplation of the beauty round her, observed every variant of light and shift of cloud with the eyes not only of an artist, but of a close watcher of the skies. She recorded later:

I was struck by Miss Brontë's careful examination of the shape of the clouds and the signs of the heavens in which she read, as from a book, what the coming weather would be. I told her that I saw she must have a view equal in extent at her own home. She said that I was right, but that the character of the prospect from Haworth was very different; that I had no idea what a companion the sky became to any one living in solitude,—more than any inanimate object on earth—more than the moors themselves.[2]

Upon this, Charlotte's fourth consecutive encounter with Sir James, she was able with her genius for analysis, shrewdly to define the man. She wrote to Mr. Williams:

... his is a nature with which it is difficult to assimilate and where there is no assimilation, how can there be real regard? Nine parts out of ten in him are utilitarian—the tenth is artistic. This tithe of his nature seems to me at war with all the rest—it is just enough to incline him restlessly towards the artist class, and far too little to make him one of them. The consequent inability to *do* things which he *admires*, embitters him I think—it makes him doubt perfections and dwell on faults. Then his notice or presence scarcely tend to set one at ease or make one happy; he is too worldly and formal.[3]

Almost exactly similar were Mrs. Gaskell's findings after a three-day scrutiny of her host. She wrote to her intimate friend Tottie Fox,[4]

Lady K-S was confined to one room, so she (CB) and I had much of our day to ourselves with the exception of some lectures on art, and 'bringing ourselves down to a lower level' and 'the beauty of expediency', from that eminently practical man Sir James, who has never indulged in the exercise of

[1] CB to WSW, 5 Sept. 1850: *W & S* iii. 155–6.
[2] *Life*, 310.
[3] CB to WSW, 5 Sept. 1850: *W & S* iii. 155.
[4] Mrs. G. to Mrs. Fox, 27 Aug. 1850. *Letters of Mrs. Gaskell*, p. 130: op. cit.

any talent which could not bring a tangible and speedy return. However, he was very kind; and really took trouble in giving us, Miss Brontë especially, good advice; which she received with calm resignation.

However outwardly submissive, Sir James's 'bohemian ladies' seethed with rebellion inside, and rightly diagnosed the tyrannous quality of his benevolence. 'After dinner we went a drive to Coniston', Mrs. Gaskell told Catherine Winkworth,[1] 'to call on the Tennysons who are staying at Mr. Marshall's Hunt Lodge—Sir James on the box, Miss B & I inside very cosy; but alas it began to rain so we had to turn back without our call being paid, which grieved me sorely and made me cross.'

To Tottie Fox Mrs. Gaskell confided rather more: 'Do you know I was as near as possible to seeing Tennyson. He and Mrs. are staying at Coniston and Sir James, Miss B. and I were on the Lake there, when we heard it; and Sir James knows him; and said he would go and call; and then looked up at the sky and thought it was going to rain, so he didn't. I held my peace and bit my lips.'[2]

The indisposition and non-appearance of Lady Shuttleworth throughout Mrs. Gaskell's stay was cheerfully and humorously accepted by that lady. As Lady K. S. was ill, she explained to Catherine Winkworth:

I made breakfast all the time I staid; and an old jolly Mr. Moseley Inspector of Schools came to breakfast [an echo of Sir James's years with the Committee of Council on Education] who abused our Mr. Newman (brother of the Cardinal) soundly. . . . After breakfast we 4 went on the lake; and Miss B. & I agreed in thinking Mr. Moseley a good goose; in liking Mr. Newman's Soul—in Liking Modern painters (Ruskin's book), and the idea of the Seven Lamps . . . and she told me about Father Newman's Lectures in a very quiet concise graphic way.[3]

The absence of a hostess afforded the two lady guests the best and swiftest opportunity for making acquaintance. Apart from the excursions organized by Sir James, the days were theirs till the evening and to great profit they put their time, Mrs. Gaskell's sympathy drawing from Charlotte the tale of her life. Then, as later, it appeared not only pitiful to Mrs. Gaskell, but barely credible. Were it not for the scrupulous honesty of the speaker, there were times when Mrs. Gaskell would have doubted what she heard. She wrote to Mrs. Froude:

[1] *Letters of Mrs. G.*, p. 124: op. cit.
[2] Mrs. G. to Tottie Fox, *Letters*, p. 130: op. cit.
[3] *Letters of Mrs. G.*, p. 124: op cit

Miss Brontë I like. Her faults are the faults of the very peculiar circumstances in which she has been placed; and she possesses a charming union of simplicity and power; and a strong feeling of responsibility for the gift which she has given her. She is very little and very plain. Her stunted person she ascribes to the scanty supply of food she had as a growing girl, when at that school of the Daughters of the Clergy.[1]

'Such a life as Miss Brontë's I never heard of before' was Mrs. Gaskell's verdict on the confidences she received in those few days with Charlotte. The contrast between the implacable nature of Charlotte's destiny and surroundings and the smiling sunny landscape of her own home and circumstances were too pronounced for her to keep a balance when the time of assessment came. The first impressions, derived in the heat of revelation, were necessarily simplified, the subtle tones obscured. Charlotte's 'undeveloped' person, her poignant griefs, her stoic acceptance of life as, at best, a 'mixed cup' of blessings —these roused every maternal instinct in Mrs. Gaskell to redress the wrongs that, she felt, had been heaped on this frail creature. Pity was always to remain her predominant feeling towards Charlotte.[2]

Their differences of taste and outlook Mrs. Gaskell accepted, stimulated by Charlotte's fire to defend the causes she had at heart: 'She is very silent—very shy;' Mrs. Gaskell wrote Mrs. Froude, 'and when she speaks, chiefly remarkable for the use she makes of simple words, & the way she makes language express her ideas. She and I quarrelled and differed about almost everything—she called me a democrat; & cannot bear Tennyson—but we like each other heartily, & I hope we shall ripen into friends.'[3]

Charlotte gave her impression of Mrs. Gaskell in a letter to Ellen after her return: 'Lady Shuttleworth never got out, being confined to the house with a cold, but fortunately there was Mrs. Gaskell, the authoress of 'Mary Barton', who came to the Briery the day after me. I was truly glad of her companionship. She is a woman of the most genuine talent, of cheerful, pleasing and cordial manners, and, I believe, of a kind and good heart.'[4]

Mrs. Gaskell's age at the time of her first meeting with Charlotte was just 40.

Of social ordeals Charlotte had only, in the event, to submit to the

[1] Mrs. Gaskell to Mrs. Froude, c. 25 Aug. 1850: *Letters of Mrs. G.*, p. 128: op. cit.
[2] The impression created of CB's ill health was the one generally accepted in society; it caused CB some complications. See Additional Notes.
[3] Mrs. G. to Mrs. Froude: *Letters of Mrs. G.*, p. 129: op. cit.
[4] CB to EN, 26 Aug. 1850: *W & S* iii. 147–8.

one while at Windermere, the visit to the widow of Dr. Arnold, living at Ambleside with her daughters. The Arnolds' house, Fox How, built by Dr. Arnold as a holiday home in 1833, stands by the Rotha off the Rydal Road, towered over by the wooded slopes of Loughrigg Fell, and was plainly visible from Harriet Martineau's house, The Knoll. Miss Martineau was away, to Charlotte's regret, escaping as she did each year from the tourist season, which disturbed the regular residents even in those days.

Charlotte knew nothing as yet of the reputation of Arnold of Rugby, and confessed as much to James Taylor when he lent her the newly published *Life* of the Doctor by Dean Stanley in the autumn. To him she described the charm of Fox How as she saw it on the occasion of her summer visit.

It was twilight as I drove to the place, and almost dark ere I reached it; still I could perceive that the situation was exquisitely lovely. The house looked like a nest half buried in flowers and creepers, and, dusk as it was, I could feel that the valley and the hills round were beautiful as imagination could dream . . . I had not then read Dr. Arnold's Life; otherwise, the visit would have interested me even more than it actually did.[1]

Wordsworth, perhaps the most loved poet of Charlotte's adolescence—as Byron had been of her childhood—no longer trod those shady lanes and wooded hillsides between Grasmere and Ambleside when Charlotte came to the Lakes in August 1850. He had died on 23 April of that year. Of his grave in Grasmere churchyard, easily accessible by Sir James's carriage, neither Mrs. Gaskell nor Charlotte made any mention. Humbler mementoes, however, of his fifty years' residence in that particular area of the lakes and of his friendships for some among his illustrious neighbours, Charlotte certainly saw: notably the chimneys of Fox How which were Wordsworth's 'architectural creation and special care' (so the architect averred) under the eastern gable of which the date, 1833, and the initials of Thomas and Mary Arnold were carved; and the sundial on Harriet Martineau's terrace, for which Wordsworth chose the motto: 'Come, Light, visit me.' He it was, also, who in 1846 planted the two sentinel pine trees that guard The Knoll on the terrace side, 'digging and planting in the most experienced manner', as Harriet Martineau recorded in her *Autobiography*; 'then washed his hands in the watering pot, took my hands in both of his, and wished me happy days in my new abode'.[2]

[1] CB to James Taylor, 6 Nov. 1850: *W & S* iii. 178.
[2] *Autobiography* of HM: op. cit.

During the days at Briery Close Charlotte again had opportunities of meeting the Shuttleworth children's German governess. She told Ellen afterwards:

I saw the governess at Sir J. K. Shuttleworths, she looked a little better and more cheerful. She was almost as pleased to see me as if we had been related, and when I bid her good-bye, expressed an earnest hope that I would soon come again. The children seem fond of her, and on the whole obedient: two great alleviations of the inevitable evils of her position.[1]

Charlotte's visit to Windermere lasted exactly a week—18 to 25 August. On the 26th she wrote to Ellen from home: 'You said I should stay longer than a week in Westmorland; you ought by this time to know better. Is it my habit to keep dawdling at a place long after the time I first fixed on for departing? . . . My visit passed off very well; I am very glad I went.'[2]

The easy relationship instantly established with Mrs. Gaskell can clearly be felt in the first note Charlotte addressed her on reaching home: in it one perceives the various strands of their interrupted talks taken up one by one, and debated at greater length than their limited time together at Windermere allowed. Mrs. Gaskell had championed Tennyson, Charlotte Wordsworth: the proof of their critical 'positions' had to be reinforced by an exchange of books. Dissimilar in taste, they both knew quality when they met it, and for Charlotte the opportunity to talk of literary matters with an intellectual equal was always precious. She wrote on 27 August:

Papa and I have just had tea; he is sitting quietly in his room, and I in mine; 'storms of rain' are sweeping over the garden and churchyard: as to the moors, they are hidden in thick fog. Though alone I am not unhappy; I have a thousand things to be thankful for, and, amongst the rest, that this morning I received a letter from you, and that this evening I have the privilege of answering it.[3]

To Mrs. Gaskell she had told the tale of her sisters' achievement and early deaths; in sending her the volume of their *Poems* now, she characteristically denigrated her own share in the production. She wrote to Mrs. Gaskell:

The little book of rhymes was sent by way of fulfilling a rashly made promise, and the promise was made to prevent you from throwing away four

[1] CB to EN, 2 Sept. 1850: *W & S* iii. 151–2.
[2] CB to EN, 26 Aug. 1850: *W & S* iii. 147.
[3] CB to Mrs. Gaskell, 27 Aug. 1850: *W & S* iii. 149–50.

shillings in an injudicious purchase. I do not like my own share of the work, nor care that it should be read; Ellis Bell's I think good and vigorous, and Acton's have the merit of truth and simplicity. Mine are chiefly juvenile productions, the restless effervescence of a mind that would not be still. In those days the sea too often 'wrought and was tempestuous' and weed, sand, shingle—all turned up in the tumult. This image is much too magniloquent for the subject, but you will pardon it.[1]

The very next week after writing to Mrs. Gaskell, a proposal was made by Smith, Elder which would bring her sisters' achievement even more vividly present to her mind: she was asked to edit a reprint of their literary *Remains*, and preface it with a biographical notice of their lives. 'I should much like to carry out your suggestions', she wrote Mr. Williams on 5 September, 'respecting a reprint of "Wuthering Heights" and "Agnes Grey" in one volume, with a prefatory and explanatory notice of the authors. . . .'[2]

To Mr. Williams's query whether her sisters had left any unpublished material that could now be included in a definitive edition of their works, Charlotte returned so ambiguous an answer that it has left Brontë scholars uncertain and divided in opinion ever since. 'As to additional compositions,' Charlotte wrote Mr. Williams, 'I think there would be none, as I would not offer a line to the publication of which my sisters themselves would have objected.'[3]

That sentence is no decided negative. Newby's letter to Ellis Bell of 15 February 1848 is sufficient proof that Emily *was* engaged on a new novel some time before her death. Charlotte's ambiguous 'giving out', if it means anything, must be an admission that her sisters *did* leave material, but in so unfinished a state and of so personal a nature that she thought it was better to suppress it.

That is, in effect, what she did, save for a very small selection of their poems. She chose seven of Anne's (out of a *known* remaining total of 25 unpublished poems). In her life-time Emily had published 21 poems (her part in the joint volume); to-day her published poems number 193. Of this important poetic legacy Charlotte chose only 18 to represent her sister's genius and, moreover, drastically 'edited' them, as well as Anne's; altering and shortening the texts, suppressing the original Gondal titles, eliminating, in fact, the key to their inspiration and confusing their sense.

---

[1] CB to Mrs. Gaskell, 26 Sept. 1850: *W & S* iii. 162.
[2] CB to WSW, 5 Sept. 1850: *W & S* iii. 155–6.
[3] Ibid.

In the case of Anne, Charlotte confessed to withholding much from publication because of its religious melancholy; there must have been as much in her papers relating to her love for the Revd. Mr. Weightman—to which barely seven poems attest—and to the ordeal of her years at Thorp Green. Charlotte's choice, however, concentrated on her religious outpourings, the *least* personal aspect of Anne's poetry.

In the 'Memoir' prefacing Anne's poems in the new edition, Charlotte wrote: 'In looking over my sister Anne's papers I find mournful evidence that religious feeling had been to her but too much like what it was to Cowper. . . . Some perhaps would rejoice over these tokens of sincere though sorrowing piety in a deceased relative; I own, to me they seem sad, as if her whole innocent life had been passed under the martyrdom of an unconfessed physical pain.'

In her 'Memoir' to the selection of Emily's poems, Charlotte admitted to eliminating all but a very few of the remaining pieces.

It would not have been difficult to compile a volume out of the papers left by my sisters, had I, in making the selection, dismissed from my consideration the scruples and the wishes of those whose written thoughts these papers held. But this was impossible. An influence stronger than could be exercised by any motive of expediency, necessarily regulated the selection. I have, then, culled from the mass only a little poem here and there. The whole makes but a tiny nosegay, and the colour and perfume of the flowers are not such as fit them for festal uses.[1]

While paying a noble tribute to her sisters' characters and lives, and respecting their reticences to the full, Charlotte's editing of their works added nothing to their stature as writers; in her keeping, the vestal flame was so shielded from the contact of air as almost to go out. (Annotators of the text of *Wuthering Heights* know how systematically Charlotte weakened and restrained the language, which has no equal outside Elizabethan literature.)

Several problems were raised by the reprint of *Wuthering Heights* and *Agnes Grey*—the claims of Newby, to begin with. Of his business methods Charlotte had the lowest opinion. 'For my own part,' she wrote Mr. Williams on 13 September, 'the conclusion I drew from the whole of Mr. Newby's conduct to my sisters was that he is a man with whom it is desirable to have little to do; I think he must be needy as well as tricky.'[2] Entering into the conditions of his contracts with Ellis

---

[1] *Memoir of Ellis and Acton Bell* prefixed to posthumous edition of their *Poems*, 1850.
[2] CB to WSW, 13 Sept. 1850: *W & S* iii. 156–7.

and Acton Bell, Charlotte told Smith, Elder that Newby had neither refunded the original £50 paid by her sisters, which became due on the sale of the first 250 copies, together with an equal share in the £100 royalty; *nor* had he ever paid Acton more than £50 out of the contracted £150 for *Wildfell Hall*.

Mention has already been made of Charlotte's definite discouragement of the projected reprint of *Wildfell Hall*:[1] 'Wildfell Hall it hardly appears to me desirable to preserve', she wrote Mr. Williams, and conveyed so strongly her dislike of the book and its subject (too hastily identified as representing the case of Branwell) that Smith, Elder could not well go against her feelings. They waited till 1859, four years after her death, to reprint the book in a Post 8vo single volume edition.

One of the purposes to be served by the Smith, Elder reprint of the works of Ellis and Acton Bell was to settle once and for ever the subject of their true identities. In laying before the world the picture of her sisters' individual natures and qualities, their separate intensely personal responses to the glories of Nature round their home, and to the tribulations of their early lot, Charlotte hoped to establish in the minds of their readers and of posterity for ever an image of their touching genius. This she succeeded in doing.

In Emily's nature the extremes of vigour and simplicity seemed to meet. Under an unsophisticated culture, inartificial tastes and an unpretending outside, lay a secret power and fire that might have informed the brain and kindled the veins of a hero. . . . Anne's character was milder and more subdued. . . . Long-suffering, self-denying, reflective, and intelligent, a constitutional reserve and taciturnity placed and kept her in the shade, and covered her mind, and especially her feelings, with a sort of nunlike veil, which was rarely lifted.[2]

Even as she wrote of the peculiar genius of each sister, Charlotte realized that they were too different from the world of their time for the world to comprehend them: 'for strangers they were nothing', she summed up her tribute; 'for superficial observers less than nothing; but for those who had known them all their lives in the intimacy of close relationship, they were genuinely good and truly great'.[3]

Wuthering Heights and Agnes Grey by Ellis and Acton Bell, 'with a

---

[1] CB to WSW, 5 Sept. 1850: *W & S* iii. 156.
[2] *Memoir of Ellis and Acton Bell*: Smith, Elder, 1850.
[3] Idem.

biographical notice of the authors, a selection from their best literary remains, and a preface by Currer Bell', was published 10 December 1850 in a single volume, price 6s., by Smith, Elder & Co. Though he had not yet, by publication date, bought the authors' rights from Newby, George Smith succeeded in doing so shortly after.

On 8 December Charlotte sent a copy of the new book to Sydney Dobell, author of the article in the September issue of *The Palladium* which, under the title 'Currer Bell', paid such high tribute to the author of *Wuthering Heights* and *Jane Eyre*, while rejecting the separate identities of the Bells.

I offer this little book to my critic in the 'Palladium' . . . not so much for anything he has said of myself as for the noble justice he has rendered to one dear to me as myself—perhaps dearer—and perhaps one kind word spoken for her awakens a deeper, tenderer sentiment of thankfulness than eulogies heaped on my head. As you will see when you have read the biographical notice, my sister cannot thank you herself . . . it revived me for many a day to find that, dead as she was, the work of her genius had at last met with worthy appreciation.[1]

Despite his unshakeable belief in the oneness of the Bell genius, and of his consequent blindness to the divergences of thought and style that informed *Wuthering Heights*, *Jane Eyre*, and *Wildfell Hall* (divergences which he attributed to the times at which they were written), Sydney Dobell had a remarkable insight into Charlotte's genius. He saw that quality which Harriet Martineau discerned in the living woman, and of which she disapproved: the incessant need to be loved. In the *Daily News* review of *Villette* that so wounded Charlotte, Harriet laid her finger on the motivating power of all the action in Charlotte's novels, the medium through which she saw and presented all events and persons: the medium of the passion of love. In Charlotte's heroines what Harriet so deplored was the disregard paid to the 'other substantial, heart-felt interests for women of all ages' that modern life offered them. Not in censure but just as surely, Sydney Dobell with no inside information recognized the *woman* in Currer Bell by the evidence of her attitude to love. 'Every word she utters is female', he wrote. 'Not feminine, but female. . . . It is not merely improbable, but impossible that a man has written "Jane Eyre". Only a woman's eye could see man as she sees him. . . . Never since or before the destruction of the cities has man looked on man with

[1] CB to Sydney Dobell, 8 Dec. 1850: *W & S* iii. 186–7.

this romance of latent love.' Like the pilot light, Sydney Dobell saw this 'latent love' in Charlotte waiting for ever to leap into devouring flame.

Currer Bell, then, is a woman, and a young woman, with a heart, when she wrote 'Jane Eyre', as yet disengaged, though perhaps not wholly unsmitten ... and with powers which have already drawn the best eyes in England ... who, if she can endure the trial of early success, will work one of the richest fields which the world ever offered to labour, and, hand in hand with one or two other poets, may have to carry down to posterity the ideal literature of our day.[1]

Dobell could not have rated Charlotte more highly. He credited her with abilities to sway the course of contemporary history, thought, society. But he feared she might burn herself out if she had not the patience to WAIT—as he impressively implored her. Already in *Shirley* he perceived signs of exhaustion, comparing it and *Jane Eyre* to the 'fat kine and the lean kine'. '. . . it is the prerogative of genius', he declared, 'that its very leaves may be for the healing of the nations. . . . It will be well for the possessor of genius if he can keep silence till that time. These things we commend in love to the authoress of "Shirley". . .'.

'. . . The article in the "Palladium"', wrote Charlotte to James Taylor, 'is one of those notices over which an author rejoices with trembling. . . . I am counselled to wait and watch. D.V. I will do so. . . .'[2] For the time being she had no alternative; the power to create had entirely abandoned her.

The work of reading, sorting, and transcribing her sisters' remaining manuscripts had borne heavily on her spirits and nerves. It revived the full pang of bereavement, as she confessed to Ellen. '. . . I found the task at first exquisitely painful and depressing; . . . it is work that I cannot do in the evening, for if I did I should have no sleep at night. . . . For one or two nights, I scarcely knew how to get on till morning; and when morning came, I was still haunted with a sense of sickening distress. I tell you these things, because it is absolutely necessary to me to have some *relief*. . . .'[3]

The pattern of her life had become one of unrelieved loneliness, whether she was able to work or not. Only the absolute necessity for

---

[1] *The Palladium*, Sept. 1850.
[2] CB to James Taylor, 5 Sept. 1850: *W & S* iii. 153–4.
[3] CB to EN, 3 Oct. 1850: *W & S* iii. 166.

change and companionship, which drove her from time to time away from home, and made her admit, however half-heartedly, the court-ship of such men as James Taylor, altered its course in any way. During the lifetime of her father, to whom she clung as the last spar from the great wreck of her world, no radical alteration could be expected.

In early December Mrs. Gaskell invited her to join her on a visit to her friends the Shaens at their house at Crix, near Chelmsford, for a quiet stay in the country. Charlotte wrote her on 13 December:

My dear Mrs. Gaskell, Miss Shaen's kindness and yours is such that I am placed in the dilemma of not knowing how adequately to express my sense of it. This, I know, however, very well—that if I *could* go with you for a week or two in such a quiet south-country house, and with such kind people as you describe, I should like it much. I find the proposal marvellously to my taste; it is the pleasantest, gentlest, sweetest temptation possible; but, delect-able as it is, its solicitations are by no means to be yielded to without the sanction of reason. . . . Meantime, the *mere thought* of it does me good, and I tell you this because I know that feelings like yours find gratification in the consciousness of having benefitted anybody.[1]

In this instance Charlotte's refusal to join Mrs. Gaskell in the south arose from a pre-engagement to visit Harriet Martineau at Ambleside, which that lady had been urging since October. The task of editing her sisters' papers having made her really ill (as she confessed to Laetitia Wheelwright) she accepted the necessity of a change and travelled to Ambleside on Monday, 16 December.

Harriet's house, The Knoll, which she had built for her at the lake-head just outside Ambleside, was barely two miles from Briery Close, a mile and a half from Rydal Mount, the Wordsworths' home, and within sight of Fox How and Loughrigg Holme, where the Arnolds and Edward Quillinan, the widower of Dora Wordsworth, respectively lived. It was what Emerson called 'a well-neighboured house'.

For Harriet it represented true emancipation: it was her first home, built with her own earnings, after years of drudgery in London lodg-ings, and years of incapacitating illness in relations' homes. She loved the house, and had the good fortune to live in it for thirty years.

It is still[2] there today, built of dark grey Westmorland stone, in

---

[1] By courtesy of the Librarian, Manchester Univ. Lib.
[2] My knowledge of The Knoll has been made possible by the kindness of the present occupiers.

Elizabethan style with gables and clustering chimneys, and with the addition of large bay windows (that cost Harriet £5 per annum in Window Tax). The editor of her *Autobiography*, her friend Maria Chapman, described it as 'overgrown to the very eaves with ivy, jasmine, passion-flowers and climbing roses—which make a harbourage for the birds'. It stood in a two-acre domain, enclosed by a cross-pole fence of larchwood entangled with rose-bushes. A low stone wall circled the terrace, from which stone steps led down to an orchard-slope below, where stood the famous sundial.

Inside, the house was just as pleasant, and Charlotte found the genial chatelaine pleasanter still. Harriet Martineau was a woman of immense humanity. She was deeply concerned for the welfare of others, adopting rather than employing the young village girls she engaged to serve her. Their education, happiness, and health were her active concern, and more than one, after years of devoted service, was married from The Knoll. Charlotte wrote to Ellen on 18 December:

I am at Miss Martineau's for a week. Her house is very pleasant, both within and without arranged at all points with admirable neatness and comfort. Her visitors enjoy the most perfect liberty; what she claims for herself she allows them. I rise at my own hour, breakfast alone (she is up at five, and takes a cold bath, and a walk by starlight, and has finished breakfast and got to her work at 7 o'clock). I pass the morning in the drawing-room, she in her study.[1]

Along one entire length of the drawing-room wall was a bookcase filled with complimentary copies presented by Harriet's author friends. As her acquaintance included almost the entire range of contemporary writers, Charlotte was at no loss to find reading to her taste. On the bookcase stood a French clock and, hanging on the wall facing the drawing-room door, was Harriet's own portrait in crayons by Richmond.

Though her time was her own until 2 o'clock when her hostess put aside her work for the day, Charlotte was fetched most mornings by Sir James Kay-Shuttleworth for a drive (a form of exercise that Harriet execrated and never accepted) and was shown still more of the lakeside now in winter. As a means of placating Sir James, who had counted on her visiting Briery Close on leaving Miss Martineau, Charlotte found the drives effective. Lady Shuttleworth, who was

[1] CB to EN, 18 Dec. 1850: *W & S* iii. 189.

'near her confinement' and did not go out, Charlotte did not see at all.

Harriet was busy on her *History of the Thirty Years Peace 1815 1845* and, realizing perhaps for the first time Charlotte's intense interest in politics, military matters, and, above all, the Duke of Wellington, consulted her as her work progressed. 'She has just been into the room to show me a chapter of her history which she is now writing', Charlotte told her father on 21 December, 'relating to the Duke of Wellington's character and his proceedings in the Peninsula [*sic*] She wanted an opinion on it, and I was happy to be able to give a very approving one—she seems to understand and do him justice.'[1]

Harriet, recalling the same incident for Mrs. Gaskell years later, left a memorable cameo of the scene.

One morning I brought her the 1st part of the chapter on the Peninsular War in my Introductory History, and said, 'Tell me if this will do for a beginning, etc.' I read the page or two to her as we stood before the fire, she looked up at me and stole her hand into mine, and to my amazement the tears were running down her cheeks. She said, 'Oh! I do thank you! Oh! we are of one mind! Oh! I thank you for this justice to the man!' I saw at once there was a touch of idolatry in the case, but it was a charming enthusiasm.

From 2 o'clock the two women walked, talked, and worked together at their embroidery (as Charlotte told Ellen) till the five o'clock dinner hour, after which they spent the evening together. 'It was delightful to sit near her in the evenings and hear her converse,' Charlotte told Mr. Williams, 'myself mute. She speaks with what seems to me wonderful fluency and eloquence. Her animal spirits are as unflagging as her intellectual powers.'[2]

At ten o'clock Charlotte retired to her own room (the bedroom over the dining-room, it is said) and Harriet wrote letters till midnight.

In this close yet unconfined intimacy, they learnt a lot about each other in a few days, Charlotte in particular liking, wondering at, and admiring what she saw, and marvelling at the health and energy of her hostess. 'She appears exhaustless in strength and spirits,' she told Ellen, 'and indefatigible in the faculty of labour. She is a great and a good woman; of course not without peculiarities, but I have seen none as yet that annoy me.'[3]

Harriet's avowed atheism, the subject of daily dissension between

[1] CB to Revd. PB, 21 Dec. 1850: *W & S* iii. 190.
[2] CB to WSW, 3 Jan. 1851: *W & S* iii. 193.
[3] CB to EN, 21 Dec. 1850: *W & S* iii. 191.

the two, neither then nor later caused a real rift between them. *That* was provoked by a far more personal consideration, arising out of Harriet's strictures of the love-interest in *Villette*.

During Charlotte's visit to The Knoll, the proofs of Harriet's forthcoming book—*Letters on the Laws of Man's Social Nature and Development* (which consisted of the correspondence with her close friend Mr. Henry G. Atkinson)—were coming in, which gave Harriet the opportunity of discussing her standpoint with Charlotte. Charlotte was 'very far indeed from sympathising in our doctrine,' Harriet recorded in her *Autobiography*, 'and emphatically said so; but this did not prevent her doing justice to us.' Charlotte was not drawn to what she heard of Mr. Atkinson; she derived an impression, as she said, of a 'cold slow-beating heart' and reported of him that 'he serenely denies us our hope in immortality and quietly blots from man's future, heaven and the life to come. That is why a savour of bitterness seasoned my feeling towards him'.[1] But not towards Harriet. To her she wrote after the book's appearance: 'Having read your book I cannot now think it will create any outcry. You are tender of others; you are serious, reverent and gentle. Who can be angry?'[2]

Nevertheless, the outcry was deafening in the event, and left Charlotte, for once, undecided in her views. She told James Taylor:

It is the first exposition of avowed Atheism and Materialism I have ever read.

In judging of such exposition . . . one would wish entirely to put aside the sort of instinctive horror they awaken . . . and to consider them in an impartial spirit. . . . This I find difficult to do. The strangest thing is that we are called on to rejoice over this hopeless blank. . . . Sincerely—for my own part —do I wish to find and know the Truth, but if this be Truth . . . Man or Woman who beholds her can but curse the day he or she was born.[3]

The atheism of her hostess never blinded Charlotte to her entire honesty and goodness. Charlotte wrote to Taylor after her visit to Ambleside:

Of my kind hostess herself I cannot speak in terms too high. Without being able to share all her opinions, philosophical, political or religious . . . I yet found a worth and greatness in herself, and a consistency, benevolence and perseverance in her practice such as wins the sincerest esteem and affection.

[1] CB to James Taylor, 1 Jan. 1851: *W & S* iii. 193.
[2] *Autobiography*: op. cit.
[3] CB to James Taylor, 11 Feb. 1851: *W & S* iii. 208.

She is not a person to be judged by her writings alone, but rather by her own deeds and life—than which nothing can be more exemplary or nobler.[1]

To her father Charlotte said: 'As to Miss Martineau, I admire her and wonder at her more than I can say. . . . She is very kind to me, though she must think I am a very insignificant person compared to herself.'[2]

Harriet thought no such thing. Recalling Charlotte's visit in her *Autobiography*, she wrote:

Between the appearance of 'Shirley' and that of 'Villette' she came to me—in December 1850. Our intercourse confirmed then my deep impression of her integrity, her noble conscientiousness about her vocation, and her consequent self-reliance in the moral conduct of her life. I saw at the same time tokens of a morbid condition of mind, in one or two directions;—much less than might have been expected . . . under circumstances so unfavourable to health of body and mind as those in which she lived . . . her permanent temper was one of humility, candour, integrity, and conscientiousness. She was not only unspoiled by her sudden and prodigious fame, but obviously unspoilable. . . .

She was somewhat amused at her fame but oftener annoyed; at least when obliged to come out into the world to meet it.

It was impossible for Charlotte staying at the genial Harriet's not to be obliged to 'come out into the world' occasionally. There was Edward Quillinan, Wordsworth's son-in-law, living close by. Poet, translator, and traveller, he was sensitive and distinguished-looking, and he had invited Harriet to dinner for the Monday of Charlotte's arrival. She told him that she expected 'Miss Bronti', and was too busy 'with work all the week to finish'. However, 'I promised to take Miss Bronti with me one day,' Harriet recorded, 'if he would dine early enough to enable my delicate guest to return before nightfall. That was a very pleasant day—no one being there, in addition to the family, but Mrs. Arnold from Fox How, and ourselves.'[3]

To Mrs. Arnold's at Fox How the friends were invited to dine on Saturday, 21 December. As it happened, Matthew Arnold, then aged 28 and until recently a master at Rugby, was at home for the Christmas holidays, and was prepared to put himself out to entertain his mother's illustrious guests. His impressions, red-hot from the experience, were dispatched that very night to his fiancée, Miss Wightman:

At seven came Miss Martineau and Miss Brontë (Jane Eyre); talked to Miss Martineau (who blasphemes frightfully) about the prospects of the Church of

[1] CB to J. Taylor, 1 Jan. 1851: *W & S* iii. 192.
[2] CB to Revd. PB, 21 Dec. 1850: *W & S* iii. 190.   [3] *Autobiography*: op. cit.

England, and, wretched man that I am, promised to go and see her cow-keeping miracle to-morrow—I, who hardly know a cow from a sheep. I talked to Miss Brontë (past thirty and plain, with expressive grey eyes, though) of her curates, of French novels, and her education in a school in Brussels, and sent the lions roaring to their dens at half-past nine, and came to talk to you.[1]

The bright young man who could flippantly dispose of a couple of lionesses in this strain, did not, however, get away without a mauling by one of them. Charlotte, who sat throughout the evening as though she alone was not enjoying the party (so said Miss Arnold in after years), was at her most watchful in the drawing-room at Fox How. She noted how Mrs. Arnold, however good and amiable she might be, lacked both genuineness and simplicity of manner on first acquaintance, and, moreover, how Matthew inherited 'his mother's defect'. Charlotte told James Taylor afterwards:

Striking and prepossessing in appearance, his manner displeases from its seeming foppery. I own it caused me at first to regard him with regretful surprise; the shade of Dr. Arnold seemed to me to frown on his young representative. I was told, however, that 'Mr. Arnold improved upon acquaintance'. So it was: ere long a real modesty appeared under his assumed conceit, and some genuine intellectual aspiration, as well as high educational acquirements, displaced superficial affectation. . . . Most unfortunate for him, doubtless, has been the untimely loss of his father.[2]

On Thursday, 19 December, Sir James dined at The Knoll and Charlotte managed to get out of staying with him 'by a promise to come some other time', as she told Ellen. Relatives of Harriet's and other guests being expected for Christmas, Charlotte left Ambleside on 23 December, but instead of going straight home went to Brookroyd for three days, returning to Haworth on the 26th.

Charlotte confessed with a rare enthusiasm how 'exceedingly' she had enjoyed her visit to Harriet Martineau. She told Mr. Williams on 3 January, 1851:

A visit more interesting I certainly never paid. If self-sustaining strength can be acquired from example, I ought to have got good. But my nature is not hers; I could not make it so though I were to submit it seventy times seven

---

[1] Matthew Arnold to his fiancée Frances Lucy Wightman (whom he married in 1851) 21 Dec. 1850: *Letters of Matthew Arnold*, ed. George W. G. Russell, 1895, i. 13.
[2] CB to James Taylor, 15 Jan. 1851: *W & S* iii. 199.

to the furnace of affliction, and discipline it for an age under the hammer and anvil of toil and self-sacrifice. Perhaps if I was like her I should not admire her so much as I do.[1]

The daily spectacle of Miss Martineau's industry, made possible by her exceptional physique, left Charlotte more than ever conscious of her own painfully limited powers. Sickness and headache (the result of chronic liver deficiency), the all-too recurrent colds and coughs, loneliness, and deep depression—these were the constant handicaps with which she had to contend. The creative impulse languished and the new work, for which her publishers were waiting, was hardly ever mentioned between them, except to dispel any premature hopes on their side. To Mr. Williams, in thanking him for his care in editing her sisters' *Remains*, she made a rare mention of the position in a letter of 2 October 1850:

I feel to my deep sorrow, to my humiliation, that it is not in my power to bear the canker of constant solitude. I had calculated that when shut out from every enjoyment, from every stimulus but what could be derived from intellectual exertion, my mind would rouse itself perforce. It is not so. Even intellect, even imagination, will not dispense with the ray of domestic cheerfulness, with the gentle spur of a family discussion. Late in the evening and all through the nights, I fall into a condition of mind which turns entirely to the past—to memory.... This will never do, and will produce no good. I tell you this that you may check false anticipations.[2]

To Ellen, she added the sad confession: 'I thought to find occupation and interest in writing, when alone at home, but hitherto my efforts have been vain: the deficiency of every stimulus is so complete ... the deadly silence, solitude, desolation, were awful; the craving for companionship, the hopelessness of relief, were what I should dread to feel again.'[3]

To Harriet Martineau she made an even more revealing confession of the paralysing influence of grief: 'I think I would rather hire myself out again as a governess than write against the grain, or out of the mood. I am not like you, who have no bad days. I have had bad days, bad weeks, aye! bad months.'

In solitude she waited for the sign without which, scrupulous artist that she was, she would not write a line.

[1] CB to WSW, 3 Jan. 1851: *W & S* iii. 193.
[2] CB to WSW, 2 Oct. 1850: *W & S* iii. 167.
[3] CB to EN, 23 Oct. 1850: *W & S* iii. 173–4.

THE LONELY HEART

THE new year—1851—did not touch Charlotte's sleeping powers into life; the lethargy of the spirit persisted. A frank confession of her inability to work brought a generous and understanding response from Cornhill, to which she replied on 1 February:

I cannot lose any time in telling you that your letter ... gave me heart-felt satisfaction, and such a feeling of relief as it would be difficult to express in words. The fact is, what goads and tortures me is not any anxiety of my own to publish another book ... but a haunting fear that my dilatoriness disappoints others. Now the 'others' ... reduces itself to my father and Cornhill, and since Cornhill ungrudgingly counsels me to take my own time, I think I can pacify such impatience as my dear father naturally feels. Indeed, your kind and friendly letter will greatly help me.

Since writing the above, I have read your letter to papa. Your arguments have weight with him: he approves, and I am content.[1]

But something more than the inability to concentrate on her writing was at work to unsettle her. Ever since the return from Scotland the previous summer her feelings had been constantly roused by echoes and rumours of a disturbing influence that kept her watchful and unnerved. On 14 September 1850 she wrote:

I wish, dear Ellen, you would tell me what is the 'twaddle about my marrying, etc' which you hear. If I knew the details I should have a better chance of guessing the quarter from which such gossip comes; as it is I am quite at a loss. Whom am I to marry? I think I have scarcely seen a man with whom such a union would be possible since I left London. Doubtless there are men whom if I chose to encourage I might marry, but no matrimonial lot is even remotely offered me which seems to me truly desirable: and even if that were the case, there would be many obstacles; the least allusion to such a thing is most offensive to papa.[2]

Ellen's report coincided curiously with a resumption of the correspondence with James Taylor which, Charlotte had to confess to her

[1] CB to WSW, 1 Feb. 1851: *W & S* iii. 206.
[2] CB to EN, 14 Sept 1850: *W & S* iii. 157–8.

friend, had ceased for some nine months past—ever since her London visit of the previous December. On that occasion, it is evident from her own admission, she was conscious of treating Mr. Taylor 'with injustice and unkindness', and though she had since 'endeavoured to remedy the wrong she once did him', 'both to himself and in speaking of him to others, Mr. Smith to wit', she was convinced, firstly, that Mr. Smith had never passed on the soothing message, and secondly, that Mr. Taylor had not forgiven her.

She was surprised, therefore, in early September, to receive a letter from him and a copy of the literary journal he had formerly sent her regularly. The ostensible object of his letter was to draw her attention to the article in *The Palladium*, whose tribute to Emily, Taylor knew well enough, would rejoice her beyond any tribute to herself. From the time of their meeting at Cornhill in December 1849, Taylor (who had first met her in her home when fetching the manuscript of *Shirley*) had sought to reach Charlotte's heart through the medium of sympathy over the loss of her sisters. Writing to Ellen then, Charlotte had said: 'Mr. Taylor—the little man— . . . tries to be very kind and even to express sympathy sometimes, but he does not manage it.'

Towards his revived offer of friendship Charlotte responded gently now. Thanking him in a letter of 5 September for his letter and the journal, she wrote: 'I need not say how I felt the remarks on "Wuthering Heights"; they woke the saddest yet most grateful feelings . . . they are full of late justice—but it is very late—alas! in one sense too late . . . Whoever the author of this article may be, I remain his debtor.'[1] (The author, as Harriet Marineau shortly after informed C, was Sydney Dobell.) The tender chord had been touched, and in the renewed correspondence Taylor did not lag behind with expressions of feeling. 'The interest you so kindly express in my sisters' works touches me home', Charlotte wrote him after a four-month exchange of letters on 15 January 1851. 'Thank you for it, especially as I do not believe you would speak otherwise than sincerely. The only notices that I have seen of the new edition of "Wuthering Heights" were those in the "Examiner", the "Leader" and "The Athenaeum". That in "The Athenaeum" somehow gave me pleasure; it is quiet but respectful —so I thought, at least.'[2]

The resumed correspondence with Taylor seldom deviated from

[1] CB to James Taylor, 5 Sept. 1850: *W & S* iii. 153–4.
[2] To the same, 15 Jan. 1851: *W & S* iii. 199–200.

literary discussions of books and people—notably the Arnolds, and Harriet Martineau and her atheism, with occasional eulogies of Scotland, his native land. There was little more.

At the same time Charlotte was engaged in a wittier, livelier, far more genial and personal correspondence—that with George Smith of which all too few specimens have been preserved. Only by a few allusions and references can something of their interest to Charlotte be divined.

That she read more than their surface meaning into George Smith's letters is shown by her calling on Ellen for her judgement of them. On 8 January 1851 Charlotte wrote to her: 'Enclosed is a letter received a few days since from Mr. Smith; I wish you would read it because it gives a very fair notion both of his temper and mind. Read, return, and tell me what you think of it.'[1]

Ellen, who would shortly be roundly snubbed for her romantic interpretations of the correspondence, was prepared to see far more than Charlotte admitted to seeing in it. Charlotte answered her on 20 January:

Your last letter but one, dear Ellen, made me smile. I think the undercurrent simply amounts to this—a kind of natural liking and sense of something congenial. Were there no vast barrier of fortune, etc., etc., there is perhaps enough of personal regard to make things possible which are now impossible. If men and women married because they liked each other's temper, look, conversation, nature, and so on, the chance you allude to might be admitted as a chance, but other reasons regulate matrimony, reasons of convenience, of connection, of money. Meantime, I am content to have him as a friend, and pray God to continue to me the common-sense to look on one so young, so rising, so hopeful, in no other light.[2]

George Smith, who had startled his mother and sisters the previous summer by insisting on taking Charlotte to Edinburgh, was now advancing a further suggestion for the coming summer, that Charlotte should join him and his family on a trip up the Rhine. How to interpret this caprice to the prudent Ellen, let alone to herself, Charlotte found difficult indeed. 'That hint about the Rhine disturbs me,' she continued in the same letter, 'I am not made of stone, and what is mere excitement to him is fever to me. However it is a matter for the future, and long to look forward to. As I see it now, the journey is out of the

[1] CB to EN, 8 Jan. 1851: *W & S* iii. 197.
[2] CB to EN, 20 Jan. 1851: *W & S* iii. 201–2.

question, for many reasons. I cannot conceive either his mother or his sisters relishing it, and all London would gabble like a countless host of geese.'[1]

The invitation to the Rhine, coupled with the sight of George Smith's letters, encouraged Ellen to hazard some facetious remarks in return. 'You are to say no more about "Jupiter" and "Venus", Charlotte commanded her in reply. 'What do you mean by such heathen trash? The fact is, no fallacy can be wilder and I won't have it hinted at even in jest, because my common sense laughs it to scorn. The idea of the "little man" shocks me less—it would be a more likely match if "matches" were at all in question, which *they are not.*'[2]

The parallel of this passage occurred 18 months later in the eventual discussion with her publisher over the ending of *Villette*, when Charlotte wrote to George Smith (3 November 1852): 'Lucy must not marry Dr. John; he is far too youthful, handsome, bright-spirited, and sweet-tempered; he is a "curled darling" of Nature and of Fortune, and must draw a prize in life's lottery . . . he must be very happy indeed. If Lucy marries anybody it must be the Professor.'[3]

What Charlotte was admitting to herself already in January 1851 was that *because* the 'little man' was nothing like her ideal of a lover, and she had no right to expect more from life's lottery, her common sense could allow her to contemplate *him* as a suitor but *not* the dazzling George Smith.

Telling Ellen of Taylor's renewed attentions, she wrote:

He still sends his little newspaper—and the other day there came a letter of a bulk, volume, pith, judgement and knowledge, worthy to have been the product of a giant. You may laugh as much and as wickedly as you please—but the fact is there is a quiet constancy about this, my diminutive and red-haired friend, which adds a foot to his stature—turns his sandy locks dark, and altogether dignifies him a good deal in my estimation. However, I am not bothered by much vehement ardour—there is the nicest distance and respect preserved now, which makes matters very comfortable.[4]

The word 'now' makes it clear enough that previously there had been 'vehement ardour'—until extinguished in that first London encounter. The unfortunate Mr. Taylor was still only the lightning-conductor for a flame that could not strike where it willed.

[1] CB to EN, 20 Jan. 1851: *W & S* iii. 201–2.
[2] CB to EN, 30 Jan. 1851: *W & S* iii. 204–5.
[3] CB to Geo. Smith, 3 Nov. 1852: *W & S* iv. 16.
[4] CB to EN, 30 Jan. 1851: *W & S* iii. 205.

On the heels of Mr. Williams's kind, soothing letter on the subject of her work came an invitation to Charlotte from George Smith for another visit to London. Charlotte's reply of 5 February is in her best vein, both of raillery and of firmness in putting aside a temptation. It is a letter that both Jane Eyre and Lucy Snowe might have written, so revealing is it of the need for firmness with herself.

Something you say about going to London, but the words are dreamy, and fortunately I am not obliged to hear or answer them. London and summer are many months away: our moors are all white with snow just now, and little redbreasts come every morning to the window for crumbs. One can lay no plans 3 or 4 months beforehand. Besides, I don't deserve to go to London; nobody merits a change or a treat less. I secretly think, on the contrary, I ought to be put in prison, and kept on bread and water in solitary confinement—without even a letter from Cornhill—till I had written a book. One of two things would certainly result from such a mode of treatment pursued for 12 months; either I should come at the end of that time with a three-volume MS in my hand, or else with a condition of intellect that would exempt me ever after from literary efforts and expectations.[1]

Throughout February and much of March Charlotte was in fairly constant correspondence with Mr. Taylor, receiving each week the copy of his journal and analysing with him the character and quality of the books he regularly chose and sent for her to read. She invariably commended his choice and praised his letters.

Without preamble, or any intimation from the person concerned, Charlotte suddenly learnt from George Smith in the third week of March that James Taylor was shortly sailing to Bombay on the firm's affairs. The fact that the news was not conveyed by himself obviously doubled the shock for Charlotte. She hastily made up a parcel of the Cornhill books and periodicals and returned them to him, writing under separate cover the following day (22 March) a letter whose very reserved tone sufficiently betrayed her offence. Thanking him for the books and periodicals she said:

The article to which you particularly directed my attention was read with pleasure and interest, and if I do not now discuss it more at length, it is because I am well aware how completely your attention must be at present engrossed, since, if I rightly understood a brief paragraph in Mr. Smith's last note, you are now on the eve of quitting England for India.

[1] CB to Geo. Smith, 5 Feb. 1851: *W & S* iii. 206–7.

I will limit myself, then, to the expression of a sincere wish for your welfare and prosperity . . . and to the hope that the great change of climate will bring with it no corresponding risk to health. I should think you will be missed in Cornhill, but doubtless 'business' is a Moloch which demands such sacrifices.

I do not know when you go, nor whether your absence is likely to be permanent or only for a time; whichever it be, accept my best wishes for your happiness, and my farewell, if I should not again have the opportunity of addressing you.[1]

Such an outcome to their relations was wholly unexpected by Charlotte. She knew of Smith, Elder's important trade with India (it included a postal service using Lieut. Waghorn's 'overland route' to India via Suez) which had so increased of recent years as to surpass in the volume and variety of exports the transactions of all the other Anglo-Indian agencies. She knew too of Mr. Taylor's responsibility for that side of the business, but little had she expected that it would take him overseas. The suddenness and finality of the event shook her.

Meanwhile, James Taylor, who never supposed his important news would reach her by other channels, wrote from Scotland the very next day to announce it and to ask her permission to call on his way south. Charlotte's reply, written 24 March, was couched in very different terms from her letter of the previous day. 'My dear Sir—I had written briefly before I received yours . . . I will now only say that my father and myself will have pleasure in seeing you on your return from Scotland—a pleasure tinged with sadness certainly, as all partings are, but still a pleasure.'[2]

The need to open her heart to Ellen and receive her advice on her affairs even before this crisis had prompted Charlotte to invite Ellen at rather short notice for a brief visit to Haworth. The visit occurred during the second and third weeks in March. Evidence of it, and also of Charlotte's feelings for her friend, is contained in a letter to Mrs. Gaskell of 25 March. Thanking Mrs. Gaskell for yet another kind invitation, Charlotte wrote:

Kind, pleasant and cordial is your little note, and you are thanked for it. If it had come a week ago, I should just have obeyed its injunctions simply and at once—and gone straight over to Manchester for a few days; but I have an old friend and schoolfellow staying with me just now . . . so that at present I am bound at home.

[1] CB to J. Taylor, 22 Mar. 1851: *W & S* iii. 213–14.
[2] CB to J. Taylor, 24 Mar. 1851: *W & S* iii. 214–15.

You do not know—you cannot tell what a relief is her society; not that she boasts any special superiority of character—but she is at least truly good and kind and we have many quiet subjects of interest in common, and her attentions—her affection—her very presence give me a sort of new life—a support and repose for which I cannot be too thankful. Then it does me good to have to look after her comfort in return, to be called on to amuse her and make her happy; my rest at night has been calmer and more continuous since she came; she benefits me indeed in many ways.[1]

Ellen had returned home by the time Mr. Taylor came to Haworth on Friday, 4 April. The upshot of the visit was wholly negative. How this could be Charlotte found difficult to explain, too shaken in mind by the occurrence to adhere to a single line of conduct. All too obviously, in the presence of the man who had come to engage her troth, she had been unable to give him the one sign he waited for. To his advances she had not only been dumb, she had recoiled. She wrote to Ellen on the 9th:

... each moment he came near me, and that I could see his eyes fastened on me my veins ran ice. Now that he is away I feel far more gently towards him, it is only close by that I grow rigid—stiffening with a strange mixture of apprehension and anger—which nothing softens but his retreat and a perfect subduing of his manner. I did not want to be proud, nor intend to be proud, but I was forced to be so.[2]

James Taylor had found nothing to say that could evoke a response. Like her own Jane Eyre she could only repeat: 'My heart is mute—my heart is mute!'

His absence was to be for five years. This alone militated against him: '. . . An absence of five years—a dividing expanse of three oceans —the wide difference between a man's active career and a woman's passive existence—these things are almost equivalent to an eternal separation. . .' she declared to Ellen. But the real barrier, the one that was 'more difficult to pass than any of these' was simply the man himself: 'Would Mr. Taylor and I ever suit? Could I ever feel for him enough love to accept him as a husband?'[3] On the very evening of his departure Charlotte had plainly seen the impossibility:

As he stood near me, as he looked at me in his keen way, it was all I could do to stand my ground tranquilly and steadily, and not to recoil as before.

[1] By courtesy of the Librarian, Manchester Univ. Lib.
[2] CB to EN, 9 Apr. 1851: *W & S* iii. 222.
[3] Idem.

It is no use saying anything if I am not candid—I avow then, that on this occasion, predisposed as I was to regard him very favourably—his manners and his personal presence scarcely pleased me more than at the first interview.[1]

Even after the passage of several days, the impression was as strong:

It would sound harsh were I to tell even *you* of the estimate I felt compelled to form respecting him; dear Nell, I looked for something of the gentleman— something I mean of the *natural* gentleman; you know I can dispense with acquired polish, and for looks, I know myself too well to think that I have any right to be exacting on that point. I could not find one gleam, I could not see one passing glimpse, of true good-breeding; it is hard to say, but it is true. In mind too; though clever, he is second-rate; thoroughly second-rate. One does not like to say these things, but one had better be honest. Were I to marry him, my heart would bleed in pain and humiliation; I could not, *could* not look up to him. No—if Mr. Taylor be the only husband fate offers to me, single I must always remain.[2]

Yet the decision brought no relief. How she had rested on the possibility of such a union she let appear. '. . . Something at my heart aches and gnaws drearily. . .' she confessed on the very day of his departure; 'Certainly I shall not soon forget last Friday and *never*, I think, the evening and night succeeding that morning and after- noon. . . .' In a few days she had to own: 'a more entire crumbling away of a seeming foundation of support and prospect of hope than that which I allude to, can scarcely be realised. . . . We will say no more about it. . .'.[3]

One thing emerged from their meeting. Taylor admitted to going to India very much against his wish; and from that and other hints he let drop, Charlotte derived the impression that there was a certain mystery about the whole transaction, as she wrote to Ellen on 5 April. This suspicion was heightened by the circumstance that he 'studiously avoided reference to Mr. Smith individually—speaking always of the "house"—the "firm". . .'.

She wrote Ellen a few days later:

There is still a want of plain, mutual understanding in this business, and there is sadness and pain in more ways than one. My conscience, I can truly say, does not *now* accuse me of having treated Mr. Taylor with injustice or unkindness. What I once did wrong in this way, I have endeavoured to

[1] CB to EN, 4 Apr. 1851: *W & S* iii. 220–1.
[2] CB to EN, 23 Apr. 1851: *W & S* iii. 228–9.
[3] CB to EN, 12 Apr. 1851: *W & S* iii. 223–4.

remedy both to himself and in speaking of him to others, Mr. Smith to wit, though I more than doubt whether that last opinion will ever reach him.[1]

The inference broadly admitted here that Messrs. Smith and Taylor did not pull well together, and that Cornhill was too small to hold them both, was inescapable.

From Mr. Williams on more than one occasion, Charlotte received eulogies of James Taylor, but from George Smith—who yet was left 'loaded with work by the departure of Mr. Taylor'—she heard only complaints about his temper.[2]

Mr. Taylor gave Charlotte a book at parting, 'requesting in his brief way, that I would keep it for his sake, and adding hastily, "I shall hope to hear from you in India—your letters *have* been, and *will* be a greater refreshment than you can think of or I can tell."'[3]

From London he wrote to her on 23 April announcing his departure for 20 May and hoping that he might yet see her there before he sailed. This, Charlotte told him, was unlikely since her projected visit to London was not until June.

Mr. Taylor found a champion in an unexpected quarter, in no less a person than Mr. Brontë himself. Charlotte wrote to Ellen on 5 May:

I discover with some surprise Papa has taken a decided liking to Mr. Taylor. The marked kindness of his manner when he bid him good-bye, exhorting him to be 'true to himself, his country and his God', and wishing him all good wishes, struck me with some astonishment. Whenever he has alluded to him since, it has been with significant eulogy. When I alluded that he was no gentleman, he seemed out of patience with me for the objection. You say papa has penetration. On this subject I believe he has indeed. I have told him nothing, yet he seems to be 'au fait' to the whole business. I could think at some moments his guesses go further than mine. I believe he thinks a prospective union, deferred for 5 years, with such a decorous reliable personage, would be a very proper and advisable affair.[4]

A marriage deferred for five years, when he himself might no longer be alive to need a daughter's care, was the sort of calculation that Mr. Brontë's detractors over the years have not failed to accuse him with. The facts are probably quite different. Martha Brown and her family were witnesses that Mr. Brontë feared marriage[5] for his tiny daughter chiefly for the dangers of child-bearing (and in this proved himself a

[1] CB to EN, 23 Apr. 1851: *W & S* iii. 228–9.
[2] CB to EN, 2 June 1851: *W & S* iii. 241. [3] CB to EN, 4 Apr. 1851: op. cit.
[4] CB to EN, 5 May 1851: *W & S* iii. 230–1. [5] Chadwick 477.

wise father). Taylor's absence till a time when Charlotte might be beyond child-bearing was far more probably Mr. Brontë's motive in supporting his courtship. Taylor appeared moreover to be the sort of man to provide adequate security and companionship for Charlotte when she was bereft of her father. For these reasons he alone of all Charlotte's suitors received Mr. Brontë's vote.

Without knowing all his motives, Charlotte had yet a profound respect for her father's judgement. If James Taylor did not appear ungentlemanly to him, she had deeply to question her own, perhaps unjustifiable, reactions. But months after he had sailed, and had written a few times from India, Charlotte was still as uncertain of her feelings for him. She wrote to Ellen (4 November 1851): '. . . This little man with all his long letters remains as much a conundrum to me as ever. . . .' The 'conundrum', as it concerned her, was never resolved. When James Taylor returned to England in 1856, Charlotte was dead.

As the projected time for her visit to London approached, Charlotte was relieved of one difficult decision she might have been called on to make: George Smith wrote to say that the trip up the Rhine that summer was called off, for purely business reasons. (In the event, he allowed himself only one day's holiday that year.) In reply to his letter of regrets Charlotte wrote on 19 April:

> Your project, depend on it, has been quite providentially put a stop to. And do you really think I would have gone to the Rhine this summer? Do you think I would have partaken in all that unearned pleasure?
>
> Now listen to a serious word. You might *possibly* have persuaded me to go (I do not *think* you would, but it does not become me to be very positive on that point, seeing that proofs of inflexibility do not abound). Yet had I gone I should not have been truly happy; self-reproach would have gnawed at the root of enjoyment. . . . Ergo, though I am sorry for your own and your sister's sake that your castle on the Rhine has turned out a castle in the air, I am not at all sorry for mine.[1]

When the tone of her letters to George Smith is compared with that of her letters to James Taylor, the world separating these two men in her estimation becomes all too evident.

Several letters were exchanged between her and her publisher before the date of her visit was fixed. To Ellen, on 26 May, she wrote to announce it: 'Next Thursday is the day now fixed for my going. I have heard again from Mr. Smith and his mother. I would send you the notes, only that I fear your comments; you do not read them by my

[1] CB to Geo. Smith, 19 Apr. 1851: *W & S* iii. 227–8.

lights and would see more in an impetuous expression of quite temporary satisfaction, than strict reality justifies.'[1]

Ellen might indeed have judged mistakenly of the 'impetuous expressions of satisfaction' had she seen only one side of the correspondence, for Charlotte's side was also necessarily withheld from her; and Charlotte's side revealed a degree of intimacy and ease that Ellen had probably never found in her before. Never was Charlotte less sententious, less guarded, less pompous than in her letters to George Smith. He had a gift for infusing her with life, and frequently with gaiety that no other correspondent achieved. She could not but recognize how exhilarating she found his friendship.

Her letter of 12 May is a good example of her manner with him. Opening with a comparison of Thackeray's sneering approach to his art and Ruskin's earnest one, she continued on the theme of her forthcoming visit:

I wondered to myself once or twice, whether there would be any chance of hearing his [Thackeray's] lectures. No doubt they will be blent throughout with sarcasm calculated to vex one to the heart—but still—just out of curiosity one would like to know what he will say. . . .

Of course I am not in the least looking forward to going to London—nor reckoning on it—not allowing the matter to take any particular place in my thoughts: no: I am very sedulously cool and nonchalant—Moreover—I am not going to be glad to see anybody there; *gladness* is an exaggeration of sentiment one does not permit oneself; to be *pleased* is quite enough—and not too well pleased either—only with pleasure of a faint tepid kind—and to a stinted penurious amount. Perhaps—when I see your Mother and Mr. Williams again—I shall just be able to get up a weak flicker of gratification—but that will be all. From even this effort—I shall be exempt on seeing *you*. Authors and publishers are never expected to meet with any other than hostile feelings and on shy and distant terms. They never ought to have to shake hands; they should just bow to each other and pass by on the opposite sides—keeping several yards distance between them. And besides if obliged to communicate by Post—they should limit what they have to say to concise notes of about three lines apiece—which reminds me that this is too long and that it is time I thanked you for sending the Dividend—and begged with proper form to be permitted to subscribe myself—respectfully yours—[2]

Confirming her arrival to Mrs. Smith in a letter of 20 May, she gave one of those sudden personal revelations that make her life—and

[1] CB to EN, 26 May 1851: *W & S* iii. 237.
[2] CB to Geo. Smith, 12 May 1851: *W & S* iii. 232-3.

suffering—so real to her readers: 'I will not say much about being glad to see you all', she wrote. 'Long ago, when I was a little girl, I received a somewhat sharp lesson on the duty of being glad in peace and quietness—in fear and moderation; this lesson did me good and had not been forgotten. . . . If I do not hear from you, I shall conclude that it [the day fixed] is approved. I should come by the express train which arrives at Euston Square at 10 p.m.'[1]

However much Ellen might be deprived of a sight of the 'impetuous expressions of satisfaction' addressed to Charlotte by her host, she was kept informed of Charlotte's shopping at Leeds in preparation for her visit, where she bought a bonnet at Hunt & Hall's 'which seemed grave and quiet there amongst all the splendours, but now it looks infinitely too gay with its pink lining', and where she also saw 'some beautiful silks of pale sweet colours but had not the spirit or the means to launch out at the rate of 5/- per yard, and went and bought a black silk at 3/- after all. . . .' Charlotte added the doubly touching admission that she regretted this 'because papa says he would have lent me a sovereign if he had known. . . .'[2]

The evidence of the pink-lined bonnet and of the silk gown, that *should* have been of a 'pale sweet colour' even by Mr. Brontë's reckoning, inclined the little circle that cherished Charlotte to draw its own conclusions: answering Ellen's banter on the theme, Charlotte wrote her on 21 May: 'Your poor mother is like Tabby—Martha and Papa—all these fancy I am somehow, by some mysterious process, to be married in London, or to engage myself to matrimony. How I smile internally! How groundless and impossible is the idea! Papa seriously told me yesterday, that if I married and left him, he should give up house-keeping and go into lodgings!'[3]

In beautiful weather Charlotte travelled up to London on Wednesday, 28 May, the date being advanced by one day to allow her to attend Thackeray's second lecture[4] on the English Humorists on the Thursday afternoon. She wrote immediately the next morning to announce

---

[1] CB to Mrs. Smith, 20 May 1851: *W & S* iii. 234.

[2] CB to EN, 10 May 1851: *W & S* iii. 231.

[3] CB to EN, 21 May 1851: *W & S* iii. 236.

[4] CB attended four of Thackeray's six lectures, those of 29 May, 5 June (postponed to 12 June), 19 June, 26 June. The advertisement announcing them gave the ticket agencies where seats could be booked; these included 'Messrs Smith, Elder, Cornhill'. The third lecture scheduled for 5 June was postponed to 12 June at the petition of fashionable ladies of T's audience, who wished to attend Ascot Races on the former date. CB mentioned the postponement in the letter of 14 June to her father (*W & S* iii. 246–7), with sarcastic comments on T's snobbery and submission to his 'Duchesses'.

her safe arrival—'without any damage or smash in tunnels or cuttings' —to her anxious father. Waiting for her at Euston Square Station, though it was 10 o'clock at night, were George Smith and his mother, who gave her a 'kind and cordial welcome. . .'.

The next afternoon her round of engagements began with the most stimulating of all to her thinking: Thackeray's lecture. It was devoted to Congreve and Addison. The lectures were given on successive Thursdays in Willis's Rooms, King Street, St. James's, 'where Almack's balls are held, a great painted and gilded saloon with long sofas for benches. . .', as Charlotte described to Ellen in a letter of 2 June, adding that 'the audience was said to be the cream of London Society, and it looked so'. Charlotte was accompanied by Mrs. Smith. As she entered the room, Thackeray recognized her and came forward to greet her, and took her up to his mother, 'a fine, handsome, young-looking old lady', who was very gracious, Charlotte told Ellen. Thackeray's mother, Mrs. Carmichael Smyth (whose husband stood for the proto-type of Colonel Newcome), was only 19 years older than her famous son, and was in fact 59 when Charlotte remarked on her youthful looks.

In a later account of the meeting Charlotte added the comment: '. . . His mother who (he says) is the original of Helen Pendennis, came to see me the other day. I liked her better than I thought I should. . . .'[1]

Within five minutes of meeting Currer Bell again, Thackeray was guilty of a solecism compared with which his flight from the reception in her honour the previous year was nothing. Leading Charlotte up to his mother he said, 'Mother, you must allow me to introduce you to Jane Eyre.'—All eyes were turned towards Charlotte who, according to George Smith, 'was very angry'.

She was sufficiently able to master her anger to enjoy every moment of the lecture, however. She wrote to her father next day that it was 'truly good; he has taken pains with the composition. It was finished without being in the least studied, a quiet humour and graphic force enlivened it throughout'.[2] The ease with which he addressed his fashionable audience did not escape the painfully shy author of *Jane Eyre*. 'The audience was composed of the elite of London society', she told her father. 'Duchesses were there by the score, and amongst them the great and beautiful Duchess of Sutherland the Queen's Mistress of the Robes. Amidst all this Thackeray just got up and spoke with as

[1] CB to Amelia Ringrose, 7 June 1851: *W & S* iii. 244.
[2] CB to Revd. PB, 31 May 1851: *W & S* iii. 239.

much simplicity and ease as if he had been speaking to a few friends by his own fireside.'[1]

Charlotte herself received more attention than she liked. 'Just before the lecture began', she wrote Ellen, 'somebody came up behind me, leaned over and said, "Permit me, as a Yorkshireman, to introduce myself." I turned round, saw a strange, not handsome face, which puzzled me for half a minute, and then I said, "You are Lord Carlisle." '[2]

Richard Monckton Milnes (later Lord Houghton and the biographer of Keats) made the same claim to her acquaintance, and Dr. Forbes, whom she had consulted by post when Emily was dying, came forward also and introduced himself. Charlotte 'was sincerely glad to see him'.

Mrs. Gaskell[3] has described how Thackeray, when his lecture was ended, left the platform and came down the hall to Charlotte to ask what she thought of it, and how taken aback she was by the *naïveté* of the gesture. Transposing the incident into the setting of *Villette*, where Paul Emanuel shows a similar lack of self-control and reticence, Charlotte described her own feelings thus: 'He should not have cared just then to ask what I thought, and what anybody thought; but he *did* care, and he was too natural to conceal, too impulsive to repress his wish. . . . I would have praised him; I had plenty of praise in my heart; but alas! no words on my lips. Who *has* words at the right moment.'[4]

Thackeray's unfortunate gaffe in blurting out the name of 'Jane Eyre' exposed Charlotte to a considerable ordeal in leaving the hall. As she and Mrs. Smith moved to go, Mrs. Smith became aware that the packed audience was respectfully making a lane 'of eager and admiring faces' down which Charlotte had to pass to reach the exit. The hand on Mrs. Smith's arm trembled terribly, but otherwise Charlotte did not flinch. The shyest of women, exposed to a wholly unsought demonstration of respect, may have reflected that it was not just for her, but for her creation and also for her sisters that the tribute was paid.

Thackeray did not escape unscathed for his levity. The next morning Mrs. Carmichael Smyth 'and one of her grand-daughters' (presumably Anne, now aged 14) called on Charlotte, and shortly afterwards the 'Titan' himself appeared. George Smith, who came in later,

[1] CB to Revd. PB, 31 May 1851: *W & S* iii. 239.
[2] CB to EN, 2 June 1851: *W & S* iii. 241.
[3] Gaskell 335–6.   [4] *Villette*, ch. 27.

recorded what he had observed. As he entered the drawing-room, he saw Thackeray

standing on the hearth-rug looking anything but happy. Charlotte Brontë stood close to him, with head thrown back and her face white. The first words I heard were 'No, Sir! If *you* had come to our part of the country in Yorkshire, what would you have thought of me if I had introduced you to my father, before a mixed company of strangers, as "Mr. Warrington"'? Thackeray replied, 'No, you mean Arthur Pendennis.' 'No, I *don't* mean Arthur Pendennis—I mean Mr. Warrington, and Mr. Warrington would not have behaved as you behaved to me yesterday.' The spectacle of this little woman, *hardly reaching* to Thackeray's elbow, but, somehow, looking stronger and fiercer than himself . . . resembled the dropping of shells into a fortress.[1]

To her home correspondents Charlotte did not mention Thackeray's indiscretion towards her, but reported his call, and having 'a long talk with him...', and added: 'I think he knows me now a little better than he did; but of this I cannot yet be sure; he is a great and strange man.'[2]

With the exception of the first lecture in the series, on Swift, and the last on Sterne and Goldsmith, Charlotte was able to attend all Thackeray's lectures while in London. When they appeared in book form two years later, she wrote to Mr. Williams:

I thought well of them when I heard them delivered, but now I see their real power, and it is great. The lecture on Swift was new to me; I thought it almost matchless. Not that by any means I always agree with Mr. Thackeray's opinions, but his force, his penetration, his pithy simplicity, his eloquence— his manly, sonorous eloquence—command entire admiration . . . I was present at the Fielding lecture; the hour spent in listening to it was a painful hour. That Thackeray was wrong in his way of treating Fielding's character and vices, my conscience told me. After reading that lecture I trebly felt that he was wrong.[3]

With the ruin of Branwell in mind, Charlotte's heavy condemnation of Thackeray's cynicism takes on a meaning that best explains why she always took so personal an interest in his moral vagaries, and why she both feared and rejected his philosophy of life. 'Had Thackeray owned a son, grown or growing up, and a son brilliant and reckless—would he have spoken in that light way of courses that

[1] *George Smith, A Memoir*: by his widow. Privately printed (1902), 99–100.
[2] CB to EN, 2 June 1851: *W & S* iii. 240.
[3] CB to WSW, 17 May 1853: *W & S* iv. 66–67.

lead to disgrace and the grave? He speaks of it all as if he theorised; as if he had never been called on . . . to witness the actual consequences of such failings; as if he had never stood by and seen the issue, the final result of it all.'[1]

To the end of her life, Charlotte would be puzzled by Thackeray— the trivialities, the vulgarities even, of his nature, blending so ill with the native distinction, the profuse endowments, the genial warmth, and the fundamental sentimentalism of the man. Reports of his extravagance, his buying of carriages and horses, his pursuit of money, puzzled and saddened the ascetic little 'Joan of Arc', as he called her. '. . . He stirs in one both sorrow and anger,' she wrote Mrs. Gaskell (22 January 1851). 'Why should he lead so harassing a life? Why should his mocking tongue so perversely deny the better feelings of his better moods. . . ?' The report that he had accepted an engagement to appear with Barnum's Circus roused her true contempt. 'If he has— let him speak of it with what levity and sarcasm he may—he has done wrong . . . better be very poor than make money thus. . . .'[2] The report, of course, was false; but Charlotte herself saw her hero to almost equal disadvantage on the occasion of his dining at the Smiths' during her stay in town. She wrote to her father on 14 June:

I almost wonder the Londoners don't tire a little of this vast Vanity Fair— and, indeed, a new toy has somewhat diverted the attention of the grandees lately, viz. a fancy ball given last night by the Queen. The great lords and ladies have been quite wrapt up in preparations for this momentous event. Their pet and darling, Mr. Thackeray, of course, sympathises with them. He was here yesterday to dinner, and left very early in the evening in order that he might visit respectively the Duchess of Norfolk, the Marchioness of Londonderry, Ladies Chesterfield and Clanricarde, and see them all in their fancy costumes of the reign of Charles II before they set out for the Palace![3]

Commenting on the financial success of his lectures, estimated by Mr. Smith as £4,000, Charlotte added that Thackeray was a 'good deal spoiled by all this . . . and indeed it cannot be otherwise. . . .'.

Towards herself Thackeray was exceedingly kind and attentive. 'He has offered two or three times to introduce me to some of his great friends,' Charlotte told her father, 'and says he knows many great ladies who would receive me with open arms if I would go to their

[1] CB to WSW, 17 May 1853: *W & S* iv. 66–67.
[2] CB to Mrs. Gaskell: by courtesy of the Librarian, Manchester Univ. Lib.
[3] CB to Revd. PB, 14 June 1851: *W & S* iii. 246–7.

houses; but, seriously, I cannot see that this sort of society produces so good an effect on him as to tempt me in the least to try the same experiment, so I remain obscure.'[1]

Thackeray and Charlotte did not meet again after that summer in London, though they exchanged occasional letters. What he really thought of her, as a woman and as an artist, he partially revealed in letters to friends, to Mary Holmes notably, to whom he made two important confidences respecting Charlotte. Forwarding a letter from Charlotte on 25 February 1852 he wrote:

> You see by Jane Eyre's letter don't you why we can't be very great friends? We had a correspondence—a little one; and met, very eagerly on her part. But there's a fire raging in that little woman, a rage scorching her heart w[hich] doesn't suit me. She has had a story and a great grief that has gone badly with her. 'Tis better to have loved and lost than never to have loved at all.' I said the same thing before I read it in Tennyson.[2]

Thackeray had the insight to penetrate to the heart of Charlotte's suffering before the publication of *Villette*, when many other perspicacious readers did the same.

As an artist, Thackeray found fault with Charlotte for 'writing in a passion about her characters'. Discussing her further in a letter to Mary Holmes of 10 August 1852, he said: 'I think Miss Brontë is unhappy and that makes her unjust. Novel writers should not be in a passion with their characters as I imagine, but describe them, good or bad, with a like calm.'[3]

Before Charlotte met Thackeray what she admired about him more than anything else as a novelist was precisely this Olympian calm. Writing to W. S. Williams on 29 March 1848 about *Vanity Fair*, then coming out in monthly parts, she said: 'Thackeray is a Titan, so strong that he can afford to perform with calm the most herculean feats; there is the charm and majesty of repose in his greatest efforts; *he* borrows nothing from fever, his is never the energy of delirium—... Thackeray is never borne away by his own ardour—he has it under control.'[4]

In such fundamental differences of temperament lay, all too evidently, the inability of these two geniuses to agree. The fact remains that Charlotte's opinion was important to Thackeray, and he quoted

---

[1] Idem.
[2] *Letters and Private Papers of W. M. Thackeray*, iii. 12.
[3] Idem, iii. 63.
[4] CB to WSW, 29 Mar. 1848,: *W & S* ii. 201.

her strictures or approbation in letters to his mother and his friends, with pique or satisfaction, as the case might be.[1]

Apart from Thackeray's weekly lectures the high-light of Charlotte's London visit in 1851 was the performances of Rachel, the great French tragedienne. Considerably against her taste and inclination she was also obliged to visit Paxton's 'fabulous' Crystal Palace in Hyde Park, where she was taken five times.

Though usually attending the services at the Chapel Royal, St. James's, on Sundays, Charlotte's curiosity after other forms of religious observances prompted her to explore and experiment. She made a point of attending two services conducted by the recently elevated Roman Cardinal of Westminster, Nicholas Wiseman, and sent her father blazing hot reports on them. She wrote Mr. Brontë on 17 June:

Yesterday I saw Cardinal Wiseman and heard him speak. It was at a meeting of the Roman Catholic Society of St. Vincent de Paul; the Cardinal presided. He is a big portly man something of the shape of Mr. Morgan; he has not merely a double but a treble and quadruple chin; he has a very large mouth with oily lips, and looks as if he would relish a good dinner with a bottle of wine after it. He came swimming into the room smiling, simpering and bowing like a fat old lady, and sat down very demure in his chair, and looked the picture of a sleek hypocrite.

On 22 June, Sunday, Charlotte went to a confirmation service at the Spanish Ambassador's chapel, at which Cardinal Wiseman officiated 'in his archi-episcopal robes and mitre. . . . The whole scene was impiously theatrical', as she told Ellen.

She derived a very different stimulus from hearing the French Protestant preacher, D'Aubigné, on her first Sunday (1 June) in town, and confessed to Ellen that 'it was pleasant—half sweet, half sad—and strangely suggestive, to hear the French language once more. . . '.[2]

Her curiosity and determination to pursue the truth wherever it might be found, prompted her also to ask George Smith to take her to a yet different form of worship: to a service at the Friends' Meeting House in Leicester Square. 'I am afraid this form of worship', commented George Smith, 'afforded her more amusement than edification. . . .'

[1] *Letters and Private Papers of W. M. Thackeray*: op. cit.
[2] Charlotte made a strange reference to the experience of that day, writing of it as 'a day to be marked with a white stone—though most of the day I was very happy without being tired or over-excited . . .': CB to EN, 2 June 1851: *W & S* iii. 241.

The great French tragedienne, Rachel, was in London that summer, giving a number of performances from her repertoire at the St. James's Theatre, the success of which extended the season from 2 June to 26 July. Charlotte's letters to her various friends show that she saw Rachel twice—in both her classical and modern vein; in the contemporary Scribe's *Adrienne Lecouvreur*, and in Corneille's *Les Trois Horaces*, with Rachel playing the part of Camille. Charlotte's comments both at the time and in the famous passage in *Villette* where she describes the performance of 'Vashti', convey the fascination rooted in horror, incredulity, and wonder that the great French artist awoke in her. Charlotte, however, saw Rachel in two of her 'mildest' roles. One wonders what her epithets would have been had she seen her in *Phèdre* or *Athalie*. Rachel appeared in *Phèdre* on her opening night in London, 2 June, the English press commenting that she 'was as passionate and artistic' in the role as ever. As 'Adrienne' (which she saw on 7 June) Charlotte found her acting 'something apart from any other acting it has come in my way to witness—her soul is in it—and a strange soul she has—it is my hope to see her again. She and Thackeray are the two living things that have a spell for me in this great London—and the one of them is sold to the Great Ladies—and the other—I fear—to Beelzebub.'[1]

Rachel's diabolical inspiration affected Charlotte still more powerfully in the part of 'Camille'; 'I shall never forget her—She will come to me in sleepless nights again and again . . . I would go every night for 3 months to watch and study its manifestation . . .'[2] she told Sydney Dobell. To her other correspondents she also confessed her subjection to the great actress's thrall. 'On Saturday [21 June] I went to see and hear Rachel,' she told Ellen, 'a wonderful sight, terrible as if the earth had cracked deep at your feet, and revealed a glimpse of hell. I shall never forget it. She made me shudder to the marrow of my bones; in her some fiend has certainly taken up an incarnate home. She is not a woman; she is a snake.'[3]

Incorporating the experience of that night (with so much else derived from her London visits) into the texture of *Villette*, Charlotte greatly elaborated her reactions to the acting of Rachel. 'Before calamity she is a tigress,' she wrote there, 'she rends her woes, shivers them in compulsed abhorrence. Pain, for her, has no result in good;

---

[1] CB to Amelia Ringrose, 11 June 1851: *W & S* iii. 245.
[2] CB to Sydney Dobell, 28 June 1851: *W & S* iii. 253.
[3] CB to EN, 24 June 1851: *W & S* iii. 251.

tears water no harvest of wisdom: on sickness, on death itself, she looks with the eye of a rebel. Wicked, perhaps, she is not, but also she is strong.'[1]

The range of voice and gesture, of expression and pose required of a consummate actress of the Comédie Française school, were both too conventional and too immoderate for Charlotte to distinguish the degree of truth attained. To her the artifice of Rachel's effects was inhuman, its extravagance obscene. In blaming the ferocity of the presentation, Charlotte forgot that the passion depicted was not of Rachel's creation, but of Corneille's before her. That the performance struck Charlotte as larger than life, titanic in scale, is all too evident; but then, as she confessed to Amelia Ringrose, 'as yet it has not been my lot to set eyes on any serious acting for which I cared a fig'.[2]

In *Villette*, as no doubt in the theatre itself, Charlotte was concerned to penetrate the feelings of her companions at the spectacle, 'Dr. John' in the one instance, George Smith in the other; and what she found in that scrutiny gives in great measure the key to their true relations. Had all other things been equal between them—age, fortune, health—this *lack* of depth in the man would effectually have prevented a true union between him and this particular woman: Charlotte wrote of Dr. John:

His heart has no chord for enthusiasm. To bright soft, sweet influences his eyes and lips gave bright, soft, sweet welcome . . . for what belonged to storm, what was wild and intense, dangerous, sudden, and flaming, he had no sympathy, and held with it no communion. When I took time to glance at him, it amused and enlightened me to discover that he was watching that sinister and sovereign Vashti, not with wonder, nor worship, nor yet dismay, but simply with intense curiosity.[3]

The visit to Gloucester Terrace, though filled every day with absorbing engagements, must after all be judged, from Charlotte's viewpoint, by the extent to which it contributed to her friendship with George Smith. In this respect the visit was certainly illuminating: 'Mr. Smith is somewhat changed in appearance,' Charlotte wrote Ellen immediately on arriving in town; 'he looks a little older, darker and more careworn, his ordinary manner is graver, but in the evening his spirits flow back to him. Things and circumstances seem here to be as usual.'

Yet, even in writing this, Charlotte was compelled to admit:

---

[1] *Villette*, ch. 23.
[2] CB to Amelia Ringrose, 7 June 1851: *W & S* iii. 244.   [3] *Villette*, ch. 23.

'I fancy there has been some crisis in which his energy and filial affection have sustained them all; this I judge from the fact that mother and sisters are more peculiarly bound to him than ever and that his slightest wish is an unquestioned law.'[1]

We are bound to ask ourselves whether the realization of 'his slightest wish' had been obtained at the price of just one sacrifice. Had George Smith submitted to his mother's wishes and to the financial necessities of his firm, and waived the dreams of cultural success which a union with the renowned but portionless and delicate Currer Bell might have advanced? The answer, if it was ever clearly expressed, has been deleted from all records, unless it is hidden in the pages of *Villette*.

Several indications of a change of plan are discernible in Charlotte's correspondence of those days. Her visit began inauspiciously, by her own confession, both on the physical and the emotional planes; her health and spirits were constantly affected during the first fortnight of her stay. Describing a couple of days of 'rampant headache' and sickness Charlotte wrote to Ellen on 11 June: 'I had hoped to leave my headaches behind me in Haworth, but it seems I brought them carefully packed in my trunk, and very much have they been in my way since I came.'

To Ellen, who knew something—perhaps too much—of her relations with Smith and whose eager credulity had constantly to be checked, she had to speak a warning, if also a cryptic language respecting the true cause of her depression:

You seem to think me in such a happy enviable position; pleasant moments I have, but it is usually a pleasure I am obliged to repel and check, which cannot benefit the future, but only add to its solitude, which is no more to be relied on than the sunshine of one summer's day. I pass portions of many a night in extreme sadness.[2]

Sadness, low spirits, sickness, the words recur in every letter. She reported again to Ellen on 18 June:

I cannot boast that London has agreed with me this time, the oppression of frequent headache, sickness and a low tone of spirits, has poisoned many moments which might otherwise have been pleasant. Sometimes I have felt this hard, and been tempted to murmur at Fate, which compels me to comparative silence and solitude for eleven months in the year, and in the

[1] CB to EN, 2 June 1851: *W & S* iii. 240–1.
[2] CB to EN, 11 June 1851: *W & S* iii. 246.

twelfth, while offering social enjoyment, takes away the vigour and cheerfulness which should turn it to account. But circumstances are ordered for us, and we must submit.[1]

She fixed her return home on three occasions, prolonging her stay each time for a different reason; the first of these, reported to her father, sufficiently accounting for the rest. Having twice announced her return home for the 'end of the week' (by 21 June) she wrote to Mr. Brontë on the 17th: 'in haste to tell you that I find they will not let me leave London till next Tuesday'.

'They' were, of course, her host and hostess, George Smith and his mother who, very understandably, did not like her to depart so out of sorts and spirits, and prevailed on her to remain a few days more. Her departure was then fixed for Tuesday, 24 June, when she was to go to Manchester for a short visit to Mrs. Gaskell on her way home.

To Ellen was given as an added reason for her further stay the sudden discovery of her presence in town by Sir James Kay-Shuttleworth, who instantly pressed on her an invitation to 'take up her quarters' at his house on leaving the Smiths. Mrs. Smith, Charlotte reported, helped her to get off this invitation which finally resolved itself into spending a day with the Kay-Shuttleworths.

Since the previous winter when, staying at Harriet Martineau's, Charlotte had allowed herself to be driven about by Sir James, her attitude towards him had decidedly hardened. She made no secret of wishing to avoid his attentions in London and bluntly told Mrs. Gaskell, just before her presence in town was discovered, 'I have not called on Lady Kay-Shuttleworth, and indeed don't see why I should. Cui bono?'[2]

Mrs. Smith's timely support in preventing the change of domiciles, though redounding to her credit as a hostess, is only fully explained in a letter of Charlotte's of 24 June, when she again announced a deferment of her departure to Ellen and gave the full reason for it. 'I cannot now leave London till Friday [27 June]. Tomorrow [25 June] is Mr. Smith's only holiday. Mr. Taylor's departure leaves him loaded with work. More than once since I came he has been kept in the city till three in the morning. He wants to take us all to Richmond, and I promised last week I would stay and go with him, his mother, and sisters. I go to Mrs. Gaskell's on Friday.'[3]

[1] CB to EN, 18 June 1851: *W & S* iii. 250.
[2] CB to Mrs. Gaskell: by courtesy of the Librarian, Manchester Univ. Lib.
[3] CB to EN, 24 June 1851: *W & S* iii. 251.

To Mr. Brontë, not only was no reason for the further deferment given ('I have not yet been able to get away from London' was all she told him on the 26th) but a strange omission made. Her letter to him written on 26 June makes no allusion to the excursion to Richmond, which had taken place the previous day. Yet the letter is full of accounts of her latest social engagements (her invitation to one of Samuel Rogers's breakfasts, a fifth visit to the Crystal Palace, private views of art collections, further courtesies from the Kay-Shuttleworths) and it contains, moreover, an illuminating reference to her improved health: 'During this last week I have seen many things, some of them very interesting, and have also been in much better health than I was during the first fortnight of my stay in London.'[1]

Though it brought no tangible assurance of any sort, the visit obviously ended on a happier note than it began. With her increased knowledge of George Smith's character, however, there is no proof that Charlotte would have accepted him had he proposed. She knew his limitations now, and she may not yet have fully realized her own bitter plight. But for the time being she was prepared to defer decisions and to preserve her friendship with a man rich in personal charm. It was pleasant, too, to reflect that her life as an author was inextricably bound up with the firm of which George Smith was so able a manager. It was incumbent on both to maintain the most cordial business relations.

Meanwhile, he insisted on taking her to Richmond. Richmond was not the Rhine, but as a centre of excursion and pleasure (as readers of Thackeray know) it was accounted highly by Londoners. George Smith, ever more committed to the gruelling demands of an expanding business, had still enough of the schoolboy in him to plan a treat well ahead, especially when the only holiday he could look for in his year was for one day. The man Charlotte Brontë described in *Villette* would be the happier in feeling that he was conferring a pleasure by including her; he would also, perhaps, be impervious to the fear of conferring pain by extending the invitation no further.

The excursion to Richmond was made on Wednesday, 25 June; only one allusion to it occurs in Charlotte's writings. Two days later she travelled to Manchester on her way home.

[1] CB to Revd. PB, 26 June 1851: *W & S* iii. 252.

WRITING *VILLETTE*

Since their meeting at Windermere the previous August Elizabeth Gaskell and Charlotte Brontë had corresponded with a degree of warmth and freedom that had advanced their friendship as much as though their letters had been personal encounters. 'I wonder what it was I said that suited you;' Charlotte wrote after that first meeting; 'in vain have I puzzled my memory to make out what it could be.'[1]

There was a lack of formality about Mrs. Gaskell that cut through Charlotte's social inhibitions; to no other correspondent was she herself less formal. The attraction, for Charlotte, was largely due to the ease and liveliness of Mrs. Gaskell's manner, to which she naturally responded. The famous Gaskell charm, to which all who knew her were susceptible, was based on something that Charlotte—the avowed enemy of insincerity in all forms—instantly recognized. Mrs. Gaskell was genuine; and Mrs. Gaskell was kind.

Her very first letter to Charlotte after their meeting at Windermere enclosed some wild flowers. It was the simplest gesture, but one to which Charlotte was unaccustomed. 'Thank you for your flowers,' she wrote back on 28 September 1850; 'when put in water they revived and looked quite fresh and very beautiful. I kept them for more than a week; the bit of heliotrope I especially prized for its incomparable perfume.'[2]

Comparing the personalities and endowments of her two fellow authoresses and friends, Mrs. Gaskell and Miss Martineau, Charlotte wrote to George Smith on 4 August shortly after her visit to Manchester that Harriet Martineau 'has faults, but she has, too, a fine mind and noble powers. She can never be so charming a woman as Mrs. Gaskell but she is a greater writer.'[3]

Mrs. Gaskell was seen to advantage in any company, but nowhere more so than in her own home. The image left of her by her great

---

[1] CB to Mrs. G, 26 Sept. 1850: *W & S* iii. 162.
[2] Idem.
[3] CB to Geo. Smith, 4 Aug. 1851: *W & S* iii. 266.

friend Susanna Winkworth conveys something of the wealth of her outward and inward endowments:

She was a noble-looking woman with a queenly presence, and her high, broad serene brow, and finely-cut mobile features, were lighted up by a constantly-varying play of expression as she poured forth her wonderful talk. It was like the gleaming ripple and rush of a clear deep stream in sunshine. Though one of the most brilliant persons I ever saw, she had none of the restlessness and eagerness that spoil so much of our conversation nowadays. There was no hurry or high-pressure about her, but she seemed always surrounded by an atmosphere of ease, leisure, and playful geniality, that drew out the best side of everyone who was in her company. When you were with her, you felt as if you had twice the life in you that you had at ordinary times.[1]

(The latter quality would explain why Charlotte always felt the better for being in Mrs. Gaskell's company.)

With all her abundant gifts, Mrs. Gaskell's outstanding quality was still as a home-maker; and dearly did she love and grace the house at 42, as it then was, Plymouth Grove, to which the family moved at the beginning of 1850.

Situated in the Victoria Park district of Manchester, which at that time was well on the outskirts of the city, and set in 1,500 square yards of its own grounds and surrounded by open fields, the house was the first the family inhabited that was away from the smoke and slums of the central areas where the social work of both husband and wife lay. It must have seemed an act of great extravagance for a junior Unitarian minister, even though he had private means, and the acquisition of the house was hailed by Mrs. Gaskell with a sense of adventure and delight. 'We've got a home. Yes! we really have,' she wrote her friend Tottie Fox in the winter of 1849–50. 'And if I had neither conscience nor prudence, I should be delighted, for it certainly is a beauty.'

The rent was £150 per annum and Mrs. Gaskell knew that it must seem both extravagant and selfish to indulge themselves thus when 'so many are wanting'. But, she added, with characteristic reasoning: 'I must try to make the house give as much pleasure to others as I can and make it as little a selfish thing as I can.'

Few houses have more fulfilled their promise. The home of the Gaskells, and after them of their remaining unmarried daughters up to 1914, became a centre not only of civilized living where almost every

---

[1] Hopkins 312.

illustrious Victorian was entertained, but of social service and charitable enterprise for over 60 years.[1]

The house had the advantage of standing on the corner of two shady lanes planted with overhanging trees at that time—Plymouth Grove and Swinton Grove—and was a Georgian structure set well back from the road and surrounded on all sides by a garden. It had, and still has to-day in its diminished state, a fine façade with alternating flat and rounded columns and a solid double-door with Adam moulding. Solidity and grace are, throughout, its qualities. A square entrance-hall gave access on the right to Mr. Gaskell's study and library, and on the left to Mrs. Gaskell's morning-room. An archway at the rear of the hall framed in the drawing-room on the left and the dining-room doors straight ahead, with the staircase rising to the right. All the rooms had high Georgian window-panes, Mrs. Gaskell's in particular being well sited to catch the sun. The famous drawing-room, with its conservatory at the further end and two high windows piercing the left wall was, to our modern eyes, overcrowded with bric-a-brac, ornaments, and cabinets; but it was to the taste of the day, with its heavily draped and curtained windows and doors—even the marble mantelpiece was draped with heavy embroidered cloth with chenille bobbles. For all that, it was a gracious, restful room, furnished with Chippendale chairs and Sheraton tables, with Wedgwood and Delft ware in the recesses and cabinets, and water-colours by Ruskin covering the walls.

There all the giants of the contemporary literary scene were entertained at one time or another. No literary celebrity visiting Manchester was ever suffered to lodge at an hotel; a standing invitation being extended to all to make Plymouth Grove their home while in the city. There came Thackeray, Dickens, the Brownings, Matthew Arnold, Ruskin, the Carlyles, Emerson, the Froudes, Forster, Crabb Robinson, Harriet Beecher Stowe, and many others. They were lavishly entertained to dinner off Mrs. Gaskell's beautiful Minton dinner-service, or to breakfast off her Coalport Ware. The dining-room had a grand bow window at the farther end from which steps led down into the garden beyond.

Upstairs there were seven bedrooms, and two attics; the usual domestic staff was five servants, including a coachman and a boy, and Mr. Gaskell kept his own carriage.

[1] For data concerning the Gaskell's home see *Manchester Guardian*, 22 Feb. 1910; *Manchester Quarterly*—'Mrs. Gaskell: A Manchester Influence', W. Henry Brown; Catalogue of Gaskell Sale, 9 Feb. 1914, Manchester Cent. Lib.

THE DRAWING-ROOM OF THE GASKELLS' HOME, 84 Plymouth Grove, Manchester

Charlotte Brontë was charmed with the house, as well she might be. Writing to George Smith on 1 July after her visit, she said:

The visit to Mrs. Gaskell on my way home [from London] let me down easily; though I spent only 2 days with her they were very pleasant. She lives in a large, cheerful, airy house, quite out of Manchester smoke; a garden surrounds it, and, as in this hot weather the windows were kept open, a whispering of leaves and a perfume of flowers always pervaded the rooms. Mrs. Gaskell herself is a woman of whose conversation and company I should not soon tire . . . her husband is a good and kind man also.[1]

The presence of books in great numbers in all the rooms (at the Gaskell sale in 1914 between four and five thousand titles were catalogued), the display of pictures, porcelain, and plate (the Gaskells brought home art-treasures from every trip abroad), the old and easy furniture, the grand piano in the drawing-room—diffused an atmosphere of beauty and civilized living that Charlotte may not have expected to find in the home of a Unitarian minister. Yet Plymouth Grove was, at the same time, a refuge for the unfortunate and the dispossessed. Despite her five servants it must still seem remarkable to the career-woman of this servantless age how Mrs. Gaskell managed to do all she did, and to be so many active and complete persons in one. For the charming hostess, and the hard-pressed novelist contributing for over thirteen years to Dickens's *Household Words*, was the same Mrs. Gaskell who carried on rescue-work in Manchester in collaboration with her friends the Winkworths, and who held weekly classes in her home for girls from the slum-areas of the city, and corresponded at exhaustive length with Dickens and Angela Burdett-Coutts on ways and means of shipping her protégées out to Australia. *Cranford* may be a cameo-masterpiece, but its author knew how to live and work upon a wide front. The pace of life at Plymouth Grove was set by the pulsation of a singularly feeling heart, as all who experienced its hospitality discovered.

Mrs. Gaskell was careful to invite no other guests to meet Charlotte on that first visit, knowing her friend well enough already to realize that coming to terms with a large family of strangers was as much as Charlotte's nerves could compass without undue strain. There were the long, lean scholarly husband to contend with, and the four girls: Marianne, who was nearly 17; Margaret Emily (Meta) 14; Florence Elizabeth, not yet 9; and Julia, whose birth in September 1846 had

[1] CB to Geo. Smith, 1 July 1851: *W & S*, iii. 255.

coincided with Charlotte's visit to Manchester on the occasion of her father's eye-operation.[1] Mrs. Gaskell's own estimate of her children at about the time of Charlotte's visit is a vivid commentary on their characters and ways. She wrote to her friend Tottie Fox:

> Now about the children. It is delightful to see what good it has done Ma [Marianne] sending her to school. . . . She is such a law unto herself now, such a sense of duty, and *obeys* her sense . . . I wish you could hear Ma sing. It is something *really* fine; only at present she sings little but Italian and Latin Mass music. It is so difficult to meet with *good* English songs. . . .
>
> Now to turn to Meta who is a great darling in another way. . . . Meta is untidy, dreamy and absent; but is so brimful of I don't know what to call it, for it is something deeper, and less showy than talent . . . her drawings are equally thoughtful and good. She is *quite* able to appreciate any book I am reading. Ruskin's Seven Lamps of Architecture for the last instance. . . .
>
> Florence has no talents under the sun; and is very nervous and anxious; she will require so much strength to hold her up through life; everything is a terror to her; but Marianne at any rate is aware of this, and is a capital confidante for all Florence's anxieties. . . .
>
> Julia is witty, and wild and clever and droll the pet of the house; and I often admire Florence's utter absence of jealousy, and pride in Julia's doings and sayings. These are my 4 children; for you *must* go on knowing them as they are, not their mere outsides.[2]

Charlotte Brontë, the keen analyst, became quickly and deeply absorbed in Mrs. Gaskell's children. After staying at Plymouth Grove she wrote to Mrs. Smith: 'Mrs. Gaskell's family consists of four little girls—all more or less pretty and intelligent—these scattered through the rooms of a somewhat spacious house—seem to fill it with liveliness and gaiety.'[3] In point of fact Charlotte did not see Marianne on that first occasion, because Marianne had been at boarding-school in London since the previous January, and the holidays had not yet begun. Marianne might have met Charlotte at one of Thackeray's lectures that summer, had she not been too shy to approach the famous Currer Bell. When Charlotte heard this she wrote to Mrs. Gaskell: 'I wish Marianne had come to speak to me at the lecture; it would have given me such pleasure. . . .'

Meta was 'inclined to be overcritical and fastidious with everybody

---

[1] The Gaskell children were born: Marianne, 12 Sept. 1834; Meta, 5 Feb. 1837; Florence Elizabeth, 7 Oct. 1842; Julia, Sept. 1846.

[2] Mrs. G. to Anne Robson, 1 Sept. 1851. Gaskell Letters, 160–1: op. cit.

[3] CB to Mrs. Smith, 1 July 1851: *W & S* iii. 254.

and everything,' her mother reported, 'so that I have to clutch up her drawings before she burns them': she did not follow Marianne to school till the following year, when her letters home, lent to Charlotte by Mrs. Gaskell, drew from Charlotte warm praise.

> And to see how that little maiden—Meta—has inherited Mamma's gift. What is her age? it cannot be more than fourteen, and with a few strokes she can put on paper a lively little pen-and-ink sketch of character. I read her letters with pleasure—they seem to me remarkable: I might well use the word 'companion' in speaking of her; there is something specially conversible, *companionable*, interesting in these letters.[1]

Of all her daughters Meta was, perhaps, her mother's closest confidante and companion in later years; certainly the one who entered most fully into her work on the 'Life' of Charlotte Brontë.

But of all Mrs. Gaskell's children, Charlotte's own favourites were undoubtedly Florence and Julia. Julia in particular captivated her heart. This singular experience surprised, as much as it overwhelmed, Charlotte herself. Never before had she—the former nursery-governess of the little Sidgwicks and Whites—met children like this; they absorbed her attention not only during the visit, but in retrospect for many days to come. Charlotte wrote Mrs. Gaskell the following year:

> Whenever I see Florence and Julia again, I shall feel like a fond but bashful suitor, who views at a distance the fair personage to whom, in his clownish awe, he dare not risk a near approach. Such is the clearest idea I can give you of my feelings towards children I like, but to whom I am a stranger. And to what children am I not a stranger? They seem to me little wonders; their talk, their ways are all matter of half-admiring, half puzzled, speculation.[2]

After her visit to Plymouth Grove she wrote to Mrs. Gaskell on 6 August: 'Remember me kindly and respectfully to Mr. Gaskell, and though I have not seen Marianne I must beg to include her in the love I send the others. Could you manage to convey a small kiss to that dear but dangerous little person Julia? She surreptitiously possessed herself of a minute fraction of my heart, which has been missing ever since I saw her.'[3]

'What you say of that small sprite Julia amuses me very much,' Charlotte wrote in her next letter, of 20 September 1851: 'I believe

---

[1] CB to Mrs. G, 22 May 1852: Manchester Univ. Lib.
[2] Idem.
[3] CB to Mrs. G, 6 Aug. 1851: *W & S* iii. 269.

you don't know that she has a great deal of her mamma's nature (modified) in her, yet I think you will find she has as she grows up.'[1] Julia, it was evident, had taken Charlotte's fancy in no small way and intently had she noted the child's exceptional sensibility and original ways. It would be so on each successive visit to Plymouth Grove. Writing to Mrs. Gaskell on 9 July 1853, after her second visit in April of that year, and sending messages to the girls who had just started on a continental holiday, she said:

Give my kind love to Meta and Marianne, dear happy girls as they are. You cannot now transmit my message to Flossy and Julia. I prized the little wild-flower—not that I think the sender cares for me; she *does* not, and *cannot*, for she does not know me; but no matter. In my reminiscences she is a person of a certain distinction. I think hers a fine little nature, frank and of genuine promise. I often see her, as she appeared, stepping supreme from the portico towards the carriage that evening we went to see 'Twelfth Night'. I believe in Julia's future; I like what speaks in her movements, and what is written upon her face.[2]

Only once, in all Charlotte's writing, did she express herself in such terms about a child, and that was 'Paulina' in *Villette*. It is strange that in seeking an original for the rare perfection of that character Brontë biographers and commentators have always harked back to a long-past experience of Charlotte's—to her stay at Easton with the Hudsons in 1839, when her fancy was greatly taken by their little seven-year-old niece Fanny Whipp. They have wholly overlooked the recent and powerful impression that Julia Gaskell had made upon her at the very time she was writing the opening chapters of *Villette*. It seems much more likely that she was the original of 'Paulina'. Both the child's indirect advances and Charlotte's passive but intensely self-conscious responses recall the interplay between Paulina and Lucy Snowe.

Mrs. Gaskell recalled in her 'Life' of Charlotte the instinctive yet mute attraction that sprang up between Charlotte and Julia during that visit:

The child would steal her little hand in Miss Brontë's scarcely larger one, and each took pleasure in this apparently unobserved caress. Yet once when I told Julia to take and show the way to some room in the house, Miss

Brontë shrunk back: 'Do not *bid* her to do anything for me,' she said, 'it has been so sweet hitherto to have her rendering her little kindnesses spontaneously.'[1]

References to Julia in Charlotte's correspondence with Mrs. Gaskell show admiration, amusement, concern—always the liveliest interest. 'Poor little Julia!' she wrote on 6 February 1852: 'How terrible that moment you describe must have been! I trust there will be no return of the alarm.' And in September 1853, after two further visits to Plymouth Grove: 'The incident you relate of Julia is very characteristic. What a brave little soul it is! My true love to her—and not less—in a different way—to Flossy.'[2]

It was not Mrs. Gaskell's habit to interpret or appropriate her friend's sources of inspiration; the manner in which she excluded herself from Charlotte's biography was, indeed, exemplary. Hence she would not say, even if she suspected it, that her own minute daughter was the model on which Charlotte Brontë drew for 'Paulina'. Yet, the porcelain fragility of portrait and original is too strikingly similar in its rarity and freshness not to evoke the comparison.

It was Ellen Nussey (who, of course, had not met Julia Gaskell) who insisted on Fanny Whipp being the prototype for 'Paulina', though twelve years had passed since Charlotte had seen her. But then Ellen Nussey was all too fond of finding originals for Charlotte's characters and incidents in which *she* had a part. There is, surely, in the character of 'Paulina', both as child and countess, a quality of fastidiousness, innate distinction, pride, restraint, and courage that pertain more naturally to Julia Gaskell than to Fanny Whipp.

Charlotte herself was extremely reticent in admitting to the existence of any originals of her characters. It was only because George Smith was slow to acknowledge the manuscript of *Villette* that she confessed herself afraid, to Mrs. Gaskell, that he had been 'offended' at the close likeness to himself and his mother in the characters of Graham and Mrs. Bretton. George Smith himself later acknowledged the truth of the portraiture in both characters, and said that several of his mother's usual expressions were given 'verbatim' to Mrs. Bretton.[3] It would not be surprising, then, if Charlotte, already deeply involved in the beginning of her tale when she went to Manchester, incorporated

---

[1] *Life of Charlotte Brontë*, ch. 24, p. 375.
[2] Letters of CB to Mrs. G, 6 Feb. 1852, and 30 Sept. 1853: Manchester Univ. Lib.
[3] *Cornhill Magazine*, Dec. 1900: op. cit.

Julia Gaskell in the Bretton scenes for which she was even then making mental notes.

Villette has for so long been associated with Charlotte's Brussels experience and in particular with the evocation of Monsieur and Madame Heger in the characters of Professor Emanuel and Madame Beck that her readers have tended to overlook the biographical and factual origins that supplied its secondary theme—that which relates to Lucy Snowe and Graham Bretton. Though *Villette* marks the end of the road back from Brussels (it is Charlotte's noble valediction to her one-time 'Master') and was a book that could not have been written earlier, it was not merely a tale of experience past; it was, as a study of its plot and characters will reveal, an exploration of the present—a present so unpredictable that it left the author continually in suspense as to the issue. This uncertainty in Charlotte's actual circumstances and state of mind was the main reason why *Villette* proved so arduous a task.

Uncertainties and doubts no longer besieged Charlotte on the score of her feelings for Monsieur Heger. She had long since recognized them for what they were—and hence the passionate righteousness of her retort to Harriet Martineau when accused of giving too much prominence to the theme of love in the book: 'I know what *love* is as I understand it,' she wrote Harriet in reply; 'and if man or woman should be ashamed of feeling such love, then is there nothing right, noble, faithful, truthful, unselfish in the earth, as I comprehend rectitude, nobleness, fidelity, truth and disinterestedness.'[1]

What delayed the writing of *Villette* were the uncertainties and doubts immediately confronting her—the fearful problem of her solitude—bereft of family as she was and living at a great distance from friends—and the few straws of hope and comfort at which she had to decide whether or not to clutch. That is why there is so much suffering in *Villette*, and why critics like Harriet Martineau, protesting at the suffering and unaware of its origins in the author's personal circumstances, complained of it as of an artistic fault: 'under all, through all, over all, the book is almost intolerably miserable', Harriet Martineau wrote in her review of *Villette* in the *Daily News* of 3 February 1853. '. . . An atmosphere of pain hangs about the whole which forbids that repose which we hold to be essential to the true presentment of any large portion of life and experience. In its pervading pain, the book reminds us of Balzac.'[2] The wonder to present-day readers, better

---

[1] CB to HM: *SBC* 429; also *W & S* iv. 42.
[2] HM in *Daily News*, 3 Feb. 1853: *W & S* iv. 42–44.

informed of Charlotte's circumstances than her contemporaries were, is less at 'the pervading pain' than at the lively and often joyous passages in *Villette*; for the book was certainly engendered in darkness and despair.

The true subject of *Villette* is in any case not love but loneliness, the theme that most obsessed the writer's mind during the period—probably sixteen months in all—she was writing the book. Viewed in chronological order, the facts are as follows: the London visit which started off with some unease between Charlotte and her publisher, ended with an increase of cordiality on both sides. Abandoned by his family, who went to Hastings on holiday, George Smith took the initiative in resuming a correspondence with Charlotte, the frequency and cordiality of which over the next few months coincided, it is worthy of note, with a period of steady progress in her work and with a decided improvement in her health.

The first of these letters reached her, to her surprise, while she was at Plymouth Grove where, as she told George Smith in her answer, she had expected no letters, having given the address to nobody: 'I went to Church by myself on Sunday morning (they are Unitarians)' she wrote him on 1 July back at home. 'On my return shortly before the family came home from Chapel the servant said there was a letter for me. . . . Of course I was not at all pleased when the small problem was solved by the letter being brought; I never care for hearing from you the least in the world.'[1]

A week later, after receiving a further letter in which Smith enclosed the 'Characters' for which he and she had sat to a noted London phrenologist (they had gone together 'incognito', taking the names of Mr. and Miss Fraser), she told him that she could not now expect any more letters for some months, knowing how overworked he was, but confessed that she was 'jealous of becoming dependent on this indulgence'. The expectation of the post-hour, so poignantly described in *Villette* and once before experienced in a manner never to be forgotten by Charlotte when Monsieur Heger ceased corresponding with her, was an addiction she hoped never to fall victim to again. Even so, she lacked the resolution completely to discourage Smith from writing: 'since you say that you would like to write now and then I cannot say "never write" without imposing on my real wishes a falsehood which they reject . . .'.[2]

---

[1] CB to Geo. Smith, 1 July 1851: *W & S* iii. 255–6.
[2] CB to Geo. Smith, 8 July 1851: *W & S* iii. 261.

Harriet Martineau, who approached Charlotte to negotiate an agreement with Smith, Elder for her next book, furnished the subject of several exchanges of letters between Smith and Charlotte during July and August, into which more personal matters were naturally introduced. Writing on 4 August, Charlotte told him that she was 'much better in health than when I was in London . . .', and on 9 August she wrote again: 'It was kind of you to write that last letter; I could hardly believe when I opened it that it was all for me. . . .'[1]

George Smith had described the incident (incorporated in *Villette*) of the alarm created by an outbreak of fire at private theatricals at Devonshire Place, when he escorted a young lady to safety. 'Mr. Fraser,' wrote Charlotte, giving him his 'incognito', 'and the panic-struck young lady both revealed themselves according to their different natures. It is easy to realise the scene. . . .'[2]

Charlotte often expressed concern about his overwork and urged him to take reasonable care of his health; she referred to Mrs. Smith, her daughters, and young Alick 'all enjoying themselves by the seaside this fine weather; doubtless they wish you shared their enjoyment'. She was concerned, too, for his success as a business man, and over-anxious lest she prove a financial loss rather than a profit to his firm. Her normal slow rate of progress, even under such good conditions for work as existed then, made Smith suggest she should consider serial-publication, to keep her name before the public. This she always reso-lutely refused, declaring that she would never publish any work 'of which the last number is not written before the first comes out'.

It pleased her extremely to hear that several new authors were ap-proaching Smith, Elder with their work, feeling that in *their* success George Smith might recoup what he was losing with her. 'I am sure I am not low-spirited just now,' she wrote him on 22 September, 'but very happy, and in this mood I will write to you. . . . Can I help wishing you well when I owe you directly or indirectly, most of the good moments I now enjoy?'[3] (There is a painful echo in this passage of her letter to Monsieur Heger of 24 October 1844.)

Referring yet again to his suggestion that she adopt serial-publica-tion, she added: 'But though Currer Bell cannot do this you are still to be *his* friend. You are to keep a fraction of yourself—if it be only the end of your little finger—for *him* and that fraction you will neither

---

[1] CB to Geo. Smith, 9 Aug. 1851: *W & S* iii. 270.
[2] Idem.
[3] CB to Geo. Smith, 22 Sept. 1851: *W & S* iii. 279.

let gentleman or lady . . . take possession of, or so much as meddle with.'

Though she had been in London as recently as June, George Smith now suggested that she make a further short stay to 'break the interval between this and Christmas'. In her reply, Charlotte exposed a good deal more of her feelings than she had done before, or was to do again. She continued in her letter of 22 September:

What is it you say about my breaking the interval between this and Christmas by going from home for a week? No; if there were no other objection, (and there are many) there is the pain of that last bidding good-bye, that hopeless shaking hands, yet undulled and unforgotten. I don't like it. I could not bear its frequent repetition. Do not recur to this plan. Going to London is a mere palliation and stimulant; reaction follows.

Meantime I really do get on very well; not always alike, and I have been at intervals despondent; but Providence is kind . . . a cheering sunrise so far ever followed a night of peculiar vigil and fear. Hope, indeed, is not a plant to flourish very luxuriously in this northern climate, but still it throws out fresh leaves and a blossom now and then.

A letter to Mrs. Gaskell of almost identical date, 20 September, reveals a less assured state of mind: it would, indeed, be always a principle with her to keep her most despondent moods hidden from George Smith. She feared not only to appear physically delicate before him, but also to seem too often afflicted with depression. 'You charge me to write about myself', she answered Mrs. Gaskell. 'What can I say on that precious topic? My health is pretty good. My spirits are not always alike. Nothing happens to me. I hope and expect little in this world, and am thankful that I do not despond and suffer more.'[1]

Interruption to her work came in October, first by the visit of a Branwell cousin from Penzance and then by the deferred visit of Miss Wooler, who stayed ten days at the Parsonage, from 29 September to 8 October. It was a visit which proved such a pleasure to her that she said later she had not for many years known such enjoyment.

The rapprochement with Miss Wooler, which this visit consummated, erased the unfortunate impression made on Charlotte by her former teacher's comments on *Jane Eyre*: 'Miss Wooler is and has been very pleasant', Charlotte told Ellen during the visit. 'She is like good wine; I think time improves her, and really, whatever she may be in person, in mind she is younger than when at Roe Head. Papa and

[1] CB to Mrs. Gaskell, 20 Sept. 1851: Manchester Univ. Lib.

she get on exceedingly well; I have just heard Papa walk into the dining room and pay her a round compliment on her good sense.'[1]

Miss Wooler was touched by her old pupil's attention, reconciled to her new status as successful novelist, and reassured by the spectacle of Charlotte's constant devotion to duty that her excursions to London had not undermined her principles. It became one of Miss Wooler's great pleasures from then on to follow the stages of Charlotte's growing celebrity, and also the course of her family trials, and quietly to lend her help when help was needed. The friendship ended with a truer mutual appreciation than its beginnings foreshadowed.

The spell of uninterrupted work and tolerable health that Charlotte had enjoyed since leaving Manchester was further broken by a period of sickness affecting the whole household in October. Tabby and Martha had influenza, and Mr. Brontë had one of his periodic attacks of bronchitis. The manuscript of *Villette* was laid aside.

Something more than the care of her invalids now spoiled Charlotte's peace. She was assailed by a return of the intense depression she had known every year since the deaths of her sisters. Of its power to reduce her mentally and physically she wrote to Mrs. Gaskell on 6 November, a letter which strangely harmonizes with the most tempestuous passages of *Villette*; those like the death of Miss Marchmont, and the final pages of all, in which is revealed the strange and close affinity that existed between her mercurial temperament and the weather. Few writers have confessed so freely to the domination of the elements, not only over their nervous system, but even, as Charlotte certainly believed, over her destiny. Romantic writer that she was, Charlotte never overlooked the affinities binding Nature and Man.

She wrote in reply to a kind invitation from Mrs. Gaskell:

If anybody would tempt me from home, you would; but, just now, from home I must not, will not go. I feel greatly better at present than I did three weeks ago. For a month or six weeks about the equinox (autumnal or vernal) is a period of the year which, I have noticed, strangely tries me. Sometimes the strain falls on the mental, sometimes on the physical part of me; I am ill with neuralgic headache, or I am ground to the dust with deep dejection of spirits (not, however, such dejection but I can keep to myself). That weary time has, I think and trust, got over for this year. It was the anniversary of my poor brother's death, and of my sister's failing health: I need say no more.

[1] CB to EN, 3 Oct. 1851: *W & S* iii. 282.

As to running away from home every time I have a battle of this sort to fight, it would not do. Besides the 'weird' would follow.[1]

To Ellen she had merely admitted, in a letter of 30 October, to 'Some painful mental worry I have got through this autumn, but there is no use in dwelling on that.' To Laetitia Wheelwright, whom she seldom saw, she drew a less restrained picture than to Ellen:

It cannot be denied that the solitude of my position fearfully aggravated its other evils. Some long, stormy days and nights there were when I felt such a craving for support and companionship as I cannot express. Sleepless, I lay awake night after night: weak and unable to occupy myself, I sat in my chair day after day, the saddest memories my only company. It was a time I shall never forget, but God sent it and it must have been for the best.[2]

It would be easy to over-emphasize the effect on her spirits of her relations with George Smith at this time. In her loneliness she found comfort in the tiny grains that his friendship offered; but she may not have mistaken them for the seed of life.

George Smith had an undoubted capacity for hurting her, which he neither intended nor even knew about. (This she freely elaborated in *Villette*.) She had the courage, partly, to tax him with it. Acknowledging an unexpected royalty on 7 November, which she obviously feared might be disguised charity—though she recalled his mentioning 'something at Richmond about having some money for me'—she excused her scepticism on the score of his habit of 'raillery' which she described as 'an inaudible laugh to yourself, a not unkindly but somewhat subtle playing on your correspondent or companion for the time being—in short, a sly touch of a Mephistopheles with the fiend extracted'.[3]

Did George Smith but realize it, Mephistopheles complete with his fiend would have been less of a strain at times for Charlotte than the cool detachment of his manner. (Had she not 'domesticated' with Zamorna very well?) Their true natures, though neither had as yet acknowledged it, were as oil and water.

Too much of George Smith at a time was what her intense sensibility could not endure; she knew herself well enough to dread depending on the fitful sunshine he shed. It was thus that she quite firmly declined the kind invitation to visit Gloucester Terrace again so soon.

[1] CB to Mrs. Gaskell, 6 Nov. 1851: Manchester Univ. Lib.
[2] CB to Laetitia Wheelwright: 12 April 1852: *W & S* iii. 330.
[3] CB to Geo. Smith, 7 Nov. 1851: *W & S* iii. 286.

She wrote him on 20 November and again on 28 November to clarify the two outstanding issues between them: her progress with *Villette* and the invitation to London. She had told him in the earlier letter:

I have been able to work a little lately, but I have quite made up my mind not to publish till Mr. Thackeray's [*Esmond*] and Miss Martineau's [the projected 'Oliver Weld'] books have had full career . . . [these were both due from Smith, Elder]. So you will not think of me till next autumn or thereabouts; is not this for the best? Meantime, it is perhaps premature in me, even to allude to the subject, but I do it partly to explain one of my motives for remaining at home this winter . . . Winter is a better time for working than summer; less liable to interruption. If I could always work, time would not be long, nor hours sad to me; but blank and heavy intervals still occur, when power and will are at variance.[1]

On 28 November she wrote further: 'Your Mother and sisters are very kind to think of my coming to see them at Christmas, but you must give them my best regards and say that such a step is not to be thought of. Tell your Mother not to ask me, because I could only repeat what I have said above.'[2]

The decision, though firmly made and adhered to, led to precisely contrary effects to those reckoned on by Charlotte: for the next four months she was almost constantly ill and incapable of work.

There were material reasons for this—the intense cold affected her liver and provoked a severe attack of jaundice, and the death of Keeper, Emily's inseparable companion, on 1 December, revived poignant memories of her sister. She was reminded of her death and burial at which Keeper had played so memorable a part. His life stretched back for over twelve years of the family's fortunes; his huge figure looming in every retrospect of their walks on the moors, and of their fireside evenings. Ellen Nussey recalled winning Emily's goodwill on one such occasion:

Poor old Keeper! Emily's faithful friend and worshipper—he seemed to understand her like a human being. One evening when the 4 friends were sitting closely round the fire...Keeper forced himself in between Charlotte and Emily and mounted himself on Emily's lap. Finding the space too limited for his comfort he pressed himself forward on to the guest's knees making himself quite comfortable—Emily's heart was won by the unresisting endurance of the visitor.[3]

---

[1] CB to Geo. Smith, 20 Nov. 1851: *W & S* iii. 293.
[2] CB to Geo. Smith, 28 Nov. 1851: *W & S* iii. 296.   [3] *SBC* 163.

Keeper's death was a sorrow in which Mr. Brontë shared; Charlotte did not forget the time at Manchester when he believed his life in danger after his eye-operation, and he grieved aloud at the thought of never feeling Keeper's head on his knee again. Charlotte wrote the news to Ellen on 8 December:

Poor old Keeper died last Monday; after being ill all night, he went gently to sleep. We laid his old faithful head in the garden. Flossy is dull and misses him. There was something very sad in losing the old dog; yet I am glad he met a natural fate; people kept hinting he ought to be put away, which neither papa nor I liked to think of.[1]

Causes of yet deeper perplexity and disturbance were at work to bring the writing of *Villette* to a standstill. As autumn advanced she did not see the way ahead either in her life or in her work. Greatly to her surprise she received, through the offices at Cornhill, two letters from James Taylor from Bombay; in her reply to the second, on 15 November, she frankly expressed her surprise. Commenting on the points of interest his letters had contained, she said:

My father I am thankful to say, continues in pretty good health. I read portions of your letter to him and he was interested in hearing them. He charged me when I wrote to convey his very kind remembrances.

I had myself ceased to expect a letter from you. On taking leave at Haworth you said something about writing from India, but I doubted at the time whether it was not one of those forms of speech, which politeness dictates; and as time passed, and I did not hear from you, I became confirmed in this view of the subject.[2]

Her answer was less than noncommittal; it was decidedly cool. So much did she find herself at a loss how to interpret Mr. Taylor's renewed attentions, that she wrote to Mr. Williams for guidance. In Mr. Williams her confidence was never shaken, though it became obvious that there were times when she did not feel the same about Mr. Smith. Telling Ellen of the development, she wrote on 19 November:

Before answering his epistle I got up my courage to write to Mr. Williams, through whose hands or those of Mr. Smith, I knew the Indian letters had come, and beg him to give me an impartial judgement of Mr. Taylor's character and disposition, owning that I was very much in the dark. I did not like to continue corresponding without further information. I got the answer which I enclose.[1]

From Mr. Williams she received an 'excellent character' for James Taylor. Thanking him for it, Charlotte freely drew her own conclusions from it. She wrote on 1 January 1852:

Such a man's friendship at any rate should not be disregarded; and if the principles and disposition be what you say, faults of manner and even of temper ought to weigh light in the balance. I always believed in his judgement and good sense, but what I doubted was his kindness—he seemed to me a little too harsh, rigid, and unsympathising. Now, judgement, sense, principle are invaluable and quite indispensable points, but one would be thankful for a *little* feeling, a *little* indulgence in addition—without these, poor fallible human nature shrinks under the domination of the sterner qualities. I answered Mr. Taylor's letter by the mail of the 19th November, sending it direct, for, on reflection, I did not see why I should trouble you with it.[2]

To this letter Charlotte would appear to have received no answer. In a footnote to a letter to Ellen on 24 February, she wrote: 'The Indian mail brought me nothing.' By 4 March the case had been sufficiently debated between her and Ellen for her to fear an indiscreet confidence to Miss Wooler, then staying at Brookroyd. Charlotte wrote to her then:

Dear Nell, I thank you sincerely for your discreet and friendly silence on the point alluded to. I had feared it would be discussed between you two, and had an inexpressible shrinking at the thought; now, less than ever does it seem a matter open to discussion. I hear nothing, and you must quite understand that if I feel any uneasiness it is not that of confirmed and fixed regard, but that anxiety which is inseparable from a state of absolute uncertainty about a somewhat momentous matter. I do not know, I am not sure myself, that any other termination would be better than lasting estrangement and unbroken silence. Yet a good deal of pain has been and must be gone through in that case. . . . Understand that in whatever I have said above, it was not for pity or sympathy. I hardly pity myself. Only I wish that in all matters in this world there was fair play and open dealing, and no underhand work.[3]

[1] CB to EN, 19 Nov. 1851: *W & S* iii. 291.
[2] CB to WSW, 1 Jan. 1852: *W & S* iii. 304.
[3] CB to EN, 4 Mar. 1852: *W & S* iii. 319.

The fact that she had sent her letter direct to Bombay, without recourse to the offices of Cornhill, suggests *where* she suspected the 'underhand work' lay. She had already two years before had reason to believe that Mr. Smith bore no goodwill to James Taylor and was the last person to transmit flattering messages. She was, however, left unsure of his motives.

The silence of James Taylor now further added to the mental and physical disorders of that winter. Though she certainly did not love him, and disclaimed even feeling a 'confirmed and fixed regard' for him, the loss of even so much friendship and the insurance it offered for future security was a grave matter at a time when all her other stakes in life seemed in peril of failing utterly. Her health, about which she secretly harboured the darkest forebodings, seemed completely to give way; and the sunshine of a friendship she really cared about—George Smith's—was temporarily withdrawn. She did not love George Smith either, though she liked him well enough possibly for the friendship to evolve into something deeper at any time; certainly she came to depend on his vital flow of spirits.

The progress of the jaundice quickly reduced her strength; on 17 December she wrote to tell Ellen how ill she was:

The doctor speaks encouragingly, but as yet I get no better. As the illness has been coming on for a long time, it cannot, I suppose, be expected to disappear all at once. I am not confined to bed, but I am weak; have had no appetite for about 3 weeks, and my nights are very bad. I am well aware myself that extreme and continuous depression of spirits has had much to do with the origin of the illness.[1]

She begged Ellen to come for a few days to Haworth. 'I know a little cheerful society would do me more good than gallons of medicine', she wrote. Ellen came and stayed from 19 December for ten days, but the improvement in Charlotte's condition was only temporary, and immediately Ellen was gone she had a further relapse. The doctor, Mr. Ruddock, was treating her with mercury and only after several weeks discovered she was allergic to it. 'Mr. Ruddock', Charlotte wrote on 16 January, 'says he never in his whole practice knew the same effect produced by the same dose on man, woman, or child, and avows it is owing to an altogether peculiar sensitiveness of constitution. He expressed great regret and annoyance, but affirmed it will do me good in the end.'[2]

[1] CB to EN, 17 Dec. 1851: *W & S* iii. 300.
[2] CB to EN, 16 Jan. 1852: *W & S* iii. 307.

By 27 January she was sufficiently improved to go to Brookroyd where Ellen and her mother had been urging her to come to receive their devoted care. From there Charlotte wrote to Mrs. Gaskell: 'As the date of this letter will show—I am now from home—and have already benefitted greatly by the kind attentions and cheerful society of the friends with whom I am staying—friends who probably do not care for me a pin as Currer Bell—but who have known me for years as Charlotte Brontë—and by whom I need not fear that my invalid weakness . . . will be felt as a burden.'

To Mrs. Gaskell Charlotte confessed what she did not often mention to others—her dread lest her illness derived in reality from an affection of the lungs. So haunting was this fear that she repeatedly deferred seeing a doctor lest his diagnosis should confirm her fears. 'When at last, however,' she wrote to Mrs. Gaskell, 'a doctor was consulted, he declared my lungs and chest sound, and ascribed all my sufferings to derangement of the liver.'[1]

So great had been her dread that she had mentioned her symptoms to Mr. Williams. Writing to him on New Year's Day 1852, she said: 'My health has not been very satisfactory lately. . . . All the winter the fact of my never being able to stoop over a desk without bringing on pain and oppression in the chest has been a great affliction to me.'

Within 24 hours of Charlotte's leaving home for Brookroyd she received a suggestion from George Smith that he should call on her in the course of the next few days. The fact was that Charlotte's publishers were becoming very worried indeed at the dwindling prospect of getting a new book from her for their spring list; the last report on her health on 19 January cannot have failed to make George Smith realize that she either could not or would not settle down again to a serious spell of work. The invitations of the previous autumn, meant to cheer and revive her flagging powers, had achieved nothing; he decided, with characteristic suddenness, to see the situation for himself and visit Haworth.

Charlotte wrote immediately, urging him to make his visit rather to Brookroyd.

I *do* now wish I had delayed my departure from home a few days longer, that I might have shared with my father the true pleasure of receiving you at Haworth Parsonage. And pleasure your visit would have been, as I have sometimes dimly imagined but never ventured to realise. I shall be returning

[1] CB to Mrs. Gaskell, 6 Feb. 1852: Manchester Univ. Lib.

in about a week, but if you must make your excursion before that time, and if you came northwards and would call at Brookroyd I am desired to tell you that you would have the warmest Yorkshire welcome. My friends would like to see you. You would find me there but not exactly ill now. . . . They are hospitable people at Brookroyd and you would be made comfortable. I and my friend would do our best to amuse you; it is only 6 miles distant from Leeds; you would have to stay all night. . . . Send me a line to say whether we shall see you and when.[1]

George Smith did not go to Brookroyd. Whatever the inducements the report on her health sufficed to make him abandon the enterprise. It confirmed what George Smith, and even more his watchful mother, had already for a long time suspected: that Currer Bell's health was fundamentally unsound. This was the general view held in the circle of her London acquaintance,[2] a view innocently fostered by the concern of Mrs. Gaskell and Harriet Martineau, and which Charlotte had done her best to combat, especially in the opinion of her publisher. It had already drawn from her a strongly worded protest the previous summer, when, commenting on the invitation of Mrs. Gaskell's friends, the Shaens, she wrote to George Smith on 19 April of 'misled strangers living in Southern Counties offering accommodation suitable to an invalid lady'; and added: '. . . Why may I not be well like other people? I think I am reasonably well. . . . I have no ailment. . . .'[3]

The long-drawn-out illness of the current winter had, nevertheless, shaken Charlotte's resolution to keep silence: she wrote now to Mrs. Smith in reply to yet another very kind invitation to town, on the very day she summoned George Smith to Brookroyd. Confessing to the fear about her lungs, she explained: 'my lungs and chest were pronounced perfectly sound, and it appeared that inflammation had fallen on the liver'.[4]

The letter, among the frankest and the most affectionate she ever wrote to Mrs. Smith, ended with a repetition of the resolve not to visit London again till she had earned that pleasure by finishing her book. 'Give my true regards to all your circle,' she wrote. 'It is unavailing to say how glad I shall be when I can with a good conscience once more come and see you all. I do not, however, anticipate this event at an early date. Good-bye, my dear Mrs. Smith. Believe me Yours sincerely and affectionately.'

[1] CB to Geo. Smith, 29 Jan. 1852: *W & S* iii. 310.
[2] For reports on CB's ill health, see above, pp. 403, 448.
[3] CB to Geo. Smith, 19 Apr. 1851: *W & S* iii. 227.
[4] CB to Mrs. Smith, 29 Jan. 1852: *W & S* iii. 311.

Neither peace of mind nor greatly improved health resulted from the decision. The slow spring and late summer brought no alleviation to her condition; she could not write.

To Mr. Williams she frankly stated her case at the beginning of March:

My dear Sir—It is not at all likely that my book will be ready at the time you mention. If my health is spared I shall get on with it as fast as is consistent with its being done, if not *well*, yet as well as I can do it—*not one whit faster*. When the mood leaves me (it has left me now, without vouchsafing so much as a word or a message when it will return) I put by the MS and wait till it comes back again. God knows I sometimes have to wait long—*very* long it seems to me. Meantime, if I might make a request to you, it would be this: Please to say nothing about my book till it is written and in your hands.[1]

On 12 March she wrote in a similar vein to Miss Wooler: 'For nearly four months now (i.e. since I became ill) I have not put pen to paper—My work has been lying untouched, and my faculties have been rusting for want of exercise. . . . My publisher groans over my long delays; I am sometimes provoked to check the expression of his impatience with short and crusty answers.'[2]

On 21 March she had again to parry inquiries from Cornhill; answering a letter of George Smith's, she wrote: 'You are kind enough to enquire after Currer Bell's health. Thank you; he is better, latterly he has been much better; if he could continue so well he could look up yet—but—I say again, expect no good of him this summer.'

The expectation was indeed fulfilled; she achieved nothing. At the end of May, certain that no good would come of waiting on inspiration, she went alone to Filey for a month, and briefly announced her intention to George Smith. Thanking him for a royalty on 22 May, she wrote: 'Occupied as you are—I will not at present detain you by more than an acknowledgement. Should you write to me in the course of the next fortnight or three weeks, my address will be Cliff House, Filey, East Riding, Yorkshire.'[3]

She returned to the lodgings where she and Ellen had stayed after Anne's death—'not, however, in the same rooms, but in less expensive apartments', she told Ellen, who was spending the summer in Sussex. Charlotte was welcomed by the same kind landlady, Mrs. Smith,

---

[1] CB to WSW, 4 Mar. 1852: *W & S* iii. 320.
[2] CB to MW, 12 Mar. 1852: Allbutt Bequest, Fitzwilliam Museum: *W & S* iii. 323.
[3] CB to Geo. Smith, 22 May 1852: *W & S* iii. 334.

though the daughter who had waited on them before was just married. The cold season and her solitude did little to raise her spirits. A necessary visit to Anne's grave at Scarborough, on which the lettering was still at fault and needed correcting, revived nothing but the bitterest memories. Writing to Miss Wooler on 23 June from Filey she frankly confessed to being unable to do anything: 'I have walked as much as I could since I came here, and look almost as sunburnt and weather-beaten as a fisherman or bathing-woman, with being out in the open air. As to my work, it has stood absolutely still for a long while; certainly a torpid liver makes torpid brains; no spirit moves me.'[1]

She returned home at the end of June. After a full month she could still give no encouraging account of herself to Mr. Williams, who had written about a projected reprint of *Shirley*. Charlotte greatly feared her publishers would take the opportunity of rashly advertising a new work by the author. 'The warm weather and a visit to the sea have done me much good physically; but as yet I have recovered neither elasticity of animal spirits nor flow of the power of composition.'[2]

Two circumstances would have prevented her resuming work, even had she felt the urge to do so: her father had a slight stroke (from which he miraculously recovered) and James Taylor dropped the correspondence with her again. To Ellen Nussey, who had inquired, she wrote on 1 July, in a tone of complete finality: 'You ask about India. Let us dismiss the subject in a few words and not revive it. All is silent as the grave.'[3]

She had, earlier in the year, given Ellen an insight into the exact degree of her hopes from the Indian Mail; writing to her on 7 March she had said: 'Many Mails have come from India since I was at Brookroyd and always when the day came round (I know it now) expectation would be on the alert—but disappointment knocked her down. I have not heard a syllable, and cannot think of making enquiries at Cornhill. Well, long suspense in any matter usually proves somewhat cankering, but God orders things for us, and to His Will we must submit.'[4] She had learnt, stoically, to submit to much else already; James Taylor now went out of her life without a choice being allowed her of welcoming or rejecting what he had to offer.

The circumstances of his loss—the distance and danger of the

[1] CB to Miss Wooler: 23 June 1852: Allbutt Bequest, Fitzwilliam Museum.
[2] CB to WSW: 28 July 1852: *W & S* iv. 3.
[3] CB to EN, 1 July 1852: *W & S* iii. 341.
[4] CB to EN, 7 Mar. 1852: *W & S* iii. 321.

voyage from India, and the letters for which she waited and which came no more—became a part of the texture of *Villette*, in which the loss of one lover by shipwreck and the defection of the other, for whose letters she waited in mental agony when the post-hour came, supplied the emotional climaxes of the tale.

Charlotte's long delay in writing *Villette*, as already suggested, cannot be explained only by ill health; the subject itself, derived from the actual circumstances of her life, was in continual flux for the greater part of the year during which she was writing the book.

This is not to say that she was consciously waiting for a solution of the problems concerning her personal relationships with George Smith and James Taylor. That would not be true: the mental processes at work were of a far more complicated kind. Experience was slowly eradicating the ancient fallacies of her romantic girlhood. She was gradually moving towards a complete realization of the truth of her particular destiny, and instantly transmuting it into another truth— the truth of art. The latter could not be achieved before the other had been realized; and it took Charlotte all her life until the completion of *Villette* to accept the decrees of common existence. Only then were her evolution as an artist fully achieved and the delusions of adolescence set aside. What this realization cost her is shown in a letter to Ellen of 25 August, when in reply to complaints about her silence, she said:

I am silent because I have literally nothing to say. I might indeed repeat over and over again that my life is a pale blank and often a very weary burden, and that the Future sometimes appals me; but what end could be answered by such repetition except to weary you and enervate myself?

The evils that now and then wring a groan from my heart, lie in position, not that I am a *single* woman and likely to remain a *single* woman, but because I am a *lonely* woman and likely to be *lonely*. But it cannot be helped and therefore *imperatively must be borne*, and borne with as few words about it as may be.[1]

It is noticeable that her work on *Villette* was resumed about that time and its progress uninterrupted as the autumn advanced; by 30 October she sent the first two volumes to Cornhill and the whole finished work on Saturday, 20 November. The course of the tale, from the moment that Lucy Snowe buries the letters from Graham

---

[1] CB to EN, 25 Aug. 1852: *W & S* iv. 6.

Bretton, knowing that there will be no more, had no more problems for its author: the paths of the two principals from then on diverge, Lucy's darkening as she goes forward into the storm-wrack of the final overwhelming flood.

To achieve the isolation of her heroine Charlotte did not hesitate to make use of supernatural powers. It is the *inexplicable* nature of Lucy's early and late losses that so deepen and darken her fate, and encompass her with that sense of adverse fatality that Charlotte herself had come to believe in and to accept for herself. George Smith and Mr. Williams were quick to perceive this and to protest. To their objections Charlotte had unanswerable replies. 'You say that she [Lucy] may be thought morbid and weak, unless the history of her life be more fully given. I consider that she *is* both morbid and weak at times; her character sets up no pretentions to unmixed strength, and anybody living her life would necessarily become morbid.'[1]

In other words, Charlotte was telling her publishers that she and she alone could answer for the truth of Lucy's behaviour—since Lucy's life was hers and Lucy's feelings. She could only vouch for the veracity of what she had said and leave the rest unexplained.

Similar protests came from Cornhill about the substitution of Paul Emanuel for Graham Bretton as the eventual hero of the tale. How much George Smith knew of Monsieur Heger before the writing of *Villette* remains a moot point; and how much Charlotte herself had intended, when in introducing the figure of the professor into the opening chapters, to elaborate the part is also a mystery. What emerges with inescapable clarity is that, as the course of her own destiny unfolded in the decisive year 1852, both the memory and the lesson of her greatest experience in life—her love for Monsieur Heger—returned with new meaning and emphasis and took possession of her mind. *Villette* is the last great *devoir* Mlle Charlotte accomplished at the instigation of her Master.

Time, which had allowed her to see objectively the true nature of their unique relationship, had worked in his favour, substituting for him no image of comparable vitality. Charlotte's feeling for Monsieur Heger was the yardstick by which she measured her feelings for other men; and she knew well enough that love was not the essential part of her feelings for either George Smith or James Taylor. So recognizable was the quality of her real love, besides which her more recent emotional experiences paled, that Charlotte's first readers were left in no doubt

[1] CB to WSW, 6 Nov. 1852 : *W & S* iv. 18.

of its origin in her own experience; so Anthony Trollope[1] divined, and so too did Catherine Winkworth,[2] who wrote to her sister: 'I guess the true love was Paul Emanuel after all, and is dead; but I don't know, and don't think that Lily [Mrs. Gaskell] knows. . . .'

But there still remained the urgent need of friendship, even when love had failed. To Lucy Snowe she attributed the exact definition of the difference in the scene between Paul Emanuel and herself in the chapter 'Fraternity'. To the offer of his friendship, she was too overcome to answer him

in words, yet I suppose I *did* answer him; he took my hand, which found comfort in the shelter of his. *His* friendship was not a doubtful, wavering benefit—a cold distant hope—a sentiment so brittle as not to bear the weight of a finger; I at once felt . . . its support like that of some rock.

'When I talk of friendship, I mean *true* friendship' he repeated emphatically; and I could hardly believe that words so earnest had blessed my ear; I hardly could credit the reality of that kind anxious look he gave. If he *really* wished for my confidence and regard, and *really* would give me his—why, it seemed to me that life could offer nothing more or better . . . I envied no girl her lover, no bride her bridegroom, no wife her husband; I was content with this my voluntary, self-offering friend.[3]

Such friendship, which would have provided a satisfying substitute for what other women seek in marriage, Charlotte of course never knew. And she could not, even in fiction, permit it to her heroine; neither romance, nor solid happiness should be hers. To George Smith, who was protesting over the change of heroes before he even realized that the new hero was to be denied Lucy, she wrote with firm finality:

It is not pleasant and it will probably be found as unwelcome to the reader as it was, in a sense, *compulsory upon the writer*. The spirit of romance would have indicated another course, far more flowery and inviting; it would have fashioned a paramount hero, kept faithfully to him, and made him supremely worshipful; he should have an idol, and not a mute, unresponding idol either; but this would have been unlike real life—inconsistent with truth—at variance with probability.[4]

Upon the lesson of real life Charlotte had waited to solve the

---

[1] In his judgement of *Villette*, A. T. wrote: '. . . In *Villette* and in *Shirley*, there is to be found human life as natural and as real, though in circumstances not so full of interest as those told in *Jane Eyre*. The character of Paul in the former of the two is a wonderful study. She must herself have been in love with some Paul when she wrote the book, and have been determined to prove to herself that she was capable of loving someone whose exterior circumstances were mean and in every way unprepossessing . . .' (*Autobiography*, 211–18, World's Classics).

[2] Catherine Winkworth to Emily Shaen, 8 May 1854: *W & S* iv. 125.

[3] *Villette*, ch. 35.   [4] CB to Geo. Smith, 6 Dec. 1852: *W & S* iv. 22.

problems of her plot. The past year had proved beyond doubt that the spirit of romance was a phantom—and a fake phantom at that, like the 'Nun' in her tale. It was not through accident but design that the 'crabbed professor' was brought to the forefront in the third volume. He alone had the right to Lucy's love as Lucy's creator well knew; but to Lucy, as inexorably, she denied the fulfilment of that love.

Somehow during the summer of 1852 Charlotte learned that George Smith would never be more to her in real life than her publisher. That his mother played some part in this *éclaircissement* might be inferred from a comment of Charlotte's on the eve of her next visit to London to check the proof-sheets of *Villette*. In a note of 9 December to Ellen she wrote: 'This morning I have a brief note from Mr. Williams intimating that he has not yet been permitted to read the 3rd vol. Also there is a note from Mrs. Smith, very kind, I almost wish I could still look on that kindness just as I used to do; it was very pleasant to me once.'[1]

Mr. Brontë, who also pleaded for a happy ending to *Villette*, and George Smith, might protest and argue, but Currer Bell was not to be lulled into complacency. During the past year she had squarely faced her destiny and recognized that to certain beings suffering was pre-ordained. After all, she might have said, she had not been to Cowan Bridge for nothing. With Lucy Snowe she had accepted the decree: 'I did not, in my heart, arraign the mercy of God for this; I concluded it to be a part of His great plan that some must deeply suffer while they live, and I thrilled to the certainty that of this number I was one.'[2] The power of *Villette* derives precisely from this awareness and accept-ance of the supernal forces directing everything; it is this that places the whole drama on a cosmic level. Seldom can the reader overlook the spiritual content and implications of the story, or the mysterious influence exercised by the elements on those attuned by Nature—as were the Brontës—to receive their meaning. In passage after passage this close affinity is declared. Lucy takes the first step into her unknown future, stepping out into the clear, frosty night on a lonely path, 'which lay through still fields, and passed neither village, nor farm-house, nor cottage; I should have quailed at the absence of moonlight, for it was by the leading of stars only that I traced the dim path; I should have quailed still more in the unwonted presence of that which to-night shone in the north, a moving mystery—the Aurora Borealis'.[3]

[1] CB to EN, 9 Dec. 1852: *W & S* iv. 24.   [2] *Villette*, ch. 15.
[3] *Villette*, ch. 5.

Again, Lucy's despair in the Long Vacation:

Twilight was falling, and I deemed its influence pitiful; from the lattice I saw coming night-clouds trailing low like banners drooping. It seemed to me that at this hour there was affection and sorrow in Heaven above for all pain suffered on earth beneath; the weight of my dreadful dream became alleviated—that insufferable thought of being no more loved—no more owned, half-yielded to hope of the contrary. I was sure this hope would shine clearer if I got out from under this house-roof, which was crushing as the slab of a tomb, and went outside the city.[1]

Never before had her powers of vision and evocation been so consistently, so royally displayed. The world without, and the world within, were the illimitable stage for the drama's setting, the drama of her own life presented whole at last. The dream of Angria and the reality of Brussels were fused in one grand explosion of passion and pathos, of rebellion and acceptance, of tribulation and ecstasy. What she had been, and what she would never be, were revealed here eloquently for ever; the rest of her life could pass in silence.

Well might Charlotte scribble to Ellen on completing her work: 'Truly thankful am I to be able to tell you that I finished my long task on Saturday [20 November 1852], packed and sent off the parcel to Cornhill. I said my prayers when I had done it. Whether it is well or ill done, I don't know. D.V. I will now try to wait the issue quietly.'[2]

She need not have doubted the issue. George Eliot, on laying the book down and writing in trembling haste to her friend Mrs. Charles Bray, typified the reaction of Charlotte's first readers: 'I am only just returned to a sense of the real world about me,' she wrote, 'for I have been reading "Villette", a still more wonderful book than "Jane Eyre". There is something almost preternatural in its power.'[3]

Charlotte herself described the processes of creation, that could lend this 'almost preternatural' power to her writing, in a letter to G. H. Lewes: 'When authors write best, or, at least, when they write most fluently, an influence seems to waken in them, which becomes their master—which will have its own way—putting out of view all behests but its own, dictating certain words . . . new-moulding characters, giving unthought of turns to incidents, rejecting carefully elaborated old ideas, and suddenly creating and adopting new ones. . . .' It was thus, and not otherwise, we may be sure, that *Villette* was written. (CB to G. H. Lewes, 12 Jan. 1848. *Life*, 240.)

[1] *Villette*, ch. 15. [2] CB to EN, 22 Nov. 1852: *W & S* iv. 20.
[3] *George Eliot Letters*, ed. G. S. Haight (O.U.P. 1954), ii. 87.

CHAPTER XXVI

THE LAST ARTHUR

AFTER dispatching the manuscript of *Villette* to Cornhill, Charlotte spent a week with Ellen Nussey, from 1 to 8 December. While at Brookroyd she received a shock over the payment for her work. She had asked George Smith to invest 'the cash for the copyright in the funds', as he had always done for her, 'except £20 for which I have a present use', she wrote to him on 23 November, 'and which, perhaps, you will send me in a Bank Bill'. She fully expected, now that she was an established author, to be offered something more than for either *Jane Eyre* or *Shirley* (£500 apiece). Mr. Brontë, indeed, expected she would be offered not less than £700 and she herself, as she confided to Miss Wooler, did not 'anticipate that a lower sum would be offered'. However, when George Smith's letter came (after agitating delay) she found that he was paying her no more than £500. The decision, though it hurt her and she knew that it was 'not quite equitable', did not draw a word of complaint from her. She pocketed her pride, commenting merely to Miss Wooler that 'when an author finds his work cordially approved—he can pardon the rest'.[1]

In the present instance it was not quite correct to say that Cornhill 'cordially approved' of the third volume of *Villette*; despite their overall approbation of the work, there were such serious points of difference over the evolution of volume three (with its switch of interest from 'Dr. John' to 'Professor Emanuel') that George Smith did not sanction its being read by Mr. Williams and told Charlotte roundly that there was something 'which sticks confoundedly in his throat'[2] and about which he would answer no more questions by post.[3] On that score and the better to speed the proof-corrections,

[1] CB to Miss Wooler, 7 Dec. 1852: *W & S* iv. 23: Allbutt Bequest, Fitzwilliam Museum.

[2] CB to EN, 9 Dec. 1852: *W & S* iv. 24.

[3] CB's letter to GMS of 8 Dec. 1852 (*W & S* iv. 23), shows that she was so concerned at his silence on receiving the MS. of *Villette*, and the fact that the money order for it was accompanied by no word from him, that she had made up her mind to take the first train to London on the Monday morning and confront him. A letter from him reached her

Charlotte's presence was required in London while the last volume went through the press.

While holding herself in readiness for the call to London, she suffered an experience of a totally different and deeply disturbing nature: her father's curate, Arthur Bell Nicholls, proposed to her on 13 December.

It was a Monday evening, a time when he generally called to see Mr. Brontë on parish matters and matters concerning the National Schools, which he had wholly taken over from Mr. Brontë and where he gave 'religious instruction' every morning. To Ellen, Charlotte wrote a full account two days after the event of all that happened, enclosing a note from Mr. Nicholls which she had since received.[1]

I know not whether you have observed him specially when staying here, your perception is generally quick enough, *too* quick I have sometimes thought, yet as you never said anything, I restrained my own dim misgivings, which could not claim the sure guide of vision. What papa has seen or guessed I will not enquire though I may conjecture. He has minutely noticed all Mr. Nicholls's low spirits, all his threats of expatriation, all his symptoms of impaired health, noticed them with little sympathy and much indirect sarcasm. On Monday evening Mr. Nicholls was here to tea. I vaguely felt without clearly seeing, as without seeing I have felt for some time, the meaning of his constant looks, and strange, feverish restraint. After tea I withdrew to the dining-room as usual. As usual, Mr. Nicholls sat with papa till between eight and nine o'clock; I then heard him open the parlour door as if going. I expected the clash of the front door. He stopped in the passage: he tapped: like lightning it flashed upon me what was coming. He entered—he stood before me. What his words were you can guess; his manner—you can hardly realise—never can I forget it. Shaking from head to foot, looking deadly pale, speaking low, vehemently yet with difficulty—he made me for the first time feel what it costs a man to declare affection where he doubts response.

The spectacle of one ordinarily so statue-like, thus trembling, stirred, and overcome, gave me a kind of strange shock. He spoke of sufferings he had borne for months, of sufferings he could endure no longer, and craved leave for some hope. I could only entreat him to leave me then and promise a reply on the morrow. I asked him if he had spoken to papa. He said, he dared not. I think I half led, half put him out of the room. When he was gone, I immediately went to papa, and told him what had taken place. Agitation and anger disproportionate to the occasion ensued; if I had *loved* Mr. Nicholls

meanwhile on the Sunday morning—'and you have thus been spared the visitation of the unannounced and unsummoned apparition of Currer Bell in Cornhill. Inexplicable delays should be avoided when possible . . .': CB to GMS 6 Dec. 1852: *SLL* ii. 289.

[1] CB to EN, 15 Dec. 1852: *W & S* iv. 28–30.

CUBA HOUSE, BANAGHER, CO. OFFALY

ARTHUR BELL NICHOLLS IN 1854

and had heard such epithets applied to him as were used, it would have transported me past patience; as it was, my blood boiled with a sense of injustice, but papa worked himself into a state not to be trifled with, the veins on his temples started up like whipcord, and his eyes became suddenly bloodshot. I made haste to promise that Mr. Nicholls should on the morrow have a distinct refusal.

I wrote yesterday and got his note. There is no need to add to this statement any comment. Papa's vehement antipathy to the bare thought of any one thinking of me as a wife, and Mr. Nicholls' distress both give me pain. Attachment to Mr. Nicholls you are aware I never entertained, but the poignant pity inspired by his state on Monday evening, by the hurried revelation of his sufferings for many months, is something galling and irksome. That he cared something for me, and wanted me to care for him, I have long suspected but I did not know the degree or strength of his feelings.

How negative was her response to Mr. Nicholls's declaration is sufficiently summed up in the phrase: 'if I had *loved* Mr. Nicholls . . .'. But instantly the sense of justice and of pity was aroused, and also of conscience. She had not lived in daily contact with a man vehemently in love with her without 'dim misgivings' and 'deep concern', but on that Monday night she was made to realize how greatly she had underestimated his feelings. Irrespective of Mr. Brontë's irrational attitude to the proposal, and while convinced that poor Mr. Nicholls had nothing to hope for from her, she could pity him, as she had never pitied him before. Fortunately for her, when the moment of revelation came, the decision did not rest with her; the wounding words did not have to come from her; she had merely to make herself the mouthpiece of her father's refusal. Mr. Nicholls was a very conventional man. He did not expect (and certainly would not have advocated) rebellion in the weaker sex, and he took his dismissal without appealing to the daughter over the father's head. Having dreaded just such a rejection for months past, and even taken some half-hearted steps towards applying for a post in the Australian mission field, he handed his resignation to Mr. Brontë and waited his convenience in replacing him. Nothing could be tamer on the surface.

Till then, Charlotte had only judged him on the surface. He was 27 when he first came to Haworth in May 1845, younger than Charlotte, six months younger than Branwell, and while Charlotte consigned him to that scornful corner of her mind where she placed curates in general and local curates in particular, he was closely observing the family of his minister: 'Papa has got a new curate lately,' Charlotte wrote just after his arrival, 'a Mr. Nicholls from Ireland . . . he appears a respectable young man, reads well, and I hope will give satisfaction.'[1] Mr. Nicholls's good voice, remarked on in Charlotte's first grudging report on his abilities, lasted him into old age. Among his own folk in Ireland it was remembered that he 'possessed an unusually deep and rich voice' when he read the lessons for his cousin, the Rector of his home parish of Banagher.

How little Mr. Nicholls distinguished himself in Charlotte's eyes from his fellow curates—of whom there were three in permanent function in the outlying parishes of Oxenhope, Oakworth, and Stanbury—Charlotte's strictures to Ellen written on 18 June 1845 clearly show. Mr. Nicholls had barely been a month at Haworth. In reply to Ellen's invitation to join her at Hathersage with the offer of the local curate as an incentive, Charlotte wrote: 'I have no desire to see your medico-clerical curate. I think he must be like most other curates I have seen; and they *seem* to me a self-seeking, vain, empty race. At this blessed moment we have no less than three of them in Haworth parish, and God knows, there is not one to mend another.'[2]

Arthur Bell Nicholls entered the orbit of the Brontë family in a year of destiny for them all. It was the year of Branwell's dismissal from Thorp Green, when he returned home for good an emotional wreck, whom heart-break, drink, and drugs would kill within three years. It was also the year in which Branwell's sisters, driven within themselves by Branwell's disgrace, emerged as professional writers for the first time. However much the curate was expected to keep his distance from these doings, Nicholls noticed them, and, in as unobtrusive a way as he could, manifested his sympathy. He was an outdoor man, fond of striding the moors and, as sickness gradually bound and imprisoned the once lively inmates of the parsonage, he offered—and was authorized—to exercise the dogs. (He had, in full measure, the Irishman's love of dogs and horses and there at least found a bond of sympathy with his minister's family.) The grateful creatures went in pursuit of him to his lodgings, and to the day of his departure Flossy whined at his door for a walk; he was the last of that stricken household to run with them on the moors.

Upon Nicholls devolved the bitter duty of burying Emily in December 1848. And as Anne left home for Scarborough in the following May, it was he who stood in Church Lane and prevented Flossy from running after the gig. Charlotte may not have observed how he performed these humble services, or with what growing dedication to her image he came and went about his duties. The revelation forced upon her that Monday evening was in consequence all the more startling. Of her calamities, so stoically borne, he had been the silent witness. As time passed, and he saw how even her writing brought her but a moderate recompense for shattered nerves, sickness, and insomnia, the wish to shoulder her burdens and bring her peace—if it could not be joy—dominated his life. He waited, significantly, for her to dispatch her manuscript to Cornhill before speaking. On her return from Brookroyd he seized the first occasion of finding her alone.

The outcome cannot have greatly surprised him, for she had never given the slightest sign of responding to his hopes. But though her answer, dictated by her father, was a decided negative, it left her in the deepest perturbation. She wrote Ellen three days after her first communication:

You may well ask, How is it? for I am sure I don't know. This business would seem to me like a dream, did not my reason tell me it has long been brewing. It puzzles me to comprehend how and whence comes this turbulence of feeling.

You ask how papa demeans himself to Mr. Nicholls. I only wish you were here to see papa in his present mood: you would know something of him. He just treats him with a hardness not to be bent, and a contempt not to be propitiated. The two have had no interview as yet: all has been done by letter. Papa wrote, I must say, a most cruel note to Mr. Nicholls on Wednesday. In his state of mind and health (for the poor man is horrifying his landlady, Martha's mother, by entirely rejecting his meals) I felt that the blow must be parried, and I thought it right to accompany the pitiless despatch by a line to the effect that, while Mr. Nicholls must never expect me to reciprocate the feeling he had expressed, yet at the same time I wished to disclaim participation in sentiments calculated to give him pain; and exhorted him to maintain his courage and spirits. On receiving the two letters, he set off from home. . . . You must understand that a good share of papa's anger arises from the idea, not altogether groundless, that Mr. Nicholls has behaved with disingenuousness in so long concealing his aim, forging that Irish fiction, etc. I am afraid also that papa thinks a little too much about his want of money; he says that the match would be a degradation, that I should be throwing myself away, that he expects me, if I marry at all, to do very differently; in short, his manner of viewing the subject is, on the whole, far from being one in which I can sympathise. My own objections arise from a sense of incongruity and uncongeniality in feelings, tastes, principles.[1]

[1] CB to EN, 18 Dec. 1852: *W & S* iv. 30–31.

For Charlotte it was a great relief to be obliged to go to London just then, for no improvement could be expected in the situation until Mr. Nicholls left Haworth. Mr. Brontë was adamant, whatever Charlotte's feelings might have been.

Mr. Brontë's conduct in the affair has been the subject of universal opprobium from that day to this. Mixed as his reasons were (and fear for Charlotte's health was still the uppermost), the fact that Mr. Nicholls was a mere Irish curate was gall and wormwood to the pride of a man who had once been an Irish curate himself. If he contemplated marriage for Charlotte at all, it was with someone whose position was commensurate with her standing as one of the foremost women writers of her day; nothing less was even remotely tolerable. But when all is said for and against the paternal tyranny of Mr. Brontë, he was of his time and never doubted his absolute right to decide his daughter's happiness. The dread of losing her was, after all, a very natural selfishness from which few old people can claim to be wholly immune; Mr. Brontë showed himself in the event to be no more and no less selfish and tyrannous than the generality of fathers of his time. How he would have acted if Charlotte had declared herself in love with Mr. Nicholls from the start is an enigma.

Before going to London on 5 January 1853, Charlotte sent Ellen a last report on the state of affairs at the parsonage. Writing to her on 2 January, she said:

I am . . . preparing to go to London this week—a matter which necessitates some little application to the needle. I find it is quite necessary that I should go to superintend the press as Mr. S— seems quite determined not to let the printing get on till I come. I have actually only recd 3 proof sheets since I was at Brookroyd. Papa wants me to go too—to be out of the way I suppose—and I am sorry for one other person whom nobody pities but me. Martha is bitter against him. John Brown says *he should like to shoot him.* They don't understand the nature of his feelings—but I see now what they are. Mr. N. is one of those who attach themselves to very few, whose sensations are close and deep—like an underground stream, running strong but in a narrow channel. He continues restless and ill—he carefully performs the occasional duty—but does not come near the church, procuring a substitute every Sunday.

A few days since he wrote to Papa requesting permission to withdraw his resignation. Papa answered that he should only do so on condition of giving his written promise never again to broach the obnoxious subject either to him or to me. This he has evaded doing, so the matter remains unsettled. I feel persuaded the termination will be—his departure for Australia.

Dear Nell—without loving him—I don't like to think of him, suffering in solitude, and wish him anywhere so that he were happier. He and Papa have never met or spoken yet.[1]

The visit to London, from 5 January to 2 February 1853—which in the event proved to be Charlotte's last—was marked by none of those social highlights that had distinguished the previous ones. Neither Charlotte nor her publishers were in a mood for relaxation. The purpose of her visit was to see her book through the press, and an exacting task both she and they found it. The reason for this was not merely pressure of time, but the more subtle issue of personal suscepti- bilities.

Charlotte found George Smith greatly altered. His exhausting life was telling on his fine physique, and she was not slow to mark the deleterious effects. She wrote to Ellen:

On Mr. Smith hard work is telling early. The very lines of his features are altered; it is rather the remembrance of what he was than the fact of what he is which can warrant the picture I have been accustomed to give of him. One feels pained to see a physical alteration of this kind, yet I feel glad and thank- ful that it is merely physical; as far as I can judge, mind and manners have undergone no deterioration.[2]

Genial-tempered as George Smith had always shown himself to his author, the book did raise questions of an extremely personal nature. After all, Currer Bell had portrayed him and his mother,[3] as he was the first to acknowledge, in two of the leading characters in the tale: the procedure called for no ordinary degree of tact in both writer and publisher. In the process, something was inevitably lost that was never fully recaptured. Charlotte wrote to Ellen of 'sorrowful impressions' received during her visit; and it is obvious that, despite the mainten- ance of courteous relations in the months immediately following the publication of *Villette* (and the customary present from George Smith to his author—in this instance the portrait of Thackeray dispatched to Haworth), such a severance was reached before the year's end that Charlotte could write in the following spring: 'In the course of the year that is gone, Cornhill and London have receded a long way from

---

[1] CB to EN, 5 Jan. 1853: *W & S* iv. 32–33.
[2] CB to EN, 11 Jan. 1853: *W & S* iv. 33.
[3] '. . . In *Villette* my mother was the original of "Mrs. Bretton", several of her expres- sions are given verbatim. I myself, I discovered, stood for "Dr. John". CB admitted this to Mrs. Gaskell . . .': George Smith, 'Recollections of Charlotte Brontë', *Cornhill Magazine*, Dec. 1900.

me; the links of communication have waxed very frail and few. It must be so in this world. All things considered, I don't wish it otherwise.'[1] (In the intervening interval, George Smith had become engaged, and was married; but of that, more hereafter.)

Villette was got through the press with an expense of Charlotte's nervous energy that can be imagined. Even so, while she was brought to modify certain passages in the last volume, she resolutely refused to alter the essential lines of the plot and its ending, agreeing to give only so much comfort to her readers as to leave the actual catastrophe couched in ambiguous language. Though asked on several occasions by readers to clarify the doubt left in their minds, she always refused to do so, declaring that it would be a pity 'to spoil their sport by giving them the key'. The key, as perhaps not even George Smith realized, remained in Monsieur Heger's pocket, where Charlotte intended it should remain for ever.

How much George Smith had to be initiated into the secret shrouding the Brussels origin of the book can only be guessed from the fact that Charlotte pledged him to refuse and to *prevent* a French translation.[2] He kept his word till after her death, but it was of little avail to check the pirates: *Villette* was published in French in Brussels under the title *La Maîtresse d'Anglais—ou le Pensionnat de Bruxelles* (3 vols.) already in 1855. Mrs. Gaskell, when collecting material for her 'Life' of Charlotte, and calling on the Hegers in the following year, was made all too aware by the refusal of Madame Heger to see her how fatal had been the effect of the translation.

The discussions with her publishers and the correcting of proofs took most of Charlotte's time during the month in London. Writing to Ellen from Gloucester Terrace on 19 January, she said:

I still continue to get on very comfortably and quietly in London—in the way I like—seeing rather things than persons—Being allowed to have my own choice of sights this time—I selected rather the *real* than the *decorative* side of Life—I have been over two prisons ancient and modern—Newgate and Pentonville—also the Bank, the Exchange, the Foundling Hospital—and to-day if all be well—I go with Dr. Forbes to see Bethlehem Hospital. Mrs. Smith and her daughters are—I believe—a little amazed at my gloomy tastes, but I take no notice.[3]

---

[1] CB to Geo. Smith, 25 Apr. 1854: *W & S* iv. 119.
[2] For details concerning the French translation of *Villette*, see below, Additional Notes.
[3] CB to EN, 19 Jan. 1853: *W & S* iv. 35.

Something, surely, of the loss of cordiality towards those whose good opinion she had once so ardently courted, could be read into those lines?

George Smith remembered in after years those excursions into the *real* life of the city, on some of which he accompanied Charlotte.

At Newgate she rapidly fixed her attention on an individual prisoner. This was a poor girl with an interesting face, and an expression of the deepest misery. She had, I believe, killed her illegitimate child. Miss Brontë walked up to her, took her hand, and began to talk to her. She was, of course, quickly interrupted by the prison warder with the formula 'Visitors are not allowed to speak to the prisoners.'[1]

From such contacts, and not from her evenings at the Opera or afternoons spent in society, came that deep sense of the meaning and importance of the stir of life in a great city so memorably expressed in *Villette*; recalling her first timid introduction to the Strand, to Cornhill, to the perils of the crossings and the pressing life of the hurrying crowds, she wrote: 'Since those days, I have seen the West End, the parks, the fine squares; but I love the city far better. The city seems so much more in earnest; its business, its rush, its roar, are such serious things, sights, and sounds. The city is getting its living—the West End but enjoying its pleasure. At the West End you may be amused, but in the city you are deeply excited.'[2]

Villette was published on 28 January 1853 and was straightway acclaimed in the press. This was a matter of particular relief to Charlotte whose confidence in the book had necessarily been a little shaken by the doubts of Messrs. Smith and Williams. As the major reviews came in, Charlotte could write to George Smith: 'I have received and read the Reviews, I think I ought to be and feel I *am*, very thankful ... that in the Literary Gazette is as good as any author can look for.'[3] Whatever the reservations of her publishers, by the reception of the literary world and her readers Charlotte could feel fully justified.

Only one critique caused her pain: it was Harriet Martineau's in the *Daily News*.[4] It was the more hurtful because Charlotte had written to ask Harriet to speak freely about it just before publication: 'I know that you will give me your thoughts upon my book as frankly as if you

[1] *Cornhill Magazine*, Dec. 1900: op. cit.
[2] *Villette*, ch. 6.
[3] CB to Geo. Smith, 7 Feb. 1853: *W & S* iv. 44.
[4] See below, Additional Notes: CB and Harriet Martineau.

spoke to some near relation whose good you preferred to her gratification. . . .'[1] It was Harriet Martineau's nature to be frank, and she did
not hesitate to condemn the feature of *Villette* that she disliked—the
love interest—while enthusiastically acclaiming the rest. Unfortunately,
the offending feature was of the book's essence, and to dislike *that* was
to dislike all. Charlotte was stung to the quick. In an exchange of
letters following the review, she wrote to Harriet: 'I know what love
is as I understand it; and if man or woman should be ashamed of
feeling such love, then is there nothing right, noble, faithful, truthful,
unselfish in this earth, as I comprehend rectitude, nobleness, fidelity,
truth, and disinterestedness—Yours sincerely—To differ from you
gives me keen pain.'[2]

For Charlotte, there could be no reconciliation of principles so
divergent; though Harriet expressed great surprise at Charlotte's
reaction, and harboured no ill will herself, the friendship never
revived.

Could Charlotte but have known it, Thackeray shared Harriet
Martineau's dislike of the very same feature of *Villette*—the *double*
love interest—of which he wrote very frankly to his correspondents
but of which, of course, no echo reached Charlotte. Thackeray was in
America when *Villette* appeared, touring the States with his lectures
on 'The English Humorists', and commented in several of his letters
home on the rage the book was enjoying among lady-readers over
there. '. . . It is an excellently written book,' he commented to Mrs.
Procter in a letter of 8 March 1853, 'but a very disagreeable one. She
turns every one "The seamy side out".' To a young American friend,
Lucy Baxter, he wrote more penetratingly from his knowledge of the
author:

The good of 'Villette' in my opinion Miss is a very fine style; it amuses me
to read the author's naive confession of being in love with 2 men at the same
time; and her readiness to fall in love at any time. The poor little woman of
genius! the fiery little eager brave tremulous homely-faced creature! I can
read a great deal of her life as I fancy her in her book, and see that rather than
have fame, rather than any other earthly good or mayhap heavenly one she
wants some Tomkins or another to love her and be in love with. But you see
she is a little bit of a creature without a penny worth of good looks, thirty
years old I should think, buried in the country, and eating up her own heart
there, and no Tomkins will come. You girls with pretty faces . . . will get

---

[1] CB to HM, 21 Jan. 1853: *W & S* iv. 38.
[2] CB to HM, Feb. 1853: *W & S* iv. 42.

dozens of young fellows fluttering about you—whereas here is one genius, a noble heart longing to mate itself and destined to wither away into old maidenhood with no chance to fulfil the burning desire.[1]

Sadly perspicuous as he was of the tragedy of Currer Bell's existence, Thackeray would have been amazed to know that 'Tomkins' did exist and at that very time was pining for love of Charlotte Brontë. The justification of the author of *Villette* lay beyond reach of her critics; they saw only 'the burning desire', not the containing and fastidious pride. What George Smith and Harriet Martineau and Thackeray saw was only a particle of the truth; had it been all, the Brontë greatness would have been much diminished.

With *Villette* launched on its successful career, Charlotte had to return home and to the problems facing her there. Her father had written only twice during her month in London, and even then one of the letters was a sarcastic 'complaint' purporting to have been written by 'Flossy'. Realizing the jars that lay ahead, Charlotte begged Ellen to meet her train at Keighley and return home with her; a proof how much she dreaded the return and the long tête-à-têtes with her father. The ensuing months, indeed, showed how unequal she was to facing her father's sarcasms and Mr. Nicholls's gloom; for she took every opportunity for going away from home—even after Mr. Nicholls left Haworth at the end of May.

The restlessness that his proposal had aroused could not easily be allayed. She suffered both on his behalf and on her own, stirred as she inevitably was to a reconsideration of her lot. The loneliness of her future prospects appeared doubly threatening since his hand had been extended to her; she was back to the distractions of the previous year, when James Taylor had come and gone. Her submission to Mr. Brontë's will did not mean a renunciation of her human rights. As she did not love Mr. Nicholls she felt no compulsion to detain him; yet the sense of justice which was very strong in her demanded fair play both for him *and* for her. Meanwhile, strange to say, her health was better than in the previous year, and she could write to Mrs. Gaskell on 24 February:

For my part I have thus far borne the cold weather well. I have taken long walks on the crackling snow, and felt the frosty bracing air. This winter has, for me, not been like last winter. December, January, February '51-2 passed like a long stormy night, conscious of one painful dream, all solitary grief and sickness. The corresponding months in '52–3 have gone over my head quietly and not uncheerfully. Thank God for the change and the repose! How welcome it has been He only knows! My father, too, has borne the season well; and my book and its reception thus far have pleased and cheered him.[1]

The satisfaction Mr. Brontë derived from the success of *Villette* was a welcome relief from the one obsessing theme. Though never openly mentioned between them, it loomed in the background of their hourly thoughts; nor could they quickly dispose of it. Mr. Nicholls's departure had to depend on Mr. Brontë securing another curate, and Nicholls another curacy; neither were easily achieved. Charlotte wrote to Ellen on 6 April:

You ask about Mr. Nicholls. I hear he has got a curacy, but do not yet know where. I trust the news is true. He and papa never speak. He seems to pass a desolate life. He has allowed late circumstances so to act on him as to freeze his manner and overcast his countenance not only to those immediately concerned but to every one. He sits drearily in his rooms. If Mr. Croxton or Mr. Grant, or any other clergyman calls to see, and as they think, to cheer him, he scarcely speaks. I find he tells them nothing, seeks no confidant, rebuffs all attempts to penetrate his mind. I own I respect him for this. He still lets Flossy go to his rooms and takes him to walk. He still goes over to see Mr. Sowden sometimes, and, poor fellow, that is all. He looks ill and miserable. I think and trust in Heaven that he will be better as soon as he gets away from Haworth. I pity him inexpressibly. We never meet or speak, nor dare I look at him, silent pity is all I can give him, and as he knows nothing about that, it does not comfort. He is now grown so gloomy and reserved that nobody seems to like him . . . Papa has a perfect antipathy to him, and he, I fear, to Papa. . . . How much of all this he deserves I can't tell, certainly he never was agreeable or amiable, and is less so now than ever, and alas! I do not know him well enough to be sure there is truth and true affection, or only rancour and corroding disappointment at the bottom of his chagrin. In this state of things I must be, and am, *entirely passive*. I may be losing the purest gem, and to me far the most precious life can give—genuine attachment—or I may be escaping the yoke of a morose temper. . . . In this doubt conscience will not suffer me to take one step in opposition to papa's will, blended as that will is with the most bitter and unreasonable prejudices. So I just leave the matter where we must leave all important matters.[2]

Pity from Charlotte meant more than words or contrition; she could measure Mr. Nicholls's suffering by her own of nearly ten years

[1] CB to Mrs. Gaskell, 24 Feb. 1853, Manchester Univ. Lib.
[2] CB to EN, 6 Apr. 1853: *W & S* iv. 56.

before. The more he rejected consolation and withdrew into himself, the closer she felt drawn to him, for she had behaved in her sorrow in just the same way.

On the 22 April she went to stay with Mrs. Gaskell at Manchester for a week. It was on the occasion of this visit (mentioned in Mrs. Gaskell's 'Life') that she first met the Winkworth sisters, Catherine and Susannah, the great friends of the Gaskells, and felt instantly drawn towards them—towards Catherine ('Katie') in particular, in whom she confided over the ensuing eighteen months in a way she did not with her old-established friends. Katie indeed fully reciprocated Charlotte's rare friendliness. She had been deeply impressed by her genius and misfortunes before they met, and writing of *Villette* to Emily Shaen, her connexion by marriage, had said on 23 March 1853: 'It makes one feel an extreme reverence for any one capable of so much deep feeling and brave endurance and truth but it makes one feel "eerie" too, to be brought face to face with a life so wanting in "verschonung".'[1]

Mrs. Gaskell has related how Charlotte came out of her shell on hearing the Winkworth sisters sing in the drawing-room at Plymouth Grove. 'Miss Brontë had been sitting quiet and constrained till they began "The Bonnie House of Airlie", but the effect of that and of "Carlisle Yetts" . . . was as irresistible as the playing of the Piper of Hamelin. The beautiful clear light came into her eyes; her lips quivered with emotion; she forgot herself, rose, and crossed the room to the piano, where she asked eagerly for song after song.'[2]

Her courage was not equal, however, to calling on the Winkworths in cold blood the following morning (they lived at Alderley Edge, Manchester), because it would have meant facing a third sister (Emily who had married the Gaskell's solicitor, William Shaen); Mrs. Gaskell was left to make her excuses.

The atmosphere of Plymouth Grove worked its usual charm upon Charlotte, and on returning home she wrote to Mrs. Gaskell: 'The week I spent in Manchester has impressed me as the very brightest and healthiest I have known for these five years past.' (Since the death of her sisters, in short.)

Mr. Nicholls's departure was now fixed for the end of May, and Charlotte still further delayed her return by making a visit to Ellen on her way back from Manchester.

[1] C. Winkworth to Emily Shaen, 23 Mar. 1853: *W & S* iv. 53.
[2] Gaskell, *Life*, ch. 26, 416.

How much Charlotte anticipated with relief the coming departure, and how little she yet realized its cost for Mr. Nicholls, can best be judged by the shock she experienced on the last occasion he gave her the sacrament. The revelation of his true feelings then went far to modify her own. It is impossible to read her account of the incident, written to Ellen on 16 May, and forget that she was the same Charlotte who had written more than fifteen years before of Miss Wooler: 'If anybody likes me I can't help liking them.'

Yesterday was a strange sort of a day in church. It seems as if I were to be punished for my doubts about the nature and truth of poor Mr. Nicholls's regard. Having ventured on Whit-Sunday to stop to the sacrament, I got a lesson not to be repeated. He struggled, faltered, then lost command over himself, stood before my eyes and in the sight of all the communicants, white, shaking, voiceless. Papa was not there, thank God! Joseph Redman [the parish clerk] spoke some words to him. He made a great effort, but could only with difficulty whisper and falter through the service. I suppose he thought this would be the last time; he goes either this week or the next. I heard the women sobbing round, and I could not check my own tears. What had happened was reported to papa whether by Joseph Redman or John Brown [parish sexton]; it excited only anger, and such expressions as 'un-manly driveller'. Compassion or relenting is no more to be looked for than sap from firewood.[1]

The issue would show that Charlotte's *volte-face* concerning Mr. Nicholls started with the writing of those words: from the obligation to submit was born the compassion that would save him.

Mr. Nicholls left Haworth early on the morning of Monday, 27 May. Charlotte wrote to Ellen later in the same day:

You will want to know about the leave-taking. The whole matter is but a painful subject, but I must treat it briefly. . . He left Haworth this morning at 6 o'clock. Yesterday evening he called to render into papa's hands the deeds of the National School, and to say good-bye. They were busy cleaning, washing the paint, etc., in the dining-room, so he did not find me there. I would not go into the parlour to speak to him in papa's presence. He went out thinking he was not to see me, and indeed, till the very last moment, I thought it best not. But perceiving that he stayed long before going out at the gate, and remembering his long grief, I took courage and went out trembling and miserable. I found him leaning against the garden door in a paroxysm of anguish, sobbing as women never sob. Of course I went straight to him. Very few words were interchanged, those few barely articulate. Several

[1] CB to EN, 16 May 1853: *W & S* iv. 65.

things I should have liked to ask him were swept entirely from my memory. Poor Fellow! But he wanted such hope and encouragement as I could not give him. Still I trust he must know now that I am not cruelly blind and indifferent to his constancy and grief. For a few weeks he goes to the South of England, afterwards he takes a curacy somewhere in Yorkshire, but I don't know where.

Papa has been far from strong lately. I dare not mention Mr. Nicholls' name to him. He speaks of him quietly and without opprobrium to others, but to me he is implacable on the matter. However, he is gone—gone—and there's an end of it. I see no chance of hearing a word about him in future, unless some stray shred of intelligence comes through Mr. Sowden or some other second-hand source.[1]

Though both Mr. Sowden, Vicar of Hebden Bridge, and Mr. Grant, Vicar of nearby Oxenhope, were devoted friends of Nicholls and, in the event, rendered him capital service, it was not 'at second-hand' that Charlotte heard further from her resolute lover. It was he himself who took the initiative of writing to her.

This occurred in July. He was to take up his new post as curate to the Rev. T. Cator, Vicar of Kirk Smeaton, six miles from Pontefract, on 11 August, and wrote to tell her so; also, to implore her to authorize a correspondence. She did not reply; not till he had written six times. Then she wrote, 'exhorting him to heroic submission to his lot'. Mr. Nicholls, with more audacity and guile than might have been expected of him, wrote back to say that her letter had so comforted him that he must have a little more. The little more was accorded and before autumn was reached Charlotte found herself in regular correspondence with him.

The situation was, for her, unprecedented; she was corresponding with a man her declared lover, with whom she was not in love and, what was more, whose name was anathema to her father. Never before in her life had she acted deceitfully, and it was intolerable to her. As she later revealed to Ellen: 'The correspondence pressed on my mind. At last, sheer pain made me gather courage to break it. I told all. It was very hard and rough work at the time, but the issue after a few days was that I obtained leave to continue the communication.'[2]

What she gained was the right, not merely to correspond, but to become better acquainted. The man who wrote the letters and the morose curate she had known seemed such different beings that

[1] CB to EN, 27 May 1853: *W & S* iv. 68.
[2] CB to EN, 11 Apr. 1854: *W & S* iv. 112.

Charlotte was left in doubt as to the man's true identity. She was sufficiently moved by the one and intrigued by the other to wish to confront his image anew. Pending his next visit to the district in January (1854) Charlotte could settle to nothing. Her unusual perturbation of mind was reflected in her frequent absences from home that summer and autumn; she seemed to jump at any excuse for movement, and went with Joe Taylor, his wife, and young baby to Kirkcudbright and from there to Ilkley in the space of a week in August. She stayed with Ellen Nussey, and, in the first week of October she stayed with Miss Wooler on the East coast, at Hornsea; but her greatest pleasure was derived from the visit of Mrs. Gaskell herself to Haworth, which she made on Monday, 19 September, staying with Charlotte four full days.[1]

The timing of Mrs. Gaskell's visit—the only visit she made to Haworth in Charlotte's lifetime—at the height of Charlotte's troubles over Mr. Nicholls, must not be overlooked in assessing Mrs. Gaskell's impressions of her friend's home-life and relations with her father. Inevitably she derived a biased view of the domestic background which she saw, not under normal conditions, but at a time of crisis. In judging the accuracy of Mrs. Gaskell's portrait of Mr. Brontë (from which all subsequent portraits have been drawn) it should therefore not be forgotten that Mrs. Gaskell visited Haworth parsonage at an unpropitious moment in the relations of father and daughter. At no time in Charlotte's life, perhaps, did her father show himself more tyrannous than over the question of Mr. Nicholls's proposal; nor was Charlotte ever more at war with herself than during the period of her clandestine correspondence with Mr. Nicholls. The glances Mrs. Gaskell intercepted between father and daughter—at which she shuddered—and interpreted as permanent symbols of his despotic sway, were expressive, rather, of a particular time and issue. Mrs. Gaskell had not been a witness of the many years of close communion of ideas and scholarly tastes that had marked the family life of the parsonage. She saw the whole of Charlotte's life in retrospect coloured by a uniform drab tone, and forgot the times of promise, of youthful ambition and cheerfulness in which the father had been the instigator and the children the brilliant executants. Mrs. Gaskell saw only

---

[1] CB's letter appointing the date and time of Mrs. G's visit reads: 'Friday 16th September. I was from home—staying two or three days at Ilkley when your note came. On Monday the 19th at 2.26 a cab shall be in waiting at Keighley Station ready to bring you on. Yrs with pleasure and regard. C. Brontë.' (Manchester Univ. Lib.).

Charlotte's sorrows—her losses, her lonelinesses, her fragility—and believed her to be wholly pitiable. As her sympathy was deep and genuine, her wish to help Charlotte was energetically expressed. It is evident that she encouraged her to greater independence, and even supplied her with addresses of decent lodgings in London should she wish to get away and not be beholden to her publishers.[1]

When she had gone, Charlotte felt the loss of her invigorating presence: 'After you left,' she wrote Mrs. Gaskell on 25 September, 'the house felt very much as if the shutters had been suddenly closed and the blinds let down. One was sensible during the remainder of the day of a depressing silence, shadow, loss, want. However, if the going away was sad, the stay was very pleasant and did permanent good. Papa, I am sure, derived real benefit from your visit; he has been better ever since.'[2]

Mrs. Gaskell took with her a gift for Julia from Charlotte—a book called *New Friends or A Fortnight at the Rectory* by Mrs. Alfred Barnard, in which Charlotte wrote: 'To Julia with my love C.B. September 1853'—which Julia kept all her life and which only left Plymouth Grove in 1914 at the Gaskells' sale.

Preserved letters from Charlotte to Mrs. William Shaen (*née* Emily Winkworth), dated 21 and 24 November of that year, show that the idea of visiting London had been more than an indefinite project. She had booked rooms recommended by Mrs. Gaskell at a Mrs. Dove's, 36 Bloomsbury Square, for the 24th and wrote Mrs. Shaen (who lived in Russell Square) in anticipatory pleasure at meeting her. 'I too feel as if I knew you through Mrs. Gaskell,' she wrote her unknown correspondent, 'and look forward with sincere pleasure at the prospect of soon seeing you. Were my business in town more engrossing than it is at all likely to be I should still have contrived to make room for that gratification.'[3] The trip did not materialize. 'At the last moment when my portmanteau was packed and all ready, circumstances have taken a turn which will prevent my intended journey to London', Charlotte hastily scribbled to Mrs. Shaen on the morning of 24 November. 'I have written to Mrs. Dove and told her of course that I shall transmit at once any charge she may choose to make for the apartments taken in my name. I feel very sorry for the useless trouble you have had. Forgive it and believe me—Sincerely yours—.'[4]

[1] Mrs. Gaskell's visit to Haworth, see *Life*, 422–7.
[2] CB to Mrs. G, 25 Sept. 1853: *W & S* iv. 96.
[3] CB to Mrs. Shaen, 24 Nov. 1853: *W & S* iv. 99–100.   [4] Idem.

The incident, occurring at the height of Charlotte's disagreement with her father over Mr. Nicholls, is open to several interpretations, and her sudden decision to leave home, if only for a week, and as sudden decision to abandon her plan, has every appearance of relating to her domestic affairs. That the journey to London was nothing to do with her publishers, and furthermore that it was planned without their knowledge, would appear from a letter she wrote to Mr. Williams on 6 December. It is a sad little document, ending as it did one of the pleasantest relationships of her life. 'My dear Sir,' she wrote in what proved to be her last letter to Mr. Williams, 'I forwarded last week a box of books to Cornhill, which I trust arrived safely. To-day I received the Edinburgh Guardian, for which I thank you. Do not trouble yourself to select or send any more books. These courtesies must cease some day, and I would rather give them up than wear them out.—Believe me, yours sincerely—.'[1]

In January (1854) Mr. Nicholls stayed with his friends the Grants at Oxenhope, in the old school-house attached to the Charles I Grammar School that still stands. By then, Charlotte had made her confession to her father regarding her correspondence with Mr. Nicholls, and received his grudging permission to improve acquaintance. By that time Mr. Brontë may well have been made aware—witness the projected London journey—that if he prevented normal social intercourse between his daughter and her suitor, she might take a road to meet him that would be more unpleasant to him than the flagged field path leading from Haworth to Oxenhope.

There, in the dark January days, in the biting frosts of winter, Charlotte and Nicholls met, along a stretch of path still called 'Charlotte's Lane', which covered the mile's distance between Haworth and Oxenhope.

Charlotte found these encounters a bewildering experience. Mr. Nicholls vehemently pleaded his loyalty and devotion, certain that he could give her all she lacked in life. His very audacity aided him; he saw none of the difficulties pressing upon her. To speak to a man of his uncomplicated nature, even in the language of parables, about those regions of the soul that were precious to her was useless. He knew nothing about the 'burning clime', about the long thraldom of Zamorna—nothing of Monsieur Heger! Offering his all, he had no conception what such a heart as hers waited to receive from the declaration of love. If she were more than usually silent he, penetrating

[1] CB to WSW, 6 Dec. 1853: *W & S* iv. 100.

none of her secrets, might understandably believe he had made an impression. And this was precisely the reason why, in the long run, an impression was made.

In retrospect, the situation became simplified in Charlotte's memory and she summarized it thus for Ellen: 'Mr. Nicholls came in January; he was 10 days in the neighbourhood. I saw much of him. I had stipulated with papa for opportunity to become better acquainted. I had it, and all I learnt inclined me to esteem and affection. Still, papa was very, very hostile, bitterly unjust. I told Mr. Nicholls the great obstacle that lay in his way. He has persevered.'[1]

The 'great obstacle' by then, it is plain, was only Mr. Brontë, not Charlotte's lack of response. Assured of such a total reversal of the odds against him, Mr. Nicholls could have moved mountains.

Whether he could have moved Mr. Brontë unaided, however, will never be known. Mr. Nicholls's best ally was his successor as curate to Mr. Brontë, the Revd. George de Renzi, who so succeeded in exacerbating Mr. Brontë's nerves that, after some months, he would have welcomed almost any substitute. Charlotte, listening to her father's lamentations, would have been less than a woman had she not perceived how such a situation might be turned to the profit of her persistent lover. She reminded her father of the good service Mr. Nicholls had rendered him during his eight years' tenure of office, knowing in advance that the comparison with Mr. de Renzi was all in Mr. Nicholls's favour.

The innocent stratagem worked, thanks to the unwitting co-operation of Mr. de Renzi and Mr. Brontë's growing dislike of strangers. Between January, when he still 'showed himself bitterly unjust to Mr. Nicholls', and the beginning of April, when Nicholls spent another week with his friends at Oxenhope, and was again received at the Parsonage, the miracle was accomplished: Mr. Brontë's consent to the marriage was gained; and what was more, his respect for Mr. Nicholls.

As Charlotte wrote to Ellen on 11 April, Mr. Nicholls proved 'himself in all things disinterested and forbearing.'[1] Whereas he might secure for himself a living of £200 and serve no master, he preferred a pittance of £90 and continued servitude, because of his love for Charlotte. The increasing infirmities of Mr. Brontë laid on his curate most of the work of the parish in return for less than half his salary;

[1] CB to EN, 11 Apr. 1854: *W & S* iv. 112.

only a man infatuated with love would consent to such a bargain, and this both Mr. Brontë and Charlotte recognized.

For Charlotte to remain unmoved by such a gesture was not in her nature, though gratitude was but a poor response and left her still bewildered and unsatisfied, not with what her lover offered, but with what she found herself able to give him in exchange. She wrote to Ellen on 11 April:

> Certainly I must respect him, nor can I withhold from him more than mere cool respect. In fact, dear Ellen, I am engaged. Mr. Nicholls, in the course of a few months will return to the curacy of Haworth. I stipulated that I would not leave papa—What seemed at one time impossible is now arranged, and papa begins really to take pleasure in the prospect.
> For myself, dear Ellen, while thankful to One who seems to have guided me through much difficulty, much and deep distress and perplexity of mind, I am still very calm, very inexpectant. What I taste of happiness is of the soberest order. I trust to love my husband. I am grateful for his tender love to me. I believe him to be an affectionate, a conscientious, a high-principled man; and if, with all this, I should yield to regrets, that fine talents, congenial tastes and thoughts are not added, it seems to me I should be most presumptuous and thankless. Providence offers me this destiny. Doubtless then it is the best for me.[1]

Not so had she ever envisaged love, or aspired to marriage. The difference between the dream and the sober reality was so disproportionate in her case as to leave her not only without a spark of joy, but literally incapable of judgement. Women have doubted in fiction and in fact of the good sense of their choice in marriage, because for the most part their choice was the effect of passion. Such was not Charlotte's dilemma. She had experienced her own kind of passion to the full, and did not need a guide to trace her steps through its labyrinth. Where she was lost was in a contrary predicament: when passion was absent, what criterion was to take its place? The peculiar characteristic of Charlotte's engagement was not only the uncertainty of her sentiments towards her fiancé, but her consequent need to canvass all her friends' opinions upon a matter that concerned her only. In the absence of the correspondence that passed between her and Mr. Nicholls, her exchanges on the subject with her friends must strike the modern reader not only as sorrowful but less than fair to the man she had agreed to marry.

[1] CB to EN, 11 Apr. 1854: *W & S* iv. 112.

Ellen Nussey, the first to be consulted, long before an engagement could be contemplated, did not help by rather surprisingly espousing Mr. Brontë's viewpoint. She considered Arthur Nicholls not good enough for her friend and was ill judged enough to communicate her sentiments to Mary Taylor at the other side of the world. Absence had not made Mary any less forthright and penetrating. She answered Ellen on 24 February 1854:

> You talk wonderful nonsense about Charlotte Brontë in your letter. What do you mean about 'Bearing her position so long', and 'enduring to the end'? and still better, 'bearing our lot, whatever it is'. If it's Charlotte's lot to be married, shouldn't she bear that too? or does your strange morality mean that she should refuse to ameliorate her lot when it is in her power. How would she be inconsistent with herself in marrying? Because she considers her own pleasure? If this is new for her to do, it is high time she began to make it more common. It is an outrageous exaction to expect her to give up her choice in a matter so important, and I think her to blame in having been hitherto so yielding that her friends can think of making such an impudent demand.[1]

The reservation of Ellen, following on Mr. Brontë's long denigration of Arthur Nicholls, did not leave Charlotte wholly unaffected. She wrote openly to Ellen of her regrets that 'fine talents, congenial tastes and thoughts' were not added to her fiancé's other solid qualities. Towards Mrs. Gaskell and her friends Charlotte opened her heart on yet another aspect of her husband's limitations: his narrow religious views which she not only felt at variance with but feared would influence her against her Unitarian friends. Towards Mrs. Gaskell, the only married friend in whom she could confide, and for whom also, as for herself, the life of the intellect mattered exceedingly, she expressed herself most freely. Announcing her engagement on 18 April, she wrote:

> You remember—or perhaps you do not remember—what I told you when you were at Haworth. Towards the end of autumn the matter was again brought prominently forward. There was much reluctance, and many difficulties to be overcome. *I cannot deny that I had a battle to fight with myself; I am not sure that I have even yet conquered certain inward combatants.* Be this as it may, in January last papa gave his sanction for a renewal of acquaintance. Things have progressed I don't know how. It is no use going into detail.

[1] MT to EN, 24 Feb. 1854: *W & S* iv. 104–5.

After various visits and as the result of perseverance in one quarter and a gradual change of feeling in others, I find myself what people call 'engaged'.

Describing her father's change of heart and how he now admitted to having been unjust and declared himself happy in the matter, Charlotte had this searing comment to make on her engagement: 'I could almost cry sometimes that in this important action in my life I cannot better satisfy papa's perhaps natural pride. My destiny will not be brilliant, certainly.'[1]

To lay upon the material aspects and limitations of the case the onus of her soul's dejection at the bargain was to confess how far she had departed from the convictions of a lifetime, and explains also the sense of lost direction which appears in all her comments on the event. She had to confess that 'without knowing how', she found herself what people call 'engaged'.

Mrs. Gaskell, turning the situation in all directions and viewing it from every angle for Charlotte's benefit, put her finger, with unfailing true feeling, on Mr. Nicholls's greatest asset as a prospective husband: writing to John Forster to give him news of the engagement on 23 April, she said, after detailing all the circumstances:

He sounds vehemently in love with her. And I like his having known her dead sisters and dead brother and all she has gone through of home trials, and being no person who has just fancied himself in love with her because he was dazzled by her genius. Mr. N. never knew till long after Shirley was published that she wrote books . . . with all his bigotry and sternness it must be charming to be loved with all the strength of his heart as she sounds to be.[2]

Charlotte sent the news of her engagement also to her publishers. On 11 February 1854 George Smith had married Miss Elizabeth Blakeway, daughter of a London wine-merchant and grand-daughter of Edward Blakeway of Broseley Hall, Shropshire, and had taken his bride to live at 112 Gloucester Terrace. How little communication there had been between him and Charlotte appears in her letter of 25 April in which, thanking him for his congratulations, she said:

It gave me sincere pleasure to be assured of your happiness though of that I never doubted. I have faith also in its permanent character—provided Mrs. George Smith is—what it pleases me to fancy her to be—You never told me any particulars about her, though I should have liked them much, but did not like to ask questions . . . What *I* have to say is soon told.

---

[1] CB to Mrs. G, 18 Apr. 1854: *W & S* iv. 116.
[2] Mrs. G to John Forster, 23 Apr. 1854: Gaskell Letters, 280: op. cit.

The step in contemplation is no hasty one; on the gentleman's side, at least, it has been meditated for years, and I hope that, in at last acceding to it, I am acting right. . . .There has been heavy anxiety—but I begin to hope all will end for the best. My expectations however are very subdued—very different, I dare say, to what *yours* were before you married.[1]

Of a new work by Currer Bell there was no mention, and though at such a time her publishers might expect none, there was an unmistakable sound of valediction in the concluding words of her letter: 'I sometimes wonder how Mr. Williams is, and hope he is well. In the course of the year that is gone, Cornhill and London have receded a long way from me; the links of communication have waxed very frail and few. It must be so in this world. All things considered, I don't wish it otherwise.'

The names of George Smith and his wife, of Mrs. Smith senior and her daughters and Mr. Williams, figure on Charlotte's invitation list for her wedding. None of them, of course, attended.

On 1 May Charlotte went to stay with Mrs. Gaskell, and during her four-day visit received the most generous and understanding sympathy. The degree to which she was troubled in her mind is revealed in a letter from Catherine Winkworth to her sister-in-law Emma Shaen, of 8 May, in which she gave an almost verbatim report of her conversations with Charlotte.

Alderley Edge, Manchester.

I meant to have written to you last week, but finding that I was to see Miss Brontë this week I determined to wait till I could write about her, and her *marriage*. I suppose you will have heard that she is to be married in a few weeks to a clergyman, a Mr. Nicholls, who was for 8 years curate to her father, was then sent off in a hurry for his audacity in falling in love with the rector's [*sic*] daughter, but is now coming back to be curate and son-in-law. Alas! Alas! I am very glad for Miss Brontë's sake, but sorry for ours, for we can never reckon on seeing her much again when she is 'a married woman'. Emily and I both went over on Tuesday to see her; Emily some hours first, so as to have some talk to herself. When I came in, Lily took me in to Miss Brontë's bedroom and left me for a little bit, intending that I should speak of her marriage. I, not knowing whether I was supposed to know of it held my tongue on that subject, but we talked friendlily, chiefly she asking me questions about myself, till I thought she looked tired, so I took myself off; but at parting Miss Brontë said to me: 'I hope I shall see you again'. So I went in on Wednesday. Lily drew me in directly to the room, whispering: 'Say something about her marriage'. . . . When she was summoned away I began: 'I was very glad to hear something Mrs. Gaskell told me about you.' 'What was it?' 'That you are not going to be alone any more.' She leant her head on her hand and said very quickly: 'Yes, I am going to be married in June.' 'It will be a great happiness to you to have some one to care for, and make happy.' 'Yes; and it is a great thing to be the first object with anyone.' 'And you must be very sure of that with Mr. Nicholls; he has known you and wished for this so long, I hear.' She stopped, and then went on: 'But, Katie, it has cost me a good deal to come to this.' 'You will have to care for his things, instead of his caring for yours, is that it?' 'Yes, I can see that before-hand.' 'But you have been together so long already that you know what his things are, very well. He is very devoted to his duties, is he not? and you can and would like to help him in those?' 'I have always been used to those, and it is one great pleasure to me that he is so much beloved by all the people in the parish; there is quite a rejoicing over his return. But those are not everything, and I cannot conceal from myself that he is not intellectual; there are many places into which he could not follow me intellectually.' 'Well; of course every one has their own tastes. For myself, if a man had a firm, constant, affectionate, reliable nature with tolerable practical sense, I should be much better satisfied with him than if he had an intellect far beyond mine, and brilliant gifts without that trustworthiness. I care most for a calm equable atmosphere at home.' 'I do believe Mr. Nicholls is as reliable as you say, or I wouldn't marry him.' 'And you have had time to prove it; you are not acting in a hurry.' 'That is true; and, indeed, I am quite satisfied with my decision; still'—here Lily came in, and Miss Brontë repeated what I had been saying ending with: 'still such a character would be far less amusing and interesting than a more impulsive and fickle one; it might be dull.' 'Yes, indeed,' said Lily. 'For a day's companion, yes,' I said, 'but not for a life's; one's home ought to be the one fixed point, the one untroubled region in one's lot; at home one wants peace and settled love and trust, not storm and change and excitement; besides such a character would have the advantage that one might do the fickleness required one's self, which would be a relief some-times.' 'Oh, Katie, if *I* had ever said such a wicked thing,' cried Lily; and then Miss Brontë: 'Oh, Katie, I never thought to hear such a speech from *you!*' 'You don't agree with it?' 'Oh, there is truth in it; so much that I don't think I could ever have been so candid.' Miss Brontë said: 'And there is danger, too, one might be led on to go too far.' 'I think not,' I said; 'the steadiness and generosity on the other side would always keep one in check.' But they made a great deal of fun and laughing about this, and then Lily was called away again, and Miss Brontë went on: 'He is a Puseyite and very stiff; I fear it will stand in the way of my intercourse with some of my friends. But I shall always be the same in my heart towards them. I shall never let him make me a bigot. I don't think differences of opinion ought to interfere with friendship, do you?' 'No.' And we talked about this a little, and then I said: 'Perhaps, too, you may do something to introduce him to goodness in sects where he thought it could not be.' 'That is what I hope; he has a most sincere love of goodness wherever he sees it. I think if he could come to know Mr. Gaskell it would change his feeling.' Then, quite suddenly, she said: 'Tell me about your sister. Is she happy in her married life?' 'Yes, very happy indeed.' 'Sincerely?' 'Yes, she not only says so, but it shines out in everything that she is happier than ever before in her life.' 'And what is your brother-in-law like?' So I had to describe Will, thinking privately that it did not sound as though Mr. Nicholls would make half such a good husband, but did not say so, and to tell her a good deal about their engagement. What she cared most about hearing about Will was, whether he was selfish about small things, whether he took his share of small economies, or whether he appreciated Emily's endeavours and small self-denials, etc. Concerning which he had been praising Emily to me the last time he was here, so I edified her with reporting that, and gave him generally 'an excellent character', as people say of servants. About Emily she wanted to know what variations of mood, what doubts and fears, she had felt about her marriage beforehand. Had she felt any, or was she always light-hearted, during the time? So I said that no one could be exactly always light-hearted I thought, who was not very young and thoughtless, whereat it came out that she thought Emily not 25 now. And then we talked over all the natural doubts that any thoughtful woman would feel at such a time, and my own mother's early married life, and when Lily returned she said she felt greatly comforted; and thereupon Lily set off praising *her* husband for being a good sick nurse and so good to the children, and how very winning that was to the mother, with a great deal of kindly interest.

What I hear from Lily of Mr. Nicholls is all good. Miss B. knew him well all those 8 years. He loved her, but she refused him; he went on, but her father discovered it, went into a rage, and sent him away. He wrote to her miserably; wrote six times and then she answered him—a letter exhorting him to heroic submission to his lot, etc. He sent word it had comforted him so much that he must have a little more, and so she came to write to him several times. Then her father wanted a curate, and never liked anyone so well as Mr. Nicholls, but did not at first like to have him; sent for him, however, after a time. This was about Christmas. Miss Brontë had not then made up her mind; but when she saw him again, she decided that she could make him happy, and that his love was too good to be thrown away by one so lonely as she is; and so they are to be married. He thinks her intellectually superior to himself, and admires her gifts, and likes her the better, which sounds as though he were generous. And has very good family connections, and he gets on with her father, and all the parishioners adore him; but they will be very poor, for the living is only £250 a year. If only he is not altogether far too narrow for her, one can fancy her much more really happy with such a man than with one who might have made her more in love, and I am sure she will be really good to him. But I *guess* the true love was Paul Emanuel after all, and is dead; but I don't know, and don't think that Lily knows.[1]

Leaving Manchester on 4 May Charlotte paid a couple of visits— first to Hunsworth to Joe Taylor and his wife, and on from there to Brookroyd where the Nusseys showed her particular kindness 'of word and deed'. She was home again by 13 May and was thankful to find her father quite well, having given Mr. de Renzi his quietus.

Now that the principle of such a marriage was accepted by the main parties, Mr. Nicholls and Mr. Brontë pressed for an early date for the ceremony. Mr. Nicholls was to leave his curacy at Kirk Smeaton on 11 June, after which he would be a free man, and Mr. Brontë was eager to be rid of Mr. de Renzi. Allowing for a month's honeymoon, on which Mr. Nicholls insisted, during which Mr. de Renzi must remain, the end of June was as late as the impatient men of the family would consider. Charlotte thus found herself hurried in the end with the ordering of her clothes (her dresses were made at Halifax) and the sending out of the invitations. Mr. Nicholls, she complained laugh- ingly, had 'no end to his string of parson-friends' to whom cards must be sent. Charlotte's own list of invitations was modest enough, com- prising only 18 names. Her wish was that only her friends, Ellen and Margaret Wooler, should actually be present at the wedding. Mr. Nicholls's loyal friend, Sutcliffe Sowden, was to officiate, and with him Nicholls would stay until the night before, when they would go to the Grants at Oxenhope, and from there walk over in the morning for the early wedding. The Grants would only join the party for the breakfast, after which the bride and groom would leave for their honeymoon in Ireland.

Explaining these arrangements to Miss Wooler on 16 June, Char- lotte wrote to her old friend:

Papa seems much to wish your presence. Mr. Nicholls enters with true kindness into my wish to have all done quietly. . . . Yourself, Ellen Nussey and Mr. Sowden will be the only persons present at the ceremony. Mr. & Mrs. Grant are asked to the breakfast afterwards. . . . I hope Mr. Carter and Mr. Nicholls may meet some day—I believe mutual acquaintance would, in time, bring mutual respect—but one of them at least requires *knowing* to be

[1] C. Winkworth to Emma Shaen, 8 May 1854: *W & S* iv. 121–5. See also *Memorials of Two Sisters*, by M. J. Shaen, London, 1908.

appreciated—and I must say that I have not yet found him to lose with closer knowledge—I make no grand discoveries—but I occasionally come on a quiet little nook of character which excites esteem. He is always reliable, truthful, faithful, affectionate; a little unbending perhaps—but still persuadable—and open to kind influence. A man never indeed to be driven—but who may be led.[1]

A different note crept into Charlotte's last-minute report on final arrangements to Ellen—a first trace of humour and tolerant amusement at her lover's imaginary woes, rheumatic and emotional, as the day approached and he wrought himself to a pitch of excitement and pain. Having been alarmed by Mr. Nicholls's reports of severe rheumatic pains during his last days at Kirk Smeaton, Charlotte wrote on seeing him to Ellen:

At first I was thoroughly frightened. However, inquiring gradually relieved me. In short, I soon discovered that my business was, instead of sympathy, to rate soundly. The patient had wholesome treatment while he was at Haworth, and went away singularly better; perfectly unreasonable, however, on some points, as his fallible sex are not ashamed to be. Man is indeed an amazing piece of mechanism when you see, so to speak, the full weakness of what he calls his strength. There is not a female child above the age of eight but might rebuke him for spoilt petulance of his wilful nonsense.[2]

Mr. Nicholls's 'wilful nonsense' and Charlotte's amused recognition of it may suggest to her devotees a first faint intimation of happiness for the ill-assorted pair. A sense of humour aiding, Charlotte might in time come to a different and far happier understanding of her new role.

Barely a fortnight before the wedding she was complaining to Ellen of being behindhand with her letter-writing and her needlework, and 'sewing against time', all because of her 'worthy acquaintance at Kirk Smeaton' who had been to stay at Haworth again, 'and hindered her a full week' in her preparations.

In the absence of one enthusiastic word to describe her prospects, as she notified friend after friend of her engagement, those who cherish Charlotte's memory may reflect on the fact that the name of this stranger she was marrying with such 'moderate expectations of happiness' was Arthur—like Wellington and Zamorna before him.

[1] CB to Miss Wooler, 16 June 1854: *W & S* iv. 131–2.
[2] CB to EN, 27 May 1854: *W & S* iv. 127.

CHAPTER XXVII

EQUINOX

CHARLOTTE was married on Thursday, 29 June 1854.

Except in one important particular the marriage passed off as planned. The faithful friends, Ellen Nussey and Margaret Wooler, arrived at the parsonage the day before, and the bridegroom reached Oxenhope. Charlotte, though struggling to shake off a cold, was composed and well, and because of the early hour fixed for the service (8 o'clock), the wedding-breakfast, and the departure the next day, was busy till evening with the final arrangements. It was only then, when the household met for evening prayers in Mr. Brontë's parlour, that he declared himself unable to give his daughter away in church next day. The pretext of his feeling too unwell was recognized by all for what it was. Only Charlotte and the servants knew that behind the refusal lay more than the mere peevishness of an old man whose will has been overidden. There was genuine panic in the face of separation from his last child, an Irishman's premonition of ill fortune. He had of late developed a superstitious dislike of the marriage service and refused to perform the marriages in his own church, relegating the duty to his curate.

Argument or persuasion, as Charlotte well knew, would avail nothing while the irrational fit was on him. There was nothing to be done but seek a substitute, and after consulting the Prayer Book they found that Charlotte could as well be given away by a friend as by a parent or guardian, and Miss Wooler immediately stepped into the breach.

Absolved from the obligation of playing a major role in his daughter's marriage, Mr. Brontë recovered his spirits and by the time the bride and groom with their modest retinue of friends returned from church the next morning, he was in genial mood and, indeed, as Martha Brown later recalled, 'the life and soul of the party' at the wedding-breakfast.

When the white muslin dress with its motif of ivy-leaves bordering the veil was changed for the misty mauve of her shot-silk travelling dress, Charlotte came downstairs and passed out of her old home to the waiting cab in the lane as she had done so many times before—since the far-off day of her first desolate departure for Roe Head. If she trembled a little, as she had trembled then, there was an arm to lean on now. The wholly unaccustomed sensation gave her double support, for she was determined none of the knot of villagers waiting in the lane should detect the doubts assailing her as she stepped out into her new life.

They drove to Keighley station and took the train to Conway, where they spent the night. From there Charlotte wrote Ellen a hurried note of thanks:

Thursday Evening

Dear Ellen,—I scribble one hasty line just to say that after a pleasant enough journey, we have got safely to Conway; the evening is wet and wild, though the day was fair, chiefly, with some gleams of sunshine. However, we are sheltered in a comfortable inn. My cold is not worse. If you get this scrawl tomorrow and write by return, direct to me at the Post Office, Bangor, and I may get it on Monday. Say how you and Miss Wooler got home. Give my kindest and most grateful love to Miss Wooler whenever you write. On Monday, I think, we cross the Channel. No more at present—Yours faithfully and lovingly,

C.B.N.[1]

The next day, Friday, they went along the coast to Bangor, where they stayed till Monday, 3 July. In a letter to Miss Catherine Wooler written 18 July from Ireland, Charlotte described her brief impressions of Wales. 'The weather was not very favourable . . . yet we contrived to see some splendid scenery—one drive from Llanberis to Beddgelert surpassed anything I remember of the English Lakes.'[2]

On Tuesday, 4 July they went on to Holyhead for the crossing to Dublin. Happily, the weather 'was calm and the passage good', as Charlotte wrote Margaret Wooler on the 10th. With their landing in Dublin and the first meeting with Mr. Nicholls's relatives began for Charlotte the real discovery, not only of her husband's country but of her husband himself, his background and his people. Once she had written of his 'disingenuousness in so long concealing his aim, in forging that Irish fiction, etc', and Mr. Brontë had flatly denounced such a union for her as 'a degradation'. All that was over now, and she found herself face to face with the reality.

[1] CBN to EN, 29 June 1854: *SBC* 467.
[2] CB to Miss Catherine Wooler, 18 July 1854: *W & S* iv. 136: Allbutt Bequest, Fitz-william Museum.

Arthur Bell Nicholls[1] (Nichols or Nickles, as his father variously spelt the name) was a Northern Irishman of Scots descent. Born at Tully, his father's farm in Killead, Co. Antrim, on 6 January 1818, he was the sixth child and fourth son of his parents William Nichols and Margaret Bell (and was thus incidentally one year and nine months younger than Charlotte). The family were Presbyterians, having settled in Ireland in the 1620 'Plantation', and Arthur's forebears were buried in the Presbyterian graveyard of Killead—a curious fact when his later Puseyite propensities are remembered. His mother, Margaret Bell, came from another Scots family settled in near-by Glenavy parish since 1690, but they were members of the Established Church. Margaret's brother, indeed, the Rev. Alan Bell, was curate of Glenavy when Arthur was born. In that year, 1818, he had met and fallen in love with the vivacious and captivating Harriet Adamson while on holiday at Bray in Co. Wicklow, and brought her home to Glenavy, a bride of 17, the actual wedding taking place at Glenavy Church. The marriage, with its happy issue and numerous progeny, was of lasting importance to the young Arthur Nichols, for by the time he was seven his Uncle and Aunt Bell virtually adopted him and his immediate elder brother Alan, and took them to live with them at Banagher in far off King's County, as it was called in those days. Dr. Bell was appointed headmaster to the Royal School there (one of three Charles I foundations in Ireland) in 1824, and took his young nephews with him. It has been said that they were orphans by that time. This is not strictly correct: their mother died 12th April 1830, but their father lived till 1849, dying at the age of 80. Dr. Bell's gesture in securing a first-class education for his nephews is self-explanatory in a family where 10 children had to be provided for.[2]

At Banagher Dr. Alan Bell, LL.D., became quite a figure. He bought land which he let and farmed and came to be considered a man of wealth, his young wife, 12 years his junior, even being teased with having married 'an old man for his money'. The marriage was a very happy one from the start.

---

[1] See below, Additional Notes, p. 598, for further details relating to Nicholls's family.

[2] Arthur Bell Nicholls had four brothers and five sisters, viz: Anna Maria b. 1809; Eliza b. 1812 (married Chaplain Erskine); William b. 1813; George b. 1814 d. at Tully 1870 (both William and George remained farmers at Tully); Alan b. 1816 (Shipping Agent); Jane b. ? married Hughes, emigrated to Australia, lived to be old; Margaret b. 1821; Susan b. 1822 d. aged 4; Richard b. 1827 married Ellen McKee d. 1864. For these data concerning the Nicholls family, I am much indebted to Miss R. O'Neill, Solicitor, of Belfast.

Certainly no circumstance could have been more fortunate for young Arthur and Alan than such an adoption, for as the years passed the Bell family, numerous, large-hearted and cultured, supplied every need of their hearts and minds. Their home, Cuba House, in which the Royal School was housed after 1807, was a late seventeenth-century mansion of Palladian design standing in its own extensive grounds, and afforded them not only a gracious background but a first-rate classical education. There, as Charlotte found, the headmaster's family led the life of country gentlefolk, cultured, civilized, and kindly.

At 18 Arthur matriculated from the Royal School to Trinity College, Dublin, where he took his B.A. degree in 1844. In May 1845 he entered his first curacy at Haworth, his ordination at Ripon following in September 1846; the rest was known to Charlotte. It was her husband's antecedents that had been obscure to her, and only now on her arrival at Banagher were they fully revealed. It was a pleasant surprise.

Dr. Bell had died in 1839; a sufferer from asthma, he had been ordered to the South of France, but died when just about to embark at Kingstown. His widow, however, their five sons and two remaining daughters lived on at Cuba House, the second son James succeeding his father to the headmastership of the school. Both James and his younger brother Joseph Samuel (later Canon of St. Patrick's Cathedral) became rectors of Banagher. It was Joseph, aged 23 at the time of Charlotte's honeymoon, who, together with Nicholls's brother Alan and his favourite cousin Mary Anne, welcomed the travellers at Dublin. Charlotte wrote of them to Miss Wooler:

'Three of Mr. Nicholls's relatives met us in Dublin—his brother and two cousins. The 1st (brother) is manager of the Grand Canal from Dublin to Banagher—a sagacious well-informed and courteous man—his cousin is a student at the University [Trinity College] and has just gained 3 premiums. The other cousin was a pretty lady-like girl with gentle English manners.'[1]

As will again shortly appear, Charlotte was much astonished to find what 'English manners' the wild Irish kinsfolk of her new husband

[1] Educated with Arthur at Banagher Royal School, Alan Nicholls his elder brother also proceeded to Trinity College, entering the service of the Grand Canal, and rapidly made a position for himself as a Shipping Agent. When he died in 1890, on holiday in Paris, he left a considerable estate in trust for his two daughters Ellen and Charlotte Brontë Nicholls. His remains were brought back from Paris and he was buried in Dean's Graveyard, Dublin.

could command! Arthur's cousin, the 'pretty lady-like girl', was Mary Anne Bell, born 11 February 1830, and therefore 24 at the time. She was a true Celt in appearance, dark-eyed and dark-haired, and her temperament had the Celtic mixture of humour and melancholy. A riding accident in early life had lamed her, but in no way hampered her energy and efficiency as hostess for her mother and later as an accomplished housewife. The kindness of her welcome to Charlotte was proof not only of innate fine feeling but of a deeper sentiment still; she had always loved her cousin, and wished his happiness to be complete. Little could she have guessed then, as she complimented him on his bride and took her tiny hand in hers, that so soon she would be standing in Charlotte's place, the second Mrs. Nicholls.[1]

They arrived at Dublin late on Tuesday, 4 July. The whole of Wednesday and Thursday was spent visiting the main sites of the city: Arthur's former university—Trinity College, and its Library— and 'the museum and chapel' mentioned by Charlotte in her letter to Miss Wooler, when she added: 'and should have seen much more— had not my bad cold been a restraint on us'. But calls were made on Alan Bell and his wife, who lived in Dublin, and other relatives.

On Friday, 7 July the whole party set off for Banagher; of the two routes that offered, rail and canal, they took the railway to Birr, speed and possibly Charlotte's cold dictating the choice. (The fact that the canal route was under the management of Arthur's brother Alan—already a very successful business man—and provided a re- putedly agreeable mode of transport along the Shannon, had been an incentive.) From Birr station the party drove the seven miles to Banagher.

Banagher consists of a single street straggling uphill from the Shannon Bridge to the church. The stone of its eighteenth-century houses and their close-packed continuity of front affords a strange resemblance to those of Haworth, and Nicholls may often have made the comparison. From the church it is but another quarter mile to Cuba House.

The shell of this once imposing edifice still stands, a noble ruin. Seen from the wrought-iron gates that shut it away from the high-road, it carries the weight of its centuries with undiminished charm. It is in finely wooded ground dominating the whole region, a typical

---

[1] H. K. Bell, *Cornhill Magazine*, Jan. 1927: F. E. Bell, 'Charlotte Brontë's Irish Rela- tions': *Manchester Guardian*.

late Stuart building of brick and stone, with mansard roof, pedimented portals, and balustrade terrace; living memory yet recalls its grandeur and the scent of the daffodils that studded the grass verges of its avenue of limes. Mr. Nicholls's home was, indeed, very different from Charlotte's expectations. The school-buildings proper ran behind the house, the long classrooms below and the dormitories above. It had been founded by Royal Charter in 1638 and endowed from confiscated lands of the clan MacCoghlan, had suffered during the Fitzgerald Rebellion of 1798, been closed for eight years, and only reopened for its former purposes in 1807.[1]

Charlotte was immediately taken with the character and history of the house. She wrote Miss Wooler while staying there:

I cannot help feeling singularly interested in all about the house. In this house Mr. Nicholls was brought up by his uncle Dr. Bell. It is very large and looks externally like a gentleman's country-seat—within most of the rooms are lofty and spacious and some—the drawing-room, dining-room, etc.—handsomely and commodiously furnished. . . .

The passages look desolate and bare—our bedroom, a great room on the ground-floor would have looked gloomy when we were shewn into it but for the turf-fire that was burning in the wide old chimney.[2]

The Bells assembled at Cuba House that holiday-time to do honour to their cousin's bride were James Adamson Bell, M.A. (born 1826), his late father's successor as headmaster of the school; his brother Joseph, still a student at Trinity College, who had met Charlotte at Dublin; possibly also the eldest son, Alan, born 1824, a clergyman; Arthur, born 1828, who became a surgeon-major; and William born 1839. Only two daughters of the original family of four were present: Mary Anne and her younger 20-year-old sister Harriet Lucinda. Of them Charlotte wrote to Miss Wooler: 'Both . . . are strikingly pretty in appearance . . . and their manners are very amiable and pleasing.' In conclusion she declared, 'I must say I like my new relations.'

The most important of all, the ruling spirit of that happy house was, of course, Mrs. Bell herself, widow of the late Dr. Bell, mother of this great brood of Bells, and aunt and kind adoptive mother of Arthur Nicholls. She was 53 at the time of Charlotte's visit. She was, as has already been seen, Harriet Lucinda Adamson of Killclifden, born in her father's Dublin house in York Street on 6 October 1801. Describing her, Charlotte again remarked on her 'English manners'. 'Mrs.

[1] *Brief History of Banagher*, 1951.
[2] CBN to Miss Wooler, 10 July 1854: *W & S* iv. 134–5.

Bell', she wrote, 'is like an English or Scotch Matron, quiet, kind and well-bred. It seems she was brought up in London.'[1]

Thereby hung a tale, as her granddaughter Frances Bell liked to recall in after years:

Mrs. Bell's father, Mr. Adamson, did, indeed, take her to London with a view to leaving her at school as he felt this might be an advantage to her; but after three weeks he returned, having found life quite insupportable without his small daughter, and took her home again. In those three weeks, however, she had seen London illuminated after the Battle of Waterloo. Also when Queen Charlotte called at the school to see a child in whom she was interested, she was told: 'We have a little Irish girl here'. Evidently she was considered something of a curiosity, and was brought downstairs to be presented. 'And so' my grandmother would say as she told the story, 'I saw the little old Queen', and she would add, 'I learnt high English too.'[2]

It may have been this mysterious acquisition made during her three-week sojourn in the English capital that gave Mrs. Bell that air of English or Scots distinction noted by Charlotte. Certainly her en-counter with the 'little old Queen' in the year of Wellington's great victory was the subject of some of those confidential and delightful fireside talks between the new relations that Charlotte so much relished, and that made Mrs. Bell herself exclaim: 'Sitting together over the fire like this, I quite forget I am talking to the celebrated authoress!' It must have been then that the origin of Charlotte's nom de plume was confessed to and forgiven, and much pleasant banter exchanged with her new cousins. In that house of devoted novel-readers her genius was already prized at its true worth; and later, when copies of all her works were religiously displayed in the main rooms, the memory of her passage among them was piously preserved by each rising genera-tion of the Bells. Charlotte herself was delighted with Cuba House and its inhabitants: 'I was very much pleased with all I saw,' she wrote Catherine Wooler on 18 July, 'but I was also greatly surprised to find so much English order and repose in the family habits and arrange-ments. I had heard a great deal about Irish negligence.'[3]

Mrs. Bell would have been much amused. To the end of her life, which lasted for 101 years, she retained the manners of a great lady. ('She never struck a match in her life, and never put coals on the fire', recalled her granddaughter); but she read widely, played the piano

[1] CBN to Miss Wooler, 10 July 1854: *W & S* iv. 134–5.
[2] 'Charlotte Brontë's Irish Relations', F. E. Bell, op. cit.
[3] CB to CW: 18 July 1854: *W & S* iv, No. 906: Fitzwilliam Museum.

into old age, was an expert needlewoman, a keen gardener, and she ordered her household with humour and wisdom. Aware of her many blessings she used every night on settling into bed to recite the lines of Dr. Watts:

> Not more than others I deserve,
> But God hath given me more.[1]

The ambience of Cuba House made it easier for Charlotte to understand the origin of many of her husband's characteristics, and it brought him closer to her. The love of animals, for instance, that had always shown in his treatment of the Brontës' dogs, was common to his family. The Bells were passionate animal-lovers, and it was one of Mrs. Bell's most pathetic and favourite tales how her pet dog 'Fairy' had died 'of absolute joy' when she returned from her honeymoon. Arthur Nicholls loved wild as well as domestic animals; he would never have the trees round his later home, The Hill House, Banagher, cut down or lopped because of the shelter they afforded the squirrels.

In the care of Mrs. Bell Charlotte soon threw off her cold: 'I was not well when I came here,' she wrote Miss Wooler, 'fatigue and excitement had nearly knocked me up—and my cough was become very bad—but Mrs. Bell has nursed me both with kindness and skill, and I am greatly better now.'

Social life at Cuba House as it was in those days has been described by one of the younger generation of Bells:

> Though remote . . . Banagher was by no means dull. Friends drove long distances to visit each other, on outside cars or in phaetons, or landaus. All who came were welcome. Sometimes the young people would start dancing, and Mrs. Bell, I am sure, was often at the piano; there were picnics on the river, everyone had a boat, or could hire or borrow one, and there were concerts, in all of which amusements the officers in the barracks at Banagher and Birr, joined.[2]

It is a picture of a way of life that still has its traces today. The Shannon in its broad lazy course was then, as now, the centre of Banagher social life. In that season of fine weather, for all its brevity, Charlotte shared in the warmth and vivacity of the Bell household and drew from it a new strength.

---

[1] *Cornhill Magazine*, Jan. 1927: op. cit.
[2] F. E. Bell, 'A Hundred Years of Life', privately printed, Bath.

It is evident that she was becoming more peaceful in her mind, and viewing her marriage with something like hope. 'My dear husband', she wrote in the same letter to Miss Wooler, 'appears in a new light here in his own country. More than once I have had deep pleasure in hearing his praises on all sides. Some of the old servants and followers of the family tell me I am a most fortunate person for that I have got one of the best gentlemen in the country. His aunt too speaks of him with a mixture of affection and respect most gratifying to hear.'[1]

Comparing these tributes to her husband to her own former low estimate of his worth, she realized her need for thanksgiving and prayed she might live to repay 'as I ought the affectionate devotion of a truthful, honourable, unboastful man . . .'. The last quality had never been so apparent as in the setting of Cuba House.

Charlotte and her husband stayed at Banagher a week, going on from there to the west coast, to Kilkee in Co. Clare. There, in a remote and unspoilt little watering-place Charlotte encountered, for the first time, some of the 'Irish negligence' she had expected to find everywhere. The measure of her good humour can be judged from her account of it to Catherine Wooler:

I had heard a great deal about Irish negligence etc. I own that till I came to Kilkee I saw little of it. Here at our Inn—splendidly designated 'the West End Hotel'—there is a good deal to carp at—if one were in carping humour —but we laugh instead of grumbling for out of doors there is much to compensate for any indoors shortcomings; so magnificent an ocean—so bold and grand a coast—I never yet saw.[2]

'Such a wild, ironbound coast—with such an ocean-view as I had not yet seen and such battling of waves with rocks as I had never imagined', she further described Kilkee to Catherine Winkworth, whose letter had followed her there.

At Kilkee she found herself alone for the first time (discounting the three days in Wales) with her husband. Their knowledge of each other was still very imperfect, her fears of the difference in their aesthetic values still greatly troubling her and undermining her confidence in their future understanding. To Catherine Winkworth she wrote:

My husband is not a poet or a poetical man—and one of my grand doubts before marriage was about 'congenial tastes and so on'. The first morning we went out on to the cliffs and saw the Atlantic coming in all white foam, I did

    1 CBN to Miss Wooler: op. cit.: *W & S* iv. 135.
    2 CBN to Miss CW: op. cit.: *W & S* iv. 136: Fitzwilliam Museum.

not know whether I should get leave or time to take the matter in my own way. I did not want to talk—but I *did* want to look and be silent. Having hinted a petition, licence was not refused—covered with a rug to keep off the spray I was allowed to sit where I chose—and he only interrupted me when he thought I crept too near the edge of the cliff. So far he is always good in this way—and this protection which does not interfere or pretend is I believe a thousand times better than any half sort of pseudo sympathy. I will try with God's help to be as indulgent to him whenever indulgence is needed.[1]

An unexpected, and doubtless unintentional comment on Charlotte's letter was provided by one from Nicholls himself on his return from Ireland to his friend George Sowden. Whether Charlotte altogether misjudged his sensibility towards natural beauty, or whether he was already learning from her, he wrote of their trip: 'We had a delightful tour over nearly the same ground as you and your brother travelled, only we took the Shannon in our progress to Limerick; we also diverged to Kilkee, *a glorious watering-place with the finest shore I ever saw—Completely girdled with stupendous cliffs—it was most refreshing to sit on a rock and look out on the broad Atlantic boiling and foaming at our feet.*'[2]

Kilkee was their longest stop during a fortnight's tour through western Ireland; from Kilkee they went to Tarbert, from Tarbert to Tralee, from Tralee to Killarney.

'. . . We have been to Killarney', Charlotte wrote to Catherine Winkworth after arriving at Cork on 27 July; 'I will not describe it a bit. . . .' She had a different kind of experience to describe, and did so with characteristic Brontë stoicism:

We saw and went through the Gap of Dunloe. A sudden glimpse of a very grim phantom came on us in the Gap. The guide had warned me to alight from my horse as the path was now very broken and dangerous—I did not feel afraid and declined—we passed the dangerous part—the horse trembled in every limb and slipped once but did not fall—soon after she (it was a mare) started and was unruly for a minute—however I kept my seat—my husband went to her head to lead her—suddenly without any apparent cause—she seemed to go mad—reared, plunged—I was thrown on the stones right under her—my husband did not see that I had fallen, he still held her—I saw and felt her kick, plunge, trample round me. I had my thoughts about the moment—its consequences—my husband—my father—When my plight

[1] CBN to C. Winkworth, 27 July 1854: *W & S* iv. 137.
[2] ABN to G. Sowden, Aug. 1854: *W & S* iv. 148.

was seen, the struggling creature was let loose—she sprang over me. I was lifted off the stones neither bruised by the fall nor touched by the mare's hoofs. Of course the only feeling left was gratitude for more sakes than my own.[1]

From Glengarriff, their furthest point south, they turned eastwards and returned via Cork to Dublin where they arrived on 28 July. Writing to Ellen Nussey from there on the same day Charlotte repeated the impossibility of describing all she had seen:

I shall make no effort to describe the scenery through which we have passed. Some parts have exceeded all I ever imagined. Of course, much pleasure has sprung from this, and more, perhaps, from the kind and cease-less protection which has ever surrounded me, and made travelling a different matter to me from what it has heretofore been.

Still, Nell, it is written that there shall be no unmixed happiness in this world. Papa has not been well, and I have been longing, *longing intensely*, sometimes, to be at home. Indeed, I could enjoy and rest no more, and so home we are going.[2]

To Martha she wrote on the same day announcing their return for the following Tuesday, 1 August:

at about 7 o'clock in the evening. I feel very anxious about Papa—the idea of his illness has followed me all through my journey and made me miserable sometimes when otherwise I should have been happy enough. I longed to come home a fortnight since—though perhaps it would not have done much good—and I was sure that you would do your best for him.

Have things ready for tea on Tuesday Evening—and you had better have a little cold meat or ham as well—as we shall probably get no dinner—and Mr. Nicholls will want something.[3]

After more than a month's absence, home was reached on 1 August. Much as Charlotte had strained to leave it in the past, to try her wings elsewhere, from then on Haworth parsonage completely circum-scribed her life. Mrs. Gaskell, all unwittingly perhaps, hit on the truth when she wrote of her marriage that 'thereafter the sacred doors of home were closed upon her'. Her married life, with its hourly and

---

[1] CBN to Catherine Winkworth, 27 July 1854: *W & S* iv. 138.
[2] CBN to EN, 28 July 1854: *W & S* iv. 143.
[3] CBN to Martha Brown, 28 July 1854: *W & S* iv. 143.

intimate participation in the domestic and professional existence of her husband, anchored her to her home in a way that her writer's life had never done. Paradoxically, the presence of the stranger she had married roused in her the sense of belonging to the family that was gone to a greater degree than ever before. More than ever she clung now to her father's life; it became of immense importance to her that he should live and that he should be contented; and, indeed, her father's eventual satisfaction in her marriage became one of its chief justifications in her eyes. She put some of these new feelings into words. In her first letter to Miss Wooler after her return she wrote:

My dear father was not well when we returned from Ireland. I am, however, most thankful to say that he is better now. May God preserve him to us yet for some years! The wish for his continued life, together with a certain solicitude for his happiness and health, seems, I scarcely know why, even stronger in me now than before I was married. Papa has taken no duty since we returned; and each time I see Mr. Nicholls put on gown or surplice I feel comforted to think that this marriage has secured papa good aid in his old age.[1]

She watched him now with a mixture of anxious dread and a refusal to be blinded to the facts. 'Dr. Burnet [Vicar of Bradford] was here on Sunday,' she wrote again to Miss Wooler on 19 September—'preaching a sermon for the Jews, and he gratified me much by saying that he thought Papa not at all altered since he saw him last—nearly a year ago. I am afraid this opinion is rather flattering, but still it gave one pleasure—for I had feared that he looked undeniably thinner and older.'[2]

To Ellen on 21 November she reported: 'Papa continues pretty well, I am thankful to say; his deafness is wonderfully relieved. Winter seems to suit him better than summer; besides he is settled and content, as I perceive with gratitude to God.'[3]

The unhoped-for conciliation between her father and husband remained untroubled. Seven months after her marriage Charlotte could write of it with perfect assurance to Joe Taylor's wife (Amelia Ringrose): 'It is an hourly happiness to me dear Amelia to see how well Arthur and my Father get on together now—there has never been a misunderstanding or wrong word.'[4]

1 CBN to Miss Wooler, 19 Sept. 1854: *W & S* iv. 149.
2 Idem.   3 CBN to EN, 21 Nov. 1854: *W & S* iv. 161.
4 CBN to ART, 21 Jan. 1855: *W & S* iv. 171-2.

If Mr. Brontë was 'settled and content', so much the more was Arthur Nicholls. Charlotte's letters in the first months of marriage were punctuated by amused reports on the transformation of his spirits and health. 'Have I told you how much better Mr. Nicholls is?' she wrote Ellen on 9 August. 'He looks quite strong and hale; he gained 12 lbs during the 4 weeks we were in Ireland. To see this improvement in him has been a main source of happiness to me, and to speak the truth, a subject of wonder too.' 'Yes! I am thankful to say my husband is in improved health and spirits,' she wrote Miss Wooler on 19 September. 'It makes me content and grateful to hear him from time to time avow his happiness in the brief, plain phrase of sincerity.'

By 7 December, the growth of her domestic content could be summed up in a line: 'I am happy to say . . . my dear boy flourishes.'[1] After six months of marriage she could speak with greater assurance of its success than ever before. On 26 December sending Christmas greetings to Ellen she said: 'Arthur joins me in sincere good wishes for a happy Christmas, and many of them to you and yours. He is well, thank God, and so am I, and he is "my dear boy" certainly, dearer now than he was six months ago. In three days we shall actually have been married that length of time.'[2]

The acceptance, and recognition, of her situation was the more important that her life had undergone a complete change, not only from its pattern since the loss of her sisters, but from her girlhood. She no longer lived in the world of the creative imagination, but much more on the surface; and being the woman she was, she fully realized the implications. She wrote Miss Wooler on 18 September:

My own life is more occupied than it used to be. I have not so much time for thinking: I am obliged to be more practical, for my dear Arthur is very practical as well as a very punctual and methodical man. Every morning he is in the National School by nine o'clock; he gives the children religious instruction till half-past ten. Almost every afternoon he pays visits amongst the poor parishioners. Of course he often finds a little work for his wife to do, and I hope she is not sorry to help him. I believe it is not bad for me that his bent should be so wholly towards matters of life and active usefulness, so little inclined to the literary and contemplative.[3]

The mere fact of being wanted was a blessed change after the total solitude of recent years. To her friends she tried to explain the com-

---

[1] CBN to EN, 7 Dec. 1854: *W & S* iv. 164–5.
[2] CBN to EN, 26 Dec. 1854: *W & S* iv. 167.
[3] CBN to NW, 19 Sept. 1854: *W & S* iv. 152–3: Fitzwilliam Museum.

fort she found in performing the most ordinary tasks; she told Ellen:

Since I came home I have not had an unemployed moment; my life is changed indeed, to be wanted continually, to be constantly called for and occupied seems so strange; yet it is a marvellously good thing. As yet I don't quite understand how some wives grow so selfish. As far as my experience of matrimony goes, I think it tends to draw you out of and away from yourself.[1]

She told Miss Wooler in the letter of 19 September:

I really seem to have had scarcely a spare moment since that dim quiet June Morning when you, Ellen, and myself walked down to Haworth Church. Not that I have been wearied or oppressed; but the fact is my time is not my own now; somebody else wants a good portion of it and says, 'We must do so and so.' We *do* so and so, accordingly; and it generally seems the right thing.

The change implied a loss of many things (and one trembles to think of the masterpieces unborn as a result of this domesticity); her former leisure, even to the reading of the French newspapers that had become a habit, was gone. She explained to Ellen in a letter of 7 September:

You would almost think I had given them up, it is so long since one was despatched. The fact is they have accumulated to quite a pile. . . I wished to look them over before sending them off, and as yet I have scarcely found time. That same Time is an article of which I once had a large stock always on hand; where it is all gone now it would be difficult to say, but my moments are very fully occupied.[2]

The warning to Ellen with which she pursued the theme, bantering as it was, contained the truth as she saw it. 'Take warning, Ellen,' she wrote, 'the married woman can call but a very small portion of each day her own. Not that I complain of this sort of monotony as yet and I hope I never shall incline to regard it as a misfortune, but it certainly exists.'[3]

The unfinished fragment of her novel *Emma* (begun in November 1853) indicates how Charlotte would eventually have resolved the encroachment of the practical upon the creative life that was an essential part of existence for her; even had only a 'very small portion of each day' been her own, it is unthinkable that she would not have devoted it to the pursuit of writing, without which it had been clear since girlhood she could not live.

[1] CBN to EN, 9 Aug. 1854: *W & S* iv. 145.
[2] CBN to EN, 7 Sep. 1854: *W & S* iv. 150–1.   [3] Idem.

Her husband's attitude to her work, wilfully misrepresented after her death, can, fortunately, be clarified now once and for all. In an unpublished letter to Mrs. Humphry Ward, written 28 November 1899, he made his position both as regards that, and as Charlotte's husband, unequivocally clear. In reply to a direct question on the subject he wrote:

Since the receipt of your letter I have re-read my wife's letters written after her marriage & published by Mrs. Gaskell.

I must say that I fail to see any confirmation in them of the statement that 'I encouraged her to give up novel writing.'

There was no such understanding between us—of course. We talked of her Literary Work—on one occasion she read for me the MS (afterwards published in 'The Cornhill'); when she concluded I merely said 'I fear the critics will accuse you of repetition'—but not a word of discouragement. She replied, 'O, I shall change all that—'

I never interfered in the slightest degree with her liberty of action—I shall feel obliged if you will endeavour to remove the misconception which you say exists in this respect.

There is also another misconception, which I am told by a Literary Friend, prevails—that 'her married life was unhappy'—I should have thought that her own words written from her deathbed had made such a statement incredible but I am told it exists.

I can only say that during the few months of our married life we were never separated for a day and that during that time a hasty or unkind word never passed between us—

Thanking you very sincerely for the assurance that 'It would give you great pain to hurt the feelings of one so dear to Charlotte Brontë'.

Yours faithfully
A. B. Nicholls.[1]

The warning to Ellen, seen in its context, shows that a project of matrimony between her and Sutcliffe Sowden was being hatched by Charlotte and Arthur. The two had met at Charlotte's wedding, and a sufficiently good impression was apparently created on both sides for the matter to be seriously considered. Charlotte's many references to it in the ensuing weeks show that she countenanced it. She wished for Ellen's happiness, and knew her well enough to believe it would never be secured except through marriage.

Mr. Sowden called on the Nicholls in the first week of their return from Ireland.

[1] Quoted by kind permission of Mary Moorman, Mrs. Humphry Ward's granddaughter, to whom the original belongs.

Charlotte told Ellen: 'I really like Mr. Sowden. He asked after you. Mr. Nicholls told him we expected you would be coming to stay with us in the course of 3 or 4 weeks, and that he should then invite him over again as he wished us to take sundry rather long walks, and as he should have his wife to look after, and she was trouble enough, it would be quite necessary to have a guardian for the other lady. Mr. Sowden seemed perfectly acquiescent.'[1]

Dropping the banter, and with a characteristic display of scruple where the well-being of others was concerned, Charlotte gave her romantic friend a frank insight into the reality of marriage. The letter has long been interpreted as leaving a tragic impression of Charlotte's own experience. But it must be remembered that it was written after barely six weeks of marriage and Charlotte was speaking very differently after six months. Moreover, by being quoted out of context, the letter's emphasis has been laid where it was not intended, i.e. on Charlotte, whereas the warning was for her friend. Ellen craved for love and a home of her own. Her romantic nature Charlotte knew, and she was anxious not to disillusion her. For Sowden, a friend of several years' standing, Nicholls could vouch. He had been ordained on the same day at Ripon (20 September 1846) with Sutcliffe's younger brother George, and since then had been close friend with both brothers, through good and evil times. Both Sowdens were graduates of Magdalene College, Cambridge. By a strange chance, moreover, Sutcliffe had shown himself a good friend to Branwell. Ordained in 1841, he had been appointed curate at Mytholmroyd (parish of Halifax) at the time Branwell was clerk to the railways at Sowerby Bridge and Luddendenfoot, and through their mutual friend Francis Leyland the two became acquainted. Both were keen walkers and lovers of nature, and on many a holiday they roamed the Calder valley together. Charlotte's letter continued:

Dear Nell, During the last six weeks the colour of my thoughts is a good deal changed; I know more of the realities of life than I once did. I think many false ideas are propagated, perhaps unintentionally. I think those married women who indiscriminately urge their acquaintance to marry, much to blame. For my part, I can only say with deeper sincerity and fuller significance, what I always said in theory, 'Wait God's will'. Indeed, indeed, Nell, it is a solemn and strange and perilous thing for a woman to become a wife. Man's lot is far, far different. Tell me when you think you can come.[2]

[1] CBN to EN, 9 Aug. 1854: *W. & S* iv. 145.   [2] Idem.

Ellen's visit to Haworth, postponed on various counts till the first week in October, does not appear to have advanced matters materially. Writing to her shortly afterwards Charlotte cautiously reported, 'Arthur heard from Mr. Sowden lately—an uninteresting letter, no remarks on our vote of thanks, etc. A brother of his [George] is coming over. Arthur means to invite them both here for a night. I shall take stock of them and tell you what I think.'

The Sowdens came on 6 November; the next day Charlotte wrote to Ellen: 'Mr. Sowden and his brother were here yesterday, stayed all night, and are but just gone. George Sowden is six or seven years the junior of Sutcliffe Sowden (the one you know); he looks very delicate and quiet, a good sincere man, I should think. Mr. Sowden asked after Miss Nussey.'[1]

An unexpected turn was given the plan by the sudden irruption on the scene of Sir James Kay-Shuttleworth. He arrived at Haworth on 11 November (a Saturday) with the avowed purpose of making acquaintance with Charlotte's husband, and found him so much to his liking that he stayed till after dinner on the Monday. He ended by offering Nicholls the living of the new church at Padiham, which he had had built at the gates of Gawthorpe Hall. Nicholls, being as Charlotte reported to Ellen, 'tied to Haworth so long as papa lives, was obliged to decline for that reason, had there been none other'. He was ready, however, with a counter-suggestion that Sutcliffe Sowden should be offered the post, which carried a stipend of £200 per annum, a good house, and a 'beautiful church'.

The hopes of all appeared to have been raised by Sowden's altered prospects. Charlotte wrote to Ellen on 21 November: 'You ask about Mr. Sowden's matter. He walked over here on a wild rainy day. We talked it over. He is quite disposed to entertain the proposal, but of course there must be close enquiry and ripe consideration before either he or the patron decide. . . . I cannot help somehow wishing that the matter should be arranged, if all on examination is found tolerably satisfactory.'[2]

Sowden was interviewed by Sir James, and a month passed without Charlotte being able to give Ellen any news. 'I fear Mr. Sowden has little chance of the living', she wrote at Christmas. And by 19 January she had frankly to confess: 'I fear Mr. Sowden hardly produced a favourable impression.' Sir James had wanted Arthur Nicholls,

[1] CBN to EN: 7 Nov. 1854: *W & S* iv. 158.
[2] CBN to EN: 21 Nov. 1854 SBC 471.

husband of the famous novelist Currer Bell; he was not to be diverted from his choice.

While Charlotte and her husband were active on their friends' behalf, they themselves were still progressing in the day-to-day discovery of each other's ways and natures. Charlotte was certainly acquiring a sense of humour which, with time in her favour, might have sweetened life for her, and modified some of Arthur's more narrow ways. He was a man who abhorred ostentation of any kind and the exposure of his feelings; yet Charlotte had increasing proof of how deep those feelings could run. She was 'content and grateful to hear him from time to time avow his happiness in the brief, plain phrase of sincerity'.[1]

She herself, it is evident, was growing to value more and more her companion's scrupulous observance of the truth, and also his reticence. Commenting on the letter of Mary Hewitt—*née* Gorham and a great friend of Ellen's—telling of the birth of her first child, Charlotte wrote to Ellen: 'it is as you say very genuine, truthful, affectionate, *maternal*; without a taint of sham or exaggeration. . . . The longer I live the more I suspect exaggeration. I fancy it is sometimes a sort of fashion for each to vie with the other in protestations about their wondrous felicity—and sometimes they—FIB.'[2]

Charlotte's comments on that particular letter are the more important because she already knew, though she was keeping it secret, that she herself expected a child.

The reticence was natural with her. It was, perhaps, also enhanced by her husband's attitude to her personal correspondence: it had come as a shock to him to find how unguardedly she wrote to Ellen. The discovery deeply disturbed him. Much as he would have liked to forget that his wife was the famous Currer Bell, he could not but realize the unscrupulous use some eventual acquirer of her letters might make of them. The bare idea was repellent to him, and he insisted on Ellen's giving him an assurance that she would destroy Charlotte's letters. 'All this seems mighty amusing to me', Charlotte wrote Ellen on 7 November. 'Men's letters are proverbially uninteresting and uncommunicative. I never quite knew before why they made them so. They may be right in a sense. Strange chances *do fall* out certainly. As to my own notes, I never thought of attaching importance to them or considering their fate, till Arthur seemed to reflect on both so seriously.' Her attitude to the whole question was

[1] CBN to EN, 9 Aug. 1854: op. cit.   [2] CBN to EN, 26 Dec. 1854: *W & S* iv. 166–7.

summed up in the confession: 'I can't help laughing, this seems to me so funny.'[1] With her new-acquired tolerance she had the good sense not to make an issue of the matter with her husband; and Ellen had the greater good sense still to preserve her friend's letters for posterity.

Nicholls's alarm over his wife's letters followed Ellen's visit to Haworth in the first week of October, when the old-established friend and the new husband had their first real encounter. There was nothing very compatible in their natures, and when the cementing influence of Charlotte was lost, little remained to hold them together. In the great burst of publicity that broke around Charlotte's name after her death, it was the silent man who was made to suffer in the ultimate image created of him by the talkative friend.[2]

The fact remains that, as the days passed, Charlotte grew fonder and fonder of her husband. Their responses to certain influences, like the call of outdoor life, were identical; and completely acceptable to Charlotte were such impulses as his sudden wish to see the moors under snow one late November morning. It was 28 November and she intended writing to Ellen. Relating the incident the next day she wrote:

I was sitting down to the purpose when Arthur called to me to take a walk. We set off not intending to go far, but though wild and cloudy, it was fair in the morning. When we had got about half a mile on the moors, Arthur suggested the idea of the waterfall; after the melted snow, he said, it would be fine. I had often wanted to see it in its winter power, so we walked on. It was fine indeed, a perfect torrent raving over the rocks white and bountiful. It began to rain while we were watching it, and we returned home under a streaming sky; however, I enjoyed the walk inexpressibly, and would not have missed the spectacle on any account.[3]

The walk, however, had its consequences. Though she changed her clothes immediately on reaching home, she caught cold. A week later, she was still 'not quite well'. The confession was the sadder because she had been in so much better health since her marriage; free of headache and constant bilious attacks for the first time in her life.

Now the incipient cold, and a series of quite unrelated circumstances combined to prevent her making or receiving any more visits. She

---

[1] CBN to EN, 7 Nov. 1854: *W & S* iv. 158.

[2] EN's visit to Haworth in Oct. 1854 proved to be the last. It created CB's first dilemma since her marriage, how to accommodate two contrary elements: her oldest friend and her new husband. Walking on the moors she intimated that Ellen should walk next her, saying to her husband: 'Even you should not come between us': *BST* (1942), 99.

[3] CBN to EN, 29 Nov. 1854: *W & S* iv. 162.

very much wanted Mrs. Gaskell to come and to meet Arthur, and she had written pressingly on 30 September:

Come to Haworth as soon as you can find a fitting time. My father—all in this house who have once seen you, wish to see you again. My husband does not know you yet, but when he *does* know you, he will feel as others feel; besides I want you to see him. It will perhaps do you good to get into our Land of Silence for a little while. Beg Mr. Gaskell to come also, but a single day is too brief a space of time for such a journey—try to spare two or three days. May I look for you in the second week of October—or when?[1]

To Mrs. Gaskell's lasting regret, she allowed some 'little obstacle' to prevent her going; she was writing *North and South*, a reason that Charlotte could accept better than any with fellow feeling. Yet it was not the whole reason: Mr. Nicholls's reputed dislike of Dissenters had put—and kept—Mrs. Gaskell in a panic at the idea of meeting him, even, as she confessed to Geraldine Jewsbury, at the mere idea of writing to Charlotte. 'I've a panic about the husband seeing my letters. Bridegrooms are always curious; husbands are not.'[2] Once winter had set in, Charlotte herself preferred to defer Mrs. Gaskell's visit until the spring. Mrs. Gaskell did, indeed, visit Haworth Parsonage in July 1855, but by then there was no Charlotte to greet her.

After Ellen's visit in October it was agreed that Charlotte should pay a return visit to her before Christmas, and she wrote to say, 'When I go to Brookroyd Arthur will take me there and stay one night, but I cannot yet fix the time.' Within the week Charlotte learnt that Ellen's sister Mercy had contracted typhoid fever—a fact hidden from the Nusseys themselves by the family doctor, which Miss Wooler told Charlotte.[3] The mere mention of such a thing greatly alarmed Nicholls for his wife. Charlotte wrote to Ellen on 7 December postponing her visit till well after Christmas:

For my own part, I really should have no fear, and if it depended on me, I should come; but these matters are not quite in my power now, another must be consulted, and where his wish and judgement have a decided bias to a particular course, I make no stir but just adopt it. Arthur is sorry to disappoint both you and me, but it is his fixed wish that a few weeks should be allowed yet to elapse before we meet. Probably he is confirmed in this desire by my having a cold at present.[4]

[1] CBN to Mrs. G, 30 Sept. 1854: Manchester Univ. Lib.
[2] Mrs. G to Geraldine Jewsbury, 21 July 1854. Gaskell Letters, 303: op. cit.
[3] CBN to Miss Wooler, 6 Dec. 1854: *W & S* iv. 163.
[4] CBN to EN, 7 Dec. 1854: *W & S* iv. 164-5.

The cold, caught after her drenching on the moors, effectually prevented her visiting Ellen even after Mercy's recovery. To Ann Clapham, Ellen's married sister, she wrote on 28 December: 'I hope to visit Brookroyd about the beginning of February, but before that time I do not think it likely I shall get off. . . . Tell Mr. Clapham I have long been wanting to pay my bride visit to Brookroyd and that I shall be sincerely glad to shake hands with him once more. I want to introduce him to my husband too, and I have an idea that they would not disagree.'[1]

In the event, neither Brookroyd nor Ellen saw her again; nor kind Mr. Clapham, for whom Charlotte had a particular liking, for he died suddenly at the beginning of March.

A sequence of sad events indeed set in with the turn of the year, the effect of which was not only to isolate Charlotte but gradually to remove the old landmarks from her world. Early in December Flossy died. 'Did I tell you that our poor little Flossy is dead?' Charlotte wrote Ellen. 'He drooped for a single day, and died quietly in the night without pain. The loss even of a dog was very saddening, yet perhaps no dog ever had a happier life or an easier death.'[2]

For Charlotte the death of Anne's spoilt darling Flossy, the last of the famous parsonage pets, would have turned the knife in the yet unhealed wound, had she been alone. As it was, the sadness was something that could be shared with Arthur, who had been Flossy's friend from the first. Flossy could be laid in the garden beside Keeper with a sense that all would in time be gathered in where they belonged. As the New Year came in Charlotte could see by old Tabby's face that it would not be long before she too left her mistress. Tabby had been the only mother the Brontë children had known, but she was 84 and in a hurry now to be gone, whether or not a child was expected at the parsonage.

In the first week of January the Nicholls were invited to stay at Gawthorpe Hall, Sir James's determination to benefit Charlotte and her husband having reopened the question of the living of Padiham. While the visit had to be accepted, the living had again to be declined and the reasons repeated why, in the lifetime of Mr. Brontë, Mr. Nicholls could consider no advancement.

Mrs. Gaskell, who like Charlotte had had her opportunities for studying Sir James, told George Smith later apropos the visit to

1 CBN to Ann Clapham, 28 Dec. 1854: *W & S* iv. 167–8.
2 CBN to EN, 7 Dec. 1854: *W & S* iv. 164–5.

Gawthorpe, that Sir James had 'generally a double set of motives for all his actions', and having convened the Nicholls on a matter of patronage, profited by the presence of Currer Bell in his house to read aloud to her the manuscript of a novel he was writing and that he wished to publish, through her good offices, with Smith, Elder. (It appeared anonymously in 1860 under the title *Scarsdale*.)[1]

The continuous rain which benefited the readings aloud, also drenched the lawns of Gawthorpe, so that Charlotte, tempted to take imprudent walks in thin shoes, greatly aggravated her cold. By the time she returned home she was decidedly unwell.

A pleasure, however, awaited both her and her husband, in the visit of his cousin, James Adamson Bell, who had been their host at Banagher. Writing to Ellen on 19 January Charlotte said his visit had been 'a great pleasure; I wish you could have seen him and made his acquaintance; a true gentleman by nature and cultivation is not after all an everyday thing.' To Amelia, Joe Taylor's wife (with whom she regularly corresponded that winter during a long illness of Joe's) she added concerning Mr. Bell: 'He is a cultivated, thoroughly educated man with a mind stored with information gathered from books and travel and what is far rarer—with the art of conversing appropriately and quietly and never pushing his superiority upon you.'[2]

Still hoping to fix the deferred visit to Brookroyd, Charlotte had now to confess to Ellen that she was far from well:

I very much wish to come to Brookroyd, and I hope to be able to write with certainty and fix Wednesday the 31st January as the day; but the fact is, I am not sure whether I shall be well enough to leave home. At present I should be a most tedious visitor. My health has been really very good ever since my return from Ireland till about ten days ago, when the stomach seemed quite suddenly to lose its tone, indigestion and continual faint sickness have been my portion ever since. Don't conjecture dear Nell, for it is too soon yet, though I certainly never before felt as I have done lately. I am rather mortified to lose my good looks and grow thin as I am doing, just when I thought of going to Brookroyd. . . . Thank Mr. Clapham for his hospitable wish, but it would be quite out of Arthur's power to stay more than one night or two at the most.[3]

By 23 January the likelihood of Charlotte's being able to leave home had dwindled; it was Nicholls himself who wrote to tell Ellen so. The

[1] Mrs. Gaskell to George Smith, 5 Apr. 1860. Gaskell Letters, 611: op. cit.
[2] CBN to Amelia Taylor, 21 Jan. 1855: *W & S* iv. 170–1.
[3] CBN to EN, 19 Jan. 1855: *W & S* iv. 170.

fact was that the sickness of early pregnancy was quite dispropor-
tionate in Charlotte's case, and she had already to be put to bed.
By 29 January the symptoms had further increased and her husband
called in a second medical opinion. He sent for Dr. MacTurk from
Bradford, reputedly the best doctor in the region, and long known to
Mr. Brontë. 'I wish to have better advice than Haworth affords',
Nicholls wrote Ellen on that day.

Dr. MacTurk saw Charlotte on the 30th. He confirmed her pregnancy, but while recognizing the exceptional precautions needed in her
case—she might have to be confined to bed for some time to arrest the
sickness—did not alarm the family unduly. Neither the child's nor her
life was then pronounced to be in danger. Charlotte was left in the care
of the local doctor, Dr. Ingham, and his new young aide, Dr. Crashaw
Dugdale.

A fortnight later, however, she was making no progress. Nicholls
wrote on her behalf again to Ellen on 14 February. 'It is difficult to
write to friends', he then said, 'about my wife's illness, as its cause is
yet uncertain; at present she is completely prostrated with weakness
and sickness and frequent fever.'

To Amelia Taylor Charlotte herself wrote several pencilled notes,
chiefly to send comfort on the theme of Joe's grave illness (from which
he died in March 1857), and secondly to ask Amelia's advice since she
had not so long since had a child herself. In mid February she wrote
to her:

Dear Amelia—Let me speak the plain truth—my sufferings are very
great—my nights indescribable—sickness with scarce a reprieve—I strain
until what I vomit is mixed with blood. Medicine I have quite discontinued.
If you can send me anything that will do good—do.

As to my husband—my heart is knit to him—he is so tender, so good,
helpful, patient.

Poor Joe! long has he to suffer. May God soon send him, you, all of us
health, strength—comfort.[1]

Her own great sufferings intensified her feeling for others: to
Amelia, to Ellen, to Laetitia Wheelwright, she scribbled what messages
she could, never more affectionately worded than in those valedictory
notes. She wrote to Laetitia on 15 February:

A few lines of acknowledgement your letter *shall* have, whether well or ill.
At present I am confined to my bed with illness, and have been so for three

---

[1] CBN to ART, Feb. 1855: *W & S* iv. 163–76.

weeks. Up to this period, since my marriage, I have had excellent health. My husband and I live at home with my father; of course I could not leave *him*. He is pretty well, better than last summer. No kinder, better husband than mine, it seems to me, there can be in the world. I do not want now for kind companionship in health and the tenderest nursing in sickness. Deeply I sympathise in all you tell me about Dr. Wheelwright and your excellent mother's anxiety. I trust he will not risk another operation. I cannot write more now; for I am much reduced and very weak. God bless you all![1]

On the afternoon of Tuesday, 13 February, Charlotte scribbled a note to Dr. Ingham, which speaks for itself: 'Dear Sir,' it ran, 'I regret to disturb you at a time when you are suffering from illness, but I merely wish to ask if you can send any medicine for our old servant Tabby. Yours faithfully.'[2]

With the whole care of the house centred on Charlotte it had been decided, much to Charlotte's regret, to send Tabby down to her sister's cottage in Stubbing Lane at the foot of the hill; there, on the 17th she died.

It was the same day that Charlotte made her will. The clauses providing for a possible child, or children, would appear to show that it was not drawn up as a measure *in extremis*. The whole of her estate was left to her husband. She wrote to Ellen on the 21st:

I am not going to talk about my sufferings, it would be useless and painful —I want to give you an assurance which I know will comfort you—and that is that I find in my husband the tenderest nurse, the kindest support—the best earthly comfort that ever woman had. His patience never fails, and it is tried by sad days and broken nights . . . Papa thank God! is better. Our poor old Tabby is *dead* and *buried*. Give my truest love to Miss Wooler. . . . May God comfort and help you.[3]

On the very day of that letter, 21 February, Tabby was borne to her grave at the foot of the parsonage wall. She had been with the family ever since the return from Cowan Bridge in 1825, but not one of them was there to follow her to her rest. The 'childer' had all gone before, except the one now lying in the first floor bedroom, so weak that she would have to be raised on her pillows if she were to see the little cortège enter the churchyard and Arthur, the only spokesman for them all, performing the last rites.

[1] CBN to LW, 15 Feb. 1855: *W & S* iv. 172.
[2] CBN to Dr. Ingham, 13 Feb. 1855: *W & S* iv. 171.
[3] CBN to EN, 21 Feb. 1855: BPM.

Charlotte lay now in the mahogany four-poster bed that had been her parents', then her aunt's, then her own shared with Anne, and, since her marriage, once again the 'state' bed in the sense it had when her parents were young and the whole family future yet to make.

Kind Martha and her sister Tabitha (working full-time now at the parsonage) tried to bring back her will to live with thought of the coming child, but she found it difficult to envisage the future. She had always lacked what she called 'animal spirits', and the effort of bringing another life into the world derived from her own was beyond her. She had had a plentiful creation, she might have told them, but they had been born of the spirit; for *her* it was more natural so.

The servants compared her to a tiny bird in the great bed, a 'throssel' opening its beak for food. Her hand when it was raised appeared quite transparent, they said.[1]

Though she could see her own condition (she described her 'skeleton emaciation' to Ellen), she did not appear to recognize its meaning. To her father, indeed, she kept up to the end the pretence of improvement, forcing herself to rally when he came into the room and to say: 'See, Papa, I am better today', even when speech was generally beyond her. In a last pencilled note to Ellen she wrote: 'I cannot talk—even to my dear, patient, constant Arthur, I can say but a few words at once.'[2]

It has been reported that she spoke in surprise when, overhearing her husband pray for her recovery, she exclaimed: 'Oh, I am not going to die, am I? He will not separate us—we have been so happy.'[3]

With March there came a sudden improvement in her condition. The sickness stopped, she 'craved food and eat eagerly', as Mrs. Gaskell heard from the servants later,[3] and for a few days it looked as though she would rally. Then, by the middle of the month she relapsed. 'The bad weather has thrown her back', wrote Mr. Nicholls to Ellen on the 13th in a letter of sympathy for the sudden death of her brother-in-law Robert Clapham. It is significant that Charlotte's husband should attribute her collapse to the effect of the weather, sheltered from it as she was in her curtained bed; but the affinity was an undeniable fact and one that, could she have spoken, she would have corroborated. The March gales had come in, and to those who know the district their gathering force is a phenomenon not to be underrated. Their mounting fury rocks the sky and shudders in the hollows of the hills; every object in their path is swept aside; the waterfalls are tossed

---

[1] Chadwick.
[2] CB to EN, 21 Feb. 1855: BPM.
[3] Gaskell 400.

into the air, the rocky boulders hurled into the becks, the solitary trees on the bare hillsides are tattered and torn. In the narrow village streets the windows rattle in their frames, the wooden shutters crash, the chimneys roar, and the very key-holes are a vent for eerie cries. To stand between the front and back doors of the old houses in Haworth at such a time is to hear banshee voices shrieking in the gale.

Well did Charlotte know these voices; they had powerfully worked upon her spirits in the past. Few people were more susceptible to the effects of weather than she. To Mrs. Gaskell she had confessed to an almost psychic response to the elements: 'For a month or six weeks about the equinox (autumn or vernal) is a period of the year which, I have noticed, strangely tries me. Sometimes the strain falls on the mental, sometimes on the physical part of me, I am ill . . . or I am ground to the dust with deep depression of spirits.'[1]

There had been times when sitting alone on winter nights in the empty dining-room, the plaint of the storm had taken on the very tones of her sisters' voices. Then, indeed, there had been mortal conflict, and it had not been easily resolved by the victory of the forces of life. In happier times, especially in her visionary girlhood, the call of the elements had been the preliminary requisite for her spirit's release preceding each creative experience. At Roe Head had she not written?:

There is a voice, there is an impulse that wakens up that dormant power. . . . That wind pouring in impetuous current through the air, sounding wildly unremittingly from hour to hour, deepening its tone as the night advances . . . is heard at this moment far away on the moors at Haworth. Branwell and Emily hear it and as it sweeps over our house down the church-yard and round the old church, they think perhaps of me and Anne. Glorious! that blast was mighty it reminded me of Northangerland. . . . O it has wakened a feeling that I cannot satisfy.[2]

Such a summons she heard now. She recognized in its majestic tones the prelude to yet another liberation, such as formerly had heralded her finest flights. This time the call was not for one magic hour, but for eternity. In times of health, in the few settled moments even of content that she had known with those she loved, the genius that inhabited her had held but a precarious lodging; its wings were always set for flight. The little girl who had set out to find the Celestial City and had had to abandon course, vowed that next time she would not

[1] CB to Mrs. Gaskell, 6 Nov. 1851: Manchester Univ. Lib. By courtesy of the Librarian.
[2] Roe Head Journal: Bonnell (98), BPM.

fail to find it. That time had now come. Despite the loving hands stretched out to hold her, the adventurous spirit leapt to get away.

The equinoctial storms of 1855 came in early. Charlotte was attached to earth by a mere thread of life. It needed no such multitudinous array of elements, as in her strength she had described, to bear her away. It cannot be doubted that she gave herself up to the summons now, assured at last of reaching the heart of the storm where she believed lay peace, and where with her sisters and brother she had faith that she belonged.

Charlotte Brontë died in the night of Saturday, 31 March 1855. Her death certificate made no mention of her pregnancy; it gave 'Phisis' as the sole cause of death, uniting her thus, as if proof of any closer ties were needed, with the sisters and brother who had gone before, and of whose lives her own was an integral part; bone of their bone, flesh of their flesh, soul of their soul.

Little Dr. Dugdale, barely beginning his long career as the village accoucheur, carried into old age the regret and humiliation of losing his first—and most illustrious—patient. Of all the babies he lost, he used to say, the one that grieved him most was Charlotte Brontë's.

She was buried on 4 April in the family vault in the old church, where all but Anne were reunited and where in due course the bereft father would join them. Sutcliffe Sowden, who had married her just nine months before, was the officiating minister.[1]

Thus did Mr. Brontë's predictions come true. Though he said nothing to his son-in-law, to the servants he didn't hide his thoughts: 'I always told you Martha,' he said when Charlotte was gone, 'that there was no sense in Charlotte marrying at all, for she was not strong enough for marriage.'[2]

By one of those profound strokes of irony with which the Brontë story is scored, Mr. Brontë and his unwanted son-in-law were left in a six-year tête-à-tête, during which Arthur Nicholls scrupulously kept his promise to Charlotte. The uneasy partners did not always see alike—especially on questions of church observance, the old evangelical minister finding much to laugh at in the formalism of his curate. But they shared a common sorrow, and remained true to it.

---

[1] In accordance with local tradition and custom a funeral sermon was preached in Haworth Church on the Sunday following CB's funeral. The preacher was Dr. Cartman from Skipton, an old friend of Mr. Brontë's: his text was from Luke viii. 52—'. . . And all wept, and bewailed her; but he said, Weep not; she is not dead, but sleepeth . . .' Whiteley Turner, op. cit. 199.

[2] Chadwick 477.

The detractors of Arthur Nicholls interpreted his devotion to his wife's old father to the expectation of inheriting the living of Haworth. If that was so, he was disappointed, because the living depended on the nomination of the Church Trustees whom he offended by his unbending ways, and who bestowed it elsewhere. He had, luckily, the loving family at Banagher to withdraw to, and left Haworth in October 1861 with all that remained to him of his vehement love for Charlotte—her dresses and manuscripts and drawings—which into extreme old age he refused to regard as anything but tender keepsakes concerning none but himself. Towards the last living inmates of the parsonage he continued to show the humanity of his nature, taking with him to Ireland Mr. Brontë's last dog, 'Plato',[1] and Martha Brown, who stayed at Banagher for long periods at a time, more as a valued friend to the second Mrs. Nicholls than as a servant; initiating her into the culinary secrets of Haworth Parsonage and leaving behind her famous recipe for sponge-cake.[2]

When Arthur Nicholls died on 2 December 1906, his devoted cousin and second wife, who had known him better than anyone all his life, had his coffin carried into the dining-room of the Hill House, Banagher (where they lived 40 years), and placed under Richmond's portrait of Charlotte, which he had hung there on first returning from Haworth.

He would often, in old age, fall into an abstraction and be heard, by the younger generation of nieces and nephews growing up round him, to say of that reunion towards which he looked with certainty: 'I wonder how it will be?'

[1] See below: Additional Notes, p. 598.
[2] F. E. Bell; 'A Hundred Years of Life': op. cit.; F. E. Bell, 'Charlotte Brontë's Irish Relations': op. cit; H. K. Bell, 'Charlotte Brontë's Husband': *Cornhill Magazine*, January 1927; Marjorie Gallop, 'Charlotte's Husband': *BST*, 1954.

MRS. GASKELL AND M. HEGER

It was John Greenwood, the Haworth stationer, who informed Mrs. Gaskell of Charlotte's death. They were not total strangers to each other, having certainly met during Mrs. Gaskell's visit to Haworth in September 1853. Charlotte had spoken of him when staying in Manchester and told Mr. Gaskell that he was 'the one friend I have in Haworth', and the Gaskells had subsequently sent messages to him through Charlotte. His letter reached Mrs. Gaskell in London from where she wrote him on 4 April: 'My dear Sir—I can not tell you how *very* sad your note has made me. My dear dear friend that I shall never see again on earth! I did not know she was ill. I had heard nothing of her since the beginning of December when she wrote to a mutual friend saying that she was well, and happy.'[1]

She wrote immediately to Mr. Brontë and received in reply a letter dated 5 April, in which he said among other things: 'The marriage that took place seemed to hold forth long and bright prospects of happiness, but in the inscrutable providence of God, all our hopes have ended in disappointment and our joy in mourning.'[2]

The death of Currer Bell brought from the daily and periodical press tributes and assessments of her work in great number, but among the valuable contributions, such as Harriet Martineau's in the *Daily News*, there crept in far too many ill-informed and speculative notices purporting to supply data about the lives of the three Bells. Ellen Nussey was the first to realize the danger to Charlotte's reputation if such extravagant reports remained unchecked, and wrote to Mr. Nicholls on 6 June to draw his attention to the June issue of *Sharpe's Magazine* which carried an article called 'A Few Words about *Jane Eyre*' which she declared to be full of 'malicious misrepresentations', and urged on him to engage Mrs. Gaskell to 'undertake a reply' and 'give a sound castigation to the writer. Her personal acquaintance with Haworth,' Ellen considered, 'the Parsonage, & its inmates, fits her for

[1] Mrs. G to J. Greenwood, 4 Apr. 1855. Gaskell Letters, 335–6: op. cit.
[2] Lock & Dixon: Life & Letters of the Revd. Patrick Brontë, 479.

the task. . . . Will you ask Mrs. Gaskell to undertake this just and honourable defence? I think she would do it gladly. She valued dear Charlotte, and such an act of friendship, performed with her ability and power, could only add to the laurels she has already won.'[1]

Such was the genesis of Mrs. Gaskell's 'Life' of Charlotte Brontë. At the outset, she was merely to refute an ill-mannered magazine review; there was no thought as yet of a full-scale biography.

Mrs. Gaskell herself, however, early entertained the idea. Writing to George Smith on 31 May 1855 for permission to have a copy taken of the Richmond portrait (which she believed Smith to possess) she said: 'I cannot tell you how I honoured and loved her. I did not know of her illness, or I would have gone straight to her. It seems to me that her death was as sad as her life. Sometime, it may be years hence—but if I live long enough . . . I will publish what I know of her and make the world . . . honour the woman as much as they admired the writer.'[2]

After reading the article in *Sharpe's Magazine*, Mr. Nicholls and Mr. Brontë did not, at first, think it merited a reply. Mr. Brontë's reactions to the remarks concerning him in it were indeed hilarious: 'I have not seen him laugh as much for some months as he did while I was reading the article to him', Nicholls wrote to Ellen on 11 June.[3]

Some weeks later, however, having considered the matter in its further implications, Mr. Brontë wrote direct to Mrs. Gaskell (16 June) formally asking her to undertake an authoritative account of Charlotte's life and works.[4] He gave as his reason: 'a great many scribblers, as well as some clever and truthful writers, have published articles . . . and seeing that many things that have been stated are untrue, but more false; and having reason to think that some may venture to write her life who will be ill-qualified for the undertaking, I can see no better plan than to apply to some established author to write a brief account of her life'. He assured Mrs. Gaskell that he and Mr. Nicholls would give her 'all such information as she might require'.

Mrs. Gaskell accepted the task, though realizing at once, as she wrote to George Smith, that it was a 'far more serious task than the one which, as you know, I was proposing to myself'. The request having come

[1] EN to ABN, 6 June 1855: *W & S* iv. 189.
[2] Mrs. G to GMS, 31 May 1855: Gaskell Letters 345: op. cit.
[3] ABN to EN, 11 June 1855: *W & S* iv. 191.
[4] Revd. PB to Mrs. G, 16 June 1855: Lock & Dixon, op. cit., 493.

from Charlotte's father, Mrs. Gaskell realized that she would have now 'to omit a good deal of detail as to her home, and the circumstances which must have had so much to do in forming her character. All these can be merely indicated during the lifetime of her father, and to a certain degree, in the lifetime of her husband'.[1]

The existence of both must lay a kind of moral embargo on Mrs. Gaskell's outspokenness; so she estimated the difficulties that lay ahead of her, unsuspecting as yet the greater ones to follow.

Her first step was to visit Haworth Parsonage, where she went on 23 July. Telling her daughter Marianne of it next day she wrote: 'It was a most painful visit. Both Mr. Brontë and Mr. Nicholls cried sadly. I like Mr. Nicholls.'[2]

She said this though realizing at once that Mr. Nicholls was against the whole enterprise; it was rendering public what to him was personal and sacred; as Mrs. Gaskell wrote to Ellen Nussey the following day: 'He yielded to Mr. Brontë's impetuous wish', and gave her what material he had to start on 'in the shape of a dozen letters, addressed principally to her sister Emily, one or two to her father and brother, and one to her aunt. The dates extend from 1839–43. But Mr. Nicholls said that he thought you were the person of all others to apply to; that you had been a friend of his wife's ever since she was 15'.[3]

Had Ellen Nussey been less anxious to secure an authoritative work on her friend's life, she might have thrown the ball back at Mr. Nicholls and said that Charlotte's letters to her were not for publishing, as she had always declared when refusing to destroy them at his request. In the event, she allowed Mrs. Gaskell to see some 300 of them.

To that initial material Mrs. Gaskell gradually added the main collections of Charlotte's voluminous correspondence, applying to George Smith, who further introduced her to Mr. Williams and put her in touch with far-away Mr. Taylor, G. H. Lewes, Harriet Martineau, and others of her literary acquaintance. Though the Gomersal Taylors gave her what help they could, Mary Taylor herself, when applied to, declared sadly enough that she had destroyed the whole of Charlotte's letters to her, not having felt that it was 'safe' to keep them. The Miss Woolers, too, gave her access to the thirty-four letters addressed to them; she visited Laetitia Wheelwright in London and was full of questions about Charlotte's school-days in Brussels. Visiting

[1] Mrs. G to Geo. Smith: 18 June 1855: Gaskell Letters, 349: op. cit.
[2] Mrs. G to MG: 24 July: 1855 Gaskell Letters, 364: op. cit.
[3] Mrs. G to EN: Gaskell Letters, 361: op. cit. 24 July 1855.

everybody connected with Charlotte became, indeed, the rule in her pursuit of data, so that she could gain not only *facts*, but *insight* into the people who had in any way influenced Charlotte's life. With the exception of Mary Taylor in New Zealand, she visited them all, not hesitating to go across to Brussels to visit the Hegers.

Prepared as Mrs. Gaskell had declared herself to be to encounter great difficulties in writing the life of a still young woman whose relations and friends were all mostly alive, she had not foreseen the problem that Charlotte's relations with the Hegers was going to create in the writing of her life-story. Mrs. Gaskell had read *Villette* and cannot have ignored the inner truth it contained even if Charlotte had told her nothing more. Her friends, the Winkworths, it will be remembered, conjectured how much Lily knew about 'the real Paul Emanuel' at the time of Charlotte's marriage. Whatever she anticipated in the way of a difficult situation, what Mrs. Gaskell found when she rang at the door of the Pensionnat Heger far surpassed it. To begin with, directly she heard that Mrs. Gaskell was a friend of Miss Brontë's, Madame Heger refused to see her. From this it is plain that the pirated translation of *Villette—La Maîtresse d'Anglais ou Le Pensionnat de Bruxelles*—published in 1855, had already reached her. This is likely because Mrs. Gaskell's visit to Brussels was in the early summer— April or May of 1856.

Monsieur Heger's conduct was very different from his wife's. He received Mrs. Gaskell 'and very much indeed I both like and respect him . . .' was her comment on the meeting.[1] Of importance is the 'respect' that his conduct at that meeting awoke in her, for she received proof then and there that what he *knew*, and the material he possessed, was gunpowder in unscrupulous hands, and could blow Charlotte Brontë's reputation sky high.

It has long been a matter of conjecture *how* Mrs. Gaskell obtained the extracts from Charlotte's letters to Monsieur Heger that she published in the 'Life', and how much she knew of their *entire* text. Yet the evidence is plain and has been to hand for years, and reposes in the University Library at Manchester. It is contained in a letter from Monsieur Heger to Mrs. Gaskell dated 22 May 1856 (written after her visit) in which he states that *at her request* he is sending her some specimens of Emily's and Charlotte's *devoirs* in French, together with 'quelques extraits textuels des lettres que Mlle Charlotte m'a écrites. . .'. The extracts themselves are headed by him: 'Extraits des lettres *que*

[1] Mrs. G to EN: 9 July 1856: *W & S* iv. 201–3.

j'ai promis.' The selection, as might be supposed from the tenor of the *later* letters, was confined to the first two letters, those of 24 July and 24 October 1844. They bore entirely upon Charlotte's accounts of her continuing study of French and plans for setting up school, reports of her own and her family's health, and the conventional messages she addressed the members of his household: nothing, in short, that any pupil could not write to any master. When Mrs. Gaskell came to use these excerpts in the 'Life', she further confused the context by mixing up those of one letter with those of the other.

Her motive in doing so came from her knowledge of the full text of the letters. These, it is evident, Monsieur Heger showed her or read to her, and she instantly realized their danger if ever published. This appears plainly from her correspondence with George Smith over the posthumous publication of *The Professor*, whose editing he asked her to undertake. Before reading the manuscript she dreaded lest, like *Villette*, it again dealt with Monsieur Heger, and wrote to George Smith: 'I could not undertake the editing (which would to a certain degree seem like my sanctioning it) *after receiving M. Heger's confidence and hearing her letters*, if, as I fear, it relates to him.'[1]

After reading the manuscript she was reassured and wrote to her friend Emily Shaen: 'I dreaded lest the Prof. should involve anything with M. Heger . . . and I thought if he were again brought before the public what would he think of me? I believed him to be too good to publish those letters—but I felt that his friends might really with some justice urge him to do so.'[2]

Monsieur Heger had no intention of ever making Charlotte's letters public (other than the emasculated extracts he gave Mrs. Gaskell) but he realized the importance of his *own* letters to Charlotte being known, and was very insistent with Mrs. Gaskell that she should ask to see them. He was convinced Charlotte would have kept them, he said, as they contained good advice for her health and studies.

The implication was clear enough to Mrs. Gaskell: he wished to prove that no improper subject had ever been discussed between him and his former pupil.

The letters, however, had disappeared. One hesitates to say disappeared *for good*, recalling the strange incident of the burial of Dr. John's letters at the foot of the tree 'Methusaleh' in *Villette*. Charlotte had cryptic ways of revealing, while concealing—truths that touched

---

[1] Mrs. G to GMS: 1 Aug. 1856. Gaskell Letters, 401: op. cit.
[2] Mrs. G to ES: 8 Sept. 1856. Ibid. 409.

her closely in her novels, and it would be in character for her to have buried them rather than destroy them when the time came to tear them from her heart.

Ellen Nussey, when applied to by Mrs. Gaskell, could only tell her that Charlotte had declared 'that she would destroy all former correspondence before her marriage'.[1] The fact that she intended doing so made it evident to Mrs. Gaskell that the letters of Monsieur Heger had had a meaning and a value for Charlotte that she could no longer allow them to have as the wife of another man. Their very importance to her made their destruction necessary. Her reasoning in the matter can be deduced by analogy with Charlotte's conduct over another correspondence, that with James Taylor. It appears (from a letter of Ellen Nussey's to George Smith of 27 February 1869)[2] that Charlotte kept Taylor's letters, and that immediately after her death Nicholls found them and in great agitation of spirits hurried over to Brookroyd to learn from Ellen what there had been between his wife and Taylor. Ellen assumed complete ignorance both then and later, when Nicholls returned to the charge; as did Miss Wooler to whom he similarly applied. They might well have allayed his misery by telling him that the mere fact of the letters' preservation was proof of their *want* of value in Charlotte's eyes.

The disappearance of Monsieur Heger's letters confirmed for Mrs. Gaskell the need to hide the truth of Charlotte's feelings for her Master at all costs. Hence the major difficulties in her way when she came to describe Charlotte's experiences in Brussels and the resultant omissions and chronological errors she had to resort to in explanation of certain facts. Hence the total omission of the crucial letter Charlotte wrote to Emily about her act of confession at Ste Gudule; hence the strict editing of every reference to Madame Heger in Charlotte's letters home; hence the ante-dating of Branwell's ruin—advanced by 18 months—to account for Charlotte's low spirits after her return from Brussels.

Mrs. Gaskell had perception enough to know that nothing dishonourable had ever been mooted between Monsieur Heger and Charlotte; her meeting with him had shown her, moreover, that he also had perception enough to judge of the rare quality of Charlotte's feelings for him, and not to misinterpret them. But while they two might understand and pity, the world of the mid nineteenth century would not be prepared to give Charlotte the benefit of the doubt if even the shadow of the truth was allowed to appear; so it must be

[1] EN to Mrs. G, July 1856. [2] EN to GMS, 27 Feb. 1869: Hopkins *W & S*, iv.

suppressed, even at the cost of weakening the portrait of Charlotte that emerged. To suppress her sufferings over Monsieur Heger, was also to diminish her triumph over herself, and the miracle of re-created experience she achieved when she came to write of her love.

In connivance with Ellen Nussey and all Charlotte's other kind friends, Mrs. Gaskell set out to present a picture of a good and admirable woman, as a corrective to the harsh views taken by some contemporaries of Charlotte's so-called 'coarse' writing. Ellen, even, urged the reproduction of Richmond's portrait of her friend as showing her in a different light from general belief. 'It has been a surprise', she wrote to Mrs. Gaskell, 'to every stranger, I think, that she was so gentle and lady-like to look upon.'[1]

While proclaiming her aim at whitewashing Charlotte, Mrs. Gaskell also betrayed the *need* to do so; on the theme of James Taylor's proposal (she does not name him of course) she wrote:[2] 'I shall now quote an extract from one of her letters. . . . I quote it because it relates to a third offer of marriage which she had, and because I find that some are apt to imagine from the extraordinary power with which she represented the passion of love in her novels, that she herself was easily susceptible of it.' (Harriet Martineau had condemned *Villette* on that very score.)

The world has become less censorious in the century since Mrs. Gaskell first presented Charlotte's 'Life' and more concerned with psychological truth, and it has become a paradoxical comment on Mrs. Gaskell's loyal covering-up of Charlotte's greatest experience that her novels are most admired and read today precisely because of their analysis of love.

In the troubles that she brought upon herself in writing Charlotte's biography (a threatened lawsuit with Mrs. Robinson, attacks by Carus Wilson's son, displeasure at Haworth), Mrs. Gaskell had not reckoned that harm could come so long as the central figure escaped censure. In her judgement of Mr. Nicholls she showed herself mistaken: he did not hesitate to defend her account of his wife's sufferings at the Clergy Daughters' School, when Carus Wilson's son entered into the controversy; in five letters that he contributed to the *Halifax Guardian*—between 23 May and 8 August 1857—he warmly maintained the truth of Mrs. Gaskell's descriptions.

As to the threatened libel action brought by Mrs. Robinson's lawyers and the official retraction and apology imposed on Mrs.

---

[1] EN to Mrs. G, 22 Oct. 1856: *SBC* 20.   [2] 'Life' 331.

Gaskell, and the deletion of the offending passages from the third edition of her book, the last word did not remain with the enemies of Mrs. Gaskell—and the Brontë family—but with their friends: Mary Taylor who had loved them all (and especially Branwell Brontë) wrote to Ellen Nussey from the antipodes on hearing of the scandal on 28 January 1858: 'As to the mutilated edition that is to come, I am sorry for it. Libellous or not, the first edition was all true, and except the declamation [on p. 195 *re* Mrs. Robinson] all, in my opinion, useful to be published. Of course I don't know how far necessity may make Mrs. Gaskell give them up. You know one dare not always say the world moves. . . .'[1]

---

[1] Mary Taylor to EN, 28 Jan. 1858: *W & S* iv. 229.

CHARLOTTE BRONTË'S PHRENOLOGICAL CHARACTER[1]

During her visit to London in May–June 1851, Charlotte went with George Smith to a phrenologist then much in vogue, Dr. J. P. Browne, to have her 'talents and disposition' estimated. She and George Smith presented themselves as Mr. and Miss Fraser. Writing to him afterwards (1 July 1851) Charlotte said: 'Somehow I quite expect that you will let me see my "character" though you did not promise that you would. Do you keep it back on account of my faults; remember Thackeray seems to think our faults the best part of us. I will tell you faithfully whether it seems to me true or not.'

Smith sent both his own and her 'character' to Charlotte. She refused to comment on hers, but trusted him enough not to need to 'give him directions nor impose restrictions' on its use. On Smith's she commented enthusiastically, telling him it was so *'like, like, like . . .'* that he could throw away the lithograph of himself by Ford, and keep the 'character' as a portrait instead.

The text of Dr. Browne's 'Phrenological Estimate' of Charlotte reads:

Temperament for the most part nervous. Brain large, the anterior and superior parts remarkably salient. In her domestic relations this lady will be warm and affectionate. In the care of children she will evince judicious kindness, but she is not pleased at seeing them spoiled by over-indulgence. Her fondness for any particular locality would chiefly rest upon the associations connected with it. Her attachments are strong and enduring—indeed, this is a leading element of her character; she is rather circumspect, however, in the choice of her friends, and it is well that she is so, for she will seldom meet with persons whose dispositions approach the standard of excellence with which she can entirely sympathise. Her sense of truth and justice would be offended by any dereliction of duty, and she would in such cases express her disapprobation with warmth and energy; she would not, however, be precipitate in acting thus, and rather than live in a state of hostility with those

[1] *W & S* iii. 256–8.

she could wish to love, she would depart from them, although the breaking off of friendship would be to her a source of great unhappiness. The careless and unreflecting, whom she would labour to amend, might deem her punctilious and perhaps exacting: not considering that their amendment and not her own gratification prompted her to admonish. She is sensitive and is very anxious to succeed in her undertakings, but is not so sanguine as to the probability of success. She is occasionally inclined to take a gloomier view of things than perhaps the facts of the case justify. She should guard against the effect of this where her affection is engaged, for her sense of her own importance is moderate and not strong enough to steel her heart against disappointment; she has more firmness than self-reliance, and her sense of justice is of very high order. She is deferential to the aged and those she deems worthy of respect, and possesses much devotional feeling, but dislikes fanaticism and is not given to a belief in supernatural things without questioning the probability of their existence.

Money is not her idol, she values it merely for its uses; she would be liberal to the poor and compassionate to the afflicted, and when friendship calls for aid she would struggle even against her own interest to impart the required assistance—indeed, sympathy is a marked characteristic of this organisation.

Is fond of symmetry and proportion, and possesses a good perception of form, and is a good judge of colour. She is endowed with a keen perception of melody and rhythm. Her imitative powers are good, and the faculty which gives manual dexterity is well developed. These powers might have been cultivated with advantage. Is a fair calculator, and her sense of order and arrangement is remarkably good. Whatever this lady has to settle or arrange will be done with precision and taste.

She is endowed with an exalted sense of the beautiful and ideal, and longs for perfection. If not a poet her sentiments are poetical or are at least imbued with that enthusiastic glow which is characteristic of poetical feeling. She is fond of dramatic literature and drama, especially if it be combined with music.

In its intellectual development this head is very remarkable. The forehead is at once very large and well formed. It bears the stamp of deep thoughtfulness and comprehensive understanding. It is highly philosophical. It exhibits the presence of an intellect at once perspicacious and perspicuous. There is much critical sagacity and fertility in devising resources in situations of difficulty, much originality, with a tendency to speculate and generalise. Possibly this speculative bias may sometimes interfere with the practical efficiency of some of her projects. Yet since she has scarcely an adequate share of self-reliance, and is not sanguine as to the success of her plans, there is reason to suppose that she would attend more closely to particulars, and thereby prevent the unsatisfactory results of hasty generalisation. This lady possesses a fine organ of language, and can, if she has done her talents justice by exercise, express her sentiments with clearness, precision, and force—sufficiently eloquent but not verbose. In learning a language she would investigate its spirit and structure. The character of the German language would be well adapted to such an organisation. In analysing the motives of human conduct, this lady would display originality and power, but in her mode of investigating mental science she would naturally be imbued with a metaphysical bias; she would perhaps be sceptical as to the truth of Gale's doctrine. But the study of this doctrine, this new system of mental philosophy, would give additional strength to her excellent understanding by rendering it more practical, more attentive to particulars, and contribute to her happiness by imparting to her more correct notions of the dispositions of those whose acquaintance she may wish to cultivate.

J. P. Browne, M.D.

367 Strand
June 29th, 1851

CHARLOTTE BRONTË'S LAST
MANUSCRIPTS

IN addition to the mass of her unpublished juvenile prose fiction—
stretching over the years 1829–39—Charlotte left in manuscript the
completed novel *The Professor* and fragments of two new tales begun
since the publication of *Villette*. These were: *Emma*, begun 27
November 1853, of which the first twenty 8vo pages remained,
written in pencil; and an untitled fragment begun in the summer of
1853, called for the sake of convenience *Willie Ellin* from the main
character—a young boy.

Her entire estate having been left to her husband, the copyright of
Charlotte's published and unpublished works became vested in him,
and his consent had therefore to be obtained to quote from or publish
any part of them. Judging him more averse than he was to proper use
being made of his wife's literary remains, Mrs. Gaskell doubted gaining
his consent even to a sight of Charlotte's last manuscripts, and took
with her Sir James Kay-Shuttleworth when calling on Mr. Nicholls
and Mr. Brontë for that purpose, in the August of 1856. She reported
on the outcome of the visit to her friend Emily Shaen on 8 September
1856:

[Sir J. P. K. S.] He had not the slightest delicacy or scruple: and asked for an
immense number of things, literally taking no refusal. Hence we carried away
with us a whole *heap* of those minute writings of which William showed you
one or two at Alderley: the beginning (only about 20 pages) of a new novel
which she had written at the end of 1854, *before* marriage and I dare say
when she was anxious enough. This fragment was excessively interesting;
a child left at a school by a rich flashy man, who pretended to be her father;
the school mistress's deference to the rich child—her mysterious reserved
character evidently painfully conscious of the imposition practised; the non-
payment of the bills; the enquiry—no such person to be found, and just
when the child implores mercy and confesses her complicity to the worldly
and indignant schoolmistress the story stops—for ever—[1]

[1] Mrs. G to ES, 8 Sept. 1856: Gaskell Letters 408: op. cit.

Mrs. Gaskell's hurried résumé of the tale perfectly corresponds to *Emma* which Mr. Nicholls later authorized George Smith to publish in the new *Cornhill Magazine* (edited by him) with an introduction by Thackeray.[1] Mrs. Gaskell was mistaken only about the date of composition; it was not at the end of 1854, but of 1853 that Charlotte began it, as Mr. Nicholls was able to prove in the accompanying details with which he supplied George Smith and Thackeray, and which Thackeray incorporated into his Introduction.

One evening, at the close of 1854, as Charlotte Nicholls sat with her husband by the fire, listening to the howling of the wind about the house, she suddenly said to her husband, 'If you had not been with me, I must have been writing now.' She then ran upstairs, and brought down, and read aloud, the beginning of a new tale. When she had finished, her husband remarked, 'The critics will accuse you of repetition.' She replied, 'Oh! I shall alter that. I always begin two or three times before I can please myself.' But it was not to be. The trembling little hand was to write no more.[2]

The existence of a novel subsequent to *Villette* was thus not only proven, but Charlotte's manner of composition disclosed: her habit of making several beginnings to a new book. The fact that the fragment of *Emma* was as yet written only in pencil was evidence also of its early stage, for she only copied corrected manuscripts in ink.

The fragments of *Willie Ellin*—begun in the summer of 1853—demonstrate Charlotte's manner of making several beginnings at a tale; there are three attempts in which occur variants of the principal names (the housekeeper is variously called 'Mrs. Widdup' or 'Mrs. Hill', the family home 'Ellin Hall' or 'Ellin Balcony', and the narration written in the first and third persons) which sufficiently show that Charlotte had not settled down at all to the definite presentation of her tale. The possibility, even, of *Emma* and *Willie Ellin* forming parts of the same story cannot be ruled out, for the name 'Ellin' occurs in both tales.

The incidence of this name, together with the plots of both as far as they were developed, suggests a further connexion between the two: a common origin in Charlotte's and Branwell's earliest Angrian novels. *Willie Ellin* was yet another of the 'Brother-enemies' themes which had their origin in the earliest 'Tales of the Islanders', where the two Wellesley boys, Arthur and Charles, introduced the long line of brother figures dominating Charlotte's stories for over ten years, culminating in the rival Edward and William Percy pair whom she finally introduced into *The Professor* as the Crimsworth brothers. Similarly, Mr. Fitzgibbon and his daughter Matilda were familiar figures to the Angrian cycle of tales—the devoted father-and-daughter pair who began with the Percys—went through *Caroline Vernon* and came to triumphant perfection in Mr. Hume and Paulina in *Villette*. When Mr. Nicholls judged that his wife's critics would accuse her of repetition in her choice of plot, he little knew how right he was: the plots of *Emma* and of *Willie Ellin* held hackneyed elements, but only Charlotte knew what variations she could play on them.

In addition to the manuscripts already mentioned, Mrs. Gaskell and Sir James Kay-Shuttleworth took away with them from their visit to Haworth, the manuscript of the finished *Professor*. About this work Mrs. Gaskell felt great anxiety, as she confided to Emily Shaen:

lest it should involve anything with M. Heger—I had heard her say it related to her Brussels life—and I thought if he were again brought before the public what would he think of me? I believed him to be too good to publish those letters—but I felt that his friends might really with some justice urge him to do so—so I awaited the arrival of the Prof. . . . with great anxiety. It does relate to the School; but not to M. Heger, and Mme or Madame Beck, is only slightly introduced; so on *that* ground there would be no objection to publishing it. I don't think, [Mrs. Gaskell strangely considered,] it will *add* to her reputation.[1]

Sir James, on the contrary, thought highly of the book, though taking exception to 'certain coarse and objectionable phrases' and offered himself, indeed, to revise and expurgate the text for publication. The idea of Sir James Kay-Shuttleworth 'editing' a work of Charlotte's would, Mrs. Gaskell felt keenly, have been peculiarly distasteful to Charlotte. She wrote Emily Shaen:

I don't know if you remember some of the passages I copied out in her letters relating to Sir J. and there were others I did *not*, all making me feel she would have especially disliked *him* to meddle with her writings. . . . Mr. N. quite agreed with me, and wrote to Sir James declining his proposal, saying privately to me that he feared Sir J. would be hurt (he, Sir J. evidently wants to appear to the world in intimate connexion with her) but that knowing his wife's opinion on the subject, he could not allow any such revisal, but that he would himself look over the 'Professor' and judge as well as he could with

[1] Mrs. G to ES, 8 Sept. 1856. Gaskell Letters 400: op. cit.

relation to the passages Sir J. and I had objected to. So there it rests with Mr. Nicholls, to whom the MS of the Prof. was returned a fortnight ago. With regard to Mr. Smith of course he jumped at the idea.[1]

The Professor, originally called *The Master*, finished 27 June 1846 and offered for publication to six successive firms, laid aside while *Jane Eyre* made its author's name, twice again offered to George Smith and rejected, reached the public only ten years later on 6 June 1857, when the just-published *Life of Charlotte Brontë* had brought its author to the fore on a tide of pathos, publicity, and near-scandal. Arthur Nicholls had added a short foreword to his wife's earlier preface:

The foregoing preface was written by my wife with a view to the publication of 'The Professor', shortly after the appearance of 'Shirley'. Being dissuaded from her intention, the authoress made some use of the materials in a subsequent work—'Villette'. As, however, these two stories are in most parts unlike, it has been represented to me that I ought not to withhold 'The Professor' from the public. I have therefore consented to its publication.

A. B. Nicholls

Haworth Parsonage
September 22nd 1856.

Mr. Brontë lived to see both the publication of *The Professor* and of *Emma*, under the title: 'The Last Sketch', with Thackeray's tribute to Charlotte appearing in the *Cornhill Magazine* for April 1860. Thanking George Smith for his complimentary copy of the latter he wrote on 26 March 1860:

My dear Sir—Though writing is to me now something of a task I cannot avoid sending you a few lines to thank you for sending me the magazines, and for your gentlemanly conduct towards my daughter in all your transactions with her, from first to last. All the numbers of the magazines were good; the last especially attracted my attention and excited my admiration. 'The Last Sketch' took full possession of my mind. Mr. Thackeray in his remarks in it has excelled even himself. He has written 'multum in parvo, dignissima cedro'. And what he has written does honour both to his head and heart. Thank him kindly both in Mr. Nicholls' name and mine. . . . If organless spirits see as we see, and feel as we feel, in this material clogging world, my daughter Charlotte's spirit will receive additional happiness on scanning the remarks of her Ancient Favourite.[2]

[1] Mrs. G to ES, 8 Sept. 1856: op. cit.
[2] Revd. PB to Geo. Smith, 26 Mar. 1860: Lock & Dixon, 491–2, op. cit.

THE FRENCH TEXTS OF THE HEGER LETTERS

I. LETTER FROM CB TO M. HEGER, 24 JULY 1844: BM

French text of letter translated on pp. 268–70

Monsieur,

Je sais bien que ce n'est pas à mon tour de vous écrire, mais puisque Mde Wheelwright va à Bruxelles et veut bien se charger d'une lettre — il me semble que je ne dois pas négliger une occasion si favorable pour vous écrire.

Je suis très contente que l'année scolaire soit presque finie et que l'époque des vacances approche — j'en suis contente pour vous Monsieur — car, on m'a dit que vous travaillez trop et que votre santé en est un peu altérée — C'est pourquoi je ne me permets pas de proférer une seule plainte au sujet de votre long silence — j'aimerais mieux rester six mois sans recevoir de vos nouvelles que d'ajouter un atome de poids, déjà trop lourd, qui vous accable — Je me rappelle bien que c'est maintenant l'époque des compositions, que ce sera bientôt celle des examens et puis, des prix — et pendant tout ce temps, vous êtes condamné à respirer l'atmosphere desséchante des classes — à vous user — à expliquer à intérroger, toute la journée et puis le soir vous avez toutes ces malheureuses compositions à lire, à corriger, presqu'à refaire — Ah Monsieur! je vous ai écrit une fois une lettre peu raisonnable, par ce que le chagrin me serrait le cœur, mais je ne le ferai plus — je tâcherai de ne plus être égoïste et tout en regardant vos lettres comme un des plus grands bonheurs que je connaisse, j'attendrai patiemment pour en recevoir jusqu'à ce qu'il vous plaira et vous conviendra de m'en envoyer. En même temps je puis bien vous écrire de temps en temps une petite lettre — vous m'y avez autorisée.

Je crains beaucoup d'oublier le français, car je suis bien persuadée que je vous reverrai un jour — je ne sais pas comment ni quand — mais celà doit être puisque je le désire tant, et alors je ne voudrais pas rester muette devant vous — ce serait trop triste de vous voir et de ne pas pouvoir vous parler; pour éviter ce malheur — j'apprends, tous les jours, une demie page de français par cœur dans un livre de style familier: et j'ai un plaisir à apprendre cette leçon — monsieur — quand je prononce les mots français il me semble que je cause avec vous.

On vient de m'offrir une place comme première maitresse dans un grand pensionnat à Manchester, avec un traitement de 100£, i.e. 2500 frs par an — je ne puis pas l'accepter — car en l'acceptant je dois quitter mon père et cela ne se peut pas — j'ai cependant mon projet — (lorsqu'on vit dans la retraite le cerveau travaille toujours — on désire s'occuper — on veut se lancer dans une carrière active). Notre Presbytère est une maison assez grande — avec quelques changements il y aura de la place pour cinq ou six pensionnaires — si je pouvais trouver ce nombre d'enfants de bonne famille je me dévouerais à leur education — Emilie n'aime pas beaucoup l'instruction mais elle s'occuperait toujours du ménage et, quoiqu'un peu recluse, elle a trop bon cœur pour ne pas faire son possible pour le bien-être des enfants — elle est aussi très généreuse et pour l'ordre, l'économie, l'exactitude — le travail assidu — toutes choses très essentielles dans un pensionnat — je m'en charge volontiers.

Voilà mon projet Monsieur — que j'ai déjà expliqué à mon père et qu'il trouve bon. Il ne reste donc que de trouver des élèves — chose assez difficile — car nous demeurons assez loin des villes et on ne se soucie guère de franchir les montagnes qui nous servent de barrière — mais la tâche qui est sans difficulté est presque sans mérite — il y a un grand intérêt à vaincre les obstacles — Je ne dis pas que je réussirai mais je tâcherai de réussir — le seul effort me fera du bien — il n'y a rien que je crains comme la paresse — le désœuvrement — l'inertie — la léthargie des facultés — quand le corps est paresseux, l'esprit souffre cruellement.

Je ne connaîtrais pas cette léthargie si je pouvais écrire — autrefois je passais des journées, des semaines, des mois entiers à écrire et pas tout à fait sans fruit puisque Southey et Coleridge — deux de nos meilleurs auteurs, à qui j'ai envoyé certains manuscrits en ont bien voulu témoigner leur approbation — mais à présent j'ai la vue trop faible pour écrire — si j'écrivais beaucoup je deviendrais aveugle. Cette faiblesse de vue est pour moi une terrible privation — sans cela savez-vous ce que je ferais Monsieur? — j'écrirais un livre et je le dédierais à mon maitre de litérature — au seul maitre que j'ai jamais eu — à vous Monsieur. Je vous ai souvent dit en français combien je vous respecte — combien je suis redevable à votre bonté, à vos conseils, je voudrais le dire une fois en Anglais — Cela ne se peut pas — il ne faut pas y penser — la carrière de lettres m'est fermée — celle de l'instruction seule m'est ouverte — elle n'offre pas les mêmes attraits — c'est égal, j'y entrerai et si je n'y vais pas loin ce ne sera pas [par] manque de diligence. Vous aussi Monsieur — vous avez voulu être avocat — le sort ou la Providence vous a fait professeur — vous êtes heureux malgré cela.

Veuillez présenter à Madame l'assurance de mon estime — je crains que Marie — Louise — Claire ne m'aient déjà oubliée. Prospère et Victorine ne m'ont jamais bien connue — moi je me souviens bien de tous les cinq — surtout de Louise — elle avait tant de caractère — tant de naïveté tant de *vérité* dans sa petite figure. — Adieu Monsieur — Votre élève reconnaissante,

C. Brontë

Je ne vous ai pas prié de m'écrire bientôt, puisque je crains de vous impor-
tuner — mais vous êtes trop bon pour oublier que je le désire tout de même
— oui — je le désire beaucoup — c'est assez — après tout — faites comme
vous voudrez Monsieur — si, enfin je recevais une lettre et si je croyais que
vous l'aviez écrite *par pitié* — celà me ferait beaucoup de mal.

Il parait que Mde Wheelwright va à Paris avant d'aller à Bruxelles — mais
elle mettra ma lettre à la poste à Boulogne — encore une fois adieu monsieur celà fait mal de dire adieu même dans une lettre — Oh c'est certain que
je vous reverrai un jour — il le faut bien — puisque aussitôt que j'aurai
gagné assez d'argent pour aller à Bruxelles j'y irai — et je vous reverrai si
ce n'est que pour un instant.

2. LETTER FROM CB TO M. HEGER, 24 OCTOBER 1844: BM

French text of letter translated on pp. 274–5

Monsieur —
Je suis toute joyeuse ce matin, ce qui ne m'arrive pas souvent depuis deux
ans — c'est parce que un Monsieur de mes connaissances va passer par Bruxelles et qu'il a offert de se charger d'une lettre pour vous — laquelle lettre
il vous remettra luimême, ou bien, sa sœur, de sorte que je serai certaine que
vous l'avez reçue.
Ce n'est pas une longue lettre que je vais écrire — d'abord je n'ai pas le
temps — il faut que celà parte de suite et ensuite je crains de vous ennuyer.
Je voudrais seulement vous demander, si vous avez reçu de mes nouvelles au
commencement du mois de Mai et puis au mois d'Aout? Voila six mois que
j'attends une lettre de Monsieur — six mois d'attente c'est bien long, cela!
Pourtant je ne me plains pas et je serai richement récompensée pour un peu
de chagrin — si vous voulez maintenant écrire une lettre et la donner à ce
monsieur — ou à sa sœur qui me la remettrait sans faute.
Quelque courte que soit la lettre j'en serai satisfaite — n'oubliez pas seulement de me dire comment vous vous portez Monsieur et comment Madame
et les enfants se portent et les maîtresses et les élèves.
Mon père et ma sœur vous présentent leurs respects — l'infirmité de mon
père augmente peu à peu — cependant il n'est pas encore tout à fait aveugle
— mes sœurs se portent bien mais mon pauvre frère est toujours malade.
Adieu Monsieur, je compte bientôt avoir de vos nouvelles — cette idée
me sourit car le souvenir de vos bontés ne s'effacera jamais de ma mémoire et
tant que ce souvenir durera le respect qu'il m'a inspiré durera aussi. —

Votre élève très devouée

C. Brontë.

Je viens de faire relier tous les livres que vous m'avez donnés quand j'étais à Bruxelles; j'ai un plaisir à les considérer — cela fait tout une petite bibliothèque — Il y a d'abord les ouvrages complets de Bernardin St. Pierre — [*sic*] Les Pensées de Pascal — un livre de poésie, deux livres allemands — et (ce qui vaut tout le reste) deux discours de Monsieur le Professeur Heger — prononcés à la distribution des Prix de l'Athénée royal —

3. LETTER FROM CB TO M. HEGER, 8 JANUARY 1845: BM

French text of letter translated on p. 278

Mr. Taylor est revenu, je lui ai demandé s'il n'avait pas une lettre pour moi — «Non, rien.» «Patience» — dis-je — «sa sœur viendra bientôt» — Mademoiselle Taylor est revenue. «Je n'ai rien pour vous de la part de Monsieur Heger» dit-elle «ni lettre ni message.»

Ayant bien compris ces mots — je me suis dit, ce que je dirais à un autre en pareille circonstance. «Il faut vous résigner et, surtout, ne pas vous affliger d'un malheur que vous n'avez pas mérité. Je me suis efforcée à ne pas pleurer à ne pas me plaindre —

Mais quand on ne se plaint pas et qu'on veut se dominer en tyran — les facultés se révoltent — et on paie le calme extérieur par une lutte intérieure presque insupportable [.]

Jour et nuit je ne trouve ni repos ni paix — si je dors je fais des rêves tourmentants où je vous vois toujours sévère, toujours sombre et irrité contre moi —

Pardonnez-moi donc Monsieur si je prends la partie de vous écrire encore — Comment puis-je supporter la vie si je ne fais pas un effort pour en alléger les souffrances?

Je sais que vous serez impatienté quand vous lirez cette lettre — Vous direz encore que je suis exaltée — que j'ai des pensées noires &c. Soit Monsieur — je ne cherche pas à me justifier, je me soumets à toutes sortes de reproches — tout ce que je sais — c'est que je ne puis pas — que je ne veux pas me résigner à perdre entièrement l'amitié de mon maître — j'aime mieux subir les plus grandes douleurs physiques que d'avoir toujours le cœur lacéré par des regrets cuisants. Si mon maître me retire entièrement son amitié je serai tout à fait sans espoir — s'il m'en donne un peu — très peu — je serai contente — heureuse, j'aurai un motif pour vivre — pour travailler.

Monsieur, les pauvres n'ont pas besoin de grand'chose pour vivre — ils ne demandent que ces miettes de pain qui tombent de la table des riches — mais si on les refuse ces miettes de pain — ils meurent de faim — Moi non plus je n'ai pas besoin de beaucoup d'affection de la part de ceux que j'aime je ne saurais que faire d'une amitié entière et complète — je n'y suis pas habitueé

— mais vous me témoigniez, autrefois, *un peu* d'intérêt quand j'étais votre élève à Bruxelles — et je tiens à conserver ce *peu* d'intérêt — j'y tiens comme je tiendrais à la vie.

Vous me direz peutêtre — Je ne vous porte plus le moindre intérêt Mademoiselle Charlotte — vous n'êtes plus de ma Maison — je vous ai oubliée.

Eh bien Monsieur dites moi cela franchement — ce sera pour moi un choc — n'importe ce sera toujours moins hideux que l'incertitude.

Je ne veux pas relire cette lettre — je l'envoie comme je l'ai écrite — Pourtant, j'ai comme la conscience obscure qu'il y a des personnes froides et sensées qui diraient en la lisant — «elle déraisonne» — Pour toute vengeance — je souhaite à ces personnes — un seul jour des tourments que — [a portion of paper is covered by a fragment torn from another part] j'ai subis depuis huit mois — on verrait alors s'elles [ne] déraisonneraient pas de même.

On souffre en silence tant qu'on en a la force et quand cette force manque on parle sans trop mesurer ses paroles.

Je souhaite à Monsieur le bonheur et la prospérité.

C. B.

4. LETTER FROM CB TO M. HEGER, 18 NOVEMBER 1845: BM

French text of letter translated on pp. 291–2

Monsieur,

Les six mois de silence sont écoulés; nous sommes aujourd'hui au 18 Novbre, ma dernière lettre était datée (je crois) le 18 mai, je puis donc vous écrire, sans manquer à ma promesse.

L'été et l'automne m'ont paru bien longs; à vrai dire il m'a fallu des efforts pénibles pour supporter jusqu'à present la privation que je me suis imposée: vous ne pouvez pas concevoir cela, vous, Monsieur, mais imaginez vous, pour un instant, qu'un de vos enfants est séparé de vous de 160 lieues de distance et que vous devez rester six mois sans lui écrire, sans recevoir de ses nouvelles, sans en entendre parler; sans savoir comment il se porte, alors vous comprendrez facilement tout ce qu'il y a de dure dans une pareille obligation. Je vous dirai franchement, qu'en attendant, j'ai tâché de vous oublier, car le souvenir d'une personne que l'on croit ne devoir plus revoir et que, pourtant, on estime beaucoup, harasse trop l'esprit et quand on a subi cette espèce d'inquiétude pendant un ou deux ans, on est prêt à tout faire pour retrouver le repos. J'ai tout fait, j'ai cherché les occupations, je me suis interdit absolument le plaisir de parler de vous — même à Emilie mais je n'ai pu vaincre ni mes regrets ni mon impatience — c'est humiliant cela — de ne pas savoir maîtriser ses propres pensées, être esclave à un regret, un souvenir, esclave à une idée dominante et fixe qui tyrannise son esprit. Que ne puis-je avoir pour vous juste autant d'amitié que vous avez pour moi — ni plus ni moins? Je serais alors si tranquille, si libre — je pourrais garder le silence pendant six ans sans effort.

Mon père se porte bien mais sa vue est presque éteinte, il ne sait plus ni lire ni écrire; c'est, pourtant, l'avis des médecins d'attendre encore quelques mois avant de tenter une opération — l'hiver ne sera pour lui qu'une longue nuit — il se plaint rarement, j'admire sa patience — Si la Providence me destine la même calamité — puisse-t-elle au moins m'accorder autant de patience pour la supporter! Il me semble, monsieur, que ce qu'il y a de plus amère dans les grands malheurs physiques c'est d'être forcé à faire partager nos souffrances à tous ceux qui nous entourent; on peut cacher les maladies de l'âme mais celles qui attaquent le corps et détruisent les facultés, ne se cachent pas. Mon père me permet maintenant de lui lire et d'écrire pour lui, il me témoigne aussi plus de confiance qu'il ne m'en a jamais témoignée, ce qui est une grande consolation.

Monsieur, j'ai une grâce à vous demander: quand vous répondrez à cette lettre, parlez-moi un peu de vous-même pas de moi, car, je sais, que si vous me parlez de moi ce sera pour me gronder et, cette fois, je voudrais voir votre aspect bienveillant; parlez-moi donc de vos enfants; jamais vous n'aviez le front sévère quand Louise et Claire et Prosper étaient près de vous. Dîtes-moi aussi quelque chose du Pensionnat, des élèves, des Maîtresses — Mesdemoiselles Blanche, Sophie et Justine restent-elles toujours à Bruxelles? Dites-moi où vous avez voyagé pendant les vacances — n'avez vous pas été sur les bords du Rhin? N'avez-vous pas visité Cologne ou Coblentz? Dites-moi enfin ce que vous voulez mon maître mais dites-moi quelque chose. Écrire à une ci-devant sous-maîtresse (non — je ne veux pas me souvenir de mon emploi de sous-maîtresse je le renie) mais enfin, écrire à une ancienne élève ne peut-être une occupation fort intéressante pour vous — je le sais — mais pour moi c'est la vie. Votre dernière lettre m'a servi de soutiens — de nourriture pendant six mois — à present il m'en faut une autre et vous me la donnerez — pas parceque vous avez pour moi de l'amitié — vous ne pouvez en avoir beaucoup — mais parceque vous avez l'âme compâtissante et que vous ne condamneriez personne à de longues souffrances pour vous épargner quelques moments d'ennui. Me défendre à vous écrire, refuser de me répondre ce sera de m'arracher la seule joie que j'ai au monde, me priver de mon dernier privilège — privilège auquel je ne consentirai jamais à renoncer volontairement. Croyez-moi mon maître, en m'écrivant vous faites un bon [*sic*] œuvre — tant que je vous crois assez content de moi, tant que j'ai l'espoir de recevoir de vos nouvelles je puis être tranquille et pas trop triste mais quand un silence morne et prolongé semble m'avertir de l'éloignement de mon maître à mon égard — quand de jour en jour j'attends une lettre et que de jour en jour le désappointement vient me rejeter dans un douloureux accablement et que cette douce joie de voir votre écriture, de lire vos conseils me fuit comme une vaine vision, alors, j'ai la fièvre — je perds l'appétit et le sommeil — je dépéris.

Puis-je vous écrire encore au mois de Mai prochain ? j'aurai voulu attendre une année — mais c'est impossible — c'est trop long.

C. Brontë

I must say one word to you in English—I wish I could write to you more cheerful letters, for when I read this over, I find it to be somewhat gloomy—but forgive me my dear master—do not be irritated at my sadness—according to the words of the Bible: 'Out of the fulness of the heart, the mouth speaketh' and truly I find it difficult to be cheerful so long as I think I shall never see you more. You will perceive by the defects in this letter that I am forgetting the French language—yet I read all the French books I can get, and learn daily a portion by heart—but I have never heard French spoken but once since I left Brussels—and then it sounded like music in my ears—every word was most precious to me because it reminded me of you—I love French for your sake with all my heart and soul.

Farewell my dear Master—may God protect you with special care and crown you with peculiar blessings.

C. B.

Haworth, Bradford, Yorkshire.

French text of letter translated on p. 253

Ma Chère Charlotte,

Veuillez me faire le plaisir d'accepter cette petite boite en souvenir de moi. J'ai trop bonne opinion de votre cœur, pour oser supposer qu'il vous faille la vue d'un objet quelconque pour me rappeler à votre doux souvenir; non, je suis convaincue que l'amitié que vous m'avez toujours témoignée, a sa source dans les plus nobles sentiments. Néanmoins, vous me feriez de la peine si vous refusiez de me donner encore cette marque de votre affection. Adieu, ma bonne Charlotte; j'aime à croire que je ne vous perdrai pas entièrement dans 15 jours et que vous daignerez encore de temps en temps, lorsque vous aurez revu le sol natal, tourner votre pensée vers la triste Belgique, où plus d'une personne pensera à vous.

Tout à vous,
Votre amie Sophie

Bruxelles, le 17 Décembre 1843.

French text of letter translated on p. 208

Letter of Louise de Bassompierre:

Miss Emily était beaucoup moins brillante que sa sœur mais bien plus sympathique. Elle voulait se perfectionner dans l'étude du dessin et y avait acquis un véritable talent. Elle m'a donné un joli paysage signé de son nom et que je garde avec soin.

Letter of Baronne Willmar:

French text of letter translated on p. 216

Madame Heger, une femme d'élite, vraiment pieuse, mais de cette dévotion qui ne blesse pas, au contraire. Je l'ai vue obliger et soulager bien des infortunés, sa physiognomie semble refléter un rayon de bonheur autour des personnes qui l'approchent.

French text of letter translated on pp. 271–2

Letter to CB from 'Mathilde', undated

Ma chère Demoiselle,

Si je l'avais pu, il y avait longtemps que j'aurais profité de l'adresse que vous m'avez donnée et dont l'envoi m'a fait tant de plaisir.

En pension le mois d'août approchant, nous avons plus d'ouvrage que de coutume, mais ce ne serait rien si je n'avais encore des maîtres à la maison, et de plus l'obligation d'étudier mon piano de toutes mes forces, car par les maladies un grand déficit se trouve dans nos pianistes, et il a bien fallu, faute de mieux, me prendre pour jouer à la fête de Madame. Je ne sais comment je m'en tirerai; pour mon malheur malgré toute ma bonne volonté, l'idée que quelqu'un m'écoute ou me regarde suffit pour me faire perdre la tête et je crains bien que ce début ne soit pas heureux. Cependant, je désire de tout mon cœur réussir; une de mes cousines, qui a eu les plus grands malheurs, est maintenant ma maîtresse de piano elle a beaucoup d'élèves chez Mme Heger mais dans le pays des aveugles les borgnes sont rois, et par conséquent je suis la meilleure de toutes. Nous chérissons notre bonne maitresse comme elle le mérite, bien réellement et c'est beaucoup — Vous sentez combien je puis lui faire de peine et de tort en ne répondant pas à son attente. Allons, il faut prendre courage et espérer que Dieu me protégera dans une chose de si peu d'importance en elle-même, mais qui peut avoir des résultats bons ou mauvais pour ma cousine.

Il y a dans votre lettre, Mlle Charlotte, un mot qui m'a fait bien plaisir.
J'ai tort, j'en suis sûre, car peut-être l'avez-vous mis sans y ajouter une
aussi grande signification que moi: vous souvenez-vous m'avoir dit, I shall
not cease to think of you with affection and even with estim [*sic*]. Eh! bien,
ce mot estime vous ne pouvez vouz imaginer combien il m'a fait plaisir je
dirai meme, il m'a rendue heureuse. Il m'avait semblé jusqu'ici que parfois je
pouvais bien espérer aspirer à l'amitié de certaines personnes qui ont mon
estime, mais à l'estime c'est selon moi bien plus que l'amitié, quoique cependant je ne crois pas jusqu'à cette heure, avoir, malgré toutes mes fautes, rien
fait qui puisse me rendre méprisable. Ce mot dit par vous, ma bonne maîtresse,
m'a fait un bien! — tenez, vous ne pouvez vous en faire une idée.

Si vous saviez, il n'y a de celà que bien peu de temps, les pensées noires que
j'avais! J'étais certaine par exemple, que personne ne pouvait jamais m'aimer,
quoique une de mes anciennes compagnes, m'en ait bien désabusée; c'était
de véritables accès de misanthropie, au point que Maman m'a cru malade.
Heureusement, si cela n'a pas entièrement disparu, cela a du moins beaucoup
diminué.

Ma chère demoiselle, permettez-moi de vous gronder, vous ne me donnez
aucune nouvelle de votre santé! J'espère que si vous m'en direz quelques
mots la Ière fois que vous pouvez m'écrire, et pour vous en donner l'exemple,
je vous dit que moi je jouis d'une santé si bonne pour le moment que je
souhaite que vous vous portez de même. Adieu, Mlle Charlotte, adieu, permettez-moi de vous embrasser de cœur, puisque je ne puis même le faire
en perspective.

Votre toute dévouée
Mathilde

Mlle Charlotte, excusez-moi pour cette folie, mais il me semble que lorsque
je vous écris la porte de mon cœur s'ouvre et toujours le temps et le papier
me forcent à le refermer.

ADDITIONAL NOTES

CHAPTER I

p. 4. *Ann Evans*. CB remembered Miss Evans with gratitude and regard and pictured her as 'Miss Temple' in *Jane Eyre*. Like Miss Temple, Miss Evans left school to be married on 6 July 1826 at Tunstall Church, the Revd. W. Carus Wilson officiating. Miss Evans married the Revd. James Connor of Oswestry who later espoused Unitarian tenets and migrated to America. On the publication of Mrs. Gaskell's 'Life' of CB, both husband and wife (returned to England by then) entered into the controversy opened in the press over the account of the Clergy Daughters' School, and gave evidence in favour of the school and its founder. Miss Evans was succeeded as superintendent of the school by Miss—or Mrs.—Harben, a close friend of Carus Wilson. The courtesy title of 'Mrs.' was given her in consideration of the tragic circumstance of her bridegroom having died in church on her wedding day. Mrs. Harben remained at the school until 1843. See: 'Notes on the Clergy Daughters' School' by Miss Williams, 1935. I am indebted for the data concerning the marriages of Miss Evans and of Miss Harben to the Vicars of Tunstall and Casterton churches.

CHAPTER IV

p. 45. *Martin's engravings in the Brontës' home*. The presence of large engravings (41 in. × 27 in.) in a home where luxuries did not abound makes their price of interest: it was £2. 12s. 6d. each. Their success, following the exhibition of the original paintings at the Royal Institute and RBA Galleries between the years 1812–32, was phenomenal. They also enjoyed a brisk export to the Continent, to France and Belgium especially, the result maybe of a strange reversal of fortune that had made Martin the landlord to the once poor and unimportant Leopold of Saxe-Coburg while at Chelsea in 1814, later first King of the Belgians, and Martin's keen patron to the end of his life.

p. 45. *Features of Martin's pictures influencing the Brontë Juvenilia*. Features especially mentioned are: his Tower of Babel (*Young Men's Magazine*, Dec. 1827), his Tower of Babylon (*Young Men's Magazine*, Dec. 1829), his Palace of All Nations (Conversations in Bravey's Inn, *Young Men's Magazine*, Oct. 1830), supposedly painted by Edward De Lisle the Verdopolitan painter, who would appear to represent Martin himself in the Brontë saga. His reputed painting of 'The Four Genii in Council' is patently copied from Martin's illustration for 'Paradise Lost' featuring Satan presiding at the Infernal Council (*Young Men's Magazine*, Dec. 1829).

CHAPTER V

p. 76. For further data on the Roe Head district and CB's friendships formed there see: W. W. Yates, *The Father of the Brontës,*' 1893; J. Erskine Stuart, *The Brontë Country*, 1888; Armitage Goodall, *Spenlandia*, Dewsbury, 1953;

H. Ashwell Cadman, *Gomersal Past & Present*, Leeds, 1930; H. C. Cradock, *History of the Ancient Parish of Birstall*, SPCK, 1933; T. W. Thompson, *The Spen Valley*, Heckmondwike, 1925; 'Pilgrimage to Shirleyland' in *The Reporter* for 31 July 1897; 'Reminiscences of Batley during the last 30 years', *Batley News* (1882), p. 112–13; The Registers of Mirfield and Birstall Churches; The Wooler family graves, and the Nussey family graves in Birstall churchyard.

CHAPTER VI

p. 109. *The letters to Southey and Wordsworth.* How the young Brontës struck their illustrious correspondents is seen from the letter of Southey to Caroline Bowles of Easter Monday, 1837 (*W & S* i. 156), in which he mentions 'the sister' with kindness, and quotes Wordsworth's annoyance at the ill manners of 'the brother' and adduces this for W's not answering him. Nearly twenty years later Mrs. Wordsworth, hearing that Mrs. Gaskell was then engaged in collecting material for her 'Life' of CB, sent her Branwell's letter. Wordsworth had died in 1850. (See *W & S* iv. 209, Mrs. Gaskell to Emily Shaen, 8 Sept. 1856.)

CHAPTER XI

p. 163. *Charlotte's reply to Mr. Weightman's valentine.* In the *Whitehaven News* for 17 Feb. 1876 appeared the following: *A Valentine*. An Appleby correspondent sends the following: A perusal of the under-written valentine may, at this season, prove interesting to some of your readers. Thirty-six years ago the verses were written by the celebrated authoress whose name appears at the foot of them, and addressed to a clergyman, a native of Appleby, and educated at the Appleby Grammar School, who was then officiating in the West Riding of Yorkshire. The original is now in my possession and is signed by the authoress and three of her friends [*sic*] and relatives.

> A Roland for your Oliver
> We think you've justly earned;
> You sent us each a valentine
> Your gift is now returned.
>
> We cannot write or talk like you;
> We're plain folks every one;
> You've played a clever jest on us,
> We thank you for your fun.
>
> Believe us when we frankly say
> (Our words though blunt are true)
> At home, abroad, by night or day
> We all wish well to you.
>
> And never may a cloud come o'er
> The sunshine of your mind;
> Kind friends, warm hearts, and happy hours
> Through life we trust you'll find.

Where'er you go, however far,
In future years you stray,
There shall not want our earnest prayer
To speed you on your way.

A stranger and a pilgrim here,
We know you sojourn now;
But brighter hopes, with brighter wreaths
Are doomed to bind your brow.

Not always in these lonely hills
Your humble lot shall lie,
The oracle of fate foretells
A worthier destiny.

And though her words are veiled in gloom
Though clouded her decree,
Yet doubt not that a juster doom
She keeps in store for thee.

Then cast hope's anchor near the shore,
'Twill hold your vessel fast,
And fear not for the tide's deep roar,
And dread not for the blast.

For though this station now seems drear,
'Mid land-locked creeks to be,
The helmsman soon his ship shall steer
Out to the wide blue sea.

Well officered and staunchly manned,
Well built to meet the blast;
With favouring winds the bark must land
On glorious shores at last.

                                                    Charlotte Brontë
February 1840

The correspondent who sent this poem was a Mr. A. H. Saltaire.

It is notable that Mrs. Gaskell made no mention of Mr. Weightman in her 'Life' of CB other than as one of Mr. Brontë's curates designated by an initial only and confounded with the other curates figuring in *Shirley*. Mr. Weightman is not among these, and Mrs. Gaskell, who had seen all CB's letters to EN, must have been aware of his intimacy in the domestic circle. The suppression of this friendship can only be interpreted as a wish not to add to the number of CB's male friends, of which her reference to the proposal of James Taylor (Gaskell 331) is symptomatic. Towards Branwell the suppression was unfair, since Branwell tended his dying friend with devotion and sincerely mourned him. See his letter to Grundy of 25 Oct. 1842. SLL I 242–3.

CHAPTER XIII

p. 196. *Charlotte's French* devoirs. The titles of some that have been presented by the Heger family are: 16 Mar. 1842, L'Ingratitude; 18 Apr. 1842, La Jeune Fille

Malade; 31 May 1842, La Mort de Napoléon; 31 July 1842, Portrait de Pierre l'Hermite; 11 Aug. 1842, La Chenille; 6 Oct. 1842, La Justice Humaine; 16 Oct. 1842, La Palais de la Mort; 30 Mar. 1843, La Chute des Feuilles; 27 July 1843, La Mort de Moïse; 6 Oct. 1843, Athènes Sauvée par la Poésie.

CHAPTER XIV

p. 262. *The letters of M. Heger to Meta Mossman.* The original of these and several other letters addressed by M. and Mme Heger to two generations of pupils in the family have been generously lent me by Walter Cunliffe Esq.

CHAPTER XVIII

p. 336. *Newby's defence.* On 30 Nov. 1859 George Eliot had occasion to write to *The Times* to complain of the publication by Newby of an anonymous work *Adam Bede, Junior*, the wording of whose advertisement might lead readers to suppose it to be a sequel to her own book. '. . . I am not the first writer', said George Eliot, 'who has had to suffer from this publisher's method of trading. The readers of Currer Bell's life will remember a very unpleasant illustration of it.' On 5 Dec. Newby replied in *The Times*: 'I published the novels of Ellis and Acton Bell. No disagreement ever took place between those ladies and me, and long after the publication of *Jane Eyre* Miss Anne Brontë [*sic*] brought me a work *The Tenant of Wildfell Hall* which I published in due course. If George Eliot had confined himself to describing truly the terms of my announcement of *Adam Bede, Junior, a Sequel*, he would neither have required to trouble you with a protest against what never happened, nor to reproduce a most palpable misrepresentation levelled at a publisher whose name the author of Miss Brontë's "Life" declined to give, but whom "George Eliot" for the first time identifies with me. . . .' (*The George Eliot Letters*, ed. Haight, iii. 220 n.)

CHAPTER XIX

p. 347. *Miss Rigby and the authorship of* Jane Eyre. '. . . various rumours, more or less romantic, have been current in Mayfair', wrote Miss Rigby, '. . . as to the authorship of *Jane Eyre*. For example, *Jane Eyre* is sentimentally assumed to have proceeded from the pen of Mr. Thackeray's governess, whom he had himself chosen as his model of Becky, and who, in mingled love and revenge, personified him in return as Mr. Rochester. In this case, it is evident that the author of *Vanity Fair*, whose pencil makes him grey-haired, has had the best of it, though his children may have had the worst having, at all events, succeeded in hitting that "vulnerable" point in the Becky bosom, which it is our firm belief no man born of woman, from her Soho to her Ostend days, had ever so much as grazed. To this ingenious rumour the coincidences of the 2nd edition of *Jane Eyre* being dedicated to Mr. Thackeray has probably given rise. . . .' (*Quarterly Review*, Dec. 1848, 174–5.)

p. 366. *The Brontës at Covent Garden.* It has been stated (Ada Harrison, *Anne Brontë: her Life & Work*, Methuen, 1959) that Jenny Lind sang in the Barber of

Seville at the performance attended by CB and AB. I am informed by the Historical Records Dept. of the Opera House that Jenny Lind did not come to England at all that summer (1848) and that, moreover, she never sang at Covent Garden, always at the Haymarket, during her London engagements.

Notices of the performance appearing in the papers of the day gave the cast as follows:

Rosina	Mde Persiani
Bertha	Mde Bellini
Almaviva	Signor Salvi
Figaro	Signor Tamburini
Bartolo	Signor Revere
Basilio	Signor Tagliafico
Fiovello	Signor Soldi

Conductor: Mr. Costa

The performance was scheduled to commence at 8 o'clock, and was to be followed by a scene from the opera of Betly, with Madame Alboni and the ballet 'La Rosiera' with Mlle Robert.

CHAPTER XXI

p. 404. *The Wheelwright family.* In 1857 the family moved to 2 Campden Grove, where Dr. Wheelwright died on 12 Aug. 1861. Together with his wife, his three daughters Laetitia, Frances, and Sarah, and his son William, he was buried in Old Brompton Cemetery where the family graves are still in good preservation. For those people who wish to search them out, they are: 27892/112175/171110/ 171860/152936/163798. Emily was the only daughter to marry; her husband was Daniel Perry Poulter. Her daughter married a Mr. J. J. Green of Godwyn Lodge, Clive Vale, Hastings, and it was there that her aunt Frances died in Mar. 1913 (buried at Brompton as stated above). Laetitia died in 1911. Before then the sisters lived together after their mother's death at 17 Ladbroke Grove, where Clement Shorter visited them in 1896.

CHAPTER XXII

p. 429. *CB at Newman's lectures.* Coinciding with C's visit to London that summer was a series of lectures given by 'Father' John Henry Newman, several of which she attended. Their subject was 'The Difficulties of Anglicans', delivered twice weekly on Thursdays and Fridays at the Oratory Church, King William St., Strand, beginning 9 May. The object of the lectures delivered by the brilliant convert only returned to England three years before and filled with fresh missionary zeal, was to carry along with him his former associates in the Tractarian Movement who had stopped short of taking the final step towards Rome. Starting from their common disillusionment with the Church of England, which he described as without antecedents in the Churches of other lands, and no more than a Government department, he called on his listeners to by-pass the High Church compromise, and go straight back to Rome. With his charm, his wit, his dialectics, he made an immense impact on his hearers, as the cartoons of Punch attest; conversions followed in numbers, the sanguine Cardinal Wiseman forecast the general return of England within the fold. Such a wave of feeling provoked the inevitable reaction; by the following November the Guy Fawkes celebrations were marked by scenes of violence and the burning in effigy of the Pope and Cardinal Wiseman. Only the politic action of the Cardinal in writing to the entire press on 23 Nov., steadied public opinion and won him respect. Amidst the heated arguments of the day, Charlotte Brontë was, as usual on religious questions, remarkable for the sobriety of her views. This Mrs. Gaskell noted on their first meeting at Windermere that summer. On 25 August she wrote to Catherine Winkworth of their talks together and of Charlotte's account of Newman's lectures given 'in a very quiet, concise, graphic way . . .' (*W & S* iii. 142). Charlotte commented further to George Lewes on 23 Nov. on Cardinal Wiseman's letter to the press (*W & S* iii. 183), showing how the subject had quickened her interest. This was not merely on her father's account (for whom she acted as a purveyor of news) but obviously on her own; the experience of Brussels had left, for all the bias, a lasting fascination with the theme.

CHAPTER XXIII

p. 448. *The reports on CB's ill health.* Mrs. Gaskell's first impressions of CB's ill health were responsible for the view held in society and in literary circles that she was chronically ill; a view she sought on many occasions to combat. Mrs. Gaskell wrote on first meeting her: '. . . There seems little doubt that she herself is already tainted with consumption. . . .' See letter to C. Winkworth, 25 Aug. 1850.

Catherine Winkworth forwarded Mrs. Gaskell's letter to her sister Emily, who commented: 'Crix, August 30th 1850. Thanks for Mrs. Gaskell's. Poor Miss Brontë, I cannot get the look of the grey, square, cold, dead-coloured house out of my head. She has friends though now, surely? I wonder whether she has any unmarried ones; people who could go and look after her a little if she were ill. Oh dear, if the single sisters in this world were but banded together a little so that they could help each other out as well as other people. . . . One feels that her life at least *almost* makes one like her books, though one does not want there to be any more Miss Brontës. . . .' (*W & S* iii. 151).

CHAPTER XXVI

p. 520. *The Pirated French edition of* Villette. The actual copy, 3 vols in 8vo, read by Mme Heger and preserved by her granddaughter, Mme Beckers-Heger, was placed in my hand when the latter so kindly received me at her home in Ucclelez-Bruxelles in Sept. 1962. The book's imprint reads:

La Maîtresse d'Anglais

ou

Le Pensionnat de Bruxelles

par

Currer Bell (Charlotte Brontë)

Bruxelles et Leipzig
Kiessling, Schnee et Cie Editeurs
Rue Villa-Hermosa 8
1855

p. 521. *CB and Harriet Martineau.* HM's review of *Villette* in the *Daily News*, 3 Feb. 1853, contained many eulogies of the work and of its author ('she can touch nothing without leaving on it the stamp of originality . . .') but attacked its sentiment and moral atmosphere. '. . . An atmosphere of pain hangs about the whole, forbidding that repose which we hold to be essential to the true present-ment of any large portion of life and experience. In this pervading pain the book reminds us of Balzac and so it does in the prevalence of one tendency, or one idea, throughout the whole conception and action. All the female characters, in all their thoughts and lives, are full of one thing, or are regarded by the reader in the light of that one thought—love. It begins with the child of six years old . . . a charming picture—and it closes with it at the last page; and, so dominant is this idea—so incessant is the writer's tendency to describe the need of being loved, that the heroine, who tells her own story, leaves the reader at last under the un-comfortable impression of her having either entertained a double love, or allowed one to supersede another without notification of the transition. It is not thus in real life. There are substantial, heartfelt interests for women of all ages, and under ordinary circumstances, quite apart from love. . . .'

p. 523. *Thackeray's comments on* Villette. His further comments are contained in five letters written from America, dated 8, 11, 25–28 Mar., 4, 5 Apr. 1853. As with *Jane Eyre* he was impressed by the writing: '. . . the book is like a fine Dutch picture the painting is as minute and delicate' (8 Mar. to Mrs. Proctor). '. . . The good of *Villette* in my opinion . . . is a very fine style; and a remarkable happy way (which few female authors possess) of carrying a metaphor logically through to its conclusion. . . .' '. . . That's a plaguy book that *Villette* [4 Apr. to Mrs. Proctor]. How clever it is! and how I don't like the heroine. . . .' What he disliked was what he called its 'vulgar' subject. '. . . I don't make my *good* women ready to fall in love with two men at once; and Miss Brontë would be the first to be angry and cry fie on me if I did . . .' (25–28 Mar. 1853 to Mrs. Carmichael Smyth): *Letters & Private Papers,* op. cit.

CHAPTER XXVII

pp. 542 and 567. *Arthur Nicholls.* Old Haworth inhabitants still remembered up to the First World War the religious instruction given by Mr. Nicholls in the National School, and certain traits of his kindness. He was always accompanied by Mr. Brontë's dog 'Plato', and it was a regular recompense to attentive scholars to get a ride on his back across 'Parson's Fields' after school hours. (See *BST* 1942. Also: 'Whiteley Turner', 'A Springtime Saunter' p. 212.) In Jan. 1962 there died at Haworth an old lady of 94, Mrs. Eleanor Stanton (niece of Martha Brown and daughter of Tabitha Brown) whom I knew very well, and who remembered with vivid admiration and gratitude Mr. Nicholls's kindness to her aunt. She charged me with energy to 'speak fair of Mr. Nicholls' if I wrote of him, for he was 'a right gentleman'.

p. 567. *Charlotte's memorial.* The old Brontë family tablet carrying the names of Mrs. Brontë, her four daughters, and Branwell, was so crowded by the time

Charlotte died, that a separate one was placed in the wall beside it to her memory; it read:

ADJOINING LIE THE REMAINS OF

CHARLOTTE, WIFE

OF THE

REV. ARTHUR BELL NICHOLLS, A.B. INCUMBENT.

AND DAUGHTER OF THE REV. P. BRONTË, A. B. INCUMBENT.

SHE DIED MARCH 31ST, 1855, in the 39th

Year of her age.

On the death of Mr. Brontë, 7 June 1861, both tablets were removed and, by order of Mr. Nicholls—who dreaded the souvenir hunters—broken up and the pieces buried in the Parsonage garden, and a new and comprehensive tablet to the memory of the whole family erected in their place.

SOURCES OF EVIDENCE

I. ORIGINAL DOCUMENTS

The letters, juvenile and adolescent MSS. of Charlotte Brontë preserved in the following centres: Brontë Parsonage Museum, Haworth; British Museum; Manchester University Library; Leeds University Library; Fitzwilliam Museum Library, Cambridge; Berg Collection, New York Public Library; Harry Elkins Widener Memorial Library, Harvard University, Cambridge, Mass.; Wrenn Library, Texas University; Henry Huntington Library, San Marino, California; J. Pierpont Morgan Library, New York City; the Bonnell Collection, Philadelphia.

The letters, juvenile and adolescent writings of Branwell Brontë preserved in the following centres: Brontë Parsonage Museum, Haworth; British Museum; Brotherton Library, University of Leeds.

The letters, diary-papers, and poems of Emily Jane and Anne Brontë, preserved at the Brontë Parsonage Museum, Haworth; British Museum; and the above-mentioned American collections.

The diaries of Elizabeth Firth 1812–25 and 1829, Sheffield University Library.

The autograph letters of M. and Mme Heger to Kate and Marion Douglas and Meta Mossman, by courtesy of Walter Cunliffe Esq., of Uckfield, Sussex.

The autograph letters of M. Heger to the Comte de Villermont 1863–6, by courtesy of the Comte de Villermont.

Autograph letters of the Dixon family, Leeds City Museum; by courtesy of Miss Maidie Rathbone, Ashford, Kent.

II. OFFICIAL DOCUMENTS

Registers, ledgers, and record books of the Clergy Daughters' School, Casterton, Westmorland.

Matriculation records of Trinity College, Dublin.

Extracts of the Diocese of Ripon Act Books.

Registers of births, deaths, marriages of the following churches: St. Michael and All Angels, Haworth; Tunstall Church, Lancs.; Casterton Church, Westmorland; Mirfield, Kildwick, Lothersdale, Birstall Parish churches, Yorkshire; St. Lawrence's, Appleby, Westmorland; the Wesleyan registers of the Keighley Round, 1798–1825; St. Paul's, Banagher, Co. Offaly, Ireland.

The Manor Rolls of Batley, Yorkshire.

Pedigree of the Greenwood family of Swarcliffe; pedigree of the Sidgwick and Benson families of Skipton and Stonegappe; Report on the State of Children Employed in Manufacture 1816; Minutes of the Manchester–Leeds Railway Co., Historic Records Dept., BTC, London, W. 2; Archives of the Town of Brussels; Police Register of Foreign Residents; Records of the Athénée Royal of Brussels; Kensington Borough Rate Books.

III. PUBLISHED DOCUMENTS

Contemporary newspapers preserved in the British Museum Newspaper Library; Belgian Newspaper Files, Bibliothèque Royale, Brussels; Whitehaven Reference Library; Keighley Reference Library; County Library, Bridlington;

County Library, Beverley; Enthoven Theatre Collection, Dept. of Prints and Drawings, V. and A. Museum, South Kensington; Catalogue of the Sale of Household Effects at the Parsonage, Haworth, 1 Oct. 1861, BPM; Catalogue of the Gaskell Sale, 9 Feb. 1914, Manchester Central Library; Catalogue of the Library of Ponden House, Cartwright Memorial Hall, Bradford; text of the Funeral Sermon for the late Revd. William Weightman, M.A., preached by the Revd. P. Brontë 2 Oct. 1842, printed Halifax, 1842.

IV. TOPOGRAPHICAL AND LOCAL INFORMATION

Derived on the spot at the following places connected with CB (see also Acknowledgements): Casterton School, Westmorland, by courtesy of the Headmistress; Brontë Cottages, Cowan Bridge, Lancs., the original site of the Clergy Daughters' School; Mr. Brontë's home at Hightown, Hartshead; Roe Head (by courtesy of the Father Superior, Verona Fathers); Rydings, Brookroyd (Birstall), Ellen Nussey's homes; The Red House, Gomersal; Oakwell Hall, Birstall; Heald's House, Dewsbury Moor; The Green House, Stocks Bank Road, Mirfield; Lascelles Hall, Huddersfield; Stonegappe, Lothersdale; Swarcliffe Hall, Harrogate; Bridlington, Scarborough, Filey, and the houses there connected with CB. For the varied sources of evidence pursued at Brussels, see detailed notes for Chapters XIII, XIV, XV.

V. WORKS BY THE BRONTËS: PUBLISHED TEXTS

Poems by Currer, Ellis and Acton Bell. Aylott & Jones, London, 1846.
Jane Eyre; An Autobiography, by Currer Bell. Smith, Elder, London, 1847.
Wuthering Heights and *Agnes Grey,* by Ellis and Acton Bell, 3 vols. T. C. Newby, London, 1847.
The Tenant of Wildfell Hall, by Acton Bell, 3 vols. T. C. Newby, London, 1848.
Shirley, by Currer Bell, 3 vols. Smith, Elder, London, 1849.
Wuthering Heights, Agnes Grey, together with a selection of Poems by Ellis and Acton Bell. Prefixed with a Biographical Memoir of the authors by Currer Bell. Smith, Elder, London, 1850.
Villette, by Currer Bell, 3 vols. Smith, Elder, London, 1853.
The Professor, by Currer Bell, 2 vols. Smith, Elder, London, 1857.
Emma: A Fragment, by Currer Bell with Introduction by W. M. Thackeray, *Cornhill Magazine,* vol. i. 1860.
And the Weary are at Rest, by Branwell Brontë. Privately printed, 1924.
The Odes of Horace. Book I translated by Branwell Brontë, edited by John Drinkwater. Privately printed, 1923.
The Poems of Charlotte Brontë and Patrick Branwell Brontë, edited by T. J. Wise and J. A. Symington, 1 vol. Oxford, 1934.
The Complete Poems of Emily Jane and Anne Brontë, ed. idem.
The Complete Poems of Emily Jane Brontë, ed. by C. W. Hatfield, Oxford, 1941.
The Miscellaneous and Unpublished Writings of Charlotte and Patrick Branwell Brontë, ed. by T. J. Wise and J. A. Symington, 2 vols. Oxford, 1934.
The Brontës: their Lives, Friendships and Correspondence, ed. by T. J. Wise and J. A. Symington, 4 vols. Oxford, 1932.

The Twelve Adventurers and Other Stories, by Charlotte Brontë, ed. by C. W. Hatfield. Hodder, 1925.
The Spell, by Charlotte Brontë, ed. G. E. MacLean. O.U.P., 1931.
Tales from Angria, by Charlotte Brontë, ed. Phyllis Bentley. Collins, 1954.

VI. UNPUBLISHED TEXTS

'Charlotte Brontë's Roe Head Journals': Bonnell Collection, BPM.
'Caroline Vernon', July 1839: Harvard.
'Henry Hastings', Mar. 1839: Harvard.
'Mina Laury', Apr. 1836–Jan. 1838. Harvard.
'Julia', June 1837: Wrenn Library, Texas.

VII. WORKS ON THE BRONTËS: IN ORDER
OF PUBLICATION

1857 Gaskell, E. C., *The Life of Charlotte Brontë*, 3 vols. Smith, Elder.
1871 Nussey, Ellen, 'Reminiscences of Charlotte Brontë', *Scribner's Magazine*, May. (Reprinted in *BST*, 1899.)
1877 Wemyss-Reid, T., *Charlotte Brontë, A Monograph*. Macmillan.
1879 Grundy, F. H., *Pictures of the Past*. London, Griffith & Farrar.
1883 Duclaux, Mary (Robinson), *Emily Brontë, a Memoir*, English Women of Letters Series. London.
1886 Leyland, F. A., *The Brontë Family with Special Reference to Patrick Branwell Brontë*. London.
1887 Birrell, A., *Life of Charlotte Brontë*. London.
1894 Macdonald, Frederika; 'The Brontës in Brussels', *Woman at Home*, July.
1896 Shorter, C. K. *Charlotte Brontë and her Circle*. Hodder.
1905 — *Charlotte Brontë and her Sisters*. Hodder.
1908 — *The Brontës: Life and Letters*, 2 vols. Hodder.
1912 Sinclair, May, *The Three Brontës*. London.
1914 Chadwick, Ellis, *In the Footsteps of the Brontës*. Pitman.
1914 Macdonald, Frederika, *The Secret of Charlotte Brontë*. T. C. & E. C. Jack.
1914 Shorter, C. K. *The Brontës and their Circle*. Dent.
1915 Green, J. J. 'The Brontë/Wheelwright Friendship', *Friends Quarterly*, Nov.
1916 *A Centenary Memorial: Charlotte Brontë*, ed. Butler Wood. Fisher Unwin.
1919 Spielmann, M. H., *The Inner History of the Brontë–Heger Letters*. Chapman & Hall.
1930 Moore, George, *Conversations in Ebury Street*. London.
1932 Benson, E. F., *Charlotte Brontë*. Longmans.
1936 Cooper, Irene Willis, *The Authorship of Wuthering Heights*. Hogarth Press.
1937 Harrison, G. Elsie, *Haworth Parsonage*. Epworth.
1941 Ratchford, F. E., *The Brontës' Web of Childhood*. Columbia University Press.
1947 Christian, Mildred, *A Census of Brontë MSS in the USA*. Reprinted from The Trollopian. London.
1947 Hinkley, Laura, *The Brontës: Charlotte and Emily*.

1948 Harrison, G. Elsie, *The Clue to the Brontës*. Methuen.
1948 Raymond, Ernest, *In the Steps of the Brontës*.
1959 Gérin, Winifred, *Anne Brontë. A Biography*. Nelson.
1961 — *Branwell Brontë. A Biography*. Nelson.
1965 Lock, John, and Dixon, W. T., *A Man of Sorrow*. The Life, Letters & Times of the Revd. Patrick Brontë. Nelson.

The *Transactions of the Brontë Society*, with special reference to the following years, authors, subjects:
1895 Yates, W. W., 'The Brontës at Dewsbury'.
1896 Lee, P. F., 'Charlotte Brontë and the East Riding'.
1898 Scruton, W., 'The Reminiscences of Ellen Nussey'.
1899 'Reminiscences of Ellen Nussey' (*Scribner's*, May 1871).
1906 Wroot, Herbert E., 'The Persons and Places in the Brontë Novels.'
1907 Wroot, H. E.: The late Rev. A. B. Nicholls.
1910 Welldon, Rt. Revd. J. S. C., 'The Brontë Family in Relation to Manchester.'
1912 Bache, Rev. K., 'Biographical data concerning A. B. Nicholls.'
1913 'Two Brussels School-Fellows of the Brontës.'
1916 'Mrs. Gaskell & Charlotte Brontë.'
1919 Wood, Butler, 'The Connection of Charlotte Brontë with the Lake District'.
1921 Hopewell, Donald, 'Cowan Bridge'.
1921 — 'The Suppressed Passages from Mrs. Gaskell's "Life" of C.B.'
1922 'Bibliography of Charlotte Brontë's Early Writings.'
1923 Hambley-Rowe, J., 'The Maternal Relations of the Brontës'.
1923 de Knevett, Edgar, 'Charlotte Brontë's School in Brussels'.
1930 Payne, Revd. George, 'Charlotte Brontë's Biographer'.
1937 Edgerley, C. M., 'Miss Branwell'.
1939 Hatfield, C. W., 'The Relatives of Maria Branwell'.
1940 Edgerley, C. M., 'Ellen Nussey'.
1941 — 'Tabitha Aykroyd'.
1942 — 'The Revd. A. B. Nicholls'.
1944 — 'Mary Taylor'.
1945 Spielmann, Percy E., 'The Brontë–Heger Mystery'.
1946 Weir, Edith, 'Cowan Bridge'.
1946 M. C., 'Memories of Ellen Nussey'.
1947 Weir, Edith, 'Contemporary Reviews of the Brontë Novels'.
1948 Bentley, P., 'Charlotte Brontë's Sketch-book'.
1950 Whone, Clifford, 'Where the Brontës Borrowed Books: the Keighley Mechanics Institute Library'.
1951 Preston, A., 'John Greenwood & the Brontës'.
1952 Blakeley, Max, 'Memories of Margaret Wooler and her Sisters'.
1953 Curtis, Dame Myra, 'Cowan Bridge School'.
1954 Gallop, Marjorie, 'Charlotte's Husband'.
1955 Charlier, Gustave, 'The Brussels of Charlotte Brontë'.
1955 Huguenin, Dr. C., 'Bronteana at Princeton University'.
1956 Fielding, K. J., 'The Brontës and *The North American Review*'.
1958 Cortazzo, E., 'Recollections of Nancy Wainwright'.
1959 Holgate, Ivy, 'The Brontës at Thornton'.
1962 — 'The Structure of *Shirley*'.

VIII. TOPOGRAPHICAL WORKS

1824 Pigot & Co.: City of Dublin & Hibernian Directory.
1837 Lewis's: Topographical Directory of Ireland.
1853 Prichard, E. W., *A Guide to Filey & Scarborough*.
1867 Shaw, G., *Rambles about Filey*.
1868 Pettit, Revd. A., *The Filey Hand-Book*.
1879 Keighley, W., *Keighley Past & Present*.
1888 Stuart, J. Erskine, *The Brontë Country*.
1897 Turner, J. Horsfall, *Haworth Past & Present*.
1894 Rawnsley, H. D., *Literary Associations of the English Lakes*.
1898 Scruton, William, *Thornton and the Brontës*.
1913 Turner, Whiteley, *A Springtime Saunter*.
1916 Rawnsley, H. D., *Past & Present at the English Lakes*.
1930 Cadman, H. Ashwell, *Gomersal Past & Present*.
1933 Cradock, Revd. H. C., *History of the Ancient Parish of Birstall*, SPCK.
1949 Pearson, F. R., *Charlotte Brontë on the E. Coast of Yorkshire*.
1953 Goodall, Armitage, *Spenlandia*.

BIBLIOGRAPHY OF GENERAL WORKS CONSULTED

LITERARY AND ARTISTIC

GASKELL, *The Letters of Mrs Gaskell*, ed. J. A. V. Chapple and Arthur Pollard. Manchester University Press. 1966.

THACKERAY, W. M., *The Letters & Private Papers of W. M. Thackeray*, ed. Gordon N. Ray, 4 vols. O.U.P., 1945.

ELIOT, GEORGE, *The Letters of George Eliot*, ed. Gordon S. Haight, 6 vols. O.U.P., 1954.

ARNOLD, MATTHEW, *Letters of Matthew Arnold*, ed. G. W. E. Russell, 2 vols. London, 1895.

TROLLOPE, ANTHONY, *Autobiography*. World's Classics, 1961.

— *Thackeray* (the first biography). English Men of Letters, 1880.

TILLOTSON, GEOFFREY, *Thackeray: The Novelist*. Oxford Paperbacks, 1962.

TILLOTSON, KATHLEEN, *Novels of the 1840's*. Oxford Paperbacks, 1955.

THACKERAY, ANNE ISABELLA (LADY RITCHIE), *Chapters from some Memoirs*. London, 1894.

HOPKINS, A. B., *Elizabeth Gaskell: Her Life and Work*. John Lehmann, 1952.

GASKELL, E. C., *Mary Barton* and *Ruth*.

SHAEN, MARGARET J., *Memorials of Two Sisters*. [Winkworth.] London, 1908.

MARTINEAU, HARRIET, *Autobiography*, 3 vols., 1877.

— *Deerbrook*, 1839.

WHEATLEY, VERA, *Harriet Martineau*. Secker & Warburg, 1957.

SMITH, MRS., *George Smith: A Memoir by his Widow*. Privately printed, 1902.

HUXLEY, DR. LEONARD, *The House of Smith, Elder*. Privately printed, 1923.

OLIPHANT, MRS., *Annals of a Publishing House*. Macmillan, 1897.

SMITH, FRANK, *The Life & Work of Sir James Kay-Shuttleworth*. Murray, 1923.

BROOKFIELD, CHARLES and F., *Mrs. Brookfield and her Circle*. Pitman, 1905.

LEE, AMICE, *Laurels and Rosemary: The Life of William and Mary Howitt*. O.U.P., 1955.

BUNTING, T. P., *The Life of Jabez Bunting*, 2 vols. Longman, 1859, 1887.

EWBANK, JANE, *The Life and Works of William Carus-Wilson*. Titus Wilson, Kendal, 1960.

WILSON, WILLIAM CARUS, 'The Children's Friend'—monthly parts, 1826–34. A. Foster, Kirkby Lonsdale.

— 'The Child's First Tales'. A. Foster, Kirkby Lonsdale, 1836.

— 'The Friendly Visitor'—monthly parts, 1825–43. A. Foster, Kirkby Lonsdale.

WARD, MARY (MRS. HUMPHREY), *A Writer's Recollections*. 1918.

WARD, WILFRID, *Life of J. H. Newman*, 2 vols. Longman, 1912.

NEWMAN, J. H., *Lectures on 'The Difficulties of Anglicans'*. Longman, 1908.

DOWDEN, E., ed. *Letters of Robert Southey to Caroline Bowles*. Dublin, 1881.

BENSON, A. C., *Life of Edward White Benson, late Archbishop of Canterbury*, 1895.

MOORE, GEORGE, *Conversations in Ebury Street*. London, 1930.

SIMMONDS, JACK, *Southey*. Collins, 1945.

BALSTON, THOMAS, *John Martin 1789–1854: His Life & Work*. Duckworth, 1947.

PENDERED, MARY, *John Martin, Painter*. London, 1923.

BEWICK, THOMAS, *A History of British Birds*, 2 vols. Blackwell & Co., Newcastle, 1797, 1804, 1847.

MORELL, SIR CHARLES, *Tales of the Genii*. London, 1764.

— *The Arabian Nights' Entertainment*, translated from the French of Antoine Galland, now done into English from the last Paris edition. London, 1787.

CROXALL, SAMUEL, *Aesop's Fables*, 1825.

HISTORY AND SOCIAL BACKGROUND

HAMMOND, L. L. and B., *The Bleak Age*. Pelican, 1947.

YOUNG, G. M., *Victorian England*. O.U.P., 1956.

WOODHAM-SMITH, CECIL, *The Great Hunger*. Hamish Hamilton, 1962.

THOMSON, PATRICIA, *The Victorian Heroine*. O.U.P., 1956.

HOWE, BEA, *A Galaxy of Governesses*. Derek Verschoyle, 1954.

McCARTHY, JUSTIN, *Sir Robert Peel*. Sampson Low, 1891.

THURSFIELD, J. R., *Peel*. Macmillan, 1901.

DISRAELI, B., *Coningsby* and *Sybil*.

HOWARTH, T. E. B., *The Citizen King*. Eyre & Spottiswoode, 1961.

ROWSE, A. L., *The English Past: Evocations of Persons and Places*. Macmillan, 1951.

PERIODICALS

The Methodist Magazine, 1798–1812.

Blackwood's Edinburgh Magazine, 1822–8.

Cornhill Magazine, 1860, 1900.

Quarterly Magazine, Dec. 1848.

Friendship's Offering, 1827–34.

Forget-Me-Not, 1826.

The Keepsake, 1828, 1832, 1833.

BRUSSELS BIBLIOGRAPHY

Almanach de Poche de Bruxelles pour l'Anneé 1844.

Guide de Bruxelles et ses Environs.

DES MAREZ, *Guide*. Touring Club de Belgique, 1928.

Indicateur Belge pour l'An 1840.

Guide Pittoresque dans Bruxelles: Beaux Arts, 1846.

Guide Indispensable du Voyageur sur les Chemins de Fer, 1842.

HYMANS, LOUIS, *Bruxelles à travers les Ages*.

QUIEVREUX, LOUIS, 'Bruxelles, les Brontës et la famille Heger', *La Lanterne*, Avril 1950.

DEPAGE, HENRI, 'Les Origines du Pensionnat Heger', *Revue Edelweiss*, Juin 1956.

— *La Vie d'Antoine Depage: Son Histoire*, 1950.

SLOSSE, AUGUSTE, *Paul Heger 1846–1925*: Éditions de l'Université.

DORCHY, HENRI, *L'Athénée Royal de Bruxelles: son histoire*, 1950.

LANDOY, EUGÈNE, 'Le Salon de 1842', *Revue Complète*.

CHARLIER, GUSTAVE, 'Passages', *Renaissance du Livre*, 1947.

— 'Le Bruxelles de Charlotte Brontë'. *BST*, 1955.

COSTYN, ARTHUR, *Sites Brabançonnes*. Touring Club de Belgique.

Registre des Etrangers (Police Registers) pour l'Année 1842, Archives de la Ville de Bruxelles.

Prospectus pour 1844 du Pensionnat de l'Athénée Royal de Bruxelles, Directeur: M. Lebel. Imp., J. J. Sorez, rue du Beurre, Bruxelles.

Statuts de la Société Royale de la Grande Harmonie de Bruxelles, 1890.

Registers of Births, Deaths, Marriages for the United Anglican Churches of Brussels.

Registers of Births, Deaths, Marriages of l'Eglise Protestante du Musée.

Le Journal de Bruxelles for 1842 and 1843.

L'Indépendant for 1842 and 1843.

Le Journal de Belgique for 1842 and 1843.

L'Indépendance Belge for 4 Sept. 1886, 9 May 1896. (Golden wedding, and death of M. Heger.)

INDEX

ABBREVIATIONS

AB	Anne Brontë	EN	Ellen Nussey
CB	Charlotte Brontë	MT	Mary Taylor
EJB	Emily Brontë	GMS	George Murray Smith
PB	Revd. Patrick Brontë	CDS	Clergy Daughters' School
PBB	Branwell Brontë	WSW	William Smith Williams
G	Mrs. Gaskell		

Abbot, Jane, pupil at CDS, 2.

Ackermann, Rudolph, 42.

Agnes Grey, novel by AB, recollections of governess life in, 21, 140, 161, 168, 312, 323, 332, 336, 339, 350, 382, 451, 452, 453.

Agnes Grey, heroine of novel, 161.

Andrews, Miss, teacher at Clergy Daughters' School, 11, 12, 14.

'Angria', setting of Brontës' juvenilia, 82, 87, 88, 89, 93, 94, 100.

'Annuals', vogue in, 41, 42, 43, 44, 49, 51, 52.

Arabian Nights, early influence on Brontës of, 25, 26, 27, 28, 30, 45.

Arnold, Matthew, meeting with CB, 460-1.

Arnold, Mrs., 449, 460, 461.

Atkinson, Revd. Thomas, Vicar of Hartshead, CB's godfather, 18, 54, 67, 101.

Atkinson, Mrs. (*née* Frances Walker), CB's godmother, 18, 54, 64, 66, 68, 101, 397.

Aykroyd, Tabitha, 'Tabby', Brontës' servant, 19, 20, 22, 30, 31, 37, 38, 39, 160, 236, 245, 368, 441, 474, 498, 563.

Aylott & Jones, publishers, 307, 308, 310, 311, 312, 321, 322, 371, 372.

Beck, Madame, character in *Villette*, 277, 494.

Bell, Dr. Alan, and family, of Banagher, 542-8. *See* Nicholls.

'Bell, Currer', CB's professional pseudonym, 40, 75, 161, 235, 309, 310, 312, 322, 335, 337, 338, 347, 349, 357, 358, 363, 364, 366, 369, 370, 371, 372, 397, 398, 399, 400, 401, 403, 404, 408, 411, 413, 414, 415, 416, 418, 419, 420, 424,

430, 435, 436, 437, 455, 475, 483, 496, 504, 505, 506, 535, 556, 557, 561, 568.

'Bell, Currer, Ellis and Acton', Brontës' pseudonyms, 307, 309, 310, 312, 322, 323, 335, 341, 347, 350, 370.

Benson, Edward White, 146, 147.

Blackwood's Magazine, early influence on the Brontës of, 23, 24, 28, 29, 30, 31, 41, 47, 97, 108.

Branwell, Elizabeth, CB's aunt, 19, 20, 21, 22, 23, 33, 34, 35, 37; helps nieces financially, 37, 54, 116, 172, 173, 175-6; ignorant of Brontës' writing, 37; sponsors nieces' plan to open school, 171, 172, 173; finances nieces' education in Brussels, 175-6, 177; death of, 213, 214; CB's letter to, 175-6.

Brett, Dr. Edward Samuel, Burlington doctor, 385.

Brocklehurst, Mr., character in *Jane Eyre*, 12, 39.

Brontë, Anne ('Acton Bell'), CB's first story written for, 5, 6.

godmothers, 18.

twin-like devotion to Emily, 20, 86, 116-17.

aunt's religious influence on, 21, 34.

early collaboration with sisters, 25, 26, 27, 31.

George Moore's views on, 40.

pupil at Roe Head, 95, 96, 98, 102, 108, 113, 114.

illness at school, 113-14.

governess at Blake Hall, 140, 141, 160, 161.

love for Mr. Weightman, 166, 168, 211.

governess at Thorpe Green Hall, 169, 211, 217.

resigns her post, 288.

PRINTED IN GREAT BRITAIN
AT THE UNIVERSITY PRESS, OXFORD
BY VIVIAN RIDLER
PRINTER TO THE UNIVERSITY